Handbook of Sports and Recreational Building Design
Volume 2

HANDBOOK OF SPORTS AND RECREATIONAL BUILDING DESIGN

Volume 2 Indoor sports

Second edition

THE SPORTS COUNCIL
TECHNICAL UNIT FOR SPORT

Edited by Geraint John and Kit Campbell

Linacre House, Jordan Hill, Oxford OX2 8DP
225 Wildwood Avenue, Woburn, MA 01801-2041
A division of Reed Educational and Professional Publishing Ltd

ℛ A member of the Reed Elsevier plc group

OXFORD AUCKLAND BOSTON
MELBOURNE JOHANNESBURG NEW DELHI

First published 1981
Second edition 1995
Reprinted 1996, 1997, 1999

British Library Cataloguing in Publication Data
Sports Council
    Handbook of Sports and Recreational
    Building Design. – Vol. 2: Indoor Sports. –
    2 Rev.ed
    I. Title   II. John, Geraint
    III. Campbell, Kit
    725.8043

Library of Congress Cataloguing in Publication Data
Handbook of sports and recreational building design.
    'The Sports Council, Technical Unit for Sport.'
    Includes bibliographical references and indexes.
    Contents: v. 1. Outdoor sports – v. 2. Indoor sports.
    Handbooks, manuals, etc. I. John, Geraint.
    II. Campbell, Kit.   III. Sports Council (Great Britain).
    Technical Unit for Sports.
    GV413.H36   1993   725.8   92-35106

ISBN 0 7506 1293 2 (v. 1)
ISBN 0 7506 1294 0 (v. 2)

Typeset by TecSet, Wallington, Surrey
Printed and bound in Great Britain by Bookcraft (Bath) Ltd

Volume 2   Indoor sports

A note about the Sports Council

The Sports Council was incorporated by Royal Charter in 1972 and its main objectives are to increase participation and excellence in sports and physical recreation, to increase the quantity and quality of sports facilities, to raise standards of performance, and to provide information on sports and sports facilities. It is currently focusing on the development of excellence, sport for young people, and the effective distribution of Lottery funds.

Back Row *1 Geraint John 2 Robin Wilson 3 Peter Clapp 4 Dave Bosher*
Centre Row *5 Eifion Roberts 6 Patricia Smith 7 Veronika Mhatre-Rolvien 8 Peter Ackroyd*
Front Row *9 Lynda Taylor 10 Gordon Stables 11 John Davies 12 David Butler*
Not included in photograph: Jennifer Millest, Christopher Harper

Foreword

Since the Sports Council began its work in 1972 sports participation has risen steadily in Britain. In some areas more women participate in indoor sports than men. The increased sophistication of the sporting public, as well as improving sporting standards, has raised our expectations of sports buildings. Throughout, the Sports Council has continued to provide authoritative design advice, much valued by the building professions, the building industry, and clients and developers.

This further volume of the Handbook is the result of many years of hard work by our Technical Unit for Sport, working closely with a number of authors, all experts in their various subjects. This is the second volume of the new, completely revised edition of the Handbook which was first published, in four volumes in 1981. I am proud of the reputation it acquired as a work of reference.

I expect the new edition to acquire a similar status serving another generation of sports buildings which will be given an added impetus in the UK by the introduction of the National Lottery. Properly designed buildings of the right quality, offering a wide range of uses, and capable of withstanding wear and tear have been shown to provide value for money in operation and construction. The sports centres of the 1970s are, like many of us, greying at the temples and in need of rejuvenation or refurbishment to bring them into an acceptable condition. I commend this Handbook to all who have the exciting task of getting us, and them, fit for the next century.

Rodney Walker
Chairman, Sports Council

Preface

This is a new edition of a book which has established itself as the definitive practical handbook for architects, clients and providers of sports and recreational buildings. The original edition, which was written in 1981, has been substantially revised, rewritten and updated. Like its predecessor, this book aims to provide practical advice and guidance on the design of new facilities and the conversion, adaptation and upgrading of existing buildings.

In short, this publication is designed to be the new edition of the major textbook on the subject. It is a new statement bringing together a wide range of reference works, including those which have been written since the first edition, to make the book as comprehensive as possible. New material has been added as appropriate. Because of the quantity of information, the book has been split into three volumes, with Volume 1 covering outdoor facilities, Volume 2 indoor dry sports and Volume 3 swimming pools and ice rinks. This three volume format is a change from the four volumes of the previous edition.

Dimensions and specifications are given for some 80 sports in the three volumes.

This book would not have been possible without the help and encouragement of a wide range of people involved in the sport and recreational field.

Individual authors and sources are credited within the book, but thanks are also due to colleagues in the Sports Council working closest with the Technical Unit for Sport, namely the Facilities Unit, the Information Centre and the Research Unit, for their contributions. Mention must also be made of the help given by the Sports Council's regional officers, staff in the National Sports Councils and others who have given their time and assistance.

The relevant Governing Bodies of Sport and other sports organisations have made a significant contribution in helping to ensure the accuracy of the information contained in this book.

Geraint John
1995

Contributors to Volume 2

Peter Ackroyd Dip Arch RIBA MILAM is a Senior Architect in the Technical Unit for Sport of the Sports Council.

Sylvester Bone BA, RIBA, AA Dip, Dip TP, FASI is a Principal of The Camden Consultancy, a grouping of independent consultancies in the construction, planning and information fields.

David Bosher is the Environmental Services Engineer in the Technical Unit for Sport of the Sports Council.

Kit Campbell B Arch, MSc, RIBA ARIAS MRTPI MILAM is an architect and planner, Principal of Kit Campbell Associates, Leisure Recreation and Tourism Consultants, Edinburgh.

David Carpenter is a Senior Development Officer with the Sports Council in London. He has carried out extensive world-wide research into the operation of tennis facilities and worked on the development of the UK's Indoor Tennis Initiative programme since its inception in 1986.

James Clough is an exercise and physiology lecturer, leisure consultant and writer. A regular presenter at major conventions and in popular demand on instruction training courses, he has recently been appointed Lecturer in Sport and Exercise Sciences at Cheltenham and Gloucester College of Higher Education.

John Davies is a Senior Quantity Surveyor in the Technical Unit for Sport.

Barry Dawson Dip Arch (Dist) is an architect, previously of Miller Associates.

Ken Farnes is a consultant architect and a member of the Sporting Installations Commission of the Union Cycliste International.

Ian Firth is a Partner with the Flint & Neill Partnership, consulting engineers, and provides specialist advice on the design, construction and maintenance of fabric membrane structures.

Mike Fitzjohn is a Senior Research Officer in the Sports Council.

Mark Foley is a partner of Burrell Foley Fischer and has a specialist interest in theatre spaces and facilities for the arts.

Christopher Harper is a Senior Architect in the Technical Unit for Sport of the Sports Council.

Rick Holmes is a Director of Curtins Consulting Engineers plc.

Colin Jepson is a Director of Verde Sports (Bowls) Ltd.

Geraint John Dip Arch UCL, RIBA, MILAM, CISRM is Chief Architect and Head of the Technical Unit for Sport at the Sports Council.

Philip Johnson MA, BEd(Hons), Dip PE Adviser to British Athletics Federation on Indoor Facilities, and Consultant and Lecturer in Recreation and Leisure.

Rose Macdonald BA, MSSP, SRP is Director of the Sports Injury Clinic at the Crystal Palace National Sports Centre.

Jim Meikle ARICS is a Partner in the Davis Langdon Everest Consultancy Group.

Jennifer Millest is an Architect in the Technical Unit for Sport of the Sports Council.

David Payne is Head of the Facilities Unit of the Sports Council.

Roger Payne is the British Mountaineering Council's National Officer and has had special responsibility for the development of climbing walls.

Eifion Roberts is a Senior Building Surveyor in the Technical Unit for Sport.

John Roberts is Head of the Communications Unit of the Sports Council.

Charles Smith is an architect with many years' experience in sports and leisure building design.

Peter Sutcliffe MSc, PhD was cricket's first Director of Coaching, and subsequently Head of the Facilities Unit for the North West Region of the Sports Council. He now works as a freelance consultant.

Neil Thomson BSc(Hons), MA, Dip Arch, RIBA is an architect and Principal of Neil Thomson Associates, Architects & Designers, London and Malvern.

Maritz Vandenberg BA Arch(Hons) is an architectural writer, editor and publisher.

Michele Verroken is head of the Sports Council's Doping Control Unit.

Part I   Overview

1

The case for sport

Geraint John (drawing on material for the Sports Councils in the UK)

1 Introduction

Sport is for all. Millions of people take part in sport or physical recreation (in the UK half of the entire population participates in sport at least once a month). Millions more watch or follow sport. Sporting successes – local or national – bring pleasure and pride to all of them.

Many nations recognise the economic benefits of sporting success as well as its value to national prestige. They have invested heavily in new sporting developments.

Sport is a major source of local and national pride. How often in recent years have we seen the millions of lights still burning in the small hours of the night in homes all over the world. The dramas of a World Cup or an Olympic Games have closed offices early and emptied commuter buses and trains.

It is not only international events that stir the hearts of nations. Weekend after weekend millions of people go out to support, or to play for, their local side. Every town, every village, every school, draws some part of its spirit and identity from the performance of its sporting teams.

Sport offers the opportunity to millions of adults to maintain and improve their health and find companionship. It also provides a ladder of fulfilment and success to youngsters who may otherwise be crowded in uncomfortable housing or tempted to a wayward life on the streets. It offers positive role models. It provides a context of discipline, self-awareness and self-satisfaction to many who might be tempted to selfishness or even petty crime. For every individual it offers the experience of working with and for others and achieving goals that seemed beyond reach.

The pace and intensity of modern life impose great stress on many individuals. The pressures of the workplace offer little scope for exercise and too little chance to escape from desk or factory bench. Sport and recreation offer a unique outlet from the pressures of daily life.

Sport opens a path to relaxation which we rarely find at work. Physical exercise improves a person's mood, decreases anxiety and improves self-image.

Above all, sport brings people together whether in personal competition or in team play. Parents and children, partners and friends, all can take pleasure in each other's achievements. To realise the best results every sportsman or woman must work for and depend on others.

The standards of conduct, respect for common rules and teamwork which are inherent in successful sport at any level are also vital for our well-being as nations.

The Sports Council believes that the sense of national cohesion and common interest which can result from sport can be a major binding force in society as a whole. Sport is of far greater value than simply the enjoyment and excitement it gives to those who play it and those who follow it.

Sport is its own justification. It is a vital element in national culture. In addition, sport:

- Contributes to greater fitness, better health, and a sense of personal well-being
- Plays a vital part in a rounded education for children
- Offers opportunities for varied experiences and new fellowship in the community
- Generates large sums of money for national economies (in the UK in 1990 it generated the equivalent of 1.7% of the gross domestic product)
- Provides a large number of jobs
- Promotes and enhances a nation's standing in the world.

More facilities, better use of them and the targeting of groups less likely to take part in sport and recreation (such as women, older people and disabled people and teenagers leaving school or college) are necessary to promote recreation in the future. In the UK, the Sports Council's primary aim is to increase the level of participation, to widen understanding of its benefits and to remove social and economic constraints on taking part. The sport or recreation of an individual's choice is the most attractive way of taking the exercise he or she needs, **1.**

Regular recreation is part of a healthier life-style which millions of people need no pressure or incentive to choose. Between 1977 and 1986, the proportion of adults taking part in sport rose in the UK by nearly 7%. Given the chance, millions more might follow them.

Sport offers particular fulfilment and health benefits to people with disabilities. The achievements of men and women in the Paralympics are among the most inspiring in all sport. Advances in sports medicine are bringing discoveries of benefit to all. The promotion of sport should be part of any worthwhile programme of preventive healthcare.

Table 1.1: Average number of occasions of participation per adult per year (1)

Walking	37.9
Snooker/billiards/pool	11.4
Swimming	6.9
Darts	6.5
Keep fit/yoga	10.1
Cycling	11.3
Athletics – track and field	0.3
Other running (including jogging)	4.5
Football	2.8
Weightlifting/weight training	4.7
Golf	2.1
Badminton	1.4
Squash	1.3
Table tennis	1.3
Fishing	0.9
Tenpin bowls/skittles	0.5
Lawn/carpet bowls	1.3
Cricket	0.5
Water sports (excluding sailing)	0.5
Horse riding	0.9
Self-defence (excluding boxing)	0.7
Ice skating	0.2
Basketball	0.2
Sailing yachts/dinghies	0.2
Motor sports	0.2
Rugby	0.2
Netball	0.2
Gymnastics	0.3
Boxing/wrestling	0.2
Hockey	0.1
Field sports	0.1
Climbing	0.1
Curling	0.0
Other	0.3

Note (1): Source – Jil Matheson, Office of Population Censuses and Surveys, *General Household Survey 1987: Participation in Sport*, HMSO, London (1991).

Derived from the *General Household Survey* and calculated by multiplying the number of participants for an activity by the number of days on which they took part in that activity in the 4 weeks before interview, multiplying this figure by 13 and dividing by the total number of people interviewed in the year.

Persons aged 16 or over: Great Britain 1987.

1 *Participation in basketball*

2 Sport and health

More and more people have sedentary occupations. The number of people in non-manual jobs has increased in the UK by approximately 20% over the last 20 years, whilst the number of people in manual employment has fallen in the UK by around 35% over the same period (source: Social Trends 1990).

Regular exercise for men and women of all ages can provide the essential complement to programmes of preventive health care evolved by governments and health authorities.

Costs of remedial care in the health service rise inexorably year by year. In England they went up from £6.5 billion in 1978–79 to £26.6 billion in 1990–91 (source: *Hansard*, 14 May 1991, col. 129). Investment in sports development is likely to pay back in the reduction of many avoidable illnesses.

3 Sport and schools

If the numbers of people participating in sport are to be raised, no setting is more important than school. Sporting skills gained at school will be an asset for life. A loss of playing fields and a lack of commitment to school sports can deprive youngsters of their birthright. This is a loss to a nation as a whole, **2**.

Team work and achievement in sport impart a spirit of self-discipline, personal achievement, and respect for others. The implications of policies on the availability of modern sports facilities to schools and communities need careful study. Errors made now would cost huge sums of money to repair; for many young people opportunities may never recur.

It is important that people who leave school in further education have continuing access to sports facilities.

The Sports Council believes that sharing facilities between schools and local people confers positive benefits. Such a partnership should be a factor in all local strategies for sports developments. It is important that maximum use is made of sports halls, pools, and pitches, but it is equally important that physical education should have a full role properly to create literacy in movement, as vital to every person's literacy as verbal expression itself.

Many sports clubs provide opportunities that school children might not otherwise have. Sports policy should promote such arrangements between clubs and schools, and schools and the community. The aim should be to promote self-confidence among children, to encourage school-leavers to maintain sporting activity in later life and to identify and develop special talent.

4 Sport and the economy

Sport, even when its costs are considered, gives far more than it consumes. In the UK each year, total income to the Treasury from sports and sports-related sources is nearly £3.3 billion. For every £1 in grants received, sport gives back £9 in taxes. Even this figure takes no account of the invisible gains – through tourism, lower calls on the health service and greater fitness in the workforce. Even excluding betting, people choose to spend far more on sport and

2 *A young try scorer in a junior rugby game*

Table 1.2: Selected categories of UK consumers' expenditure in 1989 (1)

	£ million
Motor vehicles	17,363
Sport, including gambling	10,677
Cigarettes	7244
Sport, excluding gambling	6368
Furniture and floor coverings	6005
Electricity	5787
Bread	5575
Menswear	5412
DIY goods	4655
Spirits	4641
Wines and ciders	4500
Gas	4424
Newspapers and magazines	2949
Pets	2014
Records	1653
Books	1088
Bingo admissions	229
Cinema	187

Note (1): Source – CSO, Henley Centre.

recreation than on other leisure interests such as hi-fi, DIY or video.

The benefits are not only national. Partnerships between local authorities, developers and sports bodies, with or without the use of public money, create new facilities for local communities. In the UK in 1989–90 alone, 55 sports halls and 21 indoor swimming pools were completed, with 49 halls and 48 pools under construction; 32 new artificial outdoor pitches were added, increasing by more than one-sixth the nation's stock.

The Sports Council believes that investment in sport and recreation is worthwhile, in hard times as well as in good.

5 Sport and employment

Sport and recreation have become great national creators of jobs. A Council of Europe study in 1985 suggested that sports-related employment in Council countries reached some 2 million jobs. More recent studies in the UK alone point to almost 400,000 jobs being related to sport. For every job created directly in sport, another job is created elsewhere. The market for sports gear is expanding (expenditure on sports clothing and footwear has more than doubled over the last 5 years).

Recreation is also important to the workplace. It is good for morale and good for fitness. Regular exercise has been proved to reduce the number of working days lost and hence to increase the overall productivity of a firm. Both managers and workforce should give greater attention to these factors and to the sense of cohesion that can come from involvement with a works sports team.

6 Sport and the nation

The UK is not the only country with reason to know that sport has a significant effect on its standing in the world. That effect can be positive or it may be negative. Well-publicised examples of hooliganism have done much to

Table 1.3: Average annual growth rates of selected categories of UK consumers' expenditure, 1985–89

	Real increase per year (%)	Overall real increase 1985–90 (%)
Sport, including gambling	7.1	40.9
Sport, excluding gambling	4.7	25.8
Motor vehicles	4.7	25.8
Recorded music	13.2	85.9
DIY goods	5.7	31.9
Pets	9.4	56.7
Books	6.4	36.4
Cinema	5.4	30.1
Furniture and floor coverings	4.1	22.3
Bread and cereals	2.0	10.4
Wines and ciders	3.0	15.9
Menswear	2.7	14.2
Womenswear	4.3	23.4
Newspapers and magazines	0.2	1.0
Beer	0.2	1.0
Spirits	0.3	1.5
Electricity	0.5	2.5
Cigarettes	0.3	1.5
Bingo admissions	2.5	11.6
Gas	1.3	6.7
Total consumers' expenditure	4.7	25.8

Source – CSO, Henley Centre.

undermine the national image of 'fair play', which the development of sport itself had created. The negative aspects must be urgently addressed by all involved – through firm controls, better facilities and the encouragement of more young people to direct their energies to being players as well as spectators of sport.

However, governments should recognise that far more good is done, within the nation and abroad, by sporting success than through any harm which may be suffered by the bad aspects, like hooliganism.

Four out of five people in a MORI poll in the UK believed that sport helped to break down problems of different race, colour and creed. Three-quarters of all British people affirmed that they felt a sense of pride when a local team or sports person did well.

Sport not only breaks down barriers, it builds new bridges. Men and women make an equal contribution and take out equal benefits. People from different backgrounds, regions and nations come together to play under a common international code. Even people with different languages can establish immediate understanding.

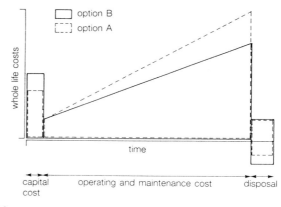

2

2
Whole life costs

Jim Meikle

1 Introduction

The planning and design phases of any building project involve a multitude of decisions. Many of these may have physiological, social, political and environmental consequences; nearly all have economic consequences also. In money terms, the big decisions tend to be made early: where to build and when; whether to build new or refurbish existing; how much money is available; and so on, **1**.

As decisions are made, each succeeding one tends to have a narrower impact on total costs. The facility owner and his professional advisers (most notably the designer) make many of the key decisions. They are made early in the process when both the widest range of choices and the least amount of information are available. If 'value for money' is to be achieved then the right decisions will be the ones which achieve the best balance between initial and operating costs and revenue, assessed over the lifetime of the facility. This is the purpose of life cycle, or whole life, costing.

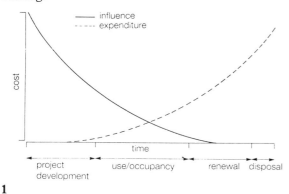

1

2 The technique

Life cycle cost analysis is a technique. It is an aid to, rather than a process of, decision making. The technique may be used in two ways: to determine the consequences of making a decision, or to allow an informed choice to be made from among options. Life cycle costing generally considers only those factors that can be measured in money terms.

Life cycle costing allows both present and future costs to be compared on a common basis. **2** illustrates two design options, one of which has low initial costs but high operating costs (option A) and another with higher initial costs but lower running costs (option B). There is a trade-off implied here between capital costs and running costs. By carrying out the analysis it is possible to identify such a trade-off – if it exists. It should not be assumed, however, that spending more now leads inevitably to lower overall costs and improved value for money. Costly assets often need to have a lot spent operating and maintaining them.

Identifying and quantifying all relevant costs and revenues (cash flows) over an asset's life is what life cycle costing is all about. To assess the whole life cost of an asset it is necessary to add together cash flows now to cash flows at some time in the future. Money declines in value over time, however, so that its value now is more than its value in the future. All payments and receipts (now and in the future) therefore need to be converted to today's money, ie its present value.

If £1 is invested today at a 10% rate of interest it will accumulate to £1.10 after the first year, £1.21 after the second year, and so on. Put another way, £1.21 in 2 years time has a present value of £1. The rate at which future amounts are discounted is made up partly by inflation and partly by the real rate of return over and above inflation. For capital investments such as those involving a sports facility, the rate at which future sums are discounted is often the rate at which the finance is borrowed. The higher the discount (or interest) rate, and the further into the future the analysis seeks to forecast, the less significant are sums of money in present day terms. As an example, at an annual interest rate of 10%, £11 receivable in 25 years is worth only £1 today.

Another example could be a piece of equipment costing £2000 which is cleaned annually at a cost of £50, is overhauled every 3 years at a cost of £500, and undergoes major replacement of its component parts every 9 years at a cost of £1500. The unit is installed in a facility built to last 30 years and the annual rate of inflation is 5%. The stream of payments (compounded at 5%) over the 30 year period is indicated in **3a**.

If the payments are discounted to today's values at a real discount rate of 5% (ie after the effects of inflation have been removed), the profile looks very different, **3b**. It is clear that, after about 20 years the present value of even relatively substantial future amounts is becoming quite small.

The total costs over the operating life of the asset can now be added together, **4**. This of itself provides a fairly meaningless result but can be used to compare alternatives so that informed choices may be made. This is where the life cycle costing technique is most useful.

3 Applications

A life cycle costing approach to appraising investment in sports facilities is particularly appropriate. For example, some surfaces may require replacement sooner than others with considerable economic consequences. Additionally, certain types of materials may have to be maintained more frequently. The consequences of higher than normal maintenance levels and the presence of maintenance personnel may also be disruptive to use and have a discouraging effect on users.

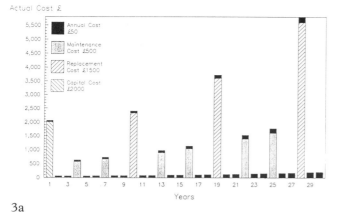

3a

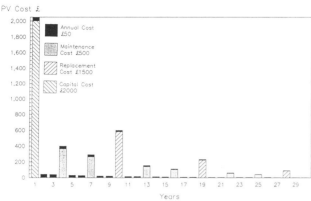

3b

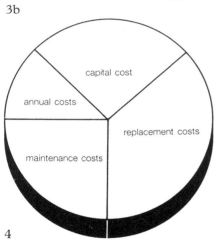

4

fashion. Many capital investments – in the retail sector, for example – are based on life expectancies of less than 10 years. Analysis periods can also be based on expectations of obsolescence. This may affect the whole facility or only part of it. Generally, the results from life cycle cost analysis comparisons are not sensitive to changes in the appraisal period over about 40 years.

The owner and his advisers must identify the options to be examined, bearing in mind that life cycle costing is applicable to options at the level of detailed specification as well as at the level of complete buildings. The streams of costs and incomes associated with each option are then calculated and converted to today's money so that the options can be compared and a choice made.

Cash flows which must be considered, **5**, include:

- Capital costs, finance charges and professional fees at the project development stage
- Staff and administration costs, annual maintenance and cleaning, routine replacement costs and when these might be incurred, energy costs, water charges and other consumables such as chemicals
- Major repairs and replacement (eg boiler plant, sports surfaces) and when these are likely to occur
- Revenue income
- Any costs or income arising from the eventual demolition or disposal of the facility.

For example, for a 20 m swimming pool over a 30 year period, a typical cost breakdown, **6**, shows that capital costs, amount to only about one-fifth of total costs over the life of the facility. The largest proportion is accounted for by staff costs, but note that maintenance, repair and replacement costs may amount to more than the initial costs of the facility.

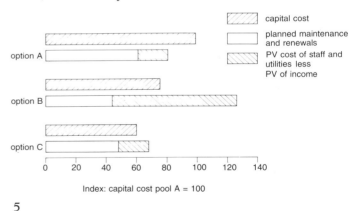

Index: capital cost pool A = 100

5

Life cycle costing may also help answer the questions 'When should we refurbish an existing facility?' and 'When should we decide to build a completely new facility?' Such questions are not easily answered and really depend on a detailed appraisal in each case. Some facilities, for example, may have inherent characteristics which may make refurbishment the most desirable or indeed the only option. If, for example, refurbishment costs are beginning to rise above 75% of newbuild costs then the newbuild option should seriously be considered.

Assuming the need for an improvement in the level of provision has been identified – to be met by refurbishment or newbuild – the owner needs to set key criteria relating to capacity, performance standards and so on. This is important prior to detailed analysis as the more comparable are the different options being considered, the more robust the technique is for the basis of selecting them.

The owner and his advisers must consider the period over which an analysis is to be carried out. This can be related to the expected duration of the owner's interest in the building (his time horizon); it can also be based on expectations of changing consumer requirements and

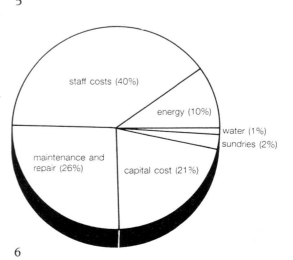

6

3
Environmental issues

David Bosher

1 Overview

Environmental or 'green' issues reflect widespread concern for the future of the world's climate, wildlife and environment. They are likely to remain important for the foreseeable future as they encompass anything and everything that affects the local or global environment in any way.

The exact definition of a good or bad environmental effect may be somewhat unclear, but it is generally accepted that practices and measures which on all the best available evidence appear, on balance, likely to alter the climate or environment in a significant and harmful way should be modified so as to be more environmentally friendly. Some of the areas causing most concern are:

- The destruction of the tropical rain forests
- The discharge of ozone depleting gases into the atmosphere
- The emission of greenhouse gases
- All forms of pollution to the air, land or sea
- Use of the Earth's finite resources.

Sport and recreation can affect the environment in a number of ways, including the direct effect of the activity on the local environment and the method of transport of participants, spectators and staff to and from the location where the activity is taking place.

Buildings account for over half of the annual energy use in the UK, **1**, and therefore production of the main greenhouses gases together with other pollutants. The materials used and consumed in the construction and operation of a building also have a substantial effect on the environment. People spend an average of 90% of their lifetimes inside buildings and therefore they are an important medium through which to confront environmental issues. There are a number of positive things that can be done to produce buildings that are more environmentally friendly.

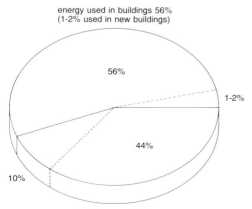

energy used in buildings 56%
(1-2% used in new buildings)

56%

1-2%

44%

10%

energy used in industry, agriculture etc 44%
(10% used in building materials' production)

1 *UK annual energy consumption*

Careful selection of fuels and effective energy conservation will reduce the emission of greenhouse gases and limit global warming. The use of insulation materials and refrigerants that do not utilise chlorofluorocarbons (CFCs) will reduce the damage being caused to the ozone layer. Pollution can be restricted by appropriate specification and treatment of discharge. Care should be taken to utilise non-toxic biodegradable materials than can easily be maintained and replaced and do not impose an unacceptable drain on finite natural resources.

Incorporating concepts that are more environmentally friendly will generally result in natural, simple and resourceful characteristics taking precedence over high technology, complex design and overcomplication. This will generally involve making optimum use of natural energy via effective planning utilising landscaping and building location and orientation to control natural light, solar gain and wind exposure. Designers should seek to maximise natural light and ventilation where appropriate and incorporate long useful life with adaptability and flexibility without undue built-in obsolescence. This is not to suggest that all new technology is inherently bad but rather to emphasise that technology is best applied where its impact may be identified clearly as being beneficial to the environment.

Energy use, materials and technology are all important components in achieving environmentally friendly buildings but good design alone is not enough. Designers, operators and users of buildings all have a responsibility towards protecting the environment. Building operators and users should also acknowledge their personal responsibility in this area and realise that what may appear to be individual, small-scale, insignificant decisions and actions may collectively produce large-scale, significant effects. Finally it is vital that designers, operators and users alike have a constant awareness of the environment outside of the building and the effect that their actions and decisions may have on the quality of that environment.

In order to reduce and hopefully halt and reverse the trend of environmental damage that mankind has apparently embarked upon, action will be needed on a wide range of issues including environmental sustainability, human health, building design quality and responsibility in building operation and use. A substantial improvement in the design, operation and use of buildings will be a big step for mankind in the right environmental direction.

2 Energy and the environment

Sport and recreation facilities make a major contribution to local communities but they also have a significant environmental impact locally and globally. This is due to the fact that they are often substantial buildings using considerable quantities of energy to operate, especially if they include a swimming pool or ice rink.

The materials and energy used in the construction of the facility will have an impact on the environment as will the mode of transport used by customers and staff to get to and from it.

The main area addressed in this section, however, is that of the energy used in operating the facility and how this affects:

- The internal environment (eg temperature, ventilation, lighting levels)
- The local external environment (eg local pollution, light, noise)
- The global environment (eg global warming/greenhouse effect, ozone depletion).

Most of the energy used in operating sports and recreational facilities is utilised to produce and maintain a suitable internal environment to enable the various activities to be carried out comfortably, safely and effectively. The selection of optimum values for temperatures, lighting levels and ventilation rates for each space and activity within that space is therefore critical in order to achieve maximum energy efficiency.

The local external environment is obviously affected by the operation of a facility in a number of ways. In the main this takes the form of pollution by light and noise but it may also include some local atmospheric pollution by fumes from heating plant. The most important element of pollution from the heating (or cooling) of the facility, however, will be the global pollution caused by the production of greenhouse gases and their contribution to global warming.

2.1 Global warming

Of the Sun's energy reaching the earth's surface, 80% is absorbed and radiated back mainly in the form of long-wave infra-red radiation. 'Greenhouse gases' in the atmosphere trap and retain much of this energy and in the process of this 'greenhouse effect' raise the surface temperature of the planet from what would be $-30°C$ to the present average of about $15°C$.

Scientific opinions differ, but it is generally agreed that concentrations of the main greenhouse gases are increasing, largely due to the actions of industrialised areas of the world, and this is likely to result in overall global warming. Some estimates indicate an increase of between $1.5°C$ and $5.5°C$ by 2030 unless action is taken to halt or reverse the trend. The United Nations Inter-Governmental Committee on Climate (IPCC) forecasts an increase of $1°C$ by 2025 and $4°C$ by 2100 unless corrective action is taken.

The following illustrations indicate the contribution that energy use makes to global warming and the relative contributions of different types, of energy use and building types with particular emphasis on sports facilities.

2.2 Greenhouse gases

The IPCC suggests that cuts of 60% in carbon dioxide emissions are needed to maintain the atmosphere at its present condition. This emphasises the importance of carbon dioxide in general and energy use involving fossil fuel burning in particular in controlling global warming. Table 3.1 and **2** summarise the relative contribution to global warming of different gases.

The amount amount of carbon dioxide delivered into the atmosphere per unit of delivered energy in the UK (1987 figures) is shown in Table 3.2. It indicates that using

Table 3.1: Relative contribution to global warming

Nitrous oxide	6%	Fertilisers, fossil fuel combustion, biomass burning, changing land use
Ozone (low level)	12%	Reactions from other pollutants and sunshine
CFCs	14%	Refrigeration, air conditioning, plastic foam, solvents, food freezants, aerosols, etc
Methane	18%	Biological decay, animal waste, fermentation, etc
Carbon dioxide (CO_2)	50%	Fossil fuel combustion, deforestation, erosion, etc

Table 3.2: Carbon dioxide emitted per unit of delivered energy (UK 1987)

Fuel	CO_2 emitted (kg/Gj)
Natural gas	55
Oil	84
Coal	92
Electricity	231

one unit of electricity for energy produces two-and-a-half times as much carbon dioxide as coal, nearly three times as much as oil and four times as much as natural gas for the same amount of useful delivered energy.

The UK energy use in buildings is given in **3** by fuel. Over 50% is electricity use (heating, lighting, power, etc.).

The UK energy use in buildings is given in **4** by end use. Over 60% is used for space and water heating and 30% (all electric) for lighting and power.

The main sources of energy use in dry sports buildings and swimming pools are identified in **5** and **6**. In the former, three-quarters of all energy consumption is used for space heating, and this figure rises to 86% if fans and pumps are included. In pools, three-quarters of energy consumption is used for heating and ventilating the pool hall and water.

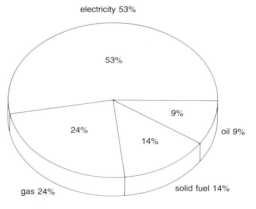

3 *UK energy use in buildings (by fuel)*

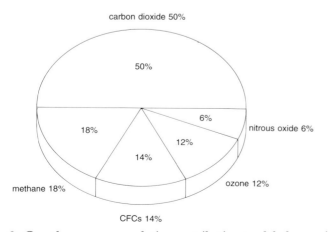

2 *Greenhouse gases – relative contribution to global warming*

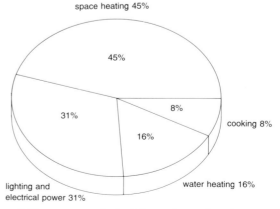

4 *UK energy use in buildings (by end use)*

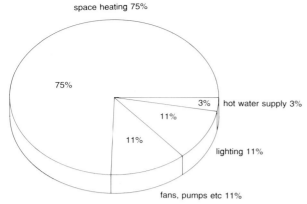

5 *Energy use in a typical dry sports centre (without a swimming pool)*

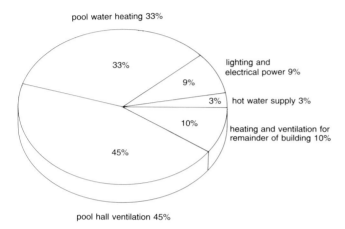

6 *Energy use in a typical swimming pool*

Comparative energy use targets in various building types are expressed in Table 3.3 as an annual energy figure per square metre of gross floor area. From this it is clear that swimming pools are by far the highest energy user, consuming five times as much energy per sqare metre as an office, school or dry sports centre and twice as much as a hospital or sports centre with pool.

2.3 Factors influencing energy use
Getting the initial brief correct for the type of facility, its use and management is vital. The following factors will then apply:

- Location, orientation, exposure, etc. – making optimum use of natural energy (light, solar heat, shelter from wind, etc.)
- Building insulation – 1990s UK Building Regulations are equivalent to 1930s Scandinavian levels. These should be improved upon whenever possible
- Type of fuel – overall fuel efficiency and comparative carbon dioxide production – electricity least efficient,

natural gas most efficient in overall terms (primary fuel to end use efficiency consider combined heat and power)
- Services design – services must be appropriate for building and use – flexible and energy efficient
- Energy recovery – heat reclaim, heat pumps, air recirculation
- Effective control – ensure design criteria are efficiently maintained and conditions can vary to suit load and occupancy without wasting energy
- Installation – well designed systems and buildings must be installed and constructed effectively
- Commissioning – services installations must be properly commissioned and control systems set to appropriate values for systems to function effectively
- Maintenance – it is vital that systems, controls and buildings are properly maintained in order to maximise system efficiency and maintain customer satisfaction
- Management – it is essential that the facility and its building services are managed effectively and with energy efficiency as a priority (eg in programming activities of similar environmental requirements together and ensuring that only areas in use are heated, lit and ventilated to the necessary standard as required)
- Users – facility users have a role to play in energy efficiency in their use of a building (switching off lights, closing doors, etc).

Energy use plays a major role in the influence that leisure facilities have on the global environment as well as overall operating costs. Simple measures to produce improvements include better planning, better design, better insulation, better control, better management and better maintenance.

3 Buildings and materials
The materials used and the energy expended in constructing a building will obviously have a substantial impact on the environment. It is not sufficient when designing buildings and choosing materials simply to consider the building as currently envisaged and during its anticipated useful life but to consider the much broader perspective of the life-span of the building and materials in relation to the local and global environment.

There is now a recognised need to consider the complete life cycle of buildings and materials with regard to the overall effect on the environment. The extraction of the raw materials and the production processes involved in the manufacture of materials used together with the energy and associated environmental pollution produced all need to be taken into account, as well as the actual on-site construction process. The performance of the building and materials during the actual life of the building need to be assessed and allowance made for possible changes of use as well as any maintenance, replacement and refurbishment that may be required.

Environmental considerations do not stop, however, when the building and materials reach the end of their useful life. It is important to consider what happens to the structure and finishes of buildings when the use for which they were primarily designed and selected is ended. Wherever possible recycling of materials should be allowed for and buildings should in general be designed so as to be flexible and easily adaptable so that they can be simply converted and/or refurbished and their useful life maximised. Where there is no other viable alternative to disposing of materials and/or demolishing buildings it is important that the waste material produced can be

Table 3.3: Energy use in different building types

Building type	Annual energy use – (kWh/m^2 total floor area)		
	Good	Fair	Poor
Office – air conditioned	<225	225–360	>360
heated	<215	215–270	>270
Hospital	<500	500–710	>710
Health centre	<270	270–350	>350
Primary school (no pool)	<180	180–240	>240
University	<325	325–355	>355
Dry sports centre (no pool)	<200	200–340	>340
Sports centre (with pool)	<570	570–840	>840
Swimming pool	<1050	1050–1390	>1390

disposed of without pollution or damage to the environment.

In order to make buildings more environmentally friendly it would appear that there may be a need to return to a more natural method of heating, lighting and ventilating together with greater use of natural materials. An essential part of better overall control of the environment may include consideration of returning to methods of building which are based upon treating the fabric of a building as a 'third skin' – ie after human skin and clothing. In the same ways as traditional clothing materials were dramatically affected by the development of nylon and other man-made fibres in the 1950s and 1960s, so were building materials influenced by similar scientific developments, especially in the fields of plastics, resins, rubbers and man-made fibres. It seems likely that the move back towards more natural clothing materials that are more comfortable and allow the human skin to breathe will be complemented by similar moves in building materials and methods.

This is not to suggest that progress should be reversed or that development of new materials and systems should cease but simply that mankind and science should try to work in harmony with nature and not fight against it. New developments and materials should be properly assessed over their complete life cycle and utilised with caution until long-term overall environmental effects are monitored and documented. It is important that the overall environmental impact of a facility (including the complete life cycles of all buildings and materials involved) is fully and properly assessed at the earliest practical stage in the design process in order that adequate consideration can be given to all the environmental issues involved.

4
Refurbishment projects

Charles Smith, Stuart Miller and Kit Campbell

1 Introduction

No sports building can continue to meet changing market needs without regular refurbishment. In some instances major repairs may be needed simply to keep a building in a safe and usable condition; in others upgrading may be needed in order to attract new user groups. This section offers a checklist of those items which should be assessed whenever refurbishment is under consideration.

2 The decision to refurbish

The factors which influence the decision to refurbish an existing building are likely to include:

- Substandard construction:
  - (a) Roof
  - (b) Walls
  - (c) Floor
  - (d) Structure
  - (e) Ineffective thermal insulation
  - (f) Ineffective sound control
  - (g) Excessive internal condensation.
- Substandard services:
  - (a) Heating
  - (b) Ventilation
  - (c) Electrical power and lighting
  - (d) Water treatment
  - (e) Drainage
  - (f) Communications
  - (g) Security system.
- Substandard support facilities – users often judge sports buildings by support areas as much as the main activity areas. When finishes in changing rooms, locker rooms, showers, public toilets, circulation and social areas deteriorate beyond a certain point, no amount of cleaning can make them presentable.
- Substandard facilities for people with disabilities:
  - (a) Inadequate disabled public toilet facilities
  - (b) Inadequate or unsuitable changing and locker facilities
  - (c) Inadequate or unsuitable shower facilities
  - (d) Unsuitably designed reception desk
  - (e) Inadequately sized lobbies
  - (f) Unsuitable access to upper floors.
- Poor energy management – energy cost savings of over 60% have been achieved in some buildings. Even where systems operate efficiently energy cost savings of up to 10% can sometimes still be made. For effective energy cost savings to be made, the fabric of a leisure centre building should first be upgraded to at least the minimum standards set out in the Building Regulations 1990 or current amendment. If budgets allow, thermal insulation should be increased above the basic building regulations standard.
- Poor energy performance of the building fabric:
  - (a) Rising damp in external walls and floors
  - (b) Water penetration through walls and roof
  - (c) Excessive air penetration through walls and roof
  - (d) Cold bridging between the internal and external structural elements of both walls and roof.
- High staffing costs – inefficient planning can result in unacceptably high staff costs. Some key areas which should be reviewed are:
  - (a) The reception area – does it allow good visual security control over visitor movements, and easy access to staff areas?
  - (b) Changing areas – are they easy to supervise and control?
  - (c) Bar/cafeteria serveries – can they be staffed efficiently?
- Dated image:
  - (a) Finishes and decoration
  - (b) Graphics
  - (c) Fixtures and fittings

3 The objectives of refurbishment

Before starting to draw up plans for refurbishment it is important to identify clear objectives. This is very much a client responsibility, possibly with assistance from a specialist consultant. It will often also be desirable to undertake a market assessment in order to prepare a brief for the refurbishment. An existing building, particularly a fairly old one such as some pools, may not be located in the best position to take optimum advantage of the available market. If this is likely, it may be sensible for the owner to commission a market study. The results of this may suggest that the existing building should be closed or converted to some other use.

Refurbishment projects can be considered as repairs, improvements or a mixture of both. Repairs are fairly simple and do not normally involve major changes to the building.

With improvements, however, the key factor is what the building owner wants to achieve. For example, is the objective to provide a better service for existing users, or is the intention to increase use and therefore income, or reduce operational costs? If so, an appraisal of market potential, operational costs and customer profile will be required as well as a technical assessment.

The main objectives of refurbishment can be considered as being:

- *To provide a new image* throughout the building by graphics, colours, fabrics or other means.
- *To provide new facilities within the existing building* – this may involve changing the use of some areas within the building to accommodate new activities (for example, converting a squash court to a fitness studio) or re-allocating existing uses within the building (for example, creating a new social area adjacent to the main entrance).
- *To extend the building* in order to provide additional sports or recreation facilities.
- *To improve energy efficiency* – when the structure, fabric and services of a building become inefficient through age or disrepair running costs can rise astronomically. However, when a building is refurbished and the external fabric has been transformed into an energy efficient high performance envelope requiring a minimum of energy to maintain comfort levels internally,

1–2 *Bramley Baths, Leeds, a late Victorian listed building which has been completely restored to its original appearance both internally and externally. The pool was closed in 1988 following a roof collapse. A structural survey revealed that most of the defects were caused by foundation settlement/movements and damp penetration through the roof and walls. The majority of the original features were found to be intact and have been retained: for example the stained glass leaded windows to the pool hall; the glazed panels to doors and the reception counter,*

3; *the ornate balustrade to the pool hall gallery. Architects: Leeds Design Consultancy. Photos: Derrick, Wade and Waters*

4 Preliminary investigations

4.1 Building condition

All buildings eventually reach the end of their useful lives and either have to be replaced or their use changed to suit the market. The point at which this happens depends upon a number of factors which are often interrelated. The principal elements to be considered are normally:

- External envelope – roof and walls
- Internal fabric and structure (including the pool tank in pools)
- Environmental services and communications
- Plant
- Problems arising from the existing construction
- The success or otherwise of any past repair works.

The building's structure, fabric and systems should be assessed against current building regulations, relevant codes and standards and all other appropriate safety or other guidelines. If original drawings and specifications are available they can be used for guidance, but the actual contents of facilities should be verified by physical checks – very few buildings remain completely unaltered for long – and if necessary a measured survey undertaken. A thorough understanding of the building will enable the designer to plan the refurbishment works more effectively. It is therefore desirable for the condition of the building to be assessed by the design team which will be responsible for any upgrading, although it is often helpful to obtain

care should be taken to review internal air movement levels to ensure that sufficient fresh air is circulated to all internal areas as recommended by the Chartered Institution of Building Services Engineers (CIBSE) code and the relevant chapters of this volume (see in particular Chapters 60 and 61).

- *To allow new uses of existing facilities* – for example, to make school sports facilities suitable for public use.
- *To improve internal environmental conditions.*

specialist help in relation to wet and dry rot and animal or insect infestation.

Finally, a detailed schedule of dilapidations should be prepared.

4.2 Constraints

Every refurbishment project will have far more constraints than a project on a green field site. These should be identified and understood at an early stage. The factors to consider normally include:

- *Budget* – the budget may be predetermined or generated by the design team. It should be based on an evaluation of existing operational costs against post-refurbishment costs. In that case it may be important to produce several alternative basic designs for capital and operational cost comparisons.

  Short-term financial considerations are often the major controlling factor in refurbishment projects. However, when the refurbishment works are complete, financial considerations and appraisals will change from short to long term. It is therefore important to evaluate the long-term logic of short-term repairs from the start of the project. If the refurbishment project is costing more than about two-thirds or three-quarters of the cost of rebuilding, a new building will probably be a better option.

  Building design teams have traditionally considered building costs without reference to the many other cost inputs. For refurbishment projects additional costs must also be evaluated and may include, for example, staffing costs, redundancy payments arising from prolonged shutdown periods plus start up and funding costs.
- *Shutdown period* – the building team will always benefit from a total shutdown during the work. The client/operator will often prefer to minimise this period but normally a compromise is achieved. Particular care is required for buildings that are both in use and at the same time are being refurbished. Safe separation of customers and staff from builders and their supplies is often difficult, but always necessary.
- *Appearance* – some parts of the existing building may be valued for their appearance, others will be unwelcome. Often the most unwelcome are important functionally. Chimneys, fuel tanks and delivery areas are difficult to disguise and expensive to replace.
- *Physical constraints* – a check should be made that the existing building, surrounding space, car park, access roads, service supply lines and drains are adequate for the proposed refurbished building and its future servicing requirements. In particular, a check should be made of the dimensional requirements for the different sports to be accommodated, including the standard of play to be achieved. Spaces can be filled and reduced far easier than extended. Diving facilities in pools will need special care.
- *Requirements of specific user groups*, for example schools, clubs and people with disablties. Accommodating some groups' requirements into a refurbished building can be difficult. In particular, the legislation affecting provision for the disabled in public buildings may require standards that are not easy to achieve. Compromises often have to be made and therefore it will be appropriate to involve key user groups so that they can participate in establishing priorities.

5 Progressing a refurbishment project

5.1 Contract documentation

Well considered contract documentation will always result in more accurate costing and a smoother construction process. However, for refurbishment projects, the prudent team will always allow for the possibility of hidden problems by including a sensible contingency and appointing an experienced Clerk of Works. Problems will then be identified with enough lead-in time for a capable design team and builder to devise a solution.

It is particularly important to incorporate particulars related to partial closure and resultant restricted working into the agreement with the contractor.

5.2 Constructional pitfalls

Common pitfalls which should be identified before work starts if at all possible include drains/structure/plant not being in the expected position, not being operational, not being the expected size, or being partially corroded but just operational. Not all of these pitfalls may be revealed in an initial survey while the building is in use.

The long-term shutdown of a pool complex will mean that consideration must be given to keeping the pool empty or full. Apart from a leaking pool tank, usually the most important factor relating to this area is the state of the pool tank finish. Is it to be retained or replaced? If it is being retained, then serious consideration should be given to keeping the tank full. Over a prolonged period of work, however, pool water will become stagnant and full of debris if left without protection or treatment.

Safety is also an important factor. Pools, empty or full, can be a major hazard in an unlit building site. Adequate precautions must be taken and included in the specification.

Protection of finishes to be retained is difficult if not adequately considered. Suspended ceilings are susceptible to physical damage and changes in temperature or humidity. Ceramic tiles are brittle and it can be difficult to remove building site debris. All removable items must be stored safely or they will be stolen.

It is easy for the responsibility for unnoticed defects arising from the original construction work to be passed on to the designers and builders involved with refurbishment projects. Any existing defects in the building which come to light at any time should be noted and investigated. It should not be assumed that simple remedies will always be adequate to overcome defects. For example, movement problems in brickwork can indicate a shortage of expansion joints; they could also mean lack of wall ties or inadequate foundations.

5.3 Phased projects

Refurbishment contracts that require phased handover will generally have a higher cost that those where a complete shutdown for the duration of the contract is acceptable. However, the operator may need to know the cost of both in order to evaluate the costs and benefits of a phased handover or the implications of keeping some facilities open to the public throughout the refurbishment process. If this is the case the contractor must be instructed to take particular care to protect the public during the contract period. Ideally this should involve regular liaison with the local authority Health and Safety Officer.

5.4 Commissioning and handover

Client pressure to speed up the handover of an almost completed building is often encouraged by contractors seeking release of retention monies. The design team should always resist this and insist on proper commissioning and completion of the works. Everyone should be warned of the consequences if this advice is disregarded.

5.5 Feedback

The completed building should be monitored so that the design team can evaluate and improve their service. The original objectives should be remembered.

5.6 General

Communications and records are critical in all complex projects. Letters should be circulated to all parties involved so everyone has the opportunity, obligation and responsibility to comment. A detailed record should be made of what is agreed, and circulated. It is essential that the client knows and approves of what he is getting and that the builder, including the subcontractors, know what they are providing. No grey areas should be left for misinterpretation.

5
Converted buildings

Geraint John

1 Background

The use of converted buildings for sport is expanding; other uses of the existing building stock are declining or changing and it is natural, therefore, that existing buildings provide a possible resource for the creation of new sport and recreation facilities.

However, this is a much deeper issue than simply putting old buildings to new uses: there is a whole layer of emotional, cultural and social factors which are involved. There is a growing concern within the population for its dwindling architectural heritage, and familiarity with surroundings is becoming more important in a changing world.

The opportunities for conversion, rehabilitation or re-use should be evaluated under three broad headings: the aesthetic/cultural, the community/social and the economic. There is a great deal of interest in recreational provision within the decaying inner-city areas, the areas of urban deprivation: the places where quality of life is low. It is, of course, precisely these areas where a large reservoir of disused existing building stock exists, where buildings lie derelict for want of a new use.

In England there is priority for schemes which are local in character. The answer for these 'round the corner' facilities can often be found by conversion or adaptation.

2 Aesthetic/cultural aspects

It has already been suggested that redundant buildings can represent a resource of labour and materials which we may ill afford to squander. It is impossible to quantify the value of preserving an architectural landmark in our changing society: even an aesthetically ugly building can be regarded with affection by a local community and certainly represents an existing economic investment. There may also be a contribution to a townscape. Society has already decided that it must make efforts to preserve some of its significant architectural buildings (in the UK by listing and grading them) and re-use may be the only practical answer to conservation. When buildings are of architectural importance, the design problems of conversion become more difficult to solve as the aesthetic character must not be spoiled. This obviously limits the potential. Building for recreational use can make heavy demands: big spaces, heavy robust use, good lighting and services will all need to be incorporated.

3 The needs of sport and recreation

Any building with the potential for re-use must be looked at in terms of the need and location: the proposed facility should be justified by a demonstrable need. Nevertheless, sometimes opportunities are taken that ultimately create and satisfy a demand which would have been difficult to predict.

1 *St Marks, Deptford, London, is a redundant church which was retained as a landmark in an area redevelopment scheme. The conversion inserted an extra storey into the nave to provide an activity space in the upper level. An interesting aspect of the conversion is the retention of part of the original building as a chapel; thus the building retains something of its original identity. Architects: Raymond J Cecil & Partners*

2 *Pocklington Station, Yorkshire, was built in 1845 and closed in 1965. It was listed Grade II because of its historic and architectural interest. The building was purchased from the local authority by Pocklington School, which converted it into a sports building for the school and local community. A sports hall was created where the tracks had run, with changing, refreshment and storage areas in the waiting rooms, booking hall and other accommodation. Architects: Arthur Quarmby Associates*

Some buildings are located at traditional assembly sites, well served by existing public transport and close to public services. Demolition and rebuilding on such a site could well mean that the costs, especially land costs, would put a scheme beyond the resources available to recreation.

A conversion may dictate that standards lower than those demanded by the Sports Council(s) or the equivalent National Sports Agency and the governing bodies of sport will have to be tolerated. This must be judged on the specific case. Occasionally the introduction of local rules can adequately provide for recreational play: after all, this is a function of the essentially local provision (though there may be notable exceptions), which most of these facilities will represent.

3 *Interior of Pocklington Sports Hall*

4 Economics

Cost is obviously of crucial importance, both in capital and recurrent terms. Low capital-cost conversions can mean high running costs in terms of management, maintenance, supervision, heating and ventilation. If, at the same time, the overall nature and dimensions of the building produce a limited result for the user the project must be questioned.

If also the limited capital cannot produce an aesthetically sound scheme, then the disadvantages may begin to outweigh the advantages. It is not possible to generalise about conversion costs because of widely differing situations, but this aspect should not be underestimated.

The basic construction should be sound and worthy and capable of conversion.

5 Statutory controls related to conversions

As well as sometimes providing facilities themselves, local authorities, together with other statutory bodies, control the development as a planning authority and administrator of regulations and local byelaws concerning constructional, environmental and safety standards. Though not exhaustive, the following sections give an indication of some aspects of conversion schemes that might be affected.

5.1 Planning

Buildings of architectural or historic interest are given special protection and assistance in many countries. Legislation should be checked with the relevant local and national bodies.

5.2 Building construction

Standards of construction, including structural stability and fire resistance, are controlled by local authorities (in the UK through the Building Regulations).

5.3 Public health

Means of escape from public buildings, including standards of provision for escape routes and emergency lighting, must be considered. Advice on these standards and on appropriate fire-fighting equipment should be sought from the local fire authority and fire prevention officer at an early stage. They may be particularly important where the building is likely to be used for public entertainment or where additional floors are proposed.

5.4 Licensing

Where a building is to be used as a place of public entertainment, for such activities as film shows, dances and discos, an entertainments licence must be obtained.

4 *Fort Regent. The conversion of a nineteenth-century Fort in Jersey, built in the Napoleonic wars, roofed and converted into a sports hall. Photo: British Steel Corporation*

5 *External view of mill buildings converted to recreational use at Rayleigh, Essex. Photo: Geraint John*

6 *Exterior view of Hexham Swimming Pool. This nineteenth-century wool warehouse was a building of some quality in an historic town. It has been converted into a 25 m indoor swimming pool, learner pool, and hall with ancillary accommodation. Architects: Napper, Errington & Collerton. Photo: James Riddell*

7 *Interior view of the converted warehouse. Photo: James Riddell*

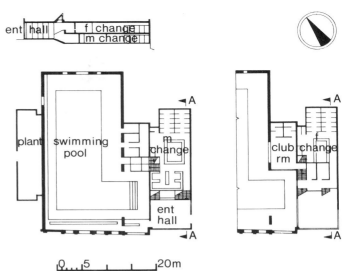

8 *Ground and first floor plans of Hexham Swimming Pool*

For a full licence in the UK the requirements of the licensing authorities with regard to toilet and escape provision may well exceed those of the Public Health and Fire Precautions Acts. If, as in most cases, such use is likely to be intermittent, there would be some advantage in basing provision on applications for an occasional licence where the requirements are less onerous. If a licensed bar

is to be provided, approval must be sought from the licensing justices or court.

5.5 Users with disabilities

All public buildings must allow reasonable access to and provision for people with disabilities, including appropriate signposting. Many older buildings with stepped entrances and narrow doorways may demand special consideration in detailing. Ideally a converted building should meet the standards required for a new facility. (Refer to Technical Study 7.)

5.6 Administration

Whether or not the building is permanently staffed, some office space will be needed for administration and bookings. In such cases, office and toilet space must be provided in accordance with the requirements of the relevant legislation.

5.7 Statutory undertakers

A change of use may entail the provision of new gas, water and electricity supplies which will have to be installed in accordance with the relevant authority's regulations.

5.8 Parking

Adequate parking will sometimes create a difficulty in dealing with converted buildings, particularly in urban sites. The solution to this must be considered in consultation with the local planning authority.

6 Redundant churches and chapels

The greatest need for local facilities exists in inner-city areas and sparsely populated country districts. It is precisely in these areas where, precipitated by population shifts, many churches and chapels are being made redundant. This building type had the advantage of representing a recognisable and central meeting place for local communities, many of which do not want such buildings demolished.

In the UK churches and chapels are becoming redundant in substantial numbers and some are dimensionally suitable for sports use – particularly the larger Victorian churches in decaying urban areas. One good example of a church which has survived by converting parts of its premises to other activities is St Mark's at Deptford in London. Threatened with demolition, the

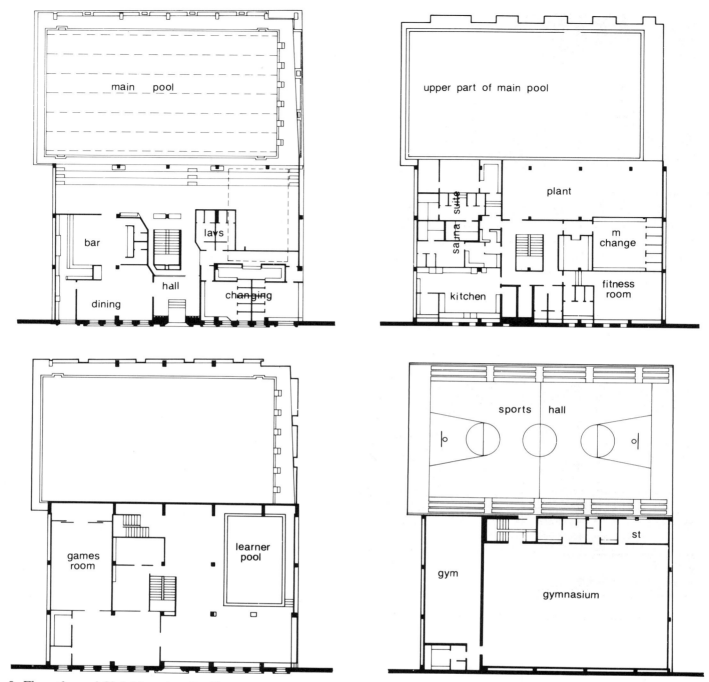

9 *Floor plans of Club Natacion, Seville, which was converted to provide a community sports building.*

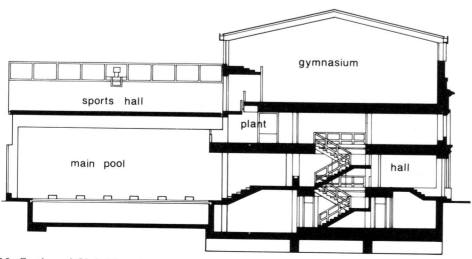

10 *Section of Club Natacion*

11 *Vethoulder Verheij. An interesting conversion of an obsolete gasholder in Amsterdam into a sports centre. The circular roof was inspired by Nervi's structures for the 1960 Rome Olympics. Photo: Helen Heard*

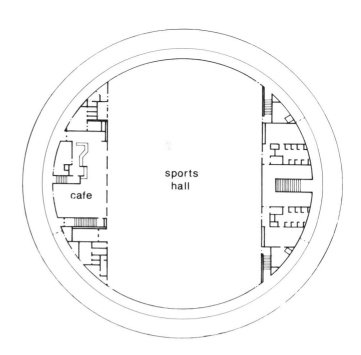

12 *Interior view of the sports hall. Photo: Helen Heard*

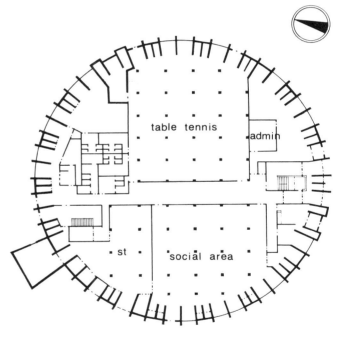

13 *Plans of the upper and lower floors of Vethoulder Verheij*

church decided on this radical solution and the original use survives in partnership with new life.

Parking provision demanded by the planning authority should be considered.

Religious buildings of different denominations may be protected by legislation and this needs to be investigated.

There is also the question of appropriate use and the design for the new uses in dealing with former religious buildings. The architectural handling of this situation must be undertaken with some sensitivity. It may well be that some former religious buildings are simply not suitable for a sports and recreational re-use and the designer will have a key role in helping to make what may sometimes be very difficult decisions.

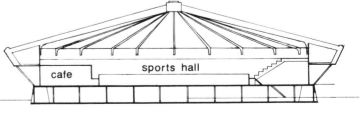

14 *Section of Vethoulder Verheij*

6
Maintenance

Eifion Roberts

1 Introduction

There are about 1300 public swimming pools in the UK; about 125 were built before 1914 and a similar number between 1914 and 1940; only a handful between 1940 and 1960 and almost half of all existing pools between 1961 and 1990. Indoor sports centres are a comparatively new feature in the UK and few were built prior to about 1968; thereafter, some 350 were provided between about 1968 and 1974. The synthetic sports surface is also a relative newcomer to the UK; it is estimated that about 320 have now been laid, about 120 athletic tracks and 200 pitches, most during the 1980s.

Sporting activities are infinitely varied and some are also of a highly specialised character. These days, a number of sports activities take place in buildings that are supplied with very sophisticated plant and services. Given these circumstances it is not possible in a volume of this kind to set out details of maintenance operations that will be required within these richly varied circumstances.

Provided the general principles indicated later are followed however, there should be little difficulty in dealing with maintenance issues. Such action should lead to facilities that will be at all times safe to use, fit for their purpose and a continuing asset to both the community and the sports people they are intended to serve.

2 Characteristics of maintenance

2.1 Definition

Building Maintenance is defined in BS 8210: 1986 *British Standard Guide to Building Maintenance Management* as,

> Work, other than daily and routine cleaning, necessary to maintain the performance of the building fabric and its services.

An earlier definition, contained in BS 3811: 1964 *Glossary of Maintenance Management Terms in Terotechnology*, referred to work undertaken to keep or restore a facility to an acceptable standard.

2.2 Factors affecting the need for maintenance

It is not possible to construct a building that is entirely maintenance free. All the elements of a building deteriorate at varying rates, depending upon such matters as component quality, location, juxtaposition to other elements, the degree of exposure and the use.

In this regard, the original design, specification and construction are all of crucial importance to future performance and maintenance liability. For this reason it is highly desirable to obtain some appropriate specialist maintenance input into the design process. Unhappily, this rarely occurs.

2.3 Types of maintenance

Maintenance can be characterised as either planned, preventative activity or unplanned. BS 8210: 1986 defines planned maintenance as:

> Maintenance organised and carried out with forethought, control and the use of records, to a predetermined plan based on the results of previous condition surveys.

Planned maintenance is usually more effective in terms of quality and cost, although it would probably be uneconomic to remove the need for unplanned activity altogether. The art is to seek the most effective economic balance between the two. In particular, the former has the added benefit of allowing work to be carried out at the most suitable time and within an agreed budget framework. It also avoids abortive work by taking into account such matters as proposed alterations and improvements, plant shutdown periods and cyclical repainting. Over a period of time it should also reduce the incidence of unplanned activity.

2.4 Standards of maintenance

Standards are difficult to define. Where there are statutory requirements they are clearly the minimum acceptable standard. Within the context of building maintenance generally, however, except perhaps in relation to engineering equipment and services, legislation tends to be silent in regard to standards. Standards are either dealt with indirectly by reference to health, safety or welfare issues or by a typically British reference to reasonableness.

The long-term utility and value of any building or structure depend, crucially, upon the following factors:

- The quality of the original design and specification
- The quality of the original construction
- The effectiveness of maintenance.

It therefore follows that the minimum acceptable standard of maintenance is that which sustains the utility and value of the facility at all times. Furthermore, the consideration of standard will also need to take account of periodic upgrading and improvement as technical developments occur and social factors change, if the primary considerations are to be fully satisfied.

3 The general maintenance situation

It is an unfortunate fact that maintenance is a sadly neglected charge. The results of this neglect are often easy to confirm by casual observation. Examples abound: dilapidated buildings of all kinds; dirty, poorly decorated and outmoded facilities; unreliable transport and litter. Sports facilities do not escape this general criticism.

A number of publications have sought to highlight the huge backlog of maintenance and the serious consequences arising from this, both of which are direct and inevitable results of a lack of concern. In the UK an Audit Commission report on local authority property management, for example, highlighted the problems resulting from underfunding of housing maintenance, as well as the woeful lack of knowledge by authorities concerning their estate of properties generally. This report forecasts that maintenance expenditure will have to rise dramatically as the stock of properties ages. It referred to this as a 'maintenance time-bomb ticking away'.

Other publications lend support to these views. They also make the point that the size of the maintenance backlog represents poor asset management.

There are suggestions that further research into maintenance issues could be a catalyst for improvement in maintenance generally. Indeed, it might be noted that there appears to be very little research directed towards strategic maintenance issues.

3.1 Developments in the maintenance of sports facilities

The UK Audit Commissions's point about the ageing of the building stock has a particular application to sports facilities.

As indicated in the opening paragraph, the UK has, by and large, an ageing stock of sports facilities. Many of these now require both major repairs as well as upgrading. The question of upgrading is particularly relevant not only in terms of the building fabric but also energy management and environmental factors.

The world is currently passing through a period of severe recession and there is extreme pressure on spending right across the board. This is having, and likely to continue to have, a severe impact upon the availability of sports facilities. At the same time there is rising public demand for quality provision coupled with changes in demography, trends in working and leisure patterns and a host of other factors which lead to a need for additional provision. The only reasonable conclusion to be drawn is the need to put in place, as a matter of urgency, a phased programme of major repairs and renovations to existing facilities throughout the next decade. The objective should be to extend their useful life into the first decades of the next century. But of equal importance is the need to press the case for sound ongoing maintenance. Whether a new facility comes on stream, or an upgraded facility comes back into full use, the maintenance of that facility needs to be recognised as a priority commitment throughout its economic life cycle. Only by pressing this case shall we break the past cycle of large capital investment, followed by neglect, leading to underutilisation or total loss to the community, then a further large injection of capital at the start of yet another depressing cycle.

The bottom line is that sound regular maintenance makes economic sense.

3.2 Maintenance management for sports facilities

The maintenance of sports facilities, discounting the need for upgrading referred to before, is generally little different in character to the situation already outlined.

An effective maintenance management process for sports facilities will therefore require the following:

- *Detailed knowledge of the facility*. This applies to the structure, plant and engineering services, equipment and the land within the curtilage. With an existing facility, this will include a knowledge of its current condition – including commissioning condition surveys if necessary – and a study of its past maintenance history. For a new facility, it is essential that 'as built' drawings should be provided by the design/construction team. These should include the layout of all plant and services with the position of all valves, controls and the like shown; full schedules of all plant and equipment installed; details of manufacturers' recommended maintenance procedures; and plant and equipment operating manuals. Together, these documents should identify in detail all materials and components incorporated into the facility. It is of the utmost importance that the supply of the above items is incorporated as a term within the contracts drawn up with the design and construction teams. It is equally important that these terms should be rigorously enforced.
- *An appropriate level of budget for all maintenance matters*. This must be based upon the carefully established needs of the facility and not upon some hypothetical historic basis – where management decrees, for example, that it shall be last year's figure plus a bit for inflation.
- *Skills*. Responsibility for maintenance to be vested in, or delegated to, someone with the appropriate knowledge and skills to discharge the duties in an effective way.
- *Systems*. A satisfactory management accounting system to plan and control the volume, quality and cost of the work required and to provide feedback to inform future planning.

7
Facilities for people with disabilities

Neil Thomson

1 Introduction

1.1 Changing attitudes

The last two decades have seen a significant change in the social position of people with disabilities and this has led to generally beneficial legislation. Regulations and guidelines relating to access within the built environment are being continually improved and extended. Thus, building designers are being encouraged to design for the whole community rather than just the average man or woman. New legislation is also beginning to look at the need to improve existing buildings and facilities.

A consideration of the needs of people with disabilities should now be a natural part of any design and planning process and all building management and maintenance policies. The following recommendations and comments are not intended to repeat regulations or provide comprehensive guidance but simply to serve as a reminder of some of the more important points to be considered. Designers are advised to consult *Sports and Recreation Provision for Disabled People*, edited by Neil Thomson, for more detailed guidance.

1.2 Sport for all

Sport is an activity which can be enjoyed by people of all ages and abilities, whether by participation or through spectating. All sports buildings and spaces should therefore be designed to cater for all potential users whatever their degree of mobility or impairment. Everyone can experience difficulties in coping with the built environment in certain situations. A well designed barrier-free environment will benefit everyone and not just those who are conventionally labelled as 'disabled'.

Very few sports and recreational activities are exclusive to so-called able-bodied people. It is now accepted that blind and partially sighted people, wheelchair users, people with deafness or hearing impairment, limbless people and those with other mobility restrictions and people with learning difficulties all participate in water sports, field and track events, outdoor pursuits and indoor games. This ranges from casual leisure activity to serious international and Olympic competition.

1.3 Consultation

A programme of consultation with disabled people at all critical stages in the planning and design process is perhaps the most important requirement. Even with close adherence to the latest regulations and guidelines mistakes can still be made by a designer working in isolation.

Consultation should take place with organisations of disabled people interested in sport and the local authority's Access Officer who can be a key figure in obtaining planning approval. National bodies (such as the British Sports Association for the Disabled in the UK) can be approached who will either advise directly or put forward more local or specialised groups. Local groups will often have particular needs and preferences which should be taken into account in the design of local community facilities.

2 Differing needs

The needs of people with different disabilities and who use different mobility or sensory aids can vary enormously. There is not space here to describe these needs properly, but the following notes will provide some useful pointers.

2.1 Wheelchair users

These can range from being independently mobile athletes to elderly people needing to be pushed at all times. Three common constraints determine basic design requirements:

- Lower level and limited reach – determines heights of controls and counters
- Width of wheelchair – wider than standing person – determines door and passage widths
- Can only go where wheels can go – determines need for lifts and shallow ramps to negotiate level changes.

2.2 Ambulant disabled

People who are able to walk may depend on other mobility aids or be unable to manage stairs or door handles and other fitments. Most improvements made for wheelchair users will be beneficial but sometimes different provision is required, for example steps as well as ramps and narrower WC cubicles.

2.3 Deaf and hard of hearing

There are many variations in quality and amount of hearing loss. Good acoustics are necessary for people who

1 *There are many kinds of disabilities in those who participate*

are hard of hearing to distinguish speech from background noise. Good lighting is necessary for deaf people to lip read, through ticket office screens for example.

Good communication is perhaps the most important issue; clear consistent signposting and visual information and warnings are essential. Use of induction loops and amplifiers should be considered for users of hearing aids particularly in stadia and arenas.

2.4 Blind and partially sighted
The majority of people with visual impairment have some sight, and good lighting, large clear signs and colour contrast are important. Avoidance of hazards is essential, especially projections between waist and head height, loose obstacles and columns in circulation routes. Changes in surface textures on floors and pavements can indicate hazards. Raised letters and braille on signs and lift controls should be provided.

Sound clues are useful for orientation. Avoid large open-plan and non-rectangular areas if possible. Good acoustics and clear audible information announcements and warnings are essential. Consider producing raised tactile maps for large buildings and outdoor areas. Allow for guide dogs to accompany some blind people. Sports facilities should be well serviced by public transport as blind people obviously cannot drive. Safe comprehensible external routes and footpaths are essential.

2.5 People with learning difficulties and other special needs
Buildings and spaces should be easily comprehensible and good signposting and avoidance of hazards will benefit everyone. Facilities such as toilets and changing rooms should allow for accompanied use.

3 External areas

3.1 Site, vehicle access and parking
Whenever possible, sites for sports facilities should be selected to be level rather than hilly or undulating and well served by nearby public transport.

There should be generous parking provision and at least 5% of bays should be clearly marked as reserved for disabled users. Reserved bays should be as close as possible to the building or facility entrance and never more than 40 m away. There is a case for grouping them separately from the main car park as this lessens the risk of unauthorised use. The surface should be tarmacadam or similar and well drained but virtually level, and should preferably be level with adjoining footpaths, or well provided with ramped kerbs.

There should be good vehicle access to the site and a clearly marked drop-off point for cars and coaches provided adjacent to the main entrance, preferably with a weather protective canopy.

3.2 Footpaths and ramps
If changes in level along external routes are unavoidable then ramps should be provided which should not normally be steeper than 1 in 20. Ramps should *never* be steeper than 1 in 12 and if more than 1 in 20 steps should also be provided alongside; handrails should be provided to both sides of the ramp and steps.

Footpaths and ramps should be a minimum width of 1.2 m (approx 4 ft) and preferably a minimum of 2 m (approx 6.5 ft), to allow for wheelchairs to pass safely. Surfaces should be firm, smooth and slip-resistant. Jointed surfaces such as paving slabs are not recommended, but where provided should be laid flush on a well consolidated base.

Ramps should have a 100 mm (approx 4 in) kerb on all exposed edges. Level areas at least 1.8 m (approx 6 ft) long should be provided at every 10 m (approx 33 ft) in length and at the top and bottom of any ramp.

If footpaths are level with vehicle and activity areas they should have clearly marked edges with colour and texture contrasts. If there are raised kerbs, ramped kerbs should be provided at crossings, with a maximum 1 in 10 gradient and a contrast in colour and surface texture. Seating should be provided at regular intervals and all routes should have good external lighting.

3.3 Signposting
All external areas should have clear and consistent signposting with a minimum of wording. Signs should indicate all accessible routes, entrances, activity areas and facilities.

3.4 Outdoor sports and recreational areas
All outdoor activity areas can normally be made accessible to disabled users. Athletics tracks, for example, need no adaptation for wheelchair racing so long as there is suitable level access on to the track and it has a synthetic surface. Stands, terraces and viewing or resting areas should all be provided with a sufficient amount of level area with good unobstructed views. Toilets and changing areas should all be accessible.

Many other kinds of outdoor activities can be enjoyed by people of all abilities if proper care is taken at the design and planning stage. To mention a few examples, accessible fishing platforms can be provided on river banks and canal sides; ramped mounting platforms can be provided in riding schools; adventure play areas can be designed to stimulate children with very limited mobility and learning difficulties; countryside nature trails can be provided with tapping rails and listening posts for blind people and bird-watching hides can be designed with ramped entrances and wheelchair height viewing slots.

4 Indoor facilities

4.1 Entrance
Main entrances should be clearly recognisable, well signposted and protected from the weather. Approaches should be level if possible and with alternative steps and handrails if ramped. Thresholds should be level and a minimum 900 mm (approx 3 ft) clear opening width should be provided. Care must be taken in detailing door furniture, matwells, closing devices, etc to allow for easy use by all potential users. Automatic sliding doors should be installed in larger buildings. Entrance doors should be glazed for good visibility from a sitting position but not fully glazed without warning bars or stripes.

Draught lobbies should be of sufficient size to allow unimpeded access for wheelchair users. Reception areas should be spacious to allow for orientation and waiting. Desks and counters should be in obvious positions and at a usable height from a wheelchair (and for children). Provide adequate seating. Telephones should be at wheelchair accessible height and with special facilities for people with sensory disabilities.

4.2 Internal circulation
All areas should be fully accessible, including staff areas. Small changes in level should be avoided and lifts as well

as staircases should be provided to all floors and levels above or below entrance level. Staircases should be designed in accordance with current Building Regulations.

Building layouts should be designed in full consultation with Fire Officers and should allow for 'refuges' and other precautions allowing easy escape in case of fire for people with disabilities. (See BS 5588: Part 8 *Means of Escape for Disabled People* for relevant UK legislation.)

Lifts should have internal dimensions of at least 1.4 m depth × 1.1 m width (approx 4.5 × 3.6 ft), to accommodate a single wheelchair and helper. Larger lifts with 1.4 × 1.6 m (approx 4.5 × 5.25 ft) internal dimensions are preferred, particularly in centres where teams of wheelchair users may be playing in a match and may wish to travel to a refreshment area on an upper level. Controls should be at a height of 1–1.4 m (approx 3.3–4.5 ft) and have raised digits; doors should give a clear opening width of 800 mm (approx 31 in) minimum and be controlled by a photo-electric cell and audible floor level announcements should be provided for blind people.

Corridors should be a minimum of 1.2 m wide (approx 4 ft, although 1.5 m (approx 5 ft) is preferable, and handrails should be provided on major routes.

Doors should not normally open on to corridors although this does happen with some activity areas. In such cases adequate protection and space for manoeuvre must be provided. Doors between corridors should also be easily accessible.

Standard 900 mm (approx 3 ft) wide doorsets will satisfy most situations. Door closers where required should be adjusted to low pressure and preferably of the delayed action type. Lever handles should be fitted in preference to knobs and most doors should incorporate toughened or wire glazed vision panels down to a maximum height of 1.01 m (approx 3.3 ft) above the floor, as well as kick plates 400 mm (approx 16 in) high.

To assist people with impaired vision all projections from walls such as litter bins should be avoided. Flooring should be smooth but non-slip. Contrasts in floor finishes (colour and texture) can be helpful to indicate circulation routes and different activity areas.

4.3 Changing rooms, toilets and showers

Open plan and team changing rooms with bench and transfer seating are adequate for many disabled users, although some family sized unisex changing rooms which incorporate shower, WC and basin should also be provided. These are obviously appreciated by families as well as people with disabilities who may have helpers of the opposite sex.

Access from changing areas to activity areas should be level and as short as possible. Shower areas should have level access and incorporate handrails, folding seats and controls at a height accessible from wheelchairs. Toilets in changing areas should incorporate at least one designed for wheelchair use.

All public buildings should incorporate at least one unisex wheelchair accessible toilet compartment designed to BS 5810, preferably adjacent to the main entrance area. Babycare facilities should also be provided for parents and carers of both sexes.

4.4 Signposting

Clear and consistent directional signposting is essential to all users of sports buildings and especially for people with sensory disabilities. Of particular importance are signs for accessible routes, toilets, lifts and any special services for people with disabilities. Notice boards giving details of current and special events and programmes should be

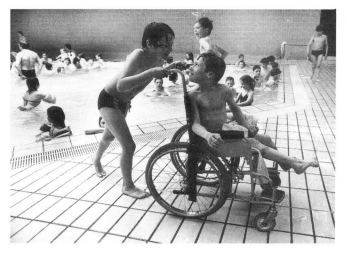

2 *Access to swimming pool facilities is important*

3 *Wheelchair basketball is a very popular and demanding sport*

prominently displayed, well lit and at a height readable by people in wheelchairs.

4.5 Activity areas

Detailed guidance on the design of particular areas can be found in *Sports and Recreation Provision for Disabled People* edited by Neil Thomson.

Swimming pools are of particular importance, water being an element which allows many people to be mobile when they would otherwise be confined to a wheelchair or have to use some other aid or prosthesis. The entrance, changing rooms and poolside should all be on the same level and obstructions such as footbaths must be avoided. Hoist sockets should be provided on the poolside. The pool edge must be clearly defined (colour and texture contrast). Ramped entry to the water (with handrails each side) is useful in addition to steps, and electric platform lifts have now been designed which can operate under water, giving direct wheelchair access. Where pools are fitted with movable floors these can be constructed so that the upper level is flush with the poolside, thus enabling easy access.

Most indoor sports halls and other activity areas need little modification, but wall surfaces must be flush and special equipment and markings can be provided for activities such as goal ball for blind players, wheelchair basketball and wheelchair fencing. Bowls is an activity which people with disabilities can take part in on equal terms with able-bodied people so long as wheelchair access is provided on to the green.

4.6 Social areas and spectator facilities

Social areas such as restaurants, snack bars and licensed bars have gained significantly in importance and must be accessible to all visitors with disabilities. In viewing galleries, rails should be positioned so as not to interrupt views for people in wheelchairs. All spectator areas should include provision for wheelchair users and be accessible without steps.

5 Stadia and arenas

Stadia and arenas are spectator facilities with special requirements for people with disabilities. These are set out in Vol. 1, Technical Study 22 and in *Designing for Spectators with Disabilities*, published by the Sports Council.

6 References

Barker, P, *Key Features of Good Design*, Royal National Institute for the Blind, London (1992).

Council of Europe, *European Charter on Sport for All: Disabled Persons*, Council of Europe, Strasbourg (1987).

Football Stadia Advisory Design Council, *Designing for spectators with disabilities*, Football Stadia Advisory Design Council, London (1992).

Lawn Tennis Association, *Tennis Centres: Designing for People with Disabilities*, Lawn Tennis Association, London (1994)

Sports Council, *Sports and Recreation Provision for Disabled People*, Sports Council, London (1984).

Thomson, N, *Sports and Recreation Provision for Disabled People*, London: Architectural Press/Disabled Living Foundation, London (1984)

Thorpe, S, *Sports and Leisure Facilities*, Centre for Accessible Environments, London (1992).

US Dept of Health Education and Welfare, *Recreation and Leisure for Handicapped Individuals*. Resource guide, US Dept of Health Education and Welfare (1979).

8
Planning for sport and recreation

Mike Fitzjohn and David Payne

1 Introduction

The purpose of the section is to provide a summary checklist of relevant considerations in planning for sport and recreation; it is necessarily wide ranging, seeking to embrace planning from the national/strategic to local facility levels in a world-wide context. It is important to stress, however, that irrespective of context, the planning *process* for sport and recreation is no different from any other form of planning.

2 Why plan?

At its simplest a plan sets out a considered way forward to guide future development. There are many reasons why a planned approach to the development of sport and recreation is necessary and beneficial. They include:

- Political and social systems which believe in intervention to help ensure that resources are owned and distributed equitably amongst the population. In short, a planned approach will help to create and develop opportunities for people to participate – the philosophy which underpins 'Sport for All'
- To set clear directions and accommodate change. A planned approach will present a clear view of key longer-term goals, thereby enabling short-term changes to be evaluated in a broader context
- To make clear to others what is important in sport and recreation and to indicate courses of action which they should pursue to implement the plan

2.1 Whose plan and who does the work?
If the plan affects the interests of several organisations, it will often be sensible for them to come together at the outset in order to prepare it jointly; this will improve the 'ownership' of the plan and help ensure its successful implementation. Whether or not the plan has such multiple sponsors it will be necessary to give early consideration to who might do the work. If the sponsoring agency has sufficient resources of money, time and staff expertise it may wish to carry out the work itself. Alternatively it may wish to place a contract with a consultant, which will have the advantage of bringing an independent view to the task. A third approach is to combine the independent and technical skills of consultants with the practical and detailed knowledge of the sponsor's staff jointly to carry out the work.

2.2 Setting objectives
The decision to prepare a plan will have been triggered by a perceived problem, eg a shortage of stadia, insufficient water space or the need to improve sports centres. One or more objectives should be derived for the plan; they should

be as clear and precise as possible. They might include such issues as:

- Whether the plan is designed to cater for high level performers and competition, for community participation, or both
- Whether there is a need for additional new provision or for improving existing provision
- Whether the plan should deal with built facilities, improved management (especially for countryside issues), other relevant matters, such as the needs for coaching staff, or a combination of these
- The specific sports, geographical areas and people for which the plan is designed.

2.3 Context
No plan can be produced in a vacuum; there will be a wide range of factors, most external to sport, which will need to be considered and may affect the plan. They might include such matters as:

- Climate and geography; particularly for outdoor facilities
- Political priorities – eg the wish to bid for an Olympic Games or other major international competitions
- The state of the economy and the availability of financial, human and material resources
- Demography – eg size, distribution, age structure, ethnic groupings, role of women
- Natural resources – their availability for sport and recreation and the convergence/divergence with other policy goals for such resources
- Other policy goals, opportunities and constraints – eg health, planning, agricultural diversification
- Relevant legislation – eg education, recreation, health and safety
- The existing framework of national, regional and local plans – the plan will need to be consistent with broader scale plans and also set a clear framework for more detailed plans.

It will be necessary to examine recent trends, the current position and likely future trends in each of these factors. In the light of this analysis it may also be necessary to modify the objectives.

2.4 Sporting background
Having examined the external environment it will be necessary to consider the more detailed sporting background. This might include such matters as:

- Sporting structures – history and traditions
- Sectoral mix – public, voluntary and commercial; partnerships and relationships amongst the three
- Client markets – the 'public' generally or specific groups
- Identification of requirements – eg surveys of need, consumer preferences
- Existing participation rates – how many, who, what, when, why?
- Existing facility provision: eg condition, costs, competition
- Related resources – management, coaching and administrative staff availability and skills
- Market trends – eg short term 'fads' or long-term interests, conventional versus leisure pools
- Constraints and conflicts – competing claims on resources, eg other land uses in the countryside.

As with the external environment, past and future trends will need to be analysed and, as a result, it may be necessary to modify objectives.

2.5 Preparing the plan

A wide range of techniques, from the simple to the sophisticated, are available for analysing the assembled material and developing the plan. However, all such techniques are based on one of two broad approaches:

- A 'standards' approach, such as one facility per 50,000 population. This has the advantage of clarity and simplicity, but is likely to miss local nuances and detail.
- A 'local assessment', essentially based on a more sophisticated modelling of local factors which affect the demand for and supply of facilities. This approach is more sensitive to local circumstances, but is more costly of resources than the first alternative.

2.6 Key planning concepts

In preparing the plan there are a number of key planning concepts which are likely to feature. These include:

- Multiple use – the ability to integrate the planned use with both other sporting uses and other land uses, eg agriculture or nature conservation in the countryside
- Accessibility – both physical, eg for people with disabilities and for relevant transport modes, and social, eg for potential users who may, for whatever reason, find it difficult to identify with the planned provision
- Environmental considerations – the aesthetics of the built environment and sustainable uses of the natural environment
- Whole life costs – both of buildings, and their costs in use, eg management, staffing, pricing structures
- Location and site suitability – this should be determined by the planning process outlined above and not simply by considerations of land availability and cost
- Liaison and consultation – the chances of any plan proving effective in achieving its objectives and acceptable to relevant interests will be greatly enhanced if those most directly affected by it, eg sports users or the local community, are genuinely involved in its preparation rather than presented with a 'fait accompli'.

2.7 Developing alternatives and choosing the optimum

In many cases it will be possible to identify more than one plan which relates the identified needs to the objectives set and the resources available. In such instances it will be necessary to choose the optimum solution. This will in part be a technical process, involving greater detailing of the options in order that they can be more thoroughly evaluated, and in part a political process involving the community, its elected representatives and other relevant interests.

3 Implementation

Depending on the scale of the plan, implementation will vary from achieving national political and policy change at one extreme to the detailed briefing of the architect/designer at the other. The speed with which any plan can be implemented will be crucially dependent on the resources of finance, manpower and materials.

4 Monitoring and review

Once implemented it is important that performance is monitored against the objectives established at the outset. Again dependent on scale, such monitoring may involve the implementation of policy, the achievement of management objectives (such as for natural resources in the countryside), the performance of buildings and the satisfaction of users. In the light of such monitoring it may be necessary to amend the objectives, modify buildings or management regimes and possible recommence the planning process with a view to making additional provision to meet unmet demand.

5 References and further advice

The Sports Council, and related organisations, have published many detailed reports on planning for sport and recreation at the national, regional and local levels. The reader seeking specific advice is advised to obtain such publications. See for example:

Sports Council, *Sport in the Community: Into the 90s*, Sports Council, London (1988).

Regional Councils for Sport and Recreation, *Regional Recreation Strategies* (1985–1991).

Sports Council, *District Sport and Recreation Strategies – A Guide*, Sports Council, London (1991).

Sports Council/The National Playing Fields Association/The Central Council of Physical Recreation, *The Playing Pitch Strategy*, Sports Council, London (1991).

9
Joint provision and dual use facilities

Geraint John

1 Joint provision

'Joint provision' and 'dual use' are terms which refer to the development and use of facilities by school and community. They represent an integrated approach to the planning, design and management of sports and recreation facilities so that both may use and benefit from them: the educational establishment itself and the wider community of which it forms part.

Joint provision schemes can ensure optimum use of expensive facilities and enable the community to share the benefits flowing from the large capital investment in educational buildings and sites. The concept is by now well established and proven by use.

The Education Acts of 1986 and 1988 in England and Wales, and the introduction of the local management of schools, is changing the relationships in current and new joint provision schemes. There is a new role for Governors and Head Teachers and potentially a new independence from the Education Authority. The exact legal position remains unclear and could affect existing and planned schemes. The latest information sources should be consulted before embarking on a scheme.

2 Finance

A good joint scheme between an education authority (or, alternatively, the governing body of a grant-maintained school) and other authorities can offer facilities which none of the parties could afford separately. Such a scheme also constitutes a desirable use of limited resources both in terms of capital investment and of land. Education authorities and local councils can therefore win considerable benefit for themselves and the community whenever new schools are planned, or existing facilities replanned, by incorporating the joint provision principle.

In England and Wales the administrative background to such schemes is that the Education (School Premises) Regulations set minimum requirements for schools. Between the lower limit set by these Regulations and the upper limit set by the financial resources available, the local education authorities have room to manoeuvre in the detailed design and construction of schools. The funds which the local education authority devotes to facilities for physical education depend on the educational brief and local factors. But it must be understood that extra finance for the provision of a joint sports/recreational facility must come from the other partner(s) in the scheme. This may include contributions from voluntary sources.

Maintenance costs should be shared on an agreed basis, which should reflect the degree of use made of the facilities by each member of the joint enterprise. Consultation and co-operation between the local education authority, any

partner authority, and third or other partners in the enterprise will clearly be essential.

2.1 Phased development

In a climate of financial restraint there can be difficulties in co-ordinating local authority and educational budgets, but every attempt should be made to overcome them.

One means of achieving this is by creating a phased development, so that the school facilities can be provided to fit in with the educational budget, but the opportunities are not lost for a properly conceived community scheme to follow later when funds become available. The Sports Council's Technical Unit for Sport's scheme at Belgrave, 7 and 9, is an example of this procedure: the original intention was to create a full joint provision scheme on the same site and at the same time as the school extensions were being constructed.

The scheme was planned so that later parts can be added to create a full community sport and recreational centre, including a swimming pool, squash courts, and possibly other facilities. There is also the possibility of integrating a youth and community centre with the scheme.

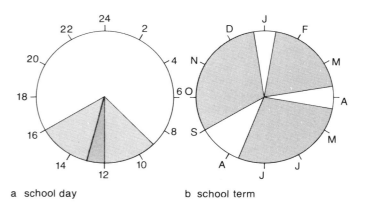

a school day   b school term

1,2 *Examples of utilisation circles. Areas without tone show:*
(1) those hours during the day when a school is underutilised;
and (2) the proportion of a year that a school remains empty

2.2 Upgrading existing facilities

Where the location is suitable, existing school facilities can be developed and upgraded for community use. Such schemes should meet the same financial criteria as those outlined above for new facilities. Such extra facilities can often be financed by local authorities out of their general funds. Failing this, other sources such as Parent Teacher Associations and Trusts should be investigated.

An example of such a scheme is the school swimming pool at Ellesmere in the UK, which was upgraded for full public use. A refreshment lounge was created to overlook the pool, the changing areas were improved to adult use standards and a new reception area was provided. The building was also given improved roof insulation.

2.3 Educational use of facilities off the school site

There has been a long established practice of schools using facilities outside the school site, eg playing fields and public indoor swimming pools. Obviously if a sports centre were nearby, this would affect the kind of provision for physical education made at a school; it is precisely this kind of co-ordinated planning which is needed. Many public swimming pools and sports centres would be under-used without school use during weekdays. The decision as to whether it will be best to provide them on or off the school site will be crucial; there is a great need to ensure that money is spent to the greatest effect. There is also the possibility of alternative multi-funding arrangements through trusts to bring in and co-ordinate any available finance and similar, usable facilities.

2.4 School landscape

With thoughtful design, school grounds can support and enrich the education of all pupils instead of being the barren expanses of asphalt too often seen. They can, for example, provide a wide range of ecological interests, enabling young people to observe wildlife and nature, thus stimulating the interest not only of school children but also the wider community.

In the UK, Hampshire County Council has followed the inspiring 'Learning through Landscapes' movement which sets out to integrate buildings, landscape and education so as to create the richest possible learning environment for pupils and public alike. Bordon Whitehill Primary School is an early instance, with many more schemes under development. These are evidence of the excellence that can be achieved in school building.

See also Department of Education and Science Building Bulletin 71 *The Outdoor Classroom*. This includes information on the 'Learning through Landscapes' project.

3 Examples of development

An early significant joint provision scheme in the UK was Bingham Sports Centre, completed in 1969, which accommodated a sports hall, swimming pool (main pool and learner pool), activity area, gymnasium and other ancillary spaces. Nottinghamshire County Council tended to take the lead in providing for school and community and a number of schemes followed Bingham, the most notable being Carlton Forum completed in 1969. There accommodation included a sports hall with upper activity areas, learner and main pools and squash courts. These areas had separate entrances but were also integrated into the main school buildings.

In some areas the concept of joint provision has caught on and developed. The Binford Church of England Primary School in Bracknell has extended its school hall

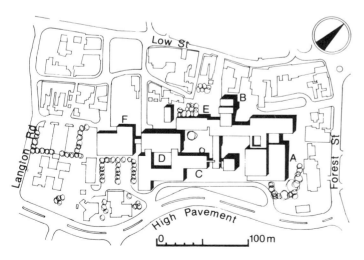

3 *Sutton-in-Ashfield Centre, Nottingham. The various elements are as follows: A, sports centre; B, theatre; C, maths and day centre; D, liberal studies; E, adult education, upper school and youth centre; F, lower school. The new centre is planned as an extension to the shopping and commercial centre, linked through by a pedestrian mall. The playing fields are on a separate site*

for use for badminton and other activities with funding from the local Parish Council.

The success of joint use projects depends to a large extent on how they are managed. Where a shared facility is funded by more than one authority, it is important to develop a management structure which will allow each partner an appropriate share in determining the overall policy for use. Joint management committees have been established at many centres.

4 Secondary schools

In general there are two approaches to providing for sport and recreation facilities at schools on a shared school and community basis.

4.1 Integrated facilities

Larger schemes can embrace a much wider range of activities than sport and physical recreation activities; for example, the DES development scheme for the Abraham Moss Centre in Manchester, where school and community activities are fully integrated and, in addition to a sports centre, facilities include hairdressing, shops, and an old people's centre. Another example is the Sutton Centre in Sutton-in-Ashfield, Notts, **3, 4** and **11**. This concept tends to produce a school conceived as part of the total community and less easily identified as a separate educational establishment. The prospects are wide and include shared activities with the arts and a wide range of further educational activities with any partner.

4.2 Separate facilities

These are community facilities on the school site, but separate enough to be recognised as a distinct community block. This approach is favoured by some as it avoids the feeling that one is going 'back to school', a factor which might discourage recent school leavers and others from using dual provision schemes (though Sports Council research does not reveal this as a significant factor). An example is the project for a centre at Belgrave in Tamworth by the Sports Council's TUS, where the centre is shared by a local school and the community. The first phase consisted of a 17 × 32 m sports hall, an arts workshop, social areas and offices, as well as lavatories and changing rooms. Later phases included a swimming pool, squash courts and youth club, as well as an ancillary hall and additional changing and social facilities.

Other examples in the UK include:

- Victoria Centre, Crewe, Cheshire. This is still attracting a third of a million customers a year and has a very full programme of activities (see *A & B Paper No. 8*, and *Building Bulletin 39*) **11**.
- The Dukeries Centre, Ollerton, Nottinghamshire. This is a modest community school breathing new vitality into a building halfway through its useful life (see *Design Note 42: The Dukeries Complex – a Place for the Family*).
- The Bacon CTC, Docklands, London. This scheme with extensive sports and social facilities caters for the community living within the docklands redevelopment area.

5 Primary schools (and other possibilities)

There is now a healthy trend to widen the possibilities of dual provision to include primary, junior and other educational establishments. Primary schools, particularly,

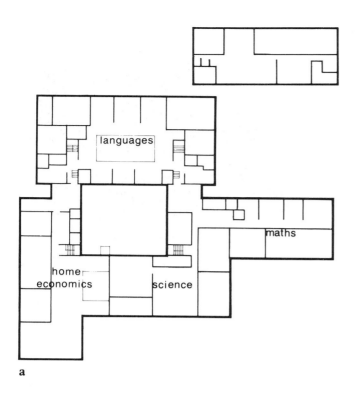

a

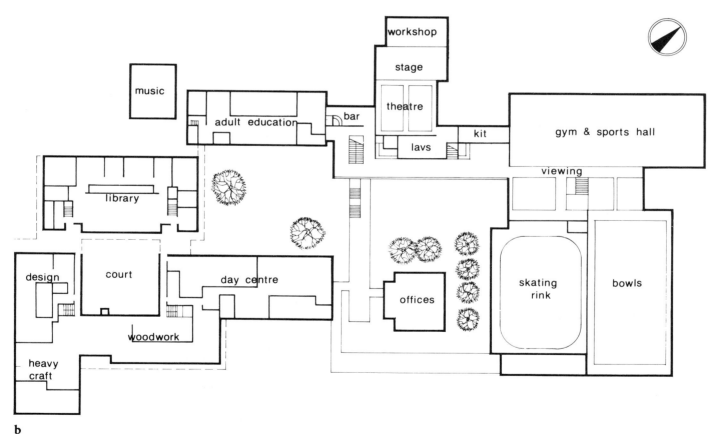

b

4 *Upper (a) and lower (b) floor plans of the Sutton-in-Ashfield Centre*

can act as centres for local and rural requirements. They usually serve a population of about 2000 persons and, in urban and suburban areas, are often within walking distance for the majority of children – true 'round the corner' facilities.

It also seems that some of the educational objectives tie in closely to serve the community for social reasons. The Department of Education and Science development project for an infant and nursery school at Ilkeston,

Derbyshire, includes a family centre which can be self-contained. The aims of the centre are:

- To encourage adult members of the community, particularly parents, to take part in the work of the school to understand better the development of young children
- To provide a place where parents can meet one another and members of staff, informally

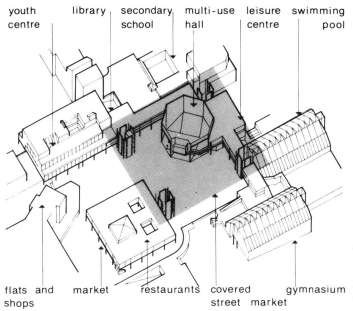

youth centre | library | secondary school | multi-use hall | leisure centre | swimming pool

flats and shops | market | restaurants | covered street market | gymnasium

5 Marne-la-Vallée (Le Quartier de L'Arche Guedon), near Paris, France, is a new town to the east of Paris which is divided into four urban units each with 100,000 to 180,000 inhabitants. Axonometric of the central area, with roof to the central market space shown in tone

- To make possible the fuller use of combined school and community provision for both school and a wide variety of community activities
- To provide accommodation and a base for holiday and after school activities.

This scheme obviously raises the possibility of further opportunities. The accommodation was produced primarily for educational reasons but could prove to be a base for wider activities, on a joint provision basis – the round-the-corner provision of sports and recreational activities. A hall, large enough to take a single badminton court, could be supplied for the community and then be used for a wide variety of other sports. The difference between this and the school provision could be met by the local authority. Walsall developed a policy of building primary schools on a joint provision basis and a notable example is the Park Hall Primary School which includes two squash courts in its dual use block.

6 Design features

There are no regulations for the design of joint provision sports and recreation buildings and each particular circumstance will have characteristic features requiring its own solution. The following are some of the main design features:

- The facilities should be designed to ensure that the needs of children during school hours are fully met.
- The scheme should be accessible by public transport to allow children to reach the centre easily.
- Adequate car parking for sports centre staff and users, in addition to that provided for school staff use, should be created. Peak loads will generally occur at weekends and evenings when the school places are not needed.
- The centre should be sited so that the community use does not conflict with school use during the day.
- The siting should be such that the community facilities are recognisable and able to be identified by the public, whether they are an integrated part of the school buildings or a separate block.

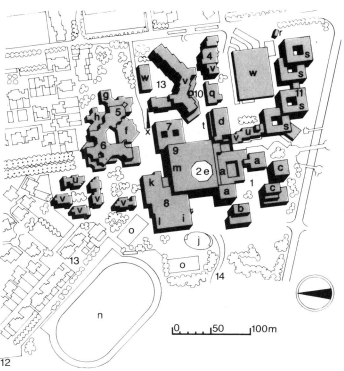

0 . . . 50 . 100m

6 Block plan of the centre of L'Arche Guedon:
1 A student centre:
(a) secondary school (900 pupils);
(b) special studies (96 pupils); and
(c) technical college specialising in economics and commercial vocations.
2 A leisure centre:
(d) youth club;
(e) multi-use hall; ⋆*club rooms, 30's club and TV centre.*
3 A public library.
4 A family centre:
⋆ *social centre and day nursery.*
5 An infant centre:
(f) primary school;
(g) nursery school;
(h) creche; and ⋆ *children's social centre and day hospital.*
6 A health centre:
⋆ *mental health clinic, student hygiene, TB and VD clinics, etc.*
7 School restaurants *(open to the public)*
8 A sports centre:
(i) indoor swimming pool;
(j) outdoor swimming pool;
(k) gymnasium;
(l) training rooms;
(m) exercise floor space;
(n) stadium; and
(o) various pitches and playing fields.
9 A covered market *(360 m²).*
10 A commercial centre:
(p) shops; and
(q) a supermarket.
11 An office complex:
(r) information centre; and
(s) offices.
12 An artists' centre *(15 studios).*
13 Accommodation:
(t) hostel for young workers;
(u) staff housing; and
(v) houses and flats.
14 A park
15 Car parking:
(w) covered parking; and
(x) underground parking.
⋆ *not individually shown on block plan, 8.*

7 *Drama class in the sports/arts workshop at the Belgrave Centre. Photograph: David Butler*

8 *School use of changing rooms. Photograph: David Butler*

9 *The sports hall at Tamworth in the UK was designed as a blind box illuminated solely by artificial means with economy in mind, while at the same time creating a suitable environment for people to enjoy their sport. Photograph: David Butler*

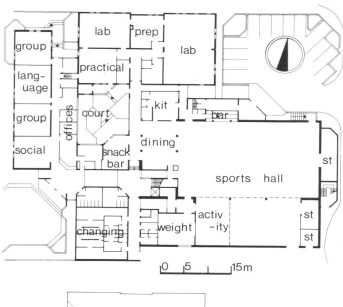

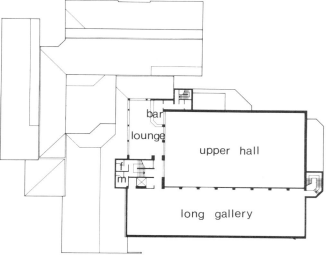

10 *Plans for one of the new buildings in the Crewe Central Area project which is being built jointly by the Department of Education and Science Development Group, Cheshire County Council and Crewe and Nantwich District Council as a means of exploring the potential contribution of schools within the process of urban renewal.*
a *Ground floor plan;*
b *the first floor*

- The public entrance to the facilities should be welcoming and easily visible to the public including those who are disabled, and provide an opportunity to display information about current activities, classes, sporting and social events.
- Separate entrances can be provided to the sports centre and to the school, although these may combine in the entrance foyer. Where this arrangement is appropriate, doors should be provided so that the school premises may be locked from the public at evenings, weekends and holiday times. This latter point is critical to the security of expensive equipment used in workshops and laboratories in schools. The entrance will justify a reception desk if the scheme is of any size, and this will provide efficient control of access to the centre. Here fees will be paid, enquiries answered, courts and pitches booked and equipment hired. Depending on the size and nature of the centre, this desk may be manned either full-time or at certain hours for the more local centre.

11 *Sutton in Ashfield indoor bowls hall being used by the community*

12 *Burnham Copse Infant School at Tadley, Hampshire, has a circular plan; at the centre is a lofty shared space, surrounded by a ring of classrooms which open on to the landscape on the far side. The shared space, shown on this photograph, has a striking structural form and is painted in rich colours to provide a stimulating environment which is much enjoyed by the children. It is under the apex of a tent-like roof which slopes down over the surrounding classrooms, providing a visual landmark in the landscape. Photograph: Peter Cook*

- Offices and staff rooms should be provided to meet the different needs of the sports centre. In addition to these needs, an office may be required for the person in charge of physical education.
- Storage areas for equipment are needed for any centre used by the public. In addition to this storage, some schools may require separate storage for their own equipment not utilised by the public. Foam mats require a separate store for fire protection.
- The specification and materials used to build the joint provision scheme will often need to be upgraded from school standards. They will take heavier wear and, in general, the standards of caretaking and cleaning, possible during the hours that a school is closed or on holiday, will not be feasible at a fully used community centre.
- As with sports centres generally, staffing should be kept to a minimum and the relationship of elements carefully considered, together with circulation routes, to produce an easily managed centre.
- Car parks (and approach paths and signposts thereto) should be well lit for night use.

7 Design checklist
The following is a useful checklist for the designer:

7.1 Site/existing building
Is the proposed site/existing building situated so as to be:

- Convenient for access by pupils, parents and school buses?

- Accessible to the general public?
- Convenient for public transport routes?
- Convenient for access to other educational institutions and related community facilities in the area?

7.2 Site planning
- Are the principal buildings readily accessible by foot and vehicle from the public highway?
- Has provision been made for external signposting designed to assist infrequent visitors to the site?
- Has provision been made for exterior lighting?
- If any of the site is to be adopted by the local authority do the standards and specification of roads, footpaths and exterior lighting conform to their requirements?
- Does the site meet the statutory requirements for school outdoor physical education? If not, can alternative provision be made in the area, or alternative covered provision be made on the site?
- Can the use of outdoor physical education facilities by the community be extended by improved specification, floodlighting or additional provision?
- Can covered waiting areas be provided adjacent to the buildings?
- Is the design and standard of external planting etc appropriate to public as well as school use?
- Can any of the areas around or between the buildings be exploited to contribute to the stock of public open space in the area?
- Are any of the external areas required to be enclosed to safeguard young children or for security?
- Are the buildings sited, or designed in detail, to avoid vehicles disturbing noise sensitive areas, eg study areas, medical facilities, administration offices?
- Has provision been made for disabled drivers' vehicles and access to the building by wheelchairs?
- Can adequate parking provision for community use be made on the site or is space available in the neighbourhood, eg shopping centre, car park?

7.3 General disposition of buildings
- To what extent can the general disposition of the buildings allow for alterations in the size of contribution from non-education partners during the design process?
- Can major changes in utilisation or ownership of all or part of the buildings be accommodated?
- Can major additions or extensions be made to the buildings?
- Are the elements of the building most heavily used by the public readily accessible with adequate means of escape and egress routes?

7.4 Ancillary accommodation
- Has provision been made for the coats of public and pupils?
- Is toilet provision appropriate for the needs of the public as well as the pupils?
- Has provision been made for the special needs of the physically handicapped?

7.5 Catering
- Has provision been made for coffee and light snacks in addition to school meals?
- Can school meals provision be extended to provide meals for the public at weddings, parties and dinners?
- Is provision to be made for alcoholic refreshment and, if so, does the accommodation meet the appropriate licensing requirements?

7.6 Staff accommodation
- Has provision been made for the increased staffing establishment associated with joint use?
- Can school staff accommodation be extended or must separate accommodation be provided for non-school staff?
- Is accommodation required for a resident caretaker?

7.7 Caretaking and maintenance
- Have the caretaking and maintenance implications of extended use been considered?
- Is accommodation required on the site for large-scale ground maintenance equipment?

7.8 Storage
- Have the increased storage requirements of multiple use been considered?
- Can separate provision for the various user groups be made?
- Has separate provision for storage of foam filled equipment been considered with the Fire Prevention Officer?

7.9 Young children
- Can provision be made for informal social space to meet community as well as school needs?
- Can social accommodation be associated with catering facilities?
- Is a crèche needed for staff and public use?

7.10 General teaching accommodation
- As well as extended use for adult education, is any of the accommodation suitable for community use for such activities as committee meetings, discussion groups, advisory clinics and voluntary associations?
- Can furniture be cleared or stacked to allow flat floor activities such as ante-natal classes, yoga, karate, junior youth club activities, etc?
- Is it necessary to allow for the separation of certain areas of accommodation which are unsuitable for community use or where community use would disrupt teaching programmes?

7.11 Specialist accommodation
- As well as extended use for adult education, is the accommodation suitable for community use for such activities as car maintenance, DIY workshops, individual use of specialist equipment, music practice, etc?
- Can the accommodation be used by organised local groups, eg scientific or horticultural societies, or aero modellers?
- Is it necessary to allow for the separation of certain areas of accommodation which are unsuitable for community use, or where community use would disrupt the teaching programme?

7.12 Large group spaces
- Are any large halls suitable for public performances and assemblies and if so do they have adequate means of escape?
- Have the differing and sometimes conflicting requirements of multiple use been considered, eg music, dance, speech, drama, films?
- Are there any spaces suitable for such diverse community activities as car boot sales, bazaars, political meetings, public inquiries, exhibitions, dog shows and the like?

- Is the ancillary accommodation associated with large spaces adequate to allow for extended community use, eg crush spaces, lavatories, etc?

7.13 Physical education facilities
- Is the accommodation suitable for community recreation as well as physical education, including the disabled?
- Does the ancillary accommodation allow for extended community use, eg changing rooms, cash and control desk, etc?
- Can the accommodation be upgraded and is it designed for safety?

7.14 Finishes
- Is the specification and standard of finish adequate to meet extended community use?
- Can routine cleaning of floors be carried out while the building is in use?

7.15 Lighting/power
- Will emergency and secondary lighting be required to meet extended use?
- Do sections of the accommodation require separate metering and controls?

7.16 Heating/ventilation
- Will heating controls allow independent use of parts of the building?
- Does the system's speed of response allow economic intermittent use?
- Where a central boiler house is provided, is separate metering required for sections of the accommodation?
- Will mechanical ventilation be required to meet intensive public use/smoking?

7.17 Furniture
- Is the furniture selected appropriately sized and sufficiently robust to meet community as well as school use?
- Is there a need to reserve certain areas exclusively for use by children because of furniture requirements?
- Is furniture selected adaptable and dimensionally co-ordinated to allow multiple utilisation?

7.18 Internal signposting
- Have the needs of occasional users of the buildings been considered?
- What special emergency signposting will be required to meet community use and licensing considerations?

7.19 Security
- Has the need been considered for certain areas to be closed to provide privacy/security?

- Will consideration of security conflict with emergency escape requirements?
- Are any secure stores required for special items of equipment?
- Will a safe be required?
- Will the individual partners in joint use schemes require special lock suiting arrangements?
- Can the sports/recreation facilities used by the community outside school hours be made available and accessed without affecting the security of the rest of the buildings?
- Can the public gain access to facilities during school hours?

8 Acknowledgement

The assistance of the Department of Education is acknowledged and, in particular, that of Michael Hacker for his original material.

9 References and further advice

A & B, The Victoria Centre, Crewe: An Update, *A & B Paper No. 8*, Department of Education and Science, London (1985).

British Standards Institution, *BS 5500: Fire Precautions in the Design, Construction and Use of Buildings: Part 6: Code of Practice for Places of Assembly*, BSI, Milton Keynes (1990).

Department of Education and Science, 'Outdoor Classroom, Education Use, Landscape Design and Management of School Grounds', *Building Bulletin 71*, gives information on school grounds, HMSO, London (1990).

Department of Education and Science, *Design Note 14: School and Community 2* (1976). (This Note, written by Michael Hacker, provided much of the original background to this chapter.)

Sports Council, *Designing for Safety in Sports Buildings*, *Factfile 5*, Sports Council, London.

Sports Council/Health and Safety Commission, *Safety in Swimming Pools*, Sports Council, London (1988).

Sports Council, *Community Use of Primary Schools*, *Data Sheet 62*, Sports Council, London (1993).

Sports Council and ILAM, *The Community Use of Sports Facilities on School Sites*, Sports Council, London (1994).

Sports Council, *Guidance Note: Educational Facilities – Design for Community Use*, Sports Council, London (1995).

Weston, R., *Schools of Thought*, Hampshire County Council (1992).

10
Design briefs

Kit Campbell

1 Introduction

The best sports and recreation buildings are generally the result of an enlightened client working closely with an experienced design team to a clear brief.

Traditionally many design briefs for the modernisation of an existing sports building or the design of a new one have been very simple documents. Sometimes they have contained little more than a list of the main areas or facilities required within a proposed building; and in some instances they have simply been a broad instruction to a design team to design a building with little guidance as to its scale or content. Frequently briefs have evolved at the same time as the design of a project and in some instances it is difficult to avoid the suspicion that the design has come first and the brief second.

This was understandable when sports and recreation facilities were a fairly new building type for both clients and design teams were 'feeling their way'. The consequences of early decisions will affect the performance of the resulting building for 50 or 60 years, however, and as clients are increasingly seeking competitive fee bids from potential design team members, it is essential for them to be clear from the outset as to what they want to build, for whom, why, where and at what capital and operating costs. They also need to specify in advance the 'ground rules' which will apply to any design commission. In short it is up to clients to set objectives; and design teams to find cost-effective ways of meeting them.

This section suggests one flexible model for the contents of a design brief and is intended primarily for clients. It is written in the context of a new build proposal but can readily be adapted for modernisation projects.

2 The objectives of briefing

Briefing generally has to serve a number of purposes and it is usually appropriate to split up the brief accordingly. For public sector projects, if required the various sections can even be prepared by a working party of officials from different departments such as Leisure and Recreation, Planning and Technical Services.

The main objectives of a comprehensive brief are:

- To set the administrative 'ground rules' for the design and construction of the project – referred to below as the administrative brief
- To specify the planning context within which the project is to be set – the planning brief
- To set objectives and priorities for the project and specify in broad terms its scale, content, capital and revenue costs, and performance in use – the design and performance brief
- To set the broad principles of future management policy insofar as they might affect either the design or construction of the project – the management brief

- To specify a broad programme for the design and construction of the proposed project – the programme brief.

3 The nature of the design brief

The nature of the design brief and the level of detail it should contain will depend upon the method of procurement to be adopted.

With a consultant design team, or an in-house one, the design will evolve in discussion between client and designers and the initial brief may not need to be highly detailed. On the other hand, a vague or non-existent brief may allow the appointed design team to make too many decisions; the design team should be expert at designing buildings within predetermined social, recreational and sporting objectives, not at setting those objectives.

It is clear from the experience of many authorities that it is desirable to have management input both into design briefs and the design of the building which results. This can best be obtained by appointing the manager of a proposed centre during the design period but if this is not possible for some reason general advice and assistance is available from the appropriate Sports Council.

4 Content of the brief

4.1 The administrative brief

For many public clients such as local authorities the administrative brief will probably be governed by standing orders or policies relating to the administration of capital projects. It should include:

- The title of the project, together with any standard abbreviations which will be used when referring to it.
- The name, address and telephone number of the client.
- The name, address and telephone number of the person who will co-ordinate the project on behalf of the client. For all projects there should be a single channel of communication between the design team and the client and all instructions should be issued through this person. For large projects, or when a tight programme is set, a deputy project co-ordinator might also be appointed. It will also be important to specify the limits of authority of both project co-ordinator and design team – for example, in terms of authority to approve variations to the contract and additional costs.
- Details of how client instructions will be issued and to whom. Formal instructions should always be confirmed in writing.
- A statement of the terms and conditions on which the design team is appointed, and setting out their responsibilities, fees and how and when they will be paid. Very often one of the standard Memoranda of Agreement published by professional bodies such as the Royal Institute of British Architects or the Association of Consulting Engineers is used. Some clients have additional requirements, such as for the amount of professional indemnity insurance particular members of the design team should have.
- A clear statement of the status of the brief, or the stages through which the brief will pass – for example, a draft for discussion, a sketch design brief, or a final brief.
- A list of useful contacts who will have to be consulted as the project develops: for example, relevant officials in the planning or finance departments of the local authority, or in any grant-aiding bodies.

The administrative brief will often be prepared by the council's technical services department (if it has one) and may be based on a standard document.

4.2 The planning brief

All building projects take place within a planning context which affects such things as the choice of site, access to it, and the nature of building which is acceptable. The main purpose of the planning brief is to define this context in order to avoid the possibility of abortive work by the design team. In addition, if the proposed project is being funded or provided through a planning obligation (see Chapter 8 in this volume) it is also important to specify at the outset exactly who is to pay for each element of the project and how any joint or cross-funding is to work. The planning brief will often be the responsibility of the planning department.

4.3 The design and performance brief

The most important task of the design and performance brief is to set objectives for the development: for example, if the over-riding objective is to provide facilities for competitive swimming at regional level this should result in a very different building from situations where the overall objective is to provide facilities for local recreational swimming.

When setting objectives the key points to consider are:

- What are the social, economic and recreational aims?
- For whom are the proposed facilities being provided and what priority should be given to each different market segment?
- What standards or levels of performance should the facilities accommodate?

When writing a brief, initially it is best to think in terms of performance or results – in other words, for example, 'What sports development or other purposes are intended to be achieved by this project?' – rather than facilities. This avoids preconceptions about the actual design. If the required outcome can be stated clearly and unequivocally it can be translated into a particular mix of facilities at a particular scale, with specific priorities.

The actual design and performance brief should state clearly:

- The objectives of the proposed project
- The proposed philosophy of use and management
- The range and scale of facilities required
- Key design features and factors
- Priorities, in case the cost of the project exceeds the budget available
- The performance required from different elements of the project
- The approximate throughput anticipated and the overall pattern of use
- The acceptable financial implications
- The 'building policy'.

Most of these items will have been determined during the initial feasibility study and should be self-explanatory with the possible exception of the last two. The acceptable financial implications have to be stated in a way which is absolutely clear and relate, for local authority projects, to spending plans. It is fairly common for a capital cost limit to be set, although often this emerges as the result of the preparation of initial design studies. It is important to identify those items which must be included in the capital cost. These might include site acquisition costs, survey costs, fees for statutory applications, the provision of public utilities, external works, professional fees and expenses, and – often overlooked in the early stages of a project – furniture and loose equipment. It is sensible also to relate capital costs to operating costs and specify how trade-offs from one to the other will be evaluated.

Building policy is less common a concept. It refers to a diverse range of subjects related to the client's attitudes to the sort of building wanted but is not intended to determine the actual design. Building policy might therefore cover such things as the quality of finish required, the wish or need to 'theme' the building and phasing or expansion requirements. In addition it should also include such basic requirements as accessibility for people with disabilities.

The Sports Council has published a detailed design and performance brief with cost guidance notes for a SASH type dry sports centre (1) and a 25 m pool addition (2) both of which can be used as models.

The design and performance brief will normally be the prime responsibility of local authority leisure and recreation and technical services departments, perhaps assisted by outside consultants in some instances.

4.4 The management brief

The broad principles of the way in which the proposed building is to be managed should also be determined at the outset and related to the objectives set in the design and performance brief. At this stage the management brief will probably contain outline views on:

- Pricing policies
- Opening hours
- Programming, including sessions for clubs
- Key target groups and how they will be attracted to the pool
- Catering policy
- Image and possible need for 'theming'
- Quality of finish
- Promotion.

The preparation of the management brief will normally be the responsibility of the client side of the council's leisure and recreation department.

4.5 The programme brief

Finally, the programme brief should set out the time-scale planned for the implementation of the project and set target dates as appropriate – for example, in relation to cash flow in particular financial years, or to the need to open at a particular time of year in order to cater for a major competition. As a rule of thumb, the length of time needed for the pre-contract stages of a major project (initial planning, feasibility work, preparation of design brief, design and preparation of detailed drawings and specification) normally takes at least as long as the post-contract stage (ie the length of time needed to build the proposed building).

At the initial stage, the programme should contain as few key dates as possible and have considerable 'float' or flexible, unallocated time built in. The detailed programme will have to be discussed and agreed with the design team and, eventually, the contractor. The main purpose of including key dates in the initial brief is to provide a basis for the design team to plan its work programme. A particularly tight programme may also have financial implications which should be assessed at an early stage in the project.

The preparation of the programme brief will normally involve the local authority finance and leisure and recreation departments; it may also involve technical services and planning departments.

5 Expansion of the brief

These five elements form the draft brief – the starting point for the design team. It should be regarded not as 'tablets of stone', but as a working document which will guide rather than determine the final design. It should nevertheless be a clear statement of purpose against which design proposals can be tested. As the design evolves, however, so will the brief. The extent to which it may need to be expanded and amplified depends largely upon the experience and knowledge of the appointed design team. The brief is nevertheless always the responsibility of the client and not the design team.

6 Conclusions

Briefing can be a long, tough, often argumentative process which is conducted properly far too rarely. Without good, comprehensive briefing, providers run the risk of getting the wrong sort of building to the wrong level of quality.

But with clear thinking and achievable objectives it should be possible to achieve what the Audit Commission has dubbed 'a more effective product':

> In some authorities, the specification of design, including the range of facilities to be provided, has been left in the hands of the appointed architect. Other authorities have developed an architect's brief; this has tended to result in a more effective product. (Department of the Environment Audit Inspectorate 1983.)

7 References and further advice

Department of the Environment Audit Inspectorate, *The Design and Operation of Leisure Centres*, HMSO, London (1983).

Sports Council, TUS, *SASH Design Guide 1: Indoor Dry Sports Building (Brief, Design, Performance Specification and Cost Guidance Notes)*, Sports Council, London (1985).

Sports Council, TUS, *SASH Design Guide 2: Swimming Pool Option (Brief, Design, Performance Specification and Cost Guidance Notes for the Swimming Pool Addition to the SASH Sports Centre)*, Sports Council, London (1985).

11
Facilities for TV and radio broadcasting

Geraint John

1 TV requirements

1.1 General

Wherever possible the requirement for broadcasting should be incorporated at the planning stage of the building design, although only after a venue has become established is it likely that events held at the proposed facility will attract broadcasting or film-making interests.

Where operating TV companies undertake to broadcast sports activities, it is always important to have discussions as early as possible with them to ensure that their latest requirements are met and verify the current sizes of vehicles and equipment to be used.

Generous notice is usually needed for any event so that the programme for the centre can be arranged. About one month before an outside broadcast takes place, a survey should be carried out by the TV company to schedule the necessary equipment and to establish its position within the facility to ensure a minimum of inconvenience to spectators. This procedure applies to indoor and outdoor transmissions and requires the full co-operation of management and other staff. Approximately 2 days may be required to deliver and set up the equipment for transmission although this time will depend upon the complexity of the TV coverage and on the facilities available. A day may be needed to dismantle and remove equipment.

1.2 Safety

Although TV companies have their own safety regulations, the local authority is ultimately responsible. The district authority's surveyor or building inspector should be consulted as soon as TV transmissions are contemplated.

1.3 Vehicles required for indoor and outdoor transmissions

The following is a list of vehicles required for an outside broadcast and gives some idea of their size and weights so that adequate parking facilities may be provided. The figures given are for British Broadcasting Corporation (BBC) vehicles and the height of their largest vehicle is approximately 3.5 m. The dimensions of vehicles used by other television companies vary in length and they are generally 200 mm (8 in) higher than BBC vehicles owing to a built-in roof rack. However, the figures given can be used as planning sizes for vehicles. Amendments to the size of vehicles can occur from time to time and designers are therefore advised to check with the TV authorities before design decisions are made.

Colour mobile control room (CMCR)
This is usually divided into three compartments:

- Sound control
- Production control
- Vision control.

Size: 12 x 2.50 m
Weight: 20 tonne
Side and rear opening doors: allow 1.30 m for doors
Total size for planning: 14.30 × 4 or 5 m
Many vehicles now have expanding sides up to 1.0 m each.

Camera vehicles
Cameras carried on each side of the vehicle are removed by sliding them out from side lockers
Size: 9.20 × 2.50 m: allow minimum of 1.30 m on each side for removal of cameras
This vehicle also carries additional equipment and it is desirable to park it adjacent to the CMCR vehicle
Total size for planning: 10.50 × 4.00 m
Weight: 13 tonne.

Cable tender vehicle
Size: 13 x 2.50 m including tractor
Low loading, side and rear doors: allow minimum of 1.30 m on each side and 4 m to the rear
Once the equipment has been delivered this vehicle may be parked elsewhere if required: in some circumstances the cable drums are left on the ground for the duration of the broadcast.
Total size for planning 17 × 4 m
Weight: 20 tonne.

Electrical generator vehicle (if 200 kW)
Size: 8 × 2.5 m
Weight: 17 tonne
One or more generators may be required depending on the capacity of the existing power supply.

Other vehicles which may be required
- Radio link vehicle
- Mobile video tape vehicles
- Aerial vehicle for telescopic aerial unit. Many companies use Simon hoists with the working platform at 20–60 m. The 60 m Simon hoist (S6000) weights 35 tonne and requires a parking space of size 14.0 × 8.0 m with *no overhead obstructions such as power cables*.
- Supplementary lighting equipment delivery vehicle
- Mobile catering facilities – kitchen and dining bus (when required)
- Toilets
- Security caravanette.

Parking requirements
A level hardstanding is required, particularly for the aerial vehicle, capable of carrying the weight of the vehicles. The area for parking may be incorporated within the public or staff car parks provided they are adjacent to the main building, thus keeping cable runs to a minimum. Temporary parking areas for these vehicles may be provided if transmissions are not to be frequent.

The turning circles required by the largest vehicles are between 25.9 and 27.4 m. Access roads should be wide enough to accommodate these vehicles, bearing in mind the vehicle heights.

Where a unit is on site overnight, the TV company will usually provide security staff. The numbers of TV staff employed on an outside broadcast will vary, but in general 40 people should be allowed for.

Note: in covering big events, more than one TV company may be involved, with consequent effect on support areas.

1.4 Weight, cable access and location of equipment
The difficulty of access for cables and equipment represents one of the greatest problems experienced in the setting-up for an outside transmission.

Equipment
- Lamps vary in size and can weight from 1.5 to 77 kg for internal or external use. Many lamps may be used and a considerable superimposed structural load results
- Cameras are about 900 mm long x 600 mm wide x 460 mm high. Some cameras weigh up to 70 kg including the zoom lens
- Fixed camera mounting 900 mm wide base weighing up to 100 kg
- Camera cable drums
- Microphone cable drums
- Mobile camera dollies of various sizes and weights from 26 kg. The heaviest of these dollies weighs approximately 3 tonne. Dollies can be fitted with various types of wheels according to the types and condition of the floor finish, eg solid rubber or pneumatic wheels.

All the above equipment can easily be taken through a pair of double doors (approximate size 1650 × 1980 mm) located adjacent to the parked vehicles and as close as possible to the equipment inside the building. This does not include the more specialised equipment available from hire companies.

Cable access
Access routes for cables vary considerably. A lockable hatch approximately 300 × 300 mm should be provided within easy reach in an outside wall to allow cable access into the building and to avoid cables having to pass through doorways and fire escapes. All cable access from the vehicles to the equipment inside the buildings should be kept separate from the access provided for the general public and away from main circulation and escape routes.

Corridors must be wide enough to move all types of equipment and negotiate changes of direction. The corners of walls should be protected by metal or rubber angles to prevent damage. Cable trays may be provided but require to have long radius bends (approx 600 mm) as some cables may be 25 mm in diameter. An allowance should be made for cable junctions and sockets in addition to cable diameters. Cables may also be supported from the walls using suitable brackets fixed well above door head height, spaced up to 3 m. Where it is impossible to run cables away from public routes, overhead cables should be run out of normal human reach at, say, 3.5 m above floor level. Wherever possible, cables crossing escape routes at floor level must be in a duct and not just protected by ramps. Because of increasing use of a.c. discharge lighting and portable electric dimmers, separate cable ducts or wall cleats should be provided for lighting cables.

Location of equipment
Although some sports halls and swimming pools have incorporated fixed positions for cameras as part of the building design (eg above scoreboards or platforms in galleries) these predetermined positions are not always the most suitable or practical. The location of cameras depends on the type of coverage to be provided and the choice of the TV company.

Camera positions and lighting equipment must be isolated from public access. Hydraulic platforms or purpose-made scaffolding platforms can be used for cameras and commentary positions, or a section of the spectators' gallery may be set aside and a temporary platform erected to take a load of approximately 2 kN/sq m minimum. After several transmissions the equipment positions become known and more permanent provision may be made. It is therefore advisable to consult the TV companies regarding equipment locations at the design stage of a new complex before selecting permanent positions. TV companies will supply and erect platforms for occasional transmissions.

Provision of access to high flat areas of roof is useful for facilities for mounting radio links equipment. Ideally the area should have a 360 degrees unobstructed view.

Small shoulder-mounted cameras are now regularly used on a roving basis and are required to move around relevant areas.

1.5 Electrical power and lighting

Power
A three-phase 50 Hz supply, typically 200 A per phase with appropriate neutral and earth connections, is usually adequate for general technical and lighting requirements and depends on the size of the area to be illuminated and the prevailing lighting conditions. Two phases may be used for lighting, together with the residual capacity on the third phase after the technical requirements are met.

A main 'take off' point is preferred, terminated in a switch and bus bars capable of accepting lugs or terminals. The three-phase supply and the switches for technical and lighting supplies can be connected to the bus-bars. An alternative is to provide a power cabinet adjacent to the vehicle hardstanding, fitted with three-phase and neutral isolator. Suitable switches (to current practice) for power can then be installed.

Lighting requirements
A considerable amount of lighting for activities in sports buildings and swimming pools is mainly directional. Lighting for TV transmissions requires techniques used in photographic lighting. The type of lamp used depends very much on camera positions, the type of event to be televised and the existing lighting conditions. The basic requirements of TV lighting are outlined in the *CIBSE Publication LG4, Lighting Guide: Sports* and *International Commission on Illumination (CIE) Publications Nos 67 and 83.*

It must be remembered that the evaluation of an existing or proposed installation for sport requires design or checking by TV and lighting engineers.

Most existing lighting has to be supplemented with special lighting provided and installed by the TV companies. The cost of this equipment does not allow permanent provision to be made for only intermittent use, although a permanent access, such as a moving gantry, may be suspended below ceiling level for easy fixing of temporary lighting. A TV company will provide the various special lamp mountings they require on each occasion. Ceiling access and fixing provision to take wires for scaffold rigs should be considered.

The colour of daylight varies continually so natural light must be reduced as much as possible; it is difficult to match the different colour temperatures of natural and artificial light. In some existing sports halls and swimming pools side glazing presents a particular problem. Screens can be erected, usually to a height of 3.00 m, in order to reduce glare and also prevent people peering in from outside. Although glazing should never be placed behind a diving board in a spectator swimming pool, some existing diving towers are placed in front of a large window.

In televising a diving event, the background (the whole area behind the diving board), if glazed, must be screened. A grey/fawn/beige coloured fabric should be used for screening. Such colours are in the A and B colour group (high grey content) set out in BS 5252.

Illumination less than the requirements will limit the effective coverage of outdoor events such as horse jumping, soccer and rugby because the illumination will be insufficient for close-up shots. The depth of field will be restricted for cameras placed near the touch-lines and players at varying distances from the camera will appear out of focus. Lighting plot agreements for various sports have been agreed with the TV companies (eg the BBC).

1.6 Colour schemes
When selecting colour schemes, the use of highly saturated or strong colours (for a definition see BS 4727: Part 4) should be avoided as much as possible as this adversely affects the quality of the pictures. Matt surfaces are also preferred to reduce reflections as much as possible; this should include flooring.

1.7 Sound quality
Some sports halls and swimming pools have long reverberation times and poor acoustic conditions because of their internal large areas of flat, hard surfaces and often large windows. Ideally, as short a reverberation time as possible is required and in a well-designed pool this should be between 1 and 2 seconds. A high-quality multi-speaker audience reinforcement system is recommended to ensure good sound reproduction. So that the transmission of routine calls by the centre's public address system is not made during critical phases of a TV broadcast, it is essential to have a communications link between the commentary position and the centre's control point. Provision should be considered for TV companies to link into and out of the public address system.

1.8 Timing devices
Timing devices are used for many events. Consideration should be given to a coded feed for the TV company.

1.9 Interview rooms
On completion of an event or match, some participants may be interviewed. This happens mostly at major events, particularly where those being interviewed are well known. At the majority of sports facilities the provision of a room reserved solely for interviews is unnecessary. There is usually sufficient room on the pitch or court to hold these discussions or, if more appropriate, the manager's office may be used. A suitable area is about $4 \times 3 \times 2.5$ m high.

1.10 Commentary boxes
For coverage of major events it is usual to provide formal commentary positions. International commentary positions are usually grouped and compartmented so that commentaries can be given in different languages without distraction. Depending on the importance of the event and media interest in it, however, this formal approach may be unnecessary, and successful commentaries be made from reserved areas in the spectator seating or other vantage points. When not needed for press functions these areas may be returned for use by ordinary spectators.

Up to 50% of a television broadcast commentary is made using the monitor installed adjacent to the com-

mentator. A clear space of about 3 x 2 m is suitable for this purpose.

1.11 Cost implications
The cost of providing permanent TV facilities depends on the extent of the desired coverage and the size and the complexity of the facilities to be provided. Because of these factors it is not possible to give cost indicators. If provision for TV is to be made at the design stage of sports facilities it is wise to seek advice at the earliest opportunity so that costs of permanent fixtures can be established. Advice may be sought from the Head of Outside Broadcast Production Resources, Television Outside Broadcasts of the British Broadcasting Corporation and the Chief Engineer of the commercial TV companies.

2 Film production requirements

2.1 General
In this section the requirements of film-making companies are considered. There is generally no problem in making films in a sports facility which complies with the recommendations previously made for TV, but if film production only is to be considered then there can be a reduction in those recommendations.

2.2 Lighting
For film production it is often unnecessary to reduce the level of daylight entering a hall through windows or roof lights. It may, however, be necessary to screen large windows if they form the background to the scene. This is because the glare from the windows makes it impossible for details to be filmed and players will show only as silhouettes.

To enable good quality films to be made under artificial illumination, care must be exercised not only in the disposition of the luminaires but in the type of lamp used, particularly if high-speed photography is to be used to produce slow-motion sequences.

An illuminance of not less than 500 lux should be provided over the whole activity area and if this is to be provided by discharge lamps the stroboscopic effect may have to be reduced. Stroboscopic effects are caused by the cyclic variation of the alternating current supply which, when used with some discharge lamps, shows as a 'ghost image' on fast-moving objects. It is important, therefore, when considering making films, and especially when employing high-speed photographic techniques, to reduce this effect by connecting adjacent lamps to different phases or considering alternative lamp types.

2.3 Electrical power
The equipment used is battery operated and so requires no special generating equipment, but if it is necessary to increase the level of artificial illumination and this additional electrical load is not available from the installed switch gear a generator may be necessary. See Section 1.3 above for its size and weight.

2.4 Access for electrical equipment
The equipment required is delivered to the site by a vehicle which is unloaded and then driven away. All the equipment will pass through a pair of double doors (approximate size 1.65×1.98 m). Where an electrical generator is required it should be parked as near the film location as possible and will require a space of approximately 5×2.2 m and weigh about 3.2 tonne (3 ton). For recommendations on cable access see Section 1.4 above.

The operating area required for the camera is approximately 1 m square.

2.5 Sound
There are no special requirements for sound in film production but background music may be a source of annoyance to film crews when they are working. If background music is picked up on the film sound track then 'performing rights' may have to be paid when the film is projected.

3 Radio broadcasting requirements

3.1 General
With the growth in the number of small commercial radio stations it is possible that broadcasting from relatively local sporting events will increase and sponsors should consider this possibility when centres are being planned. In addition there is a likelihood of increasing radio coverage, particularly at football matches.

Because radio commentary is received audibly, rather than visually and audibly as in TV, it is important that the radio commentator can see clearly the events he or she is describing. There are four broad categories of radio broadcasting:

- Reports with or without interviews
- Full commentary broadcast
- Interviews
- Full programme presentation including commentary.

The requirements of these are briefly discussed separately as are the special requirements of the overseas broadcast.

3.2 Commentary positions
Commentary positions should be provided in an agreed area. These positions will vary according to the event taking place but will be the same whether the activity is taking place indoors or outdoors. In tennis and badminton, for example, the commentary position should be at the end of the court. For soccer, rugby and hockey, the commentary position should be in line with the halfway line. When commentating on cricket, behind the 'bowler's arm' is considered to be the best position, while for horse racing the commentary position is set opposite the starting and finishing lines with extra positions as necessary to see as much of the course as possible. For boxing, a ringside position near a neutral corner is desirable.

3.3 Control point
This may be a room within the complex which should be at least 4.5 × 3 m. With bigger events one or more vehicles will probably be used. The largest vehicle is a mobile studio which has the following dimensions:

- Length 11.0 m
- Width 2.5 m
- Height 3.5 m
- Weight 13.0 tonne.

With side and rear opening doors the total size is 12.4 × 4.0 m.

Other vehicles that may be required are:

- Foreign commentary control vehicle
- Caravan for production facilities
- Radio link control vehicle
- Mobile generator

- Security caravanette.

Programme output will be by British Telecom (or equivalent) circuits or by radio link. Increased use of satellite communications may require an additional vehicle on site.

3.4 Combined radio and TV
Where radio and TV broadcasts are to be made simultaneously it is usual for the two services to work independently. On some occasions, however, there may be some interconnections to allow radio commentators to receive vision and sounds from effects microphones to supplement their commentary.

In all cases it is advantageous, from a setting-up point of view, if radio and TV commentary positions are in the same general area. It is also of advantage for security and management reasons.

3.5 Categories of radio broadcasting

Report
This is the simplest form of broadcasting and is made from a spectator seat or a press area which commands a good view of the arena. The report is made over British Telecom or equivalent lines during or after the event. These reports may or may not include interviews with participants.

Full commentary broadcast
This is made at the time of the event and under the control of the technical staff of the broadcasting company. The equipment is installed by the broadcasting company in the control area and microphones in the commentary positions. Whether or not cables are permanently laid will depend upon the frequency of use and the venue, but in both cases the same precautions should be taken as described in Section 1.10 above.

Interviews
Interviews may be broadcast 'live' or, if more convenient for the radio programme, recorded and broadcast later. If a new major facility is to provide space for interviews, there are obvious advantages if radio and TV share interview rooms. For sound broadcasting, extensions for microphones will be required from the control area to the commentary positions.

Overseas broadcasting
The BBC usually provides the technical facilities for overseas radio organisations. These require commentary positions and control facilities similar to domestic radio. At international events and world championships of mixed sports up to 20 additional commentary positions may be required. Three or four extra commentary positions may be required where an international single-sport event is held. However, the details of requirements for overseas broadcasting are outside the scope of this study and information should be obtained from the BBC.

Where operating companies undertake to broadcast sports activities and shows the recommendations made in this section should be implemented. It is always important to have discussions as early as possible with the interested companies to ensure that their latest requirements are met and verify the current sizes of vehicles being used.

4 Stadia and arenas

The facilities for radio and TV broadcasting in stadia and arenas have special needs. For stadia, refer to Vol. 1, Part V, Technical Study 22. For indoor arenas, refer to Vol. 2, Technical Study 50.

5 Sources of information

The main sources of information for this study were:

The British Broadcasting Corporation's Television and Radio Outside Broadcasts Departments
London Weekend Television
Thames Television
Independent Broadcasting Authority.

The TUS thank these organisations for their help.

5 References and further advice

Chartered Institution of Building Services Engineers, *CIBSE Lighting Guide LG4: Sports*, CIBSE, London.
International Commission on Illumination, *CIE 83: Guide for the Lighting of Sports Events for Colour Television and Film Systems*, CIE.
International Commission on Illumination, *CIE 67: Guide for the Photometric Specification and Measurement of Sports Lighting Installations*, CIE.

Part II Multi-purpose facilities

12
Dry sports buildings

John Roberts

1 Introduction

Internationally, more and more sport tends to be going indoors, even in favourable climatic conditions. As standards rise, indoor conditions offer longer hours of play and more controlled conditions of lighting, ventilation and temperature as well as better event control.

Tennis is an international example. Many more tournaments are held in indoor arenas than only a few years ago and even the major outdoor facility in Flinders Park, Australia, has been equipped with a movable roof to permit play to go on at all times. Specialist facilities for practice and training have also been built in great numbers.

There has been a trend for more specialist facilities for particular sports to be built, reflecting the desire for higher standards and greater control.

The multi-purpose indoor sports space still has its secure place for community use and will be a continuing feature, but it will feature as part of a pattern of balanced provision.

The following paragraphs set out the provision for indoor sport in the UK. The provision will probably reflect the position in many developed countries.

2 Provision for indoor sport in the UK

Participation in indoor sports and recreation activities in the UK continued to grow through the 1980s. This trend is expected to continue through the 1990s but with the changing age structure of the population, the size of households and their geographical distribution, there will be shifts in the demand for specific types of activity and increasing emphasis on the quality of both facilities and service.

The most significant change has been the increase in women's participation, reflecting an international trend. This has been largely concentrated on a relatively small number of activities such as swimming, badminton, keep-fit, aerobics and movement and dance. Access to a car remains a major factor in participation, although a study in Belfast has shown that high levels of local provision and/or a local authority policy of supporting participation by socially and economically deprived groups through selective marketing and pricing can overcome low levels of car ownership.

The next 10 years will also see major changes in the financing and management of sports facilities. Local authorities have been the traditional providers of most indoor facilities from small community centres servicing rural populations of 2000 or less up to very large leisure centres with annual attendances exceeding 1 million. Buildings provided in the 1960s and 1970s are now facing the need for major refurbishment. Coupled with the restrictions placed on local government finance, this has

inevitably meant a major cutback in new facility building programmes. The private sector has invested in some commercial sports but this rarely extends beyond major population centres or economically viable sports such as tenpin bowling and snooker or health and fitness clubs. Public sector grant aid will encourage investment in facilities for more marginal activities, typically ice or roller rinks, tennis, squash and bowls.

Many sports develop through small voluntary clubs with their own specialist facilities. Traditionally this sector has been dominated by outdoor sports where the cost of facilities is less. There are however many examples of successful clubs with their own specialist indoor facilities, although most have been developed with assistance from grant-aid sources (eg Sports Council, local authority, Foundation for Sport and the Arts). Indoor shooting ranges can be built for a relatively modest cost, if used only for small-bore or air weapons. Gymnastics is another sport requiring highly specialised facilities with permanent equipment and pits sunk in the floor for training. These sports highlight the need for a proper awareness of safety in the planning and design of facilities; this is essential as sometimes fatal accidents can occur. British Standards (BS) have been developed for the more important areas and many of these will soon be adopted into European Standards (CEN) linked possibly to European Directives on design, management and use.

Sports which require much larger indoor spaces such as tennis and bowls have investigated lower cost means of provision within voluntary clubs. This has led to the widespread use of industrial components (eg metal cladding) or lightweight structures (eg PVC membranes). Planning authorities will inevitably be more concerned about the location of what might be considered as environmentally less attractive buildings suitable for an industrial estate rather than a residential urban fringe area.

Central government programmes have and will continue to focus on urban regeneration in the country's more deprived areas. Programmes like City Challenge in England and Wales have provided opportunities to look constructively at the needs of local populations. There will often be unused or derelict buildings which are suitable for conversion into centres for sport and recreation, but they must be assessed very carefully. The most appropriate activities are those requiring smaller or less defined spaces and good examples can be found of use for gymnastics, fitness training, movement and dance, boxing, judo, martial arts and table tennis.

The use of a facility will be determined primarily by its management. The introduction of compulsory competitive tendering (CCT) for the management of local authority facilities has required much greater attention to be given to programming and pricing policies with contracts being let for between 4 and 6 years. Although more than 80% of contracts have been won in the first place by the local authority's own in-house team (known as a DSO or DLO), the management will inevitably seek to generate additional income wherever possible. This has already led to refurbishment of catering and social areas and the development of health and fitness suites. There is a danger, however, that unless the local authority provides the capital, there will be a concentration on areas generating quick financial returns.

Other government legislation that has affected the management of sports facilities involves schools. The Education (No 2) Act and the Education Reform Act have changed the way in which schools are managed. School governors have been given much greater responsibility for both budgets and premises under the scheme of Local

Management of Schools (LMS). The option of applying for 'Grant Maintained Status' also provides for schools to become independent of local education authorities. The dual use of school premises by both school and community has been very successfully implemented in a large number of authorities, with leisure services departments often funding and/or managing community use out of school time. Management agreements will, in the future, need to be negotiated with individual schools, rather than education authorities, and this could provide many opportunities, although there are some disadvantages. Governors are being encouraged to look at ways of developing closer links with their local community and generating more income.

The potential for use of existing school sports facilities has been demonstrated in a number of recent publications. A starting point may be a link with local clubs for regular lettings, but moving eventually to a managed recreation centre. The latter may need modifications such as a reception area, improved changing rooms, lockers, larger stores and social/catering areas. Not all school buildings will be suitable for adaptation and designers must also consider: *locational issues*, eg secure access to regular public transport; *planning issues*, eg neighbouring properties, car parking, road access, layout of buildings; and *management issues*, eg school staff, local authority staff, voluntary clubs, private companies, catering contract, indoor and outdoor lettings.

3 Conclusions

The four most important factors in sports building design are accessibility, attractiveness, functionality and manageability. An understanding of how a building is intended to be used, and the level of sports participation expected, will be prerequisites for a brief to be interpreted effectively. Most buildings will be a compromise of some sort, whether of shared activity, cost or scale, but establishing accepted boundaries at an early stage will save valuable time in developing a design and will increase the chances of end-user satisfaction.

The second half of the 20th century has seen the building of sports facilities on a large scale in many countries. The next decade will see an extension of this programme, including an emphasis on upgrading and refurbishment to bring these facilities up to modern standards.

13
Standards of provision

Christopher Harper

1 The hierarchy of provision

This section sets out the broad range of sports building types from the most modest up to complexes capable of holding events for 1500–2000 spectators. The hierarchy starts with village halls and local community recreation centres, **1**, then spans multi-sports facilities with or without indoor pools, ice rinks or other specialised features and terminates with large centres of sub-indoor sports arena size, **2**. The most convenient method of describing this stage-by-stage progression is to relate the overall content of a facility to its main activity space, the hall, and to describe it according to the number of badminton courts accommodated. Chapter 49 gives details of the courts which can be accommodated within halls of different standard sizes.

1 *Banham Community Centre, Norfolk. Photo: C J Harper*

In determining the requirements for a particular location, the sponsor should be aware of the full multi-use potential of facilities and the economies which can result from increased scale. There must be a clear appreciation of the role the building is to fulfil and whether it is geared primarily to sport or leisure use. Although the schedule of accommodation may be similar, standards of finish and the general ambience of the centre will be different according to the market it seeks to satisfy. There must be a clearly defined strategy of provision. Overlapping catchment areas should be avoided so that each new sports/leisure building slots in between existing facilities and provides for a focus on a particular sport or an expanded range of leisure pursuits.

The hierarchy of provision discussed in this section assumes multi-use, in terms of both a range of indoor sports and the possibility of arts, community and other events. Multi-use often provides the best value for money in both capital and recurrent expenditure terms and can enable centres to offer the flexibility to accommodate changes in fashion in leisure interests. Multi-use also means more appeal across a given community and the opportunity to persuade the uncommitted or casual visitor to try new sports.

Sports orientated centres are less prone to changes in the dynamic leisure market than are community leisure centres. The committed sports person will invariably support an appropriately located facility and will not be so sensitive to ambience and environment as the average leisure or family group user. The leisure market is in a state of constant change and subject to the forces imposed by commerce, the media and increasing consumer expectation. Buildings and their managements must be responsive to these demands. This will mean periodic changes in decor, lighting, furniture and equipment, particularly in the foyer and social areas. The image the building conveys will be of the utmost importance in a highly competitive market and this will extend to the exterior where a strong identity, good graphics and ease of access will all be of importance. The desirability of accommodating change should be recognised at the site selection/feasibility study stage where the opportunity for long-term structural change can be met by planning for growth zones accessible from the main circulation spine.

The following notes describe different sizes of main hall and the types of accommodation normally associated with them, together with alternative/additional options. This is not an exhaustive list of examples; its purpose is to help prospective sponsors define their requirements in the light of 30 years development of indoor sports facilities and a far longer experience of buildings for small communities. Each of the types covered is categorised primarily by its sports content but can equally well provide for extensive community and arts use. Even the village hall, based around a badminton court, can hold audiences of up to 200 people and function as a concert room, lecture hall, exhibition space or theatre when required.

2 Village halls/community recreation centres

These facilities, normally based on 1–2 badminton court sized halls are regarded as appropriate for catchment populations of up to about 6000. They will inevitably be multi-functional and have a wide range of ancillary accommodation options, according to the social needs of often rural and sometimes isolated communities. They may be located on an education site, to the benefit of a school, and provide a standard of facilities unlikely to be achieved in other ways, or associated with outdoor games areas. Refer to Chapter 68 for further details.

3 Small sports centres

The small sports centre, most usually based on a four-badminton-court hall, is by far the most numerous category of sports building and capable of serving populations of up to about 25,000. It is also the best documented dry sports building and perhaps the easiest to brief as sports use invariably predominates. Community and leisure use are enhanced by incorporating multi-use smaller halls and the addition of facilities such as snooker rooms, sauna suites and indoor pools. Spectator or arts use of the main hall is rare.

2 *The Link Centre, Swindon. Photo: Sports Council Publications*

4 Medium/large sports centres

Larger centres with principal halls of 6–9 or more badminton courts capacity are often combined with indoor pools, ice rinks and other leisure attractions. They may have a regional status for competitive sports with significant amounts of mobile spectator seating. They also offer considerable scope for the performing arts and for trade shows and exhibitions. Their design brief can be extremely challenging. Where large-scale events are held, the need for separate entrances to the building and separated circulation routes have to be taken into account so that different facilities can remain in use concurrently.

14
Safety in sports buildings

Sylvester Bone

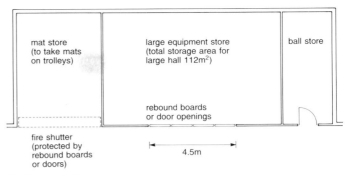

1 *Separate foam mat store*

1 Introduction

Statutory requirements focus the designer's attention on certain aspects of designing for safety such as emergency escape, conditions relating to alcohol sales, first aid and safe means of access. Other safety considerations may not come to the designer's attention until after the building is occupied. In certain cases the manager may require an alteration to correct a potential hazard, sometimes after an accident has occurred.

This section is based on a series of data sheets published by the Sports Council as *Factfile 5: Designing for Safety in Sports Buildings*. Where subjects related to safety are covered by other sections of this Handbook - such as designing for children, designing for the disabled, spectator seating, design and dimensions of courts and pitches to allow adequate safety margins – the safety aspects of these topics have been included in them and are not dealt with here.

2 Fire safety

Most new sports buildings are likely to be classed as assembly buildings under both the England and Wales and Scottish Building Regulations. If the public are invited to a sports building as spectators a licence will be required under the Fire Safety and Safety of Places of Sport Act 1987. Both the Building Regulations and the licence impose safety requirements. For new buildings designers should consult the Building Regulations (in England and Wales Part B; in Scotland Parts S and T; and in Northern Ireland Parts E and EE) and the British Standards to which they refer, particularly BS 5588: Part 6 (see References and further advice below). If the building conforms with these regulations it should also meet the licensing requirements. For work to existing buildings designers should consult the Home Office *Guide to Fire Precautions in Existing Places of Entertainment and Like Premises*, which is intended to give the requirements for local authority licensing.

Fire safety includes the control of the spread of fire and smoke, the protection of the structure, means of escape, access for the fire brigade and provision of fire extinguishing equipment. In sports buildings particular attention should be paid to the following.

2.1 Storage of combustible equipment

As was shown by the tragic fire at the Maysfield Leisure Centre in Belfast, the storage of foam filled mats used for gymnastics and other sports creates a serious hazard. Stringent requirements for management of mat stores are published in the *Fire Service Circular 1/1988*. The recommendations for the design of the store includes a 1 h fire resisting enclosure, smoke detectors wired to the

fire control panel and the store door not to open on to an escape route. Foam filled pits used in gymnastics and foam filled play shapes in children's crèches are also a hazard.

It is recommended that combustion modified foam should be used but this does not entirely eliminate the hazard. Once ignited, such foam will burn fiercely and give off lethal fumes. The storage of plastic stacking chairs can also be a fire hazard.

2.2 Accumulations of litter

Inaccessible voids, such as those beneath some forms of retractable seating, can allow rubbish to accumulate. Although this is primarily a management problem, if the design creates voids that are hidden and difficult to clean litter is likely to accumulate.

2.3 Escape routes

The principles for means of escape design are the same as in other buildings. Occupants should be able to turn away from a fire and move quickly and easily to a place of safety. However, certain features of sports buildings or combinations of them can require special consideration. The users of the building may not be familiar with its layout. There may be groups of children who cannot read signs or instructions and groups of disabled people who cannot easily negotiate stairs. Before evacuating the building parents will want to collect their children from crèches (or at least know that they are safe). The large undivided spaces in sports buildings may make the travel distances to exits longer than is normally allowed. These large spaces will have to accommodate different seating arrangements for different activities. Escape routes must be considered separately for each arrangement.

In sports complexes several audiences may be watching simultaneous activities in separate parts of the building. Conflicting traffic flows in escape routes must be avoided. Where spectators are on galleries escape routes must lead away from a fire in the area overlooked by the gallery and the escape route should not normally lead through the overlooked area. Open galleries should not be used as escape routes from other parts of the building. Clear signing and good lighting of escape routes are essential. The provision of illuminated exit signs and emergency lighting is normally a condition of an indoor sports licence. The provision of adequate storage has a bearing on escape. If storage is crowded or inaccessible there is a risk that bulky items such as trampolines and access towers will be left where they obstruct escape routes.

2.4 Alarm and communication systems

Orderly evacuation of a sports building depends on conveying the right information to occupants at the right time. Detector systems, internal telephones and closed circuit television (CCTV) can help to identify hazards that warrant evacuation; they include threatening behaviour,

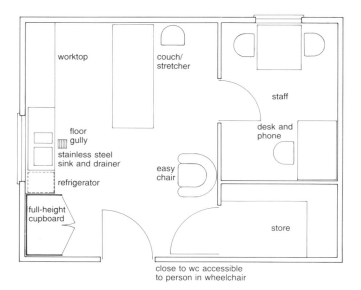

worktop

couch/
stretcher

staff

desk and
phone

floor
gully

stainless steel
sink and drainer

easy
chair

refrigerator

store

full-height
cupboard

close to wc accessible
to person in wheelchair

2 *First aid room to serve a medium-sized or large hall. Area to be at least 20 m²*

fumes, bomb scares and lighting failure as well as fire. There is then a need to let occupants know that they must leave the building and which routes to use. In many sports buildings staged (or staff) alarms are installed allowing staff to be alerted to move to predetermined positions to control evacuation before the general alarm is sounded or an announcement is made over the public address system. As sports buildings are normally unoccupied at night fire detectors are often linked to an alarm system which can automatically call the emergency services.

2.5 Emergency services

Easy access for the fire brigade, police and ambulances is essential and must be considered by the designer from the outset. Access routes which may be obstructed by vehicles, people evacuating from the building or stored materials (either on the site or on approaches to the site) should be avoided. The extent to which the perimeter of a sports building should be accessible to fire appliances depends on the size of the building. For example, if the floor area is less than 7000 cu m only 15% of the perimeter needs to be accessible, but if it is over 85,000 cu m the brigade must have access to 100% of the perimeter. Clear signing of the access route and a plan of the building inside the main entrance will help the emergency services. *Sports Council Data Sheet 60.11* gives advice on how to develop a co-ordinated signing system for sports building which can integrate the various categories of safety and information signs that will be required.

3 Accidental injury and first aid

The most usual cause of injury in a sports building is a result of the sports activities – people may be kicked, collide, fall, strain muscles or hurt themselves on equipment. First aid equipment, therefore, must be available close to where sports activities take place. There should also be a convenient route to an ambulance access. People with serious injuries must usually be left unmoved until the ambulance arrives. People with minor injuries may be treated in a first aid room before returning home or going on to hospital. In small sports buildings a dedicated first aid room is seldom likely to be used and may therefore be taken over for another purpose. In such buildings first aid equipment in the office will be adequate. In larger sports

buildings different levels of first aid provision should be made depending on the numbers using the building.

Accidents can also occur where people move about the building or engage in activities which cause them to collide with parts of the buildings. A number of design measures can increase safety and reduce the incident of this type of injury.

3.1 Flush detailing

Injuries can result from active occupants in light sports clothing colliding with projections. Doors and jambs in sports areas should be brought flush with adjacent walls by fitting panels. Fire extinguisher and other low level fittings should be recessed. Doors opening into traffic routes should be avoided. Lever door handles should be of the type that turn towards the door at the end to avoid catching clothes.

3.2 Glazing

Building regulations now require safety glazing in doors, side panels and at low level. They also require full height glazing to be 'manifested' by some stripe, rail or mark to prevent people walking into it. In general low level glazing should be avoided in sports buildings, and all glazing should be considered to be in an area of 'special risk' when applying the recommendations of BS 6262: 1982 *Code of Practice for Glazing for Buildings.*

3.3 Lockers

Open metal locker doors can cause collision injuries. Large lockers should not be provided at low level as children may become trapped inside them.

3.4 Loose equipment

Unbagged nets hanging across a sports hall can be hazardous for active users of the hall, as can gymnasium equipment and five-a-side goals if they are not put out of the way when not in use.

3.5 Storage of chemicals

A secure store should be provided for any chemicals that may be required for plant maintenance or cleaning. The Control of Substances Hazardous to Health (COSHH) Regulations will apply and management will need to control the use and storage of chemicals.

3.6 Flooring

Both the initial specification of the flooring and the maintenance it receives will affect the slipperiness and therefore the safety of flooring – this topic is dealt with more fully in Chapter 64.

3.7 Kitchens

Injuries in kitchens are relatively frequent. They should have their own first aid equipment to deal with burns, cuts, etc. Adequate space must be provided around cooking appliances.

3.8 Access to plant

The operation and maintenance of plant requires adequate access. BS 8313: 1989 gives recommended dimensions for working on services in ducts. Maintenance instructions should always be provided for plant, but if access is inadequate the essential maintenance may not be done which can in some cases lead to health problems such as *Legionellosis* or kitchen infestations.

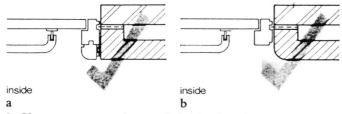

inside
a

inside
b

3 *Sharp corners may be rounded either by a hardwood fillet, **a**, or a bullnose brick, **b***

PUSH BAR TO OPEN

4 *Rebound panels are fitted above and below the panic bolts for five-a-side football to protect players' shoulders and heads from striking exposed door frames. Photo: David Butler*

4 Violence and security

The managements of sports buildings must protect their staff and the users of the building. They also protect cash and valuables in the building.

4.1 Protection of valuables

Alcohol licences are likely to specify a requirement for secure storage. If cash is collected at various points in the building (eg cafés, vending machines, equipment hire, crèches, bars and concession trading points) it can be stored in a single safe in a position which is under surveillance and gives easy access to a security firm for collection. Wages may also need to be stored in the safe.

4.2 Exclusion of intruders

Sports buildings containing anything of value are likely to be equipped with intruder alarm systems designed by specialists. However, the building designer can contribute to security by making the intruder's work more difficult and therefore more likely that a 'softer' target will be chosen. Public surveillance of entrances may discourage an intruder. Secure locks on doors and windows, avoidance of easy routes on to roofs and openable rooflights, good site lighting and avoidance of hiding places within the building will all reduce temptation. Lighting and surveillance are particularly important in parking areas to discourage theft from and of cars.

4.3 Protection from violence

Staff may be subjected to threatening behaviour and violence in any part of the building. Internal telephones will allow them to call for assistance. Surveillance of one space from another will help to discourage such behaviour. The most vulnerable point in the building is likely to be the reception desk. A personal attack alarm should be installed which, when operated, can summon help by flashing lights (rather than by sounding a bell or siren). Some managements insist on glazed screen protection for reception staff. The reception staff need to be able to control who is allowed into the building, both to exclude unwanted visitors and to prevent overcrowding. Turnstile systems are therefore often fitted. The designer needs to be aware that the reception desk and entry control may well be altered as one management regime succeeds another. The basic design should be spacious enough to allow for change.

5 Safety and the designer's role

Management – and more particularly the manager in charge of a sports building at a particular time – carries the direct responsibility for the safety of people in and around the building. However, management has to rely on the designer for information and advice. The designer should see that attention is paid to safety during the various stages of design, handover, maintenance and alteration and information provided in a form management can understand and use. Designers should bear in mind that the original client for a sports building, with whom the management options were first discussed when the brief was prepared, may well have little to do with the organisation which eventually takes on the management responsibility. It is important that the eventual managers know what was originally intended, particularly any limitations applying to the original scheme.

Table 14.1 lists some of the safety aspects to be considered at different stages.

6 References and further advice

British Standards Institution, *BS 5588: Fire Precautions in the Design, Construciton and Use of Buildings. Part 6: Code of Practice for Places of Assembly*, BSI, Milton Keynes.

Table 14.1: Safety aspects to check at each stage of design and construction

1 At initial briefing

Schedule of accommodation to include areas and numbers of users or staff, stating:
- Capacity for spectator events
- No. of persons with disabilities – including participants
- Anticipated non-sports multi-uses
- Social and local organisation spaces
- Restrictions on construction programme and access to side
- Provision of crèche facilities.

Use of outside spaces, for example:
- Coach and other heavy vehicle access
- Access for bringing in heavy items of equipment
- Supervised and controlled car and coach parking
- Access for emergency vehicles
- Access for dray supplying bar.

Booking and payment system policy established for:
- Reception entrance control and cash handling
- Waiting areas
- Equipment hire and retail outlets.

Standards required for sports activities:
- Whether national/international, club/country, recreation or practice standards are required and that dimensions suit
- Type of lighting required (eg 'blind box' or natural)
- Check the required position of stores for major items of equipment
- Establish mat store size.

First aid:
- Level of provision, ie separate room or use of office or other room.

2 At outline design stage

Details of accommodation – check:
- Ramps and separate toilet for people with disabilities
- Seating and alternative escape routes
- Adequate heights and safety margins for sports activities.

Layout of outside spaces – check:
- Traffic routes for different vehicles
- Provision of bay for ambulance to stand-by
- Adequacy of pedestrian routes to and from building (including places of safety outside building after evacuation)
- Access from street and disabled parking spaces into building, eg ramps, handrails, suitable paving (consider access for blind and partially sighted)
- Access for pushchairs.

Design of inside spaces – check:
- Reception and control to be suitably positioned for function
- Secure space (office) for cash handling and storage
- Secure routes to bring in and take away cash
- Fire separation to be adequate for mat storage
- Access to hall clear of corners and not restricted by wall mounted goals
- Glare from daylight avoided around and above courts
- Requirement of licensing authorities for separation of bar area
- Containment of areas where glasses can be used
- Approval of fire department to escape routes and exits
- Layout of first aid room and space to stand and move stretchers
- Approval of management to exit and entrance arrangements for staff, participants and the public
- Provision required for storage of chemicals
- Adequate and well positioned storage space for sports equipment, vending machine refills, etc.

- General policy on evacuation routes and alarm system to be adopted
- General policy on signing system, including external signs, for the building.

3 At final scheme stage

Design of outside spaces – check:
- Height and type of fencing has adequate strength and resistance to climbing while allowing for surveillance from routes used by the public
- Opportunity is taken for traffic calming to reduce risks to pedestrians
- Potential climbing routes giving access to rooflights and high level openings are avoided (eg rainwater pipes, hedges and adjoining structures).

Design of inside spaces – check:
- Details of fire prevention scheme approved, eg emergency lighting, fire fighting equipment, detector alarm systems
- Potential for unauthorised high level viewing perches is avoided
- Access and accommodation are acceptable to the police and ambulance services
- Flush details are used throughout sports and circulation areas. This means rebound panels across any doors in the hall that are not flush with the walls and no projecting door furniture (handles, overhead door closers, etc) or fire fighting equipment
- Floor finishes are of suitable quality for areas of most wear (eg hall, circulation, changing rooms or showers)
- Use of C or B class safety glazing or protection wherever glazing is vulnerable
- Critical safety dimensions for different sports given in Chapters 15–46 and 70–102.
- Water supply system for features promoting growth of *Legionella* (eg warm water in dead legs or storage feeding showers)
- Intruder alarm system and control
- Adequacy of natural ventilation and its resistance to intruders (window restrictors, etc)
- Public address or intercom system
- Kitchen design to include first aid, lavatory basin and adequate space around appliances
- Type of lockers for security and to avoid sharp edges or possibility of entrapment
- Detailed, co-ordinated signing system for the building.

4 At handover

Provide designers' input to maintenance and operation manual to include:
- Requirements or conditions in approvals (eg planning and building regulations)
- Licensing requirements (eg what licenses are required – any record of consultation with licensing authority)
- Test certificates (eg electrical, emergency lighting, fire and intruder alarm systems, floor sockets for gym equipment)
- Names and addresses of installers and suppliers of components and equipment eg windows, sanitary ware, ironmongery, service installations, cooking equipment, floor surfaces
- Maintenance instructions for equipment, surface finishes, services installations (including records of any discussion or offers for maintenance agreements)
- Separate list of outstanding defects related to safety and warnings about use of equipment or spaces before defects are put right.

5 When making alterations

Establish working restrictions (eg what parts of building will be closed and what this will affect):
- Ensure existing safety measures are not reduced (eg replacement of safety glass, additional travel distances for means of escape, loss of first aid facilities)
- Check effect of works on safety (eg access and parking of vehicles, storage areas for plant and materials, protection of the works, work programme, access for workmen to rest of building, restrictions on particular types of work while building is in use).

15
Indoor sports data

Compiled by Peter Ackroyd with David Bosher (Internal environment), Kit Campbell (badminton), Christopher Harper (Gymnastics), Mark Foley (Movement and Dance) and Maritz Vandenberg in collaboration with the governing bodies of sport and many others whose assistance is gratefully acknowledged.

1 Introduction

The chapters in this part of the Handbook give fundamental technical information for over 50 sports and different disciplines which can share a sports hall floor, based on standards used in the UK. Data for other sports which need dedicated floor space are given in Chapters 70–90 inclusive, including a few sports such as roller skating which may be practicable in a multi-sports space, subject to circumstances and local constraints.

The minimum overall space required for each of the relevant standards of play takes into account any necessary run-out or safety margins, team bench and officials' control spaces around the playing area. These together amount to the *overall areas* shown by a broken line surrounding the space diagram in each chapter.

Refer to Volume 1 for details of outdoor sports data.

2 Standards of play

A space table for most of the sports sets out dimensions grouped under one of the following alternative formats with the bracketed notations used in the tables:

Standard of play
International   Regional (Rg)   Recreational (R)
National (N)   County (Cy)
                 Club (C)

Where club and county standards differ (as with badminton), with club and recreational being the same, the format used is:

Standard of play
International   Regional (Rg)   Club (C)
National (N)   County (Cy)   Recreational (R)

It is important to stress that a growing number of sports seek the same standard of space provision for both regional/county and national training and competition. These are recognised by identical or very similar dimensions given in the tables. For a few, such as badminton, the minimum height is the only acceptable difference.

3 Metrication

In keeping with European practice, imperial conversions are given following each metric dimension. By far the majority of governing bodies now publish and mark-out using metric dimensions. Some have rounded off former imperial dimensions; others have converted exactly.

4 Acknowledgements

We would like to thank the following for their help: the Scottish Sports Council and Sports Council for Northern Ireland; the governing bodies of sport and other organisations named in the references for each sport with contributions from many officials; the Sports Council's Development, Facilities, Information and Publications Units and Regional Officers; the sports equipment trade; recreational consultants; architects; and many others who have supplied illustrations.

5 Further advice

The data and dimensions in each of the following chapters are partly based on the rules of each sport and some may have been changed by their governing bodies since their preparation. See also Chapter 49.

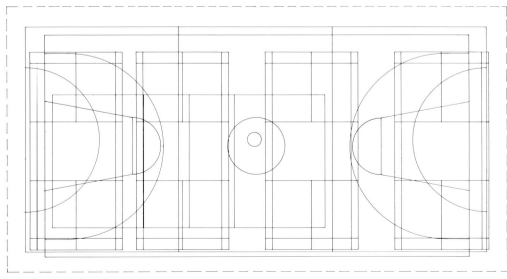

1 *Markings network graphic: TUS*

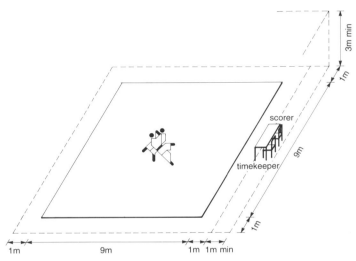

16
Aikido

Peter Ackroyd

1 Introduction

There are two different forms of aikido. Tomiki aikido is a competitive combat sport, based on an ancient Japanese system of self-defence. Force is met not with counter-force but with avoiding action, enabling the defender to take advantage of the attacker's temporary loss of balance to score with a successful aikido technique.

Orthodox aikido, on the other hand, is a strictly non-competitive discipline based on a traditional system of self-defence, aimed at physical, mental and spiritual development. There are no contests or bouts of sparring and therefore many of the recommendations below do not apply. Also, the safety requirements for the non-combative activity are not so stringent. Requirements for traditional aikido are generally the same as for judo, except that no special provisions are necessary for contests or spectators.

1.1 Critical factors
- The overall area of space including safety margins around the combat mat
- The distance of spectators from the mat
- For this bare-footed sport the floor surface, cleanliness and personal hygiene are important
- Flush walls, and safety padding where necessary
- Fire precautions for mat storage.

1.2 Space
The mat can be placed anywhere in a common sports space having a minimum clear area of at least 9 × 9 m, preferably with a surrounding safety area, and a minimum clear height of 3.0 m, **2**. For competitions at least three combat areas are required in a minimum overall space of 33 × 13 m.

Space table

	International National (N)	Regional (Rg) County (Cy) Club (C)	Recreational (R)
Combat mat	9 × 9 m	9 × 9 m	9 × 9 m
Minimum safety area around mat	1.5 m	1 m	1 m
Additional officials' table margin at one side	1 m min	1 m min	–
Minimum overall area	13 × 12 m	12 × 11 m	11 × 11 m

2 *Space diagram. Spectators should be at least 1.5 m from the mat or officials' seating*

1 *Photo: British Aikido Association*

1.3 Storage

Storage will be required for mats on trolleys, officials' table and scoreboards. Mats may be a fire risk and require storage in a separated fire resistant store.

1.4 Floor mats

Consult specialist equipment suppliers. Sectional mats must be prevented from slipping or opening up.

Preferably a 'soft floor' without need for mats should be considered. This could be particularly suited to practice halls or specialist training and combat rooms where other activities such as gymnastics and movement and dance would also benefit from the surface resilience.

1.5 Surrounding enclosure

Hall walls or netting. In small practice halls, walls should be padded by upstanding mats or mattresses to a minimum height of 1 m.

1.6 Internal environment

As for judo. For general details of environmental services recommendations refer to Chapters 60 and 61.

1.7 Competitors and judges

Allow changing space for five persons per contest.

1.8 Spectators

Some mat-side chairs can be arranged in the spaces on both sides of the officials' table or on tiered units around the safety area. Spectators should be at least 1.5-2 m from the mat depending on the standard of competition. The sport is developing and could possibly attract 1000 or more spectators and devotees at major events and championships.

References and further advice

The British Aikido Board.

17
Archery

Peter Ackroyd

1 Introduction

Indoor shooting ranges must not share a hall with other simultaneous sports activities, even if separated by a net or barrier. Any sports or practice hall which is compatible with the dimensional and other requirements given below is probably suitable for archery.

1.1 Critical factors

- The 20 yd round is the only remaining UK official distance kept in Imperial measurement
- Archery must not share a space with any other simultaneous activity or users; see safety notes below
- Overall area of space including the safety margins and nets surrounding the shoot
- The increased minimum height above the shoot, clear of all obstructions and fittings
- Access and viewing must be only from the rear of archers
- Other safety precautions, including location of unlocked doorways, balconies and danger notices.

1.2 Space

The official distances of rounds for all standards of archery are:

- 18 m (approx 59 ft)
- 20 yd (18.29 m)
- 25 m (approx 82 ft)
- 30 m (approx 98 ft 6 in).

Note that there is no longer a 15 yd Imperial distance.
A minimum clear ceiling height of 3 m is required and preferably higher.
The official diameters of target faces are:

- At 18 m, 400 mm diameter
- At 20 yd, 600 mm diameter
- At 25 m, 600 mm diameter
- At 30 m, 800 mm diameter.

The most economical and usual space allowance is for four archers per target, shooting in two shoots of two archers shooting at once. To conform with competition rules, the minimum intervals between target centres for the number of archers at a time on the shooting line, are:

- For two (or four) archers per target (the more usual number), 2.5 m
- For three archers per target (less usual), 3.66 m.

1.3 Layout and safety

The general layout of an indoor range is shown in **2**. Spectator provision must be behind the archers and raised if this is possible. Access must be from behind the archers.

1 *Photo: Grand National Archery Society*

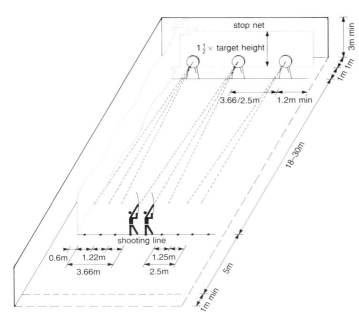

2 *Diagrammatic setting-out of targets and archer positions for the various recognised lengths of rounds*

There must be no shooting towards a balcony or viewing area and there must be no spectators alongside the shooting range, even on a balcony. All doors except those behind the archers must be kept locked during shooting to prevent people entering.

Safety nets
Safety nets must be made of white archery mesh and should be as high as possible, preferably up to beneath the roof; but if this is not feasible, 3.5 m (11 ft 6 in) is an absolute minimum height for distances up to 30 m and 6.1 m (20 ft) the preferable minimum height. The stop net behind the target should be at least 3 m high, or half a target higher as viewed from the shooting line, whichever is the greater.

1.4 Floor and markings
The floor finish should preferably be wood. Marking lines are required to represent the shooting line and the target line (see diagram), with space markings for the targets and archers. The markings at the target stands should be non-slip.

1.5 Storage
There should be storage provision large enough to allow stacking of targets on their face, rather than on edge. A tackle box shelf measuring at least 750 × 300 × 75 mm, provided the zone is behind the shooting line, is an advantage. Also secure storage for demountable target lighting, if provided.

1.6 Environment
For general details of environmental services recommendations refer to Chapters 60 and 61.

Targets must be well-lit in the interests of the sport and safety. General illumination levels in multi-use facilities may be too low for archery, especially where targets are situated against end walls. Provision for additional lights directed at the targets (and away from the archers) is recommended.

2 References and further advice
Grand National Archery Society and 1990 Rules of Shooting.
Volume 1, Chapter 38, for archery outdoors.

18
Sportshall athletics

Peter Ackroyd

Introduction

Sportshall athletics has developed since 1976 to provide vital competition for young athletes during the winter period. It is meant to be fun and encourage team participation. Whilst most of the events are unique, some are based on past events; an example is the standing long jump which was an Olympic discipline and the forerunner of the modern long jump.

The principal age groups for the regional and national competitors are under 13 and under 15, but local leagues involve other age groups. Under 11 boys' and girls' team competitors help to emphasise the importance of taking part and working together. Championships are not held for this age group. Pairs races and relays replace individual track events and the scoring of the jumps and throws is based on the summation of the performances by two, three or even four team members.

1.1 Critical factors

- Participation should be fun for youngsters attracted to athletics
- Layout and dimensions must provide safe distances
- Reversaboards and team mats are essential for track events
- Consultations for the provision of adequate barriers around shot put area and protection of floor.

1.2 Space

Suitable layouts are shown in **2** and **3**. Disciplines and events are grouped and illustrated as follows:

Track

Races include one or two lap sprints (one lap equals two lengths of hall), four and six lap middle distance races, eight lap time trials and relay races. A lane width is twice the norm for athletics and the combined start/finish line is at the centre point **3**. Reversaboards and team mats are fundamental and should be carefully positioned (see also equipment below). For the obstacle relay an equipment layout is shown in **4**.

Field

Comprising the vertical jump, **5**, standing long jump, **6**, and standing triple jump, **8**. These 'standing start' disciplines all require special equipment as described with the diagrams, but occupy little space, **2**, **3**. Field events are always positioned on the far side from spectators.

1 *Relay race showing reversaboards against rear wall. Photo: John Evans*

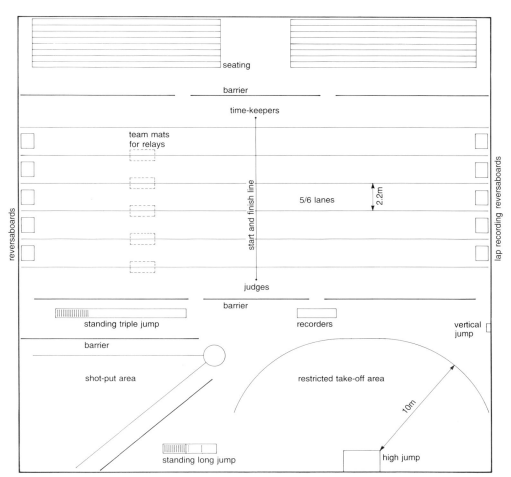

2 *A typical large hall layout. Always position 'field' events on far side from spectators*

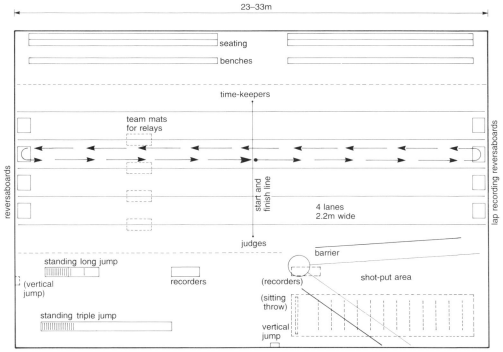

3 *A typical medium hall layout showing alternative field event locations including sprint and 4 × 2 lap relay layouts. Team mats are essential to avoid team members from getting in the way of runners*

High jump

Normal high jump rules apply except for restricted take-off of 10 m (approx 32 ft 10 in) radius, **2.** Details of foam filled landing beds and storage precautions are given in Chapter 70.

Shot

Normal shot competition rules apply using 2.75–4 kg shots. Also refer to Chapter 70. It must be emphasised that for safety reasons sportshall athletics bodies should be consulted about the type and dimensions of safety barriers and margins to protect adjacent activities and users of the hall. See also Section 4 and 5 below.

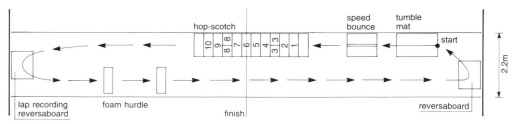

4 *Equipment layout for 4 × 1 lap obstacle relay. The lower reversaboard is moved over to allow competitor to turn clear of other team members before the touch take over*

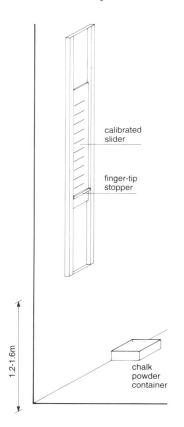

5 *The vertical jump is an internationally recognised measurement of fitness relating leg strength to body weight. The event uses a magnetically held calibrated slider (in a wall mounted frame) which is adjusted to the competitors extended finger tip height beforehand and against which the jump height is measured*

Speed bounce

A foam based speed bounce mat with a 200 mm (approx 8 in) high foam wedge dividing it into two equal halves must be used. For further details, consult athletics bodies.

1.3 Other events

There are also under 11 year olds fun-in-athletics events, **9,** over–under relay and sitting throw **10**.

2 Equipment and storage

The most important equipment for track races are the reversaboards, **2, 3**. Both the fully automated and mechanical versions measure 813 mm (32 in) wide by 1.22 m (4 ft) deep. Units are placed at each end of a sprint lane and are used by athletes for turning – in much the same way that a swimmer uses the wall of a pool to push off for the return length. They are set at a 50° angle to the end wall and are designed with a 686 mm (27 in) wide by 381 mm (15 in) deep target area which runners hit with their feet when turning.

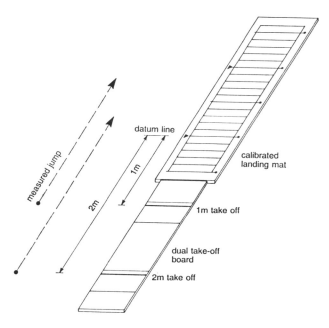

6 *Standing long jump is a test of co-ordination and leg strength. A special calibrated landing mat is used for recording jumps. It is attached to a take-off board which has two standing blocks, one at 1 m for the under 11 years and one at 2 m for the over 11 years age group*

With the automated 'contactor' reversaboard, a wall-mounted electronic device, clearly visible to both judges and competitors, indicates the number of laps to be run by each competitor in each lane. The final lap is signalled by means of a large white light.

A card indicator system is also available. This requires the manning of the lane by monitors who hold up large cards showing the number of laps to be completed. Card systems are much less costly than the automated contactor reversaboard and enable fixed reversaboards to be utilised at either end of a sportshall.

A considerable amount of other equipment must be stored securely or brought in from other facilities.

Track Events
Reversaboards:

- 5 or 6 contactor recording boards
- 5 or 6 fixed non-recording boards
- 5 or 6 indicator panels with brackets
- 1 power unit.

Relays:

- 5 or 6 relay mats
- 5 or 6 batons.

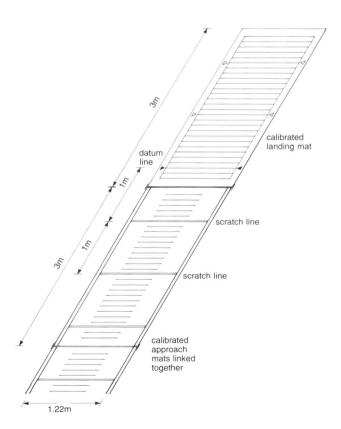

7 Standing long jump. Photo: John Evans

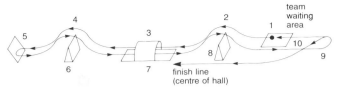

9 Fun-in-athletics for under 11 year olds includes an over–under relay which starts at (1) with a mat tumble, then (2) over a foam hurdle, (3) through tunnel, (4) over second hurdle, (5) runner turns on the reversaboard and retakes the three obstacles to turn again on reversaboard (9) for shoulder touch takeover at (10). The last member of team runs back to centre of hall finish line

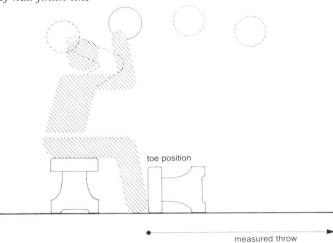

10 Sitting throw. The under 11 year old sits on a standard gym bench with both feet against another bench. The throw is as a soccer throw-in using a size 4 football. The throwing area is premarked at 250 mm intervals from and parallel to the bench

8 Standing triple jump equipment consists of a semi-rigid approach mat with a selection of starting lines suitable for all ages and abilities. The landing mat is calibrated in centimetres for instant reading of the jump

Judging:

- 2 finishing posts
- 1 set of judging discs
- Judges' stands (if available).

Obstacle relay
- 3 or 4 tumble mats
- 3 or 4 bounce mats
- 3 or 4 hop-Scotch mats
- 6 or 8 foam hurdles.

Field events
Vertical jump:

- Measuring board (screwed to wall)
- Powdered chalk tray.

Standing long jump:

- Calibrated mat and take-off board.

Standing triple jump:

- Calibrated mat.

Bounce mat:

- See Obstacle relay.

Shots:

- Shot circle
- 2 × 2.72 kg, 2 × 3.25 kg, 2 × 4.00 kg shots
- Marking tape for quadrant.

High jump:

- Landing bed
- Stands
- Bar (plus spare).

Other equipment
Officials and competitors, tables and chairs for marshals, track and field judges, competitors coloured discs, recorders and timekeepers equipment.

3 Floor and markings
Footwear is not spiked and therefore a multi-sports surface is satisfactory, but grip and bounce are important criteria. The floor may need protection from shot putting (refer to Chapter 70). Lane lines are marked using coloured tape which on a multi-sports floor must contrast clearly with other sports markings.

For general information, see Chapter 64.

4 Environment
For general details of environmental services recommendations refer to Chapters 60 and 61.

There are no special requirements, except that the reversaboards should be clearly seen and not in shadow, for example from bunched netting.

5 References and further advice
Athletics governing bodies.
Chapter 70, Athletics training halls.
National Sportshall Athletics Championships: Rules of Competition.
Sports Council, *National Lottery Sports Fund Guidance Note 335.* Sports Council, London (1995).

19
Badminton

Kit Campbell

1 Introduction

Badminton is one of the most popular racquet sports in the UK, parts of Europe and much of Asia. Players have to be able to sight the fast moving shuttlecock against both wall and ceiling surfaces, **1**, and provision for the game is likely to have a particular impact on the height of halls, colour schemes and ventilation and lighting design. Badminton courts may be provided in purpose-designed badminton halls, **2**, or in multi-purpose spaces provided that the particular needs of players are not compromised. Short tennis is also played on badminton courts – see references.

1.1 Critical factors
- Adequate overall area, including safety margins around and between courts

1 *Badminton between the beams in a SASH hall. The fluorescent light fittings are protected by translucent covers and mounted each side of the roof beams over the space between courts. Note that the additional light fittings for other sports are placed on the diagonal ties and shielded to prevent glare. They are on a separate circuit so that they can be switched off when badminton is played. Design & Build: Nicholas Grimshaw & Partners and Bovis Construction Ltd. Photo: David Butler*

- Adequate height and lighting over the whole of the court
- Plain medium to dark background colour to contrast with shuttlecock
- Uniform, glare-free side lighting
- Lights arranged to be compatible with court layout (generally outside court area)
- Lighting designed to avoid stroboscopic effects
- Design and type of heating and ventilation system
- Avoidance of shuttle trap ledges on walls and in the roof structure
- Non-slippery floors.

1.2 Space and layout

Basic dimensions
Court and overall space dimensions are given in the space table below and in **3**. Hall capacities and critical layouts are illustrated in the section on the 'Layout of Courts' below.

Roof profiles
Suitable roof profiles are critical to play and affect both capital and heating costs. The apparent greater height beneath a pitched roof is seldom of significant benefit for badminton except when the eaves height is only 6.7 m (the recreational minimum). The lower slopes of a pitched roof can actually inhibit the flight of the shuttle, particularly on service, because its parabolic trajectory reaches a maximum height approaching the baseline. A hipped or mansard roof profile can provide greater height over the back of the court. Roof trusses or beams located between badminton courts must provide a minimum height of 7 m for other sports along the length of the hall.

Heights of halls and levels of provision
Tests for height carried out by the Sports Council confirm that halls of 7.6–8.4 m (approx 25–27.5 ft) are adequate for badminton at club and league matches. Halls of less than 7.6 m (25 ft) from the floor at a point over the baseline are unsuitable for the game to be played to a high competitive level. They will be acceptable for children's and recreational play. On the basis that in sparsely populated areas a low hall is better than no hall at all, 6.1 m (20 ft) height is the recommended absolute minimum for small community centre halls designed only for recreational play.

Space table

	International/ National (N)	Regional (Rg)/ County (Cy)	Club (C) and Recreational (R)
Clear minimum height over length of court (see also Section 3.4)	9.1 m	8.4 m (1)	C: 7.6 m R: 6.7–7.6 m (2)
Playing area (doubles court)			
Length	13.4 m	13.4 m	13.4 m
Width	6.1 m	6.1 m	6.1 m
Wall from baseline, min	2.3 m	2.3 m	1.5 m min
Wall from side-line, min	2.2 m	2.2–1.2 m(3)	1.2 m min(4)
Between parallel courts, min	2.0 m	2.0–0.9 m(3)	0.9 m min
Minimum overall area (minimum dimensions)			
For a single court	18 × 10.5 m	As National	16.4 × 8.4 m min
For a parallel pair(4)	18 × 18.6 m	Space	16.4 × 15.5 m min
For each additional court	+18 × 8.1 m min	Standards	+7.0 m min

Note (1): Badminton Association of England (BAoE) revised County (Cy) height introduced in 1987.
Note (2): For one or two badminton court halls (in local community or village halls) the BAoE accept 6.1 m (approx 20 ft) height as the absolute minimum for recreational play.
Note (3): Absolute minimum for practice/coaching in existing halls or where it is impractical to remark courts with wider side margins. Umpire's chair between match play roll-down courts should not be less than 2.0 m.
Note (4): Where halls are subdivided by netting, a full side margin of 1.2 m should be allowed along both sides of the net when setting out adjacent badminton courts.

2 *The synthetic-surfaced courts at the Telford Racquets and Fitness Centre. Increasingly halls may be planned for badminton alone, for example the purpose designed High Wycombe Badminton Centre and the English National Badminton Centre at Milton Keynes. Note the dark sight screen curtains surrounding the hall. Preferably, the screen colour should match that of the background wall seen above to avoid shadow contrast which increases the difficulty of following a fast-moving shuttle across the sight screen height. Photo: SC Publications*

Layout of courts

Figures **5** to **8** relate to the hall sizes and multi-sports layouts shown in Chapter 49, Multi-purpose halls for sport and the arts. Figures **6** and **7** illustrate critical sizes and court layouts to ensure that the minimum dimensions for the surrounding safety margins are provided. They also show courts 2 m apart for English County (Cy) play in order to allow space for umpires' chairs.

In a multi-sports hall where other games may be programmed to take place at the same time as badminton, there are usually conflicting demands of compatibility to be resolved by management. Basketball, volleyball and most martial arts, for example, are noisy and will disturb even recreational badminton play. Tennis, table tennis (providing netting is drawn between the two spaces to stop balls running into the badminton courts), fencing and judo are satisfactory simultaneous activities.

Distractions caused by lights, movement and noise can largely be overcome by curtains of netting drawn between different activity zones and at the back of courts where they are not near walls.

The entrance to a hall should be at the side and not at the back of a court so that people using it do not distract players. This applies particularly to multi-court halls. In small halls where courts are placed across the width, it is more difficult to avoid doorways in side walls along the ends of courts.

1.3 Floor and court markings

The floor may be of wood, composition or synthetic materials, but it must not be slippery. The finish should be dull to avoid reflected light which adds to the difficulty of sighting the shuttle. Some 'give' in the floor surface is extremely desirable to prevent injuries.

Regulation court markings are matt finish white lines 40 mm (1.5 in) wide included within overall court dimensions. Where tennis has been marked in white, yellow has been recommended for recreational badminton. However, on multi-sports floors this results in the majority of all lines glowing in the brightest colour which

can be very distracting for other sports. It is now good practice to re-mark all badminton courts in white using a colour for tennis, if provided. The increasingly popular game of short tennis, played on badminton courts, then has the benefit of white lines. Refer to Chapter 88 for the preferred indoor location of tennis.

Lay-down mat courts are also available. Roll-down PVC and other sheeting has been tried out but problems experienced include rucking and the rolled weight. Special storage rollers can be supplied to ease storage and removal. The size of roll-down courts should be checked against the overall area given in the table above, particularly the length. A change of surface level within the minimum overall space should be avoided if possible.

1.4 Walls

A suitable background against which a fast-moving shuttle can be seen easily is *critically important and this point cannot be overemphasised*. Badminton ideally requires a hall with four plain walls with no windows or glass. If viewing windows are necessary in walls at court ends, then curtains or blinds must be fitted to avoid distracting match players. For top standards of play, games nets and other distracting attachments should be removable. For all standards of play there should be no ledges or other projections which will trap shuttles and practice basketball backboards behind a court should be removable.

Walls behind the ends of courts should be finished in medium to dark shades with a matt surface. For reflectance values and guidance see the *CIBSE Lighting Guide*. A gloss finish is too reflective. This applies equally to side walls as many shots are played to the side of the body looking towards the side of the court. Walls at opposite ends of court should be identical. In Sports Council SASH sports halls, **10**, Cornflower Blue BS 20E51 has been found excellent by international and recreational players, and provides a cheerful environment for other hall users. The SASH programme developed a blue-coloured net with curtains to match the walls, **10**.

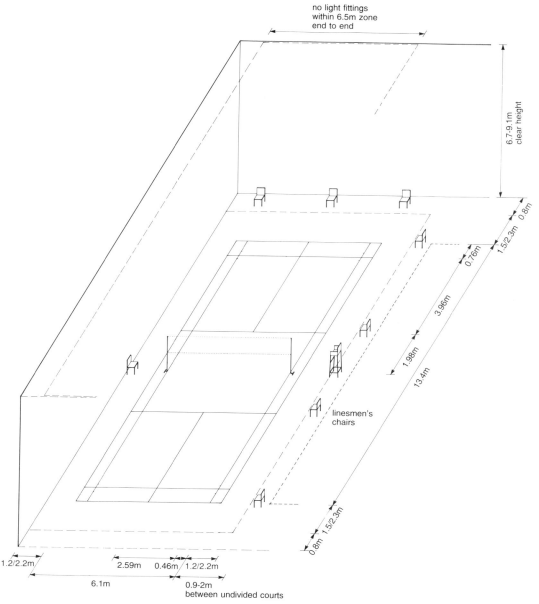

no light fittings
within 6.5m zone
end to end

6.7-9.1m
clear height

0.8m
1.5/2.3m
0.76m
3.96m
1.98m
13.4m

linesmen's
chairs

0.8m 1.5/2.3m

1.2/2.2m
2.59m 0.46m / 1.2/2.2m
6.1m
0.9-2m
between undivided courts

3 *Badminton space diagram. Dimensions for the different standards of play are given in the space table. Note the critical minimum dimensions specified in the footnotes. For multi-court layout for national standard play, see* Arenas *publication in References*

2 Environment

2.1 General
For general details of environmental services recommendations refer to Chapters 60 and 61.

2.2 Lighting
Players must be able to follow the flight of the shuttlecock against the background without being troubled by glare or having their attention distracted by bright light sources near their sight lines. The shuttlecock is seen by light transmitted by, and reflected from the translucent 'feathers'. Natural lighting, if any, should be confined to roof lights designed and positioned to give even lighting free from glare and sun penetration. Illuminated signs, doors and windows to other lit areas, **11**, are all distracting and should be capable of temporary screening by curtains or able to be switched off. Lighting should be as 'uniform' as possible. The recommended lighting level is 500 lux for levels of play up to club/county and 750 lux for national and international level.

2.3 Heating and ventilation
The minimum temperature should be about 16°C (61°F). Warmer air can affect the flight of shuttles and so different types of shuttle are available to suit different temperatures in playing halls.

Any ventilation system which moves the air can deflect the shuttlecock. A draught-free atmosphere is therefore essential. The location and protection of all air input and extract grilles or openings, and the resultant air movement produced, must be carefully considered particularly in relation to the flight path of shuttlecocks (see grille locations, **10**). For further details see Chapters 60 and 61.

3 Equipment
When the court is permanently in use for badminton, the most satisfactory and convenient net posts are those with a metal base which can be screwed to the floor on the side lines. Where this is not possible, posts with well weighted bases which will hold the net taut at its correct height can be obtained. A satisfactory modern design can be wheeled into position.

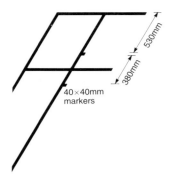

4 *Detail of corner marking: shuttle test markers in two diagonally opposite corners of the court*

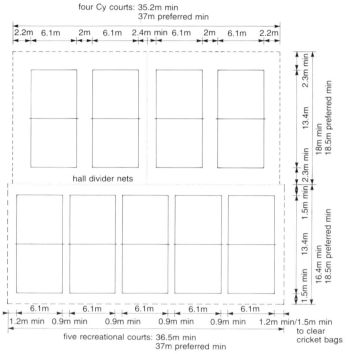

5 *Eight or 10 marked-out courts with space for net dividers. Two lots of four parallel courts are spaced apart for county preliminary rounds (with few spectators) but are also spaced from the quarter-net to provide a pair of recreation courts when three-quarters of the hall is in other sports use. A further alternative is a nine-court layout as drawn, with four county plus five club/recreation courts (over which the four lay-down courts are used for county prelims)*

4 Storage

Storage space close to the courts is required for posts and nets. As the posts are heavy, trolleys are often employed for easier movement when setting up apparatus. Two trolleys occupying a space 3 × 3 m (approx 10 × 10 ft) accommodate all the apparatus required by four badminton courts.

5 Spectators

Badminton has developed as a major spectator sport in the past decade and attracts TV coverage to its premier events. Adequate space for spectators is therefore desirable in all halls providing first-class facilities. In large halls a total width of at least 18 m (approx 59 ft) is recommended in the lengthways direction of the court. This leaves space at each end for two rows of spectators and chairs for players

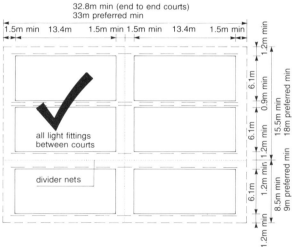

6 *This outdated and poorly lit layout provides two courts which are end-to-end with resultant reduced run-backs without a sight screen divider net between courts, acceptable for recreational play only*

7 *Development of six-court hall adjusted in size 33 × 27 × 7.6 m. This end-to-end layout needs a minimum length to 32.8 m for full club standards of play. A net divider across the hall is essential. An interesting development of this plan form at Claremont Sports Hall, Newcastle University is shown in **9***

between games. At the other extreme, the potential capacity at major events is estimated at between 2000 and 15,000 (see Chapter 50 and other references).

Regional and subregional centres need to accommodate at least 1000 spectators. For tournaments and 'centre-court' matches, spectator accommodation is normally in the form of demountable or mobile seating units arranged in any position required although the best viewing position is at the ends of courts.

6 Building conversions

The critical factors to be examined for recreational badminton include clear heights and the shape of the ceiling, the floor space, lighting and background.

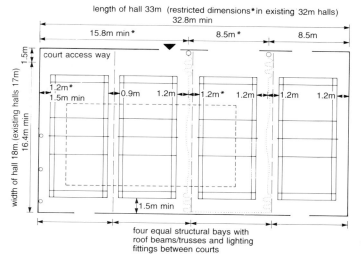

length of hall 33m (restricted dimensions* in existing 32m halls)

32.8m min

15.8m min* | 8.5m* | 8.5m

court access way

1.5m

width of hall 18m (existing halls 17m)

16.4m min

1.2m*
1.5m min | 0.9m | 1.2m | 1.2m* | 1.2m | 1.2m | 1.2m

1.5m min

four equal structural bays with
roof beams/trusses and lighting
fittings between courts

8 *A four-court small multi-sports hall: improved layout. the recommended minimum area has been increased to 33 × 18 m. Setting out of four badminton courts and alternative locations for the coloured space divider net, on a U-shaped track (based on SASH developments)*

- *Draped cricket nets at one end of the hall often catch the flight of shuttlecocks. The end margin is therefore increased to 1.5 m.*
- *Hall space divider nets also often obstruct the use of one court, even for singles. Nets should be positioned to provide maximum flexibility in use of space, not simply for structural convenience. This layout aims to provide maximum flexibility.*
- *Check the needs of other users of the multi-sports space on court 4, particularly for table tennis and the martial arts, before deciding location of the hall dividing nets*
- *In halls of 18 m width with at least 8.4 m clear height (see Section 3.4) the spacing between courts 2–4 (and the 1.5 m end margin) is adequate for umpires' chairs for county standards of play on three out of four courts.*

9 *This scene in Claremont Sports Hall, Newcastle University, relates to the notes to 7. It shows interesting developments in the roof form, which slopes 7–9 m across a 26 m span, to provide for top competition play along one side. Note the mansard eaves (top right) over the side margin. The walls appear to be too light in tone and show up the pattern of blockwork joints. Matching coloured joints are advisable. The sightscreen net (bunched right) is drawn across between the end-to-end courts for club play. (The lengthways net is the dark one bagged top left.) A building study of this hall appeared in* The Architects' Journal, *28 March 1984. Photo: Jeremy Preston, Architect: Faulkner Browns*

10 *SASH at the School & Community Gladesmore Sports Centre, Tottenham, in the London Borough of Harringay. The large armoured glass viewing window withstands footballs and is fitted with blinds to reduce distraction to badminton players from reception lighting. The illuminated exit signs (over doors) are too bright. Hall lighting is mounted along roof beams except that the end lights, beyond the courts, do not switch off during badminton play. In the photograph one such light, on the centre beam, is not working. This shows clearly the resultant darker tone of the adjacent wall, with less reflected light (as preferred for higher standards of play) and makes an interesting comparison with the shadow-free wall in **1**. The dividing net is seen drawn across in location B in **8**. Photo: John Hovell. Design & Build: Nicholas Grimshaw & Partners and Bovis Construction Ltd*

- *Height*: any obstruction (such as roof structure or light fittings) is undesirable but those along the length of the court are likely to be less serious than those across it. Courts should be arranged to fit between beams on to which side lighting can be mounted. For children's and recreational play, the acceptable minimum clear height is in the region of 6 m (approx 20 ft), ideally with more height between the existing structure and beneath a pitched roof.
- *Shape*: long, narrow halls may dictate an end-to-end court location, where courts must be screened by a curtain or blinkered net, with an absolute minimum baseline distance of 0.9 m (approx 3 ft) and preferably 1.5 m (approx 5 ft). Side margins can be reduced to an absolute minimum of 0.9 m (approx 3 ft) from a wall or any projection. The minimum reasonably safe space for recreational badminton in such cramped conditions is 15.2 × 7.9 m (approx 50 × 26 ft), or 15.2 × 14.9 m (approx 50 × 49 ft) for a pair of side-by-side courts, subject to the position of doorways and protrusions such as columns. These margin reductions could also apply in wider spaces, where it is just possible to place courts across a hall. Side margins between courts are the least

critical dimension, so that in a purely recreational hall, marred perhaps by other impediments, it would be worth accepting a common outside line for two adjacent courts in order to squeeze an extra court in, giving a minimum width for two courts of 14 m (approx 46 ft).
- *Floor*: the problems most likely to need attention are worn and uneven surfaces and distorted timber finishes.

7 References and further advice

Badminton Association of England, *Annual Handbook. Halls for Badminton – Conditions and Technical Data.*
Chapter 38, Short tennis.
Chartered Institution of Building Services Engineers, *Lighting Guide: Sports LG4*, CIBSE, London (1990).
International Badminton Federation, *Flooring*, IBF.
Scottish Sports Council, Demonstration Indoor Sports Centre (DISC), *Information Digest FD24*, The Sports Council, Edinburgh (1989).
Sports Council, *TUS Datasheet 51: Short Tennis*, Sports Council, London (1985).

Sports Council, *TUS Datasheet 56: Badminton*, Sports Council, London (1987). (Gives further detailed guidance and BAoE recommendations.)

Sports Council, *Arenas: A Planning, Design and Management Guide*, Sports Council, London (1989).

Sports Council, *TUS Design Note 10: A Guide to Visibility and Lighting in Small Multi-purpose Sports Halls*, Sports Council, London.

Sports Council, *Small Sports Halls: A Value for Money Approach to Design*, Sports Council, London (1994).

20
Basketball and mini-basketball

Peter Ackroyd

1 Introduction

For recreational purposes, courts situated in school gymnasia are being brought back into use subject to safety factors. A reduced minimum size of court is recommended in footnote (1) to the space table. Also, as part of their development plan, the English Basket Ball Association (EBBA) continues to promote outdoor basketball to increase the game's popularity and widen its take-up opportunities, as outlined in Chapter 41, Volume 1. For further details of indoor basketball and mini-basketball, see References and further advice below.

1.1 Critical factors

- Proportionate court dimensions, surrounding safety margins and other space criteria (see the footnotes to the space table)
- Clear height for competition play
- Small halls should be wide enough for match officials' space and team areas, unless restricted to recreational play
- Colour of line markings to contrast with the floor. Additional lines mark the extent of team areas
- The two goal units, backboards and supports must be of an identical type
- Spectator facilities and safety
- Noise
- Storage and labour needed for a portable court.

1.2 Space

The following space table and diagrams are revised from FIBA and EBBA Official Basketball Rules 1990–1994 for the following standards of play:

- N   International/national
- NL   Divisions of the national league
- Rg   Regional including leagues
- Cy   County
- C(TD) Club including top divisions of local leagues
- C(LD) Club including lower divisions of local leagues
- R   Recreational.

1.3 Floor

The playing court must be a flat surface free of obstructions. The flooring should provide suitable ball-to-surface resilience, be slip-resistant and non-splinter.

The EBBA uses a portable beech floor for international and national championship matches. This court is made up of easy-to-assemble sections and laid on top of an existing floor. Roll-down portable courts are available with permanent court markings but roll sizes should be considered carefully together with the other critical factors of rolled weight and storage space. For further advice consult the basketball governing bodies.

1.4 Court markings

Court markings are measured to the *inside* of the 50 mm wide boundary lines but the out-of-bounds surrounds are measured from the *outside* of these lines. Lines to mark out the team bench areas are shown in **3**. These four 2 m (approx 6 ft 7 in) long lines shall be of a contrasting colour to that of the side and end lines.

The governing bodies advise that the colour of the markings should contrast strongly with the court surface (see Further advice below). In halls with a wide variety of other sports markings basketball is often seen to be marked in black or dark blue, the colours recommended by the Sports Council in the first edition of this Handbook.

Another development is an almost lineless court marking developed for colour television. This has contrasting coloured panels for the court, the restricted area, the jump circle and out-of-court area.

2 Equipment

A matching pair of goal backboard support structures will be portable or fixed to the end wall or roof structure as shown in **5**. Suppliers should be consulted for loadings and fixings. When a portable backboard support is used for top competition, it must be placed at least 1 m (approx 3 ft 3 in) from the outer edge of the end line in the out-of-bounds area. In addition, it must be suitably padded and contrast in colour with the background so as to be clearly visible to the players and officials.

Three practice goals mounted along each side wall, provided they are clear of doorways, nets and other equipment, can be used to create three cross-hall practice courts. The wall colour should contrast with the white painted backboards. Preferably, these practice goals should also side-fold against the wall.

All the scoring equipment must be operable from the scorer's table which should be placed just off the court opposite the halfway line. Power socket outlets are needed nearby. The following scoring equipment should be placed as in **3**, where it can clearly be seen by officials sitting at the scoring table, players, coaches and spectators:

- A scoreboard capable of recording the scores of two teams up to 199:199.
- A stop/start clock capable of recording passing time in seconds, a countdown mechanism with a preset facility and at least in the last 60 seconds of each half and extra period indicating time remaining to one-tenth of a second.
- Two loud sounding devices, distinct from each other, incorporated into the scoreboard/clock. (Note: experience shows that these devices are invariably not loud enough.) One of them should sound automatically when the countdown clock reaches zero. Both of these devices should have the facility to be operated manually.
- A 30 seconds clock operated from the scorer's table is required at each end of the court. They should have a sounding device distinctive from the scoreboard sounds. For major matches, four clocks may be required.
- It is advisable for the time-keeper to have a separate control panel from that of the scoreboard operator. A combined control panel is not desirable.

3 Spectator facilities

Basketball is a spectator growth sport and its attraction is increasing as standards of play improve and with expanding European competitions. The EBBA advise that amenities for a minimum of 250 spectators should be

1,2 Basketball is as much a sport for women . . . as it is for men and boys. Photos: Ian Weightman

allowed for at all competition venues (see space table). For national league matches a minimum of 1500 seats are required. For major national and international events, the potential capacity is now estimated at 8000 plus. Spectators and advertising boards must be placed at least 2 m from the court. The best viewing is from the sides, although the use of transparent backboards lessens the obstruction of view from the ends.

The EBBA publishes *Guidelines for Control and Safety of Spectators*. Detailed design advice on all aspects of spectator provision is given in Chapter 50 (see References and further advice below).

4 Internal environment

For general details of environmental services recommendations refer to Chapters 60 and 61. Background heating is required for players and substitutes to be able to sit for long periods in conditions which enable them to perform precision skills immediately upon entering the game. National league clubs should have venues with lighting levels suitable for televised matches.

4.1 Noise

The game generates noise and should not be played at the same time as quiet activities such as badminton. Walls and ceiling should be designed to reduce reverberation and provide some sound absorption.

5 Storage

If backboards are not suspended, storage is required for the two portable and, preferably, folding goal units. The match officials' table and the time-keeping and scoring equipment listed previously will also require secure storage.

6 Mini-basketball

6.1 Critical factors
- Overall area including safety margins around the court
- Reduced distance between the backboard and free-throw line
- Smaller backboard.

6.2 Space

The size of the court is now 28 × 15 m (92 × 49 ft). Other court markings are the same as for basketball except that backboards are placed only 4 m (approx 13 ft) from the free-throw lines. In small halls other variable measurements can be used provided they are in the same proportions to one another.

The main significant differences between mini-basketball and the parent sport are the reduced size of backboards and height of the basket above the floor, and the reduced free-throw distance. Note that if the mini-basketball backboard is placed directly against the front

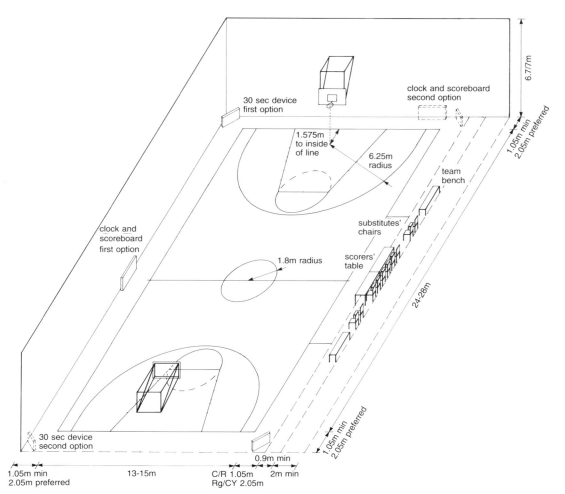

Labels on diagram:
- 30 sec device first option
- clock and scoreboard second option
- 6.77m
- 1.575m to inside of line
- 6.25m radius
- team bench
- substitutes' chairs
- clock and scoreboard first option
- 1.8m radius
- scorers' table
- 24-28m
- 1.05m min 2.05m preferred
- 1.05m min 2.05m preferred
- 30 sec device second option
- 0.9m min
- 1.05m min 2.05m preferred
- 13-15m
- C/R 1.05m Rg/CY 2.05m
- 2m min

3 *Space diagram. Note that courts are set out with a wider space along one side for the scorer's table and team benches. This is obligatory for competitions. The officials seated at the table must be able to see the court clearly. The table may be raised on a low platform which should not obstruct spectator sightlines. Different types of support for goal units are shown. In small halls, side folding, wall supported units at both ends are generally specified. In large halls, up to 5 m projections from rear walls are possible or units are hung from the roof structure. Alternatively a pair of free standing mobile units require storage space. Note that in school gymnasia all the safety margin widths should be clear of wallbar projections. Wallbars at the ends of courts should be removed or well padded to a minimum height of 3 m (approx 10 ft). See also fotnote (3) of Space Table.*

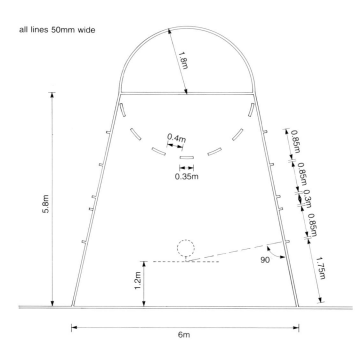

all lines 50mm wide

- 1.8m
- 0.4m
- 0.35m
- 0.85m
- 0.85m
- 0.3m
- 0.85m
- 1.75m
- 5.8m
- 1.2m
- 90
- 6m

4 *Diagram of restricted area and free throw lines*

Space table

	N/NL	Rg/Cy/C(TD)	C(LD)/R(3)
Court dimensions			
Length (1)	28 m	28–24 m	28–24 m
Width (1)	15 m	15–13 m	15–13 m (4)
Out-of-bounds surround (2)	2.05 m min	2.05 m	1.05 m min (4)
Extra one side for officials and team areas (5)	3 m	3 m	C: 0.9 m min (4)
Overall minimum dimensions			
Area (1)	32 × 22.1 m	32.1 × 22.1 m to 28.1 × 20.1 m	C: 30.1 × 18 m (1) to 26.1 × 16 m (4) R: 20.1 × 12.1 m (3)
Height, clear minimum	7.0 m	7.0 m	C: 7.0 m R: 6.7 m (6)

Note (1): All new courts should be constructed 28 × 15 m (see Court Markings below) in an overall area of 32.1 × 22.1 or 18 m minimum width for local competitions. For all domestic competitions on *existing* playing courts, dimensions which fall within the following limits are permitted: 4 m off the length and 2 m off the width, provided that the variations are proportional to each other (for example 26 × 14 m). In an EBBA modified Rule it is permissible to extend the width to 15 m subject to note (4) below where existing permanently fixed backboards make it impossible to increase the length from 26 to 28 m.

Note (2): An area free from obstruction of at least 2.00 m must be provided *outside* the boundary lines around the entire playing court. This may be varied only in respect of C/R courts as noted in notes (3) and (4) below. Taking into account the thickness of the boundary lines the out-of-bounds area extends 2.05 m around the court which is measured to the inside of the boundary lines. See Spectators below.

Note (3): *Recreational and local club competition play.* The EBBA also recommends the use of smaller sized school gymnasia, where court dimensions are reduced in proportion by 0.5 m in width for each 1 m reduction in length. However, the court should, if possible, be at least 13 m wide to give space between the corners of the court and the three-point goal arc. End out-of-bounds space must be 1 m minimum clear of wall bars and other fixtures, but side margins may be less provided all protrusions within 1 m of the lines are safely padded.

Note (4): In existing 17 m wide halls, assuming that a 1.05 m out-of-bounds area continues to be adequate for local competitions, the EBBA 'would prefer the basketball court to be marked out 26 × 14 m so as to leave adequate space around the court' for players and officials. Therefore a 26 × 14 m court should be marked out 1.05 m from one side wall. This provides a 1.95 m wide space along the other side including a narrow width for match officials and team benches, as alternatively shown in 1.

Note (5): Note that the revised recommended layout of team bench areas, scorer's table and substitutes' areas shown in 1 includes safety separation between officials' and teams' benches and spectators (EBBA *Guidelines for Control and Safety of Spectators*).

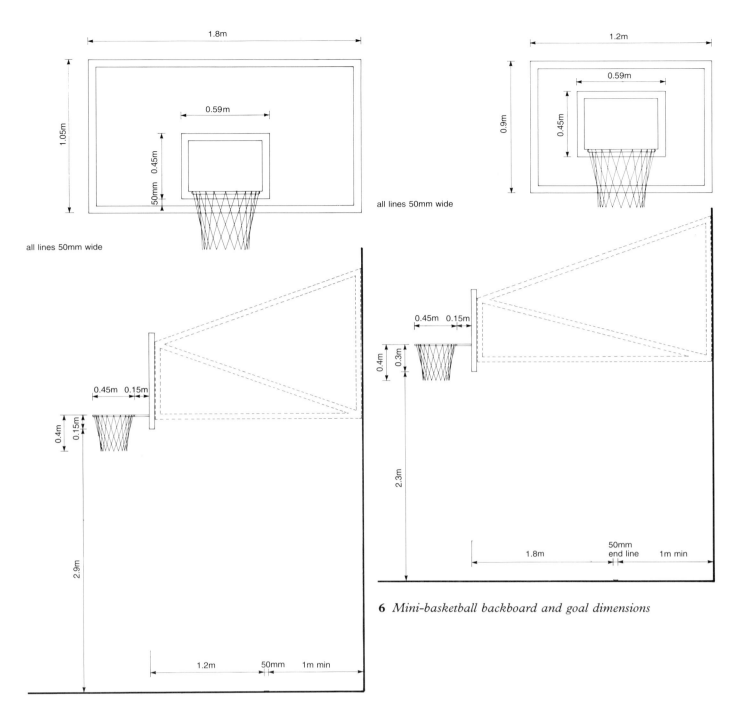

all lines 50mm wide

all lines 50mm wide

5 *Diagrams of backboard and goal (new specification, 1990–94)*

6 *Mini-basketball backboard and goal dimensions*

edge of the basketball ring, the distance to the free throw line will be the specified 4 m. Therefore no extra markings are required on the standard basketball court for the playing of mini-basketball.

7 References and further advice

The governing bodies of basketball.
Basketball outdoors: see Volume 1, Chapter 41.

British Standards Institution, *BS 1892: Specification for Basketball and Mini Basketball Equipment*, BSI, Milton Keynes.
Chartered Institution of Building Services Engineers, *Lighting Guide – Sport*, revised, CIBSE, London (1990).
English Basket Ball Association, *Marking a Basketball Court*.
Guidelines for Control and Safety of Spectators, in *Guide to Safety*, EBBA.
English Mini Basket Ball Association.
Manufacturers of sports equipment.
Sports Council, *Arenas: A Planning, Design and Management Guide*, Sports Council, London (1989).

21
Bowls: the short-mat game and roll-down carpet bowls

Peter Ackroyd

1 *National indoor short mat bowls championships at Antrim Forum. Photo: The Sports Council for Northern Ireland*

1 Introduction

Short-mat bowls, **1**, is a relatively new game which was first formally recognised in Ireland in 1961. In Wales it is known as 'short-green bowls'. The game can be played in almost any location and is enjoyed by men and women of all ages. Short-mat bowls can be played in any multi-purpose hall, village hall, community centre, social clubs, hotel or the like, provided there is both space and a level floor. Virtually all that is required is a portable mat and two lignoid bowls per player (four bowls per player for a singles match). Opportunities now exist for play at club level, in league and open competitions and in national championships. Currently, The British Sports Association for the

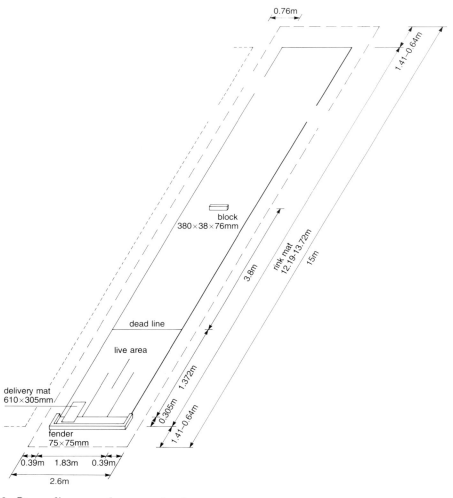

2 *Space diagram: short-mat bowls.*

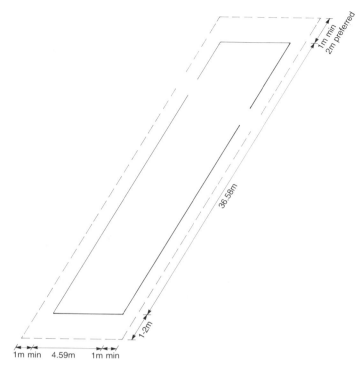

3 *Space diagram: roll-down carpet bowls. For safety of other players carpets should be stored away to avoid obstruction of safety margins around courts in use*

Disabled is negotiating rules which are aimed at making open competition easier for all bowlers.

Roll-down bowls can similarly be played in any multi-purpose hall or the like, but it uses a much larger mat in the form of a roll-down carpet. It is acceptable only at the recreational level of play, or (in England) for clubs not affiliated to the English Indoor Bowling Association (EIBA). Generally requirements are similar to those for bowls halls (see Chapter 72), except for the roll-down surface.

1.1 Critical factors
- Check whether the lack of a permanent surface may debar user clubs from certain indoor bowling competitions
- Overall area of space
- Reasonably level floor
- Storage of mats and roll-down carpet.

1.2 Space
For *short-mat bowls* there are no firm rules on minimum space, but 14.5 x 3 m (approx 48 × 10 ft) is perhaps a lower limit for a small tight space. Any number of rink mats may be placed side-by-side, but the majority of English clubs use only one mat. For dimensioned playing area see **2**.

For *roll-down carpet bowls*, **3**, the overall length of the rink is at least 35.5 m (116 ft 6 in) but preferably 38.5 m (126 ft) including an out of play ('ditch') space at each end. The overall width is a multiple of the 4.55 m (approx 15 ft) carpet roll width per green.

1.3 Floor and rink mat
For *short-mat bowls* the floor should be reasonably level and preferably of wood strip, wood block, granolithic, composition or synthetic materials. On this is laid a green rink mat consisting of a synthetic fibre pile or felt surface, on a latex-based or foam backing. The length is 12.2–13.7 m (40–45 ft) by 1.83 m (6 ft) wide. Markings on the mat are made with 12.5 mm (approx $\frac{1}{2}$ in) wide white adhesive tape. Carpeted floors may be used instead of a mat, but they tend to slow down the speed of the bowl.

For *roll-down carpet bowls* recommendations regarding the underlying floor surface are similar. The wool, felt or synthetic fibre based roll-down carpet, which would normally have an underlay, is obtainable in widths of 4.55 m (approx 15 ft) to any required length.

A green is 34.75–40.23 m (114–132 ft) by 4.5 m (approx 15 ft) minimum width. Unless some form of end ditch can be built into the floor, it is necessary to mark the out-of-play ('ditch') line with white adhesive tape and provide some form of end-stop at the end of the rink. There are no other markings on the carpet.

2 Other equipment
For *short-mat bowls*, two rubber delivery mats each measuring 610 x 356 mm (2 x 1 ft 2 in) are required for each green. Fenders and blocks are commercially available or may be made from 76 mm (3 in) square wood and painted white. Two bowls are required per player (four for a singles match), and a heavyweight jack of 0.37–0.425 kg.

For *roll-down carpet bowls* a wheeled carpet storage transporter is available that will lift and move the rolled-up carpet on rubber wheels, leaving floors undamaged.

2.1 Internal environment
For general details of environmental services recommendations refer to Chapters 60 and 61.

2.2 Storage
The mats or roll-down carpet may require to be stored in a fire-resistant store. Check with local fire officers. Carpet transporters occupy a lot of additional space in hall stores.

3 References and further advice
English Indoor Bowling Association.
English Short Mat Bowling Association.

22
Boxing

Peter Ackroyd

Space table

Ring area	International National (N)	Regional (RG) County (Cy) Club (C)	Recreational (R)
Inside ropes	6.1 × 6.1 m (international) 4.9 × 4.9 m (national)	3.66 × 3.66 m to 6.1 × 6.1 m	3.66 × 3.66 m min
Apron around ring	0.5 m	0.5 m	0.5 m
Ringside clearance around for officials and press	2 m min	2 m min	2 m circulation
Overall area	9.9 × 9.9 m to 11.1 × 11.1 m	8.66 × 8.66 m to 11.1 × 11.1 m	8.66 min × 8.66m min
Suggested floor-to-ceiling height	7.6 m min	6.7 m min	3.5 m min

1 Introduction

Fist-fighting became a modern sport with the introduction of the Queensberry Rules in 1865. Today boxing matches are fought between two men within the same weight class, either amateur or professional, in a roped enclosure. Amateur contests usually consist of three rounds of three minutes each (perhaps less for juniors), with one minute's rest between. Professional bouts may last up to fifteen rounds. Contests may take place in a common sports space or specialist boxing club facility. Contests are boxed on a raised ring, **2**, whereas recreational boxing, coaching and training usually take place at floor level.

1.1 Critical factors

- Overall area of space including safety margins around the ring
- Action is rapid and takes place at close quarters so good visibility from all directions is vital for boxers, referees, judges and spectators
- There should be separate, localised lighting concentrating on the ring
- Good ventilation is essential to counter heat from concentrated lighting.

1.2 Space

See the space table below and **2**. Additionally, a balcony or high-level vantage point for TV cameras is a great asset at any boxing venue.

Where TV lighting is provided luminaires should be mounted at approximately 6.7 m above floor level.

1 *Photo: CPNA*

1.3 Spectators

Viewing is from all around both at floor level and from surrounding stepped seating. See also References for major events requirements.

1.4 Floor

For boxing training at floor level, this should be preferably wood strip and must be covered over the entire area of the ring with a 15–19 mm ($\frac{5}{8}$ to $\frac{3}{4}$ in) thick mat of felt, foam rubber or other suitable approved material (having the same elasticity), topped with stretched canvas. If a raised platform is not used, a means of anchoring the corner posts which support the ropes must be provided. Fixing may also be required for mounting a punch ball and bag for boxing training.

1.5 Internal environment

For general details of environmental recommendations refer to Chapters 60 and 61. See also the *CIBSE Lighting Guide – Sports* for further details.

1.6 Equipment

Standards of design and manufacture are laid down in *BS 1892: Gymnasium Equipment, Part 2: Section 2.6 Boxing Rings*, 3rd revised edition, 1986.

The rules require:

- Two swivelling seats for the boxers during intervals
- Tables and chairs for officials; a gong or bell; at least one, and preferably two stopwatches; score boards and results service; scoring paper conforming to the AIBA pattern; and one microphone connected to the public address system
- For each new bout, two fresh pieces of the following equipment: mugs and water (piped or in bottles); basins with sawdust; and buckets of water
- One stretcher and first aid outfit
- Administration and meetings space
- Changing rooms for 50 competitors, 20 officials and 10 coaches
- A warm-up area consisting of two areas each of 36 m^2 and a glove-up area of 10 m^2
- Drug-testing and medical facilities, including physiotherapy and weighing-in rooms
- Hospitality and media facilities.

1.7 Storage

Secure storage is required for corner posts, ropes and floor mat, and complete demountable rings, plus all other equipment used.

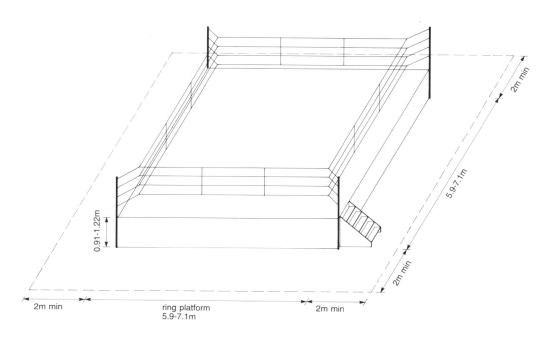

0.91-1.22m

2m min

5.9-7.1m

2m min

2m min

ring platform
5.9-7.1m

2m min

2 While most contests are held in a three-roped ring (and amateur bouts possibly in a two-roped ring), major bouts require a four-roped ring. Note the specially designed corner pads, and the necessary safety size of the apron outside the ropes and down the edge of the ring floor. At many international events steps are sited at the two 'neutral' corners for use by medical officers and others.

3 References and further advice

Amateur Boxing Association.
Chartered Institution of Building Services Engineers,
  CIBSE Lighting Guide: Sports, CIBSE, London.
Sports Council, *Arenas*, Sports Council, London (1989).

23
Cricket: six-a-side and eight-a-side games and net practice

Peter Ackroyd

1 Six-a-side game

The indoor game has developed with the increase in indoor sports centres. A national knock-out competition exists for clubs, **1**. There is a potential for this to be extended to counties, which would be very popular.

1.1 Critical factors
- Space dimensions to allow safety margin circulation around outside of net enclosure
- Protection of people at doorways
- Lighting.

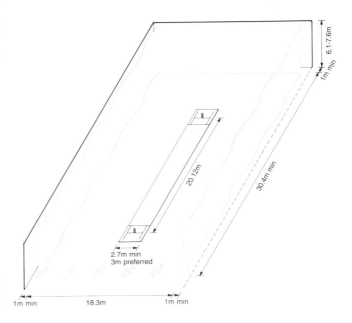

2 *Diagram of six-a-side cricket space. See also table of dimensions*

Space Table

Playing area	Maximum	Minimum
Length	35–36.5 m	30.4 m
Width	27.4–30.4 m	18.30 m
Height	7.6 m	6.10 m
Width of lines	25 mm	

Note: +0.8 m min width of safety margin around outside of net enclosure.

1.2 Surrounding surfaces and enclosure
As for cricket practice, but space must be allowed for wicket dividing nets, which are not in use, to be drawn back across the bowler's end, **2**. Doorways must be protected in a way which will stop fast balls.

1.3 Viewing
It is advisable for spectators to be protected by netting. Viewing should not be from the bowler's end, where spectators would distract the batsman's sight.

1.4 Internal environment
For general details of environmental services recommendations refer to Chapters 60 and 61.

1.5 References and further advice
National Cricket Association, London.

2 Eight-a-side game
This game originated in Australia and is now played in Britain as a commercially marketed indoor game. It uses a full-length pitch enclosed in transparent netting and is played on a synthetic surface under brilliant artificial lighting. The game is meant for the general public and not only regular players; therefore the rules have been drawn up with maximum enjoyment for everybody in mind. Players bat and bowl for an equal period of time (if you are out you lose runs but stay batting on); all equipment is supplied; and the ball is specially designed to be non-injurious.

Each match is played between two teams of eight players each, which could be mixed men's and women's teams. A match consists of one innings per team, each of 16 overs. In addition to running between the wickets, runs are scored when the ball is hit into the boundary netting, which is divided into zones which score different values.

More detailed information is available from the specialist centres listed at the end of this sheet.

2.1 Critical factors
- Space dimensions and clear height for lofted shots attempting sixes
- Non-timber floor surface
- Barrier enclosure
- Lighting
- Visit examples and consult the providers

1 *Six-a-side in Enfield Grammar School sports hall. Photo: Enfield Gazette*

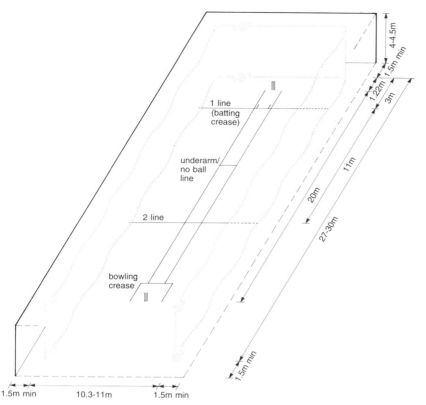

3 *Space diagram of eight-a-side. Overall dimensions only are shown; for detailed data consult the specialist centres listed at the end of this sheet*

2.2 Space

The court must be no less than 27 m and no more than 30 m in length; and no less than 10.3 m and no more than 11 m in width. The pitch is the 20 m long area between the bowling and batting creases. Two sets of wickets, each of which is 227 mm wide and 724 mm high above the floor, are pitched opposite and parallel to each other at a distance of 20 m. Each wicket consists of three stumps with bails. For all details of layout see the space diagram **3** and consult the specialist centres listed at the end of this sheet.

2.3 Spectators

Spectator areas are usually restricted to about one third of court size, with the best viewing from the side or batsman's end. It is recommended that there is a minimum of 1.5 m clear between netting and spectators.

2.4 Floor

Timber floors are generally not acceptable and a variety of synthetic finishes are used. For further details consult the specialist firms and governing body.

2.5 Barrier enclosure

The vertical netting is standardised at 4–4.5 m in height. As to netting type, various configurations of high tension netting are used **5**. Polyethylene 75 mm mesh would be a typical specification, the lower band of 1.5 m height in 10.45 gauge, the remaining vertical height in 10.39 gauge. The top net would also be 10.39 gauge.

2.6 Equipment and storage

All necessary equipment except clothing is supplied by the commercial firms who market the game and this includes wickets, bats, specially designed balls (no pads required), gloves, and probably electronic scoring equipment.

4 *Mixed cricket practice with portable roll up mats. Tracking fixed to roof structure can require a costly height of netting. Photo: John Starling*

2.7 Environment

For general details of environmental services recommendations refer to Chapters 60 and 61.

2.8 Examples

Good British examples of this comparatively new game may be seen at:

* BallPark Leisure
  Cardely Heath
  West Midlands B64 7BJ

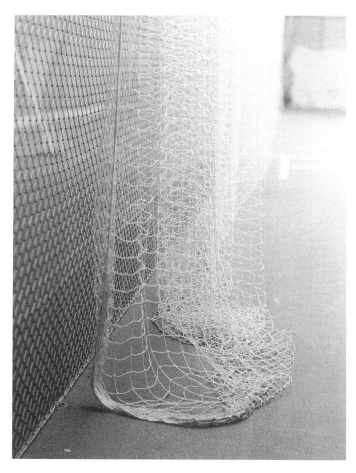

5 *Draped netting for net practice inside surrounding tensioned net (for eight-a-side game). Photo: Peter Sutcliffe*

- Indoor Cricket Stadium
  Wellingborough
  Northants NN8 6TY
- Puma-Wigan Indoor Cricket Centre
  Wigan WN5 0UY

2.9 References and further advice
Detailed information may be obtained from the management of the above-listed centres.
The United Kingdom Indoor Cricket Federation.

3 Net practice
When considering the installation of practice nets, there are three options:

- In a sports hall, 4
- In a projectile hall (see Chapter 51)
- In a specially designed indoor cricket school (see Chapter 74).

A typical installation comprises two or three roll-down surfaced pitches, three or four long, full height tracked nets, wall-mounted retaining bags with pulley and tie-off plates, winches for netbags, a continuous ceiling net and hangers, with all appropriate pulley systems, brackets and cables.

4 References and further advice
For further details, refer to Chapter 74 and extract advice and data relevant to a multi-sports hall situation.

Sports Council, *National Lottery Sports Fund Guidance Note 366*, Sports Council, London (1995).

24
Croquet

Peter Ackroyd

1 Introduction

Croquet originated in France in the 13th century as an outdoor lawn game called 'paille maille'. A modified, British form of this game became very fashionable in the Victorian era under the name 'croquet'. It is becoming popular as an indoor sport, **1**.

The full-sized 32 × 25.6 m court required for outdoor Association Croquet (see Volume 1, Chapter 46) is probably too large for most indoor locations. The dimensions below are therefore for Short Croquet.

1.1 Critical factors
● Overall area including recommended margins around the court.

1.2 Space
Dimensions are still laid down in yards, but metric equivalents are given here for convenience, **2**.

The standard short court dimensions are 21.9 × 14.6 m (24 × 16 yd). Courts smaller than this may be necessary owing to space restrictions, but it is recommended that dimensions be no less than 13.7 × 9.1 m (15 × 10 yd). Below this, so little skill is required that the appeal of the game is diminished.

Margins around individual courts
To allow players to stand back and line up shots when their ball is close to the boundary, there should be 2.7 m (3 yd) all round between the outer edge of the carpet, which forms the playing surface, and the wall, any obstruction or spectators.

An absolute minimum distance of 0.9 m (1 yd) is required to enable the carpet to be put down; and ideally at least 2.7 m (3 yd) at one end of the carpet to allow for rolling up.

1.3 Floor
The Croquet Association is anxious to extend croquet playing to those artificial surfaces used for other indoor sports so as to expand the opportunities for tournaments and coaching courses. This requires surfaces of the right

1 *Photo: Graham Hellewell Photography*

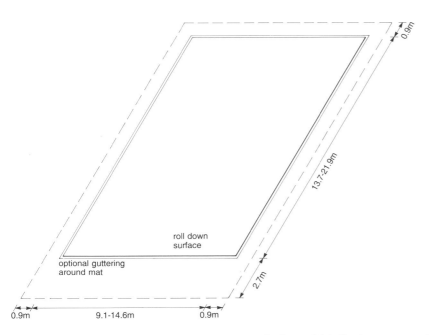

2 *Space diagram. Each hoop is fixed to a metal plate which fits into an opening cut in the carpet and rests on the floor below. A square of carpeting is glued to its upper surface to provide a smooth uninterrupted playing surface*

kind, and the ability to fix hoops so that they stand firm enough to withstand the impact of balls but are removable after the game without damage to the surface.

Two forms of non-directional rubber-backed roll-up carpet have proved satisfactory indoors.

A court can be laid in five parallel lengthwise strips, each of which is 3.3 m (11 ft) wide – about the maximum width that can be manufactured. Strips are held together using carpet 'knee-kickers'. Each such strip of carpet weighs about 150 kg (3 cwt) and can be rolled up into a cylinder of 3.3 × 0.45 m (11 ft × 1 ft 6 in). These rolls can be moved by van and carried on trolleys, or by four men using two slings. Manoeuvring such a roll through doorways, round corners and up stairs is very laborious work and courts should preferably be at ground level with wide entrance doors opening directly on to the outside parking area or driveway.

If narrower strips of carpeting are used (say nine strips of about 2 m width), handling and laying is easier, but then the surface may require more attention during play because the narrower strips tend to move apart.

Each hoop is fixed to a metal plate about 450 mm (18 in) square which fits into an opening cut in the carpet and rests on the floor below. The plate has a square of carpeting glued to its upper surface to provide a smooth uninterrupted playing surface.

Because carpeting provides a fast playing surface, it is essential that the floor surface beneath is level to an accuracy of plus or minus 3 mm (1/8 in) under a 3 m (approx 10 ft) straight edge.

1.4 Markings
Boundary lines as in **2** should be marked in white using removable Velcro tape of about 52 mm (2 in) width. The size of the court is measured to the inner edges of the boundary lines (ie the playing area excludes the lines).

1.5 Barriers
A ball barrier may be provided by means of black plastic guttering placed all round the carpet, **2**.

If there is spectator accommodation, and the spectators are on the same level as the playing surface, a second line of ball stops should be provided between the guttering and the spectators.

1.6 Changing accommodation
For big championship events there may be up to eight players with substitutes; and up to four officials per court.

1.7 Environment
For general details of environmental services recommendations refer to Chapters 60 and 61.

2 References and further advice
The Croquet Association.
Volume 1, Outdoor croquet, Chapter 46.

25
Cycle speedway

Peter Ackroyd

1 Introduction

Indoor cycle speedway is a relatively new activity in the UK and is derived from the sport outdoors (which is a bicycle version of motorcycle racing). It has become very popular, drawings crowds of several hundred spectators. National championships may attract 1000 people.

1 *Photo: Cycle Speedway Council*

1.1 Critical factors
- Overall area of space including safety margin and barriers all round separating spectators from the track
- Smooth but non-slippery floor surface, properly maintained
- Adequate lighting.

1.2 Space
The track area is a clear, flat rectangular floor surface of 35 × 25 m with no obstructions of any kind, **2**.

1.3 Safety barrier
A barrier at least 914 mm (3 ft) high is required all round the track area. It must be vertical, or very nearly vertical; and strong enough to withstand collisions.

1.4 Floor and markings
Recommended floor surfaces are hard composition, composition block or tarmacadam.

There are no floor markings unless the racing is to be televised, in which case consult the Cycle Speedway Council.

1.5 Spectators
Seating is normally required for 500 spectators and 1000 in the case of national championships.

1.6 Internal environment
For general details of environmental services recommendations refer to Chapters 60 and 61.

2 References and further advice
Cycle Speedway Council, England.
Sports Council, *Arenas*, Sports Council, London (1989).

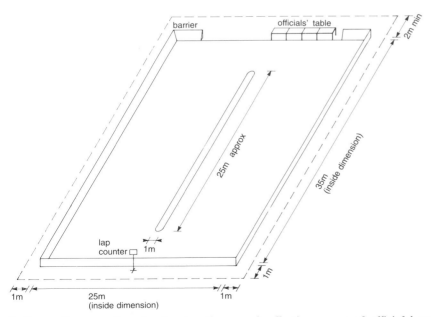

2 *Space diagram of track, showing the racers' collecting area and officials' area*

26 Fencing

Peter Ackroyd

Space table

Piste space	International National (N)	Regional (RG) County (Cy) Club (C)	Recreational (R)
Length	14 m	14 m	14 m
Width	1.8–2.0 m	1.8–2.9 m	1.8–2.0 m
Clear space (both ends)	1.5–2.0 m	1.5–2.0 m	1.5–2.0 m
Clear space both sides (including match officials' table space on one side)	3 m	1.25–2 m	1.25–2 m
Space between parallel pistes	3 m min	2.5 m min	2.5 m min
Overall areas			
Single piste	17–18 × 8 m	17 × 4.5 m min	17 × 4.5. m min
Two parallel pistes	18 × 13 m min	17 × 9 m min	17 × 9 m min
Additional piste each	18 × 4.5 m	17 × 4.5 m min	17 × 4.5 m min
Height	3.6 m min	3.6 m min	3.6 m min

1 Introduction

Fencing developed from mediaeval combat with lances, axes and heavy swords. There was a gradual shift (especially in Italy) towards lighter and swifter blades which were more elaborate and also more deadly than their cumbersome precedents. Towards the end of the 16th century several Italian teachers established themselves in London teaching the new skills. Today the sport is performed by two competitors wearing masks, protective clothing and gauntlets using either an epee (a stiff triangular blade), a foil (more flexible) or a sabre (a cut-and-thrust sword with a V-shaped blade). A bout comprises an agreed number of 'hits' on the opponent's body within a given time. The weapon may be wired to a battery, in which case the fencers wear metallic jackets and a hit registers automatically on scoring lamps.

1 *Photo: Sports Council*

1.1 Critical factors

- Overall area including safety margins around the pistes
- Action is often extremely fast and requires a high degree of viewing concentration so lighting must be adequate to enable participants quickly to discern an opponent's movements or make attacks; glare must be avoided
- A quiet situation is required, with no distractions
- Floors must be non-slip
- Floor anchors for metallic piste in specialist facilities.

1.2 Space

One of the advantages of fencing is that it can take place in any reasonably sized room or hall provided that the lighting and the floor are suitable. Fencing lessons, training sessions, practice bouts and normal fencing (or loose play) should take place in surroundings which avoid distraction and interruption. However, as fencing compe-

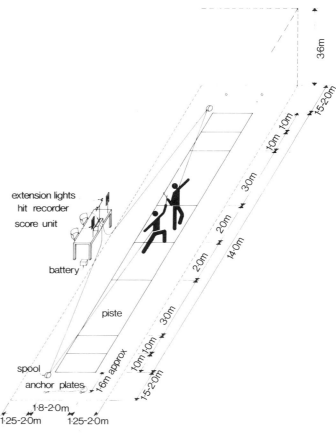

2 *Space diagram of piste*

titions will probably be held in such spaces, it is desirable to base the dimensions on the area required for competitive pistes, **2**, using the space table below. Additional accommodation for national and international events is listed in Chapter 50; see also References.

During a competition one piste will usually accommodate a pool of 6–8 competitors. A competition may start with several elimination pools and finish with a final pool. Therefore it is advisable to have as many marked-out regulation pistes as possible so that the maximum number of pools can be held simultaneously.

The minimum regulation for the overall length of the piste will fit across the widths of small sports halls given in Chapter 49.

1.3 Markings

When a metallic piste is not used, 50 mm (approx 2 in) wide white lines are marked out on the floor surface, **3**.

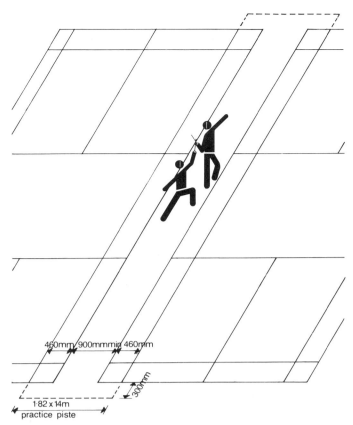

460mm / 900mm min / 460mm

300mm

1·82 x 14m
practice piste

3 *Training and recreational fencing can use the space between badminton tramlines*

1.4 Floor

It is important that the surface on which fencing takes place should be non-slip and impart a degree of person/ surface resilience when in use. A wooden floor is ideal. When the floor is excessively slippery, or of a solid construction, a special roll-down rubber piste should be used. During fencing bouts using electronic scoring apparatus a special metallic piste can be used. This prevents hits on the floor being registered by the electronic scoring apparatus. It is generally supplied as a roll of special mesh. When the floor is hard, a rubber piste can be laid directly beneath the metallic piste to minimise damage.

Provision must be made for attaching the mesh firmly in place during use. Consult specialist equipment suppliers (see References).

1.5 Internal environment

For general details of environmental services recommendations see Chapters 60 and 61.

1.6 Storage

Rolled-up rubber and metallic pistes, scoring equipment and personal equipment will need storage space.

1.7 Spectators

In the UK this activity currently attracts between 60 and 200 spectators to the majority of its major events but crowds of up to 1000 have been known and therefore the activity is potentially one which could use an indoor arena.

2 References and further advice

Amateur Fencing Association.
Leon Paul Ltd (specialist equipment supplier).
Sports Council, *Arenas*, Sports Council, London (1989) (for national and international events accommodation).

27
Five-a-side football

Peter Ackroyd

1 Introduction

The majority of five-a-side play is recreational, with games played along the length or across the width of various sizes of hall, 1. The rules available from the Football Association (FA) are for guidance only and are not mandatory. Current rules, compiled and published by the National Association of Boys' Clubs have been approved by the FA and adopted by various national organisations. For other competitions, dimensional rules and other space requirements should be obtained from the organisers.

A six-a-side game, often called 'soccer-six', is a spectator sport played within barriers resembling an ice rink. Details are given in Chapter 50; see also References.

1 *A kick-about in Rochford Sports Hall. The height of blockwork rebound surfaces aligned with doorways. Photo: Chris Harper*

1.1 Critical factors:
- This rebound game is played off the walls and rebound barrier, or 'boards'; there is no safety margin space surrounding the pitch, **2**
- Reduced size of goal circle for two pitches across a six badminton court hall, **3**
- Non-slip floor surface
- Changes to markings and colour
- Completely flush, non-abrasive surfaces for players' safety
- Very solid walls along goal 'ends' around hall
- Hall access doorways must open away from, and not on to, the pitch; escape doorways must be panelled-out flush with walls
- Stop nets above a barriered perimeter
- Noise control
- Stability and safeness of goal units stored off the hall floor.

1.2 Space
The game can be played anywhere in a common sports space having a maximum area of approx 36 × 28 m,

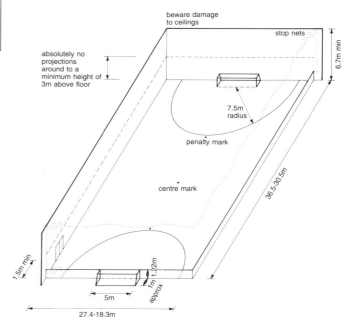

2 *Diagram of the recommended dimensions and enclosing surfaces for all standards of play. Current rules (referred to in the introduction) give all dimensions in imperial measurements with approximate metric dimensions to the nearest half-metre, but mostly converted downwards. More accurate metric equivalents (also related to sports hall sizes) are also given on the diagram beneath the arrowed lines. The goal unit at one end is shown placed behind the goal line with rebound panels along the line abutting the goal posts, **4**. Alternatively, the other goal is shown encroaching on to the playing area against a wall. In this situation the rules require the goal semi-circle to be measured from the goal line between the posts, and the semi-circle line to continue to reach the wall or barrier. (It is not clear whether it should be radiused or, as is normal, at right angles to the wall)*

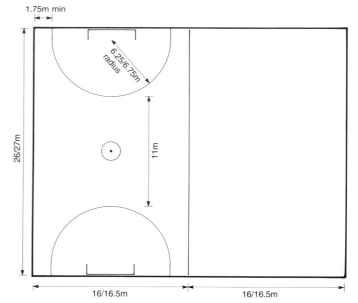

3 *Marking out a pair of five-a-side soccer pitches each in a 26 × 16 m (aprox 85 ft × 52 ft 6 in) minimum space. The goal semi-circles are 6.25 m (approx 20 ft 6 in) instead of the recommended 7.5 m (approx 24 ft 8 in); this allows 1.75 m (approx 5 ft 9 in) in the corners which is the minimum useful space outside the 'D'. It also allows a reasonable 11 m (approx 36 ft) instead of the recommended minimum between the edges of the Ds for central play*

4 *Where the pitch does not abut a hall wall, the goal line is continuous with the goal unit set flush between the enclosing rebound units. Photo: Powersport International Limited*

(approx 118 × 92 ft), **2**. There is no free space around the pitch as a feature of the game is the use of the walls as rebound surfaces. In a shared area, where the end or side lines are not wall surfaces, a portable barrier must be provided to complete the enclosure of the pitch (as detailed below). Goals may be set against end walls and protrude on to the pitch, or recessed between the barrier units along the end line, as shown in **2** and **4**.

A ball above head height (the referee, if there is one – much play is casual and not refereed – must determine that height) is out of play, nevertheless the ceiling should be high enough to minimise possible damage. See also walls below.

When the recommended minimum pitch size is applied to half of a popular six-court 'medium' sized hall, the corners outside the goal circles become useless; and the mid-field between circles becomes very restricted. Alternative dimensions in **3** are suggested as reasonable improvements.

1.3 Spectators
While five-a-side football is an important participant sport, played both competitively and as part of a training regime, the game has not developed widely as a spectator event. The indoor game, in a slightly changed form, is very popular in Europe and particularly in Holland. At major events a potential capacity of 5000 is estimated. Also,

soccer-six is mentioned above. If spectator viewing is to be at floor level, mobile seating should be provided, elevated and set back from the pitch at the sides, so that spectators in the front rows can see over the barrier. Safety netting is an added precaution, **2**.

1.4 Floor
A non-slip floor is essential. Designers should decide the extent and type of rebound barrier units, **2** and **5**, and check setting out of sockets against layout of other markings. Characteristics of rolling resistance and rebound resilience are important: refer to Chapter 64.

1.5 Markings
The Football Association's guide rules do not specify a line colour. Originally, 50 mm wide red lines were suggested by the Sports Council believing that there was sufficient similarity to netball that, for casual play, markings could be used for both sports. However, in practice these were not quite so easily marked. Also, the problem identified in the first edition of this Handbook of masking-out in white tape most of the unwanted red lines has been compounded by the change in badminton marking from yellow to white. Furthermore, five-a-side markings have also changed and are now dissimilar to netball.

Therefore, *yellow* (as specified by the Sports Council for the SASH programme) is now reaffirmed as the recommended colour for markings; see also Chapter 64 for other sports' colours.

One rule of marking must be stressed as noted beneath the space diagram, **2**. The extremities of the goal semi-circle should reach the wall, or barrier, regardless of whether or not the goal posts encroach on the field of play. When re-marking existing pitches, note the following changes to markings given in the current rules. The original centre circle is now removed, because the dropped-ball kick-off no longer applies. Also the penalty marks are now outside the semi-circle, placed as close to the centre of the arc of the semi-circle as possible.

1.6 Surrounding rebound walls or enclosure
Walls should be non-abrasive and provide completely flush, smooth rebound surfaces; there should be no

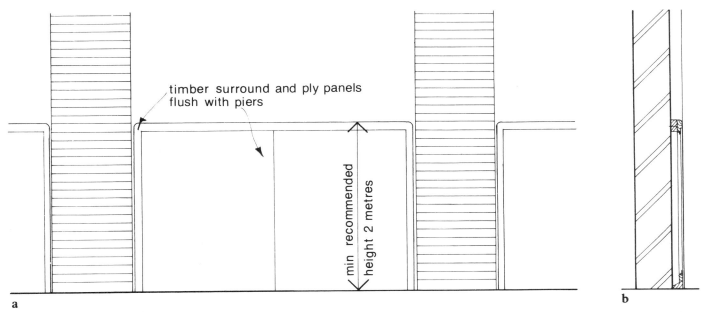

timber surround and ply panels flush with piers

min recommended height 2 metres

a

b

5 *In the conversion of buildings for sport, protruding piers are a very serious hazard and a permanent rebound surface must be provided set flush with existing walls. Refer also to Chapter 65. Details of Harben Armoury conversion, London Borough of Camden. Architect: Martin Richmond*

projections or indentations whatsoever, **2** and **5**. Alternatively, form a removable enclosure, or barrier sides of free-standing, or floor-socketed, rebound-board units to a minimum height of 1.22 m (preferably head height of, say, 2 m) as illustrated in **1** to **5** and in Chapter 65. Equipment specialists supply standard portable panels and fixings and should be consulted for detailed advice.

Background should be uniform in colour and provide a contrast to the ball. Design of blockwork walls, particularly behind goalmouths, should allow for very forceful impact of balls, which can dislodge unreinforced blockwork. Solid, not hollow, blocks are essential, as detailed in Chapter 65. In larger halls, goals may be located along four walls, **3**. Wall surfaces should be smooth and sealed to resist ball abrasion which causes grit to damage the flooring.

All door frames must be flush set. For fire exit door flush detailing refer to Chapter 65. For store openings see Chapter 55.

1.7 Internal environment
For general details of environmental services recommendations refer to Chapters 60 and 61.

The game should not be played near quieter sports such as badminton because it tends to be noisy, especially if rebound surfaces are used. Wall and ceiling surfaces should be designed to reduce reverberation and provide some sound absorption.

1.8 Storage and equipment
Storage will be required for all portable goals when not in use. As a precaution towards the safety of other users and to avoid wasting hall court space, goal units must not be left out around the hall in the safety margins of other sports' courts. Sturdiness and stability of goal units are also important safety factors.

2 References and further advice
Equipment trade.
National Association of Boys' Clubs, *Five-a-side Football Rules*, 7th edition, NABC, London.
Sports Council, *Arenas*, includes datasheets for major spectator events of five-a-side football and soccer-six, Sports Council, London (1989).
The Football Association, London.

28
Golf practice

Peter Ackroyd

1 Critical factors
- Overall area of space including surrounding safety margins, **2**
- Protective stop-nets and ceiling net
- End nets of finer mesh, located safely away from passages and doorways.

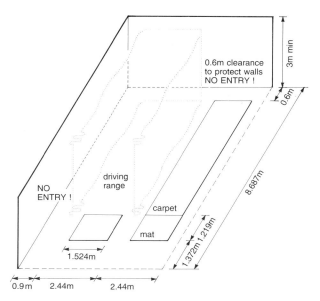

2 *Space diagram for golf practice indoors*

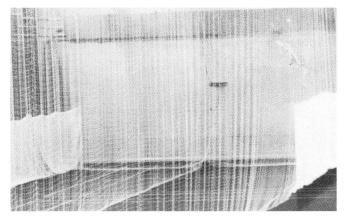

1 *Cricket nets may be used for golf practice. Photo: Central Photographic Unit, Fort Dunlop*

1.2 Space
Golf practice often uses cricket nets in halls and practice halls. A safe location away from circulation routes is important particularly across the end net, which should be clear of wall surfaces.

1.3 Surrounding surfaces or enclosure
- Floor – putting carpets and tee mats on a solid floor
- Walls – protected by nets (18 mm (approx 0.75 in) mesh) or canvas screens

- Ceiling – nets (18 mm (approx 0.75 in) mesh) to protect ceiling finish and light fittings.

1.4 Floor markings
Location line for mats taped or painted on floor.

1.5 Special fittings
Cricket nets can be used as dividers but end stop nets must be of 18 mm (approx 0.75 in) mesh. Portable golf cages are also available.

1.6 Internal environment
For general details of environmental services recommendations refer to Chapters 60 and 61.

1.7 Storage
Storage is required for framed net, mats, carpets, clubs and balls.

2 References and further advice
British Association of Golf Course Architects.
Volume 1, Chapter 24, Golf courses.

29
Gymnastics

Christopher Harper

1 Introduction

Male gymnasts compete on the vaulting horse, pommel horse, horizontal bars, parallel bars, rings and floor. Women compete on the vaulting horse, beam, asymmetrical bars and floor. Competitors perform compulsory and optional movements on each apparatus. There are separate titles for the team competition, individual combined events competition and individual events competitions. Gymnastics is a spectator sport with events taking place in multi-use halls and in sports arenas.

1 *Photo: Sportlight photography*

1.1 Critical factors

- Adequate plan and height dimensions for safety, including clear height over the podia
- A construction capable of accepting floor anchorages for stabilising equipment and ceiling mounted safety rigs
- Landing mats are required with each apparatus and require fire proofed storage.

1.2 Space

For all floor work, the official measurements of the competition mat area are 12 m × 12 m × 54 mm (approx

Space table

	International National (N) Regional (R) County (Cy)	Club (C) Recreational (R)
Length	47.5–36.5 m (156–120 ft)	36.5–32.0 m (120–105 ft)
Width	23.0 m (75 ft)	26.0 m (85 ft)
Overall Including surrounds	50.0 × 25.0 m min (164 × 82 ft)	
Height	7.6 m (25 ft)	7.6 m (25 ft)

39 ft × 39 ft × 2 in) within a 14 m × 14 m (46 ft × 46 ft) area if on a raised podium. Additional pieces of apparatus require areas of approximately 36 sq m (approx 387 sq ft) each and a minimum of 25 m (approx 82 ft) is required for vault run-up. See space diagram **2**.

Organisers of Federation Internationale Gymastique (FIG) or similar competitions must provide the double flex floor measuring 12 x 12 m (approx 39 x 39 ft) consisting of 60, 48 or 64 single tiles or mats joined together with lugs.

Whether on the flat floor or raised on to a podium, some equipment has to be anchored down.

The overall area required for Olympic competition is 73 × 33.5 m (240 × 110 ft).

The Federation Internationale Gymnastique (FIG) clear height for training areas equipped with suspended safety belts is 6.5 m.

The club and recreational length and width dimensions relate to large and medium sports hall sizes.

1.3 Equipment

All the equipment shown in the space diagram must be available, together with:

- The safety control weights and test equipment
- Landing mats 2 × 1.25 m (approx x ft) (perhaps a minimum of 20) each 65 mm (approx in) thick
- Modern rhythmic gymnastic apparatus such as rope/ball/ribbon and cane/club/hoop
- Officials' tables, etc
- Pommel covers
- Trampolines for gymnastics training
- Chalk bowls.

For dimensions of individual pieces of apparatus refer to Chapter 78.

1.4 Ancillary accommodation

Specific ancillary accommodation for gymnastics events can include:

- Storage space – for all the items listed under Equipment
- Administration and meetings space
- Changing rooms – 20 rooms and other amenities for coaches, officials and competitors
  (a) international – 40 competitors, 30 coaches and 100 officials
  (b) regional – 26 competitors, 26 coaches and 100 officials
- Warm-up area – a 33 × 17.4 m (approx 108 × 57 ft) room, fully equipped for gymnastics and adequately lit, adjacent to the competition area but out of sight of spectators and inaccessible to them
- Drug testing and medical facilities – including a massage room for gymnasts
- Hospitality facilities – including gala receptions facilities for up to 200 people
- Media facilities.

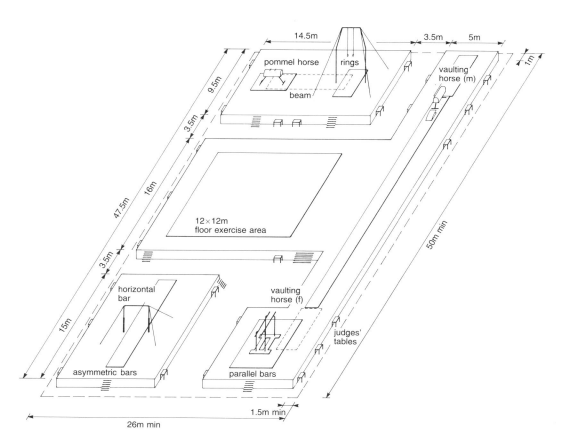

2 *Gymnastics space diagram. Championships can be set at floor level or mounted on podia 0.9–1.1 m high. A critical consideration is the anchorage of three sets of bar and ring equipment. Consult specialist suppliers for developments in equipment and fixing details*

1.5 Internal environment

For general details of environmental services recommendations refer to Chapters 60 and 61.

A minimum temperature of 21°C (68°F) should be maintained throughout an event.

Lighting requirements for individual events should be checked with FIG and the British Amateur Gymnastics Association (BAGA), particularly for international events.

For major televised events, the podium must be lit to 1400 lux at floor mat level. Practice and warm-up areas should be lit to an adequate level for gymnasts (500–750 lux).

2 References and further advice

British Amateur Gymnastics Association (BAGA).
Federation Internationale Gymnastique (FIG).

30
Handball: seven-a-side and mini-handball

Peter Ackroyd

I Introduction

The International Handball Federation (IHF) has standardised the seven-a-side court size to 40×20 m (approx 132×66 ft) but this is still longer than most UK sports halls. The Sports Council has included in its standard sizes of hall a rectangular proportioned large hall to provide full size courts for hockey, handball and korfball (see Chapter 49).

1.1 Critical factors
- Size of hall including safety margins around the court, **2**
- No unprotected glazing or breakable light fittings
- Clarity of line markings to avoid confusion with hockey markings
- Projection-free flush wall surfaces
- Adequate temperature for players on substitutes' bench.

1.2 Space

The dimensions given below for county, club and recreational levels of play are less than the standard recommended by the British Handball Association (BHA) for all levels of play but are the agreed minimum court dimensions to promote seven-a-side handball in typical UK sports halls.

The five-a-side version of the game has been discontinued by the BHA. Nevertheless in small halls, where the width is a serious restriction, team numbers are adjusted to the size of court available for recreational play.

Mini-handball has been developed for 5–11 year olds. This version of the game can take place in a sports hall or school gymnasium (if protection can be given from the projections of wall bars and other equipment), indoors or in the playground. It will fit into Sports Council small halls for local community provision, **3** and **4**.

Space table

	International National (N)	Regional (RG) County (Cy) Club (C)	Recreational (R)
Length	40 m (1)	40-34.5 m min	30 m min
Width	20 m	20-18 m min	17 m min
Side margins minimum	1 m	1 m	None (3)
Officials/team bench space, additional one side	1 m	1 m	–
End margins minimum	1 m	1 m	1 m
Minimum overall area	42 x 23 m (1)	42–36.5 × 23–21 m	32 x 17 m (3)
Height (2)	9 m	9–7.6 m	7.6-6.7 m

Note (1): British National League games may be played on 36×20 m courts in overall area of 38×22 m.
Note (2): Maximum height is an important factor: goal-keepers can attempt whole length lobs to score directly into the opponents' goal. Minimum height recommended by the IHF is 6 m (approx 20 ft).
Note (3): Side wall – side wall play in halls of 20 m (approx 66 ft) or less wide.

1 *Photo: Busser Pressefotograf, Copenhagen*

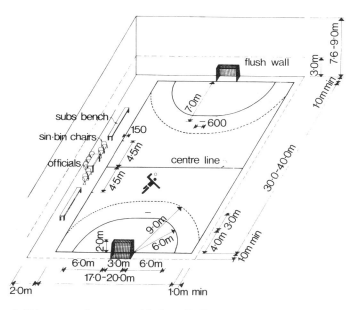

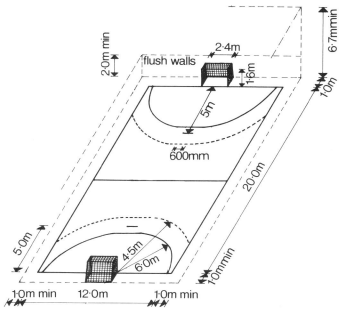

2 *Diagram of seven-a-side handball space. Note that the international maximum area of court is 40 × 20 m (approx 132 × 66 ft).*

4 *Diagram of mini-handball court. The goal size is 2.4 m wide x 1.6 m high x 1 m deep (approx 8 ft × 5 ft 3 in × 3 ft 3 in)*

3 *A sport ideal for 5–11 year old boys, girls or mixed teams, indoors or on the playground. Junior handball for 10–14 year olds is now played on a minimum full sized handball court, but with a junior ball. Photo: British Handball Association at Milton Keynes Leisure Centre*

1.3 Floor

A slip-resistant, resilient floor is preferred. Asphalt or tarmacadam surfaces are unsatisfactory for the seven-a-side game. 'Rolling resistance' is important: see Chapter 64.

1.4 Court markings

Lines 50 mm (approx 2 in) wide for seven-a-side handball are included in overall court sizes, **4**. Yellow is required for all markings under IHF regulations. The BHA will accept yellow and black striped lines, using 'hazard' tapes as an alternative for club and national matches. Orange is acceptable for recreational play. There is similarity with hockey dimensions and lines.

Mini-handball can share markings with four or five-a-side soccer in small halls if played from side-wall to side-wall. Courts marked in the centre of a hall should have a 1 m (approx 3 ft 3 in) minimum margin all round and have 50 mm (approx 2 in) wide orange lines.

1.5 Walls

Walls should be absolutely flush (as for five-a-side soccer) and up to 3 m (approx 10 ft) high without any projections such as basketball winch gears. Basketball boards should be protected. Clerestory and other windows are best avoided but if provided they must be protected, for example with steel mesh.

1.6 Spectators

Handball is a growth spectator sport in Europe and it could increase in the UK. The BHA suggests allowing for 50–250 spectators at national league and club matches with up to 1000 or more at finals and internationals. Spectators should be sited at least 2 m (approx 6 ft 7 in) from the side lines and restricted near or behind goals.

1.7 Internal environment

For general details of environmental services recommendations refer to Chapters 60 and 61.

1.8 Storage

Storage will be required for goal units made up of 80 mm (approx 3 in) square posts and cross-bar to withstand the force of ball rebounds. For recreational games dual-purpose handball/hockey units may be acceptable but thin hockey goals can be damaged by the ball.

Storage is also required for an officials' table, seven chairs, team benches, match control equipment and scoreboard.

For mini-handball storage will be required for goal units only.

2 References and further advice

British Handball Association.
Hockey datasheet, Chapter 31.
Korfball datasheet, Chapter 35.

31
Indoor hockey: six-a-side and unihoc

Peter Ackroyd

2 Women's indoor match at Crystal Palace National Sports Centre showing detail of the goal unit. Photo: Hockey Field.

1 Introduction

Indoor hockey is normally played by teams of six to rules prescribed by the Hockey Rules Board. The recommended required space of 44 x 22 m (pitch) plus the recommended clearance all round is much larger than can be provided in most existing UK halls. Therefore smaller dimensions are allowed, as given below, but they severely inhibit the game and limit the numbers of spectators.

The Sports Council has included in its recommended standard sizes of halls (see Note (1) to the space table below) a rectangular proportioned 'large' hall to provide full sized courts for hockey, handball and korfball.

1   Men's Indoor Hockey European Championships at Crystal Palace National Sports Centre. Note the white sideboard along the side line (detailed in 4), officials and team benches, officials and team benches (3) and TV cameras. Photo: Hockey Digest.

1.2 Critical factors

- Overall area of space including safety margins all round
- New halls large enough for full sized pitches, at least to club standards. Halls 36.5 m (approx 120 ft) long are no longer satisfactory for new facilities.
- Quality and condition of floor
- Side boards along both sidelines should be safely fastened and secured from lateral movement
- Solidity and detailing of enclosing wall construction to limit damage from balls and sticks
- Spectator precautions
- Adequate lighting.

1.2 Space

When new facilities are being planned and spectator provision for over 1000 is envisaged, the full size 44 x 22 m

(approx 144 × 72 ft) pitch plus clearance all round should be provided for all top standard play and, increasingly, for club play. Recommended suitable sizes of halls are given in Chapter 49. Where these cannot be achieved, recommended club minimum pitch size is 36 × 18 m (overall 39 × 22.2 m). Other possible training sizes are outlined beneath the space diagram, **3**.

There is not a prescribed minimum height for a hockey hall. In the Rules, a ball above the height of a player's shoulder is restricted from play; in addition hall height should allow for ball ricochet, adequate lighting and environmental considerations, spectator sightlines and other relevant requirements.

Refer to *Arenas* (listed in the references at the end of this chapter) for special requirements relating to major events.

The range of sizes for various standards of play, including absolute minima for *existing halls* of 36.5 m (approx 120 ft) in length, are given in the space table below.

Space table

	International National (N)	Regional (RG) County (Cy) Club (C)	Recreational (2)
Length (including back lines)	44.0–36.0 m	44.0–36.0 or 33.5 m (1)	2:1 length/width ratio
Width (including 100 × 100 mm side boards)	22.0–18.0 m	22.0–18.0 or 16.75 m (1)	See above
Run-out behind back lines	3.0 m	3.0–1.5 m min	1.5 m
Clearance outside side boards	1.5 m min	1.5 m min	1.5 m
Officials' table and team benches (additional clearance on one side)	1.2 m min	1.2 m	–
Overall area	50–42 × 26.2–22.2 m	50.0–39.0 × 26.2–22.2 or 36.5 × 21 m (1)	2:1 (See above)
Height	See text above		

Note (1): An existing hall 36.5 m long overall can provide a 'short pitch' 33.5 m in length (allowing for end run-outs). This compares unfavourably with the Hockey Association's recommended minimum overall length of 39 m for a minimum pitch 36 m long. To overcome that past problem, sponsors of 'large' hall projects should note the rectangular proportion of hall now included in Chapter 49.

It is also recommended that, whenever possible, up to the maximum width of pitch (22 m) should be marked out in order to ensure that the circle line meets the back-line in preference to intersecting the side boards.

Note (2): Team sizes can be adjusted according to the size of the pitch available but always contain at least four players.

1.3 Floor

Flooring should be firm, level, slip-resistant and completely smooth and flush to allow the ball to run true. The surface should have no pronounced texture and not produce a high bounce. A dark colour is best. Wooden floors are preferred for international competitions, but for other grades of play any finish will do that meets the above requirements. Characteristics of ball to surface resilience and rolling resistance are important. Flush inset sockets for bolt-down side boards (see below) are also required. Refer also to Chapter 64.

To safeguard the flooring, sticks that do not comply with Indoor Hockey Rules should be forbidden. Damage can also be caused by the buckles on goalkeepers' equipment. They can be taped over to avoid scratch marks on the floor.

1.4 Side boards
A kerb along side lines, reverse-splayed to limit balls from ricocheting upwards, is detailed in **4** and **5** and should preferably be made of wood. For top-class play, they require bolting securely to the floor. For lesser standards of play, lengths of side board should be joined together in such a way as to present a continuous kerb along each side of the pitch and secured from lateral movement, but should not have fasteners or supports which could be dangerous to players or umpires.

1.5 Markings
Markings are shown in **3** and must be at least 50 mm wide (except that the goal line between the goal posts may be up to 80 mm wide). White is the recommended colour for games at all levels down to recreational, where it may be orange or light blue. Yellow is sometimes used for televised games. The pitch is measured to the outside of the end lines and side boards.

For major domestic competitions, all other sports lines should be removed from within each shooting circle. In practice, this is a laborious operation and would be much less of a problem in full length halls.

1.6 Walls
Surrounding walls should be solidly built without hollows and finished to withstand the crushing impact of hockey balls and sticks. End walls should be padded (eg with matting) at both sides of the goal to prevent rebounds and injuries.

Figure **5** shows a recent development of a protective skirting course using inverted road kerbs as a damage precaution in case side boards are not used and where pitches are marked out in both directions. Refer also to Chapter 65, Detailed design: walls.

1.7 Spectators
Up to 2000 spectators may attend major events, but 100 to 200 is more usual for club matches. Raised seating is best, but level seating all round the pitch is acceptable, outside the pitch safety margins and barriers.

1.8 Barriers
If spectators may be present behind the goal lines, they must be protected by fine-mesh netting positioned at least 3 m behind the goal line, and about 5 m high. Spectators must be able to move between their seats and exit/entry doorways along a safe route, without danger from the game.

Where the pitch is part of a larger hall floor, the pitch and free zone should be separated from the rest of the hall by an enclosure of 1.2 m high portable barriers. Additionally, high nets should be fitted wherever possible.

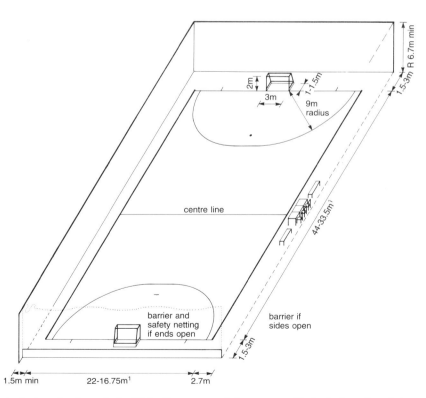

3 *Indoor hockey pitch. This diagram and the space table include reduced sizes of training pitch as relaxed by the governing bodies to fit existing 36.5 m long halls. However, the past recommended size for a large hall of only 36.5 × 32 m (1168 m²) is now acknowledged as being inhibitingly short for the development of indoor hockey. Nor is there space for spectators. To provide better facilities for these big-pitch sports, Chapter 49 includes recommended alternative rectangular proportions of hall based on 27 m, 33m, or 37 m widths of hall and up to 54 m long. These are greatly preferable shapes and possibly more economical to build. However, for community sports programmes, the rectangular form may not be so flexible as the square shape*

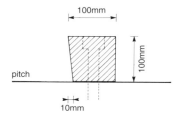

4 *Diagram of a typical side board detail showing fixing bolts (with sockets set flush into the floor surface). See also* **1**

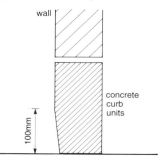

5 *Inverted solid skirting detail around the new sports hall at Christ's Hospital School, Horsham, Sussex. This detail uses concrete kerbstones to protect walls from the crushing impact of balls, which can crack and dislodge blockwork. It may possibly limit upward ricochet. Photo: David Bridges*

1.9 Internal environment
For general details of environmental services recommendations refer to Chapters 60 and 61.

1.10 Equipment
As shown in **3**:

- Goal units should be provided with side and back boards 460 mm in height for competitive hockey at any standard
- Goal units should display red and white striped markings and may have dual use for handball. Self-standing, folding and wheelaway types are available
- Outside the pitch, and along either of the side boards, there should be a bench for each team, chairs for temporarily suspended players, and tables and chairs for officials. Tables should have infilled front and side panels to guard against injury from the ball. See also space table Note (2)
- There should be a clock, scoreboard, public address system and (for higher levels of play) a hooter to signal the duration of each half-hour.

6 *Unihoc pitch markings. The length should be twice the width*

1.11 Storage
Refer to Chapter 55.

1.12 Ancillary spaces
For warm-up and other spaces for competition events, refer to *Arenas* (see References and further advice below).

2 Unihoc
This is a variation of indoor hockey usually played by teams of six but rules are flexible and allow team size to be determined to suit the available area. No maximum or minimum court dimensions are prescribed, the principal recommendation being that the length be twice the width. This flexibility allows the game to be played in many halls. In those marked for netball or five-a-side football, the already-marked area is suitable. See **6** for layout.

Alternatively, where there are no obstructions, the walls themselves can be used as boundaries.

For further advice, see below.

3 References and further advice
Indoor Hockey Rules, issued by the FIH Indoor Hockey Committee.

Sports Council, *Guidance Note: Sportshalls – Sizes and Capacities*, Sports Council, London (1995).

Sports Council, *Arenas: A Briefing and Design Guide*, Sports Council, London (1990).

The All England Women's Hockey Association.

The Hockey Association.

The International Hockey Federation (FIH).

Unihoc, En-tout-cas Ltd.

32
Judo

Peter Ackroyd

1 Introduction

Judo is derived from the Japanese word ju which means 'pliant'. The skill lies in overcoming an opponent not by weaponry or brute strength but precise action based on an understanding of the opponent's anatomical and even psychological weaknesses. With a few lessons in breakfall, judo can be made safe and highly enjoyable and in this form it has become a popular sport. Preferably, training and contests should take place in a specialised permanent 'dojo', **2**, but practice and recreational judo can be played in a multi-purpose sports hall subject to adequate space and safety conditions.

1.1 Critical factors

- Consider dedicated dojo (or training hall) provision, with suitable daytime dual-use, in preference to use of a multi-purpose zone or room; permanently laid mats also avoids a repeated, laborious and heavy job

- Overall area of flat space including safety clearways around the competition mat; and minimum clear headroom
- Fire resistant store for mats
- Special requirements for competition venues
- For this bare-footed sport the floor surface, cleanliness and personal hygiene are vital
- Flush walls, and safety padding where necessary
- Ventilation.

1.2 Space

As a guide, allow floor space of 4 sq m (43 sq ft) per participant for practice and recreational judo. A multi-purpose space, **2**, is suitable providing that it is flat, with at least the volume of space for the appropriate standards of judo participation set out in the columns of Table 32.1.

Practice halls (see Chapter 51) are preferred to main halls, though the larger spaces are satisfactory provided that other activities taking place are compatible, or preferably separated in a net-divided zone, **3**.

1.3 Equipment and storage

- Mats. One 14 × 14 m matted area requires 98 mats each 2 x 1 m (6 ft 6 in × 3 ft 3 in). A full size area takes 128 mats and the smallest competition area of 13 × 13 m uses 100 standard mats around one 1 × 1 m mat in the centre. These are best stored on trolleys ready for easy use and to avoid mishandling. Consult suppliers regarding space allowance for storage trolleys in a separated fire resistant enclosure. Foam filled mats are a high fire risk. Refer to Chapter 55 and consult fire prevention officers.

1 *Photo: Richard Gardner*

Table 32.1: Space requirements

	National (N)(1)	Regional (Rg) County (Cy) Club (C)	Recreational (R)
Contest/practice area (including danger area) (2)	9 × 9 or 10 × 10 m	9 × 9 or 10 × 10 m	9 × 9 or 10 × 10 m
Minimum matted safety space on each side	2 or 3 m	2 m	1 or 2 m
The competition mat – ie the total matted area (1 m increments)	13 × 13 m to 16 × 16 m	13 × 13 m or 14 × 14 m	11 × 11 m to 14 × 14 m
Plus officials' and competitors' space on one side	2 m min	2 m min	–
Plus clearway on three sides	0.5 m min	0.5 m min	0.5 m min (on each side)
Overall contest volume (minimum)			
A one-contest/practice area	15.5 × 14 m to 18.4 × 17 m	15.5 × 14 m or 16.5 × 15 m	12 × 12 m to 15 × 15 m
A two-contest/practice area	15.5 × 27 m to 18.4 × 33 m	15.5 × 27 m or 16.5 × 29 m	–
Or with shared safety area between (3)	18.5 × 30 m (including 10 × 10 m contest areas)	15.5 × 26 m or 16.5 × 28 m	–
For each extra contest/practice area	Add 13–16 m to overall length (4)	Add 12–13 m to overall length (4)	–
Or with shared safety areas between (3)	Add 13 m to overall length	Add 12 m to overall length	–
Clear headroom	7.6 m	4.5 m	3.5 m

Note (1): Refer to *Arenas* (see References) for fuller accommodation requirements for national events and for space and other requirements for international contest events.
Note (2): A 1 × 1 m mat is required in the centre of a 9 x 9 m contest area.
Note (3): With shared safety area it is essential to allow at least 3 m between adjoining contest areas and around each – see also note to **3**.
Note (4): Depending on chosen dimension of contest area and safety space variables (at top of table).

- Match officials' table, scoreboard, timer and pool-sheet notice board. A wall-hung blackboard is used for recreational and training sessions.
- At a competition book-in point: four tables each of minimum size 1.5 × 0.75 m (4 ft 6 in × 2 ft 6 in) are required.

2 *High Wycombe Judo Centre Dojo – built as a training dojo but at the same time suitable for small tournaments. It has a mat area of 24 × 12 m. There is a dais on one side for competition officials and 180 tiered seats on the opposite side for spectators. There are ancillary facilities of sauna, physiotherapy room, a small conference room and also an excellent bar/lounge. During the daytime the permanent mat area is used for gymnastics for children from 18 months to 9 years. The Centre is both used for area and county judo trials and as a regular training venue for the Great Britain Women's National Squad. Photo: John O'Brien*

- At the event control centre: provide two tables as above; at each table, four chairs for the tournament directors; and musical equipment, including records or tapes.
- At the weigh-in point: provide balance-type scales; screens to give privacy to male and female contestants being weighed in; and barriers to keep everyone except the weigh-in officer at least 2 m (6 ft 6 in) away from the scales.

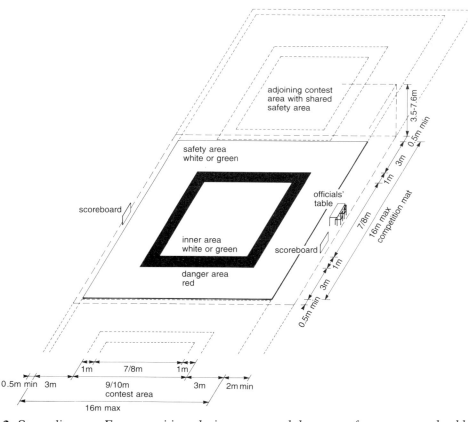

3 *Space diagram. For competitions the inner area and the outer safety area mats should be coloured green or blue. For practice and training mats covered by a white canvas may still be in use in some older sports centres*

Number of competitors	50	75	100	125	150	175	200	225	250	275	300
Number of contest areas:											
First round pools system	1	2	2	3	3	4	4	5	5	6	6
Knockout and repechage	–	1	2	2	2	3	3	3	4	4	5

Details of the above and other tournament requirements are set out in the BJA *Tournament Handbook* (see References).

2 Special requirements for competition venues

Judo competitions are extremely popular, and the BJA uses a 'star rating' to define the level of a tournament. In certain events the competitors gain points towards their gradings in the sport. Complete details of all the requirements for the various forms of Judo events are set out in the BJA *Tournament Handbook* and anyone involved in the staging of an event is very strongly recommended to obtain a copy. Below are set out some of the more important factors that can affect the choice of a venue.

Number of competitors and officials

Judo events can attract very large entries, particularly for junior events which may have up to 400 participants competing during one day. In senior events, where the individual contests are of longer duration, the maximum number of competitors is usually limited to 300. Changing areas, lockers, and shower accommodation must be adequate for the numbers of competitors participating.

The number of officials at an event will vary according to both its status and the number of competitors involved. For major competitions the numbers are likely to vary between 20, for a competition using one mat, to 64 for a competition using six mat areas. Most of these officials will be accommodated on or around the mat areas.

Number of contest areas required

The maximum number of contest areas required is unlikely to exceed six. As a guide, one mat is usually allowed for every 50 competitors. Table 32.2 gives requirements for the two major forms of competition.

Spectators and parking

The BJA *Tournament Handbook* publishes guidelines to the minimum number of spectators likely to attend an event and to the car parking required, in each case based on the number of competitors entered.

Other facilities required

Separate accommodation for:

- The Tournament Director: this official needs an office which can be used as the Control Centre. The public address system should be centralised here and the Director needs to be linked by internal telephone or runners to every table in the main competition area.
- Weighing in: a small area away from the mat area available for all competitors to be weighed in before the contest.
- Warm-up areas: two areas per day, male and female. See Section 8.
- Drug testing.
- First aid: the first aid centre should be adjacent to the matted area and should be equipped with a table and a medical inspection bed, with an external telephone nearby.

Full details of these and other events' facilities are given in *Arenas* (see References and further advice).

2.1 Flooring

Traditional flooring was Japanese rice matting, covered in vinyl. These days 2×1 m (6 ft 6 in $\times$ 3 ft 3 in) foam mats, 50–60 mm (2 to $2\frac{3}{8}$ in) thick are more common. Sectional mats must be prevented from slipping or moving apart. Modern interlocking mats, with non-slip undersurface, achieve this without the need for an outer timber-framed lock (consult specialist suppliers).

A soft floor, without the need for mats, is an advantage in practice halls or specialist training and combat rooms where other activities such as gymnastics, movement and dance could then benefit from the resilient surface. See also Chapters 36 and 52.

The International Judo Federation contest rules state that the competition area, **3**, can be mounted on a resilient platform. This should be no higher than 500 mm (19 in).

2.2 Markings

No special floor markings are used except the red coloured mats of the 1 m (3 ft 3 in) wide danger area, **3**.

2.3 Surrounding enclosure

There should be no projections such as door handles within the overall contest area. In small practice halls, where the outer safety area is restricted, walls must be absolutely flush and padded by upstanding mats or mattresses to a height of at least 1 m (3 ft 3 in). Wall mats 2 m (6 ft 6 in) high can be secured to walls by heavy strips of Velcro attached to the mats and permanently bonded to the walls before decoration.

2.4 Internal environment

For general details of environmental services recommendations refer to Chapters 60 and 61. Background heating to around 12°C only is required for participants. Adequate ventilation is essential to control humidity and prevent condensation occurring.

3 References and further advice

British Judo Association (BJA).
BJA, *Tournament Handbook*, BJA.
Sports Council, *Arenas*, Sports Council, London (1989).

33
Karate

Peter Ackroyd

1 Introduction

Karate is a practical, empty-handed fighting technique, a formal method of physical and mental training and a competitive martial art. Karate contests are held as kata, male and female competitions (introduced in 1978) and as sparring matches, in which some karate techniques are not permitted. To avoid injuries all punches, blows, strikes and kicks are controlled. Contact is permitted providing it is controlled to skin contact only.

1.1 Critical factors

- Overall area of space including the *two* safety margins: a matted area (around the central combat area) surrounded by an unmatted free-space, **2**
- Dimensions apply to all standards of this martial art, from recreational to international
- Lighting must be sufficient to enable participants to quickly discern an opponent's movements and gauge or make moves without the discomfort of glare. The speed of action in martial arts is often extremely fast.

1 *Photo: Stan Knighton, EKGB*

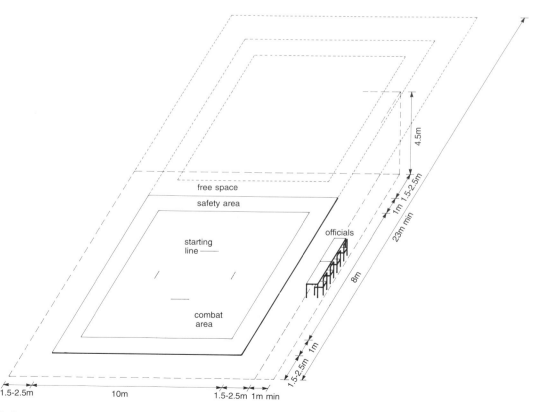

2 *Space diagram. The 10 x 10 m matted area comprises a 1 m safety area surrounding the 8 x 8 m combat area. The line between these may be broken or in a different colour (to the perimeter line on the mats). The overall area for multiple areas is given in the space table. For international events the competition area of 10 x 10 m may be elevated on a podium of up to 1 m above floor level.*

1.2 Space

Space table for all standards of competition

Length of matted area	10.0 m
Width of matted area	10.0 m
Free space, unmatted surround	1.5 (min)–2.5 m
Additional width one side for officials	1 m
Overall areas (minimum dimensions):	
One mat	12 × 13 m
Two mats (1)	22 × 13 m
Three mats for regional competitions (1)	32 × 13 m

Note (1): There is no free space between adjoining matted areas.

1.3 Floor

For competitions a firm matting which does not move apart is required.

1.4 Internal environment

For general details of environmental services recommendations refer to Chapters 60 and 61.

1.5 Other requirements

These are the same as for aikido and judo.

2 References and further advice

English Karate Governing Body.

34
Kendo (also a guide for iaido and jodo)

Peter Ackroyd

1 *Photo: British Kendo Association*

1 Introduction

Kendo is one of the traditional Japanese martial arts and is presented as a modern competitive sport. Two contestants, wearing protective armour, fight with bamboo swords. Footwork is vital – kendoka use short, fast gliding steps, and sometimes a jump for counter attacks.

The competition and practice requirements for iaido and jodo are virtually identical to those for kendo.

1.1 Critical factors

- Overall area including safety margins around the combat area
- Floor finish and maintenance must ensure no risk of damage to bare feet (mats are also a hazard)
- Action is often extremely fast and requires a high degree of viewing concentration – therefore, lighting must be sufficient to enable participants quickly to discern an opponents movements, gauge or make attacks, and perform throws without the discomfort of glare
- Walls should provide a contrast to the predominantly white or black clothing of participants
- Good ventilation is essential
- Access to first-aid box and facilities.

1.2 Space

The sport can take place in a common sports hall or large projectile hall where approximately 14 m (approx 46 ft) width and a minimum height of 4.5 m (approx 15 ft) is

Space table

Combat area	International National (N)	Regional (Rg) County (Cy) Club (C)	Recreational (R)
Length	11 m	11 m	10 m
Width	9–11 m	9–11 m	2–3 m
Minimum safety margins around	1.5 m	1.5 m	1.5–2 m
Additional width one side for officials	1 m	1 m	–
Overall areas (BKA recommended dimensions)			
Single combat area	16 × 17 m	15 × 12–14 m	–
Two combat areas	30 × 18 m	15 × 28 m	–
Three combat areas	45 × 18 m	15 × 42 m	–

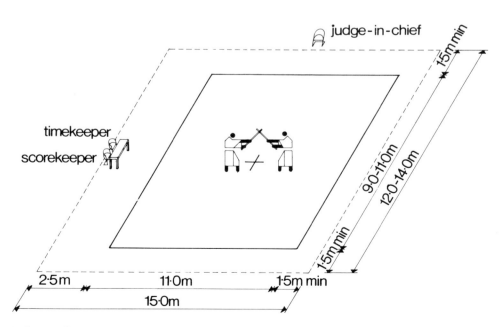

2 *Space diagram. The area shown is for contests. The minimum space for practice is approximately 10 × 3–5 m per pair*

available. Coaching and training in smaller practice halls is possible with reduced width of the combat area. The minimum practical space for five or six pairs at practice or recreational combat is approximately 30 x 13 m (approx 99 x 43 ft). See space table below and **2**.

Safety margins between combat areas must be multiple and cannot be shared.

1.3 Floor and markings
A fully sprung hardwood floor (maple, ash or birch), with a completely smooth, splinter-free surface sealed with non-slip sealant or varnish. Surface must not be waxed, and mats should not be used, as they are a hazard. The centre is marked with a cross (see **2**) and the boundary with lines 50–100 mm (2–4 in) wide. Two starting lines are also marked.

1.4 Internal environment
For general details of environmental services recommendations refer to Chapters 60 and 61.

1.5 Storage
- Space for kendo armour, allowing about 600 × 600 × 600 mm (2 × 2 × 2 ft) per outfit
- Storage for bamboo swords about 1.25 m (approx 4 ft) in length
- First aid equipment.

2 References and further advice
British Kendo Association (BKA).

35
Korfball

Peter Ackroyd

1 Introduction

Korfball from Holland was designed to give equal opportunities to both sexes: teams comprised equal numbers of males and females. Players are allowed to hinder only opponents of the same gender. Korfball uses techniques similar to basketball (see Chapter 20), handball (Chapter 30) and netball (Chapter 37), although dribbling with the ball is not allowed. The standard game is played by eight players per team, four male and four female.

The indoor game of micro korfball is now the main version of the sport in the UK. For the outdoor version see Volume 1, Chapter 62.

1 Photo: British Korfball Association

The required overall space of 44 × 26 m including the recommended clearance all round is much larger than can be provided in most existing halls. Smaller dimensions are allowed, as given in the space table, but they severely inhibit the game and limit the number of spectators. The Sports Council has included in its recommended standard sizes of halls (see Table 49.2 in Chapter 49) a rectangular proportioned 'large' hall to provide full sized courts for hockey, handball and korfball.

1.1 Critical factors
- Overall area of space and clear safety margins around
- Minimum clear height
- Non-slip floor finish with firmly stuck down marking tapes
- Flush walls and players safety factors
- No hazardous objects to be left around the hall
- Special requirements below.

1.2 Space

Korfball can be played in a large sports hall or multi-purpose sports space, **2**, as noted in Table 49.2 and diagrams in Chapter 49. The smallest recreational pitch will fit into a 34 x 18 m small hall or medium hall given 34 m length (see Chapter 49 Figures **2e-2i**). Space is comparable with those for five-a-side football (Chapter 27), handball (Chapter 30) and indoor hockey (Chapter 31); and dimensions are given in the following table. The length of the pitch is always twice the width.

A version for juniors called 'mono korfball' is played by teams of fewer than six players each, on a small court with goal posts 20 m apart and no half-way line. A version called 'macro korfball' using a court of three zones was formally discontinued in 1992.

Space table			
	International National (N) (1)	*Intercounty (Cy) Club (C) (2)*	*Junior beginners recreation (R)*
Length	40 m	40–36 m (3)	36–32 m min
Width	20 m	20–18 m min (3)	18–16 m min
Side margins	2 m	2 m	2–1 m
One side margin for table and bench space	4 m	4 m	–
End margins	2 m	2 m	2–1 m
Overall minimum area	44 × 26 m	44 × 26 m to 40 × 22 m (3)	40 × 22 m to 34 × 18 m
Minimum height	9m	9 m	7 m

Note (1): Including national league.
Note (2): Including area leagues.

1.3 Floor and markings

The surface must be resilient, even, free from dust and not wet or slippery. Clearly visible lines are at least 30–50 mm wide ($1\frac{1}{8}$ to 2 in), preferably in white for competition play. The standard colour in multi-line halls is yellow, with blue as the second choice to give excellent contrast with the floor itself. Markings should be fixed firmly to the floor and must not be slippery.

1.4 Goals

Open bottomed baskets are cylindrical 250 mm (10 in) high with an inner diameter of 390–410 mm (approx 1 ft 4 in) and preferably painted bright yellow. Its top edge must be 3.5 m (11 ft 6 in) above floor level except where otherwise decided within the rules (eg to cater for young players).

Each basket is mounted on a round metal or wooden post with an external diameter of 45–80 mm ($1\frac{3}{4}$ to $3\frac{1}{8}$ in), fixed to a circular base approximately 800 mm (32 in) in diameter and heavy enough to resist overturning. These bases must be taped to the floor to prevent their being shifted around during play. Alternatively, in specialist halls, posts can be socketed into the floor.

1.5 Surrounding enclosures

Korfball does not need to be enclosed other than for the run-off safety margins around the pitch and the minimum ceiling clearances. However, any walls should be absolutely flush and surfaces similar to requirements for five-a-side football.

1.6 Spectators

Side galleries overlooking the pitch give the best view but retractable seating even at the ends is suitable. Typical

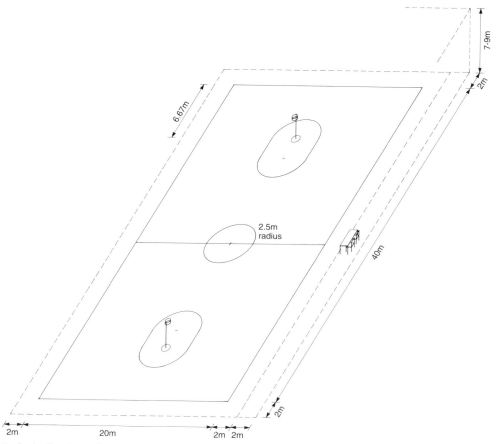

2 In halls of smaller dimensions than the official overall pitch sizes given in the space table, allow for full safety margins, but keep the pitch width around 18–20 m and make the length as near as possible to 40 m. The post positions are detailed on the diagram as fractions of the pitch dimensions. The officials' table is for scoreboard operator, microphone and records keeper

spectator numbers are 200 to 300 for league matches and 1000 to 1500 for international matches. See the large hall sizes given in Chapter 49.

1.7 Storage
Space is required for storing the goals, each consisting of a base (unless posts are sunk into the floor), a post and a detachable basket to the dimensions given above.

1.8 Internal environment
For general details of environmental services recommendations refer to Chapters 60 and 61.

1.9 Special requirements
As this game is always played by mixed teams, adequate changing and toilet facilities are required for both sexes. A first aid kit plus a supply of cold water or ice must be available at all matches.

2 References and further advice
British Korfball Association (BKA).
BKA Safety Guidelines.

36
Movement and dance

Mark Foley

1 Introduction

Activities such as movement and dance straddle the sports/arts boundary and many sports halls are used for a variety of arts and community purposes, whether this was originally intended or not. There is a great overlap of activity, particularly at local level and there can be many advantages, both economic and cultural, in providing for a number of different community activities together in a multi-purpose hall. At its most basic level the same space can house activities like table tennis, badminton, movement and dance, amateur dramatics, small concerts, meetings and a whole range of community activities. Dance studios as forms of specialist ancillary hall and commercial dance centres are described in Chapter 52. Technical data for arts workshops are given in Chapter 53.

Sports and arts activities often have common ancillary needs such as changing rooms, showers, toilets, possibly bar, refreshment and creche facilities. Movement and dance activities in particular share many of the same requirements as traditional competitive sports although they do have certain specific needs which should be taken into account. These can be accommodated within shared community provision at a reasonable cost to the participants. Much more can be done to include this growing and important area of leisure and recreation if the basic needs are appreciated. These activities encompass dance of all kinds, including aerobics and keep fit, ballet, folk, ballroom, south Asian, African peoples and modern dance and would benefit from the more sophisticated environment that design for joint use might provide, 1-3.

1 *Photo: Sports Council Publications*

This section incorporates the requirements for movement and dance drawn up by the Movement and Dance Division of the Central Council of Physical Recreation (CCPR).

2 Movement and dance organisations

The wide range of activities and disciplines are organised on a national basis and through their local organisations and members, by a large number of associations, of which the following are in membership of the CCPR:

Allied Dancing Association
Association of Health and Exercise Teachers
British Amateur Gymnastic Association – Rhythmic Gymnastics Section
British Association of Teachers of Dancing
British Council for Ballroom Dancing
British Slimnastics Association
British Wheel of Yoga
Dalcroze Society
Dolmetsh Historical Dance Association
English Amateur Dance Association
English Folk Dance and Song Society
Guild of Professional Teachers of Dancing
Health Beauty Exercise
Imperial Society of Teachers of Dancing
International Dance Teachers' Association
Keep Fit Association
Laban Guild
Margaret Morris Movement
Medau Society
National Association of Exercise Teaching
National Association of Teachers of Dancing
National Association of Teachers in Further and Higher Education – Dance Section
Northern Counties Dance Teachers Association
Physical Education Association of Great Britain and North Ireland
Royal Academy of Dancing
Society of International Folk Dancing
United Kingdom Alliance of Professional teachers of Dancing Ltd
YMCA

These organisations cater for social and recreative movement and dance activities, and have a combined membership well in excess of 100,000. Numerous activities are also organised by independent groups and community bodies. Although there are no national surveys which cover all the various aspects of movement, the 1987 General Household Survey identified that 9% of the adult population had taken part in keep fit, yoga, aerobics and dance exercise within the four weeks prior to interview, indicating that 4 million adults take part with some degree of regularity. Similarly a 1988 Mintel survey found that aerobics, keep fit and dance classes were the second most popular activity after swimming.

2.1 Critical factors
- Spacial proportions of space
- Safety precautions
- Occupancy rates and means of escape
- Licensing
- Ancillary accommodation for events
- Flexible changing/dressing rooms
- Portability of ballet barres and mirrors in a multi-use hall
- Floor surface and condition

2 *Photo: Sports Council Publications*

3 *Photo: Sports Council Publications*

- Storage
- Aesthetic quality of space and fittings
- A light, airy space with warm temperature
- Ample power sockets
- Good acoustics and sound separation
- Good ventilation without draughts
- Flexible, controllable, glare-free lighting.

2.2 Dimensions and spatial requirements

There are no dimensional rules for movement and dance except those given below. The floor area needed varies with the nature of the movement and dance activities, so a range of floor sizes is suggested below. They are generally based on a square or rectangular format to enable a clear sense of orientation to be maintained within the space.

- For rhythmic gymnastics, **2**, 14 × 14 m is required, including a 1 m safety surround (see also Section 8, below) with a clear height of at least 9–15 m.
- The space allowances for band rostra and dance equipment storage space are given below.
- It will be useful to refer to the space module for a dancer, **4**, when assessing the numbers of participants that can be accommodated within a particular space at any one time. This equates to an activity space of approximately 3.5 sq m per person. This will increase by a factor of between 2–3 for more dynamic movement across the hall but can otherwise usually be accommodated by sequencing the participants.
- For traditional ballroom dancing a minimum clear width of 10.6 m is recommended to avoid collision between the two main streams of dancers. There should be space for twelve dancers to take the floor at one time.

These activity space rates should not be confused with occupancy rates calculated for means of escape in case of fire. For these rates refer to BS 5588: Part 6: 1991 (see References and further advice) where Table 3 recommends 0.5 sq m per person as a 'floor space factor for dance areas'. This may well have been determined as a safe standard for social or disco dancing in which case it is suggested that the Fire Officer is consulted regarding the appropriate standard to be applied.

Spaces should be well proportioned, with the main movement and dance space clearly defined as a square or rectangle, free of columns, allowing good movement in all directions. Over-elongated spaces, or spaces with walls that are not square should be avoided. Recessed spaces off the main area can be useful adjuncts for storage of equipment, musical accompaniment, or even spectators, particularly in multi-use spaces.

The recommended minimum floor dimensions are 15 × 12–15 m, coinciding with the size of the smaller

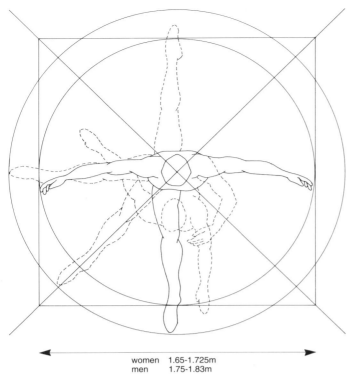

women 1.65-1.725m
men 1.75-1.83m

4 *Space module of a dancer. Rhythmic gymnastics, **3**, requires a clear height of 9–15 m, otherwise 4–6 m satisfies most of other disciplines. See also Chapter 52, diagram **5***

practice hall recommended by the Sports Council (see Chapter 51). The recommended minimum headroom for some movement and dance disciplines is 4.5 m, but it is otherwise a preferred dimension for most disciplines because it enhances the quality of space. A 9.1 × 12 m ancillary studio space would permit movement and dance activities for smaller practice groups (see Chapter 52).

The 17–20 × 15.6 m hall space suggested by the Sports Council for halls in small communities (see Chapter 68) would also be suitable for movement and dance.

A larger double-square practice hall size, 21–24 m × 12 m × 6.1 m high, can be used for movement and dance by reducing the length as necessary whereas the smaller (one badminton court) village hall size, 16.5–17 m × 8.5–10 m × 6.1 m, is less suitable in this respect (see Sports Council Datasheet 59, Small Community Recreation Centre development project).

Larger halls (see layouts in Chapter 49) can be used for movement and dance, but there may be difficulties when the hall is shared with other activities. Movement and dance (and indeed drama and music activities) generally require visual and acoustic privacy. In some cases, large halls can be subdivided by the use of appropriately designed curtain or partitioning systems, provided noise levels generated in adjacent areas can be kept at reasonable levels. (See 'Noise' below, and Acoustic considerations in Chapter 60, and Chapter 53.)

A performance space of 46 × 32 m is required for the largest events at national and international levels (refer to *Arenas* in References and further advice), but there is a greater demand for intermediate-size (minimum area 32 × 23 m) and smaller activity space. These are in great demand, especially at weekends.

2.3 Entertainments licensing
Obtaining a licence may make demands on the design beyond those of the activities themselves, for example in relation to fire precautions and means of escape. In order to permit a full range of movement and dance uses as well as other community and arts use, designers are recommended to consider the requirements for licensing from the outset, and as the regulations are for the safety of the participants, it is wise to consider them even if a statutory or local licence is not needed. See also Spectators, below.

Local authorities may treat each case on its merits and it is likely that these areas would be classed as places of public entertainment. There are now standard licensing regulations and design codes of practice for existing or, separately, newbuild premises and venues. The granting of a licence is generally subject to compliance with certain conditions contained in statutory regulations. The three principal regulatory standards and codes of practice are listed in References and further advice.

2.4 Spectators
Participants and audience are often interchangeable, particularly at festivals and rallies. Sightlines should allow for activities where the participants are stretched out on the floor. Circulation and stewarding should allow ready but safe access to and from gangways and aisles, in agreement with the safety authorities for the event. Potential spectator capacities should be checked with the relevant governing body, or through the CCPR Movement and Dance Division.

3 Ancillary spaces

3.1 Cloakrooms and changing
Adequate cloakrooms for participants who come dressed and changing accommodation with showering facilities for those who must change should be provided. For this purpose assume that at teaching and practice sessions there could be one person to 1.5–4 sq m of activity space, depending on the type and level of the activity. At local community level, movement and dance classes would, for the most part, be catering for groups of 30–40. For some activities these may be entirely women, though for others there will be equal numbers of both sexes. For social dances the capacity may be up to three times as great, but the personal changing needs will be less demanding.

For larger events and rallies allow for at least 240 people; some space could be provided on a temporary basis by conversion of other rooms by moving in portable dressing tables fitted with mirror lights, **5** and **6**. Drinking water must be readily available. One WC and shower are also required for every six dancers (50% of the provision for men being in the form of urinals). Changing rooms should interconnect for flexible use during peak periods. Indivi-

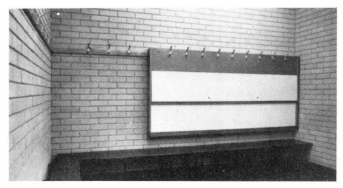

5 *Special fixture which opens up to form a make-up table at Bridgnorth Leisure Centre, Salop CC. Phoyto: Technical Unit for Sport*

6 *Fixture in open position. Photo: Technical Unit for Sport*

dual rooms are important for the use of principal performers and adjudicators in addition to staff rooms.

3.2 Refreshments
Ease of access to a refreshment and bar area should be borne in mind. For social dance activities these should ideally be adjacent to the area used. If the hall can be planned to be adjacent to refreshment areas, the space could be opened up and used more flexibly, as well as for a variety of other social and community purposes.

3.3 Crèche
A supervised creche is an important amenity for which a room should be made available. See Chapter 48.

3.4 Ancillary accommodation for events
- First aid and medical facilities.
- Administration, producers, control and meetings space off the hall.
- Warm-up areas and studios – flooring is again critical (see 'Surfaces' below). Overlay surfaces can cover unsuitable floors. These may require special fitting out with portable equipment and temporary flooring. Events organisers should also check available space when choosing a venue.
- Hospitality facilities – as the participants are likely to be spending considerable periods in the arena building, there should be lounge spaces (or a 'green room') for relaxation between sessions with nearby refreshments.
- Media facilities.
- Arena workshops – it may be necessary to repair scenery and 'props'.

For further details refer to *Arenas* (see References and further advice).

3.5 Floor surface
It is essential for most movement and dance activities that a smooth, low-slip, semi-sprung flooring system is provided as a basic necessity. Movement and dance activities, in contrast to many other sports and leisure activities, are generally practised in bare feet or dance shoes with little or no absorption to cushion the impact of the practitioners weight on the floor. Continued practice on ungiving surfaces can lead to stress of back and limbs and even permanent injury.

Different movement and dance activities will have different surface requirements, whether for barefoot, softshoe or hardshoe work. A 12 m square all-woollen carpet overlay is required for rhythmic gymnastics. The floor should also be able to withstand the hard clogs used for folk dance demonstrations.

It is also important to decide whether and where ballet shoes may be used with rosin – which can cause sticky patches to collect dirt unless regularly cleaned off the floor surface. The dance floor should not be polished.

Some activities involve lying on the floor. It is important that the floor should be kept clean and in good condition, a point which should be impressed on the designer, the management and users of facilities. Adequate steps should be taken to eliminate the introduction of grit on the floor as it is this, in conjunction with hard shoes rather than the footwear itself, which may cause damage to the surface. Such precautions may include:

- The installation of extensive entrance matting
- The sealing of any walls which may emit grit
- An intensified programme of sweeping and possibly mopping.

Subject to these measures, all movement and dance activities, including ballroom dancing, can take place on the same floor. For details see also Chapter 52 and *A Handbook for Dance Floors*. Semi-sprung timber floor constructions are also described generally in Chapter 64.

4 Equipment and services

Dance barres
A barre mounted on the wall of the hall is a useful accessory, particularly for ballet, but also for other forms of movement and dance. In multi-use halls, the permanent installation of dance barres will conflict with other uses, therefore portable barres would be a convenient way of overcoming this problem, 7 (see also dance barres in Chapter 52). Allowance should then be made to provide adjacent storage space to store equipment when not in use.

Mirrors
An area of wall-mounted mirror is of great assistance in the teaching and practice of many forms of movement and dance (see dance mirrors in Chapter 52). There is a serious conflict in multi-use halls because of the dangers and vulnerability of mirrors to damage by other sports activities. There is no easy solution to this problem. Large panels of mirror glass mounted to secure backing boards are heavy and cumbersome to move and store, particularly when many panels are involved. There are substitutes for mirror glass, such as foam-backed mirror perspex, but the reflected image definition is generally not as good as that of glass and can distort. Where the use of mirrors is important, it is suggested that a dedicated movement or dance studio is provided (see Chapter 52).

Amplification
There should be a system to provide music from a tape, cassette or music deck and, should the occasion demand, to amplify the teacher's voice and any accompanying instrument(s). For social dancing there should be provision for good quality amplification for the Master of Ceremonies/caller and a band of up to six musicians.

Teaching platform
Some teachers of movement and dance advocate a platform for teaching purposes; this can be portable and lightweight for easy movement and storage, 1. It can be used for other activities, eg drama workshop.

7 *Portable barres. Photo: Burrell Foley Fischer*

Band rostrum

For social dances a band rostrum should be provided of sufficient size to accommodate up to a six-piece band, including possibly a grand piano, and mixer and speakers for the amplification (probably about 2.5 × 6.5 m would be needed). This rostrum may also be in portable units, though one section should be of sufficient size for the piano, as this should not be carried on more than one section. Where the rostrum is a permanent fixture the controls for the amplification system and lighting should be sited on or near the rostrum.

Power

A number of flush 13-amp power points should be provided at low level, to permit the use of cleaning, amplification and other equipment.

4.1 Storage

Approximately 50 sq m will be needed for portable barres, mirrors and staging, as detailed above, if permanent fixtures are not provided. Secure storage spaces are needed for audio equipment, recorded music and tapes, and a piano (for movement and dance an upright piano is generally sufficient).

Additional storage may be needed for users' own equipment (eg balls, clubs, hoops, mats, small 'props') if the room is to permit a variety of uses. If there is no seating provision in the hall, storage will be needed for sufficient chairs for all participants. These will, of course, also be of use for meetings etc. Foam filled mats and other equipment must be stored in a fire resistant store (see Chapter 55).

4.2 Internal environment

For general details of environmental services recommendations refer to Chapters 60 and 61.

The quality of internal surroundings for movement and dance requires a higher level of comfort and sophistication than for many sports activities. Well-proportioned spaces giving a light, spacious feeling using both natural and artificial lighting are important. Spaces should try to be inspiring rather than purely utilitarian, while avoiding features that are overtly distracting.

The acoustic quality of the space should also be considered in order to provide good conditions for music and teaching.

Lighting

Lighting is one of the most important means of enhancing the quality of space and sculptural form of the dancer's body. This can be achieved through a balance between natural and artificial lighting. Glare should be avoided while diffused lighting using walls and ceilings as reflective surfaces helps to achieve this quality. Windows giving controlled natural daylight, ventilation and a view out or feeling of contact with the outside are also desirable. Tubular fluorescent lighting may not be aesthetically appropriate even though it may be economical to install and run.

The lighting installation should provide a minimum level of 200 lux at the floor (in a multi-purpose area, higher levels may be required for other activities).

Provision can be made for varying the nature and the levels of lighting by the use of dimmers and by part switching. Some fittings can be of the adjustable spotlight type to achieve a more inspiring balance. Pendant fittings should generally be avoided.

An emergency lighting system may be required.

Heating and ventilation

As the areas will be used intermittently, and as the number of occupants and the degree of activity may vary considerably, a system having capacity for a rapid response to the local environment is desirable. However, it is important that the system should not be noisy because of the masking effect on the speech communication of the teacher (see *Acoustics in Educational Buildings, Building Bulletin 51*, for fuller information). The temperature required will be 18°C (some modern and classical dancers prefer a temperature of 20°C) and fresh air ventilation in the order of 15 litres per second per person, or two air changes per hour (where the occupancy is not known), should be provided. If frequent use of the area for public dances or similar events is intended, then a higher ventilation rate would probably be required. These recommendations should be checked against local requirements.

In smaller studio spaces, it is sometimes desirable to allow users some control over their environment, either by being able to open windows for increased ventilation, or local control of the heating or ventilation. Against this, consideration should be given to the possible effect of noise disturbance on or from neighbours and heat loss through open windows.

4.3 Noise

When planning new facilities it is important that noise transmission to and from other spaces, both at the same level or on floors above and below, does not interfere with any adjacent use. The choice of materials and form of construction should be carefully considered. The sound attenuation of partitions should be sufficient to ensure maintenance of noise level of NR 30 when noisy activities such as five-a-side football or squash take place in adjacent spaces. Partitions should be taken up through suspended ceilings to the underside of floor or roof decks and be well sealed. (See also *Acoustics in Educational Buildings, Building Bulletin 51*, for fuller information.) Stores can sometimes be effectively used as sound buffers.

5 References and further advice

Action with Communities In Rural England (ACRE) publications.

Armstrong, L and Morgan, R, *Space for Dance – An Architectural Design Guide*, Publishing Centre for Cultural Resources (1984).

British Standards Institution, *BS 5588 Fire Precautions in the Design, Construction and Use of Buildings. Part 6 Code of Practice for Places of Assembly*, BSI, Milton Keynes (1991) (for newbuild premises).

Central Council of Physical Recreation (CCPR).

Chapter 52, Dance studios and workshops (including commercial dance centres).

Chapter 53, Sports arts workshops.

Chartered Institution of Building Services Engineers, *CIBSE Lighting Guide: Sport*, CIBSE, London.

Department of Education and Science, *Acoustics in Educational Buildings, Building Bulletin 51*, HMSO, London.

Fire Safety and Safety of Places of Sport Act 1987, HMSO, London (1987).

Foley, M, *A Handbook for Dance Floors*, Dance UK, National Forum for Dance (1992).

Foley, M, *Dance Spaces*, The Arts Council of England (1994).

Guide to Fire Precautions in Existing Places of Entertainment and Like Premises, Home Office and HMSO, London (1990).

National governing bodies listed in the Introduction and other organisations.

Sports Council, *Arenas: A Briefing, Design and Management Guide*, Sports Council, London (1989).

37
Netball

Peter Ackroyd

Space table

	National (N) Regional (Rg)	County (Cy)	(Club) (C)	Recreational (R)
Length	30.5 m	30.5 m	30.5 m	30.5 m
Width	15.25 m	15.25 m	15.25 m	15.25 m
Margin space along side lines (1)	2–1.5 m	1.5 m	1.2 m min	0.75 m min
Extra width along one side for match tables and team benches	1.5 m	1.5 m min	–	0.75 m min
Margin space behind goal lines	2 m	1.2 m min(2)	1.2 m min	32 × 16.75 m
Overall area	34.5–33.5 × 20.75–19.75 m	32.9 × 19.75 m min	32.9 × 17.65 –18 m min	min
Minimum height	7.6 m	7.6 m	7.0–7.6 m	6.7–7 m

Note (1): Ideally, 2.4 m between adjacent courts (where hall divider nets are not extended between courts). Also, if equipment is wall mounted, eg in a school gymnasium, then safety margin widths must be clear of all projections.
Notes (2): Minimum 1.5 m where spectators are also situated at ends.

1 Critical factors
- Overall volume of space including surrounding safety margins
- A non-slip playing surface
- Type of goalpost support and its location (see Equipment).

1 Photo: Brian Worrell

1.1 Space
Provided there is free space all round the court this game can be played anywhere in a common sports space. Refer to the caption of the space diagram, **2**, for the constraints of 32 × 17m or smaller sizes of hall.

1.2 Storage and other accommodation
The portable goals used in this game are readily and easily storable. For additional accommodation required for competition events, refer to *Arenas* in References and further advice.

1.3 Court markings
These are 50 mm wide and coloured red (or preferably white for tournament centre courts). For details see Chapter 64. Dimensions are measured to the outside of perimeter lines, ie the playing area includes the lines.

1.4 Equipment
The goalposts may be round or square, are 3.05 m (10 ft) high and 50–100 mm (2–4 in) in diameter. The new ruling from July 1991 is that the goalpost shall be placed (at the mid-point of each goal line) so that the back of the goalpost is at the outside of the goal line, **2**. Posts may be inserted into a socket in the floor or supported by *a metal base which shall not project on the court (which includes the goal line* – see Court markings above). For national matches the goalposts should preferably be inserted into a socket in the floor. For other matches each post may be supported on a metal baseplate, but which, due to the locational constraint above (in italics), must be situated behind the goal line (off the court) but with a forward mounted post on the line. This poses goalpost stability and safety problems for equipment manufacturers and for players.

1.5 Spectator facilities
Accommodation for spectators may be required. All-round seating may be unavoidable, but this game is best viewed from the sides.

1.6 Flooring
It should be noted that the International Federation of Netball Associations (IFNA) Rule 1 requires that the court shall have a firm surface. It should also be slip-resistant and preferably resilient.

1.7 Surrounding surfaces or enclosure
Walls should be non-abrasive, without windows and light in colour to contrast with the ball.

1.8 Internal environment
For general details of environmental services recommendations refer to Chapters 60 and 61.

2 References and further advice
International Federation of Netball Associations (IFNA) and the All England Netball Association Ltd.
Sports Council, *National Lottery Sports Fund Guidance Note 375*, Sports Council, London (1995).
Sports Council, *Arenas*, Sports Council, London (1989).

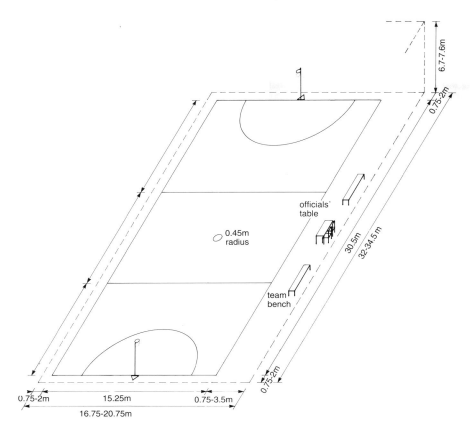

0.45m radius

officials' table

team bench

6.7–7.6m

0.75–2m

30.5m

32–34.5m

0.75–2m

0.75–2m

15.25m

0.75–3.5m

16.75–20.75m

2 *Space diagram. Note that the overall minimum area of 32.9 × 17.65 m for a club court exceeds the size of 'small' halls given in Chapter 49. If the hall area cannot be increased for a full sized court, then the court, not the surrounding safety margins, should be reduced in size. Also note the new goalpost ruling given in Section 1.4 of this chapter.*

38
Short tennis

Peter Ackroyd

1 Introduction

Tennis finds it difficult to attract the number of young recruits the game deserves – especially from non-tennis-playing backgrounds. It is a problem shared by other European countries, and so extensive research in Sweden came up with an answer – short tennis.

This game for children was piloted in Britain in 1981. It is now played throughout the country in schools, leisure centres and private clubs. This activity is supplemented by a full programme of regional, county and local competitions for the 6–11 years age range.

While short tennis is great fun it is certainly no gimmick. It is a proportionally reduced, realistic version of the full scale game. It is played indoors or out on a badminton-sized court and specially produced rackets, balls and nets.

Short tennis has a permanent, popular and important role in developing future tennis players, in that:

- It is played in exactly the same way as lawn tennis, apart from using larger service areas
- Although a simplified points-only scoring system is recommended for matches, short tennis does also

provide an ideal opportunity to introduce young children to the full tennis scoring system
- The scoring system makes it easier to introduce very young children to a structured, competitive situation.

1.1 Critical factors
- A fun game for children from the age of 6 years which also develops their tennis skills
- Can be played on a badminton court, or within it to safely maintain the surrounding run-out margins
- Changing equipment and toilets comfortable for children
- Other critical factors for badminton and tennis may apply to short tennis.

1.2 Space and rules

Court
The game should be played on a short tennis court 13.4 × 6.1 m (44 × 20 ft) or a badminton court which is exactly the same size, as shown in the diagram, **2**.

Court boundaries
The space table gives the Lawn Tennis Association (LTA) guidelines. Short tennis can certainly be played and enjoyed within more restricted boundaries. If, when using a badminton court, the side or baselines are particularly close to a wall, the inner side and/or base 'tramlines' can become the court limits.

Net
The net should be 800 mm (2 ft 8 in) in height at the centre and 850 mm (2 ft 9½ in) at the posts. Short tennis equipment is ideal but any net (eg a badminton net)

1 *Photo: Professional Sport*

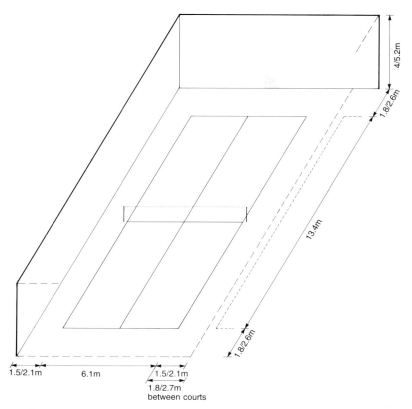

2 *Space diagram. The game is also played on a badminton court of identical size. See Chapter 19*

Space table

	General play	Competition
Court size	13.4 × 6.1 m	13.4 × 6.1 m
Minimum run-back	1.8 m	2.6 m
Minimum side-run	1.5 m	2.1 m
Minimum side-run between courts (1)	18. m	2.7 m
Minimum obstructed height over court	4.0 m	5.2 m

Note (1): Badminton courts are often spaced 0.9 m (approx 3 ft) apart.

suspended at the regulation height on badminton or other posts is quite suitable.

1.3 Floor and walls
Limited experience to date of this developing game suggests that surfaces, colour contrasting background and netting and other common factors should be the same as for indoor tennis (see Chapter 88) or badminton (see Chapter 19).

1.4 Children's changing and toilets
This is a game scaled down to the needs of the young. The height of changing equipment and toilets should reflect this. There is a growing awareness that in all sports and leisure facilities some low-level toilets and basins are now a necessity. See also References and further advice below.

1.5 Internal environment
For general details of environmental services recommendations refer to Chapters 60 and 61. Environmental requirements are the same as for tennis and badminton (with which facilities are commonly shared). Refer to Chapter 60.

2 References and further advice
Lawn Tennis Association Short Tennis Department.
Lawn Tennis Association, *Short Tennis – Rules and Teachers' Guide*, LTA, London (the complete rules and an abbreviated guide for parents or teachers).
National Children's Play and Recreation Unit.
Sports Council, *TUS Datasheet 51*, Sports Council, London.

39
Softball

Peter Ackroyd

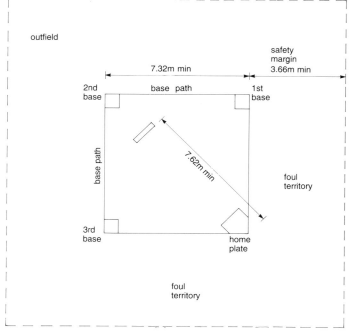

1 Introduction

Softball started as an indoor variety of baseball in Chicago in 1887, became enormously popular in both its outdoor and indoor version, and is now played world-wide. The home of the game remains North America, where some of the indoor facilities are so enormous that the game is often played to the same court dimensions and the same rules as outdoor softball. That can also be the case in Britain and Europe; but more often the rules are adjusted to suit the smaller spaces available, **1**, and make maximum use of the playing time (because of the way charges are levied on the use of indoor space). Softball is an exciting, non-stop action game to watch. Outdoor softball data are given in Volume 1.

2, 3 *Because of the different shapes and sizes of indoor halls available, two layouts are suggested. 2 is the conventional outdoor layout and can be used in 36.5 × 32 m large and square halls with conventional or adapted outdoor rules. Two minimum sized courts fit into a 36.6 × 18.3 m (approx 120 × 60 ft) hall.*

1 *Photo: National Softball Federation*

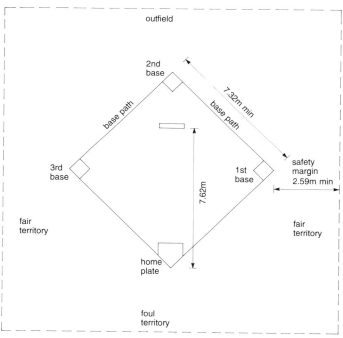

3 *was introduced by the National Softball Federation in 1989, together with special rules for its use. It is designed for rectangular halls and differs from the outdoor layout since it confines foul territory to an area behind home plate – giving a corresponding increase in fair territory. Two minimum size courts will fit into a 32 × 17 m small hall*

1.1 Critical factors

- Overall area of space including safety margins around the playing area
- Proper positioning of diamond to make best use of hall shape and available space
- Protective barrier netting
- Protection of light fittings, roof lights and other equipment.

1.2 Space

The game is fast and frenetic, with much of the energy going into running from one base to another – especially first base. The diamond should therefore be positioned in the hall for maximum distance between bases while still

allowing adequate safety margins between running lanes and walls.

Two possible layouts are recommended to allow best use of differing hall shapes and sizes, as shown in the two space diagrams. The layout in **2** is the conventional court suitable for a square hall in which play follows near-outdoor conventions. The alternative in **3** was introduced

Space table

	Practical minimum	Notional maximum
Base path	7.32 m	13.72 m
Cross-diamond	10.74 m	19.39 m
Pitching distance	7.62 m min	NA
Safety margin:		
2	Half the base path min 3.66 m	Half the base path 6.86 m
3	Third of the base path min 2.59 m	Third of the base path 4.57 m
Minimum overall area:		
2	18.06 m square (59 ft 3 in square)	33.1 m square (108 ft 7 in square)
3	15.93 m square (52 ft 3 in square)	

NA, not applicable.

in 1989 by the National Softball Federation together with special rules. It confines 'Foul territory' to an area behind the home plate, giving correspondingly more space to the 'Fair area', and introduces various adaptations to make best use of indoor conditions of play. For detailed rules contact the National Softball Federation.

The table below gives recommended key dimensions. These may be varied to suit the available space, but every effort should be made to provide safety margins at least half the distance of the base paths.

1.3 Floor
The floor finish must be smooth and non-abrasive but not slippery. It must be splinterproof and track channels for sliding partitions should not run across the playing area.

1.4 Markings
See the diagrams. Lines must be 75 or 100 mm (3 or 4 in) wide and they form part of the playing area. Orange is the recommended colour, but this may need to be changed to give adequate contrast with floor colour. Softball can in fact be played without marked lines, because the positions of the bases indicate the base paths and foul area; and in this case only a chalk line to mark the pitcher's position may be required.

1.5 Walls
Walls may also be protected by netting. More often targets are either set up or drawn on and score extra points for the defence if hit by a batted ball.

1.6 Barriers
Ceiling to floor netting to cordon off other hall users; plus protection for windows and light fittings.

1.7 Equipment
Storage is required for softball bats. Balls may be ordinary softballs, but more usually an adapted ball is used which is more suitable for indoor use; home plate and bases may be ordinary outdoor bases but more usually thinner ones are used and stuck to the floor with adhesive tape. It is useful to have a proper timing scoreboard in the hall.

1.8 Internal environment
For general details of environmental services recommendations refer to Chapters 60 and 61.

40
Table tennis

Peter Ackroyd

1 Introduction

The popularity of table tennis stretches across all ages and all socio-economic groups. It is normally played indoors by two or four players on a table of standardised size with a net across the centre.

The following data specify the different levels of facility provision which are required for accommodating everything from a beginners' session to a major international open event. Table tennis is a very safe sport, but should at all times be set out and played with due consideration to the safety of those participating and spectating.

As a sport suitable for integration of players with disabilities, there are not any official adaptations to equipment, spatial requirements or conditions, though the service law allows for disability.

1.1 Critical factors

- Overall playing area including specified clearances around and clear height above a table
- Colour, reflection, friction and resilience characteristics of the floor
- Floors and walls of dark (but not excessively so) non-reflective colour
- Uniform light over the playing area without any stroboscopic effect
- Reduced lighting intensity over spectators outside the playing area
- Good ventilation but without draughts.

1.2 Space requirements

Space requirements in comparison with many sports is small, so enabling a wide range of buildings to accommodate table tennis matches, championships and recreational play, **2**. Important dimensional and other changed requirements are included below.

The ideal venue is a purpose designed club facility (see references) or a dedicated space within a table tennis or sports centre with tables and lighting permanently available for play. However, one of the great advantages of the sport is that it can satisfactorily use ancillary spaces in sports centres and village, school, community or church halls as well as club rooms/pavilions of other sports.

1 *Photo: Charlie Wooding*

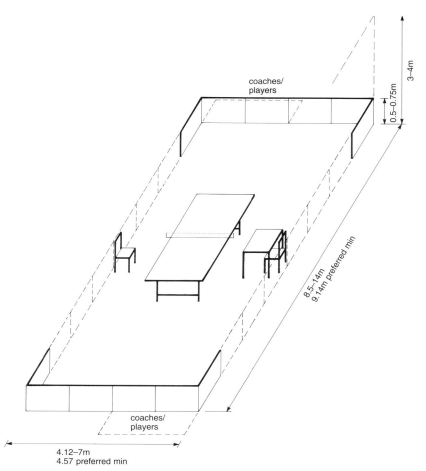

coaches/
players

3–4m

0.5–0.75m

8.5–14m preferred min
9.14m preferred min

coaches/
players

4.12–7m
4.57 preferred min

2 *Space diagram. Dimensions are ranged from the recreational minimum to the largest for grade 1 competition play: details are given in the space table. Grade 1 and 2 events require a continuous flexible barrier along all four sides of a playing area, for other standards of play see Section 1.3, Barriers. The diagram also shows the closest possible position for match officials, but if space allows, the officials' table can be located in a side bay outside the playing area. A 'pit' space of appropriate area for coaches and players is shown at the right-hand corner of both ends. Lighting and all other obstructions must be totally above the increased clear height zone, shown by the broken line at the top of the diagram*

Recreational play/coaching purposes

Spatial requirements for satisfactory play are significantly increased in the space table below and in Note (1) to that table. The range recommended allows four tables to fit on a space approximately equivalent to a badminton court. Other conditions, such as flooring, walls, environment, storage and lighting, will vary widely depending on facility availability; however, the ideals stated should be followed where possible to ensure maximum enjoyment for players. Though side by side is preferable, table layout should reflect space limitations with safety being the overriding factor.

Competitive play

Tables should be laid out side by side and not end to end, **3-4**. Each playing area should be at least the size recommended below for the three grades of play (a previous fourth grade is now obsolete). Boundaries are marked out by movable barriers. It is recommended in a multi-table venue to leave gangways between playing areas, both to enable easier player/official access to courts and to give courts total independence from each other and reduce disturbance by balls from other courts. Some major events, eg World Championships, may possibly require playing areas of 16×8 m.

There should be provision within each playing area for officials' tables and chairs each side of the table in line with the net. For some events, additional 'pit' spaces are required for coaches and in some cases for players sitting-out outside the end of the playing areas, **2**.

Championships and tournaments

For these events, there are commonly eight or more tables in use simultaneously in a single hall. Additionally, there should also be a separate working area in the playing hall of at least 9 sq m for the officials managing the tournament. This area should be slightly raised above the level of the floor of the playing hall, should be easily accessible from it, and allow a clear view of all the tables in use.

Playing area

The three grades of competitive play, each of which has related standards of playing area space, are:

Grade 1: International Table Tennis Federation (ITTF) standard for World, Continental and Open International Championships and International matches

Grade 2: English Table Tennis Association (ETTA) standard for English National Championships, 5 star and 3 star open tournaments, Premier Division matches in British League and County Championships

Grade 3: ETTA 2 star open tournaments, matches and other than Premier Division in County championships and British League

3 *A junior tournament scene with less space between tables. Photo: ETTA*

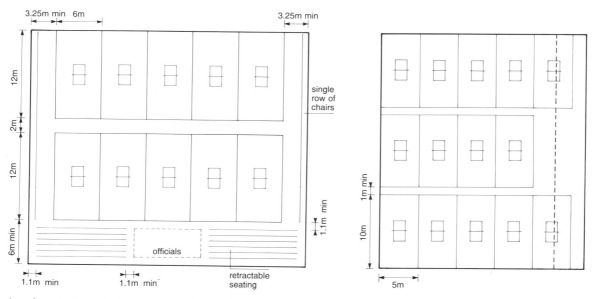

4a *A typical grade 2 tournament layout in a large sports hall. Eight or ten table layouts are normal. If twelve tables are required then space is very tight for adequate access gangways around the playing areas to more than grade 3 standards*

4b *Grade-3 10 × 5 m playing areas set out in a medium sized hall of 33, 32 × 27, 26 m or 23 m width, with table capacities. For layouts of Grade 4 and recreational/coaching tables in smaller sized halls, refer to Sports Council Datasheet 42*

Space table

	Grade 1	Grade 2	Grade 3	Grade 4	R (1)
Length of playing area	14.0 m (46 ft)	12.0 m (39 ft 4 in)	10.0 m (32 ft 10 in)	9.0 m (29 ft 6 in)	9.0–8.5 m (29 ft 6 in–27 ft 11 in)
Width of playing area	7.0 m (23 ft)	6.0 m (19ft 8 in)	5.0 m (16 ft 5 in)	5.0 m (16 ft 5 in)	4.57–4.12 m (15 ft–13 ft 6 in)
Clear height from floor to light fitting	4.0 m (13 ft 2 in)	4.0 m (13 ft 2 in)	3.0 m (9 ft 10 in)	3.0 m (9ft 10 in)	3.0 m (9ft 10 in)
Clearance from end of table to barriers or other obstruction	5.65 m (18ft 6 in)	4.63 m (15ft 2 in)	3.63 m (11 ft 11 in)	3.13 m (10 ft 3 in)	3.13–2.88 m (10 ft 3 in–9 ft 5½ in)
Clearance from side of table to barriers or other obstruction	2.74 m (9 ft)	2.24 m (7 ft 4 in)	1.74 m (5 ft 8½ in)	1.74 m (5 ft 8½ in)	1.53–1.3 m (4 ft 11 in–4 ft 3 in)

Note (1): Space standards acceptable for recreational play and coaching purposes. Increased dimensions are ranged from the ideal (maximum) to absolute minima taking into account the most economical use of small hall space and layout of tables.

Grade 4: Recommended for 1 star open tournaments, local league and club matches and championships.

For purely recreational play and coaching slightly lower space standards are acceptable; these are identified as 'R' in the space table below.

1.3 Equipment and storage
Storage facilities should be considered when building or converting a venue for table tennis use. Different table types require different volumes of space and heights of entry into storage space. Refer also to Chapter 55. Advice should always be sought with specialist suppliers and/or the appropriate governing body before making a decision. Different manufacturers have different descriptions and names for each type of table.

Tables and nets
A table tennis top measures $2.743 \times 1.524 \times 0.762$ m from the floor (9 ft $\times$ 5 ft $\times$ 2 ft 6 in). Different types and qualities of tables are required for different levels of play from coaching/recreational to international matches and tournaments.

The playability of the table is affected mainly by the thickness of the playing surface. For coaching and recreational play, the ETTA would not recommend table-top thickness of less than 18 mm. For Grades 1-4, 22 to 25 mm is recommended.

There are three types of table, differentiated by the undercarriage to suit storage and movement:

- *Free-standing type.* This is the easiest for storage and takes up least space. Used for all levels of play, it has two separate halves and eight legs, some with built-in caster wheels for easy movement. Also the easiest for handling and moving in and out of vehicles.
- *Rollaway type with playback facility.* Easy to move and erect but is much more bulky to store and requires higher headroom of 1.83 m (6 ft) for movement, being taller in its closed position than other types. An advantage is that it can be half closed so a player can practice from the horizontal end against the vertical face of the other half of the table (like a tennis player practising against a wall).
- *Rollaway type designed for mobility and economical storage but no playback facility.* Two halves fold or wheel together almost flush, with the distance between the wheels being closer than the type above. Ideal for sports centres.

Net and post sets should be sturdy, simple to assemble and easy to attach to tables of any thickness. Removable nets and posts are recommended (fixed nets can snap off and may protrude and hinder storage and safety).

Barriers
If more than one table is in use, each playing area should be divided by movable, dark-coloured, non-reflective barrier units about 50–75 cm (1 ft 8 in–2 ft 6 in) high and 1.5–2 m (4 ft 11 in–6 ft 7 in) long. Grade 1 and 2 events require a continuous barrier on all four sides. For Grades 3 and 4, barrier units should be placed along both ends and for at least 2 m (6 ft 7 in) on both sides at the corners of the playing area, **2, 5**. Where the playing area of an end table in a row does not extend to a wall, then a continuous side barrier is advisable, both to contain the ball and define gangway space. For recreational and coaching play, barriers (if available and space permits)

are useful to limit ball stray particularly from the minimum playing area. See the space table. Also, from a safety point of view, barriers help to avoid players and other centre users colliding.

Each barrier should be sufficiently stable to stay in place when struck by the ball, but it must fall easily, without toppling the adjacent barrier units when a player runs into it. Therefore, for safety reasons, barriers must not be fixed to the floor or heavily weighted.

Championships and tournaments
Scoring machines are strongly recommended, particularly for staged matches and where the general level of background noise may make it difficult for the umpires to be heard. Electronic scorers are becoming increasingly common for high profile events. The most common type of scoring machine uses manual flip-over cards and displays pairs of numerals on two faces; it is normally placed at the side of the table opposite to the umpire and operated by a match official. Draw sheets and match results should be displayed in an area accessible to spectators.

Public address facilities are necessary to notify players of play and broadcast information. Loudspeakers should also be mounted in changing rooms, refreshment and other waiting places for players. For single staged matches, the umpire should be provided with a public address microphone. For finals, British League, county or international matches, only spectators need to be addressed and the public address system should therefore have the facility to switch off loudspeakers that are not required.

1.4 Spectators
For staged or one table events, spectators should be able to sit close to the surrounds, to create an 'arena effect'. See also References and further advice.

1.5 Flooring
The floor surface must be smooth, level and able to support the table firmly. Wooden semi-sprung non-slip flooring is the ideal surface, with the main requirement being for players to be able to move rapidly and re-position their feet without slipping or affecting the table.

Solidly based, non-yielding floors are very tiring, even when surfaced with a material giving the desired friction characteristics and are therefore unsuitable. Surfaces such as concrete and some carpets are totally unsuitable.

Brightly reflecting or light colours are also precluded. Suitably dark floors are advisable which provide an adequate contrast for both spectators and players to be able easily to distinguish the ball, playing surface and surrounds.

For venues likely to stage major televised events, consideration should be given at design stage to providing underfloor ducting for power, telephone, television cables, etc. See also References and further advice, and Chapter 64.

1.6 Walls
Walls should provide a uniformly non-reflective background, without bright light sources, uncovered windows or doors letting in daylight which might affect players' vision. Ideally, the wall colour should be dark up to 2.5 m (8 ft) to provide sufficient contrast to follow clearly the flight of the small white or yellow ball. To gain maximum benefit from lighting, above 2.5 m (8 ft) walls should be light coloured. However, in multi-purpose sports halls a primary critical requirement is that walls should be of a uniform, unbroken colour (reflective value 0.3–0.5) to give

sufficient contrast to assist visibility for other sports. In this case a medium tone wall colour is usual.

Where see-through space dividing nets between tables become part of the background, they should be covered by dark 'sight screen' material up to a height of at least 2.5 m (8 ft).

1.7 Environment

For general details of environmental services recommendations refer to Chapters 60 and 61.

Ideal temperatures are in the range 15–20°C with an ideal relative humidity of around 40–50%.

Adequate ventilation is required to control humidity levels, but care must be taken to ensure that air currents do not deflect the ball in any way.

Adequate, uniform lighting is essential over the whole of the playing area. Care should be taken to avoid any stroboscopic effect when the lighting scheme is being selected and designed. Tungsten halogen quartz lighting systems are generally preferred for grades 1 and 2. Any space outside the playing area (for spectators, etc) should generally have a reduced level of illuminance to focus play and avoid distractions.

Recommended standards of illuminance measured at table level

Standard of play	Minimum maintained average illuminance over playing area (lux)	Uniformity ratio (E_{min}/E_{ave})	Uniformity ratio over surrounding playing area
Grade 1	1000	0.8	0.7
Grade 2 European draft CEN	750 min	0.8	0.7
Grade 2 ETTA prefer	1000	0.8	0.7
Grade 3	500	0.8	0.7
Grade 4	500	0.8	0.7
R	300	0.8	0.7

2 References and further advice

English Table Tennis Association (ETTA).

ETTA architect/development officers regarding club facilities and specialist centres for table tennis.

International Table Tennis Federation (ITTF).

International Table Tennis Federation, 'Playing Conditions', *ITTF Technical Leaflet T6*, ITTF.

Sports Council, *Datasheet 42*, 4th edition, Sports Council, London (March 1993).

Sports Council, *Arenas: A Planning, Design and Management Guide*, Sports Council, London (1989).

41
Tchouk-ball

Peter Ackroyd

1 Introduction

Tchouk-ball is a non-contact indoor or outdoor team game devised in the late 1960s by Dr Herman Brandt, an eminent Swiss biologist. The British Tchouk-ball Association (BT-BA) was formed in 1972. The game combines elements of handball with Basque pelota, the wall being replaced by a framed sprung net, **1**, against which the ball is thrown. A point is scored when the opposing team is unable to prevent the rebounding ball from touching the floor.

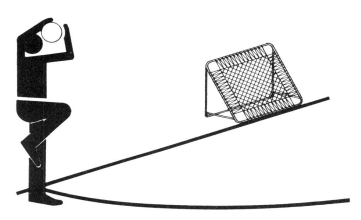

1 *The game is played against a framed sprung net*

1.1 Critical factors

● Overall area including safety margins around one-way and two-way courts, all as dimensioned below.

1.2 Space

The dimensions of the playing area can be varied to suit the space available and number of players. A high-density use is made of a limited space. There are two versions of the game: the full team international game, played with two frames, as shown in **2**; and a minor one-way recreational activity needing only half the space as shown in **3**.

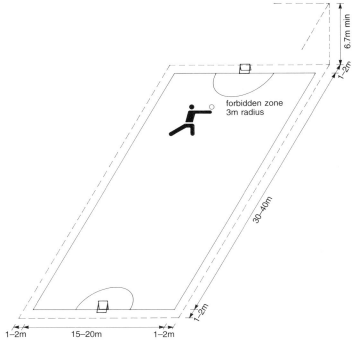

2 *Space diagram of two-way Tchouk-ball*

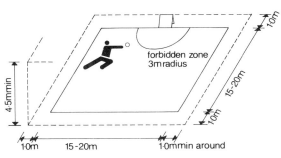

3 *One-way Tchouk-ball*

1.3 Floor

As the ball should not touch the ground, the game can be played on virtually any surface which is reasonably safe for the players. Ideally the rebound-net frames should be bolted down; for alternatives see below.

1.4 Court markings

Lines should be 50 mm (approx 2 in) wide and preferably white. All lines form part of the area which they mark off.

1.5 Equipment and storage

One or two rebound nets are required for Tchouk-ball, each consisting of a 900 mm (approx 3 ft) square frame strung with a nylon net of 40 mm (approx 1.5 in) mesh, **1**. They have the appearance of miniature trampettes inclined at an angle of 60 degrees to the floor and fold flat for storage. If not bolted down the frames must be weighted for stability.

1.6 Internal environment

For general details of environmental services recommendations refer to Chapters 60 and 61.

1.7 Changing

Allow space for 24–30 players and 2 or 3 match officials for a two-way court.

Space table			
	International National (N)	Regional (RG) County (Cy) Club (C)	Recreational (R)
Two-way game			
Pitch size	40 × 20 m	30 × 15 m to 40 × 20 m	Variable
Overall space (including minimum margins)	42 × 22 m	32 × 17 m to 42 × 22 m	Variable
One-way game			
Pitch size			15 × 15 m to 20 × 20 m
Overall space (including minimum margins)			17 × 17 m to 22 × 22 m

1.8 Spectators

This game has a growing following in Europe, Asia and South America. There are no special considerations other than the fact that spectators should not be sited along base lines.

2 References and further advice

British Tchouk-ball Association, *British Tchouk-ball Association Handbook*, BT-BA.
Volume 1, Chapter 76, Tchouk-ball outdoors.

42
Trampolining

Peter Ackroyd

1 *Trampolines are now fitted with safety spotting decks at both ends, comprising hinged leg frames to support crash mats. Photo: Allsport*

1 Introduction

Trampolining is increasingly popular both for recreation and as a high-performance championship sport. As trampolines become more advanced and performers more skilled and competitive, ever greater heights are being attained by trampolinists with implications for adequate clear headroom. The minimum recommended overhead height is steadily increasing and so are minimum safety standards for the trampoline and its surrounding area in order to safeguard trampolinists descending from heights of around 7 m (23 ft).

1.1 Critical factors
- Overall area of floor space including safety margins around the trampolines and attached safety platforms, and for operation of training rigs, **1**
- Headroom safety zone: clear height above the trampoline and surrounding margins
- Point loading of the floor
- For 'high-fall' performers, shock-absorbent mats beneath and around the trampolines
- Protective pads on bases of wheel stands of safety platforms, to avoid injury to performers who may fall on to them
- Avoid steps and raised thresholds en-route to and from trampoline storage
- Clear height of doorways to pass a folded trampoline.

1.2 Space
Space must be available to use trampolines in pairs for synchronised competitions and training. The trampolines must be parallel to each other with a distance of 2 m (6 ft 7 in) between them, as shown in **2**. The minimum height is absolutely critical to safeguard against accidents and avoid inhibiting skills and routines during practice, warm-up for regional and subregional competitions and for recreational trampolining. Guidance is given in the space table below and on the space diagram.

Two other disciplines are included within international rules:

- Tumbling, which in the UK forms part of gymnastics (see Chapter 29)
- Double mini-tramp (DMT).

This somersault discipline requires a matted run-up of 20 m (66 ft) minimum length. The DMT sprung bed, measures 2.85 × 0.72 m (approx 9 ft 4 in × 2 ft 4 in) wide, mounted 430 mm (1 ft 5 in) from the floor rising to 600 mm (2 ft) at the dismount end. Beyond the DMT there is a 300 mm (1 ft) thick shock mat landing area of 5.4 × 3.0 m (17 ft 9 in × 10 ft).

Additional height for the headroom safety zone might be gained where trampolines can be set out between overhead parallel primary roof beams where there is no ceiling, net track, bulky services or any other obstruction between beams. Clear headroom then can be measured to the underside of the roof secondary structure.

1.3 Storage and equipment
A regulation size trampoline, **2**, will fold into a space approximately 2.74 × 0.23 × 2.25 m high on roller stands, **3**. A maximum size trampoline will fold into a space approximately 3.5 × 0.25 × 2.25 m high on roller stands, but additional manoeuvring space must be allowed in the equipment store layout to select, remove and repark a particular trampoline. Overlapped storage causes trampolines to become entangled.

Storage is also required for end decks and surrounding safety mats up to 100 mm thickness (see floors below). Specialist equipment suppliers should be consulted for further details. See also 'Walls and doorways' below, particularly for clear height of access doorways.

1.4 Flooring
The design of floors should take into account the point loading from the trampoline which can be very considerable for a top performer bottoming from a height of 6.8 m. Measurements quoted by the Scottish Trampoline Association showed that, assuming an even load through the four points, there would be over a 227 kg point load. However, there is much more likely to be uneven pressure on to the floor in excess of 455 kg.

The International Trampoline Federation (ITF) competition rules require that gym mats must cover the floor around the trampoline. Thicker landing, or crash mats must be used at the ends of the frame. It is becoming a necessary practice also to line the floor beneath the trampoline with 100 mm thick crash mats to safeguard high fall performers who can bottom the bed on to the floor.

Avoid steps and thresholds. The trampoline on roller stands is heavy to manhandle, particularly for young performers if staff are unavailable. Bases of safety platform wheel stands must be padded to avoid injury to performers who may fall on to them.

1.5 Walls and doorways
All doorways en route from storage to the place of use should be wide and high enough for the easy and direct movement of trampolines on roller stands. In Chapter 55 the recommended clear height of all access openings is given at 2.7 m (2.5 m absolute minimum depending on type of equipment).

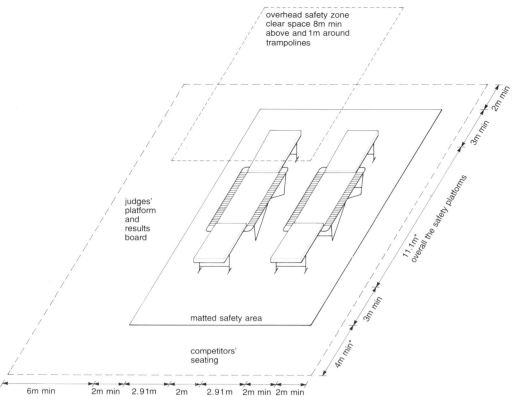

overhead safety zone
clear space 8m min
above and 1m around
trampolines

judges'
platform
and
results
board

2m min

3m min

11.1m*
overall the safety platforms

matted safety area

3m min

competitors'
seating

4m min*

6m min | 2m min | 2.91m | 2m | 2.91 m | 2m min | 2m min

2 *Space diagram: note the extended length of end frame units and other revised dimensions from those previously published*

Space table

	International National (N)	Regional (Rg) County (Cy) Club (C)	Recreational (R)
Length of frame	5.05 m (±60 mm)	4.5–5.05 m	4.5–5.05 m
Width of frame	2.91 m (±50 mm)	2.7–2.91 m	2.7–2.91 m
Height from floor	1.15 m (±5 mm)	1.05–1.15 m	0.95–1.05 m
Attached safety platforms:			
Length at both ends of trampoline	3.025 m (±25 mm)	3.025 m (±25 mm)	–
Width at both ends of trampoline	2.025 m (±25 mm)	2.025 m (±25 mm)	–
Space around (minimum):			
Clear space both sides (1)	2 m	2 m	2 m
Clear space at ends (1)	3 m	3 m	3 m
Distance between pairs	2 m	2 m	2 m
Judges' platform one side	6 m	3–4 m	–
Clear height from floor to ceiling (2)	8 m min	7.6 m min	4.88 m
Approximate overall matted areas (minimum dimensions – note 1)			
Single trampoline	7 × 17 m	6.7 × 16.5 m	–
Two trampolines	22 × 17 m	11.4 × 16.5 m	–
Three trampolines	27 × 17 m	16.1 × 16.5 m	–
Plus officials' space			

Note (1): Additional floor space is essential for training using overhead rigs – see Section 7 below.
Note (2): 6 m (19 ft 9 in) minimum for double mini-tramp competitions.

3 *Folding trampoline transporter stands. Some units allow passage through a standard 2 m (6 ft 6 in) high doorway; but some are taller (see Chapter 55). Photo: Gym-aid Ltd*

1.6 Ceiling-level equipment

A safety rig is required over each training trampoline, securely fixed to the roof or ceiling structure, **4** and **5**, at a minimum height of 5.4 m from the floor. Where ceiling heights are restricted, the overhead support may have to be placed to one side of the headroom safety zone, **2**. When setting the overhead rig, the side ropes should ideally form an angle of 45° with the performer's torso when standing on the trampoline. In 9.1 m high halls, about 14 m is necessary between the pulleys of a rig. The double pulley must not be placed against a wall since the operator will be lifted off the floor while arresting the performer's downward motion. For two adjacent trampolinists using overhead training rigs an overall space of approx 30 m is required – considerably wider than the competition space

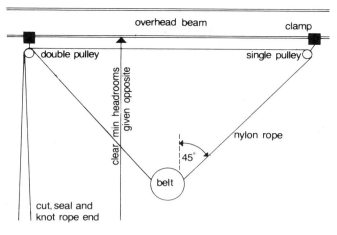

4 *Setting overhead rig*

given in the table and shown in **2**. For further details consult specialist equipment suppliers.

1.7 Spectators
Viewing is best from the ends for pairs, but otherwise all around and at a distance of about 5–6 m from the trampoline with clear views upwards at about 45°.

UK national one-day trampolining events have a potential for about 500 spectators. For international events refer to *Arenas* and consult the BTA (see References and further advice, below).

1.8 Internal environment
For general details of environmental services requirements refer to Chapters 60 and 61.

2 References and further advice
British Trampoline Federation Ltd (BTA).

5 *Overhead rig raised into the roof space in a SASH sports hall. Photo: John Hovell*

International Trampoline Federation, *International Trampoline Federation Handbook for Tumbling and Double Mini-Tramp*.

Sports Council, *Arenas*, Sports Council, London (1989) (for essential additional requirements for national and international standards of event).

43
Tug-of-war

Peter Ackroyd

1 Critical factors
- Overall area including safety margins around the pitch
- Fire precautions for mat storage.

1.1 Siting and space
Indoor tug-of-war (ToW) events generally take place on a secure mat thick enough to protect competitors from injury in the event of collapse, **1**. A space at least 35 m (approx 115 ft) long is needed which restricts indoor competition to large sports halls, **2**. Practice and club pulls can fit diagonally into medium halls and recreational pulls into small halls.

1.2 Pull surface
Artificial surfaces are used only for indoor ToW. The pull surface consists of rubber matting fixed to plywood to form a base. The interlocking sections of the mat are 1 m wide × 2 m long (approx 3 ft 3 in × 6 ft 6 in) and 25 mm (approx 1 in) thick. A complete pull surface is made up of

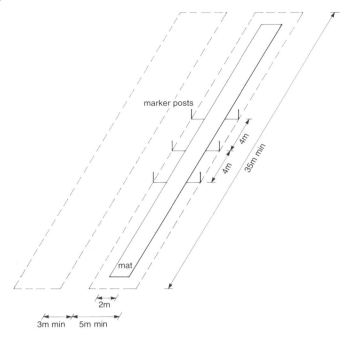

2 *Space diagram. These dimensions apply to all standards of the sport and levels of competition. There is no stipulated minimum headroom*

1 *Photo: Lee Valley Regional Park Authority/Picketts Lock Centre*

3 *Note the interlocking device. Photo: Mark Shearman*

18 mat sections which are joined together end to end by closures attached to the long sides of the base. It is heavy enough to remain stable without being tethered to the floor, **3**.

Markings
Three floor markings only are used for indoor ToW. The centre marking indicates the middle of the mat and the others are 4 m (approx 13 ft) on either side. Markings are placed directly on to the floor between six marker posts, **2**.

Rope
The rope is not less than 100 mm (approx 4 in) and not more than 123 mm (approx 5 in) in circumference and 35m (approx 115 ft) long.

1.3 Internal environment
For general details of environmental services recommendations refer to Chapters 60 and 61.

1.4 Storage
Storage will be required for the rope coil drum, marker posts and a sectional mat on trolleys. The mat may be a fire risk and will require storage in a separated fire resistant store.

2 References and further advice
Tug of War Association.

44
Volleyball and mini-volleyball

Peter Ackroyd

1 Critical factors

- Overall area including safety margins around the court
- Adequate height
- Floor surface and permanent sockets for net posts
- Siting of court to maximise multi-sports use of floor
- Environment.

1.1 Space
Provided the court has a safety margin of not less than 2–3 m (approx 6 ft 6 in–10 ft) all round, this game can be played anywhere in a common sports space. In its equipment and facilities guide, The English Volleyball Association (EVA) recommends that sports halls should be wide enough to accommodate a volleyball court width-ways to maximise the use of floor space and allow other activities to take place at the same time. For regional standard play and below this is possible in halls with a width of 24 m (approx 80 ft) or more while national standard play is possible in 28 m (approx 92 ft) wide halls with an increased clear ceiling height of 10.5 m (see Chapter 49).

When volleyball is set out in small halls so that other activities may take place at the same time, the court should be placed to one end allowing space for other sports behind curtaining (see Chapter 49).

1 *Photo: Sports Council Publications*

Space table

	International	National (N)	Regional (Rg) County (Cy) Club C)	Recreational (R)
Playing area				
Length	18 m	18 m	18 m	18 m
Width	9 m	9 m	9 m	9 m
Backline clear space	8 m	3 m min	3 m	2 m min
Sideline clear space	5 m	3 m min	3 m	2 m min
Officials' space additional on one side	3 m	2 m	2 m	–
Spectators' margin addition on the other three sides	3 m	2 m	–	–
Minimum overall space				
Area	40 × 25 m	28 × 19 m	24 × 17 m	22 × 13 m
Clear height	12.5 m	10.5 m(1)	7 m	7 m (2)

Note (1): Increased unobstructed height recommended by the English Volleyball Association from March 1994.
Note (2): 7 m is preferred but 6.7 m is acceptable for mini-volleyball with a lower net.

1.2 Floor
The main aim in volleyball is to prevent the ball touching the floor, but on many occasions players will come into contact with the floor when playing the ball. A basic technique of volleyball is the forward dive recovery shot which results in the player landing on his chest and sliding forward. This means:

- Because of the large numbers of jumps and landings by players, a slightly flexible floor of sprung wood, resilient vinyl or the like is preferable to a rigid floor
- Cork tiles, tarmacadam and felt type finishes are totally unsuitable for halls where volleyball is played
- The EVA requires that net posts be of the floor-socket type and not held down by weights; for socket details consult equipment suppliers
- The floor must be smooth and non-abrasive but not slippery
- The surface must be splinterproof
- Where floor fittings are inserted they must be flush fitting
- Channels for sliding partitions should not run across volleyball courts
- Roll-down portable courts (used for major events) can be obtained to order and size.

1.3 Net
The net, as dimensioned in **2**, is held by two heavy-duty galvanised mild steel tubes of 2.55 m (approx 8 ft 4 in) height. They must be held in floor sockets, set at a distance of between 0.5 m (20 in) and 1 m (3 ft 3 in) from each side line; they must not be held in position by weights or wires. The posts must be round and smooth, with no stays or dangerously protruding parts of any kind.

1.4 Court markings
The lines, 50 mm (approx 2 in) wide, are included in the area of the court and should be green although other colours are acceptable if there is sufficient contrast with the floor colour and other lines. Portable roll-down courts are marked in white.

1.5 Spectator facilities
Volleyball is a highly popular spectator sport in most countries of the world and particularly in Europe. Spectator facilities should be along the side of the court so that play in both halves of the court can be watched. For international matches the court is normally placed centrally within the seating.

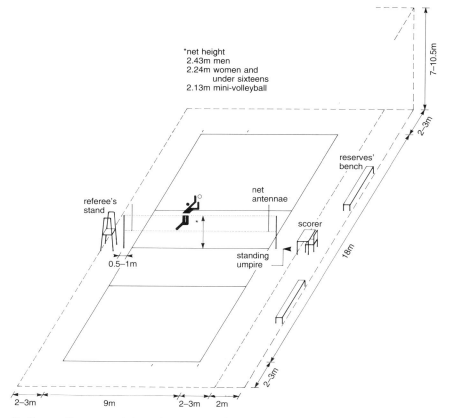

*net height
2.43m men
2.24m women and
under sixteens
2.13m mini-volleyball

7–10.5m

2–3m

reserves' bench

net antennae

referee's stand

scorer

standing umpire

0.5–1m

18m

2–3m

2–3m   9m   2–3m   2m

2 *Space diagram. A 3 m (approx 10 ft) zone is recommended all round the pitch (see space table). Note various net heights including mini-volleyball*

3 *An outdoor portable court. Photo: Spurgeon Wallis Associates and Ruberoid Ltd*

1.6 Walls

White or light-coloured walls and doors should be avoided as the ball is white.

1.7 Internal environment

For general details of environmental services recommendations refer to Chapters 60 and 61.

Background heating only is required. International rules require a minimum of 10°C for players but if spectators are to be accommodated a temperature of at least 15°C is required. For international competitions the temperature must be 16-25°C.

Lighting

Because the action is fast, good lighting levels are required. For further details refer to Chapters 60 and 61 and the *CIBSE Lighting Guide, Sports*.

Acoustics

Walls and ceiling should be designed to reduce reverberation time. The game is noisy and should not be played near quieter games such as badminton.

1.8 Storage

Storage is required for the rolled-up net, which measures approximately 1 m × 300 mm in diameter (approx 3 ft 3 in × 1 ft), posts and net height-gauge. For matches storage will also be required for officials' tables, control equipment and a referee's stand approximately 0.6 × 0.75 × 2.1 m high (approx 2 ft × 2 ft 6 in × 7 ft).

2 References and further advice

International Volleyball Federation.

Sports Council, *Arenas*, Sports Council, London (1989) (includes details of additional accommodation for national events).

The UK governing bodies for volleyball.

45
Weight lifting

Peter Ackroyd

1 Introduction

It is important to draw a distinction between the differing spaces for weight lifting (contests) and weight training. The latter requires an exclusive space, the weight training room, which is described and illustrated in Chapter 90. This section is about competition weight lifting in a common sports area; it can be accommodated anywhere its portable equipment can be installed. Theatres and public halls with a stage have been popular venues.

1.1 Critical factors
- Overall area of space including safety margins around the lifting platform
- Additional ancillary spaces for major events
- Contest platforms and separate warm-up space with non-slip surface; and supporting floor structure robust enough to withstand impact of dropped weights
- Lighting
- Ventilation to remove chalk dust
- Noise control.

1.2 Space
The basic requirement is for a competition lifting platform as shown in **2**. An additional warm-up area, adjacent weight-training room and weighing-in room are also required. For national and international competitions consult the British Amateur Weightlifters' Association (BAWLA) and refer to *Arenas* (see References and further advice) for other ancillary accommodation required for major events.

1 *Photo: Coloursport*

1.3 Equipment and apparatus
In addition to the platform mats (see **2**) an international 300 kg set of weights is required for all competitions. So are tables for officials, chairs or benches for competitors, attempt board, electronic referee's light-signalling system, an electronic score board, a results board, clocks, VHS video and a public address system.

Warm-up area mats, apparatus, chalk container, score board, extension clock, loudspeaker, doctor's table and part display of referee's light system are also required.

1.4 Floor and markings
The surface of the platform must be level and non-slip, preferably of unpolished plain wood. Platform and floor structure must be robust enough to withstand the impacts of 250–300 kg (551–661 lb) weights dropped deadweight on to the surface from approximately 2.4 m (8 ft), which is roughly the height of the bar when raised above head-height. The platform should reduce and spread the impact on the floor and structure beneath. For coloured markings, see caption notes **2**.

Adjacent areas for warm-up and spare weights must be non-slip and impact-resistant to the same specifications as above. Heavy weights room is equipped with platforms or a permanent rubber surface.

1.5 Internal environment
For general details of environmental services recommendations refer to Chapters 60 and 61.

Heating and ventilation
A background temperature of 16°C is recommended for this sport. Higher temperatures may be required for spectator areas (20°C). Weight rooms may require cooling to maintain acceptable temperatures.

Good ventilation is essential in the actual lifting area to remove chalk dust (8–10 air changes per hour minimum).

Lighting
Special lighting to provide around 500 lux may be required for the platform area.

Acoustics
Noise control is important in this sport as a quiet environment, free from background noise, is essential for concentrated lifting.

1.6 Storage
After use weights should be stored clear of the floor area, either in an adjacent weight training room or in lockable storage racks. This precaution is as much for security as tidiness.

1.7 Spectators
Seating should be allowed for 500 spectators at championship events and up to 2000 at internationals. Also refer to details in *Arenas* (see below).

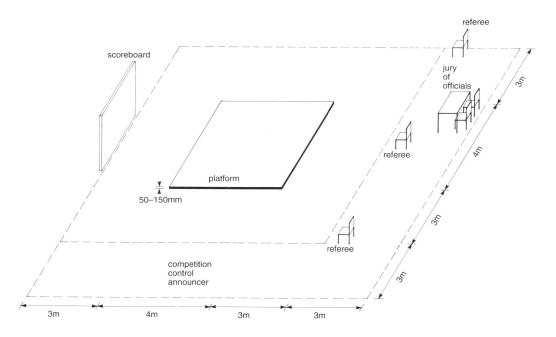

2 *Space diagram. The special platform can be raised on staging if that improves spectator viewing. If the platform and surrounding floor are of similar or same colourings, then the top edge of the platform must be marked by a different coloured line of at least 50 mm (2 in) width. At floor level line markings of other sports can be distracting to lifters and should be covered by thin matting*

2 **References and further advice**

British Amateur Weightlifters' Association (BAWLA).
International Weightlifting Federation (IWF).

International Weightlifting Federation, *IWF Handbook: Constitution, Technical Rules and Directory*, IWF.
Sports Council, *Arenas*, Sports Council, London (1989).

46
Wrestling

Peter Ackroyd

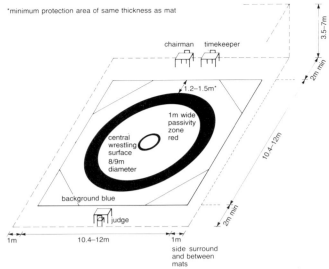

chairman timekeeper

1.2–1.5m*

1m wide passivity zone red

central wrestling surface 8/9m diameter

background blue

judge

3.5–7m

2m min

10.4–12m

2m min

1m   10.4–12m   1m
side surround and between mats

1 Critical factors

- Overall area of space including *two* safety margins: a matted border around the wrestling surface surrounded by an unmatted free space which is used by the match officials
- Fire precautions for mat storage.

1.1 Space

In a multi-sports centre wrestling training is likely to take place in a combat hall suitable for other 'combat sports' (see Chapter 52) or a practice hall (see Chapter 51).

Squad training and the training of technical officials and coaches requires a hall which can take at least one 11 m (approx 36 ft) square mat. A further safety area of 1 m (approx 3 ft 3 in) all round is advised or the walls of the hall should be protected by a suitable foam-backed material up to 2 m (approx 6 ft 7 in) from the floor.

For national and international matches a 12 m (approx 40 ft) square mat is used. When more than one mat is in use in a single hall clear spaces must be provided around each mat, 2.

National and regional championships require two, three and occasionally four mats. Spaces for all contests are set out in the space table.

2 Space diagram. The international regulation sized mat is octagonal but is not mandatory for lesser contests. An inner central wrestling area is surrounded by a 1 m (approx 3.3 ft) wide red band which together comprise the wrestling surface. The outer (octagonal or square) border is a mandatory protection area of the same thickness as the mat

Space table

	International National (N)	Regional (RG) County (Cy) Club (C)	Recreational (R)
Wrestling surface	9 m	8 m	8 m
diameter	1.2–1.5 m	1.2–1.5 m	1.2 m min
Width of surrounding border protection area of same thickness			
Length of mat	12 m	10.4–11.0 m	10.5 m min
Width of mat	12 m	10.4–11.0 m	10.4 m min
Surrounding unmatted free space			
Officials' both sides	2 m min	2 m	–
Other sides	1 m min	1 m	–
Overall area			
One mat	16 × 14 m	14.4 × 12.4 m to 15 × 13 m	10.4 × 10.4 m min
Two mats	16 × 27 m	15 × 25 m	–
Three mats	16 × 40 m	15 × 37 m	–
Four mats	16 × 53 m	15 × 49 m	–
Height	7 m	4.5 m min	3.5 m min

1.2 Equipment

At tournaments an electric scorer/timer should be provided for each mat plus two separate stop watches for time out and a gong or bell.

1.3 Competitors

International matches require residential accommodation for about 30 people. National and regional championships attract 60 to 300 competitors, some requiring accommodation.

1.4 Spectators

Wrestling is not a great spectator sport, and the number of spectators at international, national or regional matches rarely exceeds 2000.

1.5 Internal environment

For general details of environmental services recommendations refer to Chapters 60 and 61.

1 Photo: William Baxter

1.6 Storage

Storage space will be required for timing and scoring equipment. Competition mats may be a fire risk and require a separated fire resistant store.

2 References and further advice

British Amateur Wrestling Association.

139

47
General design of the building

Geraint John

1 Scale of provision

Table 47.1 details the main features required for the six major sizes of sports buildings. The national Sports Council or appropriate Regional office should be consulted at the outset to ensure that the facilities proposed complement others already existing or under development.

1.1 Floor area

Table 47.2 gives a breakdown of the floor areas of four sports centres of varying sizes. This table gives an indication of the proportions of space required for the various elements of the building.

1.2 Circulation

Grouping of elements
1 illustrates the relationships and circulation links between the main areas in a 'wet and dry' centre. **2** and **3** illustrate them for dry sports centres.

Circulation links within pool buildings are described in Chapter 98.

Changing areas
For flexibility in use and fluctuations of demand in different parts of the building, it is an advantage to group all changing rooms together. Pool changing areas should be on the same level as the pool, but dry sports facilities can be on a different level.

Table 47.1: Building features

	Large-scale sports and leisure/ rec centre	Large-scale sports centre (wet and dry facilities)	Medium-scale wet and dry sports/rec centre	Medium-scale dry only sports/rec centre	Small sports centre/ hall (dry sports only)	Small community provision
Pools	●●	●●	●●			
50 metre	○	○				
25 metre	●	●				
20 metre			○			
Free shape	○					
Learner pool	●	●	○			
Diving	●	●	○			
Sports hall(s)	●●	●●	●●	●●	●●	●●
Large hall	●	●	○	○		
Medium hall		○	●	●		
Small hall	○	○			●	
Small community hall						●
Ancillary indoor sports accommodation	●●	●●	●●	●●	○	
Practice hall	●	●	●	●	○	
Weight training/conditioning room	●	●	○	○		
Projectile hall	○	○	○	○		
Squash courts	●	●	●	●	●	●
Climbing wall	○	○	○	○		
Indoor bowls	●	○				
Billiards/snooker	○	○				
Ice rink	○					
Theatre/multi-purpose hall	○					
Ancillary accommodation	●●	●●	●●	●●	●●	●●
Changing	●●	●●	●●	●●	●●	●●
Spectator seating: fixed	○	○				
: occasional	●	●	●	●		
Informal viewing	●	●	●	●	●	●
Club meeting room(s)	○	○				○
First aid room	●●	●●	●●	○		
First aid equipment	●	●●	●●	●●	●●	●●
Crèche (separate store)	●	○	○			
Crèche facilities (alternative use, separate store)		○	○	○		
Sauna suite	○	○				
Refreshments	●●	●●	●●	●●	●	●
Cafeteria	●	●	●	●	○	
Bar	●	●	●	●	○	○
Vending machine	○	○	○	○	●	●
Staff and management						
Reception	●●	●●	●●	●●	●●	●●
Office(s)	●●	●●	●●	●●	●	●
Staff rest room	●●	●●	○	○		
Staff changing	●	●	○	○		
Outdoor associated facilities						
Grass pitches	○	○	○	○		
Hard porous/synthetic pitches	○	○	○	○		
Floodlit pitches	○	○	○	○		
Tennis courts	○	○	○	○		

Key: ●● Essential. ● Typical/desirable. ○ Possible.
This table can only be general. All buildings will of course be influenced by the area they serve, its population and by the other facilities in the area.

Table 47.2: Area analysis of four typical sports centres (support accommodation expressed as a percentage of usable area)

		Large-scale sports and leisure/recreation centre				Medium-scale wet and dry sports centre				Small sports centre				Small community provision			
Usable area	Pool hall	1831				1069											
	(Pool water area)	(1170)				(580)											
	Sports hall	1168				590				543				371	371	66	
	Activity spaces	1224	4243	47		594	2261	56		80	623	58					
Circulation		1005	1005	11	22.69	681	681	17	30.12	75	75	7	12.04	36	36	6	9.71
Ancillary areas	Sports storage	116			2.74	60			2.66	63			10.12	54			14.56
	Changing areas	955			22.51	442			19.55	113			18.14	38			10.25
	Toilet areas	163			3.85	38			1.68	24			3.86	18			4.86
	Social areas	692			16.31	263			11.64	68			10.92	25			6.74
	Management areas	492			11.60	38			1.68	32			5.14	15			4.05
	Plant area	1349	3767	42	31.80	272	1113	27	12.03	69	369	35	11.08	2	153	28	0.54
Totals			9015		112.50		4055		79.36		1072		71.30		560		50.71

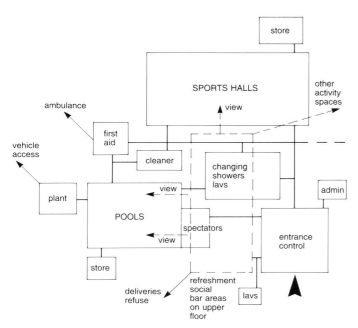

1 *Spatial patterns and circulation in a wet and dry centre.*

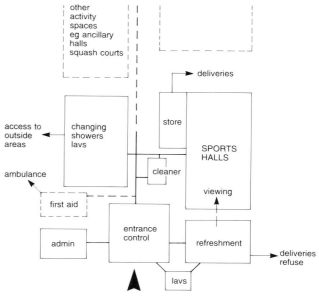

3

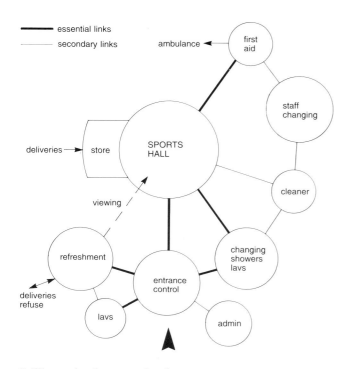

essential links
secondary links

2 *The main elements of a dry sports centre*

Entrance and control

Generally, there should be only one public access to the building although a secondary entrance may be desirable in large centres for use by spectators in connection with special events. The main entrance must be overlooked from the pay/reception desk which must also be so located as to allow reception staff to supervise access to all parts of the building.

Refreshment/bar areas

There are advantages in locating these facilities so that they have views over activity areas. The preferred choice is for snack/refreshment areas to overlook pools and bars the sports hall or other dry sports facilities. Ideally users should be made aware of the facilities as they enter and leave the building. Refreshment areas should not be located in remote or upper floor areas as this minimises usage and makes them difficult to supervise. Service areas must have direct non-public access to refuse and delivery areas.

Plant

Plant location for dry sports is not critical but air handling will be needed. For pools, see Volume 3, Chapter 30.

Sports halls/activity areas

These should be easily accessible from changing areas: delivery of equipment and its storage must also be considered. Unusually wide or high external doors may be required if a hall is to be used for non-sports purposes such as exhibitions.

1.3 Cost considerations
Refer also to Part 1, Technical Study 2: Whole life costs.

Capital cost generally
The main factors normally affecting cost, ie shape and size of the building, standard of specification, form of construction, location, time for construction and tendering climate, will always apply. However, many providers do not seem to grasp the significance of the time/cost relationship in construction. In the case of sports buildings financial incentives for the contractor to finish early will not be so important as for other building types such as commercial projects. Where completion dates are vital, eg for stadia which need to be completed for major events, the time relationship will need to be considered.

Location will often not be too significant; sports hall construction tends to be more closely related to the time/cost factor. The conclusion is that generally size, shape, standard of specification and tendering climate are the most important cost-determining factors.

Size
Considered from a geometrical viewpoint, large sports buildings ought to be less expensive in terms of cost per square metre than small sports buildings. Unfortunately there are many reasons why they are not. Factors such as height of spaces, wide spans and the wish for a high quality – which tends to attach almost automatically to a large prominent building – can all force up the size and standard of specification. In addition, the shape of a large sports building often tends to be more complex than that of a small one.

Examples of inexpensive large complexes do exist where the standard of specification appears to have been rigidly controlled at a low level in appropriate areas and the external shape of the building tends to be simple.

Relationships of activity/ancillary areas
When producing preliminary cost estimates for proposed schemes it is useful to have some idea of the likely ratio of the aggregate sports activity areas to ancillary areas. Generally the required playing spaces are known at the outset. A small low cost sports hall scheme will have a ratio of about 1:0.75 while larger schemes will have ratios of 1:1 or more and are highly variable owing in part to disparate requirements for social and management areas.

Costs – design and specification
The general principles of design economics will apply to dry sports buildings but the following points should be noted:

- Floor finishes of sports halls and other playing areas are of great concern to the users and some types can be very expensive.
- Wall surfaces in activity areas should not permit small particles of sand, cement or other particles to be rubbed off during play and the cost of sealing them should be borne in mind. Wall areas in sports halls are likely to suffer ball impacts which can generate considerable dust and make floors slippery and therefore dangerous.
- The wide spans and heights required in sports halls have significant cost implications. A comparatively minor increase or reduction in spans can have a disproportionate impact on costs.
- The cost of artificial lighting in sports halls, particularly if high pressure discharge lamps are not used, may well be high.

Table 47.3 gives a breakdown of the typical distribution of total capital cost to different elements in centres at different scales.

Costs arising from use
Maintenance costs Over the life of a sports building the total cost of repairs and maintenance are likely to be significant when calculated over the probable useful life of the building using one of the more acceptable cost appraisal methods and expressed in terms such as present values. The psychological aspects of continuing repair and replacement and the inconvenience of the maintenance processes to management may also be significant.

Vandalism Costs arising from vandalism can be an important part of maintenance costs. Two factors should be noted:

- *Management*: if the visible effects of vandalism are not removed quickly this will encourage further vandalism. Users will not respect a building which is not clean and well maintained.
- *Design and specification*: the building should be designed with fittings or other aspects which will not be prone to vandalism. It must also be planned so that staff can oversee the whole of the building in the normal course of their everyday duties.

Staffing Staffing costs are likely to be the most significant cost after capital repayments over the useful life of the building. Where capital loan periods are short they may be the most significant cost of all. The design of the building should afford the greatest possible opportunity for economic staffing consistent with the probable or intended pattern of use.

Cleaning All surfaces and finishes must be easily cleaned and access provided for cleaning and maintenance to high areas of glazing and light fittings.

Table 47.3: Average percentage distribution of capital costs

Facility	Large-scale sports/ leisure centres (wet and dry)	Large-scale sports/ leisure sports halls over 2000 sq m	Medium-scale sports halls 1000–2000 sq m	Small-scale sports halls not over 1000 sq m
No. in sample	13	24	35	35
Substructure	10	10	11	13
Superstructure	41	48	48	51
Internal finishes	10	9	10	11
Fittings	6	6	5	4
Services	33	27	26	21
Total	100%	100%	100%	100%

Schemes incorporating overgenerous circulation spaces such as extensive foyers, very wide staircases and corridors and the use of easily marked and difficult to clean surfaces will all add to the amount of cleaning work. In some cases they can necessitate extra staff. The importance of the floor finishes in activity areas has already been stated; the cleaning and maintenance of them is therefore an important consideration as is their propensity for marking and becoming dirty. The cost implications of an expensive but nevertheless inefficient floor finish (in terms of dirt and mark collection and maintenance frequency) are considerable.

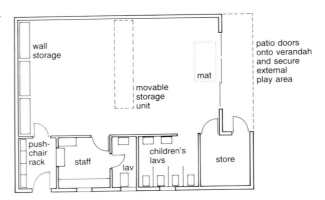

2 Crèche plan for 20 children, with no babies and a maximum stay of 2 hours. Minimum area is 50 sq m. Local authority requirements in the UK differ regarding the number of WCs. A WC suitable for staff with disabilities should be provided unless one is located nearby

48
Children in sports buildings

Sylvester Bone

1 Children in sports buildings

Children of different ages may visit sports buildings as users or spectators, in large groups, as part of a family or, in the case of older children, as individuals. All of these possibilities have to be considered.

1.1 Children as users

Children participating in sport need supervision. Changing rooms and showers and the routes to and from sports facilities should be designed for easy supervision. Mixed pool changing areas will allow control by one supervisor of either sex. Passageways which may be used as waiting spaces while rooms are being vacated or apparatus is set up should also be visible without requiring separate supervision. The lockers, particularly those at low level in changing rooms, should not be large enough to allow children to become trapped in them. Wrist bands for locker keys are safer than pins. A secure system for holding valuables such as lockers or a locked group changing room should be considered as watches and jewellery are a hazard if worn for games and gymnastics. Lockers should always have spring loaded doors that do not hang open. Sharp edges and jutting corners should be avoided. In buildings with wet and dry sides there should be showers on the dry side or children will be tempted to escape supervision to use the wet side showers provided for swimmers.

1.2 Children as spectators

Spectator seating cannot normally be sized specially to suit children except where audiences of limited numbers can be given small stacking chairs for regular use. With bench type seats there is a risk that children will squash up together and the capacity of the seating be exceeded. With individually defined seats this is less of a risk but the capacity must nevertheless be clearly marked on each tier of seats. Emergency evacuation of children presents particular problems for management, as children may not understand announcements on the public address system or be able to follow directional signs with written instructions. Pictograms can be used to make the signs more understandable and supervisors need to be available to shepherd young audiences to safety.

1.3 Children in groups

Coaches unloading children at a sports building should be able to set them down in an unobstructed space near the entrance where the direct route to the entrance does not cross traffic. The coach should not have to reverse in or out of the set-down point. Group changing rooms can be provided to make supervision easier (including checking that possessions are not left behind).

1.4 Children as part of a family

Young children may arrive with parents or older children as carers. When arriving by car there needs to be a clear area beside at least some of the parking spaces to set up pushchairs and transfer small children from car to pushchair. Within the sports building the route should be clear for a pushchair to reach spectator and cafe areas and the creche. If there are turnstiles, a gate at least 900 mm (approx 3 ft) wide will be needed for children. Where a crèche is provided the outer door to the crèche reception area should be at least 900 mm (approx 3 ft) wide to give easy access for pushchairs. The crèche itself should be located near the entrance at access level as parents are likely to make straight for where their children have been left if there is an emergency evacuation of the building. If the crèche is badly positioned parents will be struggling against the flow of people leaving the building. Some of the points to watch in the design of a crèche are given under 'crèches' below.

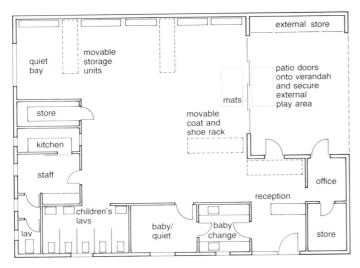

1 Crèche plan for 35 children including babies and all-day care. The minimum area is 120 sq m. Local authority requirements in the UK differ regarding the number of WCs. A WC suitable for staff with disabilities should be provided unless one is located nearby

1.5 Children on their own

The need to reinforce written signing with pictograms and for lockable storage of valuables apply particularly when children are on their own. The need for surveillance is also increased. While children are with teachers, carers and their families the staff do not have the same direct responsibility as when they are on their own. Children hanging around in circulation spaces are liable to cause damage. The risk of abduction must also be considered. There should be somewhere for children to wait in safety when there is no café in the building or when the café is closed. The reception area and entrance should be arranged to discourage loitering and allow the reception staff to see when unaccompanied children leave the building.

2 Crèche design

In addition to the safety aspects referred to above, other aspects should be considered in the location of crèche facilities. Outside play space, partly under cover, should be provided whenever possible, allowing at least 18 sq m per child. The crèche needs to be near the main areas of activity and well signposted. Its use will depend on it being an attraction that is brought to parents' attention – and its continued use will depend on monitoring by management on the flexibility within the design to make any changes asked for by users.

2.1 Space requirements

The space requirements for a crèche depend on the following factors.

The compactness of the plan

The Women's Design Group recommend a minimum area of 120 sq m of free area for up to 35 children. The total area will be considerably more than this. More space, including a babies' room, will be needed if there are babies and additional space will also be needed for a disabled persons' toilet if the creche will be open when access to such a toilet is not available. The Pre-school Playgroups Association recommend the following minimum indoor space per child:

- 3.7 sq m for each child below the age of one
- 2.8 sq m for one and two year olds
- 2.3 sq m for three to five year olds.

Crèches should not be too large, particularly if they are to be used by children under 2 years, in which case a maximum of 24 children is then recommended. The subdivision of creches intended to offer more than 24 places for small children should be considered.

Staff facilities

Staff areas must not be cramped. There should always be two staff on duty while the crèche is open. Recommended staffing levels vary from one staff member to two children to one staff member for eight children. The lower figure is that recommended by the Pre-School Playgroups Association where there are babies (under 1 year); the higher figure is the maximum usually acceptable for registration by a local authority of a crèche in a sports building. The staff will require their own cloakroom toilet, cooking facilities, office where records can be kept, and storage; wherever possible a washing machine and tumble drier should also be provided. There should be a first aid box and an external telephone for emergencies.

Storage

Storage of play equipment needs to be generous. It is difficult to provide too much space for storage. Where many foam filled play shapes are used, the storage design should recognise the fire hazard and follow the recommendations for storage of foam filled mats given in Chapter 14. Where there is an outside play area there should be at least some storage accessible from outside to avoid the need to bring equipment used outside through the indoor play area. There should be a rack for children's outdoor clothes and shoes and a rail on which to hang pushchairs that would otherwise block the entrance.

Entrance and reception areas

The entrance and reception areas of creches need to have a counter to write on, a seat for those wanting to see staff, pin up space for notices and a prominent notice on evacuation procedure telling parents where to collect their children after an alarm has been given.

2.2 Detailed design

Within the crèche, windows, doors, locks, fittings and furniture all need to be chosen to suit children's sizes and ensure their safety. Windows should be glazed with safety glass and low enough to give children a view out (but not open at levels that will allow children to fall out). Doors should have viewing panels that allow small children to be seen. Toilet doors should have a gap at the sides that will not trap children's fingers (at least 32 mm). Rooms and cupboards that are not to be accessible to children need suitably secure locks otherwise provide latches with lever or 'D' handles not more than 1 m above floor level.

The readily available child sized sanitary fittings and loose furniture should be used. *BS 7231: Part 1: 1990 Body Measurements of Boys and Girls from Birth up to 16.9 Years*, gives information in the form of tables which can be used to establish relevant dimensions. The temperature of hot water at washbasins should be controlled by group thermostat mixing valves. Radiators and hot pipes should be guarded or maintained at a low temperature by controls that are out of children's reach.

Where the crèche is intended for babies as well as children, there should be a separate baby room where babies can sleep and be changed. It needs cot space, sink, bench space, separate bin for used nappies, space for a comfortable chair for feeding and good ventilation.

The Sports Councils' *Factfile 5* contains *Datasheet 60.10* on *Designing for Children*. *Factfile 1* contains information on managing creches and gives advice on the fundamental policy issues that need to be decided when a creche is to be provided. Some of these issues such as the intended clientele and funding will affect the designer's approach and should be discussed with the client when a brief for the building is being prepared.

49
Multi-purpose halls for sport and the arts

**Peter Ackroyd and
Christopher Harper**

1 General

Only the largest sports hall will satisfy all standards of play for most indoor sports, and, therefore before determining the hall dimensions it will be necessary to decide on the range of sports and the level of play to be accommodated. Possible requirements for broader social and arts use may also be important and will vary according to local needs and be affected by the proximity of other sports centres and what they offer. Sensible use of resources necessitates planned provision and sponsors and providers should consult with their national, regional and local sports bodies on an appropriate scale of provision.

It is possible to select a floor area providing for national and international standards in one or two sports, while at the same time offering a wide variety of other activities at a lower standard of play. The following designations have been used to relate particular dimensional requirements to the hall sizes identified in the accompanying table:

International/National	(N)
Regional	(Rg)
County	(Cy)
Club	(C)
Recreational	(R)
Practice	(P)
Top divisions, local league	(TD)
Lower divisions, local league	(LD)

2 Recommended sizes of sports halls

During the last decade the Sports Council published a number of important adjustments made to the critical sizes of multi-sports halls or to some setting-out dimensions of courts, including those due to rule changes from the governing bodies of sport. Also, since the first edition of the Handbook, a large rectangular hall size has been established which recognised the needs of indoor hockey, handball, korfball and full size five-a-side soccer.

The National Lottery coincides with the beginning of a fourth decade in the evolution of sports halls in the UK. This has provided a timely opportunity to review the whole range of Sports Hall recommended sizes and to considerably reduce the many different existing sizes of hall. The current *recommended range of six sizes for new halls* are set out in the following sections and diagrams, together with the advantages gained by the *increased dimensions* of these sizes. The renaming of these sizes formally adopts names which are now in common use: that is by reflecting *the number of Badminton courts* contained in each size of hall. For example: the old term 'Small Hall' has become a 'Four-court Hall' or 'Three-court Hall'; and so on, as

named in the heading of Table 49.1. Table 49.1 sets out the new space standards for the basic six minimum sizes of sports halls for new-build projects.

The space required for most games depends upon *the standard of play* to be provided. Generally, the higher the standard, the larger the volume needed. The actual playing area, pitch or court is usually of a standard size, but the safety run-out margins around are wider for higher standards of play than for recreational (basic) standards of space. For most competition play, usually an extra zone is required for team benches and the officials' table. For major events, some sports specify a further security zone between teams and spectators. These margins of space around the playing area add up to what is known as the critical *overall space* – that is the absolute minimum area safe for each standard of play of each game. These incremental dimensions are given in Chapters 15–46 and 70–90 for each sport. Of course, budget planning should never compromise these space planning standards.

Essentially, for both the length and width of a hall there are now only *six* (previously twelve) *key critical dimensions: 18 m* (in the past 17 m). *27 m* (ex 26 m), *33 m* (32 m and 32.8 m), *37 m* (36.5 m), *51 m* and *54 m* (45 m and 50 m). Figure 49.1 shows how these are applied rationally to give modular hall sizes now recommended. These are *minimum* sizes and dimensions; in some cases, these may need to be increased:

- if extra sports needing *dedicated space* forms part of your Brief; for instances climbing and indoor athletics (Chapter 70)
- if non-sports functions combine into a *multi-purpose hall*
- to increase spectator capacities
- where the largest size of hall also services as a *regional arena*
- to fit in with structural and environmental design or building component sizes.

2.1 Which sports and how many courts fit each hall?
Table 49.1 enables you to select a hall size with activity capacity to suit the scale of provision and range of sports to be specified and written into the Project Brief.

2.2 Height of the sports hall
Badminton, tennis and trampolining require an unrestricted height of 9.1 m (approx 30 ft) for international competition and this should be provided in centres catering for regional and county competition. This height of hall will be more than adequate for games such as basketball and netball. National volleyball now requires an increased height of 10.5 m. A height of 7.6 m is necessary for club and county standard in all sports except 8.4 m for county badminton, with a stated height requirement. Where possible this should be regarded as the desirable minimum. Economies can be obtained in small halls (ie halls used for club and recreational standards of play) by positioning the main structural roof beams outside the height zone of the badminton courts. Where finance is limited, the height of the hall can be restricted to 6.7 m; this height is not ideal and severely limits participation in most sports. Badminton is regarded as the most critical sport and in conversions, Community Recreation Centres and village halls, a minimum of 6.1 m clear has been accepted.

2.3 Equipment
The equipment required for a sports hall is dependent on the sports and activities envisaged. Refer to Chapter 55, Equipment storage, for details.

Table 49.1: This table sets out the range of minimum sizes for the six new hall sizes in Fig. 49.1 and the numbers of overall playing volume for courts/pitches, of the designated standards of play, for which there is hall space. (1) Most sports with smaller space requirements have been excluded for simplification but can obviously take place in all the halls listed here. Hall grading and names reflect the maximum capacity for badminton. Tennis (excluded from multi-sports halls) is the subject of Chapter 88. One and two-court halls are the subject of Chapter 68.

	Twelve-court hall[2] 54 × 33 × 9.1 in high 1782 m² Refer to 1k			Nine-court hall[2] 51 × 27 × 8.4/9.1 m high 1377m² Refer to 1j			Eight-court hall[3] 37 × 33 × 9.1/8.4/7.6 m high 1221 m² Refer to 1g,h			Six-court hall[4] 33 × 27 × 7.6/8.4 m 891 m² Refer to 1d-f			Four-court hall[5] 33 × 18 × 7.6 m 594 m² Refer to 1c			Three-court hall 27 × 18 × 7 m 486m² Refer to 1b		
Indoor sports	Standards of play			Standards of play			Standards of play			Standards of play			Standards of play			Standards of play		
	N	Cy	C R	N	Cy	C R	N	Cy	C R	N	Cy	C R	N	Cy	C R	N	Cy	C R
Badminton and short tennis	6	6/9*	12	6	6	9	3/6*	8.4 m ht 3/6*	8	3	8.4 m ht 3	6	–	8.4 m ht 3P	4	–	–	3
Basketball	1/2*	C(TD) 1/2*	C(LD) 3	1	C(TD) 1/3P	C(TD) 1/2P	1	C(TD) 1 2P	C(LD) 2 –	1	C(TD) 1 2P	C(LD) 1 2R	–	–	C(LD) 1	–	–	C(LD) 1

Indoor sports	Standards of play			Standards of play			Standards of play			Standards of play			Standards of play			Standards of play		
	N	Cy/C	R	N	Cy/C	R	N	Cy/C	R	N	Cy/C	R	N	Cy/C	R	N	Cy/C	R
Gymnastics	1	1	3P	1	1	2P	–	P	1	–	–	P	–	–	P	–	–	P
5-a-side football	1	3	3	P	1	3	–	1	2	–	1	2	–	P	1	–	–	1
Handball	1	1	3	9 m high 1	9 m high 1	2	–	9 m high 1	2	–	–	1	–	–	1 Mini	–	–	–
Indoor hockey	1	1	3	1	1	2	–	P	2	–	–	1	–	–	1 Unihoc	–	–	–
Korfball	1	1	3P	9 m ht 1	9 m ht 1	1	–	–	1 2P	–	–	P	–	–	P	–	–	–
Netball	1/2*	1/2*	3	1	1	1/2P	1	1/2*	2	–	1	1	–	1	1	–	–	–
Volleyball	10.5 m ht 2/3*	2/4*	4	10.5 m ht 1/3*	2/3*	4	10.5 m ht 1/2*	2	2	–	1/2P	2	–	1	1	–	1 7 m ht	1
Sportshall athletics	1	1	2P	1	1	1	1	1	2P	–	1	P	–	P	P	–	–	–

(1) When considering standards of play and minimum *clear* heights, also carefully check sports' space tables of dimensions in chapters 15–46 in this volume. Sports mostly require 9 m, or 8.4 m, or 7.6 m or 7 m minimum for designated standards of play; below which play to governing body safety guidelines may be restricted to only recreational standard.
(2) Rectangular large hall or regional arena for full size pitches for hockey, handball, korfball, soccer and for gymnastics. See also *Arenas* (see References).
(3) Existing sizes are 36.5 × 32 m and 36.58 × 36.58 m (the 120 × 120 ft first generation size of UK halls c.1963). See also Chapter 4 in this volume.
(4) Existing (1975) sizes are 32 × 26 m and 32 × 23 m. However, if badminton courts are to be set out end-to-end as in **1d** then safety margins require an increased overall hall length of 33 m.
(5) Existing sizes are 32 × 17 × 7.6 m and 36.58 × 18.29 m (120 ×60 ft first generation small hall). Also the 34 × 18 m DISC size developed in 1989 by The Scottish Sports Council. The range of full size courts which the extra space now allows are shown on **1c**. See also References.
* Maximum number of courts, without spectator seating, for preliminary rounds.
   P Below space standard for competition play recommended by the governing body; but suitable for practice and training.

3 Social and arts use of sports halls

There can be many advantages in providing for a number of different community activities together in one complex and a particularly valuable area of common indoor provision, both in economic and cultural terms, is that of sport and the arts. There is a significant overlap of activity, particularly at local level where the same space can house activities like table tennis, badminton, movement and dance, amateur dramatics, concerts, meetings and a whole range of community events.

In many areas the local sports centre will be the largest and, often, the most modern facility available, and as sports and arts activities have many common ancillary needs such as changing, showers, toilets, possibly bar, refreshment and crèche facilities, the pressure for combined use can be irresistible. Movement and dance identifies the area of overlap particularly clearly and the loosening of the often artificial barrier between sport and art.

A number of large-scale leisure complexes have been developed in new towns and expanding residential areas which have sought to provide all the sporting and cultural needs of a community under one roof. The earliest examples such as Billingham Forum included a theatre alongside a sports hall, swimming pool and ice rink. Later examples at Stevenage, The Cresset in Peterborough and, more recently, the Link Centre, Swindon, have been less ambitious and the current tendency is to utilise large-scale sports halls for concerts and theatrical events. Touring theatre companies and the major orchestras as well as rock and pop bands frequently perform in local authority run leisure facilities, **3**.

3.1 Overall design implications of arts and social events

The character of the multi-faceted entertainments centre will be different from that of a conventional sports centre. The image conveyed by the building exterior should be more vibrant and its physical presence alone will proclaim that this is a venue not only for local but also for regional and perhaps even national events.

A familiar management problem with this type of leisure building is how to maintain a reasonable sports programme during times when the main internal space is let for spectator or other events. This includes the time for setting up and dismantling as well as for the event itself.

Where the scale of the building enables its continued use for sport the plan form must ensure a good degree of physical and acoustic separation. The only practical means of achieving this is to provide a separate entrance with small-scale control and support facilities.

The public areas, entrance, foyers, circulation, bars and restaurant and cafeterias must be capable of creating the appropriate ambience for large-scale events. A higher standard of finish will normally be required with, for example, greater use of carpeting both as a means of imparting a sense of quality and an acoustic moderator. The normal array of sports and user notices should be capable of being temporarily removed or screened and lighting will be selected for its decorative effect.

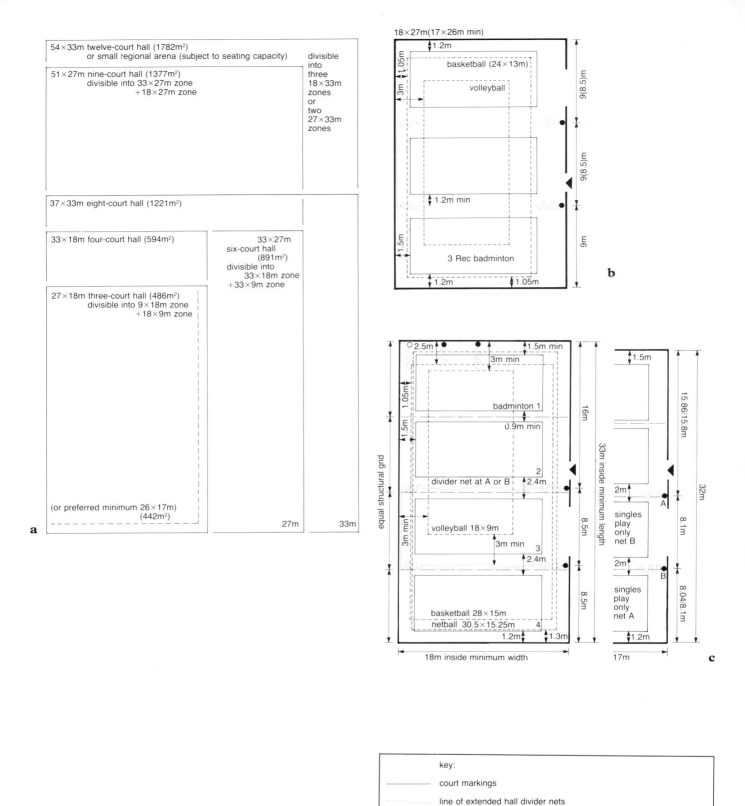

a

54×33m twelve-court hall (1782m²)
or small regional arena (subject to seating capacity)

51×27m nine-court hall (1377m²)
divisible into 33×27m zone
+18×27m zone

divisible into three 18×33m zones or two 27×33m zones

37×33m eight-court hall (1221m²)

33×18m four-court hall (594m²)

33×27m six-court hall (891m²) divisible into 33×18m zone +33×9m zone

27×18m three-court hall (486m²)
divisible into 9×18m zone
+18×9m zone

(or preferred minimum 26×17m) (442m²)

27m 33m

b

18×27m(17×26m min)

1.2m
1.05m
3m
basketball (24×13m)
9/8(5)m
volleyball
9/8(5)m
1.2m min
9m
1.5m
3 Rec badminton
1.2m 1.05m

c

2.5m 1.5m min
3m min
1.05m
1.5m
badminton 1
0.9m min
equal structural grid
divider net at A or B 2.4m
2
volleyball 18×9m
3m min
3m min
3
2.4m
basketball 28×15m
netball 30.5×15.25m 4
1.2m 1.3m

16m
33m inside minimum length
8.5m
8.5m

18m inside minimum width

1.5m
15.86/15.8m
2m
A
8.1m
singles play only net B
32m
2m
B
singles play only net A
8.04/8.1m
1.2m

17m

key:
— court markings
····· line of extended hall divider nets
•···· retracted and bagged nets
– – – clear overall space for match play without nets
—— five-a-side barrier enclosure

1 a *Examples of new, modular, sports hall sizes.* **b** *3 court hall.* **c** *4 court hall; preferred and minimum dimensions.* **d** *6 court hall; badminton layout.* **e** *6 court hall; alternative badminton court layout.* **f** *6 court hall; subdivision of 1d.* **g** *8 court hall.* **h** *8 court hall, alternative division.* **i** *10 court hall.* **j** *9 court hall.* **k** *12 court hall.*

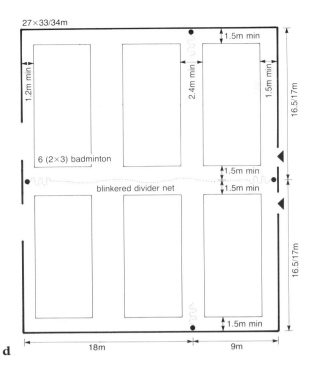

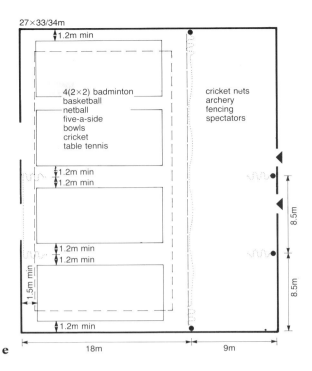

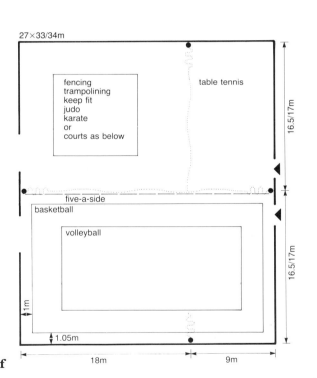

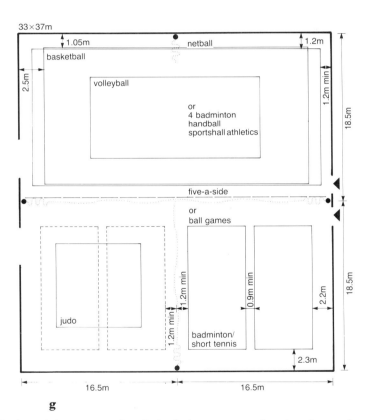

1d-f *Alternative arrangements for 6 court-sized halls. This is the minimum area for six badminton courts placed end to end.*
g *8 court hall; alternative activities in the half-hall or quarter zones.*

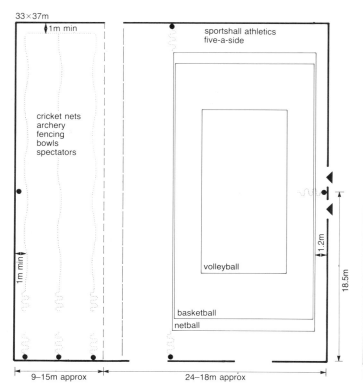

33×37m

1m min

sportshall athletics
five-a-side

cricket nets
archery
fencing
bowls
spectators

1m min

volleyball

basketball

netball

1.2m

18.5m

9–15m approx

24–18m approx

1h *Alternative court arrangements for 8 court halls*

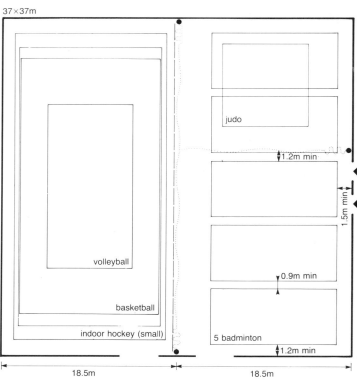

37×37m

judo

1.2m min

1.5m min

volleyball

basketball

0.9m min

indoor hockey (small)

5 badminton

1.2m min

18.5m

18.5m

1i *By widening the hall to the original 120 x 120 ft size, there is space for ten club badminton courts and more ball game spectators*

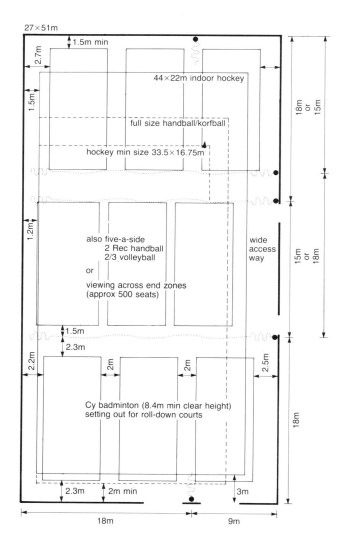

27×51m

1.5m min

2.7m

44×22m indoor hockey

1.5m

full size handball/korfball

hockey min size 33.5×16.75m

18m or 15m

1.2m

also five-a-side
2 Rec handball
2/3 volleyball

or

viewing across end zones
(approx 500 seats)

wide access way

15m or 18m

1.5m

2.3m

2.2m

2m

2m

2.5m

Cy badminton (8.4m min clear height)
setting out for roll-down courts

18m

2.3m

2m min

3m

18m

9m

1j *A 9 court hall is the smallest size for full-size indoor hockey and other big pitch sports, but limited seating space*

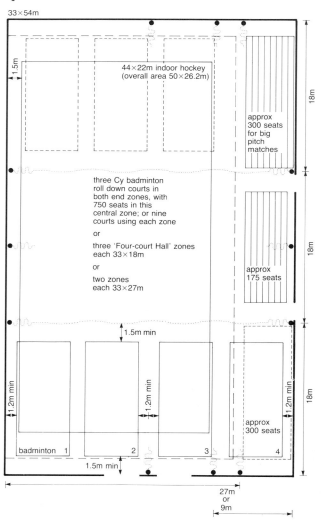

33×54m

1.5m

44×22m indoor hockey
(overall area 50×26.2m)

18m

approx
300 seats
for big
pitch
matches

three Cy badminton
roll down courts in
both end zones, with
750 seats in this
central zone; or nine
courts using each zone

or

three 'Four-court Hall' zones
each 33×18m

or

two zones
each 33×27m

18m

approx
175 seats

1.5m min

1.2m min

1.2m min

1.2m min

badminton 1

2

3

4

approx
300 seats

1.5m min

18m

27 or 9m

1k *A 12 court hall or small arena with plenty of spectator seating for hockey and centre-court ball games*

2 Gymnastics competition at the Chase Leisure Centre, Cannock. Note the permanent stage. Photo: Tony Boydon and Tri-light

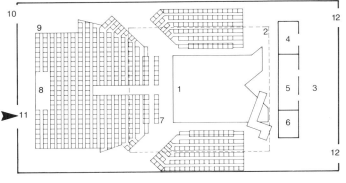

1	stage	7	possible wheelchair positions
2	tower	8	operator's position
3	backstage area	9	drape surround
4	band box	10	dressing room
5	quick change room	11	entrance
6	dimmer racks room	12	fire exit

3 Seating/stage layout for a Royal Shakespeare Company production in a 32 × 17 m sports hall

3.2 Large and medium category halls

Large and medium sized sports halls provide the space standards for a wide range of spectator, audience and community events and, if this expanded role is to be met satisfactorily, the design brief must address enhancements to the support accommodation which could include:

- Adequate access roads and overspill car and coach parking for audiences of up to 2000 for 9–12 badminton court halls.
- A plan which permits good sound control within the building, separating noisy from quiet activities. This is particularly important in large multi-function centres where an arts event may be taking place at the opposite end of the building to an evening sport programme.
- Booking office for 'on the night' admissions and a control system which combines informality and efficiency for the admission of both individuals and groups.
- A straightforward and generous access route between the foyer and events hall, planned to distribute the audience along its route and in relation to seating banks, 4.
- Cloakrooms accessed from the foyer/circulation. Cloakrooms do not form part of a normal sports centre brief,

but could be provided by emptying office or meeting room space and equipping it with temporary mobile (rag-trade) coat stands.

- Additional toilet accommodation will be required, distributed between the foyer and refreshment areas. Where additional accommodation for special event use is required it is advisable to include it as rooms which can be locked during normal use.
- Disabled persons access. Particular attention will be needed in designating safe access routes without abrupt changes in level between the car park and a designated viewing area in the hall.

4 Generous entrances and foyers are essential for large scale spectator events. Photo: C J Harper

- Additional fire exits/escape routes necessitated by the number of people using the hall. Refer to *BS 5588: Part 6 Means of Escape from Places of Assembly.*
- Temporary accommodation provided for extra security personnel and first aid staff for specific events
- Facilities for televising or broadcasting events along with rooms which are adequately serviced for use by the press.
- Changing rooms which can be transformed into dressing rooms and which must be directly accessible to any backstage area. They should include toilets and be linked into a wardrobe area.
- Extra bar and catering facilities are essential for revenue earning and customer satisfaction. Temporary bars can be set up in such spaces as equipment stores so long as noise from preparation and washing up does not interfere with the performance. A water supply and drainage point provided in appropriate storage areas at the outset will make setting up a temporary bar a simple operation. A lobby space with at least two sets of doors should be designed to prevent sound spillage. Bars must be easily accessible to the hall.
- A lighting/sound control room can be considered in a raised position opposite the performance area with a double glazed viewing panel.
- Events organiser's office – an extra office adjacent to the entrance of the hall from which setting up and derigging is controlled and from where the event is run.
- Storage – it is essential that proper storage provision is included for stowing away all items extraneous to a particular performance and ensuring that access doors into the hall permit easy transfer of bulky items of equipment and staging.

4 Hall specification and finishes

The 'workshop' interiors of most sports halls are unlikely to fulfil the basic requirement for an arts event, although they can be perfectly satisfactory for exhibitions or community activities such as 'bring and buy' and pet shows. Four aspects of the standard hall will require further consideration in order to achieve a satisfactory performance interior:

- *Equipment*: wall hung sports equipment and netting should preferably be removed or alternatively concealed behind additional wall hung drapes.
- *Lighting*: the standard sports hall system will have to be replaced (or supplemented) by lighting designed specifically for a particular event (see Chapters 60 and 61).
- *Decorative scheme*: if there is a frequent programme of non-sports events, consideration will have to be given to a compromise colour scheme. This might entail a darker wall colour than required for multi-sports spaces and also a darker ceiling colour, leading in turn to reconsideration of a satisfactory compromise for the lighting system.
- *Spectator seating*: a flexible layout is desirable and if the hall is equipped with pull-out (bleacher) units, they should be untethered so as to be usable in a number of different seating layouts. Refer to Chapter 50, Arenas.

5 Environmental services

For general details of environmental services recommendatons refer to Chapters 60 and 61 and for further information on services related to arts use to Chapter 52, Dance studios and workshops.

All aspects of the services design will have to be considered to strike a realistic compromise between standard sports and specific arts standards. This will entail:

- *Lighting*: providing fixings and additional power sockets to enable competition sports lighting or stage lighting to be located according to particular needs. A lighting control room with a view into the hall might form part of the accommodation schedule as might a projection room. Any windows or roof lights will need to be fitted with effective black-out blinds.
- *Heating*: the standard heating system should have adequate flexibility to meet the requirement of heating the hall up to comfort standards prior to audience admission, then controlling effectively to take account of user heat gains. Ducted warm air systems should be quiet in operation.
- *Ventilation*: a fully flexible, quiet and efficient system will be required, capable of providing up to three air changes per hour.

- *Acoustics*: see Chapters 60 and 61. Provision for a demountable or winched up acoustic canopy may be required for a designated performance area and could have structural implications, **5**.

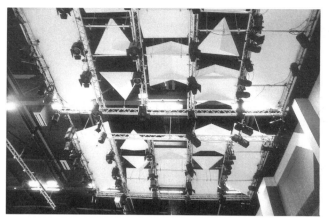

5 *The lighting and acoustic grid at the Brentwood Centre. Photo: C J Harper*

- *Power*: extra power outlets will be needed at high level and in any potential stage area. A power socket should also be provided in any temporary wardrobe space.

6 Small and community halls

These halls do not offer the same scope for events as the larger halls, but can and will host seated audiences from time to time. It is unlikely that their support accommodation will be modified from what is regarded as normal practice, but engineering services specification could require enhancement.

Ancillary halls
Refer to Chapter 51, Ancillary and projectile halls, and Chapter 68, Community recreation centres and village halls.

Sports/arts workshop
Refer to Chapter 52, Dance studios and workshops, for further details.

7 References and further advice

Arts Council/Sports Council, *Getting it Together*, Arts Council/Sports Council, London.
Chapter 11, Facilities for TV and radio broadcasting.
Chapter 52, Dance studios and workshops.

50
Arenas

Geraint John and John Roberts

1 Definitions

The Sports Council in the UK has proposed the following definitions for spectator sports venues:

- Stadium – an outdoor facility with spectators around a central activity area (see Chapter 22 in Volume 1)
- Arena – an indoor facility with spectators around a central activity area
- Velodrome – indoor cycling facility (see Chapter 75)
- Covered stadium – a recent term most associated with indoor schemes for spectator facilities of football-pitch size (see also Chapter 22 in Volume 1).

Because these four types partly overlap it is not possible to deal with each in a completely self-contained article. Therefore all the technical studies referred to above should be read in conjunction with each other.

2 Arenas

The planning and design of indoor arenas involve a complex series of decisions in order to resolve many different requirements, some of which may be conflicting.

Arenas may be expected to cope with such widely differing space requirements as boxing and cycling and the environmental conditions of ice skating and badminton. Unlike theatre, sport can rarely provide sufficient events to avoid an unacceptable number of 'dark days' for such valuable resources and alternative uses must be sought. These uses can include:

- Community sports participation programmes
- Concerts and theatre
- Exhibitions and shows
- Religious and political rallies
- Circus and entertainments
- Product launches and other promotional events
- Rallies and conventions
- Conferences and public meetings
- Social gatherings
- Animal shows.

Satisfying these demands in an acceptable manner needs an enormous variety of servicing specifications (for example acoustics, lighting, ventilation, floor surfaces and seating layouts). Sophisticated hydraulics, mechanics and electronics may allow quick conversion of lights, seats and surfaces – for example basketball and hockey events may be held in one arena on the same day – but the maintenance of state-of-the-art equipment can prove very expensive. It also requires high quality management to operate effectively.

Arena planners must recognise that 'sport is theatre where the primal things are in play – courage, passion, perfidy, endeavour, fear; where grace and sometimes incredible gifts pass in front of us', as described by David Robson, former sports editor of the *Sunday Times*.

Internal environment
For general details of environmental services recommendations refer to Chapters 60 and 61, and for details of environmental requirements for arenas refer to Part 7 of *Arenas: A Planning, Design and Management Guide*.

2.1 History of Arenas

Origins
The first indoor arena, perhaps better described as a covered stadium, was probably the Colosseum in Rome. While the remains provide a testament to this magnificent 190 × 156 m oval structure, built between AD 70 and 82, it is less well known that it had a velarium or awning drawn across the auditorium, supported by guy ropes, with a small central aperture. Life expectancy on the floor of the Roman stadia in those times was quite short, with so many gladiatorial contests alongside the horse events, archery, acrobatics, swimming, javelin throwing, wrestling and 'fly fishing'. The worst ever spectator accident occurred around AD 150 at the Circus Maximus when a stand collapsed, killing over 1000 people.

It was not until the middle of the 19th century that structures were developed to provide the roof spans necessary for large arenas. British engineers like Brunel and Telford led the way in the use of iron and two buildings in particular were significant for future developments around the world. The Crystal Palace, erected for the Great Exhibition in 1851 in iron and glass, measured 564 × 137 m, while London's St Pancras station (1868) has a huge arch span of 73 m. The Royal Albert Hall for Arts and Sciences, since its opening in 1871, has proved popular for tennis, basketball, badminton, boxing and movement and dance as well as for concerts and arts events.

The world's best known arena grew from a park off Fifth Avenue in New York called Madison Square. An outdoor arena for Barnum's Circus, boxing and even dog shows, it was eventually covered in 1879 to escape the rigours of harsh winters. The second Madison Square Garden building with a 107 × 61 m auditorium under a 24 m high ceiling lasted until 1925 and its replacement was constructed on Eighth Avenue with room for 18,500 spectators at a boxing match. An ice pad was also included for the new sport being introduced from Canada – ice-hockey.

The present Madison Square Garden rises 13 stories above Penn Station. The circular structure, 130 m in diameter, houses a 20,000-seat arena, a 48-lane bowling centre, the 5000-seat Felt Forum, an exhibition rotunda and a Hall of Fame, opened in 1968. Spectators access the building by means of 11 escalators, each manned by security staff. New events have to be built up overnight by large numbers of workers, while the ice rink has frequently to be covered and uncovered or broken out. The arena has its own TV station which contributes significantly to other revenues.

Olympic and other major games
The impetus for building many arenas around the world has arisen from the desire to stage major international multi-sport competitions such as the Olympic, Commonwealth, Asian and Pan-American Games. Among the first was the Empire Pool and Sports Arena at Wembley, built in 1934 for the Empire Games.

Some of the most outstanding arenas have been designed for the Olympic Games. The pattern was established in Rome in 1960 with two circular arenas of particularly elegant design. the Palazzetto dello Sport (Small Sports Palace) has 5000 seats around a simple oval floor. Its shallow, 58 m diameter concrete dome and good use of natural light make it ideal for a number of more intimate sporting and cultural events. The 100 m diameter Palazzo dello Sport seems like an enlarged version with a capacity for 16,000 spectators. Both set very high standards of sightlines with grace and efficiency.

The architect for the National Gymnasium for the 1964 Tokyo Games, Kenzo Tange, received the Olympic Diploma of Merit. The swimming pool on the Yoyogi field site was planned as a multi-sport arena for 15,000 spectators, in a building containing over 28,000 sq m of floor space. The building that stimulated most comment, however, was rather unromantically called the 'National Gymnasium Annex'. Four thousand spectators at a basketball match could sit under one of the most dramatic roof structures ever devised. Steel cables were draped from a single tall perimeter mast and concrete panels hung from the cables forming a semi-rigid structure. The internal wood cladding provides a warmth to the design which is perhaps typical of the Japanese philosophy and

. . . stressed the importance of the interaction between an architectural space and the human spirit, rather than emphasising questions of a technical nature.

The four following Olympics each demonstrated new technological features in arena construction, but the circular or oval 'footprint' remained similar. In Mexico, a steel space-frame gave a clear span of 132 m to the 22,000 seat Sports Palace. Environmental problems haunted the Munich Arena under the enormous net and acrylic roof, that unified it with the stadium and swimming pool. A PVC-coated polyester parasol was hung under the arena roof to shade it from the sun. Its magnificent elliptical form (113 × 85 m) was designed to accommodate a wide variety of sports and entertainments after the Games.

In Moscow, the arena built on Prospect Mira was elliptical in plan, with major axes of 213 × 174 m, over 30 m high and with a capacity for 45,000 spectators. Its most interesting feature is a 440-tonne acoustic partition that divides the arena into two smaller areas of 16,000 and 18,000 seats. Banks of seating are mounted on air cushions to allow easy movement and provide all-round viewing in both areas, **13c**.

Seoul in 1988 adopted the policy of carefully considered after-use for many of its facilities, hence the use of two small provisional arenas – at Suwon and Sangmu – and three university arenas. Five of the six major arenas have been built either at the main stadium complex or at the Olympic Park 3.5 km away.

Arenas and covered stadia
The USA led the move towards larger indoor arenas. In 1965 Houston Astrodome was opened. The 38,000 sq m of space under a steel dome can seat 53,000 for an American football match. Once proven, large covered stadia sprouted around North America. The subject of covered stadia is covered in Chapter 22, Stadia, in Volume 1. The 80,000 seat Pontiac Silverdome (1975) demonstrated the effectiveness of large air-supported roofs, **1**. A small internal pressure differential (approximately 0.25%) maintains the inflation of a Teflon-coated fibre-glass fabric, which can also be provided with a double skin to improve insulation. Steel cables maintain the roof profiles

1 *The 1975 Pontiac Silverdome in USA is an example of a large air-supported roof. It seats up to 80,000 spectators. Photograph: David Cannon/Allsport*

and support the fabric in case of collapse, as happened twice at the Metrodome in Minneapolis (once during construction in 1981, and once in 1982 when workmen were clearing snow from the roof and a large crane bucket punctured the skin). Both were safely repaired. There are arguments for and against fabric roofs, ranging from capital cost savings against longer term revenue costs and environmental problems.

2.2 Roof structures of arenas
The design of the roof structure is a key consideration for the arena designer. The roof is a very expensive capital cost element and one that can also have a profound influence on running costs. Its profile determines the volume and therefore the amount of air that needs to be serviced (ie ventilation, heating, air conditioning). It is this factor which has encouraged supporters of the saddle-shaped roofs, for which the model is the Calgary Saddledome, built in 1983 for ice events at the 1988 Olympic Games. The roof follows the contours of the seating and is produced by suspending cables from a ring beam. Concave in one dimension and convex in the other, the cables form a net in the shape of a hyperbolic paraboloid. Many arenas have a simple domed structure, eg the one in Budapest. The Tacoma dome in the USA has a timber structure.

2.3 Indoor spectator sports
Sports events that can be staged in indoor arenas can be classified into three categories:

- Sports that have developed mainly indoors, eg badminton, basketball, boxing, gymnastics, handball, snooker and volleyball
- Sports where the indoor and outdoor rules and technical requirements (apart from the surface) are virtually the same, eg American football, baseball, bowls, ice hockey, netball and tennis
- Outdoor sports of a wide international appeal which to a greater or lesser degree have been modified to suit the more limited space available indoors, eg track and field athletics, cycling, show-jumping and soccer.

It is the third of these groups which often has the most profound influence on the design of arenas. This is because they are among the most popular spectator sports, yet can be played on a variety of different-sized spaces. It is useful, therefore, to understand their historical development so that the significance of choice of size can be properly understood.

Athletics

In Europe, a number of international events are still held on 160 m tracks, but the 200 m track has become the standard with four, five or six lanes, **2**. There will be difficulties in providing 200 m tracks in North America where the majority of multi-use arenas are designed for ice skating events or other sports requiring less space.

The most recent innovation has been the development of hydraulic variable-profile tracks, where the banked bends are raised out of the floor in a matter of minutes. The first was a four-lane 154 m facility at Otaniemi, Finland, where the hall was required for a variety of training uses other than athletics. Further technical advances have been made and the savings in time and manpower are enormous. It has proved very expensive to translate the practice into six lanes, however, and a permanent spike-resistant athletics surface is impractical for a multi-event arena rather than one used for sports training and competition alone.

Show jumping

As with many sports, show jumping evolved gradually. There are records of 'leaping' events at the Dublin Horse Show of 1865 and, 10 years later, indoors at the agricultural show in Islington's Agricultural Hall. Madison Square Garden started its National Horse Show in 1883, but most indoor events towards the end of the 19th century were held in France. The first International Horse Show in England was at Olympia in 1907.

TV, sponsors and spectators clearly enjoy the intimacy, atmosphere and environment indoors, yet most arenas are very cramped compared with outdoor stadia used for Olympic and world events.

The Federation Equitation Internationale (FEI) recommends a minimum area for indoor events which now stands at 2000 sq m with a preferred minimum width of 40 m.

Indoor football

Reduced-size soccer games have always been played alongside the eleven-a-side game either as practice or for recreational activity. The size of teams is determined by the space available, and the standard sports halls of the 60s and the outdoor multi-games areas of the 1970s in the UK (based on a single tennis court) led to five-a-side being the most popular. Rules were developed using the rebound walls and convenient netball 'D' for the goal area.

2.4 A hierarchy of provision

The scale and distribution of arenas and halls is presented below in terms of several distinct groups. In practice, circumstances may dictate minor variations but, wherever possible, the minimum and optimum provisions are both presented. Solutions for specified locations should take account of populations, accessibility and existing facilities.

More detail is given in *Arenas: a Design and Management Guide* (see References and further advice).

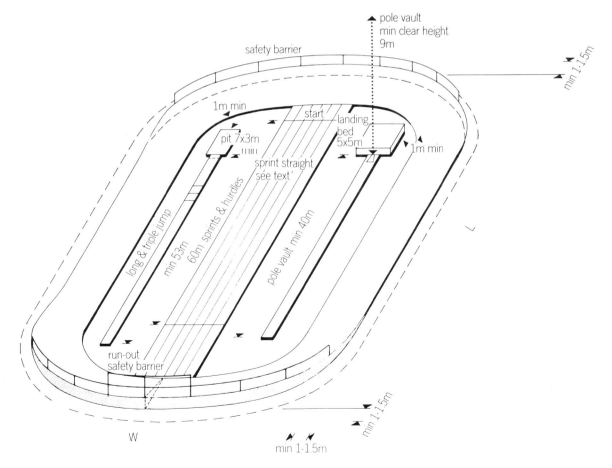

2 *Space diagram of a 200 m four-lane oval track for athletic events. Locations of shot circle and high jump can be varied depending on the size of the track, on TV or promoters' requirements, and on whether the centre area is built up or not. Shot landing sector safety precautions as specified by the IAAF must be fully taken into account. To establish the start/finish line, fix the position of the start in the outside lane, not higher than one-third the maximum height of the banking*

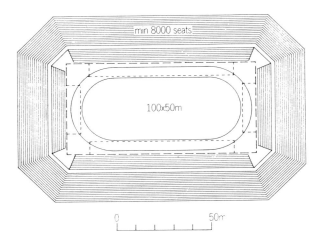

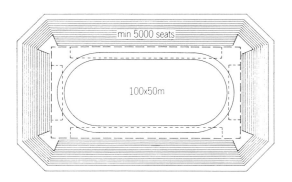

3 *Diagrammatic layout of a Type 1 National Indoor Arena. The broken line rectangle outlines the 100 x 50 m arena, which is large enough for a six-lane athletics track. The four smaller rectangles show additional pull-out seating areas. The total building area would be approximately 28,000 to 30,000 sq m*

4 *Diagrammatic layout of a Type 2 National Indoor Arena*

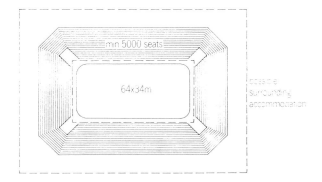

5 *Diagrammatic layout of a Type 3 National Indoor Arena*

Facility	Floor space	Minimum No. seats	Sports event, days per year (approx)
Indoor arena type 1	6-lane 200m athletic track	8000–12,000 (5000 fixed; 3000 retractable seats)	100
Indoor arena type 2	4-lane 200m athletic track	5000 (80% tiered; 50% fixed seats)	30–50
Indoor arena type 3	64 m × 34 m	5000 (80% tiered: 50% fixed seats)	30–50
Indoor arena type 4	46 m × 30 m	3000 (fixed or retractable seats)	20–40
Covered stadium	110 m × 55 m	5000 (retractable or demountable)	≥100

Note (1): In the UK the Sports Council suggests that a population of over 300,000 within a 20-minutes travel time is required to support this scale of provision. It may be worth noting, however, that a published strategy for arenas in Italy, Spaziosport, suggests this level of facility for a population of between 50,000 and 200,000.

2.5 Space planning

The two main determining factors in the production of a functional planning brief for an arena are the dimensions of the floor space and the seating capacity. From these flow the support services and infrastructure needs of the building. The inter-relationship between floor space and seating is complex. A national scale arena, for instance, with 8000 seats around a floor space approximately 100 × 50 m, could easily accommodate 10,000 for a basketball match, but the sightlines for those closest to the court would not be as good as in an arena designed for 12,000 spectators around a 36 × 22 m floor space. The flexibilities and operational economics of the arenas would also be entirely different.

Floor space

The floor space is the central area where the competitions or performance take place. The importance of each sport and the likely level of competition need to be clearly defined before an arena is planned. There are a number of critical dimensions which can help in this process.

The desirable floor space for sports events in an arena must allow for:

- The playing area
- Play safety margins
- Spaces for officials and equipment
- Team benches where necessary
- Photographers and TV cameramen
- Access for people with disabilities.

Dimensions of the playing area rarely change, although the international federations of sports do on occasion alter their rules, the most recent example being basketball.

Safety margins have increased in recent years with sports becoming faster and safety considerations paramount. Officials may operate inside or outside the playing area and, for some sports, they require chairs and tables. Timing apparatus and scoreboards may also need to be accommodated adjacent to the playing area.

The particular needs of the media are many and varied. The numbers attending an event can run into hundreds, with the majority of press photographers and cameramen wishing to be as close to the action as possible. Photographers are relatively mobile, which cannot be said for most TV cameras; their positioning, and that of their cables has to be resolved, often through experimentation and discussion. An additional hazard is the increasing use of advertising boards around a playing area. There is little problem with ice rinks, soccer-six or show jumping where vertical boards define the boundaries but the greatest care has to be taken with sports such as volleyball, tennis and basketball where players are not confined to the court boundaries.

Access around the circumference of the playing area is required for the disabled in wheelchairs, **6,** 7, unless special provision is made for them elsewhere in the building. The positioning of their access, 7, depends on the layout of the event, exits and means of escape. Particular attention should be given to obstructions such as basketball backboards, scoreboards, cameras and advertising boards.

It is not possible, therefore, to be definitive in stating the dimensions required for the floor space in a proposed arena and each case must be assessed individually. A broad indication of the critical dimensions (including safety margins) that can be used in outline planning is:

6 *Good viewing facilities for spectators with disabilities*
Photograph: Geraint John

Activity	Approximate dimensions (m)
200 m six-lane athletics track	97 × 47
200 m four-lane athletics track	92 × 42
Show jumping	70 × 40
Ice skating	64 × 34
Multi-events:	44 × 30 or
	36 × 22

See also **8**, which shows the central space of arena related to different sports and different arena sizes.

The multi-events arena is planned to provide greater space for the sports above, and in addition hockey and handball. The 30 m width is not necessarily a critical dimension, but has been included in the strategy for regional arenas as many of these would be used for community recreation programmes at other times. The 30 m allows recreational basketball, five-a-side soccer, volleyball and badminton (four courts) to be played across the hall.

---

7 *Example of location of viewing bays for spectators in wheelchairs. The diagram also cautions designers and management concerning wheelchair evacuation from floors without direct escape to the open air, where hazards could be caused to others in a crowded emergency. Escape routes for disabled people should as far as possible be on the flat, or via ramps, so that the intermediate stage of a refuge is unnecessary. Where access is by means of a suitable lift (in accordance with BS 5588: Part 9) a protected lobby to the lift may serve as a refuge*

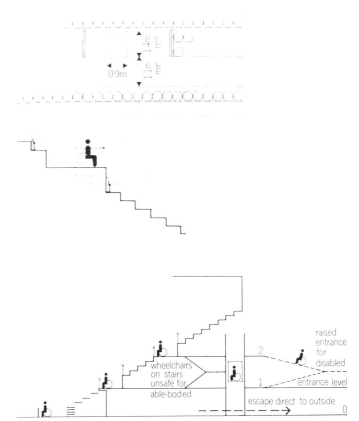

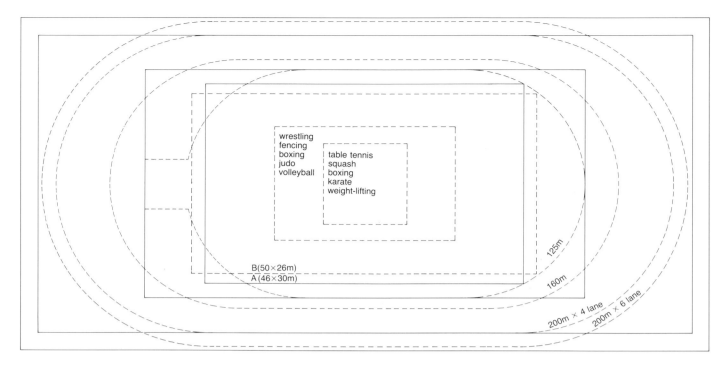

wrestling
fencing
boxing
judo
volleyball

table tennis
squash
boxing
karate
weight-lifting

B(50×26m)
A (46×30m)

125m

160m

200m × 4 lane

200m × 6 lane

8 *Diagram of central space related to different sizes of arena, and to different sports*

The multi-events arena type (B) is a relatively small space but can be used for a wide range of sports up to international level (although major national and international events in many of these activities require more space to cater for the larger number of simultaneous matches).

These include badminton, basketball, boxing, judo, netball, snooker, squash, table tennis, tennis, volleyball, weight lifting and wrestling.

The next size up is 64 × 34 m, which is large enough to accommodate an ice rink to full international dimensions (60 × 30 m) as well as a gymnastics podium. This is the space provided in most American sports arenas where ice hockey often plays an important part in the programme of events. It is interesting to note that, in the American circuit of events, several have been designed to fit into this space, eg soccer-six, ice spectaculars, circuses and rodeos.

The provision of space larger than this depends on the needs of a small number of identified sports or commercial considerations. The ability to provide as large a floor space as possible to cater for the exhibition market is tempting for many arena planners. This is achieved through the use of large numbers of retractable or demountable seating units, **10**. There are inevitable compromises in terms of quality of environment, seating comfort and how protected means of escape in the event of fire is to be achieved. A decision on choice of floor space is relatively easily reached provided the management aims and objectives are clearly defined.

Seating capacity
In defining the capacity of a building it is often helpful to state two figures: the number of seats around the *maximum* floor space and the maximum capacity around the *smallest* space user, eg boxing.

Deciding on the number of seats to include is the most difficult decision facing any arena planner. Influencing that decision are:

● Demand in the catchment area and forecasts of future demand

● Event economies
● Requirements of event promoters.

Seating and sightlines The arena must be designed so that for all practical purposes the spectator is able to see the activity area over the head of the person on the row in front.

This value, known as the *C* value, is shown in **9**. However, because of retractable and variable seating the problem in arenas is now more complex and has to be calculated on the basis of a number of situations.

A maximum rake of seating of 35° is recommended, but national regulations should be checked.

The management of seating is normally in the following categories:

● Permanent fixed seats in tiered blocks or boxes
● Variable blocks in retractable (or telescopic) seating
● Additional demountable seating in temporary tiers on part of the central space
● Additional portable seating on tiered platforms or in flat rows on the central space.

Support areas
The design and layout of spaces for these functions is a highly specialised area and beyond the scope of this book. The following checklist (and the bubble diagram, **11**) give the arena planner some idea of the critical factors:

● Catering areas are among the most capital and staff intensive areas in a building
● Catering is likely to be a mixture of fast food, self-service cafeterias, waitress service restaurants and bars
● The relative demand for different types of catering varies with the audiences and the nature of the event
● Some events have a clearly defined start, interval and end, while catering demand is continuous in others
● There are special needs for sponsors, VIPs and event receptions
● Trends and fashions in catering change quite quickly and areas need to be capable of simple and quick

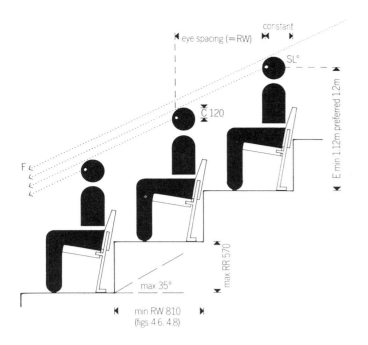

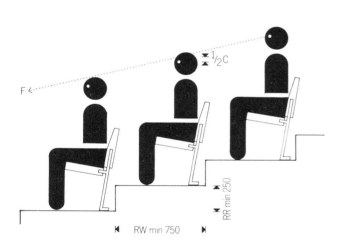

9 *Two examples of 'constant gradients'. The upper is a steep gradient, giving a good C value of 120 mm, but requiring three steps per riser. The lower needs only one or two steps per riser, but gives a less good C value. Gradients must never be steeper than 35°*

refurbishment or redesign; too many permanent structures should therefore be avoided. See also Catering and hospitality later in this section.

Toilets

The provision of toilets and cloakrooms forms part of the same planning process, linked to spectator capacity and seating access/egress. There are statutory requirements but these should be viewed as a minimum in most cases.

In large arenas, toilet facilities should be provided separately for four distinct categories of users:

- Spectators
- Staff and management
- Players, referees and events participants
- Visiting functionaries (principally the media and the police).

Spectators Toilets for spectators should be in the form of many small facilities evenly distributed throughout the

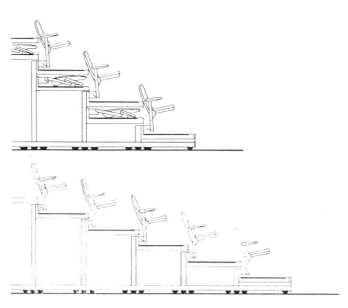

10 *Double-rake retractable seating units can be opened to 'steep rake' or 'shallow rake' positions. The top diagram shows seating opened to alternative rows only (with half the seats folded under seatways), giving a steep rake and good sightline, but smaller seating capacity. The lower diagram shows system fully extended to increase capacity and bring spectators closer to the arena (see 15), but giving shallow rake and less favourable sightlines. Diagrams: Hussey Seating Systems (Europe) Ltd*

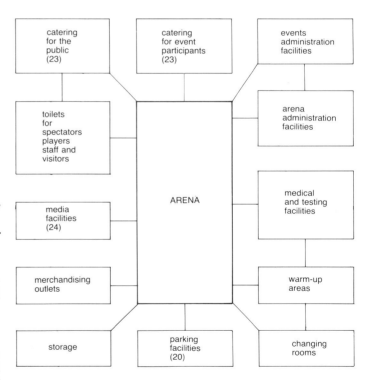

11 *Summary diagram of support areas which may be needed around arena*

spectator areas, and on all levels, not as a large centralised facility. Each seat should be at most 60 m from a usable toilet.

Because toilet provision is expensive, clients may try to cut it to a minimum; but underprovision leads to serious customer dissatisfaction and to unhygienic conditions. Adequate numbers must therefore be provided. The following scales of provision are suggested minima for stadia. Designers may well wish to improve on them after investigation.

Spectators	WCs	Urinals	Washbasins
Male	1 per 500	1 per 80	1 per 200
Female	1 per 40	–	1 per 100

The ratio of male to female users will vary with the type of audience and it may be necessary to have some toilets which can be switched from one use to the other.

Toilets should never be accessed off stairs and to avoid congestion (which is dangerous as well as inconvenient) circulation spaces leading to toilets should be generous. There should be two entrance/exit doorways to each toilet area, as wide as possible.

Surfaces should be hardwearing, impervious and easy to clean, with coved corners and angles. Floors must be capable of being washed down by hose, with a trapped outlet for draining away water.

Sanitary appliances must be robust and vandal-proof with pipework and cisterns concealed if possible. Both hot and cold water should be provided as should hand drying facilities. Frost protection should be provided to avoid the need for draining down water systems in cold weather during times of intermittent use.

Staff and management In the UK the provisions of the Offices Shops and Railway Premises Act, 1963, are an absolute minimum and are given below. The latest edition should be consulted.

Men	WCs	Urinals	Washbasins
1 to 15	1	–	1
16 to 20	1	1	2
21 to 30	2	1	2
31 to 45	2	2	3
Women			
1 to 15	1	–	1
16 to 30	2	–	2
31 to 50	3	–	3

Section 10 of the Act also requires that hot and cold running water, soap and towels (or other means of drying) be provided; and there should be space for vending machines, incinerators and waste bins.

For space planning purposes, it is suggested by Colin Cave of the firm DEGW, in *Planning Office Space*, that the overall floor areas required are 1.67 m per WC cubicle, 0.92 m per urinal, and 0.743 m per washbasin. These areas including standing space at urinals and basins; they do not include outer walls and lobbies.

Players, referees and event participants These users need toilets, baths and showers adjacent to their team rooms and changing rooms; and there must also be provision for massage and physiotherapy treatment.

Visiting functionaries In smaller arenas these people may use the staff and management toilets, but in large arenas they will need their own separate facilities close to the rooms set aside for their use. Scales of provision will be the same as for staff and management.

Restaurants Restaurants and café spaces should be provided with toilets in accordance with national codes.

Media
The growth in world-wide media interest in sport is quite astonishing. A World Athletics Championship may rank only alongside a World Cup soccer final in attracting so much interest to a single venue, but the presence of more than 3000 media people at the 1987 Rome athletics championships gives some indication of what the future might hold. An International Amateur Athletic Federation report broke down the numbers as:

- 120 press
- 230 radio and TV reporters
- 360 photographers
- 1300 radio and TV technicians.

Countries without a TV presence can take coverage either from satellite transmission or recorded tapes.

A small arena may not see the media as quite so important, but a televised snooker event requires over 60 media staff. It is likely that in the future all arenas will be looked on as large TV studios with the potential audience for events being up to 10,000 times the seating capacity. Enormous sums are being invested in the development of communications systems – around 34% of all economic activity in Europe, 45% in the USA and 54% in Japan. In the USA there are tens of millions of subscribers to cable TV, while Europe is on the verge of a massive expansion in both cable and satellite broadcasting. Language and cultural barriers have still to be overcome, but sport is universal and highly visual. New developments in optical-fibre cabling will allow programmes to be sent over 300 km without reamplification and very soon the demand for programmes will escalate in order to provide subscribers with a full choice.

Arenas will also be used to a greater extend for direct video-broadcasting such as already occurs regularly for professional boxing and occasionally for important football matches. In Stuttgart, the 1988 European Athletics Championships included an enormous colour video display board. Screens of up to 200 sq m are now available and the image quality will continue to improve as laser projectors are developed. The July 1985 Live Aid concert at Wembley was video-broadcast to several cities, including Paris where 10,000 watched a 100 sq m screen at the Bercy Arena.

There is always the danger that arenas can be left behind by advancing technical improvements and a decision needs to be taken on what is to be provided permanently and what on a temporary basis. An example of a high degree of sophisticated permanent facilities is the Centre International des Sport de Paris (Bercy Arena) on which around £13 million was spent on time-keeping, display boards, public address systems, press centre equipment, radio and television equipment and specialist lighting. If these are not permanently installed, much of the cost falls on the event budget.

Information services Not so long ago the timing of events by officials, spectator scoreboards and media information were all handled independently. Computer software can now time several races at the same time, give intermediate distance results and provide the information simultaneously to the scoreboard and VDU displays for race control, timekeepers, media and centre management. The Madrid World Swimming Championships in 1986 saw the introduction of a totally automated timekeeping, scoring and data handling service.

160

Press Space for press in an arena is normally provided in the spectator seating areas, but with a writing table and telephone points. TV monitors are also provided in the bigger arenas. The press centre need not necessarily be a permanently dedicated room but must have cabling for sophisticated electronics, including:

- Local and international telephones
- Telex and teleprinter
- Photocopying, fax and scitex (photograph transmission)
- Closed-circuit TV displaying ongoing competition, replays and results.

There is also a need for a selection of rooms for interviews, press conferences and refreshments.

Radio and TV The exchange of information is now three-way between officials, event management and the media. TV pictures can be displayed and re-run instantly on video scoreboards and in some cases are being used to assist officials. The NFL in the USA rely on an official linked to video replays to check on marginal decisions. In another example, the long jump placings at a major event were subject to scrutiny by the athletic authorities through video evidence. Video and film recordings have, of course, been used for a long time in disciplinary hearings, probably first by horse racing stewards.

Representatives from national television should be consulted at the planning stage to determine camera points, and special lighting requirements for a new arena. This is relatively straightforward in a specialist arena, but a multi-purpose arena must cater for many configurations. Cameras are becoming lighter and more easily portable, but they are being used in greater numbers at any one event. Proper power points and cabling ducts allow set-up times to be reduced, which is always in an arena's interest. Most TV companies bring their own production facilities in large vans but, for an event over a week or two, additional space for presenters may be needed. Commentators ideally require sound-proof booths with excellent views of the action, links with the production staff and arena and event information services. Interview rooms can if necessary be set up temporarily in non-dedicated spaces.

Event management The management of events staged in an arena need not necessarily be by the organisation that manages the arena building itself and the extent of outside management can be highly variable. Many governing bodies of sport use volunteers to assist in the organisation of a competition while others use professional staff or agencies. The primary requirements are for administration offices, meeting rooms and staff rooms. The functions to be serviced include:

- *Facility management* – set-up and take-down crews, specialist technicians for lighting, sound, timing and measurement, equipment control and storage
- *Competition management* – organisation of players, officials, results and media
- *Spectator management* – merchandising, stewarding and security
- *Visitor management* – sponsors, guests and international federations.

Apart from the space requirements already discussed, the designer needs to pay particular regard to how access to the main arena floor is provided for major loads of equipment. It is usually prudent to allow vehicular access as far as possible into the building. The alternative is to off-load with fork-lift trucks outside the arena, but this is time consuming, less secure, vulnerable to the weather and likely to cause disturbances to any local residents if, as often happens, the work is done at night.

Arena management
An arena will have its own management organisation irrespective of the users in the building. Its essential functions are:

- Marketing (including promotion and advertising of the arena and its events, reception and ticketing)
- Administration
- Building services (including energy control, mechanical and electrical equipment, maintenance and security).

Ticketing is becoming more and more sophisticated and all but the smallest arenas have computer-controlled systems, often linked to shops and agencies outside the immediate confines of the building. Fortunately, the space and environmental controls needed for computers are continuing to reduce. The main concerns are security for cash receipts and high speed card checking. The design of spectator access controls requires a considered analysis of people flow in and around the building. Unlike a theatre, ticket checking needs to take place at the entrance to the building as well as in the auditorium, recognising also that seating layout may vary quite considerably.

The arena management requires a suite of offices for its administration, ideally with separate access secured from all other users and visitors. It seems inevitable that once a building is open, space is at a premium and the ability to expand offices efficiently is rarely available. Other areas such as storage, toilets and catering can be distributed around the building using space voids and undercrofts, but offices must operate as far as possible as a single unit. It is useful, therefore, to locate storage or non-dedicated spaces next to the offices, so that extensions can be provided relatively easily if necessary.

Building services encompass energy sources and their control, heating, ventilation, lighting, acoustics, audio-visual aids, communications, water, sewage and refuse disposal. Their permanent staffing requirement may be small, but there also needs to be provision for a very large number of additional personnel whose functions include building maintenance, cleaning, arena equipment handling (eg floors, seating and stages) and security. The directly employed staff for these may overlap with external event management personnel and facilities must be available to ensure that the co-ordination of these activities can be accommodated effectively, eg with separate or shared staff rooms, toilets and catering. Operational requirements will inevitably change throughout the life of a building and a successful design will provide for the immediate identified need while including a degree of flexibility that does not significantly increase the capital cost.

2.6 Schedule of accommodation
The functional planning brief provides the design team with a list of space requirements, the use of these spaces and their inter-relationships. The level of detail in the brief will increase through discussions between the design consultants and representatives of funding, management and user groups. Once a site has been determined, further involvement with specialists is necessary, including statutory planners, development control officers, licensing authorities, fire, police and ambulance services, emergency control departments, traffic planners, public transport

agencies, water authorities, gas and electricity boards and radio, TV and telecommunication representatives.

The cornerstone of the brief is the schedule of accommodation, which lays down the required areas (and volumes or other dimensions where relevant) for each space or group of spaces. There is, of course, a multiplicity of design solutions to any single brief, affected by simple matters such as the slope of the site, soil conditions or planning height restrictions. The brief should therefore identify where there is flexibility or where compromises may be discussed. A typical indicative schedule of accommodation for a Type 1 national indoor arena is outlined in the table below.

Outline of a typical schedule of accommodation for a type 1 indoor arena		
Accommodation use	Floor area (sq m)	% of total
Arena	5800	20.7
Training hall, warm-up	1750	6.3
Equipment stores	2000	7.1
Plant rooms	2500	8.9
Workshop maintenance	120	0.4
Offices – administration, booking, box office, backstage	1245	4.4
Servery, food preparation, catering, cellar	1800	6.4
Toilet accommodation	1500	5.4
Changing rooms, showers, sauna, dope control, medical, physiotherapy	1100	3.9
Terraced viewing (fixed seats – on plan)	2150	7.7
Sponsors	500	1.8
Media, press	900	3.2
Circulation, multi-use, assembly, shops	6655	23.8
Total (approximate)	28000	100.0

The schedule would be supplemented with detailed technical performance requirements including the following:

Site
- Vehicular access
- Parking
- Helicopter landing
- Pedestrian access
- Services
- Landscaping.

Arena
- Purposes and uses of accommodation
- Environmental standards
- Floor specifications
- Schedule of finishes, fixtures, fittings and equipment
- Access for the disabled.

2.7 Vehicle parking

The needs of car and coach parking at an arena can be determined from an analysis of a number of factors. The principal ones are:

- Arena seating capacity
- Programme of events
- Road access to the site
- Public transport access
- Population distribution in the catchment area
- Demographics of the catchment area.

Ideally, parking should be in an area immediately surrounding the arena and at the same level as the entrances/exits. This tends to be an inefficient use of land, which can be both expensive and difficult to find in urban areas. Alternatives are multi-storey car parks, on-street parking, park-and-ride and shared parking with other

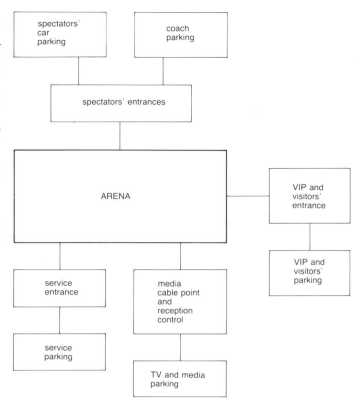

12 *Simplified bubble diagram showing parking facilities that might be required*

facilities. It is possible to consider shared use with offices and manufacturing industries, but sharing with shopping complexes is becoming more difficult with longer evening and weekend opening.

The arena's seating capacity is obviously the most important factor determining the demand for car parking, but its maximum capacity for a sport such as boxing may rarely be achieved. An optimum capacity must therefore be assessed in relation to a typical programme of use and forecast attendance. In addition, public parking spaces may on occasion be taken out for other uses. The needs of the media must be taken into account, with television in particular requiring space for several large service vehicles adjacent to the arena; but the event that causes the greatest difficulty is a horse show which may be staged over a number of days.

Different types of event attract different ratios of car to coach parking. National club finals, for example, are likely to draw a higher proportion of coach travellers with supporters' clubs and commercial companies organising group travel. A car has an average occupancy of 2.5 people, whilst a coach or bus could bring more than 20 times this number.

Car parking consumes land at the rate of one hectare for approximately 50 cars.

TV vehicles
It is essential that discussions are held with the TV authorities in the early stages of an arena design to establish the precise requirements for vehicles (and for cable access). As many as ten vehicles may be required for a major outside broadcast. Their size and weight may vary and different TV companies use different sizes.

As a general guide, and subject to the particular requirements of a specific company, each vehicle requires a parking area of 12 × 4 m. Parking areas should be level and capable of carrying the weight of vehicles up to 15 tonne. The areas may be incorporated within public or staff car parks provided that they are adjacent to the main building cable-access point, thus keeping cable runs to a minimum. Consideration needs to be given to the turning circles of larger vehicles and access roads need to be wide enough to accommodate them.

Access
In general, it is essential that public parking spaces and normal access routes do not encroach on areas required for evacuation of the arena or as manoeuvring areas for emergency services, ie fire engines, ambulances and police vehicles.

If successive events in an arena or successive 'sessions' of the same event follow closely on from each other, ideally there should be separate entrances and exits to the parking areas in order to avoid undue congestion during the changeover. Bad traffic management can have as great an effect on reducing repeat visits as anything that goes on inside the arena. Spectators arrive at a venue spread over an hour or so before the designated start time. This time may be even longer in summer, especially with the growth of 'tailgating' – a largely American phenomenon of picnicking from the back of a car. Attitudes on leaving an event are totally different. The vast majority wish to leave as quickly as possible, and space is at a premium. This is also the time when security is most difficult and clashes can occur between rival spectators and between spectators and teams or officials. In planning arenas for modern society, it is essential that the police are consulted at a very early stage.

2.8 Potential for divisible arenas
Maximum flexibility in operation should be a fundamental objective in the design of any arena. To this end, major and regional arena studies should consider the feasibility of dividing the main space with a sideways or vertical-moving screen to provide two facilities, **13a**.

Subdivision also helps to avoid the depressing appearance of rows of empty seats for events that take less space or need a smaller seating capacity.

It may sometimes be more rational to divide the length of the whole space to give two arenas of unequal size (the length of each being the width of the whole arena), thus creating a primary arena and a secondary area. Recent developments in the UK (ie Birmingham National Indoor Arena, **13**, and Sheffield Arena) support a horseshoe shape with seating on three sides only.

The advantages of dividing an arena are considered to be substantial. It should lead to a more intensive use of the building with enhanced income.

The divisible arena concept potentially offers cheaper bookings to a whole range of arena users and event sponsors. It is anticipated that many new kinds of events, sports entertainments and competitions would be generated once the facility were available.

The dividing screen
Success depends on the effectiveness of the dividing screen, on its capital cost and operating simplicity. The basic decision to be taken concerns the degree of sound separation required with the limitations that this imposes on the programme of events.

Other equipment
It is convenient to think of the two arenas as twins, and even 'identical twins', each fitted out with identical electronic score boards, commentary boxes and TV

points. However, except for major arenas this may be neither necessary nor economic. Screening off upper tiers of seats also helps to reduce the scale for smaller events.

Large sports halls and compact arenas
The current UK standard size for large sports halls of 36.5 × 32 m is prohibitively short for big-pitch indoor sports events and generally permits very limited spectator accommodation. These halls are therefore unsuitable for most of the local range of spectator events such as indoor soccer, hockey, handball and full-size gymnastics.

In many European countries, large rectangular-shaped sports halls have long been the norm, eg the IAKS Planning Guidelines for Sports Halls recommends a standard size of 27 × 45 × 7 m, divisible into three small halls.

There are advantages to be gained by lengthening and varying the proportions of new large sports halls by adopting 'medium hall' width and greater length to provide more opportunities to play the local spectator events listed above. For district and regional arenas an elongated shape offers:

- A more economic structural roof span
- Increased opportunities for sports development at levels from recreational up to national competition
- A more extensive range of spectator events and potential sponsorship.

2.9 Ancillary accommodation
An arena must have sufficient and satisfactory ancillary accommodation to support the areas devoted to competition (or entertainment) and spectators. The ancillary accommodation requirements common to all sports are outlined below and located on the circulation – or 'balloon' – diagrams, **11**, **14**, **15**. There may be specific requirements for events in a particular sport. Arena designers are advised to approach relevant national governing bodies of sport to obtain any other necessary details for a specific project.

Storage
Secure storage accommodation should be provided for all necessary sports equipment (including temporary floor surfaces), concert/convention equipment, workshop equipment, mechanical and electrical tools and the like.

Examples of typical categories of sports equipment to be stored in an arena are:

- Specialised items belonging to the arena or brought in by event promoters
- Transportable equipment relevant to a range of different sports (eg scoreboards, officials' tables and chairs, movable screens, presentation podia, barriers/restraining ropes, sectioned arena perimeter walls)
- Items not belonging to the arena but hired in association with special event contractors – to be stored securely, but for a short duration.

The minimum area of storage for a 10,000 seat arena is approximately 2000 sq m.

The storage can be on more than one level of the arena but should be located with ease of use in mind. For instance, heavy and bulky equipment should be stored at arena floor level.

The equipment storage space requirements for sports events in the arena include:

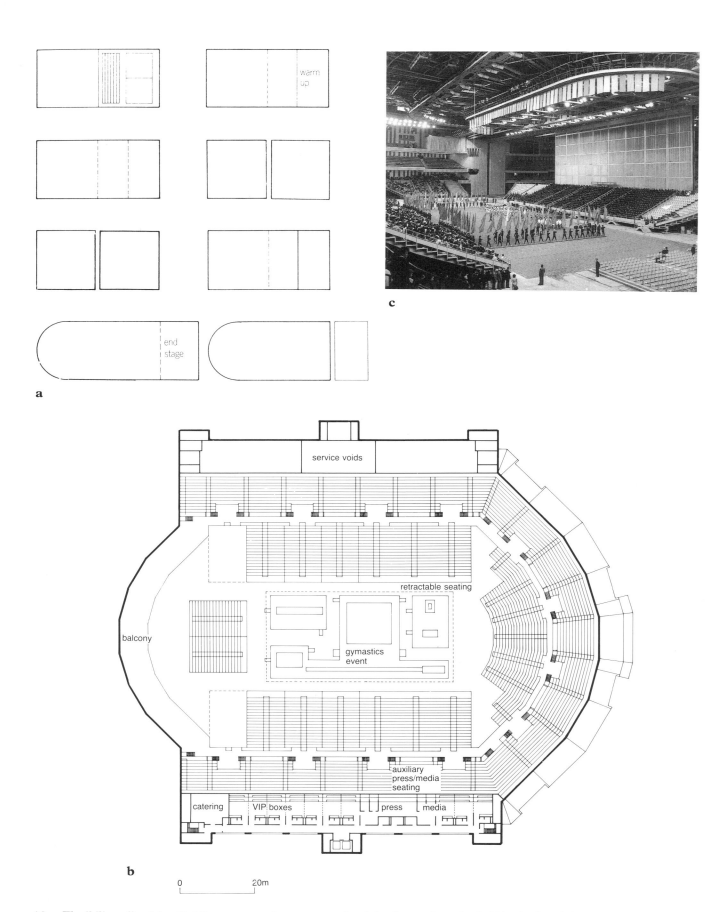

a

b

c

0   20m

13a *Flexibility offered by dividing an area;* **b,** *an example of the 'horse-shoe plan' (Birmingham's National Indoor Arena, architects HOK Inc and the Percy Thomas Partnership);* **c,** *indoor arena in Moscow showing the movable partition across the middle*

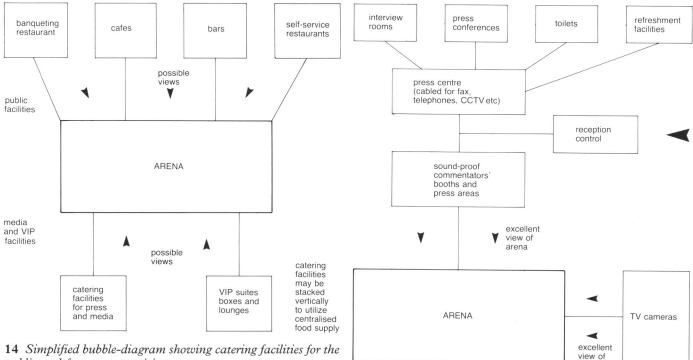

14 *Simplified bubble-diagram showing catering facilities for the public and for events participants*

15 *Circulation diagram of press and media accommodation*

- The permanent equipment storage space should be rectangular in plan and with sufficient headroom to allow access for forklift trucks.
- Direct access should be available to the storage space from outside (minimum width 3 m and a height to suit forklift trucks).
- The store should have at least two secure access points to the competition area (minimum width 4.5 m).
- Another store should be large enough to house securely all necessary itinerant equipment immediately before and after any event likely to be included in the arena programme. This overnight and short-duration storage should be separate from the permanent equipment storage space.
- Fire-resistant and protected stores are necessary to house all foam mats or other non-fire-retardant equipment. As part of the fire precautions, this storage must be situated on an outside wall of the arena building for direct ventilation and access. Only combustion-modified foam should be used and stored, as in gymnastics and other sports equipment. Permanent equipment associated with the more intensively used adjacent sports hall (see 'Warm-up areas' below) should be stored separately.
- Temporary seats, demountable staging and associated fittings and ramps should be stored separately. Separate provision should also be made for housing any transportable or retractable seating units and equipment associated with non-sports events.

As a general rule, storage space should be located and designed so that when emptied parts of it can be used as multi-purpose overflow space for other amenities, such as hospitality, displays, meetings and competition assembly points.

Administration and meetings space
It is very important to differentiate between essential space for both of the following complementary groups:

- Arena operational management staff

- Events administrators – who require additional and partially separated accommodation.

Arena operational management and staff A separate area of the arena should be provided for the arena operational staff. It should be secure and self-contained and have direct access from outside the arena. Administrative offices are for the use of the management staff in the running of the arena. Although box offices need to be accessible to the public for the purchase of tickets, other offices do not and should be capable of being made secure from the public during all events.

Staff accommodation will vary depending on the size of the arena. The following is a guide.

Administrative staff For an indoor type 1 arena, a suite of offices is needed for the arena manager and secretary, a deputy manager, two house managers plus clerk, two supervisors and a team of three secretaries, clerks and a receptionist.

Staff facilities Separate mess and locker room facilities may be required for various disciplines of arena staff (including part-time staff when the arena is in full use). These facilities may also be used as briefing rooms.

Security and control rooms An arena should have two control rooms located adjacent to a security administration room. One of them, the security room, should have closed-circuit TV monitors and house the systems relating to security, lighting and fire. It will contain up to five staff at any one time, including the arena fire officer.

The second control room should have a view of the performance area through double-glazed, one-way windows. It houses equipment for operating the air conditioning, lighting and public address systems and will also contain up to five staff at any one time.

Office accommodation is also needed for the permanent senior security officers and secretary who will administer the part-time stewards and uniformed officers involved with the spectators at any event. The accommodation should be directly accessible from outside the arena and should be used as a checkpoint if emergency teams are needed at the arena. An open access road needs to be provided for ambulance, fire brigade, police and security vehicles. Sniffer dog handlers should also arrive at this checkpoint for briefing prior to search.

Maintenance engineers/technicians accommodation An engineering workshop is required for up to 20 engineers and technicians. A separate office is required for the engineering manager, deputy manager, technical clerk, and secretary.

Cleaners' accommodation An office is needed for the supervisor (and secretary) for up to 20 cleaners, depending on the arena size.

Events administration

Administration, general office and conference space is necessary during sports events for the event organisers (who are often the international or national governing body officials, including honorary and part-timers), promoters, participants and media.

Common facilities needed for all sports are:

- Reception areas for athletes, teams and officials
- International federation office and suite
- Event organiser's offices, including fully equipped secretariat, possibly off the operational staff offices
- Event director's office and meeting room (also for governing body of sport)
- Promoters' suite
- Conference and meeting rooms for up to 250 delegates or members
- Coaching and team meeting accommodation
- Competitors' lounge
- Judges', referees' and umpires' lounge
- Marshal's room
- Jury room
- Technical rooms for checking equipment and weighing in
- Translators and interpreters office
- Photographic studio and darkroom
- Doping control rooms
- Storage.

It is not necessary to provide all this space separately, provided there is sufficient flexibly designed multi-use floor space which can be adapted during major events. The accommodation should be in a self-contained backstage area away from the general public and with a secure route to the arena areas.

Changing rooms

Changing rooms should be planned for the utmost flexibility in meeting the requirements of competitors, coaches and officials for any individual sports event likely to be held. In addition to the dedicated changing rooms, other accommodation should be available in the form of separate undesignated rooms which can be allocated as additional changing facilities or as some of the events administration spaces listed above. All these rooms should have secure access to the permanent changing rooms.

Types of changing rooms are:

- Communal changing rooms for approximately 15–20 users, with separate rooms for males, females and match officials and interchangeable male or female overflow capacity ('buffer' rooms)
- Exclusive team rooms for 10–12 players, with toilets suitable for the disabled
- Individual 'star' changing rooms for 1–2 people
- Officials and/or coaches rooms for 3–4 people (these rooms could double up as competition team offices and first aid posts)
- Small rooms to be fitted out as dressing rooms for entertainers.

Specific needs for all changing rooms include showers, toilets, lockers and purified drinking water. Sauna facilities capable of holding at least four people should be provided for weight-related sports. They may be located in one of the changing areas.

Warm-up areas

Warm-up facilities are necessary for participants' use before a competition starts. They should be totally separate from the competition area but near to it. Specific warm-up requirements for individual sports should be checked.

When not needed for warm-up, the facilities can be used:

- As a sports hall for community sports and recreation programmes
- As an overflow space for preliminary rounds of competitions which require multiple-court provision
- As a self-contained mini-arena
- For non-sports activities such as conventions and exhibitions.

The size and other details of the warm-up area depend on the scale of the arena where the events are held. Some economy of shared space is possible where dimensions and events allow.

When not being used for events warm-up, community sports use is particularly recommended for this area but the control, staffing and security implications of this alternative use must be carefully considered at the design stage.

Doping control and medical facilities

Separate facilities are needed at any arena for dope testing, medical care and physiotherapy.

Doping control A doping control station is now an essential feature of any modern arena used for sports events. It should be situated close to the competitors' exit into the arena. The details of this accommodation will be as described in Chapter 93.

Medical room The medical room should be approximately 40 sq m with a waiting room of about 20 sq m. See also Chapter 92.

Physiotherapy room The physiotherapy room should be capable of accommodating 20 people at any one time. It should have its own changing facilities for men and women. A minimum area of 80 sq m is needed.

Medical centre for general public A separate medical unit is needed for spectators, located near to the emergency checkpoint so that it can be found easily and with direct access to the outside for ambulances. It should have access to lifts (capable of taking a stretcher) and staircases linking it with other floor levels. It will also be beneficial for staff if it has easy access to the competitors' medical unit (from which the public must be strictly prohibited at all times).

An area of approximately 200 sq m is needed for a medical centre for a major arena, equipped in consultation with the local medical officer for health and bodies like the St John's Ambulance Brigade who, in the UK, will probably staff and service the centre.

Catering and hospitality
Different types of catering facilities are needed for different types of users and different occasions. The following accommodation is needed for an indoor arena type 1.

- A dedicated and comprehensive facility (ie fast food, cafeteria, restaurant and bars) to serve event participants such as players, officials and coaches in the backstage area. It should be private and secure from the public but available for public use.
- Fast food outlets and vending concessionaires selling food, ice creams and non-alcoholic drinks to the public. They should be sited in the general circulation areas and it is suggested that arena designs should allow 10 m wide circulation areas so that other people can easily move past customers using the fast food outlets and other merchandising points.
- Cafeteria-type self-service restaurants for 150 covers.
- A full banqueting restaurant to serve up to 350 covers with a bar area. It should be possible to subdivide the restaurant into three separate areas of equal size.
- A bar area for the general public (including cellar for beer storage).
- A wine bar/coffee bar meeting place.
- A catering facility to support the sponsor's boxes, VIPs' facilities, suites and lounges.
- A catering facility to support the media and press.

The location of catering facilities, particularly the banqueting restaurant, should allow good views of the arena performance area. For ease of management, it will be beneficial if the catering facilities, including the catering office but with the exception of fast food outlets, are all contained in a core block extending vertically through all levels of the arena. If and where catering areas overlook the competition space, glazing should be tinted to prevent glare and light spread into the spectator blocks when the general arena lighting is dimmed.

Merchandise outlets
In addition to the catering outlets, provision of merchandising points should be considered – at locations in the arena building which are easily accessible to the public. An appropriate area for each of these points would be 10 sq m including secure storage space. Examples of merchandise include:

- Candies, sweets and soft drinks
- Newspapers and periodicals (but not cigarettes and tobacco)
- Leisurewear and equipment
- Travel agency
- Local information and tourist centre.

3 References and further information

Essential planning guides for the layout and design of changing rooms are published in *Dossier: Palazzetti Dello Sport in Spaziosports*, Vol. II, in No. 3, September 1983 and in *SASH Design Guide 1*, Sports Council, London (1987).

IAKS, *Planning Guidelines for Sports Halls*.

John, G and Sheard, R, *Stadia: A Design and Development Guide*, Butterworth Architecture (1994).

Sports Council, *Arenas: A Planning, Design and Mangement Guide*, Sports Council, London (1989).

51
Ancillary and projectile halls

Christopher Harper

1 *Community use of the ancillary hall at the Oak Tree Lane Centre, Derby. Photo: C J Harper*

1 Introduction

In addition to the main hall, many sports centres have an ancillary multi-purpose hall, or halls, which considerably extend their use and enable a more varied and responsive programme of activities to be offered. In terms of plan form and function they fall into three categories:

- Ancillary practice hall of square or occasionally double square plan dimensions
- Projectile halls with long narrow dimensions required for linear sports
- 'Add-on' sports halls, which are usually low specification halls primarily for popular team sports.

Ancillary practice halls are by far the most numerous. They can be used for a wide range of sports, arts and social activities and are discussed in detail below. Projectile halls have a more restricted use and are unsuitable for more than a handful of sports.

1.1 Ancillary halls

Planning

These versatile spaces are appropriate for sports with less demanding spatial requirements than those normally accommodated in a main hall. Typically they include the combat sports (judo, karate, kendo and boxing and wrestling), table tennis, carpet bowls, movement and dance and practice in a number of sports ranging from gymnastics to fencing. They are also valuable for meetings, receptions, lectures, drama and music rehearsal and performance and can be suitable for pre-school playgroups. The inclusion of a hall of a friendlier scale than that of the main sports space opens up the centre to a greater range of community participation, **1**.

Plan dimensions can vary but the following sizes are suggested and have been adopted in a wide range of centres:

- 10 × 10 m (approx 33 × 33 ft) minimum 9 × 9 m (approx 30 × 30 ft)
- 15 × 12 m (approx 49 × 39 ft)
- 21–24 x 12 m (approx 69–78 × 39 ft) – sizes which can be divided.

The preferred dimensions are 10 × 10 m (approx 33 × 33 ft) which permit a 1 m (approx 3 ft 4 in) minimum safety zone for martial arts. The larger hall sizes provide generous safety margins and are sometimes capable of being subdivided. The effectiveness of subdivision, however, is entirely dependent on the specification of the partition or screen which, unlike main hall dividing netting, has to be solid, robust and of good acoustic properties. These larger halls, although useful for sport,

can be less appropriate for arts and social events and their possible inclusion should be weighed against the advantages offered by a lower cost add-on hall together with a smaller ancillary hall of good specification.

The minimum clear height required is 3.5 m (approx 11 ft 6 in) rising to 4.5 m (approx 15 ft) if drama, movement and dance and the martial arts are to have unrestricted use. If a larger 'double square' hall is considered the clear height could rise to at least 6.1 m (approx 20 ft) for recreation level badminton.

Ancillary halls require easy access from changing rooms and wherever possible should back on to the main hall store for shared use of equipment, particularly crash mats and table tennis tables. Where it is not possible to achieve direct access the hall will require its own store and a generously dimensioned circulation route for easy transfer of equipment from the principal storage area. In considering the minimum requirements for sports storage alone allow a rule of thumb figure of 10% of the hall floor area.

In order that an ancillary hall can provide full flexibility its potential for arts use and social events must not be overlooked. A location close to the main foyer with its own separate and secure entrance lobby will make it possible to programme non-sports activities with a reasonable degree of segregation. A bar and servery may also be required but where they cannot be combined with the central refreshments areas a separate space, which can be fitted out as a bar and servery for specific functions, backed by a service route may be appropriate.

If drama or dance practice or performances are proposed, **2**, the plan should ensure that there is a segregated route for performers to the back stage area. Alternatively, extra changing (dressing) rooms, toilets and an assembly area can be provided adjacent to the hall, **3**. Refer to Chapter 52, Dance studios and workshops.

The other use which can require additional support accommodation specific to the ancillary hall is pre-school playgroups. Proper provision should include a generous toy cupboard and en-suite toilets equipped for nappy changing and a sink for wet play activities. Refer to Chapter 48, Children in sports buildings.

Walls, ceilings and floors

Finishes specification requirements are similar to the main hall. There should be no low level projections but where joinery or other fittings unavoidably stand proud of the wall plane they must have radiused or splayed corners and

2 *Drama practice in the purpose-designed Sports/Arts Workshop at the Belgrave Centre, Tamworth. Photo: D J Butler*

be detailed as safely as possible. There is greater scope for introducing full natural lighting than in the main sports space, except when the hall is primarily a drama workshop when dark wall and ceiling surfaces will be preferred for total lighting control. Even then it may be possible to introduce shuttered windows at low level to give contact with the exterior. In all other cases natural lighting is essential, either introduced at roof or high level for sport or at high/low level for arts and social purposes where windows are more easily screened. These halls can be used for seated audiences and assemblies and a safely detailed bash (dado) rail may be considered to prevent a tide mark of damage to finishes from chair backs.

Ceiling surfaces should, if possible, have sound absorbing properties to control reverberation time; this is particularly important with low occupancy levels.

Floor surface selection must respond to the range of uses envisaged in the design brief. A selection based on sports requirements alone will dictate a finish that is durable, warm, easily maintained and provides sufficient slip for popular activities like table tennis. The most extreme requirement is probably posed by playgroups where these characteristics must be sought together with a degree of impact cushioning. Waterproof sheeting will have to be used to protect the floor surface if sand and water play take place and storage should be detailed to accept this temporary 'finish'. Unfortunately, carpeting is usually ruled out by the need for easy maintenance and limited

slip. Other factors inevitable with social functions are that some types of footwear will damage the floor surface and some patrons will probably smoke, despite publicised restrictions.

Environmental services requirements
For general details of environmental services recommendations refer to Chapters 60 and 61.

The minimum levels likely to be acceptable for sports are:

- Heating   15°C
- Lighting   300 lux
- Ventilation   1.5 air changes/hour

which could need augmenting for a full range of activities to:

- Heating   21°C
- Lighting   Additional decorative fittings or drama lighting
- Ventilation   3 air changes/hour or more with low background noise

The degree of sophistication required will relate primarily to non-sports use. Heating requirements will range from levels suitable for small children and adult sedentary pursuits to vigorous sports activity and the system selected will need to be highly responsive. It is better to avoid low level heat emitting surfaces but when they are specified it is advisable to set panels or radiators in recesses and ensure that they are sized for safe surface temperature. The same applies to ventilation. A wide range of air changes may be required, including the need to remove tobacco smoke and ventilate the room effectively for discos and dances. With the low background noise levels preferred for the arts it will be seen that effective heating and ventilation of the ancillary hall poses a most demanding design brief.

Lighting systems will also be influenced by the range of proposed uses. An overall illumination system is needed for sport but has to be backed up with decorative lighting for dances and social events with more specific lighting for disco and drama.

1.2 Projectile halls
Projectile halls or long galleries were once regularly included in the accommodation of large sports centres. They were specifically intended for linear sports – shooting with firearms and air weapons, archery, cricket, 4, and golf practice – and fully enclosed spaces designed to meet the standards of safety and security demanded by shooting. However, it came to be realised that the environmental problems caused by the discharge of firearms were incompatible with other activities because of the difficulties of removing particles of munitions propellant and lead, particularly from suspended tracked netting. It is now recommended that shooting indoors takes place only in dedicated ranges (see Chapter 86). Where projectile halls form part of the design brief their dimensions are weighted towards the needs of archery, cricket and bowls. Other sports which can then utilise the hall as overspill space are indoor cricket, fencing, table tennis, keep fit, martial arts and practice for golf and gymnastics. The accompanying diagram suggests dimensions compatible with these key and secondary uses, 5.

Safety remains a prime planning requirement and any lateral accesses should be limited to the end of the hall,

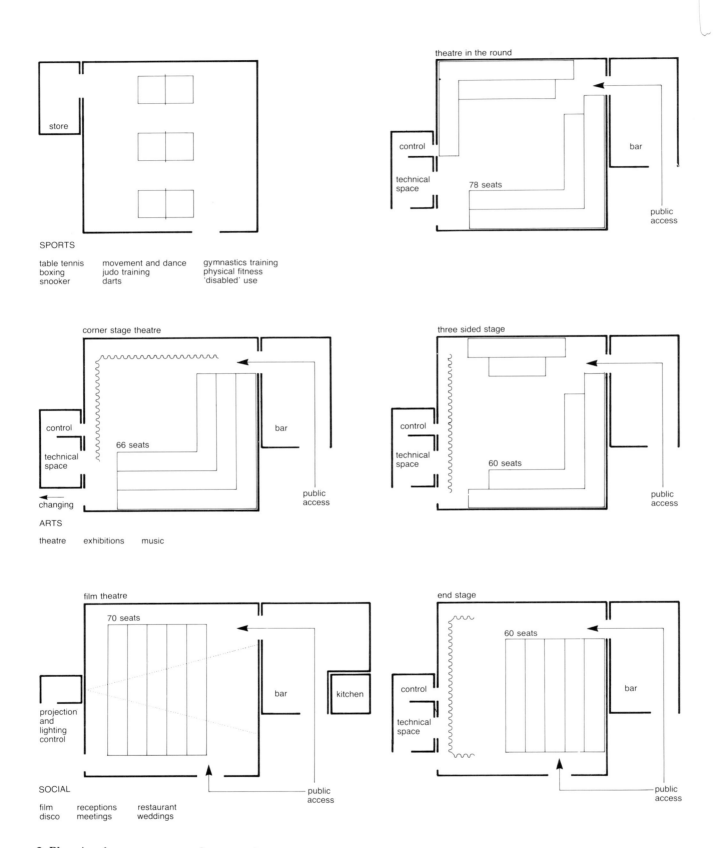

SPORTS

table tennis	movement and dance	gymnastics training
boxing	judo training	physical fitness
snooker	darts	'disabled' use

theatre in the round

control

technical space

78 seats

bar

public access

corner stage theatre

control

technical space

66 seats

bar

public access

changing

ARTS

theatre   exhibitions   music

three sided stage

control

technical space

60 seats

public access

film theatre

70 seats

projection and lighting control

bar

kitchen

public access

SOCIAL

film	receptions	restaurant
disco	meetings	weddings

end stage

control

technical space

60 seats

bar

public access

3 *Planning for sports, arts and community use*

4 *Cricket nets dictate extra height but can also be used for golf practice. Photo: Sports Council Publications*

behind the archery shooting line. An equipment store will be needed for:

- Cricket – bowlers and batting mats, wickets, balls and bats
- Archery – 1.28 m (approx 4.2 ft) bosses and stands, bow racks and tackle boxes
- Golf – mats and target tees, clubs and balls
- Indoor bowls – compromised length carpet, bowls and shoes
- Short mat bowls – 13.72 × 1.83 m (45 × 6 ft) carpet bowls and shoes
- Fencing – metallic pistes, cable drums, 'boxes' and weapons.

Additional space should be allocated if further sports are included. There are no special requirements for ceiling, wall and floor surfaces other than those of serviceability and ease of maintenance.

Environmental services should include an overall lighting scheme (with fittings designed for protection from projectiles) which is suitable for the activities proposed. An alternative form of protection is to line out the ceiling plane with netting as a permanent fixture. Heating and ventilation should be provided in accordance with the activities and occupancy rates involved. See Chapters 60 and 61 for further details.

1.3 Add-on halls

This term describes an extra sports hall, ancillary to the principal multi-purpose sports space. Add-on halls, most usually of four- but also of three-badminton court size, have been built on to established sports centres to provide extra playing area for popular games like five-a-side soccer.

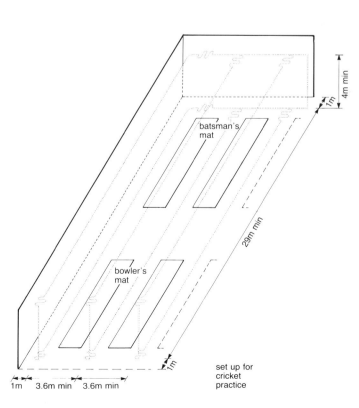

batsman's mat

bowler's mat

4m min

1m

29m min

1m

1m   3.6m min   3.6m min

set up for cricket practice

5 *Suggested dimensions for a projectile hall*

6 *Membrane structures have been used successfully as add-on halls to take team games out of the principal sports hall. Photo: C J Harper*

They may duplicate the play dimensions of the main hall but their specification is invariably lower in accordance with their more limited function. Surfaces must be durable and safely detailed but services are simplified to give only background levels of heating – 12°C with lighting and ventilation to the minimum standards of 300 lux and 1–1.5 air changes per hour. Fabric halls of even simpler environmental standards have also adequately fulfilled the need for overspill sports space and enjoyed high levels of utilisation, **6**.

52
Dance studios and workshops

Mark Foley

1 Introduction

This chapter deals with the particular needs of movement and dance where specialised spaces are required. Generally, these specialised spaces may be provided as ancillary facilities to a sports hall in which the particular requirements for dance activities cannot be accommodated without undue conflict or compromise. To a lesser extent these ancillary halls may also accommodate compact sport, eg table tennis and martial arts. Chapter 36 in this volume gives details of movement and dance activities.

Facilities may also be provided in an entirely separate context, such as a comunity or church hall (see References and further advice), or as part of commercial dance or fitness centres.

In recent years, commercial dance centres have increased in number. This can be explained not only by the current awareness of fitness but also by their function as a social centre, often mainly for women. The image of 'keeping fit' has changed over the years and newer types of exercise such as body conditioning, jazz dance, **1**, or aerobics, **2**, have become extremely popular. These activities have attracted many women principally because of their:

- Use of local facilities
- Inexpensiveness
- Good teaching/coaching structures
- Capacity to cater for all ages and abilities
- Ability to take place without predetermined numbers.

Dance activities cover a wide range of disciplines (listed in Chapter 36 in this volume), not all of which require

2 Photo: Richard J Sowersby

specialist studio facilities. However, in the struggle to attain ever higher levels of achievement and perfection, many related disciplines such as figure ice skating or rhythmic gymnastics have come to appreciate the benefits of a dance training as a means of improving technique and gaining greater control over the body's movement.

Dedicated studio spaces may be required in order that participants have sufficiently expansive space in which to move, are able to concentrate or work in privacy and have access to the facilities and equipment needed to practice a particular discipline.

Chapter 53 in this volume, Sports arts workshops, deals with movement and dance in spaces that are primarily dedicated towards community arts uses such as joint-use educational studios or theatre rehearsal spaces. For arts use of main sports hall see Chapter 49 in this volume.

2 Studio shape and dimensions

Spacial dimensions in dance studios relate to the requirements of participants when performing, for example on stage. A medium scale ballet company often requires a minimum performing area of 12 × 12 m.

It is useful to refer to the space module diagram in Chapter 36 in this volume (illustration 5) as a way of

1 Photo: Dance City

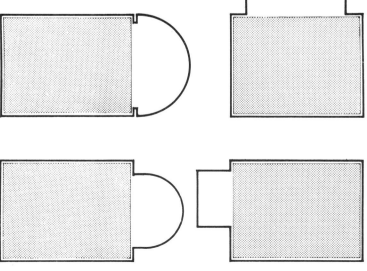

3 Examples of good dance spaces where the square or rectangle are clearly defined. Diagram: Mark Foley

assessing the numbers of participants that can be accommodated at any one time.

The importance of space proportions and quality of environment cannot be overemphasised; see Section 5 below.

Most disciplines rely on a square or rectangular space format as a means of providing basic orientation within the space, **3**. Classical ballet technique, for example, is based on a cuboidal spatial framework providing front, back, two sides, up and down. Other disciplines use space more freely, although there always remains the need to orientate within a given space. It is therefore generally desirable to avoid curving, non-parallel or asymmetrical walls, or over-elongated and badly proportioned spaces, **4**. Dance studios are generally spaces for creative work and concentration and it is important not to resolve the technical requirements of the studio into what might appear a utilitarian box. The proportions of the space and quality of lighting (both natural and artificial) are of great importance. Studios should be light, airy and uncluttered, providing an inspiring place in which to work, **5**.

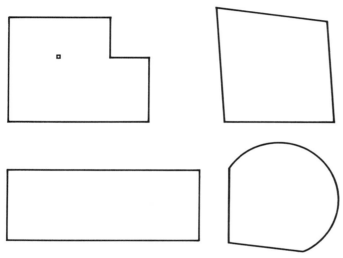

4 *Examples of unacceptable dance studio shapes. Avoid curving, non-parallel or overelongated badly proportioned spaces. Diagram: Mark Foley*

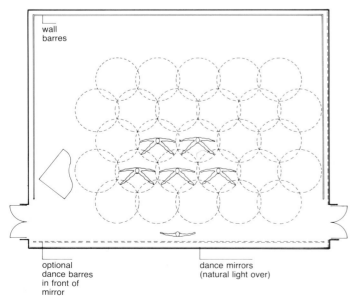

wall
barres

optional
dance barres
in front of
mirror

dance mirrors
(natural light over)

5 *Dance studios are generally for creative work and concentration. It is important not to resolve the technical requirements into a utilitarian box. Diagram: Mark Foley*

Four sizes are suggested:

- The *small practice studio* (9 × 9–12 m by 3.5 m high) will be used mostly for practice and exercise by small groups of up to 12–15 people, for personal tuition or when privacy is required. The overall dimensions of the space limit numbers and the ability to move expansively in all directions.
- The *standard dance studio*, **6** (12 × 15 by 4.5 m high), as the name suggests, is an all-purpose studio which may accommodate 30–35 people in a class with exercises ranging from lying on the floor to barre use and extended sequences of movement. The diagonal across the studio is often used to maximise the length of dance sequences in contemporary dance classes.
- The *large standard dance studio* (15 × 17 by 5.0 m high) is similar in use to the standard studio but gives additional free area for movement. It can also be used as a rehearsal space where props and sets may be accommodated or alternatively as a space for studio performances where public audiences may be admitted.
- The *large-scale rehearsal studio*, (18 × 18–20 m by at least 6 m high) is a more specialist requirement for large scale ballet companies or larger scale events such as training courses, rallies and festivals; see also Chapter 50 in this volume.

When studios are being provided in converted buildings it is important to recognise the minimum clear width dimensions given above in order not to compromise the use of the space. Columns that fall inside these dimensions are interruptive and hazardous and therefore totally unacceptable for all forms of dance.

2.1 Relationship with other spaces

When planning new facilities, it is important that noise transmission to and from other spaces does not interfere with the internal environment of each dance studio. The building layout and form of construction should be carefully considered to avoid these potential problems. The sound attenuation of partitions should be sufficient to ensure maintenance of a noise level of NR 30.

Circulation routes outside studios should also be considered from the hygiene point of view. Many dance and movement activities are carried out in bare feet or with little protection to the feet. Routes between changing rooms and studios should therefore be organised as 'clean' circulation. See also advice on floors in Chapter 64 in this volume.

Sports and arts activities often have common ancillary needs such as changing rooms, showers, toilets and possibly a bar, refreshment and crèche facilities.

2.2 Studio layout

Large dance studios will require at least two entrances or exits to the space, depending on the safe travel distance to protected escape routes. If in doubt, check with the Fire Officer. Doors should be wide enough to accept a piano, which can sometimes be a grand piano.

Viewing galleries, where provided, should be discreet and at high level in order not to distract participants.

2.3 Internal environment

For general details of environmental services recommendations refer to Chapters 60 and 61.

Lighting

Windows which provide a view out are desirable providing privacy can also be maintained. Natural daylighting must

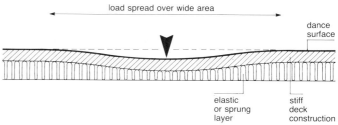

6 A dance studio with natural light windows positioned above the dance mirrors to give a good image of the dancers in the mirrors. Photo: Mark Foley

7 Area-elastic floor system. A stable surface on which to balance, with underlying cushioning. The elastic layer can be constructed in many different ways. Diagram: Mark Foley

be carefully considered. South light can be dramatic, but if uncontrolled problems of heat gain and glare will result. The ideal lighting is to have a north light positioned over the top of the dance mirrors (see above). This allows light to fall on to the front and sides of the participant when facing the mirror, producing a clear, well-illuminated image. Large areas of glazing on the opposite side will throw the participant's image into silhouette and should be avoided, **6**.

For recommendations regarding artificial lighting refer to the lighting section of Chapter 36, and to Chapter 60.

Heating and ventilation

The rapid environmental changes that can occur through intense activity in dance studios can impose heavy demands on heating and ventilation installations. Running costs may be high if installations are designed to accommodate maximum demand at all times. It may be worth considering heating and ventilating systems that can be boosted for short periods as and when necessary.

Heating by means of hot water radiators gives a balance between radiant and convected heat and generally provides the most economic and comfortable environment for dance, particularly in small studios.

Mechanical ventilation systems should run quietly, including any fans that may be fixed to convectors, and should be designed for a NR level of no more than 25.

Acoustics

The acoustics of the space are critically important and in some cases acoustic treatment may be needed to control reflected sound. The acoustics of the space should be designed for good music reproduction while also being intelligible for speech. See References and further advice below for more detailed information on the acoustic treatment of spaces. Also refer to Chapters 49 and 60.

2.4 Floors

It is vital that movement and dance activities are provided with properly designed, semi-sprung floor systems in order to avoid the development of stress and injury to dancers while also providing a level of comfort and performance that will benefit the activity. There are a few exceptions, such as clog dancing, where semi-sprung floor systems may not be required.

A variety of suitable flooring systems are available under the general heading of 'area-elastic' floors. These are floor systems with a relatively stable surface or deck and an underlying springing or elastic suspension system to absorb the impact of the dancer's body, **7**.

There are two important aspects to the design of floors for movement and dance activities:

- The surface treatement (slip or grip) of the deck on which the activity occurs
- The underlying composition and suspension system forming the area-elastic springing of the floor.

Although there are no design standards written specifically for movement and dance activities the equivalent of a floor designed to the standard DIN 1803: Part II provides an acceptable degree of 'give' and 'resilience' and level of performance for most movement and dance activities including ballroom dancing.

Movement and dance activities can be divided into what might be described as 'hard shoe', 'soft shoe' and 'barefoot' activities. The surface treatment of each of these can vary according to the particular activity, depending upon the degree of 'slip' or 'grip' required of the surface.

Traditionally, dance floors have had a hardwood surface but a wider range of flooring systems providing similar performance characteristics is now available, including the use of vinyl-type surfaces on wood composition and foam bed layers. Natural wood floor finishes should be of a close-grained splinter free timber, such as maple, with a finish treatment suited to the main activity. Dancers employing different dance forms may prefer particular floor surfaces, such as a traditional timber strip floor or vinyl dance surface. These should be checked before a final decision is made.

Where the different surface requirements of bare foot and soft shoe activities conflict, the problem can sometimes be overcome by overlaying a temporary vinyl-type dance surface dedicated to a particular use over the permanent finish. Consideration should then be given, however, to the time required to effect this change-over and the staff required to undertake the task. Storage space will also be needed to store the surface when not in use.

2.5 Equipment

Dance barres

Dance barres mounted around the walls are a useful accessory, particularly for ballet, to provide support during training and warm-up. The height of the barre may vary depending on the age groups of users. For children up to the age of about 12–14 years the barre should be at 0.914 m from floor level and for users above this age group at a height of 1.067 m. Where a studio is used by all age groups

8 *Wall barres are usually purpose designed to cater for different age groups. Photo: Mark Foley*

9 *Dance barres at the London School of Contemporary Dance. Vertical supports must be fixed through the dance floor to the structural slab below, leaving the floating surface to vibrate freely. Photo: Mark Foley*

barres at both heights can be provided through the use of purpose made brackets, **8** and **9**.

The distance of the barre from the wall should be a minimum of 250 mm. It is recommended that the diameter of the taller barre should be 45 mm while the lower barre should not be less than 32 mm. Timber barres of splinter-free wood, such as maple, with supported lap joints free of fixings on the top side are generally preferred. Wall brackets should be robust and securely fixed. Where floor supports are also provided, they should be fixed to the structural floor base leaving suspended floors to move independently of the support.

It is also important to remember that dance barres fixed along a wall will reduce the amount of activity space by 300 mm along each side.

Portable barres may be used if permanent ones would conflict with other uses. They should be designed with a stable base that does not interfere with the dancer's feet. Where good free-standing barres can be provided, they can be positioned in front of the dance mirrors to provide additional wall barre space and some physical protection to the mirrors.

Mirrors
The use of mirrors is of great assistance in the training and practice of many forms of dance. Mirrors enable the participant to watch his or her movement or body alignment while imprinting the feeling into 'muscle memory'.

One long wall of the studio should be fitted with mirrors along its length to a height of at least 2 m from the floor enabling participants to watch themselves wherever they are positioned in the studio. Sometimes a second wall at right angles to the first can also be fitted with mirrors to enable dancers to check their side view during a class. Mirrors need not be taken down to floor level but can stop at about 300 mm above floor level. See also studio layout above regarding windows in relation to mirrors.

Mirrors should be mounted on to rigid backing panels, preferably glued in position with an appropriate mastic adhesive and continuously restrained along the top and bottom edges. Point fixings drilled through the mirror glass should be avoided as this is often an area of weakness which may cause the mirror to crack. The panels should be butt-jointed side by side to provide a continuous un-distorted image from one panel to the next.

The designer should also consider the risk of accidental damage, either from shared use with other sports activities or accidental bodily impact which could result in injury (see *BS 6262: 1982 Code of Practice for Glazing in Buildings*). There are also alternatives to mirror glass comprising mirrored perspex on a foam board backing but the resulting image is not as clear.

Musical accompaniment and video equipment
Musical accompaniment is provided either live or in pre-recorded form. Live accompaniment is generally provided by a musician at a piano but can be percussion, drums, tabla or stringed instruments. The position of the musician is normally to one side, where he or she has a good view of both the teacher and class in order to be able to judge the tempo. Pre-recorded music is generally controlled directly by the teacher and is often provided by the teacher using a personal portable system. It can be an advantage to have the facility to plug into a built-in amplifier and loudspeaker system. Security and risk of vandalism are issues which should then be carefully considered.

10 *The use of video equipment as a teaching aid is now becoming more widely practised. It is used for viewing choreographed dance pieces in the studio or instant playback for improving technique. The equipment trolley can be wheeled into a secure store after the dance class. Photo: Mark Foley*

The use of video equipment as a teaching aid is now becoming more widely practised, particularly among professional dance companies, **10**. It is used for viewing dance pieces or parts that need to be learnt in the studio; or for improving technique through filming and instant playback. An effective way of housing this equipment is by mounting video recorders (and sound systems) on to a mobile trolley unit which can then be moved to where it is required and kept in a secure store at other times.

Power sockets should be provided at reasonable intervals around the perimeter of the studio for equipment.

2.6 Secure storage

Secure storage is needed for video and audio equipment, records, tapes, pianos and other musical instruments where they cannot be left in the studio. Additional storage may also be needed for users' own equipment if the room is to permit a variety of uses. Any foam filled equipment or mats, **2**, must be stored in a separate fire resistant store (see Chapter 55 in this volume).

2.7 Rest rooms and first aid

It is useful to provide resting spaces, whether in the form of a common room, lounge area with refreshment facilities or rest places off circulation routes, to allow participants to relax or recuperate after intensive sessions. These spaces should be warm, comfortable and, where possible, provide a quiet place for a short nap.

It is also advisable to provide a small first aid room of sufficient size to accommodate a bed or long couch to provide a first-stop resting place in case of stress, injury or even exhaustion. It should be equipped with a washbasin and first aid kit.

3 References and further advice

Chapter 36, Movement and dance, including references.

Department of Education and Science, *Acoustics in Educational Buildings*, *Building Bulletin 51*, HMSO, London.

Foley, M, *Handbook of Dance Floors*, Dance UK (1991).

Foley, M, *Dance Spaces*, Arts Council of England (1994).

Sports Council, *Small Community Recreation Centres*, *Datasheet 59*, Sports Council, London (1989).

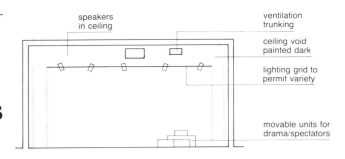

53
Sports arts workshops

Mark Foley

1 Introduction

Arts uses may include drama workshops, small music practices and recitals and possibly exhibitions within hall sizes of 15 × 12-15 and 21–24 m, coinciding with the smaller practice hall suggested in Chapter 52. Dance studios may meet the needs of some arts and community uses as well as those of some sports activities. Care must be taken, however, to assess the needs of each use independently in order not to compromise the primary function of a particular facility. Where necessary the dimensions can be adjusted to suit particular uses.

Arts workshop use will require a lighting grid with a clear headroom of approximately 6.5 m (approx 21.5 ft) and movable curtains on a track around the perimeter, **1**. It should be possible for daylight to be excluded and the room may be conceived as a 'black box' with mechanical ventilation.

1.1 General layout

It is important to establish from the outset the audience seating capacity which the hall should be designed to accommodate and whether it is to be used for public performances; if so a Public Entertainments Licence will be required. Seating capacities will affect the size and possibly influence the layout of the hall and the designer should be familiar with the technical standards that will apply for a Public Entertainment Licence and liaise with the relevant authorities at an early stage.

Where the public are to be admitted the relationship between public and private spaces should be considered. It is often helpful to think of those areas where the public have access as 'front-of-house' and those areas where they do not as 'backstage'. It is also likely there will be some no-go spaces for the public in the front-of-house areas which will be marked 'private' such as the box office and house manager's office.

In premises which will not be licensed and where only small private audiences will be admitted there may be some overlapping of facilities, such as the WC accommodation, which may result in savings. There may also be a corresponding reduction in floor areas for bar and reception areas.

1.2 External considerations

The location and siting of arts facilities are important considerations and, where the public are to be admitted on a regular basis, are fundamental to success. Ease of access, whether by vehicle or on foot is of paramount importance for participants and public alike. Consideration should also be given to car parking standards which the planning authority may set for public venues and separate service access for ease of loading and unloading stage scenery and equipment.

Where the venue is approached from a public open space or street frontage, good visibility of the public foyer

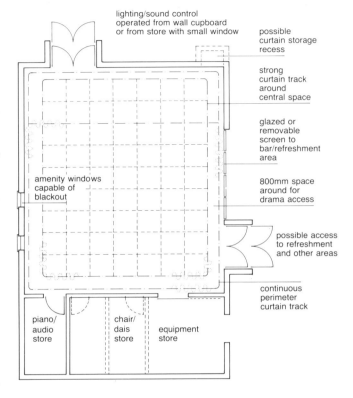

1 *Plans and section of a practice hall/arts workshop*

or reception spaces can do much to convey a sense of life and vitality within the building.

1.3 Public areas

Front-of-house areas typically consist of the main entrance area with facilities that serve as a reception desk or ticket kiosk, cloakrooms and a foyer which should also include refreshment and bar facilities. Access from these areas into the hall should lead directly to audience seating.

Front-of-house spaces should be welcoming and of sufficient capacity to hold the audience prior to entering the hall and during intervals. The public's perception of the quality of the venue will be judged largely on the standards provided and sustained in these areas.

While wishing to present a welcoming aspect to reception desks and ticket kiosks, the need for security should not be underestimated. The ticket position should also be arranged to avoid queues forming across entrance ways or extending outside into the rain.

The WC accommodation for the general public and those with disabilities should be clearly signed. The standard of provision should be calculated to accommodate peak audience or visitor capacities.

1.4 Backstage and service areas

Backstage or service areas typically comprise the dressing rooms, showers and WC facilities for participants, storage space and service access including a scene dock for large items of equipment or scenery. Direct access from these areas to the stage or performing area should be provided. Where possible more than one entrance will facilitate use and alternative layouts in the hall. Curtains or drapes can be used to provide visual masking to stage entrances, although these entrances will need to be provided with doors and possibly lobbies for sound, light and fire isolation.

1.5 The layout of the hall

The layout of the hall will primarily be determined by the relationship between stage or performing area and the audience. Alternative stage and seating formats may be decided upon – whether 'in the round' (also known as arena format), 'thrust stage' or the more conventional 'end stage' format, 2.

In practice, rectangular halls have generally proved to be more flexible than square ones because of the opportunities offered to arrange the stage along either the short or long axis.

Generally the hall will have a flat floor, 3, on which seating or staging rostra can be arranged. For each stage format seating capacities and sightlines will need to be examined.

In some situations, and where finance permits, floor pits which can be covered over when not in use can be used to accommodate small orchestras, stage traps or extended seating arrangements. The inclusion of floor pits will, however, preclude the use of semi-sprung floors and therefore movement and dance as an activity over these areas.

The position of access doorways for audiences, performers and stage equipment will need to be considered in relation to alternative seating and stage layouts, while also providing for means of escape requirements.

Access ways to and from seats and the number of seats in each row must comply with licensing requirements. It is also desirable to enable people with disabilities to sit together with able-bodied friends and not in one area designated for wheelchairs.

The control room or control positions will need to be determined in relation to the stage and seating layout, 3. Control positions require a clear view of the stage area and auditorium. They should be positioned so as not to cause a distraction to the audience. Generally this will be high up

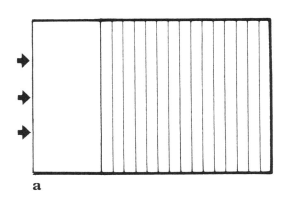

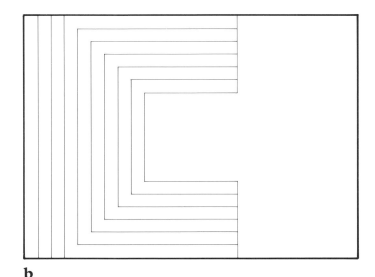

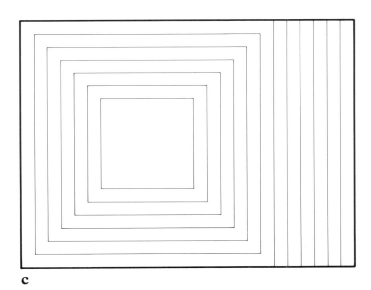

2 *Different stage and audience configurations.* **a** *End stage;* **b** *thrust stage;* **c** *in the round (arena)*

3 *The performing arts and technology studio at the University of Surrey showing wall fittings and the dividing curtain. Photo: Mark Foley*

at the rear of the seating area. Enclosed control rooms are often required to have separate escape routes outside the hall and it is sensible to check this point with the relevant authorities. Where cinema projection is required it will be useful to refer to *Theatres – Planning Guidance for Design and Adaptation* edited by Roderick Ham.

Entrance/escape doors, scene dock and service access
Some of the principles for locating entrances into the hall have already been described. When the hall is being conceived as a black box auditorium care should be given to the detail design of entrances from both front of house and backstage areas to avoid sound and light breakthrough from adjoining areas, particularly when lights are dimmed in the auditorium. Generally this can be achieved by fitting door seals and lobbying the doors or arranging an intermediate corridor space.

Doors from adjoining areas will probably have to be fire rated and fitted with door closers. Closers should be quiet and of the type that will cushion the impact of doors closing when performers gain access to stage areas or latecomers enter the rear of the hall.

Escape exits from the hall should provide good escape in at least two directions. Avoid escape exits for the public in the direction of the stage or backstage areas. These areas can be more prone to fire risk and the positioning of illuminated exit signs by the stage can be a distraction.

One set of access or scene dock doors leading to the outside are essential to enable large pieces of equipment, and even vehicles and concert grand pianos, to be brought in. Ideally, the doors should be at least 1.8 m wide by up to

3 m high. If necessary the upper panels can be hinged separately. They should be draught-proof and not rattle in the wind or be accessible to children who might play against them from outside. Where there is the space, an intervening loading bay/storage area can be a benefit.

In busy venues the value of separate rear service access to bar stores and refreshment areas should not be overlooked.

Hall seating
Alternative seating layouts have been described briefly above. Licensing and fire officers will require auditorium seating to be set in fixed positions or linked together to avoid obstructions to escape routes caused by loose furniture. Good sightlines are important and can be achieved by using mobile or demountable seating modules. These can be arranged in stepped banks using rostra units or retractable seating systems. However, conventional hard, retractable sports hall seating can be uncomfortable over long periods and liable to rattles and creaking. Care should be exercised in selecting a form of seating and support system that is firm, padded and securely braced and free from creaks and other noises. The time and manpower required to rearrange stage and seating configurations must also be considered.

Stage rostra and floors
It should not be assumed that performances or rehearsals will always take place on a raised stage. Raised stage areas are used as a means for improving sightlines and can also be used to define the performing area. Raising the stage

too high, however, sets an uncomfortable barrier between audience and performer. There are now a number of firms specialising in adjustable staging and rostra systems.

Points to watch for in the design of rostra units are strength, stability and adaptability (including height adjustment), compact storage, ease of erection and quiet operation. The masking of exposed sides to stages and rostra is also desirable.

A conflict sometimes arises with the use of semi-sprung floor systems in the arts workshop environment. Certain varieties of semi-sprung flooring systems can be used with seating and staging units that are not unduly heavy so long as they are moved at regular intervals. Heavy equipment will have a dampening effect on a semi-sprung floor, while any equipment placed on such a system will be susceptible to the transmission of impact vibrations through the floor exacerbating creaks and rattles. Where heavy retractable seating units are set up in fixed formats, for example, it may be worth considering solid support 'stops' under those areas, to prevent over compression of the floor under heavy load. Removable channels can also be laid under castors of retractable seating systems to distribute the load and prevent tramlines forming.

Floors should be warm, clean and attractive particularly where they may also be used for barefoot activities such as movement and dance. In the arts workshop environment, however, floors can suffer much abuse from audiences treading in grit from outside, as well as from pieces of equipment being dragged across the surface. Audience gangways should therefore be provided with carpets or protective roll-out surfaces of sufficient weight to prevent them slipping while areas of door matting at the entrance will reduce the amount of grit brought into the building.

There are varieties of vinyl type stage floor surfaces that can be laid over existing floors and stage rostra, providing the surface is smooth and level. They come in a number of different forms, including double-sided varieties with different colours on each side to suit different stage lighting and setting conditions. There are also cushion backed varieties to improve comfort and noise reduction on the stage floor. These surfaces can suit many forms of movement and dance activities.

1.6 Storage

Storage provision should be generous to accommodate a variety of items and pieces of equipment. The Sports Council recommends a storage area of approximately one-third of the activity space where shared sports/arts workshop facilities are provided. A storage area of 50–60 sq m is suggested in conjunction with a 15×12 m hall.

This standard will need to be reassessed where the hall includes predominantly arts uses. Adequate storage is needed for seating, staging, scenery and scaffold towers which can then also be used to accommodate sports equipment during arts events.

Separate secure storage will be required for specialist theatre equipment such as stage lighting, sound control boards, amplifiers, tape decks and microphones if these are not located in a secure control room. There may even be a need for a specially air conditioned music store for musical instruments such as an upright or grand piano. Separate storage may also be required for bar and spirits stores as well as provisions for refreshment areas. Cleaner's stores should not be forgotten.

1.7 Control rooms and theatre equipment

Sound and lighting control may operate from mobile control desks which can be positioned in a number of alternative positions or fixed in a purpose designed control room. Control equipment will normally include a lighting board (normally computerised and fairly compact in size), music replay facilities as well as public address systems so that music and other effects can be used in the hall. Internal communication systems will also be needed to relay information backstage, to technical staff, dressing rooms and front-of-house staff.

Stage and theatre equipment and technology are evolving constantly and it is recommended that specialist advice is sought regarding its layout and selection. Where budgets are limited, the hiring in of specialist equipment when required is worth investigating.

Curtains and drapes are used for a variety of purposes, from acoustic deadening to visual masking and cutting out external light sources. They should be made of heavy fire resistant fabric and stored in special curtain storage bays when not in use. Special attention must be given to the design, strength and fixing of curtain tracks.

1.8 Dressing rooms

Dressing rooms should be designed to accommodate the needs of artists and performers separately from those who participate in sports activities. They should accommodate varying proportions of male and female artists. It is often helpful to provide separate accommodation for a conductor, principal or leading soloist.

Make up worktops, mirrors and lights should be provided in each space. Locker space and security arrangements for each dressing room are essential. WC accommodation should be located close by.

It is normally desirable to provide natural daylight to dressing rooms although it should be capable of being excluded during the make up process when artificial lighting is used to simulate the colour rendition of stage lighting.

1.9 Mechanical and electrical services and environmental conditions

Mechanical and electrical services engineers should be appointed as part of the design team at an early stage. The design criteria for electrical distribution, heating and ventilation are exacting and the systems must all be integrated with the main functions of the building.

Electrical installations will need to comply with the regulations of the Institute of Electrical Engineers (IEE). Licensed premises will also need to comply with the specific requirements of licensing authorities.

The most flexible approach to theatre lighting in an arts workshop will probably best be served by installing a lighting grid over the whole area, 4. Lanterns can be suspended where required and patched into the control board. Good distribution of power around the perimeter of the hall at low level will also be required.

Access to focus and change lights suspended from the grid can be from a tallescope or scaffolding towers, although a more convenient method would be via overhead lighting galleries or crawlways, possibly as part of the grid structure itself.

The mechanical ventilation system should run quietly and a level of NR25 should be sought. The standards for the number of air changes per hour and temperature levels should be checked against Chartered Institution of Building Services Engineers (CIBSE) recommendations and local authority requirements.

1.10 Acoustics

The advice of an acoustic consultant should be sought at the outset regarding the design and control of the internal acoustics as well as guidance on the suitability of the

4 *Sports Arts Workshop at The Belgrave Centre, Tamworth. A 9 × 9 m hall predominantly artificially lit and equipped with a lighting grid. Photo: D J Butler*

proposed external envelope to meet the required standards.

Much can be done at the early design stage to avoid potential noise problems by laying out the building in such a manner as to avoid noise breakthrough from adjacent areas. This principle also extends to the location and siting of the building in relation to external noise sources such as passing traffic, trains, planes and other sources. Conflict with other considerations such as the need to maintain good public visibility of the building on a street frontage

may sometimes occur. Foyer and other spaces should then be organised to buffer sensitive areas from these noise sources. Ideally noise levels in the building should not exceed NR 30.

Internally, speech and music have different acoustic requirements. Generally for a hall accommodating no more than 300 people there should be no serious difficulties achieving suitable acoustics for the human voice.

A variety of factors will affect the acoustic performance of a hall. The volume of the space is one of the more significant; others are the shape of the hall and the amount and position of reflective and absorbent surfaces.

The design reverberation times for a hall measuring 12 × 24 × 6.5 m high (1872 cu m) should aim to achieve reverberation times of 1 second for speech and 1.6 seconds for music recitals, measured at 500 Hz.

Hard parallel walls, floor and ceiling surfaces can cause problems of flutter and standing waves. These may be reduced by the use of heavy drapes along the walls, seating arrangements and ceiling treatments to increase the amount of absorbency within the space. Good, hard surfaces close to performing areas can be used to reinforce early reflected sound and enhance musical dimension. In this respect, rectangular spaces with an end stage format using the side walls as reflective surfaces can often be considerably more successful than square spaces.

2 References and further advice

Chartered Institution of Building Services Engineers, *Lighting Guide LG4: Sports*, CIBSE, London.

Foley, M, *Dance Spaces*, Arts Council of England (1994).

Ham, R, *Theatres – Planning Guidance for Design and Adaptation*, ABTT and Architectural Press, Oxford.

Sports Council, *Data Sheet 59: Small Community Recreation Centres*, Sports Council, London.

Sports Council and Arts Council of Great Britain, *Getting it Together – Guidance on Housing Sports and Arts Activities in the Same Buildings*, Sports Council and Arts Council of Great Britain, London.

Strong, J, *The Arts Council Guide to Building for the Arts*, Arts Council of Great Britain, London.

The Association of British Theatre Technicians is also a useful body to contact regarding technical matters and information sheets. ABTT, 4 Great Pulteney Street, London, W1R 3DF (tel. 0171-434 3901).

54
Administration and control

Stuart Miller

1 *Reception area in the Arches Leisure Centre, Greenwich, London. Architects: Miller Associates. Design and build contractor: Sunley Projects*

1 General planning considerations

Poor planning and inadequate provision of administration and control facilities can have a harmful effect on the efficiency and smooth running of a centre. If basic errors in the planning and location of the administrative accommodation are to be avoided it is essential that the designer has a good understanding of the proposed management philosophy and a detailed understanding of the function of each member of staff. The key factors are likely to be charging policy, levels of use and the quality of service to be provided. In addition, because management policies tend to change and patterns of use vary over a period of time, the layout of administration areas should be flexible.

1.1 Compulsory competitive tendering (CCT)

In the UK the Local Government Act 1988 highlighted the need for clear objectives and value for money. With the market becoming increasingly sophisticated and the need to compete for leisure expenditure it is important to produce attractive buildings and provide a high quality of service with the minimum of staff. The layout of administration and control areas has a direct bearing on the level and efficiency of staffing and it has become normal practice for members of staff to carry out more than one function at off-peak times.

The introduction of closed-circuit television (CCTV) for monitoring security in the more remote areas of a centre, particularly during off-peak times, can also allow management to operate more efficiently and cost effectively, although capital installation costs may be quite high.

1.2 Entrance and control

The main entrance should be easily identified and welcoming for visitors approaching the building. Visitors arriving by car should be able to set down at the entrance and park close by. There should be parking provision for people with disabilities as close as possible to the entrance and for coach parking if the management deems it necessary. Staff parking is best provided in a separate area, away from the main public car park, possibly linked to the service yard.

Once inside first impressions are important. The entrance area should be warm and welcoming; in this lighting often plays a particularly important part. The principles and techniques used by the retail sector in shopping malls and speciality high street outlets can be used to good effect in leisure centres.

Finally the entrance foyer should be designed with sufficient space to allow the efficient movement of visitors at peak periods. Projected annual attendance figures provide the basis for an area calculation, but where possible the foyer should be as generous as possible in both area and height. It should be the heart of the centre, the hub from which, and into which, all activities are directed.

Large commercial centres with specialist facilities
In centres with a range of specialist activities likely to attract large numbers of visitors it may be necessary to remove some of the administration functions to a point further within the centre to avoid congestion. For example, where a centre contains a number of major elements such as an ice rink, ten pin bowling, multi-screen cinema, swimming pool and a multi-use sports hall, the reception area may function only as an information and advance bookings point and security control.

This method of control is becoming popular in commercial centres where visitors are allowed entry free of charge, or on the basis of a nominal charge, to the profitable food, drink and retail facilities and pay user fees only at the point of entry to each activity area.

Wet and dry leisure centres
In wet and dry centres, in addition to the general functions described below, the entrance reception should separate users of wet and dry areas. It should have distinctive yet

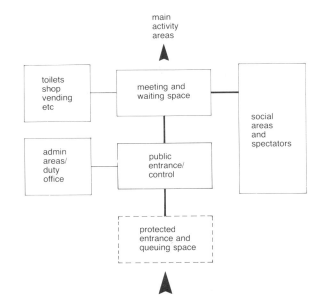

2 *Principal relationships at the public entrance/control area*

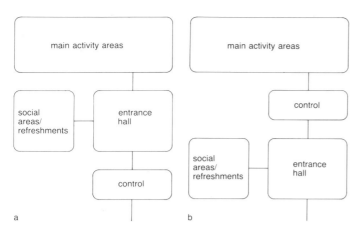

3 a *Access in cases where entrance fee is charged for all activities.* **b** *Access to controlled activity areas; other areas are freely accessible*

discreetly defined entry and exit channels which guide visitors to the reception desk and then to their respective changing or activity areas. This can be achieved by a permanent system of light barrier rails, planters or screens located to control different patterns of use during the day. Alternatively a system of demountable posts linked by flexible tape which can be located in the most practicable position can provide the best control of queues for a specific function or event.

Sufficient space should be allowed between the entrance doors and control desk to avoid external queues forming during normal use. Where this becomes uneconomic an external canopy should be provided to protect visitors from the weather.

An area for the storage of prams and pushchairs should be located immediately adjacent to the main entrance and be in full view of reception staff.

1.3 Key areas

Entrance lobby
A lobby at the main entrance will help to reduce draughts, particularly for staff on reception and avoid excessive heat loss. Doors can be either double swing or bi-parting types.

Meeting and waiting space
It is important that adequate circulation space is allowed beyond the control desk for use as a general meeting point and to allow visitors to orientate themselves. Good signage is essential to indicate directions and avoid congestion. In many centres there will also be a need for generous display boards or video walls providing information on the centre's activities. In larger centres it may be appropriate to provide casual seating at this point to form a relaxation and meeting area. At the same time visitors should be able to enjoy glimpses of some of the centre's activities from the meeting area. It may be appropriate to provide a refreshment area, vending machines or even a speciality retail shop adjacent to the meeting/waiting area.

Public toilets including a fully equipped disabled user toilet should also be located adjacent to the meeting area together with a telephone facility and a public staircase and/or lift serving upper floors.

Reception desk
The reception desk acts as the central control point for the facility and should be located so that it provides maximum efficiency for both the staff and the user.

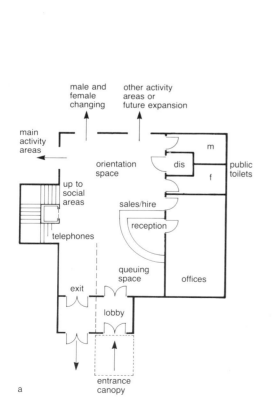

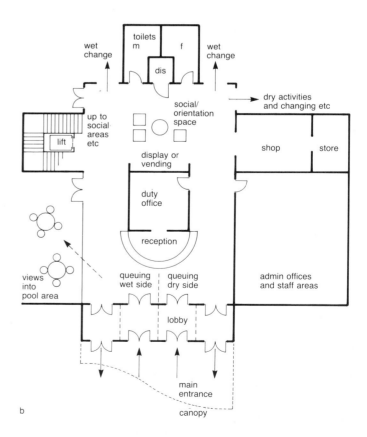

4 a *Typical small sports centre arrangement showing ideal relationship of elements and demonstrating excellent visual control over all areas.* **b** *Typical combined centre arrangement showing ideal relationship of elements and demonstrating 'island' reception*

5 *Reception area in Stirling Centre, Rochester, UK. Architects: Miller Associates. Design and build contractor: Warner Group*

6 *Island reception desk arrangement in the Hart Leisure Centre, Fleet, UK. Architects: Miller Associates. Design and build contractor: Warner Group*

The principal functions of staff at the reception desk are:

- To issue tickets to users
- To monitor season ticket holders
- To record bookings of the centre's facilities
- To hire or sell sports equipment
- To provide visual security control over strategic areas
- To monitor and action incoming telephone enquiries
- To monitor the centre's fire alarm system
- To monitor the centre's security system.

From behind the reception desk staff should be able to see:

- The main entrance doors, to ensure visitors pay on entering
- The entrance or access to changing rooms, to monitor activities and deter likely vandalism
- The entrances or approaches to the centre's main activity areas.

If possible the reception desk should be located immediately adjacent to the administration offices. In the case of larger centres it may be designed as an island unit with dedicated serving points for the centre's main activities and combined with the duty office and cashier's room.

The main factors to be considered in designing reception desks are:

- Provision of suitable space for the public to queue at pay points to cater for maximum demand
- Provision of a suitable space behind reception to allow staff circulation
- Provision of suitable space behind reception for the storage of equipment if it is to be hired or sold.

The design of the reception desk should be suitable for both users and staff. The working height of the reception desk is therefore particularly critical and should be designed to be suitable for:

- People with disabilities as well as the able bodied
- Children
- Staff working at VDU monitors.

Detailed discussions should take place with the end user management to provide suitable facilities for the storage and handling of cash. The means by which money is transferred from the reception desk to the main safe located in the duty office or administration area must be considered very carefully. Money from the tills or cash drawers is normally transferred at frequent intervals to a safe located within a secure room immediately adjacent to the reception desk. For security reasons this transfer must not involve crossing the flow of visitors. In large centres a secure cashier's room may be required.

The means by which money is transferred from the safe to security transport should also be considered carefully. The advice of a security expert and the end user's insurance company should be sought at an early stage. The aim should be to have a friendly yet tight control policy for handling money without the need for security screens.

Other factors to consider include:

- Space and suitable power points for ticket and accounting machines; in the case of computer based systems these will require 'clean' lines
- Space for telephone switchboard
- Space for control of public address system
- Space for security alarm control
- Space for fire alarm control
- Where required, space for CCTV monitoring screens; it may be preferable to locate this equipment in the adjoining duty office or security room
- Provision of a clock
- Possible display area for sports equipment where no individual shop is provided, subject to agreement with the management

- Possible display area/cabinet for sports club, subject to agreement with the management.

1.4 Management and administrative staff offices

A schedule of accommodation should be developed with management to determine the scale of staff facilities to meet the operational needs of the centre, the management and staffing structure, the administration method, programme and opening hours. The following should be considered in the planning of staff accommodation:

- Staff should be located as near as possible to the function they perform and, for economy, facilities should be grouped together.
- Office accommodation should be sited away from noisy sport activity areas to provide a quiet working environment, but should not be so isolated that management cannot respond effectively to emergency situations.
- Managerial staff should have reasonable access to the reception desk and in many centres office accommodation has been successfully located adjacent to the reception area.
- Administration offices should be accessible to the public but protected by and accessed through reception.
- In larger multi-facility centres it can be an advantage for administration offices to view over the entrance foyer or the main activity area depending upon management needs.

In the UK, office and staff accommodation must comply with the Shops, Offices and Railway Premises Act 1963 and the Health and Safety at Work Act 1974. These standards should be treated as a minimum. Discussions should be held with local authority officers to establish specific requirements.

1.5 Administration office requirements

The following examples give an indication of the office accommodation likely to be required for different sized centres. These requirements may vary depending upon specific end-user requirements and the scope of facilities offered and should be discussed with providers at the outset.

Small community recreation centres
The requirements of small community recreation centres (see Chapter 68 in this volume) and similarly scaled buildings may be met by a general office with a workstation for one person and a view over the entrance and corridors giving access to changing and other facilities. This can be achieved by:

- An extension to the staff area behind the reception desk, although some screening will be required
- An independent office adjoining the reception desk
- An independent office.

Small sports halls
The needs of small dry centres with one main hall and a total area of up to about 500–600 sq m may be met by a manager's office and either:

- An independent office adjoining the reception desk to allow direct staff communication
- An independent office.

The manager's office should be private and contain a workstation for one person and adequate space to hold meetings for up to about six people. Ideally it should be accessed through the general office.

Medium to large sports halls
Sports halls with a total area of about of area 600–1200 sq m will require broadly the same accommodation as smaller centres except that the general office should be expanded to provide space for three workstations.

Medium to large centres
Centres offering a comprehensive range of dry and wet sports facilities will need:

- *General office*: a separate office with space for three workstations.
- *Manager's office*: as for small dry sports hall.
- *Duty office*: an independent office adjoining the reception desk which can either be attached to the main administration centre or an island unit. It should accommodate up to about six people. Supervisory staff tend mainly to be involved with the activity areas for which they are responsible and use the duty office as a base. It should therefore be located so that it will allow easy access between staff and users.

Large centres offering a comprehensive range of catering and beverage facilities such as a cafeteria, licensed bar, lounge and function room may also require a kitchen and catering manager's office. This should be an independent room adjoining the lounge/cafeteria bar service area. It will be used for administrative tasks related directly to the catering operation. The space needed will be proportional to the number of restaurant seating covers.

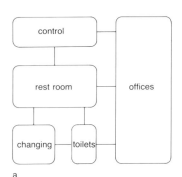

7 *Relationship of administration areas.*

8 *Typical staff room, locker room plan.*

1.6 Manual and attendant staff accommodation

There are many factors affecting staff accommodation requirements. The most important are usually:

- The range of activities provided and the layout of the centre, particularly the extent of catering facilities.
- Opening hours: where the span of a centre's opening hours is considerable, say from 06.30 to 22.00, shift working is essential. There is a corresponding need to provide a reasonable level of staff accommodation such as rest areas, changing rooms with showers and locker storage and self-catering facilities.
- Programming: a centre that maintains a constant activity programme aimed at schools, clubs and courses will normally have fairly low staffing levels.
- Location of staff accommodation: staff accommodation should generally be sited away from the main noisy activity areas so that staff can relax in relative peace and quiet.

Staff accommodation should be:

- Easily accessible to staff
- Controlled through reception
- Ideally linked with staff changing or administration offices
- Not so remote as to cause a delay in an emergency
- Provided with a reasonable external view where possible.

1.7 Attendant staff accommodation requirements

Small community recreation centres
Staff will generally use public facilities as appropriate.

Small sports halls
Small dry centres with a total area of up to about 500–600 sq m will require a staff rest room for both full and part time staff and should be equipped with a table, chairs and a means of boiling water.

Staff may use public areas for:

- Catering
- Food storage
- Washing up
- Changing
- Showering
- Storing clothes
- Toilet facilities.

Large sports centres
Sports halls with a total area of about of area 600–1200 sq m will require broadly the same accommodation as a smaller centre except that the rest room should be larger and equipped with a table and chairs, kitchen cupboards with sink unit and worktop, small cooker or microwave, refrigerator, drinking water supply and hot water supply if possible.

Staff needs for changing, showering, storing clothes and toilets may be met by sharing public facilities.

Medium to large centres
In centres offering a comprehensive range of dry and wet sports facilities the scale of facilities provided should relate directly to the number and sex of staff employed and may be met by:

- Staff rest room – as large sports centres
- Male and female changing rooms each equipped with bench seating, a locker for each staff member, toilets and cubicle or communal showers, depending upon staff numbers and sex
- Instructor's office.

Depending upon staff numbers and the complexity of facilities offered it may be appropriate to provide an instructor's office with sufficient space for workstations for two people, together with one male and one female changing space and shower cubicle.

1.8 Environmental services

For general details of environmental services requirements see Chapters 60 and 61 in this volume.

Natural lighting and ventilation
It is desirable that some natural lighting and ventilation should be provided in staff offices and rest rooms, but care must be taken to control glare and excessive solar gain.

Entrance foyer
Special care should be taken in designing entrance doors especially where double doors are not used and there may be a high rate of natural air changes or draughts. In this case a hot air draught curtain can be positioned above the doors to counteract excessive heat loss.

Artificial lighting
The design of the lighting system should be carefully considered in relation to its importance not only as a source of illumination but also for the decorative and atmospheric effects that can be achieved by well designed lighting. The benefits to management can be substantial in terms of providing a welcoming atmosphere particularly in the entrance foyer.

Power supply
The modern office is becoming increasingly dependent on electronic machines. Sports centre offices may contain computer booking systems, accounting systems, word processors and CCTV installations. Adequate power supplies with a number of 'clean lines' for computers must be incorporated from the outset.

55
Equipment storage

Christopher Harper

1 Introduction

Properly dimensioned and easily accessible storage areas are essential to enable all multi-sports and multi-functional spaces to operate effectively. Where storage is inadequate, some equipment will be stored around the walls where it will either be damaged or cause injury. Stores must be immediately adjacent to the halls or rooms they serve with opening widths and heights which do not inhibit the easy transfer of equipment. Extra area will be needed for non-sports use and for items of furniture, staging or exhibition stands.

2 Main hall storage

Storage needs

Fixed sports equipment is either wall or ceiling mounted in the hall itself and located so as not to inhibit other uses, **1**. Portable equipment is kept in the storage zone until it is required. Table 55.1 identifies the type of equipment common to multi-sports halls, together with its probable location.

The preferred location for equipment stores is centrally on the long side of the hall, ie to the sides of team games pitches. This position has three advantages: it allows access promptly to any part of the sports hall, which may itself have been subdivided by netting; it saves staff time in setting out and retrieving equipment; finally, it avoids the problems associated with the design of doors around goal areas where wall surfaces and fittings are particularly vulnerable to damage. Planning should ensure that the store depth is kept between 4 and 5 m (approx 13–16 ft) with easy access from at least two entry points. A store which is deep rather than shallow means that items of equipment placed at the front have to be removed in order to reach equipment stored at the back and poor utilisation of space and internal circulation may account for as much as 30–40% of the floor area provided, **2**.

Table 55.1: Sports hall equipment: checklist

	Fixed (or tethered)	Movable
Ceiling		
Protection for lighting	•	
Climbing ropes and trackway	•	
Climbing poles and trackway	•	
Speakers	•	
Track system for division nets:	•	
Cricket		•
Golf		•
Archery		•
Volleyball		•
Five-a-side soccer		•
Basketball		
Ceiling mounted backboards and goals (manual or electric operation)	•	•
Wall mounted backboards and goals (manual or electric operation)	•	•
Practice goals	•	
Gymnastics		
Asymmetric bars	•	•
Pommel horse	•	•
Vaulting buck		•
Vaulting horse	•	•
Horizontal bars	•	•
Rings	•	
Trampoline spotting rig	•	•
Parallel bars	•	•
Springboards, floors		•
Boxing		
Ring	•	•
Games apparatus		
Tennis		•
Volleyball		•
Badminton		•
Five-a-side soccer		•
Indoor hockey		•
Handball		•
Netball		•
Walls		
Scoreboard		•
Wall protection/padding	•	•
Seating fixings/recesses		•
Fire equipment	•	•
Protection to services/heating	•	
Wall speakers		•
Floors		
Court markings	•	•
Sockets and plates (fixed to floor or subfloor)	•	•

Portable sports equipment falls into three broad categories which must each be treated separately within the overall storage zone:

- General sports equipment and apparatus. These items demand the main floor area allocation. In joint provision schemes, it may be necessary to subdivide this space to

1 *Ceiling hung nets and fold out basketball goals in a school/community sports hall. Photo: C J Harper*

whole store can be seen and equipment is accessible via hinged rebound panels

alternatively provide at least two sets of door openings

less effective use of space; equipment becomes much less accessible – particularly bulky items

2 *The amount of storage area sacrificed to internal circulation must be taken into account. Wide vs deep plan form diagrams*

enable separate school equipment to be secured during periods of club or public use. Where tables and seating are included in the overall schedule of hall equipment, they too should be kept separately.

- Crash (landing) mats and all other equipment which might contain cellular foam. Any equipment which constitutes a fire hazard could fall into this category and will include, for example, roll down carpets or mats which are backed with foam as an anti-slip device. All equipment must be kept in a separate store constructed to give one hour's fire resistance with lockable self-closing doors. The store should be fitted with a smoke detector linked to main reception and the centre's alarm system. It should also be ventilated to outside air, either directly or through a duct. (Refer to *TUS Datasheet 60.6, Safety Fact File* for further details.)

- Small or valuable items of equipment. There should be a separate, lockable store or lockable cupboards for securing small-scale equipment which is easily mislaid or damaged if kept in the general store area. This can include: balls and bowls, shuttles, rackets, wickets, bows and tackle boxes, boxing gloves and hand-held exercise aids. It may also include toys and various types of playgroup equipment which will be kept together in separate cupboards, stacked storage boxes or steel mesh cages, and can demand a substantial amount of space. These stores and cupboards will be shelved and where balls are kept the shelves should be detailed with a reverse fall to assist stowing. An alternative is to provide suspended net ball bags.

Store size

A realistic assessment of the floor area required for halls of different size must be made at the initial briefing stage when the programme of activities is set out. New activities will inevitably be introduced during the life of every multi-use sports building and extra contingency area should be included for the acquisition of new equipment. It must also be recognised that staff and users have to move about within the store and a proportion of the space provided will be taken up by circulation. The following total areas are given as a broad guideline of what could be required. Any social, arts or exhibition use of the hall will lead to a significant increase in overall storage.

- Large hall (9 badminton courts +) storage area: 130 sq m (approx 1400 sq ft) min, to include a fire store and small equipment storage.
- Medium hall (6 badminton courts) storage area: 90 sq m (approx 970 sq ft) min, to include a fire store and small equipment storage.
- Small hall (up to 4 badminton courts) storage area: 60–65 sq m (approx 650-700 sq ft) min, to include at least a 10–12 sq m (approx 108–130 sq ft) fire store and small equipment storage

These minimum recommendations should not be accepted as read. The only realistic method of making an accurate assessment of the space required is to prepare a comprehensive schedule of equipment, calculate the spatial demands then add a contingency for later acquisitions.

Refer also to Table 55.2 for the stored dimensions and weights of a typical range of equipment.

Store access

Adequately dimensioned openings are essential to facilitate easy loading and unloading of equipment. Door openings should give direct access to the hall or room

Table 55.2: Typical schedule of indoors sports equipment (1)

	Stored dimensions (length × width × height)	Weight
Badminton		
Portable badminton court	Roll length: 6.7 m Roll diameter: 350 m	325 kg
Wheelaway posts	Height: 155 cm	35 kg
Basketball		
Wheelaway stands	Ring height 3.05 m 61 cm ring projection from posts	300 kg
Indoor bowls		
Various lengths of carpets are available between 18 and 36.6 m		
Portable rink carpet (36.6 × 4 m)	Roll length: 4 m Roll diameter: 50 cm	200 kg
Portable rink carpet (18 × 4 m)	Roll length: 4 m Roll diameter: 44 cm	100 kg
Short mat bowls		
Various lengths of carpet are available between 9.09 and 16.6 m		
Short mat carpet (16.6 m × 1.83 m)	Roll length: 1.83 m Roll diameter: 40 cm	30 kg
Short mat carpet (9.09 m × 1.83 m)	Roll length: 1.83 m Roll diameter: 30 cm	25 kg
Crash (landing) mats		
Landing mat	200 cm × 120 cm × 10 cm	
Landing mat	200 cm × 150 cm × 10 cm	
Cricket		
Indoor match wicket	Roll length: 30 m Roll width: 2 m	116.64 kg
Batting end carpet	Roll length: 9.0 m Roll width: 2 m	34 kg
Croquet		
Croquet set	Box dimensions: 110 × 28 × 18 cm	18 kg
Five-a-side soccer		
Five-a-side goals	4.87 × 1.2 m or 3.66 × 1.2 m	41 kg 37 kg
Golf practice		
Tee mat	0.920 × 1.5 m	
Practice net	1.4 × 2.28 × 0.9 m	10 kg
Chipper net	0.5 m diameter	2 kg
Gymnastics		
Balance beam	2.5 m × 10 cm × 33 cm	15 kg
Wooden bar	40 cm diameter	3 kg
Pair stabilisers	70 cm long	
Mini-springboard	77 × 40 × 14 cm	
Long box top	175 × 45 × 10 cm	
School springboard	120 × 60 × 23 cm	
Balance beam	3 m × 10 cm × 33 cm	17 kg
Mini box top	80 × 45 × 10 cm	8 kg
Bench	2.5 m × 23 cm × 30 cm	20 kg
Pommel horse	1.8 × 1 × 1.2	
Vaulting horse	1.8 × 1 × 1.3 m	
Beam 40 cm	5 × 1.2 × 1.6 m	
Ring frame	3 × 4 × 2.5 m	
Parallel bars	3 × 2 × 1.4 m	
Asymmetric bars	2.5 × 1.2 × 2.1 m	
High bar	3 m × 15 cm diameter	
Exercise bench	2.5 × 1.2 × 1.5 m	
Floor exercise carpet	13.2 × 13.2 m	
Training exercise floor 12.6 m × 12.6 m	48 pieces = 2 × 1.5 × 0.55 m	
High performance sprung floor	14 × 14 m × 11.5 m	

(Note: there are various systems of children's gymnastics equipment which might also form an additional part of a centre's inventory)

	Stored dimensions	Weight
Handball		
Handball goals (wheelaway)	3 × 2 m	
Hockey		
Indoor hockey goals	3 × 2 m	
Unihoc goals	105 × 90 cm	
Netball		
Steel posts wheelaway	3.05 m high	42 kg

Table 55.2 (*cont'd*): Typical schedule of indoors sports equipment (1) (*contd.*)

	Stored dimensions (*length × width × height*)	Weight
Rebound Panels	1.2 m high (approx 4 ft). Panels and posts for subdividing areas of the hall. Lengths vary and systems can include hinged 'gates' and be supplied with transporter trolleys	
Table tennis		
Table	1.855 × 1.83 × 0.65 m to 1.855 × 1.525 × 0.134 m	77 kg to 93 kg
Tennis		
Free-standing posts (steel)	2 posts, each 6.5 × 1.05 m	80 kg
Rebound trainer net	2.8 × 3.5 × 0.75 m	18 kg
Small rebound trainer net	2.2 × 2.4 m	8 kg
Tennis ball projector	96 × 42 × 54 cm	up to 23 kg
Short tennis		
Short tennis posts	40 × 40 × 100 cm	
Short tennis net	0.86 m × 15 cm diameter	
Trampolining		
Trampoline	Folded sizes vary but some full size models will require a clear opening height of 2.21 m (approx 7.3 ft) and are of the order of 3 m (approx 10 ft) in length	
Volleyball		
Steel posts wheelaway	2.1 m high	75 kg

Note (1): The items described are mainly based on a particular supplier's stock list and dimensions and weights should therefore be treated as approximate.

3 *Hinged rebound panel doors to a SASH sports hall store. An economical arrangement permitting access to the full width of the store. Tracked netting protects the void. Photo: D J Butler*

served and any secondary access (from the back of stores) should not, on any account, open on to a fire escape route. Clear opening height must relate to the tallest items of equipment stored, usually the trampoline at up to 2.21 m (approx 7.3 ft) high. It is important that the correct clearances are provided as injuries can result from staff or unskilled users having to tilt heavy and unwieldy equipment. Clear widths have to take account of equipment and any transporters used to ease handling. Crash mats, for example, are usually transported and stored stacked horizontally on trolleys and may require an opening in excess of 1.2 m (approx 4 ft). The most convenient, and often the least costly, method of providing unrestricted access between hall and store, is through the use of hinged 1.2 m (approx 4 ft) high rebound panels, backed by tracked netting, **3**. The only interruption of the overall width of opening is the positions of columns or piers. Alternatively, stores can be closed with full height doors, a necessity only for the foam mat store, which must have half hour side hung door leaves. All doors/frames should:

- Be robust enough to withstand the cumulative effect of both ball and body impact
- Have a smooth, flush surface without any projections and be flush with the surrounding wall surface
- Have a self-finish colour or be decorated to blend in with the surrounding surface
- Be resistant to panel distortion
- Open and close easily with hinges or door gear which maintain correct alignment with lock snibs and bolts which accurately align with striking plates and sockets.

Conventional side hung doors tend to restrict practical opening width to between 1.5 m (approx 5 ft) to 1.8 m (approx 6 ft) and take up valuable space within the store; greater widths are possible but can entail steel framing. Alternatives which have been used and may be considered are:

- *Up and over doors*: the travel rails for this type of door are generally mounted on the ceiling soffit and the clear opening height may therefore be restricted. Conventional door panels will have to be replaced with a flush, heavy duty construction back fixed to the steel frame and extra attention will need to be paid to ensuring that the panel can be securely closed and will remain flush.
- *Sliding folding doors*: this type of door enables wider openings to be considered but can result in hinges which stand well proud of the door faces and a need for heavy duty head and drop bolts to ensure the doors remain closed when impacted, **4**.

2.1 Ancillary hall and other stores

Other activity spaces and multi-functional rooms also require separate equipment stores, apart from specific single purpose stores such as those provided for cleaners. The following notes identify where these stores may occur in a sports centre and what function they may have to fulfil.

- *Ancillary halls*: these halls generally have a sports, social and arts use (see Chapter 51 in this volume). It is sensible to plan a common storage area for sports equipment, shared with the main hall. Where this cannot be achieved, a separate sports store will be required alongside furniture and playgroup equipment stores. The same evaluation of spatial requirements should be undertaken as for the main hall, but a rule of

4 *Sliding/folding panel doors to two separate 3.6 m wide openings at Moulton School, Northants. A satisfactory solution to wide openings when complete enclosure is required. Photo: C J Harper*

thumb assessment for sports equipment alone would be 1 sq m (approx 11 sq ft) for each 10 sq m (approx 108 sq ft) of ancillary hall floor area. If mats are kept here for judo or if there is foam filled play equipment, separate storage must be provided.

- *Open spectating galleries*: first floor galleries can be multi-functional and where this is the case must be equipped with a store for table tennis tables or furniture.
- *Crèche/meeting rooms*: crèche space can be utilised in the evening for meetings or club activities if provided with appropriate storage. This method of utilising underused space should always be recognised at the briefing stage.
- *Lounges and social areas*: equipped with en-suite stores, these spaces can also be used for table tennis or keep fit activities.

2.2 Wall and floor finishes

Sealed or painted blocks or bricks are suitable wall surface materials and a sealed granolithic screed is a durable and adequate floor finish. An alternative treatment is to paint the screed with a heavy duty acrylic paint which makes maintenance easier and can improve the visual quality and brightness of the store interior. The threshold between store and hall floor finishes must be level and smooth and uninterrupted by any obstruction so as not to impede wheeled equipment and trolleys, 5.

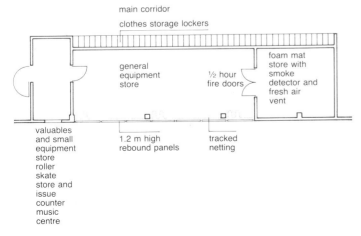

5 *Plan of the SASH sports centre showing the three principal storage zones*

Table 55.3: Ancillary hall equipment checklist

	Fixed (or tethered)	Movable
Ceiling		
Track system for curtains	•	
Lighting systems	•	•
Activities		
Judo and martial arts (mats, wall padding)	•	•
Snooker	•	
Table tennis		•
Fencing		•
Boxing		•
Boxing training	•	•
Weight/fitness training	•	•
Weight lifting	•	•
Wrestling	•	•
Movement and dance (barre mirrors)	•	
Floor		
Sockets/fixings	•	
Markings	•	
Movable floors/platforms		•

2.3 Internal environment

For general details of environmental services recommendations refer to chapters 60 and 61.

- *Heating*: stores are usually unheated although background heating may be provided if the store is on an external wall and where the hall temperature has to meet more than background levels.
- *Lighting*: luminaries should be positioned in front of shelving and along circulation routes within the store. They should be of a robust pattern and fitted with covers or protective guards.
- *Ventilation*: ventilation is not required except for the foam equipment store.
- *Power*: power sockets should be provided next to any work bench, for cleaning equipment and where, for example, balls or play equipment are inflated.
- *Water services*: in certain situations, most probably in events halls, and in community centre halls, emptied storage space can be used as a temporary bar. In these cases, hot and cold water services and drainage should be run to a permanent sink at the back of the store.

3 References and further advice

Table 55.2, produced with the assistance of En-tout-Cas plc and other suppliers, is included in order to emphasise the extent of store area required for sport alone. In addition, there could be a need for furniture and staging, playgroup equipment and a zip-up tower for safe, high-level maintenance.

It is recommended that the store is planned item by item to determine the most rational equipment layout. This should not be lost sight of once the building is open but translated into a clear system of wall labelling and taped floor markings to enable staff and users to return items to their designated position. Some steel shelving will also assist to maximise the use of the volume available, but high space is difficult to utilise without the use of machinery. Only in large multi-event halls could warehouse type storage, with mechanical fork lift machinery, be considered.

British Standards Institution, *BS 1892: Gymnasium Equipment*, BSI, Milton Keynes. (Published in several parts each dealing with a different item of equipment, eg Section 2:10:1990 Safety requirements for mats, mattresses and landing areas.)

British Standards Institution, *BS 5852: Parts 1 and 2 Methods of Test for the Ignitability of Upholstered Composites for Seating by Flaming Source*, BSI, Milton Keynes (1982).

Health & Safety Executive, *The Control of Substances Hazardous to Health Regulations*, HMSO, London (1988).

Health & Safety Executive, *Introducing COSSH (A Brief Guide for All Employers)*, HMSO, London.

Home Office, *Fire Hazards Associated with the Use of Cellular Foam in Sports and Recreational Facilities (Fire Service Circular No. 1/1988)*, HMSO, London (1988).

NATLAS (The National Testing Laboratory Accreditation Scheme for Fire Testing): this is the body by whom all laboratories testing mats and other foam equipment should be accredited.

Sports Council, *Foam Based Sports, Recreation and Play Equipment*, Sports Council, London.

56
Social areas

Stuart Miller

1 General

Social areas within sports centres have traditionally been considered as secondary to the main sports facilities. Consequently, a large number of centres exist which contain only the most basic facilities for relaxation or refreshments. As customer expectations rise, however, social areas can play an important role in providing an enjoyable and high quality leisure experience. In the case of neighbourhood centres there is also a need for facilities which fulfil the function of a social centre.

The income from bars and restaurants can contribute up to 25% of the gross income from a large centre and as much as 50% of the gross income from a small centre or squash club. The benefits of encouraging visitors to stay longer and use the social facilities are very important to the success of the centre and cannot be overstated.

In a similar way, the provision of meeting spaces for local clubs and affinity groups, together with crèche and day care centres, has expanded the scope of sports centres to appeal to a far wider market.

2 Planning considerations

The careful location, planning and detailed design of social areas is a major factor in ensuring their success.

The size and scope of the social facilities should be based on an assessment of demand within a defined catchment area. A detailed study should be commissioned by the end-user or operator to assess the anticipated use, the management philosophy, the demographics and the spending power of visitors. An assessment of other competition within the area will allow the designer to establish the most suitable size and combination of facilities for any particular location.

1 *The social area at the Arches Leisure Centre, London, UK. Architects: Miller Associates. Design and build contractor: Sunley Projects*

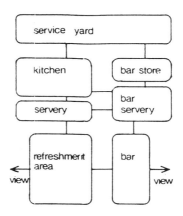

2 *Grouping of the principal social areas will allow maximum flexibility in use of both the public and service areas*

The need to maximise user spend also has a bearing on the location of the social facilities, in particular the bar and restaurant areas. Whereas it is often considered an advantage to create a view of the main activity areas, it may be more important to locate the bar and restaurant in a position where they are readily visible to the majority of visitors as they enter or leave the centre, for example adjacent to or forming part of the main entrance area. However, careful consideration should be given at the same time to siting these elements to avoid congestion at the entrance as this could detract from the warm and welcoming atmosphere. A positive approach to design will achieve both a good commercial location and also good views over some of the main activity areas.

The planning and location of facilities can also have a major influence on levels of staffing. Service facilities should be arranged so that the minimum of staff are required during off-peak times while at busy periods there is some flexibility between the two areas. Generally, areas should be planned to allow the minimum requirement for good supervision. A back-to-back situation with the bar and cafeteria serveries can provide a successful solution.

Requirements for the size and the layout of social areas tend to vary considerably during the course of the day depending on the number of users and the nature of the activities. If the management are to meet the varying demands it is important to design in as much flexibility as possible so that when necessary, certain areas can be subdivided to cater for small groups or opened up for large events. This can be achieved by an arrangement of sliding/folding acoustic screens or demountable partition systems. In the smaller centres the demand may vary from groups of 10–12 individuals up to say 100–150 for a larger social event.

Although of secondary importance to the convenience of the visitor, social facilities must be located so that they can easily be serviced from the main service yard. Adequate storage space should be allowed for restaurants and bars and suitable means of transporting heavy boxes, crates of bottles and beer kegs, possibly to an upper floor level, considered from the outset.

Means by which considerable amounts of refuse are to be disposed should also be considered and discussed with the end user and Local Authority Cleansing Officer at an early stage.

2.1 Restaurant and refreshment areas

A decision on the size and layout of these facilities should be determined by a detailed assessment of the local demand, the available capital and management philoso-

3 *Cafe/social area in the Hart Leisure Centre, Fleet, UK. Architects: Miller Associates. Design and build contractor: Warner Group*

4 *Bar/social area*

phy. Catering facilities can range from a full restaurant or cafeteria service through to a more modest self-service or snack facility. In the case of very small centres, where the cost of staffing a catering area can be prohibitive, a range of vending machines will often be more appropriate. This will also provide a service in off-peak periods.

Management philosophy will dictate whether the catering is to be managed by the in-house staff or contracted out to a specialist catering company. On the basis of the latter arrangement, the management will expect to receive an annual payment from the specialist company. This is usually based on a fixed lump sum, a percentage of the annual turnover or profits, or a combination of both. Although contracting out will to a large extent remove responsibility from the centre staff, it will also mean loss of control over the quality of the food and service.

With a few notable exceptions the restaurant and refreshment areas in most centres are regarded as complementary to the main sporting activities on offer. In this respect it is unusual for visitors to use the centre for the sole purpose of eating and drinking.

The periods of maximum demand, usually weekday evenings and weekends, can be calculated with reasonable accuracy from past attendance records of the centre and those researched from other centres. Most reasonable sized centres can justify the employment of full time catering staff.

Space allowances per diner for catering areas vary with the type of service provided and the seating and layout proposed. Typical space allowances are:

Table service

Square tables in rows seating 4	1.3 to 1.7 sq m per diner
Circular tables in rows seating 4	0.9 to 1.4 sq m per diner

Self-service

Square tables in rows seating 4	1.5 to 1.7 sq m per diner
Square tables in rows (including counter)	1.7 to 2.0 sq m per diner

The general atmosphere must be warm and relaxing with the emphasis on good quality but easily maintained finishes. In dining areas subject to light use, and where a high quality restaurant atmosphere is required, a good heavy duty contract quality carpet will be suitable. Where heavy use and frequent spillage is anticipated a more robust and easily maintained finish will be required. The interior decoration and furniture should be robust, well designed and contribute to the overall atmosphere and a feeling of quality.

2.2 Vending areas

The range, capabilities and quality of vending machines have improved dramatically over the last few years and it is now possible to provide a wide range of good quality foods and beverages to meet most demands.

In addition, it is possible to use vending machines to sell essential sports consumables and equipment such as squash balls, shuttlecocks or shampoo with the same efficiency. However, all vending machines require regular replenishment and maintenance. When they are installed on a hire basis it is essential to ensure that a service agreement is included in any contract.

The location of vending machines is dictated by the same commercial considerations as other catering areas. However, it is important that good visual supervision is maintained at all times, say from the reception desk or the duty office.

It is inevitable in an area of this intensity of use that spillages and litter will occur. It is important that floor finishes in particular can be easily cleaned and regular maintenance is carried out throughout the day. Machines should where possible be contained in purpose designed recesses and equipped with all the necessary water supplies, electricity and waste services.

The vending area should provide a pleasant and relaxed atmosphere and where furniture is to be included it should be robust and of good quality and appearance. A storage area should be situated immediately adjacent to the vending machines to allow a suitable range of refills to be stocked.

2.3 Kitchens

The kitchen area should be located immediately adjacent to and at the same level as the restaurant or cafeteria area. The size and range of equipment will be dictated by the number and frequency of meals to be served, the type of menu and the method of service. The layout of the equipment and the position of essential service outlets and

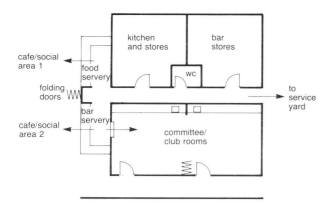

5 *Typical arrangement of social areas in relation to food and drink service, allowing flexibility of use and achieving staff economies*

drainage runs should be determined in consultation with an experienced specialist catering design company.

In designing and equipping the kitchen, in the UK the Food and Hygiene Regulations 1955 and the Food Safety Act 1991 will apply and consultation with the Local Authority Environmental Health Officer is essential. A wash hand basin with hot and cold water supply must be installed within the kitchen for staff. One may be required to service each catering outlet. A toilet must also be provided and a cloakroom for staff, but must not open directly off the kitchen.

The size and layout of back-up stores will depend on the type of kitchen and the frequency of deliveries. A dry store and a cold store are normally required but there may also be a need for a large freezer store. If so it should be installed by a specialist company. The design of these elements should form part of the expertise of the specialist catering consultant.

An enclosed service yard should be located nearby to accommodate kitchen waste and refuse from the restaurant and all other parts of the centre. This area may also act as a storage space for empty crates and containers from the bar. An unloading platform is a useful facility where regular deliveries of heavy items are expected and, if provided, should stand approximately 1 m high with a non-slip surface laid to fall to a wash down gully. For kitchens above ground floor level, a goods lift is essential.

2.4 Self-service counters
The counter length and layout of equipment depends on the scope of the menu, the frequency of service and the number and spending power of visitors and should be determined by a specialist catering consultant. A typical self-service counter of between 9 and 11 m in length, with one cashier's position, will cater for an average of 6–9 persons per minute.

Finishes should be attractive, easily maintained, robust and sufficiently hard wearing to withstand the purpose for which they were intended. Particular attention should be paid to the floor finish both behind and immediately in front of the counter. A fully vitrified ceramic tile with non-slip finish is most suitable for this purpose.

2.5 Licensed bars
Most of the factors raised in determining the size and location of the restaurant and cafeteria area apply equally to the licensed bar.

In the UK, changes in the licensing laws have resulted in a relaxation of the rigid separation of the licensed area from other social areas and allowed a far more casual physical relationship with the catering facilities. However, interpretation of the laws appears to vary between licensing authorities and no rigid rules have yet been established. Each proposal should therefore be discussed on its own merits with the local licensing authority at an early stage in the design process.

The bar should be capable of combining with the restaurant, refreshment area and function areas to provide a large and comprehensive facility that is adaptable to suit as demand dictates. Similarly, the kitchen should be located so that it is capable of serving all necessary areas and providing flexibility of use. This should provide a saving in the initial capital expenditure, economies in staff numbers and long-term running costs.

It should be possible where appropriate to combine the serveries for both food and drink to effect further savings. It is important that the size and appearance of the bar servery is in proportion to the room it serves. The length of the servery counter and the extent of the equipment provided should be directly related to the anticipated demand. The advice of a specialist consultant or the operator's preferred brewery company should be sought.

All bar fittings should be designed with a degree of flexibility that allows for future developments in equipment or changes in management requirements.

A staff toilet should be provided adjacent to the servery for bar staff as well as a wash hand basin separate from the glass washing sinks in the bar. In small centres public toilets may have to be used.

The work of equipping bars is usually carried out by specialist bar fitters, associated with a brewery.

Beer storage should be located close to the bar servery or immediately below with python pipe lines running direct to the bar pumps or with a hoist for crates and other heavy bulky items. The beer store size will relate directly to the expected sales capacity and frequency of deliveries proposed by the brewery company.

The temperature at which beer is kept and served is very important. Cooling may be carried out either in the cellar or on the python pipeline to the servery. In the case of the former, the store must be insulated locally and should generally be fitted with a sink and a wash down gully.

A separate lockable store, with alarm or security warning light linked to reception, should be located immediately adjacent to the bar servery for storing wines, spirits and tobaccos. In most centres, the space required for these items is not large, but additional space or a separate store will be required to accommodate bulk items such as cartons of crisps.

An enclosed service yard should be located nearby to accommodate refuse, empty crates, and gas cylinders from the bar. An unloading platform is a useful facility and could be combined with the service area to the kitchen and main plant area.

2.6 Committee and club rooms
There is a regular demand in most sports centres for small meeting rooms for sports club and committee use, seminars, film shows, promotions and other activities. In order to achieve flexibility and maximise the use of these rooms, consideration should be given to incorporating acoustic room dividers and links to adjacent bar or refreshment areas for larger functions. Meeting rooms offer opportunities to extend the use of the centre for more community based activities.

The addition of a sink, possibly in an ante-room, together with adequate power points, will increase the flexibility and independence of these rooms and therefore their marketing potential. It is also important that some flexibility in the control of quality of both the finishes and lighting level can be achieved to meet a variety of user requirements.

2.7 Internal environment

For general details of environmental services recommendations refer to Chapters 60 and 61.

57
Changing areas

Christopher Harper

1 Introduction

The design of changing areas should provide for good levels of user comfort allied with adequate space standards, a clear circulation pattern and finishes which ensure easy maintenance and high levels of cleanliness, **1**. With the exception of activities such as badminton, squash and fitness training, sports centres tend to attract a high proportion of team or group activities. This pattern of use dictates that sports are programmed for the principal activity spaces with the result that demand for changing occurs in a series of predictable peaks.

2 Levels of provision

Changing spaces

There are usually more male than female users for most activities other than aerobics/keep fit and the allocation of changing space must allow for flexibility and for group use by clubs and schools. This is generally provided by separate open plan changing rooms, but a small percentage of cubicle space may be considered, particularly on the female side. With this traditional arrangement buffer rooms with intercommunicating lockable doors are the best way of accommodating different levels of use and are essential for schools classes, **2**. Alternatively, several team size rooms can be provided and can be allocated for male/female or group use as required. In both cases, surplus capacity can remain locked during slack periods.

The number of changing spaces specified will relate to the maximum number of players using the centre's facilities plus an allowance for overlap. The method of assessing total capacity given below has proved to be a useful guideline although requirements for each individual centre should be adjusted in the recognition that, in some locations and for some sports, there will be a tendency for players to arrive ready changed.

- *Main hall*: calculate the maximum number of badminton players on the basis of 4 per court. In a four-badminton-court sports hall, this would result in 4 courts × 4 players = 16 players × 2 for overlap in the changing area = 32 spaces. In small centres with only a single hall an additional allowance will have to be made to cater for single sex group activities such as keep fit or aerobics. Larger centres with more activity spaces and hence a greater number of changing spaces have greater all round flexibility.

1 *The standard SASH centre changing room. An influential design with built in flexibility and good finishes. Photo: D J Butler*

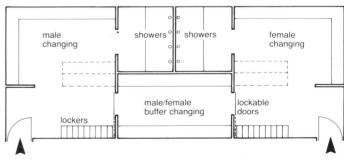

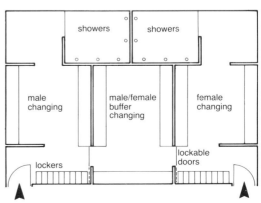

2 *Two examples of buffer room planning to meet the needs of fluctuating user levels*

- *Ancillary halls*: calculate on a floor area basis, taking particular account of the needs of martial arts, movement and dance and keep fit groups. Allow one changing space for between 5 and 10 sq m (approx 54–108 sq ft) of floor area × 2 for overlap.
- *Fitness rooms*: changing requirements relate to the number of fitness stations specified. A rule of thumb assessment is one changing space per 5 sq m (approx 54 sq ft) of floor area × 2 for overlap. This can also apply to related facilities such as sun beds, saunas and steam rooms. It is not necessary to include a factor for overlap.
- *Squash courts*: calculate on the basis of two players per court × 2 for overlap. This may be regarded as a minimum space allocation because of the typical 30–40 minute turnover rate of squash courts.

Total changing capacity can be assessed using this method of calculation but on school (joint-provision) sites, the resulting figure will invariably be over-ridden by the numbers required for school physical education classes. A 450–600 mm (approx 1.5–2 ft) run of benching is normally allocated to each changing space; 500 mm (approx 1.6 ft) can be regarded as average.

All finishes will be selected for durability and ease of maintenance and the floor should be specified to be impervious to water with good slip resistant characteristics. Changing benches and cubicles will have to be of robust construction and resistant to moisture with the detailing of floor and wall supports requiring particular attention (refer to Chapters 119 and 101 of this volume). Each bench space should be equipped with 2 rail mounted coat hooks of a snub-nose pattern. Changing room entrance doors will be provided with suitable screening and shelving, mirrors and hairdryer sockets can be located close by, **3**.

Showers

Showers will be included with male and female changing rooms and the total number of fittings should include an allowance for any additional (buffer) changing space. Shower numbers should be calculated on the basis of 1 per 7 changing spaces. In considering the overall planning, it is important to locate showers as far as possible from entry doors to avoid cross circulation and prevent water migration. It is also important that showers are provided with a dry-off zone laid to falls and with good drainage to control and contain water spillage.

Individual shower compartments are often preferred in female changing rooms, but their inclusion and the consequent need for screens or curtains and individual drainage outlets leads to greater cost. Walls should be tiled and detailing must prevent water seepage into the construction or adjoining areas (see Chapter 8 of Volume 3). Shower fittings should be robust with concealed pipework. Automatic units are recommended to prevent water wastage with a central thermostat to control temperature. Where possible, showers should be planned with a walk-in access duct to conceal pipework and master controls and permit easy maintenance. Inset soap trays should be included and the dry-off area should be fitted with towel hooks. A hose down point is best located in the shower area and a drinking water dispenser included close to established services.

Clothes storage

Clothes and personal possessions are usually stored in lockers operated with coin release/retain mechanisms. Lockers must be of robust construction and planned with sufficient clearance to prevent users obstructing access routes, **4**. The most convenient location is in the changing rooms adjacent to benches, but the most cost effective and

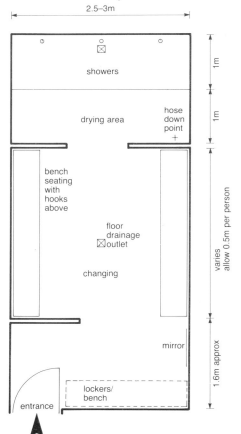

3 *This simple plan demonstrates the key principles of a changing room layout*

4 *Corridor located lockers in SASH offer maximum flexibility between male and female changing rooms and are overseen from reception. Photo: Martin Charles*

easily supervised location is in the circulation space between changing rooms and activity areas. A guideline figure of 2.5 lockers per occupant is recommended based on the occupancy assessment used for changing space calculation. Half-height lockers are usually preferred or a combination of one-half and two-quarter-height stacks. When lockers are placed in changing rooms either in central banks or as wall mounted units, they should be of a moisture resistant specification and raised from the floor on a plinth to protect against corrosion.

2.1 Services
For general details of environmental services recommendations refer to Chapters 60 and 61.

Heating
Areas should generally be maintained at 20-25°C. Underfloor or low level heating should be considered in order to help maintain warm, dry floor areas. Location and protection of the heat emitters has to be considered with regard to safety and vandalism.

Ventilation
A well distributed mechanical ventilation system providing 10 air changes per hour of fresh air should ensure that comfortable conditions are maintained.

Lighting
A general illuminance of 150 lux is recommended. All fittings should be suitably protected against moist atmosphere and potential vandalism.

Power
All outlets should be recessed with protective cover and suitable for use in potentially wet environments.

2.2 Toilets
The recommended standards related to changing spaces are:

WCs	1 per 15/20 men
	1 per 7/10 women
Urinals	1 per 15/20 men
Handbasins	1 per 15 men
	1 per 15 women

In addition, at least one fully equipped disabled persons WC will be required. This compartment can also be equipped with a changing bench and a showering facility. In small to medium sized sports centres, toilet accommodation will be planned close to changing rooms with perhaps a shared entrance lobby, **5**. In large centres or multi-sport complexes, toilets will invariably be dispersed between the foyer, refreshment areas and the changing rooms. Where there is access via changing rooms to outdoor sports facilities it is inevitable that individual toilets are included as part of the changing room brief, **6**. For services requirements refer to Chapter 60 of this volume.

2.3 Wet and dry changing
Combined changing accommodation for swimming pool and dry sports users can be considered but, although capital cost savings can result, supervision and the problems imposed by cross-circulation and different user expectations and habits are difficult to resolve. It is more difficult to devise satisfactory circulation routes in this type of plan with the result that outdoor footwear can cause

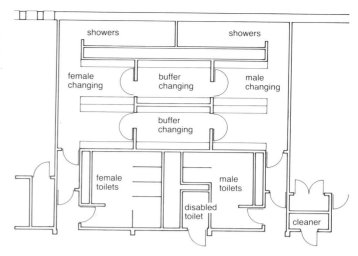

5 *SASH toilets and changing rooms share a common approach lobby. An economical solution for smaller sports centres*

6 *Toilets in SASH with easy to clean surfaces and concealed pipework. Photo: D J Butler*

floors to become dirty more rapidly and moisture transferred on to the dry side floor finishes.

2.4 Outside sports activities
In some centres, and often in joint provision schemes, changing space is shared between indoor and outdoor activities. As a general principle, this shared use should be discouraged unless the outdoor playing surfaces are of an all-weather synthetic construction. A more satisfactory

alternative is to designate separate indoor and outdoor rooms, but allocate a number of buffer spaces which can be used to give flexibility. Outdoor team sports invariably result in tougher use and finishes must be specified accordingly, for example to withstand studs. Suspended ceilings with push in panels should be avoided as they are particularly prone to vandalism. Some permanent ventilation will be needed in these rooms, capable of being boosted when showers are in operation and heating will be used intermittently. Refer to Chapter 57 of this volume, Pavilions and clubhouses, for more detail on the design of outdoor changing.

58
First aid provision

Sylvester Bone

1 Introduction

This chapter deals with first aid provision for dry indoor sports facilities with halls catering for a maximum of 2000 spectators. It does not cover wet facilities, which are included in *Safety in Swimming Pools*, or facilities for full scale sports arenas which are discussed in the Sports Council publication *Arenas*.

2 Legal requirements

Under the Health and Safety (First Aid) 1981 Regulations the management of a sports centre has a legal obligation to make adequate first aid provision for employees in the event of either illness or accident. These regulations apply only to employees but management should also ensure that first aid provision caters adequately for foreseeable types of accidents to other users of the building. The guidance from the Health and Safety Commission is that where there are regular users of a building the management may wish to make first aid provision for them.

A European Economic Community Directive 89/654 concerning minimum health requirements for the workplace stipulates (in clause 19) in that 'one or more first aid rooms must be provided where the size of the premises, type of activity being carried out and frequency of accidents so dictates'. This may lead to a more precise definition of the requirements for first aid rooms than that given in the current UK regulations, Approved Code of Practice and Guidance.

When application is made for a licence under the Fire Safety and Safety of Places of Sport Act 1987 (a requirement when the public are invited to attend sports events as spectators), the licensing authority may make the provision of a first aid room a condition of that licence.

2.1 Levels of provision

First aid provision will vary according to the size and use of the building concerned. In broad terms there is a choice between three levels of provision.

First aid box
The most basic provision is a first aid box on a wall in a convenient location – such as an office or rest room. This can be considered adequate only in very small buildings, such as village halls, and then only when they are well covered by ambulance services.

Shared use room to be available for first aid as required
In smaller sports halls, eg of the SASH type, a dedicated first aid treatment room is seldom used. A more appropriate provision would be a room normally used for another purpose, such as an office, but equipped to become an effective first aid room in an emergency and located at the same level as the main sports hall close to ambulance access. Convenient access is vital for all levels

of provision. This level of provision does not conform with the Approved Code of Practice, however, if a first aid room is a requirement. The code clearly states that the room 'should not be used for any purpose other than the rendering of first aid or health screening'.

Dedicated first aid room
In larger sports halls and in halls used by large numbers of people, either as participants or spectators, there should always be a dedicated and fully equipped first aid room. It must have easy access to the entrance that will be used by ambulances and be clear of the main activity space and public access routes.

Table 58.1 suggests the size and type of provision which would normally be appropriate for different facilities. However, types of use, the numbers of users, including users of adjacent outdoor facilities, and the cover provided by the local ambulance service should all be taken into account when deciding what first aid provision to make. Figure 1 gives three diagrammatic plans for different sizes of first aid rooms.

A dedicated first aid room will be essential:

- If stipulated in the sports licence from the local authority
- If the premises are being used for particular sporting events – eg boxing
- If the facility is used to deal with casualties from external playing fields or a swimming pool.

2.2 Use of first aid facilities

A first aid room will be used for the treatment of minor injuries such as cuts, sprains, nosebleeds, blisters and knocks. The provision of a comprehensively stocked first aid box with bandages, scissors, cotton wool, antiseptic cream, safety pins and sticking plasters and similar items will usually be sufficient to deal with such minor occurrences.

For any serious accident such as a potential fracture or heart attack an ambulance should be called immediately and treatment will generally be restricted to making the injured person as comfortable as possible. The injured person will only be moved if the first aider considers that no risk is involved. In doubtful cases it is preferable for the ambulance personnel, who have greater experience, to move the patient.

2.3 Location of the first aid facilities

It is important for the first aid facilities to be centrally located near and on the same level as playing facilities.

Table 58.1: First aid provision for sports halls of different sizes

Size and type of hall	Spectator accommodation	First aid accommodation
Dedicated first aid room		
Large sports, leisure or recreation centres	Up to 2000 None	35 people 20 people
Large-scale sports centre	Up to 1500 None	20 people 20 people
Medium scale & outdoor	Up to 1000 None	20 people 15 people
Medium scale indoor only	Up to 1000 None	15 people 15 people
Shared use room to be available for first aid as required		
Small sports hall (SASH)		Casual only
First aid box		
Small community provision (eg SCRC)		Casual only

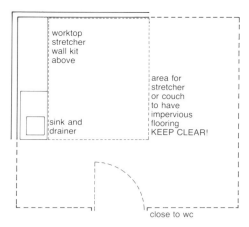

1 *First aid facility for a small sports hall, provided in an office*

Signposting

First aid facilities should be clearly signposted throughout the building. Notices should give the location of first aid equipment and facilities as well as the names and the location of the qualified first aiders in the building and how they can be contacted.

Use of WC

Ideally, first aid facilities should be close to WC facilities; disabled WCs for the disabled are particularly suitable as they are often unisex. They therefore have the advantage of being equally available to either sex and this creates less embarrassment for a first aider accompanying someone of the opposite sex who is feeling queasy and may be needing assistance.

Access routes

Routes to first aid facilities (ie corridors, lifts and doorways) and the entrance to any first aid room should be wide enough to allow access for stretchers, wheelchairs or carrying chairs. Widths of 900 mm for doorsets and 1200 mm for corridors are generally considered to be minimum dimensions.

Ambulance access

It is highly desirable for there to be a direct route out of the building from the first aid room to an ambulance outside, perhaps by the use of an emergency exit. This route should not involve passing through either an activity space or the reception area. All corridors on a potential exit route should be able to accommodate a stretcher (1900 x 560 mm) and helpers; changes of direction may need particular attention.

The site layout should be arranged to allow an ambulance to drive as close to the building as possible to reduce the journey distance of a stretcher to the ambulance. A 6-m wide access road is required for an ambulance.

2.3 Size and design of first aid room

The size and design of the first aid room will vary according to the size of the building and whether or not the building is intended to accommodate spectator events. Figures **1** to **3** show possible layouts. Table 58.2 shows the recommendations and guidance published by HMSO as an Approved Code of Practice in support of the Health and Safety (First Aid) Regulations 1981.

Under the RIDDOR 1985 Regulations (see References and further advice), specific accidents to all staff and

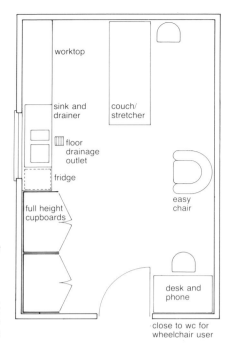

2 *First aid room for a medium-sized sports hall, minimum area 15 sq m*

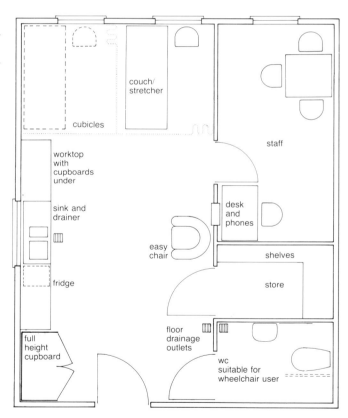

3 *First aid room for a large sports hall, minimum area 35 sq m*

visitors have to be reported to the Health & Safety Executive.

2.4 Design features

It may be preferable to provide a stretcher rather than a couch, as this can also be used to remove an injured person from a playing area if necessary. (See **2** and comments on Stretchers below.)

Table 58.2: Recommendations for first aid rooms

Recommendations forming part of the Approved Code of Practice
- Room should be large to hold a couch with space for people to work around it, and a chair
- It should contain suitable facilities
- Impervious floors (Note: a floor drain is suggested; see text)
- Effective ventilation and heating
- Easy to clean surfaces
- Effective lighting
- Be clearly identified by a safety sign
- Have an outside telephone

Guidance notes
- Have nearby toilets
- Possibly have emergency lighting
- Have sink with running water (eg stainless steel with drawer and drinking water tap)
- Drinking water and disposable cups
- Soap (and soap dish)
- Paper towels
- Smooth topped working surface (Note: also needed for writing records)
- First aid materials
- Refuse container and binliners (black and maybe yellow)
- Couch with waterproof surface (eg disposable sheets and blankets)
- Protective garments (eg disposable gloves)
- Chair
- Record book and somewhere to keep it
- A bowl
- Notice on door saying who is First Aider and where located

Other advice
- Scoop or York 4 stretcher (see discussion in text)
- Refrigerator for ice packs
- Internal telephone
- Hot water at sink
- Electric kettle and point for making hot drinks
- First aid 'snatch bags'
- Torches

Refrigerator

Although not included in the official recommendations, the availability of a refrigerator for ice packs can help first aiders to reduce the pain and swelling of some common injuries. Some experienced sports hall managers consider that a refrigerator should be an essential part of the equipment of a first aid room. However, chemical cold compresses are available as an alternative.

Floor drain

A floor drain should be provided to allow blood to be washed away with mild disinfectant solution. It is difficult to clean up blood without risk of infection if it has to be wiped from the floor.

Telephone

A telephone which can be used for direct outside calls is essential to enable the first aider to summon other help such as an ambulance. This is particularly important when:

- the first aid facility may be used out of the normal working hours; or
- is shared between indoor and outdoor activities; or
- if use of the outdoor facilities may take place at a time when staff for the building are not present (eg on a Sunday) and phones in management offices are locked up.

If there is an internal telephone system, one of the internal phones should be in the first aid room. The outside line can be a pay phone from which emergency calls can be made free of charge.

Accommodation for volunteers

If the centre has facilities for spectator events, the first aid room may be used by volunteer first aid organisations (St John or St Andrew Ambulance or the Red Cross) when dealing with any spectator casualties. Guidance should be sought from the organisers on the number of volunteer personnel to be accommodated; it should relate to the type of event and the number of spectators.

A kettle and limited tea making facilities are useful, but the facilities in the first aid room should not be used for regular tea making and should never be on a scale that could become an alternative canteen.

2.5 First aid equipment

Stretchers

The York stretcher is recommended by St John Ambulance. This is a stretcher which can be lowered to floor level to minimise the distance an injured person needs to be lifted. It can also be used in a sitting position as a chair for someone who has injured an ankle. Once on a York 4 stretcher, a person can be transported from the site of the injury to a hospital casualty department and even into an operating theatre without needing to be moved on to a different couch. The criticism made of this type of stretcher is that it is seldom used in all the intended positions and the ambulance service is not prepared to take stretchers away from a building. Some larger centres have equipped themselves with orthopaedic scoop stretchers which can be placed underneath an injured person prior to lifting them. This is a less expensive alternative and can be used to lift an injured person on to an ambulance stretcher.

Many smaller centres are equipped with folding stretchers although they seem to be used very rarely. When someone has been injured sufficiently badly to warrant the use of a stretcher, most managers would prefer ambulance personnel to be responsible for moving the injured person.

Resuscitation equipment

This is used primarily for cardiac patients. Its general provision is not recommended as it should only be used when medically trained personnel are present. Advice on appropriate provision is available from the UK Resuscitation Councils. They do not recommend the use of mechanical ventilators except by personnel specifically trained in the techniques of advanced life support.

First aid boxes

In larger buildings more than one first aid box may be needed. Additional locations are kitchens, reception, plant rooms, and adjacent to any playing facility remote from the first aid room. Snatch bags – officially called 'Travelling First Aid Kits' can be used to provide first aid materials at the spot where an accident occurs.

2.6 Internal environment

For general details of environmental services recommendations refer to Chapters 60 and 61.

59
Refuse planning considerations

Stuart Miller

1 Introduction
To allow sports and leisure centres to operate properly and offer visitors good quality facilities, the waste end of the business must be efficient.

Care should be taken in the design that:

- The refuse area is away from the public face of the building
- Ideally the refuse area should be combined with other service areas such as plant, beer store, kitchen and cleaners' stores
- The road network into the site is designed so that service vehicles are not routed past the main entrance
- Sufficient turning area is provided for refuse vehicles and where appropriate for service vehicles as well; an average turning circle for refuse vehicles is 10 m diameter, height clearance 4.2 m.

Service areas by definition deal with all the by-products from the engine room of a centre. They seem to collect all the service paraphernalia that makes a leisure centre tick. It is therefore generally favourable to screen these areas, even though they may not be directly in public view, so that they are at least contained around the perimeter.

2 Location of refuse areas
In the UK preliminary discussions should held with the relevant Local Authority's Public Cleansing Officer, Environmental Health Officer and the end-user to establish:

- The range of refuse collection services offered
- The most appropriate services for the centre
- The frequency of collections
- The design criteria for the collection system adopted.

2.1 External methods of storing refuse
Small community halls
In small centres domestic dustbins may be sufficient or, if preferred, one paladin unit, depending upon the facilities offered and frequency of collection service. Ideally refuse should be located in a contained area adjacent to the kitchen and storage areas.

Small sports halls
Paladins are normally acceptable, the numbers required depending upon the range of facilities provided in the centre, and are best located in a contained area adjacent to the plantroom, beer stores, kitchen and cleaner store.

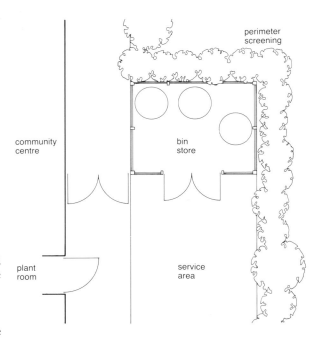

1 *Bin store adjacent to service areas*

Large sports halls offering a comprehensive range of dry and wet facilities
Refuse can be stored in:

- Standard 8 yard open type skips
- Compacting type skips
- Garbage gorger machines discharging compacted waste into plastic bags and open skips for delivery to the local authority refuse disposal unit.

The collection service can be arranged at a frequency level to suit management. Where the refuse and service yard area are quite well screened the open skip with metal cover is the most economic option. Refuse storage facilities can be positioned in a dedicated area forming part of the

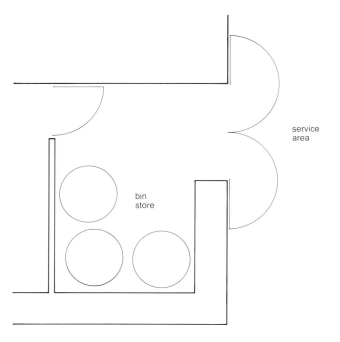

2 *An internal refuse store*

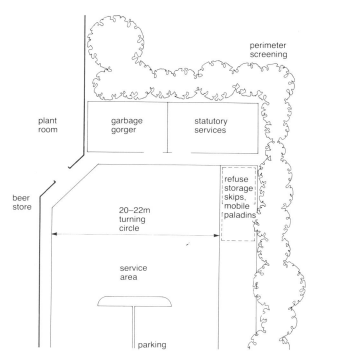

3 *Dedicated refuse area forming part of the service yard at a large sports hall or leisure centre*

general service yard and protected, if required, on three sides by bund walls.

2.2 Internal methods of storing refuse

It may be necessary to provide an internal waste storage area in centres where:

- External space is at a premium
- For environmental reasons external waste storage is unacceptable
- A refuse chute is required in the centre discharging into a storage unit inside the building.

The main factors to be considered when designing internal refuse rooms are:

- Provision of suitable internal space to allow the required number of waste storage containers to be manoeuvred to the collection vehicle
- Suitable height to allow the chosen waste storage containers to be filled
- Provision of adequate natural or mechanical ventilation to stop smells entering the main building
- Suitable specification of construction materials to resist fire: agree the level of combustibility and minimum fire resistance with building control
- Suitable specification of materials, ie robust, hard wearing, easy cleanable floor, wall and ceiling finishes
- Wash-down and drain-off facilities.

Refuse can be stored in:

- Mobile paladins
- Garbage gorgers
- Open or compacting skips.

Skips are difficult to manoeuvre and the standard skip vehicle requires a minimum 4.2 m headroom. These factors may negate the skip option.

2.3 Management monitoring and control

The storage of waste in leisure centres should be co-ordinated by management so that the refuse collection service operates efficiently. Ideally, collections should be made outside the centre's opening hours or at low times of usage.

In large centres where the refuse storage and service areas are remote from the management control, a closed-circuit TV system may be installed to enable them to be monitored continuously.

Good quality external lighting should be considered wherever facilities are used after dark and as a deterrent against unwanted intrusion and vandalism.

60
Environmental services and plant space

David Bosher

1 *Sports hall with services installations located outside the main playing zone*

1 Introduction

The provision and maintenance of satisfactory, pleasant, attractive and safe internal environmental conditions is essential in order to attract and sustain high usage levels and achieve customer satisfaction. The definition of what constitutes ideal or satisfactory conditions within an activity space will be dependent on the activity taking place and the people taking part in it. In effect this means that the actual requirements for achieving satisfactory conditions within the space will vary with changes in the activity, standard of performance and occupants.

The ideal way of meeting these requirements is through the provision of environmental services installations that are very flexible and capable of responding continually to the varying needs of the occupants. Many will be participating in sport but there will generally be a wide range of requirements depending on age, dress, standard of performance and physical activity levels. There may also be relatively inactive coaches, instructors, substitute players and casual or paying spectators.

Sports facilities are often also used for non-sporting activities such as arts use, meetings, seminars, exhibitions, exams, dances and social events and these will all introduce occupants with differing environmental requirements. It would be very difficult and extremely expensive to provide an installation that would be capable of continually adjusting to meet all potential requirements precisely. It is normally necessary, therefore, to assess the primary or most critical requirements and establish a compromise within the environmental services design that allows sufficient flexibility. At the same time the design must satisfy the most important requirements and be appropriate in terms of budget, energy use, plant space, integration within the building and operation and maintenance requirements.

The primary criteria which affect the comfort of users of a space are normally temperature, ventilation and lighting, although acoustics may also be important. The environmental services installation will generally be required to control these parameters in order to maintain the space within acceptable limits but other elements of the services installations will also be important in producing a satisfactory, safe and successful facility. These other services may include domestic water services, plumbing, drainage, electrical services, safety, security and public address and all will need to be integrated carefully with the building and each other.

The primary space within the facility with regard to the environmental services provision will be the main activity space, normally a sports hall, but it is also important that ancillary and support accommodation is adequately serviced.

In order to ensure the safety and comfort of sports participants it is important that all services distribution and items of equipment are located outside the main activity zone and, wherever possible, flush mounted or protected. The nature of the activities taking place also means that services installations are particularly vulnerable to damage from balls and other objects. All parts of the services installation should therefore be designed and installed so as to be resistant to impact. Installations should also be carefully detailed to avoid obvious traps for balls, shuttlecocks and similar objects to become lodged even when outside the normal playing zone, **1**.

2 Environmental requirements

The environmental requirements of a space are, in general, the requirements of the occupants within that space. The *CIBSE Guide: Section A1 – Environmental Criteria for Design*, states: 'The indoor environment should be safe, appropriate for its purpose and pleasant to inhabit. There should be little to cause annoyance or distraction and work or pleasure activities should be unhindered physically or mentally. A suitable environment can contribute towards a person's health, well-being and productivity.'

Table 60.1 sets out the recommended environmental criteria for the individual sports most commonly associated with indoor common space activities (see Chapters 15–46). The criteria listed are based upon the requirements of participants and do not, in general, take account of spectators, players resting or waiting to participate or non-sporting activities. Where social activities are likely to take place or there is a substantial spectator requirement, temperatures around 20°C may be necessary and ventilation rates may need to be higher than those required for sporting activities, particularly if higher occupancy of the space is involved, **2**. Special lighting and acoustic considerations may also be required for some arts or social activities and this may also be the case for certain sporting competitions such as boxing, wrestling and table tennis.

The ideal environmental services installation for a multiuse facility is obviously very difficult to define and may be expensive to achieve and could also be very inefficient in terms of energy use. It is also possible that it may be necessary to accommodate different activities within the

Table 60.1: Environmental criteria for indoor common space activities

Chap. No. in this volume	Activity	Temp. (°C)	Illuminance (lux) Recreational/ training	Club/competition	National/international
16	Aikido	12	500	1000	2000
17	Archery (1)	16	SL 200	SL 200	SL 200
			T1000(V)	T1000(V)	T1000 (V)
18	Sportshall athletics	16	200	300	500
19	Badminton	16	300	500	750
20	Basketball and mini-basketball	16	200	500	750
21	Bowls (short mat)	18	300	500	500
22	Boxing	12	500	1000	2000
23	Cricket (6- and 8-a-side and	16	500	750	750
	net practice) (3)	16	750	1000	1500
24	Croquet	16	200	300	500
25	Cycle speedway	14	200	500	750
26	Fencing	16	300	500	750
27	Five-a-side soccer	12	200	500	750
28	Golf practice	16	200	300	500
29	Gymnastics	18	200	500	750
30	Handball and mini-handball	14	200	500	750
31	Hockey (inc. six-a-side)	14	300	500	750
32	Judo	12	200	500	750
33	Karate	12	500	1000	2000
34	Kendo	12	500	1000	2000
35	Korfball	14	200	500	750
36	Movement and dance (2)	18	200	500	500
37	Netball	14	200	500	750
38	Short tennis	14	300	300	500
39	Softball	16	300	500	750
40	Table tennis	14	300	500	750
41	Tchouk-ball	14	300	500	750
42	Trampolining	14	300	500	750
43	Tug-of-war	14	200	300	300
44	Volleyball and mini-volleyball	14	200	500	750
45	Weightlifting (contests)	16	200	500	750
46	Wrestling	12	200	500	750

Note (1): SL, Shooting line; T, target; V, vertical illuminance.
Note (2): Special 'stage' lighting may be required.
Note (3): Net practice in multi-use halls only. For cricket schools see Chapter 74.

space simultaneously in order to maximise use of the space. It is generally recommended, therefore, that the environmental services installation design is based upon meeting the requirements of the activity with the highest priority whilst ensuring, as far as is practicable, that all other potential activities are catered for and there is adequate flexibility for realistic programming, **3**.

At the design stage it may be difficult to assess which activity is to have the highest priority for the environmental services design. It is likely that this will be the activity that is the primary use of the space or most critical for environmental quality. Experience suggests that in the majority of multi-use facilities badminton has the highest priority and that most other common activity requirements are reasonably satisfied by a well designed and operated environmental services installation based on badminton's requirements, **4**.

The requirements set out in Table 60.1 are generally minima but with respect to temperatures they are also, in general, the recommended operating value during the heating season. The predominant climatic conditions combined with the volume of the spaces normally involved, together with the need for adequate ventilation, mean that comfort cooling is not generally a requirement in this type of facility in the UK. Cooling may need to be considered in the particular circumstances of unusually high heat gains but these can often be dealt with by increased ventilation. Individual ventilation criteria have not been included in this table as the requirements are generally common and relate more to the space as a whole

2 Sports hall with high occupancy activity

3 Sports hall services must be suitable for a wide range of activities

4 *Services based on badminton requirements often satisfy other users*

rather than the specific activity. Ventilation requirements are therefore dealt with in the ventilation section below. Illuminance levels listed are for general guidance and are designated under three standards of activity – recreational/ training, club/county, national/international. They are given as minimum maintained average illuminance (generally horizontal at floor level) which is the value below which the average illuminance should not fall throughout the life of the installation. For full details of lighting requirements refer to lighting, below, and the *CIBSE Lighting Guide LG4: Sports.*

This information does not include television or broadcasting requirements and reference should be made to Chapter 11 of this volume, and the appropriate section of the *CIBSE Lighting Guide.*

3 Meeting the requirements

3.1 Heating

The basic thermal requirements for the various specific activities and the general common use of a multi-purpose indoor dry sports facility are given in Table 60.1. There are a number of alternative methods and systems available to meet these requirements. The most appropriate system for any particular facility will be dependent on the type of facility, range of activities, level of performance, operating and maintenance regime, energy use, fuel availability and, not least, budget.

Where mechanical ventilation is provided it may be convenient and beneficial to combine the ventilation and heating by means of a warm air plenum heating system and this is covered below. The temperature requirements for particular activities are generally minimum values but it will normally be appropriate to heat the space only to this level as higher temperatures may waste energy and could produce discomfort.

Where the heating and ventilation functions are provided separately the activity area is usually heated by warm air or radiant heating or a combination of both. In order to avoid damage and provide a clear space for sporting activities it is usual, as far as is practicable, to locate all systems and equipment outside the main activity zone. This is usually taken as the whole of the main sports hall area up to a height of around 3 m. Where it is essential to locate equipment within this zone it is generally necessary to provide recesses in order to maintain a flush wall surface and provide protection sufficiently robust to withstand

impact from balls and bodies. The difficulty of designing a conventional low level radiator or convective heating system within these restraints has resulted in most purpose designed sports halls utilising alternative systems such as high level radiant, warm air or under floor heating systems. Care must be taken in each case, however, to ensure that the system selected can be integrated effectively into the overall facility design. It must also provide the required thermal performance with the degree of flexibility that may be needed without interfering with or having a detrimental effect on the activity taking place.

Particular potential problems that may need to be considered are as follows:

High-level radiant
- Is it effective enough over required temperature range to provide the necessary flexibility?
- Is ventilation required?
- Can it provide comfort conditions around 20°C in the occupied zone?
- Are noise levels acceptable?

Warm air (high-level)
- Is distribution adequate to avoid large floor to ceiling temperature gradients which may be wasteful and inefficient?
- Are air velocities within the playing zone sufficiently low (less than 0.1 m/s) to avoid deflecting shuttlecocks, table tennis and other balls where appropriate?
- Can noise levels be controlled to within acceptable limits?

Underfloor heating
- Is response rapid enough over required temperature range to provide sufficient flexibility?
- Can it provide comfort conditions around 20°C where required?
- Can system and operating temperatures be successfully integrated into the particular floor finish and construction?
- What is the access situation and life expectancy (or guarantee) for buried pipework and/or services?

For each alternative system there will also be a choice of local or central heat generation and various alternative fuel sources. They are dealt with below but the ultimate decision should be based on a number of factors including overall energy use, maintenance, operating and life-cycle costs, the integration of services within the building, the quality of the environment produced and capital cost of the installation.

3.2 Ventilation

The wide range of potential activities and occupancy of a multi-purpose facility makes the choice of suitable ventilation rate and system very difficult. It is important to select a rate and system which satisfied the requirements of all users of the space without imposing an excessive energy burden.

The factors controlling the sizing and selection of the ventilation system are as follows:

- The introduction of adequate quantities of fresh air for the occupants
- The removal of vitiated air and odours
- The control of humidity levels for comfort and control of risk of condensation
- The control of summertime internal temperatures
- The control of internal temperature throughout the year where the ventilation system is also utilised for space heating

- The need to maintain low air movement within the playing zone (for badminton or table tennis it is recommended that air velocities are below 0.1 m/s)
- Acoustic considerations.

The fresh air requirement will generally be dependent on the number of occupants in a space unless determined by cooling needs. The *CIBSE Guide* does not define a fresh air requirement for sporting activities but a value of around 8–12 l/s of fresh air per person would seem to be appropriate in most circumstances.

Where the ventilation system also provides the heating via a warm air system the actual ventilation rate may be determined by the heating requirement and the appropriate supply air temperature. A ventilation rate of approximately 1.5 air changes per hour has been found to be appropriate for most sports halls of average height (around 7–8 metres high). This figure should perhaps be increased in facilities lower than 7 m and might be decreased in those higher than 8 m. Unless mechanical cooling is utilised, however, the rate should be checked against summer cooling requirements and occupancy rates to ensure that sufficient fresh air can be introduced. Where heat gains are particularly high (eg in a large glazed area), control of maximum temperatures is critical or if exceptionally large occupancy is a requirement it may be necessary to increase the ventilation rate up to three air changes per hour or even more.

In the majority of multi-use facilities, however, 1.5 air changes should satisfy requirements provided the air distribution is adequate. This may be difficult to achieve in that all the air needs to be distributed throughout the occupied zone to provide comfortable conditions and avoid excessive stratification, 5. Air velocities should generally be kept below 0.1 m/s within the activity zone and most of the actual air distribution and control equipment kept out of this zone (ie above 3 m). With careful design, selection of equipment, installation and commissioning this can be achieved successfully.

As long as the fresh air requirements for occupants and any existing cooling load are satisfied, the ventilation supply need not comprise only fresh air but can normally vary from a minimum of around 20% (depending on occupancy requirements) up to a maximum of 100%. This will help to minimise energy use to heat the incoming fresh air and can be achieved via automatic controls and carbon dioxide or other air quality detectors. The remaining proportion of ventilation air can be recirculated air from the space itself. In general, this can be successfully achieved only by means of centralised air handling plant and distribution ductwork. Close control of humidity is not normally a requirement in multi-use facilities and for most situations a relative humidity range of 40% to 70% is acceptable. In the UK it should be possible to control the humidity of the space within these limits reasonably easily for the vast majority of situations by means of the ventilation and fresh air control outlined in this section.

Most of the ventilation systems discussed so far have involved mechanical supply and extract and for most average sized well-used facilities these will be necessary. It is possible, however, that some of the smaller, less intensively used facilities may be able to achieve satisfactory conditions by utilising simple mechanical extract systems or occasionally even purely natural ventilation.

It is important, however, that the factors set out at the beginning of this section are always taken into account and, where extract ventilation only is being considered, there are means of replacing the extracted air. This often causes problems in that if there is no easy means of

5 *Ventilation inlets and outlets designed and located to provide good air distribution with minimal interference to the main playing zone*

replacement air to enter the building, the effectiveness of the ventilation system may be reduced. If outside air is allowed to enter freely this can result in heat loss and temperature control problems during winter periods.

3.3 Lighting
Sports facilities need to be lit so that those taking part, and those watching, can see clearly all that is going on. This entails a requirement for sufficient light in all areas, suitable brightness and contrasts over the playing area, correct distribution of light and adequate control of glare.

The lighting installation and type of lighting, including any use of natural lighting, will have a substantial impact on the design and layout of the building and it is therefore important that consideration is given to lighting design at an early stage. Surface colours and reflectances will also have an effect on the overall quality of the lighting of the space.

The extent of daylighting, if any, to be incorporated into a multi-purpose sports hall is a primary decision and should be taken at an early stage of the design process. The utilisation of daylight within a sports area can have a positive psychological effect upon participants, although the sun or bright sky seen through windows or by reflection from a glossy surface can cause unacceptable levels of disability or discomfort glare. The use of daylight in activity areas therefore requires very careful consideration and skilful design. In general it is recommended that only high level north facing glazing be installed. Rooflights and deep well glazing have been utilised in some facilities in the past. They have tended to produce serious maintenance problems. The additional problems of extra heat losses and gains brought about by installing glazing also need to be considered.

In multi-purpose facilities lighting should ideally be designed to meet the individual requirements of each activity (as set out in Table 60.1 and *CIBSE Lighting Guide LG4: Sports*). However, in the majority of cases this is neither practical nor economical and it is therefore recommended that the lighting is designed for the activity with the highest priority, provided that it will also be acceptable for other potential activities, **6**.

The layout of the playing areas and the arrangement of the lighting system should be planned together. The proposed lighting layout should be superimposed on a drawing showing all court and playing areas and arranged to be suitable for the highest priority use and checked to ensure it caters adequately for other activities.

Illuminance requirements for most activities are given in the horizontal plane (generally at floor level). It is important, however, that light distribution also ensures adequate illumination on vertical surfaces. It is usually necessary also to provide a small proportion of upward light to prevent the ceiling from appearing too dark.

Luminaires and other equipment should be protected from damage. Luminaires in sports halls should normally have wire guards or some other sort of impact resistant cover. These protection devices absorb a small percentage

of light output, however, and this must be allowed for during the design and selection of equipment.

Supplementary lighting systems may be required for special competitions (eg boxing, wrestling or table tennis) and for many non-sporting events (eg drama, exhibitions and conferences). These will generally be installed only for the particular event unless there is a special requirement to repeat an event frequently, but allowance may need to be made in the design of the facility and the electrical distribution and control circuitry.

The illuminance for a multi-purpose facility with a wide range of activities will normally need to be within the ranges stated below, dependent on priority activity and standard of play. Illuminances recommended are minimum maintained average levels (ie the value below which the average illuminance should not fall throughout the life of the installation).

- Recreational   200–300 lux
- Club/county competition   300–500 lux
- National/international competition   500–750 lux

The uniformity ratio (ratio of minimum to average illuminance) over the playing area should not normally be less than 0.7.

Table 60.1 in this section provides general illuminance level requirements for individual sports commonly played in multi-purpose facilities.

For detailed guidance on the design, installation, operation and maintenance of lighting for sports facilities refer to the *CIBSE Lighting Guide LG4: Sports*.

The above advice does not cover lighting for TV broadcasting and for these particular requirements reference should be made to chapter 11 of this volume, *CIBSE Lighting Guide LG4: Sports* and *CIE Guides 67* and *83*.

For recommendations regarding lighting requirements for non-sporting activities and ancillary non-specialised areas refer to the *CIBSE Code for Interior Lighting*.

3.4 Other requirements

Other environmental requirements necessary to ensure satisfactory, pleasant, attractive and safe conditions for activities are mainly related to acoustics, appearance and safety.

Aspects concerning safety in a multi-purpose facility including security, emergency lighting and alarm systems are covered in Chapter 14 of this volume. Reference is also made to some safety installations in 'Other services' below.

The colours and types of surface in a sports facility should be carefully selected in co-ordination with the lighting system in order to achieve the optimum visual quality for the activities taking place, particularly the priority activity. Sports halls should, in general, have light to medium coloured walls and the floors should not be too dark. Wall finishes should be matt to avoid specular reflections and walls and ceilings should not have strong patterns.

Surface reflections should generally be within the following ranges:

Walls   0.3 to 0.5
Ceilings or roofs   approx 0.9
Floors   0.2 to 0.4

The noise levels caused by mechanical services plant and equipment need to be limited to acceptable levels. The noise levels normally found acceptable for general sporting use of a facility are generally within the range NR 30 to 40. The amount of intended use for spectator events and

6 *Artificial lighting installation suitable for multi-use*

potential arts, dance or drama use may impose more stringent requirements. Noise breakout from the activity area to outside and other areas of the facility may also be an important factor and some form of acoustic insulation may be necessary. General reverberation times within the space itself can also cause problems of audibility and comfort. Once again there may be special requirements for arts or drama use but for normal sporting activities a maximum reverberation time of 2 s at 500 Hz with a background noise level of NR 50 is recommended. If sound absorption material is to be incorporated within a sports hall, it is desirable to concentrate it on the ceiling and walls above 3 metres height in order to restrict damage from impact.

For further details regarding walls, ceililng and floors see Chapters 62–67.

4 Ancillary areas

The supporting accommodation for a multi-purpose dry sports facility can generally be divided into three types of space:

- *Administrative areas* – including control points, office and staff rooms
- *Social areas* – including bars, snack bars, casual viewing, reception and meeting rooms
- *Ancillary areas* – including changing rooms, toilets, first-aid rooms and storage.

Administrative and social areas are not specific or unique to sports facilities and guidance and recommendations for the environmental services requirements for them can be found in the *CIBSE Guide and Code for Interior Lighting.*

The most critical ancillary areas with regard to environmental conditions are generally changing rooms and toilet accommodation. Changing rooms, toilets and showers should normally be lit to a minimum level of 150 lux and fittings will need to be designed and located carefully to be resistant to damage from moisture and vandalism.

The ideal temperature for changing rooms will be dependent on their use and location but it is advisable to ensure that the heating system is capable of maintaining 25°C especially where there is any shared use or links to swimming pools. It is very important that adequate ventilation is provided to maintain pleasant and comfortable conditions within changing areas and it is recommended that a minimum ventilation rate of 10 air changes an hour of 100% fresh air is achieved via a mechanical extract and supply system with good air distribution. It may be beneficial to distribute some of the air at floor level (or provide underfloor heating) in order to maintain a dry floor surface. Toilet facilities should also be provided with an all fresh air mechanical extract and supply system providing a minimum of 10 air changes per hour. The recommended temperature for toilets is 18–20°C, but this may need to be higher (21–23°C) where toilets are immediately adjacent to changing rooms maintained around 25°C.

It is important that all equipment located in toilet and changing areas is moisture resistant and that all equipment located in public areas (especially changing and toilet areas) is carefully designed and installed to minimise risk of damage from vandalism, 7.

5 Other services

Apart from the services already described, there will be a number of other environmental services installations

7 *Changing room with services located in bulkheads*

needed to maintain a satisfactory, safe and successful facility. These normally include domestic water supply, plumbing, drainage, electrical services, safety, security, telephones and public address services.

Most of these services are not specific or unique to sports facilities and guidance and recommendations regarding them can be found in standard reference works (eg *CIBSE Guide, Plumbing Services Design Guide*, IEE Regulations, Model Water Bylaws, Building Regulations). Two areas which are perhaps worthy of special attention, however, are safety and domestic water supply.

Safety is obviously a vitally important factor in any environmental services system design, particularly in a facility being used by potentially large numbers of the public who may not be familiar with the building or its services. Fire safety is critical in a public building and all elements of the fire safety services (which may include smoke control, emergency lighting, fire detection and alarm, first aid, fire fighting equipment, extinguishing systems and other fire brigade requirements) will need to be agreed with the relevant fire authority and fire insurers. General safety aspects of the facility including security, emergency lighting and alarm systems are covered in Chapter 14 of this volume.

Domestic water supplies for a multi-purpose facility will normally include mains water supply directly serving all drinking water taps and outlets to kitchens, vending machines and drinking fountains. Generally it will also provide the make-up water supply to a cold water storage system serving domestic hot and cold water distribution systems feeding sinks, hand basins, toilets and showers. The amount of water storage required will be dependent on the local water authority but is usually sufficient to meet a normal 24 hour demand. It is important that hot and cold water services are designed, installed and maintained to minimise the risk of Legionnaires disease: refer to *HSE booklet HS(G)70* and *CIBSE Publication TM13*. This, together with energy efficiency considerations, may involve careful consideration of more use of direct and point-of-use heating of hot water services and storage temperatures around 60°C where hot water storage is required.

6 Plant space and maintenance considerations

The environmental services requirements of a multi-purpose dry sports building are considerable and adequate plant and services distribution space must be incorporated. It is very important that this is considered early in the design in order that the allocation of space is both adequate and in the optimum locations in order that the services installation can be designed, installed, commissioned and maintained efficiently and effectively.

Adequate space needs to be provided for equipment to be installed and also for safe normal operation. In addition maintenance procedures and the replacement, repair or refurbishment of equipment during the life of the installation must also be considered and may have implications for the design of doorways and circulation areas.

The location of the main plant room should be chosen carefully taking into account:

- Minimising major service distribution routes
- Grouping together as much major plant and equipment as is practical
- Access for personnel and equipment
- Structural floor loadings
- Noise isolation from remainder of facility and outside
- Location of incoming mains services, meters, distribution boards, etc (fuel, water, electricity)
- Fuel and water storage locations
- Locations of boiler flues or similar exhausts
- Locations of air inlets and exhausts
- Storage for maintenance equipment, parts and materials
- Locations of maintenance staff and documentation.

8 *Adequate access is essential in plant spaces for maintenance*

Adequate access must be provided to all items of equipment and distribution systems that may need maintenance, adjustment or inspection during the lifetime of the installation, 8. Failure to do so may ensure that the installation is not operated or maintained adequately and extensive cost and disruption may be caused if the equipment needs to be adjusted, repaired or replaced at some future date.

61
Energy conservation

David Bosher

1 Introduction

The importance of energy conservation in the successful and efficient operation of a sports or recreation building arises from the fact that energy costs are generally the second highest operating cost after staffing. Energy use will also often be the only factor than can be controlled to reduce operating costs without affecting the standard of service or quality of facility. If energy use is to be optimised, the planning and design of structure, fabric and environmental services must be integrated. Energy use is also a very important factor in overall environmental considerations (see Chapter 3).

2 Thermal performance and insulation

The overall thermal performance of a building is controlled by its location and orientation, its thermal mass, the insulating properties of the building envelope or fabric and the amount of infiltration and ventilation introduced. In simple terms the more exposed a building the worse its thermal performance. It is therefore beneficial in energy terms to plan a facility in the most sheltered location available.

The better the thermal insulation of the building envelope, the better will be its thermal performance and therefore the more energy efficient it will be. All external walls, roofs and floors should be insulated as well as is practical and possible within budget limitations and areas of external glazing kept to a minimum, carefully located and double or triple glazed to reduce heat loss. Building regulations should be regarded only as a statutory minimum in this respect and improved upon wherever possible. The thermal mass of a building should be carefully matched to its systems of heating and ventilation and operational procedures in order to optimise energy use.

3 Operation and control

The selection of and operation to optimum values for internal environmental conditions such as temperatures, lighting levels and ventilation rates for each space and the relevant activities within it are critical in order to achieve maximum energy efficiency. It is also important that areas are not heated, ventilated or lit to standards in excess of those required or maintained at required levels for longer periods than necessary.

Most sport and recreation facilities are open to the public around 14 hours per day and many rooms or areas will not be in use all of that time. It is obviously beneficial if systems can be switched off or operating conditions reduced when areas are not in use. Providing that safety and risks of condensation or freezing are adequately catered for, systems should be designed to switch off or reduce in performance when spaces are not occupied and come back into full operation in readiness for the next occupation of the space. This can obviously be achieved automatically or manually or more usually by a combination of both.

Most mechanical and electrical installations will operate only at maximum efficiency if they are designed, installed, commissioned, operated and maintained properly. Every facility should have a comprehensive set of operating and maintenance instructions (including record drawings) and they should be followed carefully in order to ensure effective operation of the environmental services and minimise energy use.

4 Ventilation control

Ventilation rates should match the actual requirements of each space, particularly in relation to the supply of fresh air and infiltration. Whilst it is important to ensure that maximum occupancy can be satisfied and comfort conditions maintained by the ventilation system, it is also important to ensure that the fresh air ventilation rate is controlled to match the actual requirement at any particular time.

Sophisticated automatic control can obviously be most beneficial on larger installations but even the smallest, simplest systems can improve their energy use by sensible manual control. When only a few people occupy the space and there is no cooling requirement, fresh air supply can usually be reduced to a minimum by introducing recirculated air. When spaces are entirely unoccupied ventilation systems should normally be switched off or operate on total recirculation.

5 Heat recovery

Provided ventilation systems are correctly sized and controlled the most efficient method of improving ventilation energy efficiency is likely to be some form of heat recovery. This will be particularly beneficial on systems that require permanent all fresh air supply ventilation such as changing rooms and toilet facilities.

Ventilation heat recovery generally involves direct air-to-air recovery systems which transfer some of the available heat from the exhaust air to the cooler incoming supply air. There are a number of available systems including thermal wheels and heat pipes but the two simplest and most popular used in dry facilities are the run-around coil and plate heat exchanger.

The run-around coil is less efficient (approx 50–60% efficiency) and more complicated in that it involves separate heat exchange coils in supply and exhaust systems linked by a closed loop pipework system which circulates a heat exchange fluid. It does have the benefit, however, of being suitable for systems where the supply and extract plants are located in separate parts of the building.

The plate heat exchanger is the more efficient system (approx 70–80% efficiency) but requires the supply and extract ventilation ductwork systems to be close together and is therefore only usually practical in centralised plant systems.

6 Fuels and fuel efficiency

The choice of fuels and the efficiency of their use are obviously very important factors in the overall energy efficiency of a facility, Table 61.1.

For most facilities there will be a choice of primary fuels including coal, oil, gas (natural or bottled) and electricity and there will also be a decision whether to centralise the

Table 61.1: Typical fuel and system efficiencies

System	Appliance efficiency	System efficiency
Solid fuel boiler, non-condensing	75%	70%
Gas boiler, condensing	90%	85%
Gas boiler, non-condensing	80%	75%
Propane boiler, condensing	90%	85%
Propane boiler, non-condensing	80%	75%
Oil, condensing	90%	85%
Oil, non-condensing	75%	70%
Electric resistance heat (local efficiency)	100%	100%
Electric storage heat (local efficiency)	100%	90%

Table 61.2: Examples of typical energy consumption yardsticks (1) for sports facilities (kWh/m²)

Facility	Low	Medium	High
Swimming pool	<940	940–1355	>1355
Sports centre with pool (water area less than 20% total area)	<510	510–745	>745
Sports centre without a pool Sports club	<290	290–410	>410

Note (1): the yardsticks are based on total floor area.

use of this fuel or utilise it directly via local equipment. The decision may be controlled in some instances by fuel availability and the cost of providing it but in general the decision should be made based on overall energy efficiency and the amount of useful energy available from primary fuel.

Modern high efficiency boilers (including condensing boilers) generally provide much higher efficiencies than older conventional boilers. Once again it is important to maintain boilers and especially burners effectively in order to maintain good fuel efficiency.

Electricity is generally the most flexible and convenient fuel and will almost always be utilised for lighting and power. The efficiency of utilisation is very important, however, and the types of light fitting used and their method of control will affect the overall energy efficiency (see *CIBSE Lighting Guide LG4: Sports* for further details). It is important also to acknowledge that electricity is not really a primary fuel but is usually produced in power stations and subsequently distributed through the national grid. In environmental terms, therefore, although the end use efficiency may appear very impressive the overall efficiency of electricity is likely to be considerably lower than all the primary fuels.

7 Energy targeting and monitoring

Sensible energy targets should be assessed for any new building at the design stage, Table 61.2, and subsequently monitored in order to ensure energy efficiency.

Each facility will need to be assessed individually in order to establish anticipated energy usage. Comparison between indoor dry multi-purpose facilities is very difficult owing to wide variation in factors such as building type and size, opening hours, type of use and operating conditions. It is therefore important that energy targets are assessed as realistically as possible and then adjusted when necessary based on collected monitoring data and any variations in operating or usage.

There are a wide range of publications and information available from the Energy Efficiency Office (EEO) and similar bodies to assist in this important task (see, for example, *Introduction to Energy Efficiency in Sports and Recreation Centres*, EEO 1988).

It is vital that the energy use of a facility is regularly and sensibly monitored by separating usage of fuels, systems and areas whenever possible in order accurately to assess energy efficiency. This will enable energy use to be optimised, assessed continuously and adjusted as necessary throughout the life of the building.

62
Detailed design: general

Christopher Harper

1 General design approach

A fundamental decision affecting hall design is the method of lighting and whether natural lighting or a 'blind box' solution is required. Current sports hall lighting philosophy and techniques are discussed in Chapter 60 of this volume. Some of the more important considerations are:

- All halls require artificial lighting for night and dull weather use, but in daytime artificial lighting may be replaced or supplemented by natural lighting.
- Natural lighting can be regarded as expensive both in terms of capital and recurrent costs. Windows can be troublesome to clean and artificial lighting alone is a cheaper solution although running costs may be higher.
- Most users occupy the sports hall for a relatively short time and do not need contact with the outside world or to take advantage of the qualities of natural lighting.
- The case for natural light is sometimes made by staff and users who dislike a totally artificially controlled environment in both the hall and support accommodation.
- Halls which are used for social functions or on school sites with constant daytime use benefit most from some natural light.
- When natural light is admitted to sports halls the area of glazing has to be limited and lighting levels are consequently low. It is therefore expensive to provide in relation to the benefits offered, particularly as artificial lighting is often needed to supplement any natural sources in dull weather. However, hall ambience is invariably improved by daylight, **1**.
- The admission of daylight to activity areas eases the way to providing natural light in circulation and social spaces, giving the opportunity to create a more attractive and welcoming sports centre environment.

Different elements of sports hall envelope design are inter-related and therefore should be considered together. The roof structure should relate to the position of lighting, **2**, heating and ventilation systems and curtain and equipment supports which in turn relate to court layout. An 'integrated' design approach is therefore strongly recommended.

1.1 Colour and reflectances

The colour of surfaces also has a significant impact on the success of a hall for multi-sports use. The accepted principles for the selection of finishing materials or decorative schemes are:

Walls	Of a uniform unbroken colour with a reflectance value to give sufficient contrast with small, fast moving objects such as shuttlecocks and table tennis balls or for activities like fencing and martial arts
Ceiling	Of an unbroken light colour with a reflectance value which ensures minimum contrast with sources of illumination in order to reduce glare. White has been found to be the best background colour and it is recommended that all structural elements including purlins are painted to match the soffit.
Floor	Of a colour which gives sufficient contrast to walls to ensure satisfactory spatial modelling and provides a reflectance factor compatible with even light spread and energy economy.

Another factor which must be considered in relation to surface colour, particularly for walls, is the colour properties of the type of luminaire specified. Some types significantly distort the 'daylight' appearance of colours. The most recently published advice on multi-sports hall reflectance values is recalled in the table below together with current TUS recommendations.

	TUS design Note 10 (1984)	SASH Design Guide 1 (1986)	CIBSE Lighting for Sport (1990)	Current TUS Recommendations (1995)
Walls	0.3 (0.5 max for badminton)	0.3	0.3–0.6	0.3–0.5 (1)
Ceilings	0.9 (or more), ie white	0.8	0.6–0.9	0.9 min
Floors	0.4–0.2 (0.5 max for badminton)	0.4	0.2–0.4	0.2–0.4

Note (1): The 0.3 value is normally preferred for badminton, but lighter colours can be selected for a brighter ambience or where the floor surface is frequently covered with a roll-down darker coloured carpet, most usually for bowls. This compromise is especially relevant to sports halls with a high proportion of social use, particularly smaller community halls where values around 0.5 may be appropriate.

1.2 Methods of construction

General
The majority of sports halls are built with lightweight roof decking supported by a structural system of main and secondary beams. The walls are either loadbearing masonry or framed with masonry infill panels or lightweight cladding.

Steelwork
Although sports halls do not have such extreme environmental conditions as swimming pools, air moisture content can be high if heating and ventilation systems are not operating efficiently. Exposed and encased steelwork should therefore be protected with a suitable paint system. The structural engineer will provide information on protective systems as will the Corrosion and Coated Products Advisory Service of the British Steel Corporation. Paint manufacturers also offer advice on protective systems related to their own particular products.

Reinforced concrete
Reinforced concrete frames and beams have been used successfully in a number of sports halls. If the steel reinforcement is well protected there should be no problems with corrosion. The finish to the concrete should be smooth and easily cleaned. For further information designers are referred to the Concrete Advisory Service.

1 *Natural lighting baffled by deep 'V' beams at Immingham Sports Centre. Photo: Tri-light*

Timber

Hardwoods and softwoods, particularly in the form of laminated structural sections, have been used in a large number of sports hall designs. Natural softwood construction is adequate provided stress-graded timber is used for structural purposes and both plywood and particle board may be used for wall lining. Panel faces must be flush and adequately supported by studwork framing.

Timber finishes which can be considered are:

- Natural finishes with a clear seal
- Proprietary wood stains (without fungicide additive); if finished with a suitable clear sealant these can give a hardwearing surface.

For further information, designers are referred to the Timber Research and Development Association and BRE Princes Risborough Laboratories. All timber linings will normally be required to meet Class 1 resistance to flame spread.

1.3 Summary of basic design factors

Roof construction

- Consider roof decking construction to reduce heat loss and gain – provide adequate insulation and a vapour barrier to prevent condensation and interstitial deterioration, **3**(A).

- If practicable, provide a flush ceiling which is sound-absorbent and able to withstand impact from balls, **3**(B). Insulate at least to the standards required under current Building Regulations.
- Consider colour and surface reflectance, **3**(B).
- Consider roof structure in relation to main activity area and method of lighting, **3**(C).
- Steelwork can be encased or exposed. For protective treatment specification, consult a structural engineer, the Corrosion and Coated Products Advisory Service of the British Steel Corporation or individual manufacturers, **3**(C).
- Concrete can be left fairfaced or painted. Exposed concrete surfaces below 3 m (approx 10 ft) should be non-abrasive, **3**(C).
- Timber – refer to the Timber Research and Development Association and BRE Princes Risborough Laboratories for suitable finishes and protective systems, **3**(C).
- Consider the strength of roof structure for supporting engineering services, light fittings, netting trackways, basketball backboards and gymnastics equipment, **3**(C).
- Eliminate, as far as practicable, narrow, high level ledges where shuttlecocks and balls can get caught, particularly above structural members, **3**(D).

Wall construction

- Wall surfaces should be flush without any projections, ledges or sharp corners, **3**(E).

2 *Controlled artificial lighting arranged between badminton courts in a SASH Centre. Photo: Martin Charles*

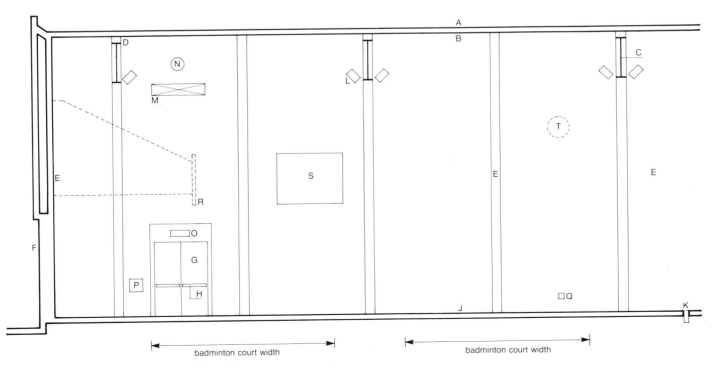

3 *Part section through a sports hall keyed in to accompanying text*

- Consider wall construction to reduce heat loss and eliminate the possibility of interstitial condensation, **3**(F). Insulate at least to the standards required under current Building Regulations.
- Consider strength of wall for body and ball impact and supporting equipment, **3**(F).
- Consider wall movement between frame and infill panels and provide movement joints as required, **3**(F).
- If fair faced blockwork is used, specify an appropriate sealant to prevent dusting, **3**(E).
- Door frames, door surfaces and ironmongery should ideally be set flush with adjoining wall surfaces, **3**(G,H).
- Wall openings should be positioned away from the corners of the hall and from goal zones and any exposed edges rounded, **3**(G,H).
- Consider acoustic properties, **3**(B).

Floor construction
- Primary requirements are traction, surface elasticity and evenness of surface, **3**(J).
- Consider colour and surface reflectance, **3**(J).
- Court markings – check recommendations of floor finish manufacturer, **3**(J).
- Consider position of sockets particularly for gymnastics equipment, **3**(K).
- Consider the thickness of floor slab in the case of suspended floors – the slab may have to be thickened locally at socket positions, **3**(K).

Environmental engineering services
For general details of environmental services recommendations refer to Chapters 60 and 61.

- Consider artificial lighting layout in relation to natural lighting (if provided) and the structural and courts layout, **3**(L).
- Where practicable, consider using the roof structure for supporting light fittings and other services, **3**(L).
- Consider location of heating and ventilation equipment and distribution and conceal whenever possible, **3**(M).
- Consider the position of wall mounted grilles and ventilation fans. Openings at low level should be avoided where possible, but if required should line through with the adjoining walls and be protected with heavy duty flush grilles, **3**(M).
- Consider position of fire alarm bell, **3**(N).
- Consider exit emergency signs and their protection, **3**(O).
- Consider position for fire alarm bell push. Set the box flush with the wall surface, **3**(P).
- Consider positions for power points in relation to cleaning and audio equipment, **3**(Q).

Fittings and equipment
- Consider design of basketball backboards and method of support whether by walls or the roof structure, **3**(R,S).
- Consider position of backboards in relation to any ventilation openings, **3**(R,S).
- Consider position (and support) of netting trackways in relation to lighting (or heating) arrangements, **3**(L).
- Consider the position of clocks and their protection, and the position of scoreboards and their support, **3**(T).
- Consider sports equipment for various activities – see individual sports data in Chapter 15 of this volume.

63
Detailed design: roof/ceilings

Christopher Harper

1 Roof form

Sports halls have been built with flat, pitched and monopitched roofs but current building economics favour the steel portal frame type of structure.

1.1 Exposed structures and suspended ceilings

Most sports halls have their roof structure exposed. The main advantages for this constructional approach are:

- Economy
- Easy structural support for engineering services, light fittings, tracks and equipment
- Easy access for maintenance and ceiling inspection.

Disadvantages include:

- The roof structure obtrudes on a flat, even soffit
- Engineering services are exposed and therefore their routing and overall design/appearance need careful consideration
- Natural light, if required, cannot be diffused or softened to provide glare-free light distribution without the use of suspended membranes or structural or applied baffles
- The roof structure and ductwork harbour dust and provide traps for balls and shuttlecocks.

The introduction of a suspended ceiling does offer some advantages to offset higher built cost:

- It can be designed to provide a flat soffit, detailed to provide some sound absorbency, together with artificial and natural lighting control, 2
- Concealed ductwork conduit and pipes can be routed as required

- Ledges and ball traps are eliminated.

But disadvantages include:

- Additional support is required for the suspended ceiling, tracks and equipment
- Access can be difficult for routine maintenance and checking the condition of roof structure
- Unless robust and adequately supported, a suspended ceiling is more prone to damage than a composite roof construction.

1.2 Detailed design considerations

The control of glare

The problem of glare in sports hall is discussed in Chapters 60 and 62. In practical terms it is difficult to prevent glare completely but the problem can be reduced by:

- Selecting a matt finish ceiling material of an appropriately high reflectance value, 2
- Careful selection of suitable colour and surface reflectance values in conjunction with wall and floor finishes and the lighting system (both artificial and natural). For detailed information, see the lighting section in Chapter 60, and Chapter 62.

The following points summarise the recommendations for multi-sport halls:

- Provide light-coloured ceilings, light/medium colour floors with walls of a medium/dark colour
- A light-coloured ceiling reduces glare from ceiling luminaires and provides better light distribution
- Colour and tone of surfaces should be selected to provide spatial definition – similar dark tones for walls and floor surfaces have resulted in drab and lifeless interiors
- Consider the colour properties of the lamps specified in relation to the colour of walls and floors.

For halls designed primarily for one sport, surface reflectances, colours and lighting need to be considered in relation to the particular requirements of that sport.

1 *A tensioned translucent membrane at a Hampshire school diffuses roof lighting and conceals luminaires. Photo: C J Harper*

2 *The sports hall at Fountains Leisure Centre, Brentford where the deep 'V' beams successfully mask the bands of rooflight*

3 *Dark ceilings and high efficiency individual lamps contribute to glare. Photo: Sports Council Publications*

Natural lighting
If badminton is an important activity, masked light sources should run at right angles to the length of the courts despite the cost penalty of longer structural spans, unless a diffusing membrane is employed, **3**.

Rooflights create shadows or dark spots particularly at the junction of the roof with the walls and, to a lesser extent, on the ceiling plane between the rooflights. These areas will always appear dark in contrast to the rooflight brightness.

Robustness
The roof construction and finishes must be capable of withstanding the impact of balls, in particular volley and soccer balls. Many standard ceiling products are therefore unsuitable for use in sports halls. Sheet materials are ruled out unless backed with a reinforcing material.

Support for equipment and access for engineering services
The roof structure must be capable of supporting these loads and, in larger roofs, the possible additional loading of catwalks. In a basic low-cost sports hall the ideal position for the fittings may not relate to the structural system adopted. In this case, services will have to be suspended or fixed to purlins or the underside of the roof deck or on supplementary structure.

Whichever method is adopted, designers need to consider:

- The position of the fittings in relation to netting trackways
- Access for maintenance, cleaning fittings and replacing lamps
- How netting trackways are to be supported – they are normally fixed to or suspended from the underside of the main structure
- How basketball backboards and items of gymnastic apparatus are to be supported; backboards can be wall-mounted if required but are normally fixed to fold down from the underside of the main structure.

1.3 Thermal considerations
Heated sports halls must comply with the current Building Regulations thermal insulation standards.

1.4 Acoustic considerations
The roof/ceiling provides the main surface for sound control and should be detailed to provide a maximum of a 2 seconds reverberation time. Noise spillage will also have to be contained on some sites.

64
Detailed design: sports floors

Jennifer Millest

1 Introduction

The success of most indoor sports facilities depends greatly on the suitability of the floor for the activities which are to take place on it. It is, firstly, the performance of the floor which provides good or bad conditions for a sport.

Unfortunately, despite other important considerations, capital cost is often a key determining factor in choosing a floor. It is frequently the case that necessary reductions in the capital cost of a building are effected by cost savings in finishes and fittings – and flooring does represent a tempting proportion of these. Naturally, the capital cost of the building is important, but it should be remembered that whilst the cost of flooring is a relatively insignificant part of the overall building cost, the floor on which a sport is played is arguably the most important element of a sports facility and this should be given due consideration when drawing up cost plans. The wrong choice of floor can significantly affect the effectiveness of a facility. While there may be opportunities to improve on fittings and furnishings at a later date, the cost of remedying the wrong choice of floor is likely to be prohibitive.

2 The choice of a sports floor

The choice of the most appropriate sports floor is rarely simple and often involves compromises between conflicting requirements. There are usually three main groups of factors to take into account:

- The proposed use of the floor for a range of sports and other activities
- The requirements of individual sports and the floor qualities they demand
- Management and other considerations.

2.1 Use of the floor

Sports activities

The choice of a suitable floor should depend principally on the range of sports activities for which the hall or room will be used. The first need, therefore, is to identify the sport or sports for which the installation is intended. For specialist rooms dedicated to a single sport this may be simple. However, it is most frequently the case that the same sports area will have to serve for a number of sports and they may have conflicting performance requirements.

Multi-sports use Many surfaces are satisfactory for a considerable number of sports, but no surface will be satisfactory for all sports, nor equally satisfactory for all the sports which could be played on it. Inevitably there has to be a compromise when choosing a surface for multi-sports use.

Priority sports Priorities will have to be identified, taking account both of anticipated maximum usage and the standards at which the various activities are expected to be played – this may vary from full international standard to a wholly recreational level. Most sports halls will cater for the recreational user. However, many of the larger centres may wish to attract county, national or even international tournaments; in such cases a suitable floor will have to be installed for the centre to gain acceptance from the sponsoring or governing body.

Main sports on multi-sports surfaces in the UK Most sports halls will need to accommodate a number of different sports, ranging from badminton to roller skating. Of the sports which are most commonly played in multi-sports halls in the UK, badminton, basketball and mini-basketball, five-a-side football, handball and seven-a-side and mini-handball, indoor hockey, movement and dance, netball, table tennis, volleyball and mini-volleyball may all be accommodated satisfactorily on the same surface.

Sports having particular requirements Roller skating and roller hockey and trampolining are among the sports which can be played on some multi-sports surfaces but impose particular requirements for stiffness and resistance to damage. Similarly, tennis and cricket are examples of sports which can be played on some multi-sports surfaces but impose particular requirements for ball bounce and spin.

Sports on mats Gymnastics, fencing competitions and the martial arts usually require the addition of mats when undertaken on multi-sports surfaces and this can also be a suitable solution for indoor bowls (the flat and short mat games) and cricket (both indoor six-a-side and nets).

Other main sports elsewhere in Europe Other sports activities which are most commonly undertaken in multi-sports halls in other parts of Europe include korfball or korbball, physical education and gymnastics (without mats).

Secondary activities Secondary activities in the UK may include fencing training, lacrosse (women's seven-a-side and box lacrosse) and tennis; and in other parts of Europe may also include cycle sports, deck tennis, fistball, gyro wheeling, pelota, powerball, rebound ball and small games and movement education. There are, of course, other sports which can be played satisfactorily on many multi-sports surfaces.

Qualities required Having identified the main sports for which the surface is required, selection of a suitable surface becomes a matter of ensuring that the most important qualities required for these sports are provided at a satisfactory level. This is addressed in Section 2.2 below.

Non-sports activities

In addition to the range of sports activities, non-sports uses should also be considered. It is almost inevitable that with a large hall at its disposal the sponsoring authority will wish to stage other non-sporting activities. An indoor sports facility may provide the only or largest hall in the locality and this may need to serve for community and arts purposes, whether or not it was originally intended for such. School sports halls may also be used for school assemblies, examinations and prize-givings. The requirement for sports centres to be commercially viable may also lead to the use of the hall for other purposes from time to time. These other uses may include exhibitions, discos, dinner dances and concerts. The floor might therefore be required to stand up to discarded cigarette ends, outdoor shoes, tables, chair legs, exhibition stands and even livestock or motor shows.

It is an aim of the Sports Council to ensure that sports activities do not become secondary to these alternative uses. However, other activities will occur and it is essential that such uses should not destroy the qualities required of the floor for its primary purpose. Hence, it is important that the possibility of such uses be taken into consideration in selecting the floor.

It should be noted that the requirements for such general activities as trade and technical exhibitions may not be compatible with, and may even be opposed to, the performance requirements for sports activities.

2.2 Qualities of the sports surface

Requirements

The characteristics required of a sports floor are those which enable activities to take place in accordance with the rules and other requirements of one or more sports, **2**, in a responsible way in relation to hygiene, health, safety and the environment, with a certain intensity, frequency and for a defined period of time, using the equipment needed for such activities.

Sports performance

The sports performance characteristics required will depend on the sport or sports for which the area is intended and relate to the interaction of the ball or player with the surface.

Ball/surface interaction

Ball rebound In the case of sports involving the bouncing of a ball, the height of rebound of the ball used for the sport must be appropriate to the sport concerned.

For sports where high ball speeds are a feature of the game (eg tennis), the loss of speed during impact with the surface, and hence the speed at which the ball returns from the surface, is also a relevant factor.

The texture of the surface and any minor irregularities, (see Acceptance criteria below) should not be such as will affect the direction of rebound of the ball.

For certain sports, such as cricket and tennis, the response of a spinning ball to impact with the surface, including the resultant spin and deviation of the ball, provides an essential subtlety of the game which will be influenced by the friction between the ball and the surface together with the surface stiffness.

Ball roll For sports such as bowls the ball roll behaviour is important.

The rate at which a rolling ball loses speed is dependent on the rolling resistance of the surface and this will affect the distance of travel in relation to the initial energy with which the ball is projected. This is not considered to be a significant factor in consideration of indoor multi-sports surfaces, most of which by their nature contribute little to reducing the speed of roll of the ball, resulting in a continuing roll to which hockey and other sports have adapted the indoor versions of their games.

However, in all sports involving a rolling ball, the flatness of the floor (see Acceptance criteria below) and the consistency of the surface will be of particular relevance to the run of the ball and should not result in deviation from its intended line.

Wheel/surface interaction

The rolling resistance of the surface is an important consideration for roller skating and other wheeled sports, including those involving wheelchair participants, though the weight of the person will bring into play to a greater degree other factors such as the need for high stiffness of the surface.

Person/surface interaction

Friction For most sports the level of friction between the player's shoes and the surface needs to be high enough to prevent accidental slipping, but not so high as to restrict foot movement either in a continuing direction or when turning. A capacity for controlled sliding of the foot is required for some sports.

In sports where sliding contact between the player's body and the surface is likely, the friction between the surface and skin or clothes may need to be taken into account.

Frictional qualities can be altered considerably by the presence of moisture which may result from cleaning of the floor, sweat, condensation or roof leaks.

Impact The dynamic interaction between the surface and the player when running, landing or falling is very complex, involving the stiffness or compliance of the surface and its shock absorbency, the force of impact between the player and the floor surface and the energy returned or lost to the player. For most sports a moderate level of stiffness is desirable: in normal running a very soft surface tends to slow the player whereas a very hard surface may jar the player. A surface with very high energy absorption is tiring and reduces performance. However, in the free fall of a player on to the surface, reduction of the force of impact between the player and the surface is important and this must be taken into consideration for sports involving bodily contact with the surface.

Safety

In practice a compromise is generally necessary between the ideal characteristics for sports performance and safety. It is incumbent on the owners and operators of a sports facility to satisfy themselves as to the suitability of the surface from a safety aspect for the sports to be played.

There are various aspects to safety, including the fire resistance and the toxicity of the surface as well as the possibility of physical injuries.

Physical injury Physical injury to the player can occur through impact or other interaction between the player and surface. For example, abrasions or friction burns might result from sliding contact between the player's body and the surface; bruising or bone fracture from severe body impact; muscle fatigue or strain from repeated foot impact (such as when running); and twisting of joints from restricted foot movement.

The likelihood of injury is dependent on a combination of properties of the surface such as stiffness, energy absorption, frictional qualities and roughness, with the nature of the sport to be played. The optimum conditions for safety in relation to physical injury, as with sports performance, will vary from sport to sport.

Abrasion from sliding body contact with the surface is influenced by surface roughness and stiffness; it is not advisable to play sports likely to involve sliding contact between the player's body and the surface on a rough, rigid surface.

Friction burns from sliding body contact are influenced by the friction and thermal properties of the surface. In general the higher the coefficient of friction the higher are the chances of friction burns in sports with the likelihood of sliding body contact with the surface, but this cannot be taken as a rule because the material and structure of the surface may significantly affect the temperature reached in sliding.

The chance of injury from impact with the floor, walls, or other players may be influenced by the frictional qualities in that inappropriate slip resistance increases the possibility of a fall or a collision.

If a severe impact occurs between a player and the floor surface, the likelihood of bone fracture or other injury is affected by the stiffness and shock absorbency of the floor. Where much body contact between the player and the surface is envisaged, very stiff surfaces should be avoided and surfaces with good shock absorbency are to be preferred.

Repeated, less severe impacts experienced in the course of running can result in long-term injury: as a general guide, the risk is least with a surface of moderate stiffness and moderate shock absorbency.

For multi-sports use, the most desirable characteristics from the safety aspect are moderate levels of friction, stiffness and shock absorption, though this may not be ideal from the performance point of view for any given sport.

Toxicity The surface must not contain any substance which is known to be toxic or carcinogenic when in contact with the skin, nor release any toxic or carcinogenic substances as vapour or dust during normal use.

Flammability A small source of fire such as a cigarette end or match should not cause the surface to burn or ignite, nor should it result in irregularity of the surface sufficient to cause a ball to deflect from its true path.

The propensity of the surface to contribute to a larger fire should be considered in the context of the flammability of surrounding materials and means of escape.

Material characteristics
The material characteristics of the surface must be such that it is capable of standing up to use for normal play (and non-sports activities if these are expected) and retaining its sports and safety characteristics over a period of time.

Durability The surface must be sufficiently durable to withstand abrasive wear resulting from use for the intended activities and the penetration and tearing tendency of spikes if spiked shoes are to be worn for the sports concerned.

It must also be strong enough to resist, and able adequately to recover from:

- Any indentation resulting from the localised static loads of portable equipment placed on the surface
- The rolling loads imposed by equipment wheeled on to the surface
- Impacts resulting from dropped equipment or occurring in the course of play.

Damage can occur from equipment dragged across the surface, but it is difficult to provide for such misuse of the surface and this is better catered for by the care and control of equipment and its handling.

The surface must be able to stand up to the ageing effects of the repeated impacts of balls and players' feet pounding the surface and of light and heat and, in intermittently occupied facilities, cold and rapid changes of temperature.

It will also need to withstand cleaning agents and water if they are used for cleaning or in the event of accidental spillage or flooding.

The surface should remain dimensionally stable, without delamination, curling, buckling, or shrinkage or stretching to an extent which will affect its use.

Other properties
Joint strength The installation should form an essentially continuous surface: joints should not significantly affect the playing performance and should be capable of retaining their integrity.

Colour transfer The surface should not transfer its colour to any other materials (such as clothing or balls) which may come into contact with it.

Colour and light reflectance The colour, tone and light reflectance of the floor should not be considered in isolation but in conjunction with the walls and ceiling, the natural or artificial lighting to be used and the specific requirements of the sports for which the area is intended.

The difference in colour or tone between the floor and walls should not be too wide as sudden contrasts increase the difficulty in following a fast moving object, but there should be sufficient contrast to give spatial definition and avoid a dull, lifeless environment.

The surface should be sufficiently light in tone to give light reflectance values which will contribute to high, even illumination levels over the playing area but it should also provide a background which will contrast in brightness or colour, or both, with any objects which need to be clearly visible in the intended sports such as balls, shuttlecocks and line markings.

Formerly, a reflectance value of 20% was suggested for sports hall floors, within the convention that floors were darker than walls which in turn were darker than ceilings. However, the pursuit of good lighting design has led to the use of lighter floors, with reflectance values up to 40% (corresponding to paint finishes of Munsell value 7) and this is the value now recommended for indoor multi-sports surfaces.

Gloss The finish should not be shiny but matt or sufficiently low gloss to avoid glare or specular reflection producing images of light sources, fittings, or players which may cause confusion and difficulty in sighting balls and may give an impression of slipperiness. Care should be taken that routine maintenance does not alter this.

The preference and expectation of clients is often for a gloss finish to the floor, but this is not in the best interests of the main uses for which a sports hall is intended.

Sound absorption For particular sports or locations there may be a need to take into consideration the sound absorbency of the surface.

Performance standards and specifications
Having established the qualities required, the qualities offered by the various products must be matched against these requirements.

Tests for most of these properties, together with specification limits for multi-sports use intended to provide a reasonable compromise between the optimum conditions for sports performance and the best conditions to reduce each type of injury, plus reasonable resistance to wear and ageing, are defined in *BS 7044 Artificial Sports*

Surfaces and were previously included in the Sports Council's *Specification for Artificial Sports Surfaces 1984* on which BS 7044 was based.

Companies whose products are under consideration should be asked to provide a copy of a report from an independent test house on the results of testing in accordance with BS 7044 so that the performance of the surface may be verified in relation to the qualities required.

Products of each of the main flooring types have been tested and shown to comply with this Standard and it is strongly recommended that selection be made from such products.

The European Standard at present in preparation is expected to cover tests and limits for all of the properties described above, plus ball rebound speed, behaviour under a rolling load, impact strength and dimensional stability which are not included in the Sports Council's Specifications nor in BS 7044, but are among the tests carried out in some other European countries. Currently this European Standard is scheduled for completion in 1998.

2.3 Management and other factors

Having established the performance characteristics of the various surfaces available in terms both of playing qualities and durability, it is necessary also to take into account various management factors and capital costs, maintenance needs and life expectancy of the products, guarantees and hence viability.

Management of the facility
Facility profile The kind of establishment, style of management and degree of control over the use of the facility should each have some influence on the type of surface selected.

The amount of regular or prolonged use by the same participants, as in schools or prisons, or for intensive training, should be borne in mind in relation to the effect of the floor on muscles, tendons, ligaments and joints. In these cases the floor should be specified as 'Impact Energy Absorbing' in the terms of BS 7044 as well as complying with the general aspects of that British Standard.

Maintenance commitment The maintenance commitment available has a bearing on the type of surface selected and the recurrent costs which may be involved in maintaining and repairing a large sports hall floor need to be considered at the outset. Some surfaces require a greater degree of regular maintenance than others to keep them in a good playable condition. For some, budgetary provision must be made for major maintenance by a specialist firm every few years, with only a relatively small amount of regular attention being needed in between.

The frequency and type of maintenance required for products under consideration should be established not only from manufacturers' trade literature but also from practical experience wherever this can be found. Local repairs of a minor nature should be within the capabilities of the centre's maintenance staff. It should also be possible to carry out repairs to the surface without the need to lift large areas of sound material which would entail high labour costs and loss of income from use of the hall.

Financial considerations The expected total hours of use have to be considered in terms of the return on the capital outlay and hence the overall costs justifiable and the capital finance available must obviously also be borne in mind. The extent to which these may affect the choice of the floor was discussed in Section 1 above.

Consideration of types of surface
The general characteristics of the various types of surface are discussed in Section 3 below.

Costs Comparison of capital costs of different products should take account of the relevant subfloor requirements as discussed in Section 4 below.

Existing installations Where possible, visits should be made by the client, key users and architect to similar installations of the products under consideration to assess how satisfactory the installation has been in practice and how well the installing firm has performed both during construction and in rectifying any defects which may have developed since. Particular attention should be paid to installational points, such as attachment to base or perimeter fixings and seams and joints, which are one of the most frequent causes of problems. The effects on the surface and its play qualities of high or low temperatures, changes of humidity and dampness caused by sweat or condensation, should also be ascertained if the hall is not to be heated and ventilated constantly by a controlled system.

Guarantee The expected standard and level of use, maintenance requirements and life of the installation should be clearly agreed at the outset and a guarantee related to them sought.

3 Surfaces for sports halls

3.1 General

The initial surge of oil-based synthetic sports flooring materials which appeared in the 1970s, in competition with the traditional timber floors and other established flooring materials, has since abated somewhat. This is due partly to the elimination from the market of substandard products following the production of the Sports Council's *Specification for Artificial Sports Surfaces*. It may also be attributed to continuing demand for qualities suitable for multi-purpose as well as multi-sports use and for multi-sports surfaces to be suitable for sports such as roller-skating which require a stiff surface.

At the same time there has been considerable movement in the availability of systems designed with the intention of reducing the stress on the body resulting from heavy impact with the surface. Most flooring materials may now be installed in this manner as an alternative to being laid directly on a solid subfloor.

The most usual way of reducing the shock of such impact is by means of some form of sprung floor. If a stiff layer such as timber, plywood, or particle board is mounted in such a manner that a fairly heavy impact will cause a large area of the floor to deflect this is generally known as a sprung or semi-sprung floor. Springing may result from wood joists themselves, cellular plastics or rubber pads or underlayers, or actual springs. Depending on the construction, a variety of sprung or semi-sprung floors can be constructed with different characteristics. As well as reducing the shock of impact the apparent return of energy may be increased. The terms 'area elastic' and 'plate elastic' are also applied to this type of floor.

The term 'point elastic' is sometimes applied to surfaces such as those of rubber and plastics which deform appreciably only at, and immediately surrounding, the point of impact. A point elastic surface may provide a degree of comfort underfoot, but a thin point elastic surface laid on a solid subfloor will contribute little to reduction of body impact stress in the case of the heavier impacts.

The more rigid materials, which deform imperceptibly on impact, will feel hard but may offer the stiffness which is required for some sports.

By a combination of materials, a floor may have the characteristics of being either point elastic or stiff, whilst also being area elastic under higher energy impacts.

It is advantageous to appreciate the general characteristics of the various types of surface which are available. They may be grouped under the headings of timber, composition floors, sheet materials (rubbers and plastics, linoleum, cork), in-situ finished polymeric surfaces and textiles, although some products may be a composite of two or more or may be used in combination as a multi-layer surface construction.

3.2 Timber floors

The traditional timber floor has been used for indoor sports for many years and offers an attractive surface for most sports.

Timber floors may be considered under the general headings of strip and block. This category also includes timber products such as medium density fibreboard, chipboard and plywood (though chipboard and plywood are used mainly as components in a system rather than as surfaces in their own right).

Timber floors may be supported by joists or battens, with or without a resilient layer or pads attached to the underside of the battens, laid over a cellular plastics sheet in the form of a floating floor or, as in the case of wood blocks, bedded directly on to the subfloor.

Timber is durable but not water resistant. All timber floors laid over a ground slab, whether direct or suspended, should be protected from latent moisture in the subfloor by a damp-proof membrane. This is in addition to the damp-proof membrane required at ground level to comply with the Building Regulations. Allowance should be made for lateral movement in the timber floor resulting from varying humidity levels by provision of an appropriate perimeter expansion gap, which must be maintained even at positions such as doorways. The advice of the flooring company should be taken in relation to the need for ventilation to any under-floor space.

When laid on joists or battens with a resilient underlayer or pads, there will generally be a degree of springing and the apparent stiffness and energy return will vary with energy of impact. Slip resistance is normally sufficient to prevent slipping while allowing some 'slide', but it will be modified by any surface treatment used.

Advice should be sought from the flooring company on appropriate maintenance regimes, and it is important that no other cleaning agents, floor emulsions, or polishes are used. Hardwood floors are susceptible to abrasion from outdoor shoes, indentation from pointed heels and marking from black-soled shoes unless measures are taken to prevent such damage.

Most natural colours are ideal for sports halls although it is essential to ensure a good quality grade for maple flooring in order to avoid unacceptable contrasts between strips. Most paint and tape markings are suitable.

Tongued and grooved hardwood strip floors are by far the most common of the timber sports floors in the UK. They are usually secret nailed to timber battens with a resilient under-layer or pads to form a sprung or semi-sprung floor. This type of floor is popular with many users. Semi-sprung hardwood strip floors are also used in squash courts. Advice on grades of timber and construction

details for squash are available from the Squash Rackets Association.

The most common choice of timber for strip floors is either 22 mm beech, which is imported in the form of boards each made up of two strips, or 19 mm maple. 23 mm laminated parquet strip boards are also available, made up of three structural layers laid crossways to each other and a wear surface 3.6 mm thick and three strips wide with a choice of various woods of different hardness. Generally beech strips are imported pre-sealed, whereas maple strips are supplied unsealed and may be left in that condition or sealed on site. Laminated boards may be delivered unlacquered or lacquered. The 22 mm tongued and grooved hardwood beech strips can also be clipped together over a rolled down cellular plastics sheet.

Solidly bedded double layered strip floors are the preference for specialist roller skating facilities. These are usually made up of a softwood base bedded in bitumen, on to which maple strip flooring is secret nailed.

Hardwood blocks are normally laid in mastic on concrete. They are very durable and are available in a range of natural colours. This type of floor is perhaps best suited for specialist weight training and weight lifting areas, but it has been used successfully for general indoor sports areas where other school activities are to take place or social events such as dances and discos are to be held. Wood mosaic finishes have also been used, stuck to the subfloor, in small multi-purpose areas as a cheaper alternative to wood block and they may also be mounted on a semi-sprung construction.

Geometrically patterned parquet laminated boards are also available, 15 mm thick for laying as a floating floor directly on to the subfloor or 23 mm laid on battens on cellular pads as a semi-sprung floor.

3.3 Composition floors

Materials used to form composition floors may include cement, wood granule, mineral or other fillers and synthetic rubber latex or other binders. They are either formed on site into a seamless floor, with or without an underlayer of rubber granules in a rubber latex matrix, or produced in the form of blocks which may be bedded on to the subfloor or mounted on a semi-sprung construction of plywood or water resistant chipboard on pads. They are hard but have good stability and water resistance.

They are reasonably resistant to wear and use for non-sporting activities and this is one of the factors that has led to the solid composition block floor being commonly used in sports halls in Britain. However, whilst the multi-use aspect is accepted as an advantage, the solid versions of these floors are not ideal for prolonged use for some sports because of the unrelenting nature of the interaction of the player with the surface. It is this which has led to the development of the semi-sprung version of the composition block floor to combine the multi-use surface with compliance to relieve body impact stress.

Pigments introduced into the basic mix of blocks provide a range of colours and seals for block floors are recommended by the flooring company. The seamless floors are usually finished with a coloured polyurethane resin layer. Slip resistance will depend on the surface treatment used and, of course, the maintenance regime. Marking of courts may be achieved by means of paint, which may be applied before the clear finishing coat so that it is sealed in, or tapes. Inlaid lines are available for composition block floors.

In the case of solid composition block floors, it is recommended that contraction joints through the composition block floor are provided in accordance with BS

5385: Part 5, to coincide with day and bay construction joints in the concrete slab or screed. Designers should discuss this with the flooring company at an early stage in the design process and consider the position of day and bay joints in relation to the positions of court markings. The joint layout should not be left to chance on site.

In the case of seamless composition floors, it is preferable to use a type of subfloor construction which will eliminate the effects of construction joints within the floor area, either by means of a reinforced slab with continuity of reinforcement through day and bay joints or by the use of a post-tensioned slab. If prestressed planks are used for the structural floor a joint may be needed at the bearing points, if they are exposed, to take account of the effects of deflection.

3.4 Sheet floor coverings

This category includes prefabricated sheet and tile materials made of rubbers and plastics, linoleum and cork.

As well as varying in constituent materials, products in this group also vary widely in quality and thickness (from 2 to 15 mm) and hence in price, and they can be laid on various subfloors. As sheet materials will follow even minor irregularities in the subfloor, this needs to be carefully specified and laying strictly supervised. (Refer to Section 4 below).

Characteristics such as durability, stiffness, ball rebound, slip resistance and impact severity will be dependent on the type, quality, thickness, surface texture and finish of the floor covering and the subfloor on which the covering is laid.

Some products are susceptible to scuff marking or cigarette burns while some have been developed specifically to resist them and others are by their nature more resistant. Welded joints can offer a more continuous and water resistant surface. A wide range of colours is available. Court markings are generally applied by use of paint or tapes.

Most sheet floor coverings require only regular sweeping and occasional mopping (damp not wet) but advice on maintenance should always be sought from the flooring company, especially with regard to the use of compatible detergents.

Thin plastics sheet materials are available with or without a backing, usually of 3 or 4 mm of cellular plastics or rubber. Such a backing is intended to increase softness. This may be advantageous for barefoot activities and activities which involve lying on the floor, but may be a limiting factor in terms of use of the facility for such activities as roller skating which demand a stiff surface without the drag which a cushioned floor may give. For the majority of sports activities, the thick cushioning now incorporated in sports shoes must throw into question the advantages (and cost effectiveness) of a relatively thin cushioned backing to the floor covering. However, plastics sheet materials are now available with a thicker cellular layer (such as 10 mm) and an intermediate stiffening layer of fibre mesh reinforced polyurethane. The principles of this type of system are outlined below under in-situ finished polymeric surfaces.

Some of the thicker rubber and plastics sheet materials offer the opportunity to extend the range of activities to include indoor athletics using short spikes.

Sheet-covered semi-sprung floors combine the principles of an area elastic floor with the variety of finish offered by sheet materials. These constructions usually comprise two or three layers of particle board laid over a continuous chip foam pad. The system reduces the shock of impact, while increasing the apparent return of energy. Such floors

are suitable for the martial arts, gymnastics and dance as well as for multi-sports use.

2 mm cigarette burn resistant PVC sheet flooring is available and a 1 mm sports surface protection sheet has been developed for use as a temporary protective covering for sports hall floors when the area is used for non-sports activities.

3.5 In-situ finished polymeric surfaces

These most commonly comprise a 10 or 12 mm cellular plastics or 4 to 15 mm prefabricated resin bound shredded rubber sheet laid over the subfloor and coated on site. The top surface, available in a variety of plain colours, is wet-poured polyurethane applied in a number of coats (according to the product) to build up a continuous layer with a thickness of between 1 and 4 mm (usually 2 mm). The 4 mm thickness is intended to provide for use with spiked shoes. A final matt finish is applied after the surface has set. Painted court markings may be used and most will also accept tapes.

In some cases a synthetic textile mesh, or even a stiff pressure distribution plate made of fibre mesh reinforced hard polyurethane, may be incorporated between the rubber sheet material and the polyurethane finish to give added stiffness to the surface, resulting in a combination of the principles of an area elastic and a point elastic floor. In the latter case it is also possible to use a sheet floor covering material as the top surface as an alternative to the in-situ polyurethane finish.

Conversely, an in-situ polyurethane finish may be used in place of a sheet floor covering on the semi-sprung construction described in the previous section.

In-situ polymeric surfaces such as those used for athletics tracks have been used on occasion for indoor halls for specialist activities but their principal market is out of doors.

3.6 Textiles

A wide variety of textile surfaces are available, including heavy woven fabrics, felts, flock, velour, fibre-bonded needle-punched and fine pile carpets, and knitted, woven, or tufted carpets. The latter group includes those with a coarse synthetic pile supposedly simulating natural grass, some having the spaces between the pile filled with a particulate material such as sand. They are generally designed for outdoor use but may be used for specialist indoor training areas for sports which normally take place outdoors on natural or synthetic turf.

Characteristics of textile materials vary considerably depending on material and construction, particularly the durability and the frictional qualities such as slip resistance and ball roll resistance.

The nature of textile surfaces has led to their use for specialised rather than general sports activities, both as permanent installations in spaces dedicated to specific sports such as tennis or bowls and as portable surfaces to provide for the needs of specific sports in multi-sports areas. The wide range of constructions and the scope for textural variation enable the requirements of specific sports to be catered for and make textile surfaces particularly suitable for sports with a high degree of contact between the ball and the surface. Their 'warmth' has led to their use for such activities as gymnastics and aerobics and their sound absorption qualities are an advantage in a teaching situation.

The use of textiles in sports areas which will also be used for non-sports activities has been limited owing to their susceptibility to cigarette burn damage which could adversely affect the sports use. Hence, examples of this type of surface in multi-sports halls are relatively few and have generally been limited to private schools where there is good control over use and users. However, textile surfaces are now available which are designed for permanent installation, using adhesive systems, in multi-sports areas and materials and treatments used in today's textiles can give fire protection to BS 4790.

The texture of some carpets may cause difficulties in providing permanent court markings if paint or tape are preferred. Inlaid markings can usually be installed but availability of colours and widths may be restricted.

Textiles may also be used as temporary coverings for sports hall floors when used for non-sports activities, to provide a 'soft' finish or to give protection to the permanent sports floor.

A somewhat hybrid flooring product, falling between the categories of sheet flooring and textiles, is made up of a 4 mm PVC load distribution layer reinforced with polyester mesh and finished with a non-woven polyester geotextile material impregnated with polyurethane, supported on a three dimensional nylon filament mesh structure cushioning underlay, bound to a polyester non-woven textile base sheet. This is offered for multi-sports and multi-purpose use.

4 Subfloor considerations and specification

4.1 General

It is important that the sports surface is considered together with its supporting layers, in terms of both cost and performance.

Some flooring materials require the provision of a screed, a high quality finish to the structural floor or particular methods of subfloor construction, while others comprise underlayers or methods of installation which obviate such needs. When comparing the costs of different flooring types, adjustments will therefore need to be made to take account of any such additional work to the subfloor. This information will also be needed when detailing the building.

Specialist sports floor companies will provide details of the standard of subfloor on which their surfaces should be laid and it is advisable to discuss this with them at the earliest opportunity. The properties of a flooring may be adversely affected by the use of the wrong type of subfloor. Incorrectly designed or constructed subfloors may cause failures of floor surfaces and standards of workmanship may also be critical.

4.2 Codes of Practice

In the UK, bases and screeds should be specified and constructed in accordance with the latest edition of the British Standard Code of Practice appropriate to the type of flooring to be installed. For in-situ floorings this is BS 8204: Part 1: 1987, for composition block floorings BS 5385: Part 5: 1990, as amended by AMD 6666 1990 and AMD 7060 1992. and for sheet and tile flooring of cork, linoleum, rubbers, thermoplastics and PVC BS 8203: 1987. The Code of Practice for flooring of timber, timber products and wood based panel products is BS 8201, and that for the installation of textile floor coverings BS 5325.

4.3 Drying out

In programming the work, allowance will need to be made for a drying period following the period of curing of concrete bases and screeds in order that sufficient of the water used in construction may be eliminated before application of the flooring. Flooring companies will advise on the level to which moisture should be reduced before their flooring can safely be laid: this will usually be 75% Relative Humidity as determined by the method given in BS 8203 Appendix A.

This is of particular relevance in the case of fast track programmes for sports halls (where many of the other elements may be prefabricated) and the time likely to be needed to achieve an adequate state of dryness within the required timescale may dictate the choice of subfloor construction, especially when sheet floor coverings are to be installed. An unbonded fine concrete or cement and sand screed isolated from the base by a damp proof membrane may be expected to be sufficiently dry within two months, but the drying period required for a concrete base on which flooring is to be fixed direct or on which a screed is laid without such isolation may be as much as a year or more. Proprietary screeds are available which are claimed to be dry enough to receive a sheet floor covering after 24 hours but this is dependent on their being laid on a base which already has a satisfactory moisture content or their being isolated from the base. See BS 8203: 1987 for guidance. If the required moisture conditions cannot be achieved within the period necessary, a proprietary surface-applied epoxy or polyurethane damp proof membrane, with a subsequent layer of at least 3 mm of a smoothing compound to provide absorbency for the adhesive used in fixing the flooring may be applied on top of the base or directly laid screed to avoid extended drying times, but this will have significant cost implications: the costs of preparation, materials and application are relatively high, but in situations where either significant savings may be made by reducing programme time, or an extension of programme to wait for drying imposes extra cost, they can be cost effective.

The time required for the hygrometer test itself must also not be overlooked. This may vary from 4 days for isolated screeds to 8 days for a concrete slab and more for thicker constructions; again, see BS 8203: 1987.

4.4 Acceptance criteria

Properties of the subfloor which will affect the performance of the finished installation should form the basis of specified subfloor acceptance criteria. For most sports floor products and systems the level tolerances and surface regularity required of the finished installation will need to be achieved by the subfloor.

Most sports require a flat and even floor, though specialist facilities for sports such as crown green bowls, indoor athletics and cycling require specially contoured surfaces. Some sports set specific requirements in these respects.

Flatness

Where no detailed requirements are specified by the sports concerned, a degree of flatness appropriate for most sports will be provided by a floor which does not deviate from the datum of a flat horizontal plane by more than ±6 mm at any point and where the difference in level of adjacent points on a 3 m grid does not exceed 6 mm. This deviation from datum corresponds to the requirements of BS 7044 Part 4 as amended by AMD 7426 1993. The additional proviso relating to adjacent points on a 3m grid constrains the floor from the possibility of differing by 12 mm in 6m which the provisions of BS 7044 would permit.

It should be noted that this is more stringent than the suggestion of ±15 mm departure from datum given in BS

8203: 1987, BS 8204: Parts 1 and 2: 1987 and BS 5385: Part 3: 1989 as being satisfactory for normal purposes. The difference in levels on a grid corresponds approximately to the recommendations for property IV in relation to floors of category 2 or 3 in the Concrete Society's technical report *Concrete Industrial Ground Floors*, which sets out a basic specification for floor flatness and gives guidance on construction techniques to achieve high standards of flatness.

Any deflection should not cause the floor to fall outside the specified limits and care should also be taken that any deflection or movement is not such as could cause cracking or failure of adhesion of the selected surface.

Surface regularity

The surface regularity in relation to localised bumps and hollows should be such that when a 3 m straight edge is placed in any position on the surface any gaps between the underside of the straight edge and the surface are no greater than 6 mm and any gaps under a 300 mm straight edge are no greater than 3 mm. This corresponds to the requirements of BS 7044: Part 4: 1991.

The former requirement is less stringent than that in the Sports Council's *Specification for Artificial Sports Surfaces* which BS 7044 supersedes and corresponds approximately to a surface regularity classification SR2 in BS 8203: 1987 and BS 8204: Parts 1 and 2: 1987.

Notwithstanding this, there should be no ridges, bumps, hollows, or abrupt changes in level (such as might occur at joints) sufficient to cause a ball to be deflected from its true path.

5 Floor fixings for equipment

Most sports hall equipment is either free-standing or suspended from the walls or ceiling. However, some sports require permanent sockets in the floor which must be covered with a flush, non-slip plug when not in use.

The most common socket or floor fixing requirements are for hockey side board fixings, volleyball and tennis posts and some gymnastics equipment such as women's asymmetrical or uneven bars, men's horizontal bar, high bar and men's rings. Sockets may also be required to anchor fencing competition pistes and any portable guard nets such as those for golf practice. Sockets will be required for five-a-side football rebound barriers in sports halls which accommodate more than one five-a-side football playing area, where spectators are accommodated alongside a playing area and where wall openings occur.

It may be necessary to thicken the floor slab to accommodate the sockets, which usually need to be drilled a minimum of 150 mm into the slab, though some may require a greater depth: for example international volleyball posts require 300 mm. Care must be taken in detailing to ensure that the effectiveness of any damp proof membranes is not destroyed.

Any underfloor heating systems and other underfloor services must be kept well clear of all socket positions.

It is essential, therefore, to consider court layouts at an early stage so that positions of sockets may be established and allowance made for them. This is particularly important where the sports hall is located on an upper suspended floor.

Most sports hall equipment manufacturers supply proprietary sockets and fixings together with setting-out and installation drawings.

Details of principal manufacturers are available from the Sports Council's Information Centre.

6 Line markings

6.1 General

Line markings are necessary for most indoor sports and consideration needs to be given to the methods which can be used with the surface. It is essential that the floor surface should be capable of marking without damage.

For specific requirements of governing bodies of sports or recommendations see Chapters 15-46 and 69-90 in this volume. Detailed requirements for major competitions are given in the sports data sheets in the Sports Council publication *Arenas*.

In some cases sports surface companies will carry out markings or recommend specialist contractors. Details of line marking products and companies are also available from the Sports Council's Information Centre.

Three types of markings are available: inlaid, painted, and self-adhesive tape.

6.2 Inlaid lines

This method is usually the most complex but also the most permanent. However this permanence can be inconvenient if changes occur in rules regarding court dimensions and markings or if alternative layouts are required at some later date.

Some types of flooring are inlaid with the same material, others are inlaid with special inlay material. Specialist flooring companies should be consulted for detailed information and advice.

Advantages:
- May be cleaned or maintained in the same way as the rest of the floor without fear of damage
- Can be overlaid by other methods
- Line widths constant
- Reference points for taped markings may be inlaid
- If the same material is used for the inlay, the qualities are likely to be the same as those of the rest of the floor; this can be particularly advantageous in relation to slip resistance.

Disadvantages:
- Permanent and therefore cannot be taken up when not required
- Adds to the number of joints and hence to any joint related problems which may be endemic in some types of material
- Colours may be restricted by manufacturers list: this should be checked before the final choice of material is made.

6.3 Painted lines

Applied by brush, spray (using a template) or machine, this is also a comparatively permanent system but is capable of adaptation in most cases.

Wear and the build-up of ingrained dirt will entail occasional repainting according to the intensity of use. It is always advisable to seek guidance from the flooring company to ensure that the paint and the surface are compatible. Some flooring companies will supply appropriate marking paint.

Characteristics, price and availability of marking materials vary greatly. Some are used direct from the container and others are two or three part systems. Drying times range from 20 minutes to 8 hours.

The durability of markings also varies and it is advisable to seek a guarantee covering the life expectancy of the markings. It may, however, be available only in relation to use solely for supervised sport and be negated by other uses.

These factors will affect the direct and indirect costs of subsequent re-marking as well as of initial line markings. They should therefore be clarified with flooring and line marking companies and taken into account at the time of the surface selection.

Advantages:
- Can be applied easily by one person using a lining machine or masking tapes, though an assistant will be needed for setting out
- Wide colour range available
- Curves as easy to produce as straight lines
- Does not tear up
- May be used on virtually all surfaces.

Disadvantages:
- Difficult to remove after application or to correct mistakes
- Cannot be played on immediately after application
- Line width may vary if equipment not properly maintained
- Continued repainting may build up an unacceptable thickness producing ridges at line positions.

6.4 Self-adhesive tapes

Though not ideal for textile floors or rough or granular surfaces, tapes are suitable for most sports surfaces and can be laid easily and removed for short term use giving the advantage of flexibility. Tapes do tend to lift under heavy usage and in some cases may need to be replaced quite regularly.

Before tapes are applied, the surface must be clean. Any surface oil or factory sheen must be removed, as well as any dust or grit which may cause future break away of the tape from the surface. Tape must be allowed to relax after it is unrolled before it is fixed to the floor, in order to avoid corners curling. Solvent based seals applied over the taped lines may cause the tape to crinkle.

Advantages:
- Easy to lay and peel off to correct misalignments, and can be put down or taken up for 'one off' events, but is not re-usable
- Straight lines can be produced easily, curved lines with only slightly more difficulty
- All standard widths available
- Area may be played on immediately after application
- Wide colour range.

Disadvantages:
- May tear during use or maintenance
- Difficult to remove after long periods
- May be stretched in application causing differences in width of line
- May not adhere to some rough or granular or textile surfaces
- Usually a two-man job to lay.

6.5 Colour

For major competitions, white lines are required for most sports – though yellow is used for handball and sometimes for indoor hockey, and basketball offers the alternative of coloured panels. The same will apply to lines in spaces dedicated to a single sport.

However, when marking out halls for a variety of activities it is necessary for different colours to be used for each sport. Factors relevant to the choice of colours for the respective sports include colour of floor (the lines must contrast sufficiently with the floor colour), dominant

Table 64.1: Colours for line markings in a multi-sports hall

Sport	
Handball	Orange
Indoor hockey	Light blue
Netball	Red
Volleyball	Green
Five-a-side football	Yellow
Basketball	Black
Badminton and short tennis	White

sports, colour of ball, importance of markings for judges and referees and speed of the game. Some governing bodies of sports specify particular colours for their sport but the majority require only that lines should be clearly visible.

As a general guide the Sports Council recommends the colours shown in Table 64.1 based on the preferred or required colours of the governing bodies of the sports. They should be laid in the sequence given in the table, which will result in the badminton lines being continuous.

The colours given in the table are appropriate for both recreational play and local matches.

It should be noted that while yellow was previously recommended for recreational badminton, with tennis being marked in white, it is now good practice to mark all badminton courts in white, using a secondary colour for tennis if required. This is because the use of yellow lines for badminton resulted in the majority of lines glowing in the brightest colour and this could be very distracting for other sports. It also has the advantage that the increasingly popular game of short tennis, which is played on badminton courts, will have the benefit of white lines. Tennis itself is only rarely played in multi-sports halls, largely because of the greater cost effectiveness of the four smaller courts which can be accommodated in the same space as one tennis court. If tennis markings are required a colour should be chosen bearing in mind the colours of other courts to be marked and the relative usage. Similarly, if lacrosse is to be played a suitable colour will need to be selected as white will not be feasible.

If a floor colour is chosen which coincides with a colour recommended for any of the courts to be marked, or does not provide sufficient contrast, it will be necessary either to use a darker tone for the line than is usual or change to another colour. This is particularly relevant to the choice of green flooring and volleyball markings.

Some types of lighting will modify the apparent colours of lines and may reduce the colour contrasts between them, resulting in a tendency for the colours to merge. Reference should be made to *CIBSE Lighting Guide LG4: Sport* for information on colour rendering qualities of different lamp types.

6.6 Widths

Most line markings are 50 mm wide. Among the exceptions is badminton, for which the lines should be 40 mm.

6.7 Match-play courts in multi-sports halls

For any match play which requires single court markings there is the option of removing or painting out all other lines or using a portable or roll-down court. The cost of removing and reinstating all other lines is high in terms of materials, man hours and loss of programme time and it is now usual to use a portable or roll-down court in order to eliminate the unwanted markings. Major events always require this, as they must not have the distraction of other court markings. Finals and semi-finals of local competitions may also require this.

7 Portable sports surfaces

There is an increasing demand for roll-out surfaces specifically to cater for competitive events, to provide both an appropriate surface for the sport concerned and a clearly marked court to ensure the best possible conditions for players, umpires and judges.

However, the development of portable sports surfaces has its origins in the fact that for some sports the qualities required of the surface may be incompatible with the requirements for other activities in a multi-sports hall. Early examples are those marketed for cricket practice and indoor bowls where the essential qualities are related to the contact between the ball and the surface. There are many situations where spaces specifically dedicated to such sports cannot be justified, for example where regular demand or the seasonal nature of the activity cannot be reconciled with the capital and recurrent costs which would be incurred, or where the space or finance for such additional facilities is simply not available. In such cases a portable court for occasional use in a hall suitable in all other respects may be a solution.

The early development of portable courts for badminton followed a similar pattern. In this case many spaces suited for the sport in spatial terms were designed to be used mainly for social events and, for instance, a highly-polished dance floor might be too slippery or permanent court markings unacceptable.

The description 'portable' or 'roll-down' surface is a loose one. In fact, with the exception of cricket and bowls strips and perhaps badminton courts, the surface area is such that its weight often makes laying, lifting and storage a laborious, time consuming and therefore expensive process. Although most manufacturers aim to produce a comparatively lightweight material, the preference for a surface which will lie flat without special fixings and not ruck in use will always entail some reasonable degree of self-weight.

The quality and nature of the floor on which the portable court is laid may have a significant effect on the performance of the portable surface. This is particularly relevant for games such as cricket where the reaction between the ball and the surface is critical. Portable floor surfaces should not differ in their characteristics from permanent specialist installations except for the fact that they are loose laid.

Portable equipment is generally available for use in conjunction with these surfaces. However, it should be noted that for volleyball, post fixings are required to be of the floor-socket type and fixing the posts to the floor by means of weights or wire is prohibited.

8 References and further advice

BS 7044, Artificial sports surfaces, British Standards Institution, Milton Keynes (1989/90/91).

BS 8201, Code of practice for flooring and timber, timber products and wood-based panel products, British Standards Institution, Milton Keynes (1987).

BS 8203, Code of practice for installation of sheet and tile flooring, British Standards Institution, Milton Keynes (1987).

BS 8204, Screeds, bases and in-situ flooring, Parts 1 and 2, British Standards Institution, Milton Keynes (1987).

BS 5325, Code of practice for installation of textile floor coverings, British Standards Institution, Milton Keynes (1993).

BS 5385, Wall and floor tiling, Parts 3 and 5. (See also AMDs 7859, 6666, 7060.) British Standards Institution, Milton Keynes (1989/90).

Chartered Institution of Building Services Engineers, *Lighting Guide LG4: Sport*, CIBSE, London.

Concrete Society, *Concrete Industrial Ground Floors*, Concrete Society, Wexham Springs (1988).

65
Detailed design: walls

Christopher Harper

2 Any form of wall glazing for daylight will produce unacceptable glare. Photo: Sports Council Publications

1 General

For detailed information on suitable methods of construction refer to Chapter 67 in this volume.

1.1 Examples of constructional methods

Sports hall walls are of either framed or loadbearing construction. The following combination of materials are examples of satisfactory internal finishes:

- Fairfaced brickwork or solid concrete blockwork with flush joints, **1**
- Fairfaced brickwork or solid concrete blockwork with flush joints, decorated with a matt paint or clear seal
- A composite construction of fairfaced brickwork or solid concrete blockwork with flush joints up to 3 m (approx 10 ft) above floor level, with either timber boarding, ply or particle board or metal faced insulating panels to roof level
- Horizontal or vertical natural timber boarding or ply or particle board from floor to roof level.

1.2 Detailed design considerations

Background contrast and the control of glare
These can be achieved by:

- Avoiding too many changes in colour and materials
- Omitting side and clerestory windows, **2**
- Considering the surface reflectances of the materials specified (see Chapters 60 and 62).

The wall construction and finishes specified should:

- Be capable of withstanding heavy impact from sports hall use, particularly during five-a-side football, volleyball and hockey, **3**

- Be non-abrasive for a height of 3 m (approx 10 ft)
- Avoid projections, eg columns, rainwater pipes, service conduits, switches and power sockets
- Provide adequate support for basketball backboards and gymnastics equipment
- Avoid ledges which harbour dust and trap shuttlecocks, **4**.

Wall openings
Structural openings will be required for access, fire exit and equipment storage doors and for air input and extract grilles, fire extinguishers and other miscellaneous items. Openings may also be required for viewing windows or galleries.

1 Wall colour should be consistent from floor to ceiling and the surface should be flush full height. Photo: Sports Council Publications

3 Lightweight membrane structures must have solid vertical rebound walls to a minimum height of 1.2 m. Photo: Chris Taylor

4 *A low budget hall with a particle board rebound zone topped with tensioned nylon mesh to protect insulation and cladding from ball impact. Photo: D J Butler*

6 *Safety glazing provides viewing panels in a SASH sports centre to give contact between the foyer and sports hall. Photo: D J Butler*

- Avoid sharp and potentially dangerous corners in the activity zone
- All doors and frames should, ideally, be flush with adjoining wall surfaces
- Determine the width and height of storage openings in relation to overall dimensions of portable equipment
- Storage openings without doors require a flush panelled rebound surface, 1.2 m (approx 4 ft) high
- Make the width, depth and height of external openings large enough to allow the delivery of bleacher seating units and other items of equipment
- Determine the position and protection of air input and extract grille openings in relation to the flight path of shuttlecocks and vulnerability to damage from ball impact
- Relate the location of viewing galleries to the main activity area layout, **5**; netting can be hung across the openings to prevent balls and shuttles from entering the gallery
- Viewing windows must be of safety glass, without projections and located so as to minimise distraction to players, **6**.

1.3 Thermal considerations

In heated halls walls must be insulated in accordance with Building Regulation requirements.

1.4 Acoustic considerations

Walls surfaces above 3 m (approx 10 ft) can be sound absorbent but must also be capable of withstanding ball impact. Slatted timber, impact resistant acoustic panels and profiled masonry blocks may be considered. The construction should take account of the need to limit noise spillage, an important issue on some sites and with some social activities.

1.5 Climbing walls

Climbing walls. Climbing walls require specialised design and are a feature which can limit the flexibility of a hall for other activities (see Chapter 73).

1.6 Doors and frames

The following notes are intended as general guidance on the detailed design of doors and ironmongery for a sports hall.

Fire escape doors

The Fire Prevention Officer (and Licensing Officer) should be consulted at the earliest possible stage to agree requirements for adequate means of escape. It is likely that internal doors will have to be fire-resisting and self-closing, while external doors will be fire escape doors. Fire escape doors must be secure from the outside but allow rapid egress in cases of emergency. Doors should be detailed to provide a suitable internal rebound surface which is flush with the adjoining wall surfaces. In reality this is difficult to achieve with external doors because of the design of panic bolts and the preference for locating frames against the outer wall face. Rebound panels can sometimes be fitted below (and also above) panic bolt pressure bars but this is not always permitted by the Fire Officer particularly for halls with spectator events or high occupancy rates, **7**. An alternative is to design lift-off panels for installation when five-a-side football or other team games are played. Where rebound panels cannot be used door jambs and reveals should be radiussed or splayed to minimise the risk of injury, **8**.

5 *Viewing galleries can also provide access to pull out seating in larger sports halls. Photo: P Elger*

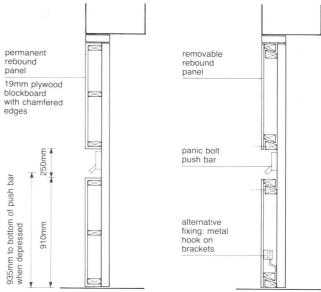

permanent rebound panel

19mm plywood blockboard with chamfered edges

250mm

910mm

935mm to bottom of push bar when depressed

removable rebound panel

panic bolt push bar

alternative fixing: metal hook on brackets

7 *Fire escape doors can be detailed with flush facing panels below and above the panic bar when permitted by the Fire Officer. Photo: D J Butler*

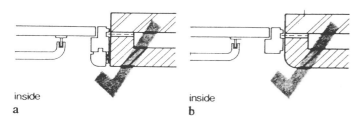

inside
a

inside
b

8 *Jambs and architraves must be rounded when a flush face to the rebound zone cannot be achieved*

Store doors
Design requirements and overall sizes of access to storage areas are discussed in Chapter 55. Storage door types which can be considered are up-and-over, straight sliding, sliding folding and side hung. Detailing must ensure:

- The rigidity and strength of the door and frame. For wide openings (eg over 4.5 m) this can be a critical factor – doors that are not sufficiently rigid may warp or twist. The door should be solid enough to withstand impact from footballs and sports hall users.
- The provision of adequate headroom for roller shutter and up-and-over doors. The overall store headroom will be reduced by the depth of the roller shutter housing or track. If headroom is critical sliding folding doors may have to be considered.
- That all ironmongery is robust enough for sports door specification. Drop bolts to secure sliding folding door leafs must be of sufficient travel to ensure positive engagement in floor and head sockets.
- That sliding folding doors do not protrude into the sports hall when opened.
- That door and frame are flush with each other and the adjoining wall surfaces.

An alternative to door protected openings is the use of hinged rebound panels to 1.2 m high, a simple solution providing convenient access across the length of the store.

9 *Rebound panels 1.2 m (approx 4 ft) high backed by a ceiling suspended roll down dividing screen. Photo: C J Harper*

Hung netting will protect the upper part of the opening from stray balls and shuttles.

1.7 Fixtures and fittings

Basketball backboards
There are a number of proprietary types available. They generally consist of the board supported by a movable steel frame which is fixed to either the wall or ceiling. When the board is not in use, the frame (and board) fold flat against the wall or roof construction. The board frame is generally fixed to wall mounted timber battens to ensure adequate rigidity.

Miscellaneous fixtures and fittings
- Fire extinguishers and hose reels. These items must not protrude into the sports hall.
- Clocks, emergency exit signs, speakers and thermostats should be designed to withstand ball impact or protected with steel grilles or cages.
- Although blackboards can be a useful teaching aid in the sports hall, an alternative location outside the hall entry doors is preferred. Posters and notices – except safety warnings – must also be excluded from the hall interior.

- Flush timber (plywood) skirtings may be considered to prevent damage to the base of walls during activities such as roller skating. For hockey an inclined concrete plinth block will prevent lofted ricochets: see Chapter 31 in this volume.

Netting tracks
Designers should consult manufacturers/suppliers at the earliest possible stage to agree fixing details, establish whether additional structural support is necessary and ascertain the method of storing nets. Typical netting subdivision layouts are shown in Chapter 49. An alternative to nets are fabric screens which fold down from ceiling mounted track and provide both a visual and an acoustic separation.

Rebound dividing partitions
These are used for dividing a sports hall to provide a rebound surface for five-a-side football or indoor hockey and they can also be used in front of wall openings for the same purpose. An alternative type is available which provides a rebound surface on each side as shown in **9**.

66
Lightweight fabric structures

Ian Firth

1 Introduction

A fundamental requirement for indoor sport is the need to cover a large area containing players and spectators with the minimum of internal supports. This leads to the requirement for lightweight roof structures spanning large distances. The use of modern fabric materials can enable this to be achieved efficiently, attractively and at low cost.

The scale of fabric structures for sport can vary from a small enclosure over a gymnasium or tennis court to a very large roof structure for an indoor arena or sports stadium. The fabric roof may be permanent or temporary, demountable or deployable and can create a wide range of opportunities for flexibility in the use of covered space. These buildings use a fabric membrane for all or part of the external envelope and can be grouped into two main categories, depending on their means of primary support:

- *Air-supported structures*, where the primary support is provided by internal over pressure of air
- *Framed fabric structures*, where the primary support to the fabric is provided by structural frames or masts.

2 Fabric materials

2.1 General

The material most commonly used is a PVC coated woven polyester fabric which combines strength and durability and provides relative ease of fabrication and handling. More expensive materials are available, such as Teflon coated glass fibre fabrics, which are more difficult to fabricate and handle but provide greater strength and durability. These are sometimes known as 'self-cleaning' fabrics because of their PTFE coating which inhibits the adherence of dust and dirt to the surface. The PVC fabrics can also be coated to improve their self-cleaning properties. These materials have been used in large stadium roof coverings and in many exotic tensile fabric structures.

The coatings provide a weatherproof matrix to protect the load carrying fibres from the degrading effects of ultraviolet radiation and can take on a wide range of colours to suit individual applications and preferences. It is possible to specify special coatings to provide added protection in particularly harsh locations, such as in an industrial or polluted environment or on sites exposed to extreme solar radiation.

Another type of membrane is a transparent Visqueen or polythene type material which is used in some low cost air-supported structures. This does not have the strength or the durability of the other materials and has to be used in conjunction with a network of stiffening cables over the outside.

Life-span

With the recent advances in materials technology, the expected useful life of the PVC coated polyester and Teflon coated glass fibre fabrics has increased to a level which enables longer design lives to be assumed than previously. It is important to appreciate that the fabric is still likely to need replacing more often than the other structural components, in much the same way as roof tiles or cladding panels need to be replaced during the life of a traditional building, and this must be allowed for in the design. It is currently considered that the expected useful lifespan may be about 20–25 years for typical structural grades of PVC coated polyester and about 25–30 years for Teflon coated glass fibre. The cheaper Visqueen materials have expected lifespans of only about 3–5 years.

2.2 Applications

Large stadia

In the USA, Japan and elsewhere, there are some very large arenas and sports stadia enclosed by lightweight fabric roof structures. These are extremely impressive structures and the principles of the air-supported cable stiffened roof in particular can be applied to cover very large areas without the need for interior supports. There are none of these covered stadia yet in the UK, partly because professional football currently has to be played on natural grass which does not grow well under permanent cover.

Small to medium size facilities

There are a number of smaller facilities in the UK, typical of those commonly used all over the world. They mostly cover about 1500 to 3000 sq m and are used for a wide range of sports, including badminton, basketball, bowls, football, golf, gymnastics, hockey, skating, swimming, tennis and volleyball.

The interior space can be subdivided if necessary with screens and there are many possible applications, **1**.

Perimeter walls

There are several advantages in using solid robust perimeter walls and keeping the fabric membrane for the roof only. They include providing greater security, deterring vandals and introducing possibilities for windows and greater architectural flexibility in the design. A perimeter wall also creates solid vertical rebound surfaces

1 *Interior of small framed fabric structure for multiple sports use. (Photo: Clyde Canvas, UK)*

which are usually desirable and reduces the necessary internal pressure in the case of an air-supported roof.

Fabric walls in framed structures present the cheapest solution, but can flap in the wind making an irritating noise and chaffing against the frames unless the membrane is properly tensioned. This is not a problem with airhalls.

2.3 Air-supported structures

General

The commonest form of air-supported structure is the airhall whose general features are indicated in **2**. The membrane is held down around its perimeter in such a way as to prevent excessive air losses and then inflated. The internal pressure is sustained by the constant running of a fan or blower system, supplying air from the outside, and must be sufficient to support the membrane under the action of imposed loads such as wind and snow, **3**.

The required internal pressure is not very high, typically less than 0.5% higher than the ambient atmospheric pressure outside, and this difference is imperceptible to most people.

The other main group of air-supported structures are pneumatics, in which two or more membranes, or two parts of the same membrane, are held apart by the pressure between them. Pneumatics may form or support a light-weight roof, with the main support off the ground typically being provided by some other means. Although not so common as airhalls, they do have several potential applications for indoor sports, particularly for deployable roof structures in cases where a mainly open air facility needs quickly to be covered when it rains.

Airhalls may be either permanent or temporary structures and it is possible to design them to be deflated, folded up and stored away to enable outdoor sports to take place during the summer. The airhall principle is also used for ground cover weather protection, such as at the All England Lawn Tennis and Croquet Club in Wimbledon where the covers can be pulled out and inflated very quickly in the event of rain.

Foundations and anchorages

Unlike most other kinds of structure, an airhall usually has to be held down and not up. The simplest way of doing this for a ground supported airhall, while at the same time providing a level top surface for attaching the anchorage, is to use a simple concrete ring beam all around the perimeter whose self weight is sufficient to counteract the upwards and overturning applied forces from the membrane. Ground anchors or tension piles can also be used and may be required to increase the holding down

3 *Interior of airhall, Europa Tennis Club, Southampton. Photo: Southern Photographic for TC Structures*

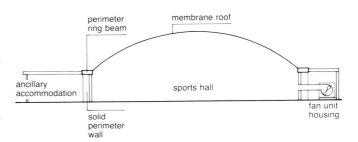

4 *Example of a sports hall with an air supported fabric roof.*

capacity of a concrete ring beam. A more complex foundation design is usually required where solid perimeter walls are used, **4**.

The membrane is commonly anchored around the perimeter to the solid foundation or perimeter wall using a steel or aluminium section or special cast-in slots. This must be designed to resist the forces from the membrane while minimising air losses and avoiding any sharp edges which could damage the material.

Cables and cable networks

In the case of cable-stiffened membranes, the cable network provides the main strength and stiffness of the airhall envelope. The cables, which are usually high strength steel wire ropes, are anchored to the perimeter

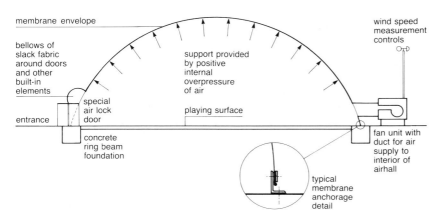

2 *Main features of a typical airhall*

236

foundation and kept in tension by the action of the internal pressure on the membrane spanning between them.

Cables are used around doors and other rigid elements 'built-in' to the membrane envelope in order to transfer the membrane tensions to the anchorage and allow a 'bellows' of slack fabric to accommodate relative movements without overstress.

Doors
Entry to an airhall has to be via special doors designed to minimise air losses. These are usually either rotating drum doors or twin 'air lock' doors where the outer door should be closed before the inner door is opened, or vice versa.

Emergency exits are usually required enabling rapid exit directly to the outside. In small air-supported structures their use results in an instantaneous loss of inflation pressure and they must be closed again immediately in order to allow the pressure to return to normal.

Fan unit or blower systems, including controls
The fan unit is generally driven by an electric motor off the mains, but the system must also have a standby alternative power source such as a diesel engine which cuts in automatically in the event of a mains power interruption in order to ensure constant reliable operation in all conditions, **5**.

The quantity of air that the fan has to deliver in order to sustain the structural support depends upon the size of the airhall, the required internal pressure and the air losses through the membrane, doors and anchorages. At high wind speeds the internal pressure needs to be increased, so the controls commonly include automatic wind speed and

pressure monitoring. The whole system should be properly maintained to reliably supply the correctly controlled quantity of air and support the structure 24 hours a day. The automatic requirements for these systems are complex and the advice of a specialist is necessary to achieve a satisfactory facility.

2.4 Framed fabric structures

General
The primary support for a framed fabric structure is provided by structural masts frames or frameworks, often with a system of cables for bracing and stability. The fabric then acts as the cladding, stretching over or between the primary structural members[9], but does not usually act structurally except in the case of some tented tensile structures.

The structural frame
Structural frames may take a variety of forms, but are commonly simple portal frames or lattice space frames in steel or aluminium, **6**. Sometimes laminated timber beams are used in portal frame construction. The components may be delivered to site in short prefabricated lengths and assembled without the need for extensive temporary works. The frames are designed with special channels or fixing details for attaching the fabric panels and it is important that care is taken to avoid chaffing of the fabric wherever it touches the frame.

Exposed internal frame members which are close to the edge of the playing area should always be protected over

5 *An airhall over two swimming pools around a building in Greece, showing the fan unit on the roof. Photo: Bingham bv, Holland*

6 *Interior of framed fabric structure for tennis. Photo: Walu Structures, UK*

the bottom 2 metres with soft material to prevent injury to players who might collide with them.

Foundations
Foundations are usually simply reinforced concrete ring beams around the perimeter, but if the frame columns are set more than 3 or 4 m apart individual pad footings may be more economic. Some form of stiff member is still required for the attachment of the fabric lower edge.

Tensile structures
So called tensile structures are typically variations of a tent type enclosure where the primary structure provides points or ridges from which the fabric is hung and stretched out to anchorages around the perimeter. These can produce a wide variety of interesting shapes and are gaining increasing popularity and application, particularly as engineers' ability to analyse their complex forms develops. Examples include the large King Abdul Aziz University Sports Hall in Jeddah and the covered Mound Stand at Lord's cricket ground in London, 7.

2.6 Environmental considerations
For general details of environmental services recommendations refer to Chapters 60 and 61.

Heating and ventilation
One of the drawbacks of fabric structures is the need for heating and ventilation systems which compensate for the low thermal insulation of the membrane materials. Pumped hot air or radiant heating systems are the most common and in the case of an airhall the heating plant is usually incorporated into the fan system which then supplies warm air. A low level of background heating is often required in winter, even when the building is not in use, in order to prevent an excessive build up of snow on the roof.

In the summer the converse is true and some kind of ventilation is usually required in order to reduce solar gain. In framed fabric structures this can be done using extractor fans and louvres mounted on the frames and the fabric sides can sometimes be lifted or rolled up like a blind in order to induce natural cross ventilation. In airhalls an increased throughput of air can be achieved by allowing excess air to escape through vents and increasing the supply flow to maintain the required internal pressure.

A second insulating membrane can be added both to airhalls and framed fabric structures and this often

7 *Tensile fabric roof covering to the Mound Stand at Lords cricket ground, London. Photo: Michael Hopkins and Partners*

significantly improves the performance by reducing heat loss, condensation and solar gain.

Lighting
The PVC coated polyester and Teflon covered glass fibre fabrics are translucent, typically transmitting about 30–40% of natural light and on a sunny day the interior is often bright enough to use without the help of artificial lighting. Even with a second insulation skin, a significant amount of natural light still penetrates to give a pleasant diffused lighting level inside.

Artificial lighting is usually required and is provided by high power lamps directed upwards to reflect off the roof fabric. The lamps may be either free standing or suspended off the structural frames and must be placed far enough away from the membrane to ensure that they do not touch it as it deflects under load.

Because of the translucent nature of the fabrics, these structures glow at night when the interior lighting is in use, particularly when only one membrane skin is used. This can be used to good effect in the design, but should be considered in the planning stages, particularly for buildings in residential areas.

Acoustics
Acoustically, fabric structures can create problems associated both with reflecting echoes on the inside and with transmission of sound to the outside. The significance of these problems will depend upon the internal activity noise level, the floor or playing surface, the overall form and shape of the building, the use of a second insulating membrane and the proximity of surrounding houses.

2.7 Design standards and regulations

Designs should be properly carried out in accordance with the appropriate standards and codes of practice applicable to the building and its location. In the UK the Building Regulations will generally apply to these structures. Only in the case of temporary buildings intended to be erected in one place for less than 28 days can the Regulations be said to be inapplicable.

The non-traditional nature of these structures has sometimes led to an inconsistency in the approach to their design and a variation in the degree of Local Authority control from one location to another. Recent events in the UK have resulted in the derivation of performance specifications, based on British Standards and they have been adopted by the Sports Council and the Lawn Tennis Association (see References and further advice). These specifications contain further information relating to the design, construction and maintenance of these structures.

2.8 Other factors

Security and vandalism

It is often necessary to erect a security fence around a fabric building in which the membrane extends down to the ground in order to reduce the risk of wilful or accidental damage to the fabric. The materials are designed to prevent a tear from developing under normal working loads so a small cut in the fabric is seldom catastrophic but always a nuisance. The fan system capacity in an airhall is usually sufficient to prevent total collapse under normal conditions, even with a fairly large hole in the membrane.

Inspection and maintenance

It is in the nature of these structures that the level of inspection and maintenance activity needs to be higher than for traditional buildings. This is particularly true for airhalls which rely on the continuous safe running of the mechanical fan system which must be serviced regularly.

The fabric needs to be checked periodically for damage or deterioration and repairs made as necessary. In the case of PVC coated polyester fabrics repairs are easily made on site, usually using a hot iron welding technique. Site repairs to Teflon coated glass fibre fabrics are not so straightforward and a whole panel of material usually has to be replaced in the event of damage.

PVC coated polyester fabrics should also be cleaned regularly as this improves the appearance and durability of the membrane.

Costs

The lowest initial cost for a typical indoor space for sports use is undoubtedly provided by an airhall. An equivalent framed fabric structure is likely to be at least 40–45% more expensive.

However, the ongoing running costs of these structures must not be forgotten. The calculation of whole life costs should include the costs of replacement of the membrane, heating, inflation equipment (in the case of an airhall), maintenance and so on and these will generally be significantly higher than for an equivalent traditional building.

On balance, it is likely that the whole life costs for an airhall, framed fabric and low cost traditional steel frame structure will be broadly similar over a period of about 50 years, with the airhall representing the lower initial capital cost.

3 References and further advice

Flint and Neill Partnership for the Lawn Tennis Association, *Performance Specification for Airhalls*, Section C of the ITI Model Scheme Specification, Lawn Tennis Association, London (1993).

Flint and Neill Partnership for the Lawn Tennis Association, *Performance Specification for Framed Fabric Structures*, Section D of the ITI Model Scheme Specification, Lawn Tennis Association, London (1993).

67
Structural considerations

Rick Holmes

1 Considerations

Unique parameters imposed by the sports hall
Of all the buildings in sports and recreational design, the sports hall presents the greatest number of structural design problems.

The clear height requirement of 6.7 m minimum even for the smallest halls demands structural solutions quite different from the more usual storey heights of less than half this. Greater heights lead to higher slenderness ratios. Therefore if a framed solution is adopted in order to maintain economy of columns and walls bracing members must be carefully integrated. Should a load bearing solution be adopted without columns, non-traditional techniques must be devised because normal solid or cavity brick/block walls are not economic at these heights. The size of the envelope, surface finishes and environmental parameters exert considerable influence on the range of structural solutions available. It is therefore important that all major structural elements are screened and co-ordinated to produce a building which is both economic and fit for its purpose.

Structure costs as a proportion of total cost
A sports hall is fundamentally a large open space surrounded by a protective shell. The cost of the structure is usually therefore a high proportion of the total cost. The combined cost of substructure and superstructure on average approaches two-thirds of the overall project cost. This is a substantial element in the total cost when compared with a proportion of one-quarter for the majority of buildings. Because of the high proportion of structure in the sports hall, it frequently follows that the structural solution chosen can, to a large extent, dictate the aesthetic and functional success of the building.

Building requirements affecting structure
The basic requirements which must be considered in the design of the structure can be summarised as follows:

Services
For general details of environmental services recommendations see Chapters 60 and 61.
- Is lighting to be natural or artificial?
- Heating and ventilation requirements (particularly when spectator facilities are included) must be incorporated. The structure must be capable of fully integrating heaters and fans as well as cables and pipework.

Fire
- The structure must have the requisite fire protection. The actual requirement can vary according to whether the hall is for public or restricted use.

Internal surfaces
- Internal surfaces should be sufficiently hard and even to permit a true bounce back for balls. Client requirements can vary the height to which internal surfaces should be robust and true. Some authorities specify full height ball bounce capabilities, others restrict to heights of 2 m or more above floor level. The 2 m height is generally regarded as adequate, and up to this height walls must also withstand body impacts.
- Restriction of projections into the hall is advisable to avoid injuries to players. For the same reason doors and cupboards should be set flush with walls rather than into recesses.
- Ledges and holes likely to trap balls and shuttlecocks should be avoided.

Maintenance
- Two aspects of maintenance should be borne in mind in the structural arrangement. It is important in a building subject to the wear and tear of sport that the fabric should be of adequate durability in order to keep down the cost of repairs. It is also desirable to ensure that routine maintenance is facilitated by such things as easy access to service valves, light fittings, ventilators, etc.
- Vandalism, both internally and externally should be discouraged by appropriate detailing and choice of materials.

Subdivision of space
- In multi-use halls floor areas will often be subdivided. This is generally achieved by large curtains hanging from the structure. More substantial barriers may be required if, for ample, archery or cricket practice is to be carried out alongside another sport. Rifle ranges can sometimes be accommodated beneath fixed spectator seating within a hall.
- The Architect may consider it necessary to relate the structure of a hall to a particular layout of courts. This enables a precise integration of such elements as dividing curtains, mechanical services and lighting within the court arrangement. Support is conveniently provided by main structural elements without recourse to extra supporting elements.

Equipment
- The structural frame must be capable of supporting fixed or movable sports equipment. The designers should also be aware that a sports hall must occasionally cater for other functions such as local concerts. Non-sports use of this nature can mean that other types of equipment may be supported from the structure, eg specialist lighting and audio equipment. In some cases climbing walls will be required. This has an important effect on the structural design of the hall.

Cladding
- Selection of cladding and perhaps, more importantly, insulation and their relationship to the structure must take into account the undesirable aspects of condensation and accidental damage. Moisture condensing on steel can cause rapid deterioration and consequently maintenance and eventually structural problems.

Rainwater disposal
- The problem of rainwater disposal from the roof must be solved in the early stages of the design process. Adequate falls, minimum 50 mm in 3 m, are needed to shed water from the roof surface into gutters. Because of the large spans involved it is more economic to frame the structure to provide the basis of falls rather than to introduce secondary elements.
- Successful integration of large drainpipes within the structure or fabric is essential to prevent undesirable visual effects.

Movement

- Sports halls are large buildings; thermal expansion/contraction joints will be required in brick or block walls and in some cases full structural movement joints are dictated by site conditions.

1.1 Range of structural solutions

General

Further technical considerations can influence the form in which the structure develops. Such items as location, character of adjacent buildings, levels across site and soil conditions, including past or future mineral extraction beneath the site, brine extraction, swallow holes etc should all be borne in mind during planning and design work. Within the normal design restraints the following structural solutions can be considered as economically viable:

- Portal frames or columns and trusses or beams with sheeting above a 2 m high wall of brick or block
- Portal frames or columns and trusses or beams with roof sheeting and full height brick or block walls
- Loadbearing brick or block walls with beams, trusses or space frame and sheeted roof.

Some combination of the above alternatives is clearly possible, for example, a framed structure and sheeted outer skin with brick or block inner skin.

Comments in the following study and drawings have generally been based on a sports hall measuring 32 x 26 x 6.7 m clear height, which is in the medium hall range of the Sports Council's recommended sizes.

Structural principles

The structural support system normally consists of roof beams or trusses supporting purlins and/or sheeting.

The beams or trusses bear on to columns or walls. Because of the height factor and lack of internal bracing walls, prime consideration must be given to lateral loading caused by wind action. The resulting forces must be resisted and transmitted to the foundations. A sequence of operations for dealing with lateral loading can be summarised as follows:

- The roof acts as a plate with stiffness in lateral directions. This is achieved by using either stiff deck sheeting (in this case it is vital to be careful about its fixing) or by adding bracing members.
- From the roof, lateral loading is transferred to the walls parallel with the wind direction.
- Walls act as shear plates and transmit forces to foundation as moments, direct forces and shears, **1**.

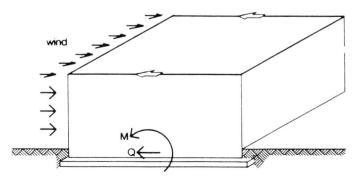

1 *Roof acting as a plate with shear forces (Q) and moments (M) acting on foundations*

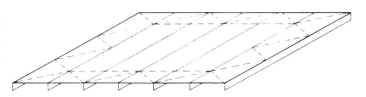

2 *Roof bracing designed to create diaphragm action in roof plate*

The diaphragm action of the roof is frequently created by the introduction of diagonal bracing similar to the illustration in **2**.

Some consideration must be given to the requirements for temporary bracings. In any structure when elements are interdependent, temporary supports or stiffeners are often need to provide overall strength during construction when some structural items are not completed. The space frame roof system usually has sufficient bracing within its framework to provide all that is necessary for roof diaphragm action.

1.2 Structural elements

Roof structure

Roof beams are usually steel sections, although laminated timber beams or timber bow trusses are sometimes used. The choice, depending upon span, roof cladding and internal suspension systems, ranges between:

- Pre-cambered universal beam sections. The camber is necessary to correct deflection tendencies in the beam but will also be used to assist in roof falls for drainage. The pre-camber is usually achieved by a mid-span 'vee' cut and weld. For large spans the weld is sometimes carried out on site to aid in transportation of the beam sections. In this case strict on-site weld testing techniques must be employed, **3a**.
- The beam may be castellated resulting in a lighter weight of steel, although of a deeper section than a universal beam. In most cases, the use of castellated roof beams will be more economic than using universal beams. Castellated beams have the added advantage of providing a ready made route for services, **3b**.
- Lattice beams can be used as roof principals with a further saving in steel weight at the expense of extra depth of section. Generally speaking the longer the span the more economic a lattice arrangement becomes. Tracks for the support of the curtains or screens and equipment can be positioned along the bottom boom of the beam and fixed at node points, **3c**.
- A refinement of the square-ended lattice beam is achieved by tapering the top members. This arrangement, by shortening a number of bracings in the beam, reduces its weight. Economies are also made in height of external wall and roof drainage is simplified and made more efficient, **3d**.
- Another variation is the three-dimensional lattice beam with natural lighting between adjacent bays, **3e**.
- Space frames are an effective means of roofing sports halls. A square on diagonal layout is indicated but several permutations are available, **4a** and **4b**. Square mansard or lattice edge details can be incorporated as required.

The use of other materials cannot be ruled out, eg reinforced or prestressed concrete or timber in either plywood box beam, glulam or truss forms. However, the

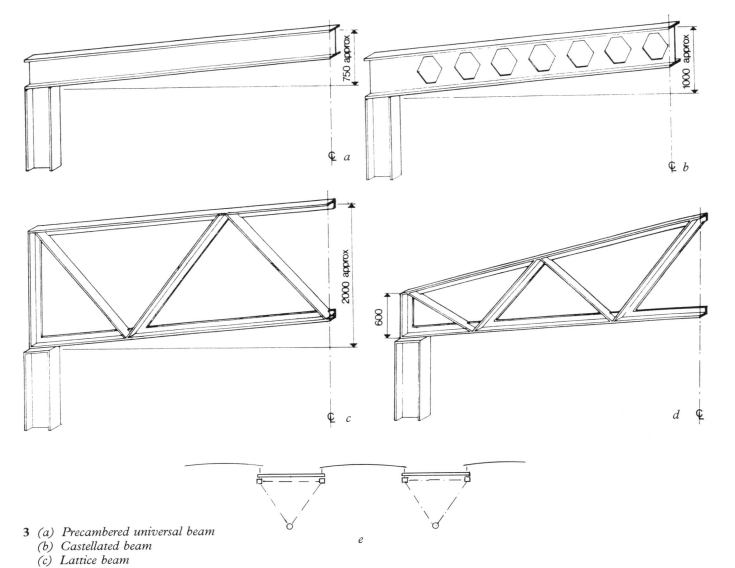

3 (a) Precambered universal beam
(b) Castellated beam
(c) Lattice beam
(d) Lattice beam with tapered rafter
(e) Three dimensional lattice beam

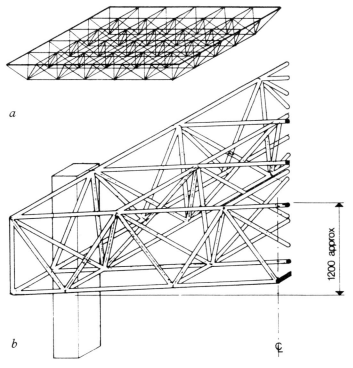

4 (a) Space frame (b) Space frame detail

long span/light load requirements of sports hall roofs unfortunately mean over-heavy concrete sizes or rather deep timber sections. The spacing of principal roof members is determined by the support requirements of the roof cladding material. In addition, economic consideration of the weights of steel members in purlins and main beams influences the spacing. A usual dimension for the spacing of main beams is around 3.5 m. The spacing of columns, which must coincide with roof principal members, has an optimum figure in the region of 3.5 m. The columns provide lateral support for cladding or walling. Excessive spacing of columns leads either to thicker walls or additional secondary steelwork, both of which increase costs.

For sports halls with fixed court layouts, overall economies may be made by basing the spacing of roof principal members and thus columns on court sizes. By arranging playing heights between the main roof beams, the total building height can be reduced. Also, secondary support systems may be omitted if dividers can be hung directly from the main steelwork.

Walls

As discussed above, the walls of sports halls function structurally in two ways: one way is to support vertical loads from roof and cladding, the other is to collect and transmit the effects of lateral loading to the foundations. The amount of vertical load is relatively small and presents few problems. Under some circumstances resolving the resistance of lateral load can be complicated.

There are broadly two arrangements of structure; framed as simple columns or portal legs; or loadbearing brick or block, either reinforced or not.

Framed walls consist usually of steel columns in universal sections with rails at requisite intervals to support cladding. If columns are widely spaced, anti-sag rods may be needed to support the rails. This arrangement necessitates the use of full bay diagonal bracing. The bracing is preferably positioned in the end bays of each of the four sides of the hall, although the need for emergency exits in these position may make this impossible, **5**.

The major task of the diagonals is disposing of forces created by wind. However, if the choice of cladding is brick or block, the need for diagonal bracing (albeit it will be required during construction) and rails can be avoided. Wall panels fixed to the columns provide the necessary bracing, **5b**.

Combinations of the two arrangements can work quite happily. For example, walls going part height with partial bracing systems above if required, **5c**.

In view of the internal requirements of flush surfaces, projections caused by structure must be accommodated within the wall thickness or project outside the hall, **6**.

With sheet cladding and internal lining it is usually convenient to position the columns between the two, but alternatively concrete casing may be possible.

Portal frames While portals can be constructed in reinforced concrete or timber the more usual sports hall construction is for steel to be used. Rafter and legs of

5 (a) Framed wall showing possible anti-sag bars and diagonal bracing in end bay
(b) Brick or block clad wall which requires no additional bracing
(c) Combination wall with braced upper section

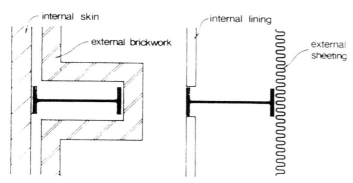

6 *Two common details used to obtain a flush inner skin*

portals are generally fabricated from universal beam sections. The use of knee and apex gussets enables a lighter section of steel to be used, producing a cost saving. The comments on bracing and secondary members of brickwork relating to beam and column construction apply in similar fashion to portal frames.

The primary concern in all cases is to protect the steel columns and rails from corrosion. Whichever covering arrangement is eventually decided upon, and there are many alternatives available, it is imperative that the steelwork be given a high grade protective treatment. Owing to the minimum height requirement for sports halls, portal frames utilising universal beam sections are not normally economic. They may be economic using a lattice portal.

Loadbearing walls Loadbearing walls can reduce the protection problem by removing the need for steel columns. With walls as high as 6.7 m between lateral supports the major problem is slenderness. The solutions below have been produced to overcome excessive slenderness.

- Fin walls. These are a development of the simple buttress principle. The fins coincide with roof beams and are therefore spaced at about 3.5 m. The shape of the fin can be adjusted to suit aesthetic requirements, **7a**. Alternatively, in order to keep projections to a minimum, post-tensioned piers can be used, **7b**.
- Diaphragm walls. These have been used successfully in overcoming the slenderness problems of high sports halls. Constructed by using two 102 mm skins and a 102 mm mid-feather tied or bonded to the skins, the diaphragm arrangement has proved an economic form of construction, **7c**. Roof beams usually sit on to a concrete ring beam going around the top of the wall. The skins of the diaphragm can be constructed in clay brick, concrete brick or concrete block according to preference. Diaphragm walls can conveniently accommodate blow heaters within the structure zone whilst maintaining a smooth internal wall finish owing to the width of the wall. Climbing walls are also easily resolved structurally.

Foundations

Site conditions and levels and subsoil strengths dictate the foundation system to be adopted for individual schemes. If conditions require the foundations to be abnormal, for example piles, rafted or heavily reinforced, the choice of super-structure arrangement has little effect on substructure costs. If, however, simple conditions are envisaged and traditional footings are possible the type of super-structure can influence foundation costs.

Framed structures involve bases for columns, usually with separate footings for walls. This sort of two-stage foundation, with elements often at different levels and requiring cast-in bolts, can complicate substructure.

If the relative difference in level between strip and base is great some economies can often be made by using edge beams to span between column casings. Experience has shown that brick/block superstructures with concrete strip or trench fill can have more economic substructures than comparable framed schemes.

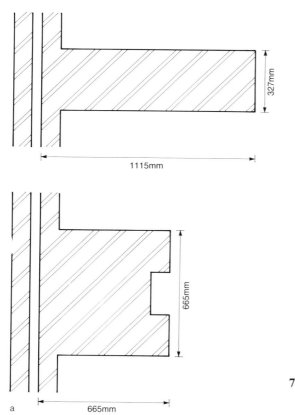

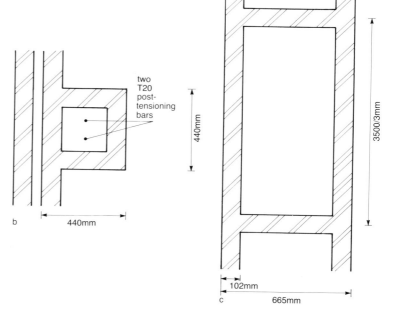

7 *(a) Alternative fins to provide a loadbearing solution*
(b) Post-tensioned pier
(c) Part of a plan of diaphragm wall

68
Community recreation centres and village halls

Kit Campbell and Christopher Harper

1 Introduction

Community recreation centres and villlage halls are the smallest types of building in which a programme of sports can be arranged alongside the customary social and arts pursuits of a rural or local community. There is an infinite range of existing provision from meagre halls of rudimentary construction with minimal ancillary accommodation and basic services up to the sophisticated community centres and village halls often found in commuter or expanding villages and in more urban areas, 1.

Many village halls in the UK were built in the years following the First World War and are approaching the end of their useful life. Finding cost-effective ways of replacing them with more modern accommodation will be a priority during the 1990s in many small communities. In addition, with the growth in popularity of living in villages it seems reasonable to expect that there will be growing pressure for small community recreation centres (SCRCs). Equally many local areas in cities will wish to have a local centre at the same scale as a SCRC.

2 Briefing

Schedule of accommodation
The potential for getting something 'wrong' at the planning and briefing stage is significantly greater for a project intended to serve a small community than a large one.

1 *The Sports Council's Small Community Recreation Centre (SCRC) demonstration project at Markfield, Leicestershire. Photo: Jim Cockayne*

A community's first preference will usually be for new-build on a virgin site but it is sometimes possible to extend existing provision, particularly a playing fields pavilion, so long as it is of a reasonable standard of construction. The main advantages of pavilion extensions are often that some social as well as changing and toilet provision already exists, the site's use is established and site dimensions may be generous, 2.

In these situations or where a traditional village hall offers scope for extension it is probably a new main hall that will be the principal requirement. The secondary need may be a general upgrading of the existing building, particularly services. In these instances the former hall will become the secondary space but may still be preferred by some user groups because of its familiarity and scale and possibly also because of some attractive architectural features.

This suggests that considerable care should be taken when drawing up a 'shopping list' of facilities at the outset. Local knowledge and consultation will normally be the best guide, but they are not infallible. In general, however, it is desirable that at least two halls should be provided on the grounds of increased flexibility in use. A single hall – almost irrespective of its size – will always be very limited. The basis for deciding the basic uses of whatever hall or halls may be provided should be the existence of organised groups, or the potential for fostering organised groups, in the area. A single badminton court size main hall is the obvious starting point but the appropriate scale of the second hall is perhaps more difficult to determine. Key activities for second halls are likely to be playgroups, keep fit, martial arts, and children's parties.

The accommodation should be selected to allow the maximum range of uses within a given size of building. Activity spaces should be dimensioned to take primary account of the needs of sports and recognised court or play areas will determine specific wall to wall dimensions. Ancillary accommodation will then be prescribed to serve these principal spaces. A suitable schedule of accommodation to provide for a fully flexible range of uses could be:

- A main hall containing one or more badminton courts
- A 9 x 9 m (approx 30 x 30 ft) minimum second hall
- A small office
- Domestic sized kitchen
- Toilets and cloakroom.

Because playgroups are likely to be important users it is important to have sufficient circulation space in entrance foyers to allow a number of buggies to be parked there. If additional funds are available consideration should also be given to the provision of a committee room, changing rooms, a bar facility, showers, an outdoor area and additional storage. It may not be necessary to have a bar but only a sink in a suitable position in a store adjacent to an activity space which will allow a temporary bar to be set up when required.

Location
The next question is the best location. Again, there is no single answer which will suit all circumstances, but a stand-alone centre will only rarely be the best option to adopt.

First it is clear that there should be linkages between recreation and other village facilities. A location which is close to as many potential users' homes is crucially important but potentially the best link is with a primary school. The advantages of access to a significant local authority budget, full time on-site staffing, local awareness

2 *Community centres come in a wide range of types and sizes.*
a *Sunningdale Community Centre, Wirral. Architects: Brock Carmichael Associates. A centre designed as part of an upgrading of a housing estate. 9+ m square hall is the smallest viable 'sports' space.*
b *Ludgvan near Penzance. Architects: Poyton Bradbury Associates. A larger than standard badminton hall flanked by ancillary accommodation. Changing rooms also serve outdoor pitches.*
c *Markfield Community Recreation Centre. Architects: TUS and Neylan and Ungless.*
d *Rothwell Community and Recreation Centre, Northants. Architects: Kettering Borough Technical Services. Similar in size to a SCRC but with an extra lounge instead of a second hall. External wall circulation facilitates later extensions.*
e *Great Bentley, Essex. Architect Bryan Thomas. A double court main hall and large lounge/meeting room. Phase 2 will add a further lounge.*
f *Lostwithiel, Cornwall. Architects: Poyton Bradbury Associates. A two-court hall, squash court and four lounges, two of which could be described as small halls. Changing for outdoor pitches.*

and a wide range of facilities are simply too important to be ignored. Accordingly the possibility of shared community use should always be explored when a new primary school is being considered. It is more difficult to adapt primary than secondary schools for joint use but the potential advantages can be substantial. Extra funding sources can ensure that the school obtains a larger hall to badminton size (or sometimes double badminton court size) but it will be necessary to add a separate community equipment store, a kitchenette and ideally also a separate entrance, with toilets, changing rooms and a meeting room. A doubling up of storage is dictated by the difference in furniture and equipment sizes used by adults and small children, **3**.

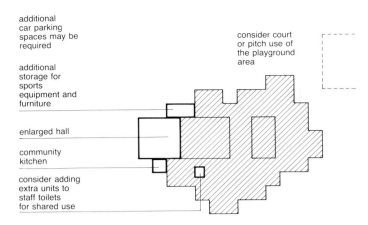

additional car parking spaces may be required

additional storage for sports equipment and furniture

enlarged hall

community kitchen

consider adding extra units to staff toilets for shared use

consider court or pitch use of the playground area

3 *The principal planning additions for primary schools adapted to community use*

A central location also seems to be very much better than a peripheral one – in terms particularly of use by women and of maximising local awareness – while the advantages of being located on a playing field or recreation ground seem somewhat nebulous unless the building is to be operated as a sports and social club. Whatever the location, particular attention should be paid to ensuring safe and well lit access if women and children are to be attracted to the centre at night.

A further amenity which should always be considered if siting permits is an outdoor floodlit multi-games area. It can allow significantly greater total sports use at comparatively low cost and relieve the building of the more robust sports. These games areas are most successful where they form part of a range of outdoor sports facilities on a playing field or recreation ground.

Standards of provision

In a village context, many potential users will have links to nearby large towns or cities and may be 'city users'. Those who wish to continue to play sport competitively may well retain their allegiance to city-based club and leisure centres, leaving village facilities to be used primarily for fairly low level participation, particularly by those people (usually women and children) without personal transport. If the majority of use – in terms of quality of participation – is simply local recreation, is there a need, for example, to provide halls high enough for competitive badminton? Alternatively, taking a longer term view, is it likely that local standards will rise if appropriate facilities are provided, and therefore that good standard facilities should be provided from the first?

The limited evidence is that the latter is likely to be the better approach if it can be afforded. Key design and specification features are likely to be:

- Adequate plan dimensions for activity halls and related storage
- Minimum overall height of at least 6.1 m in any hall intended for badminton; if badminton is not required 3.5 m will suit most other activities
- A multi-purpose floor finish such as semi-sprung hardwood in at least the main hall – but one which can accommodate some misuse during social events
- A combination of heating system, thermal insulation and thermal capacity which will allow heat to be 'stored' within the structure of the building and maintain a good standard of comfort conditions
- Adequate equipment provided from the start.

Funding

Many villages will already have some sort of existing village hall or other local facility. The greatest pressure for additional facilities is likely to come in those villages where existing facilities are at the end of their useful life, or where the population is increasing as new houses are built.

The obvious way to fund SCRC type projects in such locations is for the developers of new housing to provide them through planning agreements negotiated by the local authority, assuming of course that it is their housing which creates the need for new or additional social and recreational facilities: see Chapter 8 of this volume. Except for large developments it is unlikely that such agreements will provide all the necessary funds, but there is no reason why cross-funding from housing or some other development should not be supplemented by local funds or grants.

Uses of the building

The main users of SCRCs are likely either to be aged under 16 years or be young parents. In terms of generating high levels of use it is clearly vital to attract playgroups, social events, clubs and other organised groups. Typically a combination of a main hall and second hall will achieve an average throughput of about eight times the population within about half a mile.

At most centres the dominant use of main halls will be sport with the most popular activities probably being badminton, martial arts and keep fit. In second halls community activities will probably be the main use, particularly playgroups.

In order to be successful it is necessary to develop high levels of core group use – that is, frequent visits by a 'core' of regular users. These users will make most of the visits to the centre but it will also be important to try constantly to widen the number of users by promoting the formation of new user groups and the introduction of new activities. There is some evidence that local promotion through community newspapers and similar outlets can be effective in attracting users.

Management

Of the various management structures which might be adopted, perhaps the most appropriate for most situations will be the 'user group plus elected representatives' model.

Even more important than structure, however, is the question of management style and expertise. Any group planning a local centre should draw up a comprehensive business plan with clear objectives and then monitor results continuously against those objectives. A comprehensive business plan is important not only for good management but also to assist in persuading grant aiding bodies to invest in the project.

For those actually involved in running local centres, there is also the problem of ensuring that initial enthusiasm and offers of help at the planning stage are translated into positive help on cold wet winter nights. Many voluntary management committees consist of a handful of people who put in a lot of work and find it increasingly difficult to attract 'new blood'. If it can be afforded, it is highly desirable to appoint at least part-time staff to supplement voluntary effort.

The main benefits of staff should be:

- Additional use through the tapping of new markets. There is a clear need for coaches and activity leaders of both sexes – perhaps itinerant ones travelling from centre to centre.

- A lively and changing pro-active programme, rather than a static one which may be easy to administer but can lead to the centre becoming little more than a local club.

2.1 Site considerations

Three main factors are likely to dictate the position of a building on a proposed site:

- The position of services: gas will not be available in many rural locations and mains drainage, water and electricity may be some distance away. Service runs should be minimised to avoid excessive cost.
- Noise from cars and late evening activities can create significant nuisance for nearby residents. The location of existing or proposed housing can dictate orientation, the extent of glazing and the scope for natural ventilation.
- If the site is a recreation ground or playing fields the existing pitch layout may have to be changed to provide the best building location. The requirements of spectators may also affect the building's location and orientation.

2.2 Accommodation options

Activity/social spaces
Main halls A single badminton court size hall of 16.5–17.0 × 8.5-10 m (approx 54–55 × 28–35 ft) minimum x minimum 6.1 m (approx 20 ft) clear height will provide for badminton, band practice, boxing, concerts, dances, fashion shows, fencing, floor gymnastics, judo, keep fit, lectures, martial arts, receptions, village meetings, short tennis, table tennis and theatre, **4**.

Sports use can also be extended to teaching skills for a number of other ball games – such as football, basketball and volleyball provided that only soft balls are used. Main halls which compromise on these dimensions can still provide reasonable opportunities for sport but research has shown that examples of the Sports Council's recommended size halls have better than average use and represent good value for money.

Double badminton court halls of 17.0–20.0 × 15.6 m (approx 55.8–65.6 × 51 ft) minimum × 6.1–6.7 m (approx 20–22 ft) clear height, may be considered provided this larger size does not preclude the inclusion of a second small hall. Sports potential is then expanded to include mini-basketball and recreational level volleyball and five-a-side soccer.

4 *The single badminton court main hall, Markfield. Photo: C J Harper*

In exceptional cases a three-badminton-court hall size of 16.5 × 22.5 × 6.7 m (approx 54 × 74 × 22 ft) may be required. This size of hall will normally be provided as a sports centre designed primarily or exclusively for sports.

Small hall The smallest hall suitable for sports use is 9 m (approx 30 ft) square. Ideally it should be increased to 10 × 10 m (approx 33 × 33 ft) to provide the full safety margin for combat sports and have a 3.5 m (approx 11.5 ft) clear height. A hall of this size may be used for boxing, clinics, club meetings, craft shows, darts matches, drama workshops/rehearsals, keep fit, martial arts, old folks' luncheon clubs, painting/photo exhibitions, playgroups, table tennis, and whist drives.

In addition it is often desirable that smaller spaces are added in support of the halls to provide further flexibility in the accommodation.

Lounge/committee room The uses of these rooms can include playgroups, lectures, meetings, licensed bar, whist drives, clinics and darts.

A lounge/committee room can function as a community office when equipped with secure built-in storage. If dimensions permit then table tennis can also be considered provided there is storage for the folded table. 7.6 × 4.6 × 2.7 m high (approx 25 × 15 × 8.8 ft) is adequate.

Support accommodation
Office Even the smallest community centres run on a keyholder basis should have an office adjacent to the foyer. It will require sufficient floor area for a desk and chair and should have cupboards for records and registers and, provided it is not a multi-purpose room, a safe. All lighting and heating controls are most conveniently located in the office.

Toilets A male toilet with one WC, two urinals and two washbasins and a female toilet with two WCs and two washbasins together with a separate disabled persons' toilet represents the minimum standard appropriate to a range of centres from single to two court hall size. Separate children's toilets for playgroups may also be considered. Coat hanging space is also important and can be provided either in a lockable cloakroom or lobby or as part of any changing accommodation.

Changing rooms The provision of specific changing rooms needs careful consideration in buildings without outdoor pitches. Research has shown that changing rooms and showers have very low levels of use in neighbourhood centres where patrons often prefer to change at home although cloakroom space is essential for users to hang up outer clothing. Some provision will usually be required, but can be in the form of:

- Bench space plus a shower arranged as an extension of the toilets.
- Use of the cloakrooms where they are planned next door to toilets and can have access to a shower.
- Rooms normally used for meetings or crafts but provided with an en-suite shower and toilet and a cupboard for stored furniture, **5**.

Buildings with main and possibly secondary halls can justify between 6 and 12 changing spaces for men and women. Where there are outdoor facilities purpose designed changing rooms become essential, planned in

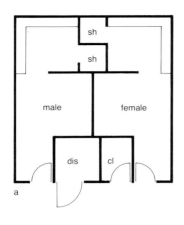
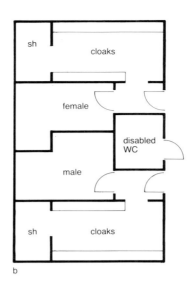
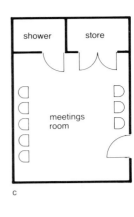

5 *Changing rooms: three alternative options to purpose designed changing rooms*

accordance with the criteria set out in Chapter 57 in this volume.

Another activity which will influence the type of layout selected is drama where it may be possible to combine changing and dressing rooms with a separate access route to the back stage area. The alternative is a further extension of the multi-use principle by utilising serviced spaces adjoining the stage.

Foyer In every community centre or village hall some circulation space is needed, even if it is only an access leading directly from the entrance to the hall flanked by an office and toilets. It should, however, be more than just a narrow corridor as large numbers of people can assemble in even the smallest community hall. Dimensions should take account of the access required for circulation, milling space and space for reading notices and using the phone. In addition there should be a place, preferably a re-entrant, for push-chairs and buggies to be parked clear of the circulation/escape route. A draught lobby should always be included at the main entrance.

Kitchen Size will vary according to the type of catering proposed but in most cases a large 'domestic' kitchen with standard appliances – four-ring cooker, fridge, freezer, and perhaps a dish washer and waste disposal unit – will meet the community's needs. Every day use will consist of the preparation of tea and sandwiches but there will be occasional catering for receptions (most usually final preparation and heating of pre-prepared food). Kitchen serveries can also double as a bar counter when occasional licenses are obtained and extra shelves must then be available for crates and kegs as well as for general storage.

Bar A licensed bar is often a valuable means of assisting rural centres to offset running costs but the need for a permanent bar must be carefully assessed. Temporary installations and licences often provide the best compromise between amenity, revenue earning and ease of operation. When a permanent bar is considered necessary great care must be taken to set up appropriate licensing arrangements, particularly if the centre is run by a charitable organisation. The proposed method of operation also needs to be scrutinised with regard to the employment of bar staff, supervision, VAT and security.

Local breweries should be approached at the design stage as they may be able to assist with the funding and fitting out of the bar.

Equipment stores Generous storage is vital to enable a full range of activities to take place unimpeded in the main and secondary halls. In older or poorly specified halls, tables often have to be stacked to one or both sides of the hall constituting both a nuisance and a safety hazard. Where there are two stores one should be accessible from both halls for access to jointly used equipment. Storage must never be underestimated, and a contingency area should always be included for extra equipment bought from time to time. The minimum provision for storage of furniture, sports equipment and club accoutrements is 50 sq m (approx 540 sq ft) in any centre with a badminton size hall and secondary hall. Youth clubs and playgroups can require considerable storage space and individual as well as general stores will be required, **6**. If an occasional bar is to be provided extra storage should be allocated and equipped with a sink, drainer and cupboards. A permanent servery with flush-fitting doors to the inside of an activity space – ideally the main hall – may also be desirable.

6 *Up and over doors to the equipment stores centred on the longside of the hall at Hadley Stadium. Note the separate mat store*

Other accommodation which may be required may include:

- A plant room – essential with gas or oil (or coal) fired boilers
- A permanent stage – an extravagant use of space but often preferred to temporary proscenium set ups or theatre in the round
- Craft workshop
- Doctor's surgery
- Separate cloakroom off the foyer
- Fitness room
- Squash court
- Billiards and snooker room
- Extra storage and changing and more meeting rooms, **7**
- Possibly also an indoor 'splash pool' or even a 12.5 or 16.6 m (approx 41 or 54.6 ft) long fitness pool.

7 *Extra small rooms are always useful. The community room at Brixton Primary School, Devon. Photo: C J Harper*

2.3 Planning
The accompanying diagrams indicate the preferred relationships between the principal accommodation, **8**. The building's massing will also have to be considered by the

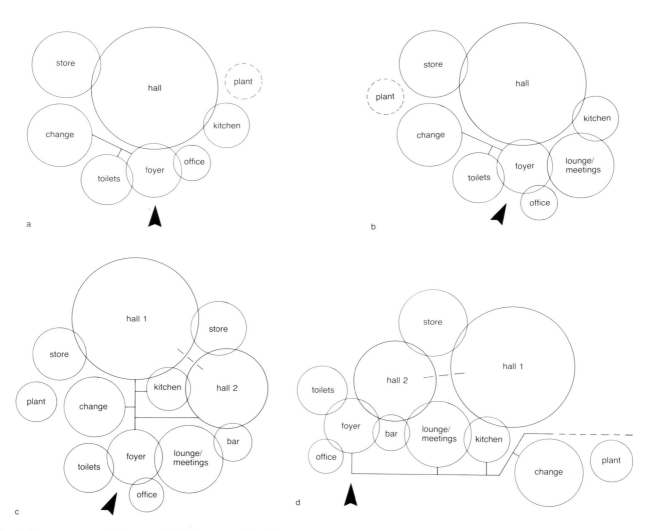

8 *Spatial arrangement diagrams for different scales of provision.*
   a *The smallest centre or village hall with basic support accomodation surrounding the principal space.*
   b *The next step up, incorporating a second activity/assembly space.*
   c *The SCRC type of arrangement. Accommodation grouped around a short central corridor and foyer. Placing the main hall on the perimeter permits a later extension.*
   d *Accommodation grouped to one side of a circulation route. The elongated plan suits many sites and provides for a range of extensions.*

architect in devising an acceptable plan form with the satisfactory integration of the high main hall a principal consideration.

Some of the key points to be considered in relation to the bubble diagrams are:

- Entrance and foyer within view of an office, kitchen or wherever the caretaker or duty keyholder is stationed
- Kitchen located to serve one, possibly two activity/assembly spaces and also perhaps the foyer
- Bar (when included) to serve two activity/assembly spaces
- Bar store planned next to the bar with direct access to exterior and secure palisaded storage.
- Principal spaces divided with a set of folding doors to create one large hall for social functions
- Equipment stores directly accessed from the halls
- Facilities for setting up a bar within the main hall serviced from a storage area
- Changing rooms located to serve indoor sports and arts needs as well as outdoor pitches (where provided).

2.4 Construction method

In most circumstances these are low budget buildings which nonetheless have to fulfil the community's aspirations for comfortable and serviceable interiors combined with an attractive external appearance.

Every possible type of construction – frame and unframed, loadbearing and clad – have been used, but it is the traditional, modified domestic, construction techniques which are generally favoured, **9**. These proven methods are both flexible and durable and often offer the best opportunity for fitting into an established town or village scape.

The clear roof spans and the height of the main hall are areas where normal domestic building practice will require upgrading but in other respects standard building methods may be used. Another advantage is that internal surfaces can conceal conduit and services, especially when a plaster finish is specified.

Many lower budget schemes, particularly sports pavilions, utilise modular buildings. There is an extensive range of products on the market, some of which would be unacceptable in planning terms in many rural locations. The robustness and maintenance characteristics of external finishes must be carefully assessed when evaluating these products as well as the suitability of internal partitions and floorings in wet areas and the acoustic separation of rooms. Any system's standard clear height

9 *Attractive materials and massing at Watchet C of E Primary School, Somerset, heightened and extended for community use. Photo: C J Harper*

and span capabilities must also be taken into account so that desired dimensions are not compromised.

The ubiquitous portal frame form of construction is sometimes selected after the span requirements of the main space and length of building programme have been considered. However, these buildings, unless carefully handled, can produce forms of an alien shape and scale in sensitive surroundings and their detailing can at times be crude. Their interiors are acceptable for sports use but unless standard components are modified or concealed a suitable ambience for social and arts uses may be all but impossible to achieve.

2.5 Detailed design considerations

It is the hall or halls which are dealt with in this section, as the rest of the accommodation does not usually pose any particular difficulties for the design team. The only possible exceptions are changing rooms, where they are required, and for the basic principles of planning and specification refer to Chapter 57 in this volume.

Badminton sized halls

The specification of small community halls differs from that of dedicated sports spaces, **10**. Sports halls must have tough durable surfaces to withstand ball and body impact, but this is not the primary requirement of spaces used for other pursuits and events. Strict sports standards therefore have to be relaxed in order to ensure that appropriate interior design standards are achieved. As a result only soft (sponge) ball games should be played in these multipurpose spaces. Most important of all is the desirability of introducing daylighting. The most satisfactory method is by a band of high-level windows to one or preferably both sides of the hall, or in the case of square halls to the sides of the badminton courts. It is impossible to eliminate glare entirely in certain lighting conditions but the problem can be controlled by the use of blinds or curtains, together with careful detailing of the window assemblies.

If viewing windows are required at low level sill height should be at 1.2 m (approx 4 ft) and glazing must be specified for safety and security. The same applies to any terrace access doors, which should ideally be protected with flush fitting shutters or alternatively heavy curtaining. If five-a-side recreational soccer or other games are being played it is advisable to face the lower part of external doors with rebound panels lining through with the wall face.

Roof lighting is invariably unsatisfactory both from the point of glare and the difficulty of blacking out the interior. If laylights are considered they should be confined to the roof perimeter, between badminton court side lines and the wall face.

Ceilings/roof Wherever possible the ceiling finish should have acoustic properties which will limit reverberation time to a maximum of 2 seconds and any exposed structure should be kept to a practical minimum. High level horizontal surfaces on beams and ties increase maintenance and can trap shuttlecocks and other projectiles. The principal artificial light sources should be arranged parallel to the line of play outside the area of the badminton court and preferably aligned to each side.

Walls Wall faces should be flush to their full height. Low-level openings must be designed to avoid dangerous projections and any frames or projecting architraves must have suitably splayed or rounded corners. All exit doors with the exception of store or intercommunicating doors should open outwards. High-level window sills should be

1	sealed roof construction can make maintenance easier and reduce volume and heating costs
2	raking struts must not encroach on clear height requirements
3	clear span structure in one external wall enables the size of the hall to be doubled
4	with some forms of construction a lower eaves height is possible as long

5	lighting fittings must be outside badminton court side lines
6	windows in end walls produce glare and are more prone to damage
7	mechanical ventilation must not interfere with shuttlecocks
8	wall hung drapes can 'soften' the hall's appearance
9	essential wall mounted fittings eg window controls must be mounted above shoulder height
10	high level sills should be splayed

11 *Fitted PE equipment in schools must fold back flush to the wall for other uses. Photo: C J Harper*

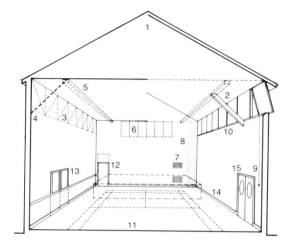

12 *Activity area floors have to withstand a wide range of uses. Photo: Sheffield City Council*

	be durable, easily maintained, and have some resilience and slip
12	doors giving direct access to a demountable stage will need extra height
13	low level side windows should be limited in area with a sill height of 1.2m so as not to interrupt the 'rebound' zone

	are essential and dado rails can save maintenance problems
15	all doors and hatches should open outwards from the hall and projections avoided. Where unavoidable eg escape door panic bolts, sharp edges should be masked from direct contact. Corridor doors should be fitted with vision panels

10 *Main hall construction and detailing notes*

splayed downwards to the interior to throw back balls and shuttlecocks. Any window control gear should ideally be located in corners above the reach of children and switches and power sockets should be flush fitting. In primary school halls with community use standard gym apparatus will need to be recessed and protected with flush and secure panels to prevent misuse, **11**. Other controls and sensors should be located where they are least likely to suffer impact damage. Wall to ceiling drapes are often introduced to soften interiors and improve acoustics. End wall drapes are preferred, and their influence on the location of other fittings must be considered both in the drawn and rolled back modes. Skirting boards should be specified and a dado or dadorail at chair back height can also be considered to reduce accidental damage and the frequency of total redecoration.

Floor Good appearance, durability, ease of maintenance and a degree of slip essential for sports use are the characteristics which must be sought, **12**. In addition, and particularly if the main hall is used by playgroups, safety and resilience has to be taken into account. The only markings generally required are for badminton; inset floor sockets are seldom specified. The heaviest point loads likely to be applied are from piano castors and this must be taken into account when timber floors on battens or sheet flooring with cushion underlays are specified.

Decorative scheme The principles of sports hall practice do not need to be adhered to in all respects but it is still advisable to provide a ceiling with a reflectance value in excess of 90% to minimise contrast with the principal light source and ensure efficient utilisation of the light provided. Wall colour should fall in the mid reflectance band, not only to ensure reasonable sighting of shuttles and balls but also to cut down on the frequency of redecoration. Floors, where possible, should be of a contrasting colour and possibly reflectance value to the walls to provide the desirable spatial definition. Refer to Chapter 62.

Small halls 9–10 m square
The foregoing comments also generally apply to smaller halls. Natural lighting is again essential but in this case will normally be provided at lower level and preferably on more than one elevation to give an even spread of illumination and the opportunity for effective cross ventilation. Wall surfaces should be flush and any low

level fittings must be selected for safety, a requirement of particular importance for play groups. Any heat emitting surfaces must have safe surface temperatures. Dado rails or bash rails should be considered to reduce maintenance as chairs are often aligned against the walls for dances and other social activities. Small children and elderly people will constitute important user groups and the floor finish should have reasonable cushioning and be slip resistant when wet.

2.6 Services – overall considerations

For general details of environmental services recommendations refer to Chapters 60 and 61.

The requirement for good standards of lighting, heating and ventilation is inevitable in modern community buildings; the inadequacy of services is one of the major criticisms of traditional halls. Prospective patrons will be reluctant to leave their own homes on winter evenings if they anticipate a badly lit, cold draughty or generally uncomfortable environment. They will also be unhappy if the centre is oppressively hot or stuffy during warm weather.

The conflict between a modest budget and onerous requirements is nowhere more apparent than in services. Domestic components are inapplicable en masse for the heating, lighting and ventilation systems. The capacity of the system as well as legislative requirements and the need to comply with codes of practice all mean that services design will have to be up to public building specification standards.

Heating

A flexible system is most desirable: heating and ventilation levels for badminton are quite different from those for a bridge tournament and heating should respond rapidly to the fluctuating demands of the centre's programme. In practice the ideal solution is seldom achievable and so the activities programme then has to group similar activities and functions to run consecutively whenever possible.

The most convenient and efficient systems generally rely on a central heat source supplying individual heat distributors throughout the building. A boiler feeding low pressure hot water circulated through pipes to a number of emitters is usually the preferred solution for community buildings giving a combination of flexibility, ease of maintenance and sustainable running and maintenance costs. Different pipework circuits can assist with economy by grouping particular compatible zones of the building together. The master control and time clocks should have restricted access and individual thermostats may need to be protected and locked.

Packaged direct fired warm air unit heaters supplying individual rooms through distributive ducting have also been used in some buildings but these systems are unlikely to be as cost effective as a water based system. Ceiling mounted direct gas fired radiant heaters, can be considered for the main hall but background noise may be a problem.

Electric heating has one clear-cut advantage over other systems - installation costs are normally lower. However, even with good insulation and time controls, running costs can be higher. A means of narrowing the operating cost disadvantages is to combine storage heaters using low tariff power with radiant heaters. This means that rooms can be maintained at background heat levels and brought up to full comfort conditions when required. The vulnerability to damage and the appearance of simple wall mounted radiant fittings must be weighed against their low cost. Individual units can be coin operated if required, as can

shower heaters so patrons pay for what they use. An alternative to individual heaters is the heat emitting surface usually achieved by incorporating electrical elements either in the ceiling or the floor construction. This system may not be ideal due to the lack of flexibility and/or unsatisfactory temperature gradients.

Whichever method of heating is selected, economical operation will be assisted by a well insulated and air tight building envelope with carefully designed and located ventilation sources. The ideal is a building which has a high thermal capacity, in which certain areas can be brought up to full operational temperature when required.

Lighting

Multi-use activity spaces ideally demand integral flexible lighting which, for cost reasons, is seldom capable of being built into community centres, 13. What must be achieved is a practical overall lighting layout appropriate to sport and general use which can be upgraded when necessary for specific functions such as dances and drama. The control of the centre's lighting should be arranged to ensure that it can be flexibly switched for economy. Centralised switching from an office or from the entrance lobby is often preferred in permanently staffed buildings. With room by room control, a master switch should be provided by the last exit for night time shut down or when the space is not in use. The energy saving potential of sensors to switch lights on or off according to occupancy is a worthwhile consideration for all buildings of this type. (Refer to *CIBSE Lighting Guide – Sports* for further details).

Table 68.1: Summary of recommended typical services performance levels for a community centre/village hall

Space	Temperature (°C)	Illuminance (lux)	Air change rate per hour
Main hall	12–20	300–400	1.5–3
Second hall(s)	18–21	300	1.5–3
Lounge(s)	21	200	
Foyer	18	200	
Office	21	500	
Bar	21	100–200	
Bar store	10	100	
Kitchen	18	500	20
Equipment store	10	100	
Changing rooms/toilets	18	100	10
Notes	1	2	3

Note (1): At −4°C external temperature.
Note (2): See *CIBSE Lighting Guide – Sports* and *CIBSE Code for Interior Lighting* for further details.
Note (3): Natural ventilation to Building Regulations requirements.

13 *Natural lighting and ceiling and wall pelmet luminaires: Chudleigh C of E Primary School, Devon*

Emergency lighting Emergency lighting will be required to illuminate escape routes and exit signs when mains power fails. Individual battery powered lights are usually sufficient but, if operating economies are considered, a central ventilated battery store powering emergency fittings may be selected.

Fire protection
Fire precaution requirements can include an alarm system linked to an indicator panel, located by the building's entrance, together with fire extinguishers. The Fire Prevention Officer should be contacted early in the design stage to discuss specific requirements particularly with regard to obtaining a public entertainments licence.

Ventilation
These buildings can generally rely on natural ventilation via openable windows, except where proximity to residential developments, high occupancy levels, or a deep plan form dictates some mechanical air extraction. The areas for which simple mechanical ventilation should always be considered irrespective of location are the toilets, changing rooms, showers and the kitchen. The need for effective ventilation of halls used for dances and discos and removal of cigarette smoke can result in a wider application of these systems. On urban sites, where security can be of particular concern, window areas may have to be restricted and this together with the need to control sound spillage from the building is likely to result in a further use of mechanical ventilation.

Main and secondary halls are the most difficult spaces to ventilate within the constraints of cost and their wide range of potential uses and occupancy. Levels of occupancy can vary from 2 or 4 people to over 150 for special events and uses can range from violent and sometimes noisy physical activity to sedentary and quiet pursuits where background noise must be kept to a minimum. Neither the basic requirements for sports halls nor the sophisticated services of a theatre are appropriate – a sensible moderate cost solution must be found.

Water services
The demand for water in these buildings is generally low, except perhaps where there are outdoor pitches and the consequent but intermittent use of showers. An economical solution may be to rely on individual water heaters or a multi-point heater for taps and showers. This can show operational advantages, particularly when outlets are grouped close together. When a hot water supply, perhaps in the kitchen or bar, is located remotely from the plant room an individual instantaneous hot water heater should be considered in order to eliminate long uneconomic pipework.

Another alternative to a central calorifier fed by the space heating boiler is to have a separate boiler or direct hot water heater to supply domestic hot water.

Power, security and communications
Power Power sockets will be located for individual items of equipment such as cassette recorders, record players, TVs and videos and for cleaning machines. By installing additional outlets in activity spaces, particularly at high level, the requirements of occasional stage, disco and exhibition lighting can be met. Residual current devices should always be considered to minimise the chances of

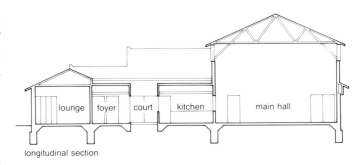

longitudinal section

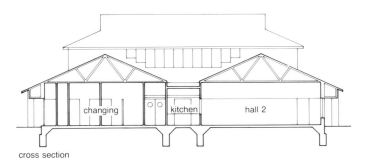

cross section

plan

0   5m

14 *Plan and sections, Markfield SCRC*

electrocution. Their incorporation is likely to be required when a licence is sought so they should be considered from the outset as part of the services brief. Power socket guards must be provided as a minimum measure where playgroups meet.

In the UK all electrical installations must comply with the current edition of the Regulations for Electrical Installations (IEE Regulations).

Telephones A coin (or card) phone is a useful amenity which can be considered for the foyer and could be regarded as vital for security and emergency purposes. A phone will always be provided if there is an office.

TV TV sockets can be considered for the lounge and smaller hall for sport transmissions, etc and a roof mounted aerial, receiver and cable TV connection may then be appropriate.

Lightning protection   In some rural locations, particularly in areas with a high incidence of recorded lighting strikes it is advisable to consider installing a complete lightning protection system.

Security   On many sites and particularly when the building includes a bar, electronic intruder alarms should be considered.

2.7 External works
The majority of users arrive at most centres by foot or car. The extent of car parking space will be agreed with the local planning authority and will vary in different locations. The provision of at least one disabled person's parking bay must be included with a ramped and kerbed division between the car park and main entrance. Everyday needs will be met by an area of metalled parking but overspill for larger social events can be provided more economically in gravel or hoggin.

External access areas and walkways should be hard surfaced and properly lit for safety and security. Light spillage from the building will also help to illuminate the immediate surroundings and provide a welcoming impression for visitors, **15**.

Any multi-use external games area will also be floodlit to ensure full utilisation within the constraints imposed by the site and local planning requirements. It is always useful if some external storage can be arranged either in the form of a purpose designed store or garage unit in which outdoor games equipment can be kept alongside other bulky items such as drama group props and scenery.

Finally, the centre should have its name displayed either in the form of wall mounted lettering or with an appropriate logo sited close to the main entrance.

15 *Playground at Markfield. Photo: Building Design*

3 References and further advice

A range of useful booklets on design and operation of community buildings can be obtained from ACRE (Action with Communities in Rural England), Strand Road, Cirencester, Glos GL7 6JR, (tel 0285-653477).

Action with Communities in Rural England, *Village Halls in England*, The Ronseal Village Halls Survey, ACRE, Cirencester (1988).

Chartered Institution of Building Services Engineers, *CIBSE Lighting Guide LG4: Sports*, CIBSE, London.

Institution of Electrical Engineers, *Regulations for Electrical Installations*, IEE, London.

Kit Campbell Associates, *SCRC Monitoring Study* (1990).

Sports Council, *SCRC Data and Fact Sheets*, Sports Council, London

Sports Council, *Community Use of Primary Schools*, *Data sheets 62*, Sports Council, London.

Sports Council, *SCRC Design Guide*, Sports Council, London (1989).

Part III Dedicated space dry activities

69
Introduction

Kit Campbell

One important feature of the development of sports facilities during the 1980s was the rise in the number of dedicated facilities – that is, facilities for a single activity or a small group of related activities, such as gymnastics and trampolining, rather than multi-purpose facilities for a wide range of activities. Some dedicated facilities have existed for many years (eg real-tennis courts, which date back several centuries) but it seems likely that this is a trend which will continue to develop.

There have been three main reasons why dedicated facilities have grown in popularity:

- To allow the development of high standards of performance in safety – examples include gymnastics training pits, indoor cricket schools and indoor athletics training halls
- To provide indoor facilities for what have hitherto been largely outdoor sports (eg tennis, cycling and bowls) so helping to boost participation and allowing these activities to be enjoyed year round
- The commercial development of some specialist facilities, for example billiards and snooker or tenpin bowling centres and climbing walls.

The basic characteristic of dedicated facilities is that they are designed to provide ideal or near ideal conditions for a single activity. It follows that there is often little room for compromise in design; indeed, some governing bodies (eg for squash, bowls and shooting) allow the designer to make comparatively few decisions relating to the detailed design or construction of the actual playing facilities. The challenge for designers is then to find way of making these largely standard facilities 'special' in some way without compromising their function. This is particularly important where several similar facilities in a comparatively small area may have to compete for users. Squash is a good example; traditional British squash centres where the courts and ancillary areas are separated are generally significantly less attractive and user-friendly than the 'open plan' centres common in Germany and some other countries.

In the future the trend towards more dedicated facilities is likely to continue; in addition, it is likely that further sports will seek dedicated facilities. The most likely ones to do so are perhaps badminton (for which there are often sufficiently high levels of local demand to sustain a dedicated facility), basketball and volleyball (which could possibly share competition and training halls), table tennis (which has highly specific requirements and can be accommodated in halls smaller than the traditional sports hall), fencing (for which specialist metallic pistes are increasingly essential), and judo or karate. There is likely to be particular pressure from regional governing bodies for the development of specialist facilities, particularly as 'new' sources of funding such as the UK National Lottery become available.

In major cities there may be scope to develop complexes of dedicated facilities. They should have lower staff costs than the equivalent area of multi-purpose space and be increasingly developable by the commercial sector if suitably cheap land can be obtained; racket centres with squash, badminton and tennis courts and possibly other facilities such as a fitness area and dance studio are a good example. Alternatively the commercial sector will probably continue to develop specialist facilities linked to accommodation in the form of holiday villages.

At the planning stage the determination of potential demand is a key step in the development of dedicated facilities; there will be little or no scope in the finished complex for one activity to cross-subsidise another. It will therefore normally be necessary to undertake a detailed market study to establish the scale and content of complexes in order to prepare a comprehensive design brief.

70
Athletics: indoor training facilities

Peter Ackroyd and Philip Johnson with acknowledgements to the former Amateur Athletic Association, Southern Counties AAA and Sports Council Working Party

1 Background information

The unreliability of the European climate means that competitors in technical and explosive events may not be able to train outdoors for long periods without considerable discomfort and an unacceptable risk of injury. Indoor provision for athletes to train and compete is therefore essential. There are indications that facility providers now consider the needs of athletes and good examples are outlined in this section.

Facilities for athletics consist of:

- *Facilities for competition* which provide for the full range of competitive indoor disciplines with spectator provision. Such facilities are outlined in Chapter 50 in this volume (see also References and further advice, below).
- *Training facilities* which are usually purpose-built or adaptations of existing halls, intended for full indoor competitions, **1**, or limited competitive use. They are best provided at or adjacent to existing outdoor tracks, **2–8**.
- Sportshall athletics in Chapter 18 of this volume.

A further important distinction is between multi-sports and specialist indoor training provision; in the former case, athletics is one of many sports sharing limited space, **4**.

The provision of training facilities for athletes indoors does not necessarily require a 200 m banked track, **1** and **7**. Many events can be simulated indoor for training purposes if the brief for the facility is thought out in advance in full consultation between providers, the appropriate governing body of athletics, development officers and coaches, **7–9**.

1 *Kelvin Hall, Glasgow – training session. This permanent track was extended to five lanes for the 1989 European Championships and is the UK's second largest competition venue. Photo: Myles Burke*

2 *New River Sports Centre and Wood Green School sports hall, London Borough of Haringey. The sports hall was a Sports Council prototype scheme for an athletics extension of a school sports hall to provide one L-shaped area capable of use for a wide range of school and community sports besides athletics training indoors, **4** and **5**. It opened in February 1980 and was the first facility of its kind in this country. It is situated opposite one of the top athletics club tracks and together they form the New River Sports Centre. The hall was a joint-provision facility located on a school site. Photo: LMGT Consultants, Harlow*

3 *Warm-up/training facilities beneath the main spectator stand at Don Valley Stadium, Sheffield. The pole vaulting bed (centre) is beneath a raised ceiling height. The high jump bed is in the bay off the straight, to the right. See also **13d**. At Wigan, a seminar and coaching room bridges and overlooks the training area. Photo: Sheffield City Council*

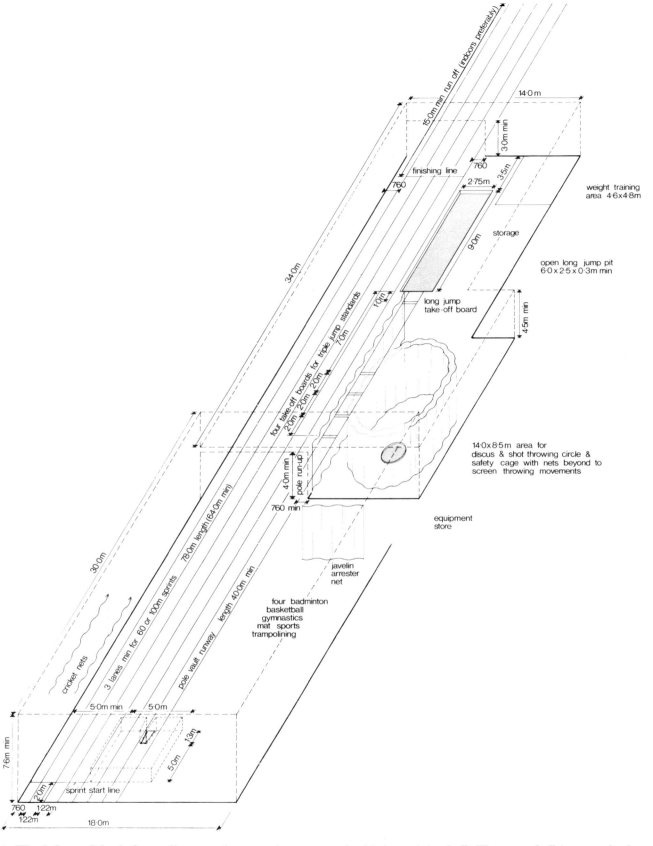

Labels within diagram:

15·0 m min run off (indoors preferably)

14·0 m

3·0 m min

760

3·5 m

finishing line

760

2·75 m

weight training area 4·6 x 4·8 m

9·0 m

storage

34·0 m

open long jump pit 6·0 x 2·5 x 0·3 m min

four take-off boards for triple jump standards

1·0 m

long jump take-off board

4·5 m min

7·0 m

2·0 m 2·0 m

2·0 m 2·0 m

14·0 x 8·5 m area for discus & shot throwing circle & safety cage with nets beyond to screen throwing movements

30·0 m

4·0 m min

78·0 m length (64·0 m min)

3 lanes min for 60 or 100 m sprints

pole run-up

equipment store

760 min

javelin arrester net

cricket nets

pole vault runway length 40·0 m min

four badminton basketball gymnastics mat sports trampolining

5·0 m min

5·0 m

7·6 m min

1·3 m

5·0 m

2·0 m

sprint start line

760

1·22 m

1·22 m

18·0 m

4 *Wood Green School. Space diagram of community sports and athletics training hall. The sports hall is a standard 32 × 17 × 7.6 m hall but with several interesting additional features:*

- *An extra 'leg' which allows a 60 m sprint to be run indoors*
- *Built-in long and triple jump pits,* **15**
- *An indoor throwing net for practice in discus, hammer (substitute) and shot. (Note that oval/circular netting, as shown, could become hazardous if the implement deflects around curved netting. See preferred square cornered layouts in* **7–10, 21***.)*
- *An outdoor run-out for the sprints*
- *Rubberised athletics floor throughout the hall and the extension*

Badminton and other court coloured markings overlapping the lanes and run-ups can distract athletes. Diagrams 7 and **11** *shows preferable multi-sports layout. Architects: London Borough of Haringey*

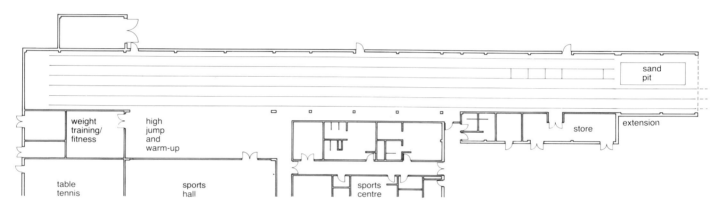

5 *The sprint straight extension of the sports hall, seen in the background and direction of diagram,* **4**. *Pole vaulting headroom is critical in small or medium size halls of only 7.6m height. Photo: Tommy Hindley*

6 *Layout of Broadbridge Heath, Horsham showing the proposed open jump pit extension in a dedicated shuttered off space at the sprint start end*

Training spaces are required for:

- Sprinting and hurdling
- Horizontal jumping
- High jumping
- Pole vaulting
- Throwing
- Weight training
- Limbering warm-up
- Wherever possible, a part bend of a 400 m track, **9**.

2 Critical factors

- Location and siting, preferably at a track
- Wintertime programmed usage
- Scale of provision
- Specialist facilities preferred: new-build, conversion or temporarily covered
- Compatible/incompatible sports and flooring in a multi-sports hall situation
- Spike resistant flooring essential
- Adequate ancillary back-up accommodation located in a flow-sequence adjacent to related training spaces. Volume for intensive use by schools
- Space requirements and safety margins for each discipline

- Run-out/run-off space at end of sprints
- Position of long jump pit and control of sand spread/containment
- Quality of sand
- In multi-sports hall floor, flush blanking boards in place of long and triple jump boards
- In multi-sports hall, flush floor cover over pole vault box
- Height for high jump, throws and increased height of pole vault run ups
- Adequate protective netting for throwing training
- Quality of netting for javelin, discus and shot
- Separate heavy weight and limbering up areas
- Security of weights and equipment in multi-purpose halls
- Adequate, separated storage for equipment
- Size of storage access doorways
- Storage racks for specific items
- Safe storage for hurdles (bulky)
- Adequate and fire resistant storage for very bulky landing beds, for high jump and pole vault and other mats
- Foam beds must not be 'stored-out-in-use' in a multi-purpose hall
- Exposed edges of walls to be well padded
- Location of doorways to avoid accidents
- Project brief agreed by designated user bodies.

263

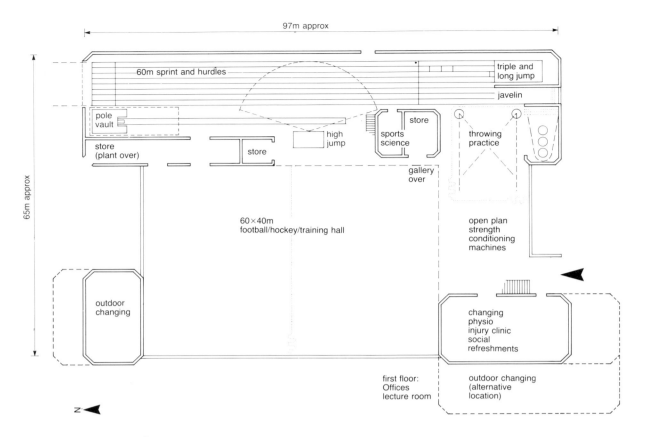

7 *Proposals for a national training centre, Belfast for SCNI. Sketch layout TUS (1991)*

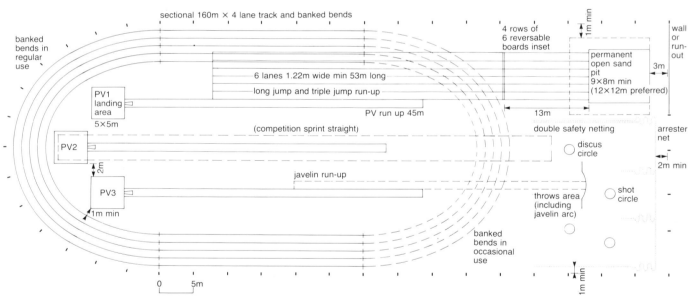

8 *Alexandra Pavilion conversion, feasibility study 1989. Sports Council/SCAAA. A 160 m training circuit was proposed. Layout: TUS (1989)*

2.1 Provision of facilities

First and foremost check local regional and national strategies for athletics provision. Athletics is a club-based sport and few towns or districts have more than one club which would require an indoor training base. For this reason, location at or near the main athletics track is desirable. Opportunities for educational joint provision and dual use should be considered.

Three types of provision are recommended:

- New specialist athletics training areas, either extensions to sports halls or located at athletics tracks (see Chapter 62 in this volume); for example, training centres located in the undercroft of the spectator seating at Meadowbank (Edinburgh), Sheffield, Hull and Wigan.
- Newbuild sports halls and projectile halls/long galleries, preferably at an educational campus or track, **2, 4, 6, 7**.
- The use of existing multi-purpose sports hall projectile ranges (see Chapters 49 and 50 in this volume), **10**.

2.2 Specialist indoor training facilities

There are a growing number of specialist facilities for indoor athletics training in the UK and their specifications vary widely. Most have been created by adapting a

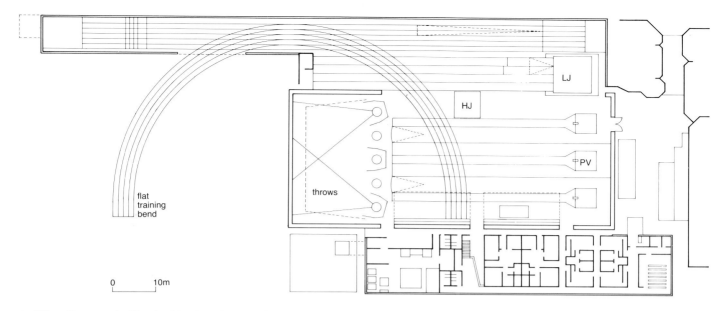

9 *West German facility in Sb 6/76 Ground floor plan showing a 400 m part-bend extending outdoors for relay baton passing practice*

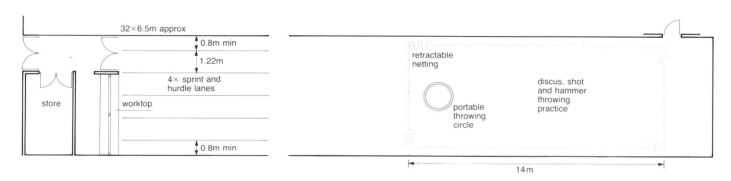

10 *Limited training in a 4.5 m high projectile hall, Lewes, Sussex. In a multi-sports space choice of floor surface is critical*

standard four, six or eight badminton court sports hall to comprise an additional area providing a 60 m straight with space for jumps and throws as at Wood Green School in Haringey, **4**, Gateshead Stadium near Newcastle, Centre AT7 in Coventry and Bedford. At Broadbridge Heath Leisure Centre in Horsham, **6**, a dedicated area 70 x 7.3 m with an additional space of 17.5 x 6 m for field events has been provided as part of a sports and retail complex. At the Don Valley Stadium in Sheffield, and at other outdoor tracks, indoor warm-up and training facilities are housed beneath tiered spectator seating. Figures **4–6** outline these examples.

Impressive examples are Kelvin Hall, **1** the Helsinki 160 m variable profile track, the Dusseldorf 200 m training/competition facility and the L-shaped Bochum shed, **9**.

2.3 Non-specialist indoor training facilities

Most clubs in the UK have access to some form of indoor facilities for training but in the vast majority of cases they comprise sports halls or school gymnasia. Whilst non-specialist facilities provide useful opportunities for athletes in the sprints, jumps and throwing events to practice during the winter months, in many instances the range of activities is constrained by the size of the facility and the nature of the flooring which precludes the use of spiked footwear. Nonetheless, during the months of October to March when the weather is not conducive to outdoor training (and non-synthetic surfaces may be unusable

owing to frost) the availability of indoor facilities is critical for many athletes. The development of *sports hall athletics* competitions for youngsters (see Chapter 18 in this volume) has demonstrated that with imagination and adaptation sports halls can provide a good environment for athletes. A further form of non-specialist indoor training facility which in many respects underlines the desperate shortage of provision is multi-storey car parks which are used by some clubs to provide covered training facilities for runners.

The increase in the provision of multi-sports halls and indoor versions of outdoor games is only beginning to have an impact on athletics. Some of the reasons for this are:

- The programming of athletics together with other sports particularly during the winter when most sports centres have their highest demands for evening usage in other activities
- The relatively long periods of exclusive use of facilities required by athletes to carry out training programmes
- The relatively large space traditionally required to train relatively small groups of athletes
- The specialist requirements for floors, pits, nets and landing mats and related technical problems in use or of storage.

Existing halls can be used for athletics training where athletes and management are prepared to exercise some degree of compromise. Where floors are unsuitable for spiked shoes, athletes should not have to train in 'flats'. Roll-out strips of 10–12 mm minimum thickness can be provided at slightly greater cost for practice with spikes. Existing halls might also be adapted and extended, **6**.

2.4 Training areas in converted buildings
Conversions of major redundant buildings which can accommodate a four-lane 125 or 160 m circuit but without the space to provide seating for a full competition facility should be considered as *regional training centres*. The technical specifications for these should be the same as for competitive facilities, except that a flat circuit track may suffice until a portable banked bend can be afforded. A full range of field events training is essential, **8**.

Conversions of smaller clear span buildings which are potentially suitable, subject to project feasibility studies, include warehouses, factories (subject to height), and hangars. The covering of outdoor training facilities at existing tracks should also be considered, eg as at Bathgate, Scotland. This could take the flexible form of tracked pull-out awning or concertina cover attached to a wall or indoor facilities. The jumps or throws area could then be opened up for summer trackside use.

2.5 Spaces
Figure **11** shows the recommended locations and juxtaposition of the following track and field disciplines and related elements of necessary accommodation. It also notes any alternatives. The following dimensioned diagrams give more detailed guidance and critical factors:

- Sprint track, including hurdles, **12**
- Part 400 m track bend, **9**
- Long and triple jump, including pit and board details, **13–16**
- High jump, **17**
- Pole vault, including floor box detail and clear headrooms, **18–20**
- Throwing practice enclosures and arrester net details, **21** and **22**
- Limbering/exercise/warming up areas, **6**, **7** and **11**
- Storage, including foam beds, **23**, **24**
- Lecture/seminar/video facility, **3**, **7**
- Sports science/performance monitoring room, **7** and **11**
- Weight training areas – a separate weight training area is essential, but free-standing machines can be shared with other sports users, **4**, **6** and **7**.

2.6 Floor surface
The most important aspect of designing for indoor athletics is the floor, including in the changing areas and approach to the track. The finish should withstand shoe spikes and be as similar as possible to the track on which athletes will compete. This is not always possible owing to a number of factors, not least of which is often the need for the special athletics facility also to provide multi-sports functions. This tends to lead to compromise but should not detract from the need to choose a surface primarily for athletics (refer to Chapter 64 in this volume).

The minimum thickness specified for permanent surfaces must take into account that the facility is for training and mainly in the explosive disciplines of track and field such as sprints, hurdles and jumps. This entails constant pounding from athletes' feet. Therefore the 'hardness' of the material may need to be a great deal lower than for the normal competition track. The surface may also need to be thicker to assist in the provision of appropriate levels of compliance and stiffness as well as accommodate the

length of spikes to be used. These qualities may also be affected by the base on which the surface material is laid. A surface thickness of 12–16 mm is recommended. In addition, when considering thickness for multi-use it is important to take into consideration the surface texture because spike resistant materials may have a very high profile. For multi-sports use a lower profile is needed and this results in different performance qualities.

The one aspect of indoor use that differs from outdoor is the constant need to clean the surface. The use of mechanical cleaners with rotating brushes, whether wet or dry, creates an extra wear factor which can cause problems with in-situ type materials with their crumb finish.

A list of the surfaces available can be obtained from the Sports Council's Information Centre. Reports of testing to the relevant performance specification should be requested from the companies concerned. Products generally can be divided into three main types:

- Wet pour in-situ polyurethane/rubber combinations similar to many outdoor tracks. It may be of variable thickness and this will give differing ball response if used in a multi-sports area. The minimum thickness required must be specified but a greater average thickness of material will need to be laid to guarantee this minimum thickness in order to allow for tolerance in laying which can only be specified to 3 mm under a 3 m straight edge. The hardness can also vary in this type of material. There is a potential health and safety factor to be taken into account in the laying process.
- Sheet material – factory manufactured rubber and polymeric to give uniform thickness and hardness. The majority of athletics specialist competition and training provision in the UK is of this type of material. Most have been developed from multi sports surfaces. A different version of the surface profile from that designed for a track surface may be needed if the facility is to be used for general sports use. There may be a health and safety factor to be taken into account in laying depending on the adhesive used.
- Carpet type factory manufactured materials used in Scandinavia but not used extensively in the UK. This type of material may be appropriate for conversion of an existing sports facility to athletics training as it can be rolled away and stored more easily than the sheet rubber and polymeric materials. It is, however, very restrictive in the spike length that can be used.

Other possible types include in-situ finished materials on sheet bases including rubber-crumb base material, or some of the outdoor materials which are made up of a wet pour finish on a sheet rubber crumb material.

For further details see References and further advice below. Also, for outdoor athletics surfaces refer to Volume 1, Chapter 13.

Markings
Generally lines are 50 mm (2 in) wide painted in white and with colour markers to IAAF colour codings. The width of each lane includes one (outside) line. Jump boards are reversible insets. Taped markings are difficult to stick to a crumb/textured surface.

2.7 Environment
For general details of environmental services recommendations refer to Chapters 60 and 61. The main advantage of indoor training is that users are 'in the dry, out of the

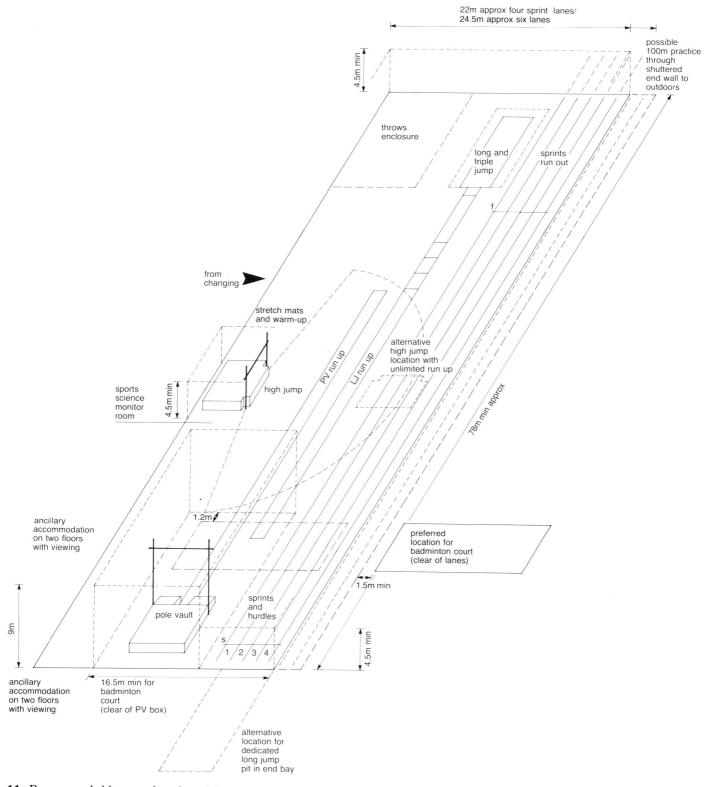

11 *Recommended layout of track and field training spaces with necessary related accommodation. Alternative locations are shown by broken lines at floor level. In a multi-sports layout it is preferable that courts should not overlap the lanes. Details of each space are given in the following diagrams*

weather'. Temperature is of less importance than fine ventilation and glare-free lighting.

A wide range of activities are included in this sport and it is therefore difficult to define ideal environmental conditions which cover all of them. A minimum design temperature of about 15°C in winter should be generally acceptable and this can probably be allowed to rise to around 25°C or so in the summer. It is important that the humidity is kept at a reasonable level and 40–50% relative humidity will generally be acceptable.

It is also important that adequate ventilation is provided to maintain a fresh, comfortable environment and remove odours but air movement must not cause excessive draughts, particularly in the vicinity of the pole vault and high jump bars.

General overall lighting of the whole arena is usually acceptable. Particular attention may need to be given to the finishing lines for track events. The pole vault bar area (6 m or so above floor level) should to be shielded from glare.

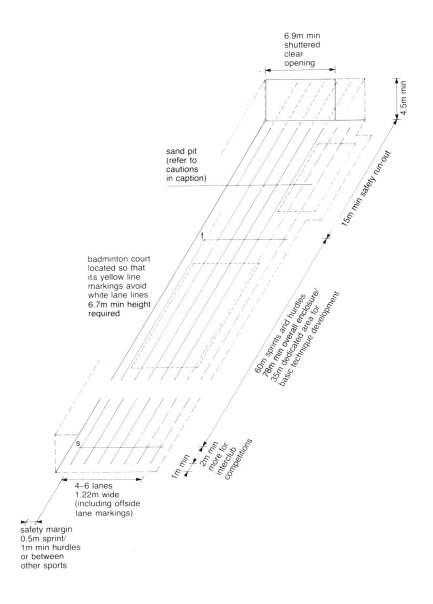

6.9m min
shuttered
clear
opening

4.5m min

sand pit
(refer to
cautions
in caption)

15m min safety run-out

badminton court
located so that
its yellow line
markings avoid
white lane lines
6.7m min height
required

f

60m sprints and hurdles
78m min overall enclosure/
35m dedicated area for
basic technique development

s

1m min

2m min
more for
interclub
competitions

4–6 lanes
1.22m wide
(including offside
lane markings)

safety margin
0.5m sprint/
1m min hurdles
or between
other sports

12 *Sprint and hurdle lanes and run-out. At least four dedicated lanes are recommended. Do not overlap a permanently open sand pit, on to sprint lanes (with shared run-ups) unless six or more lanes are provided and other critical problems noted in* **13** *are also carefully resolved. For local competition use full-length 60 m lanes are advisable. The lanes and surface should continue for at least 15 m to provide a safe, unobstructed run-out distance. Shorter run-outs must be cushioned by crash mats against the end wall*

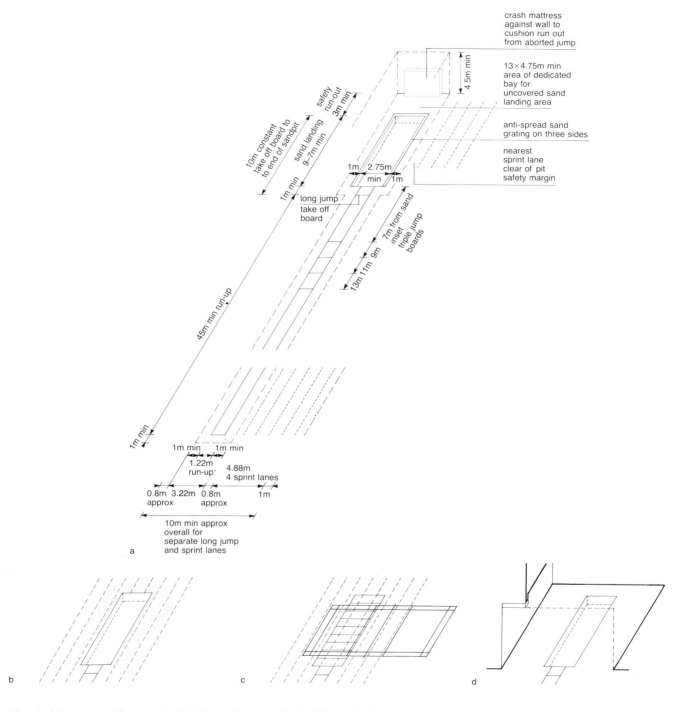

crash mattress
against wall to
cushion run out
from aborted jump

4.5m min

13×4.75m min
area of dedicated
bay for
uncovered sand
landing area

anti-spread sand
grating on three sides

nearest
sprint lane
clear of pit
safety margin

safety
run-out
3m min

10m constant
take off board to
to end of sandpit

sand landing
9–7m min

1m min

1m / 2.75m min / 1m

long jump
take off
board

7m from sand
inset
triple jump
boards

13m 11m 9m

45m min run-up

1m min

1m min / 1m min

1.22m
run-up

4.88m
4 sprint lanes

0.8m 3.22m 0.8m   1m
approx   approx

10m min approx
overall for
separate long jump
and sprint lanes

a

b

c

d

13a–d *Diagrams of long and triple jump lanes and pit. The main factors are:*
13b *Containment of sand and cleaning of surrounding textured floor surface,* **15** *and* **16**
● *Pit edge detailing,* **16**
● *Watering point nearby.*
13c *Particularly note the extremely difficult problems of the design and laborious handling of heavyweight pit covers, which are strongly inadvisable. Ten or more such heavy, deep units must be surfaced as the track and set-in flush. Weight, manoeuvrability and the resultant sunken sand level are some of the serious disadvantages of the pit overlapping the track. A cover lifting machine is used at Don Valley Stadium, Sheffield. Slow and cumbersome it is less laborious than lifting by hand, or hinging against wall (the heaviest of hinges snap eventually)*
● *Inset and reversible boards along run-ups,* **14**
● *Run-out safety margins for an aborted jump*
● *Quality of non-staining silver sand*
13d *Location in a dedicated bay and avoidance of pit covers,* **13, 16–17**.

14 *Take-off and four triple jump boards are reversed as blanking boards inset flush with the floor surface. Photo: Sports Council at AT7 Coventry*

15 *Sand is carried out of the pit and is a major nuisance. A pit edge detail which attempts to reduce the problem is shown in* **16.** *Photo: LMGT Consultants*

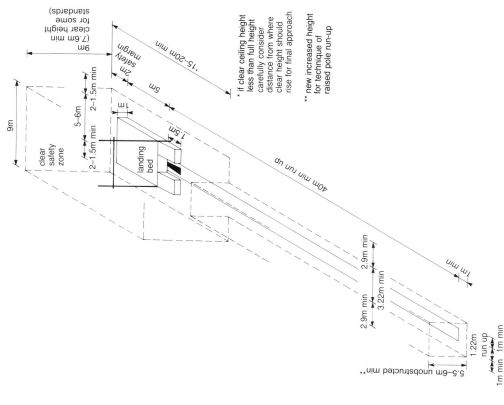

(7.6m min clear height for some standards)

9m clear height

9m

2m safety margin

5m

15-20m min

5-6m min

2-1.5m min

1m

1.5m

landing bed

clear safety zone

2-1.5m min

40m min run up

* if clear ceiling height less than full height carefully consider distance from where clear height should rise for final approach

** new increased height for technique of raised pole run-up

2.9m min

3.22m min

2.9m min

1m min

5.5-6m unobstructed min**

1.22m run up

1m min 1m min

18 *Diagram of pole vault run-up and bed. Note the essential increased headrooms, **3**, **5**. Also that the foam bed modules need approx 35 cu m of storage per bed for use in a multi-purpose space, **27***

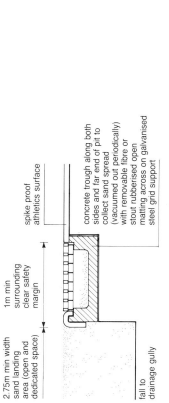

2.75m min width sand landing area (open and dedicated space)

1m min surrounding clear safety margin

spike proof athletics surface

concrete trough along both sides and far end of pit to collect sand spread (vacuumed out periodically) with removable fibre or stout rubberised open matting across on galvanised steel grid support

380mm min

fall to drainage gully

16 *A suggested sketch detail for an open pit edge. For safety, the surrounding grating should be surfaced with 'open' rubber matting (similar to door mats). This detail is developed from the National Indoor Arena, Birmingham*

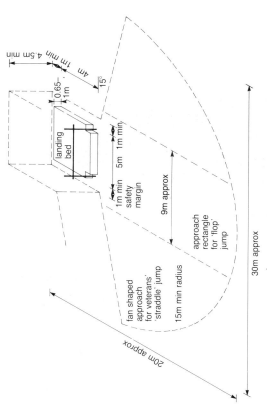

4.5m min

1m min

4m

0.65-1m

15°

landing bed

5m 1m min

1m min safety margin

9m approx

approach rectangle for 'flop' jump

fan shaped approach for veterans' 'straddle' jump

15m min radius

20m approx

30m approx

17 *High jump bed in preferred bay location. Two other options are located in* **11**. *An indoor area provided mainly for sprints and horizontal jumps is often too narrow for the run up. However, modern jumping techniques using a straight approach (making a fan shaped layout obsolete) can fit along the lanes,* **11**, *but then will restrict sprinting. There must not be a change of level or surface within the approach. The safe storage of approx 20 cu m of foam-filled bed units is a critical factor if the bed is not permanently 'stored-out-in-use' in a dedicated area, as shown. Nor should the high jump bay become a storage area for other equipment, unless safely screened off beyond the fan shaped area and surrounding safety margins*

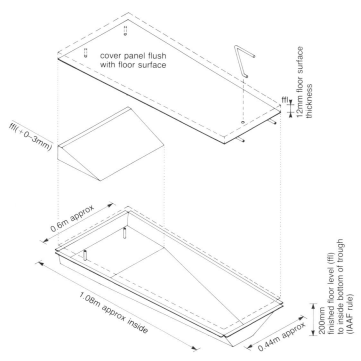

19 *Detail of pole box inset into floor. The near end wedge shaped part (centre) is removed when not in use and the cover panel, surfaced with the floor finish, carefully set flush at floor level. Note in multi-sports area the covered-in box should be located between badminton courts and clear of other court critical markings*

20 *Removable un-noticeable cover flush with floor level conceals a pole vault box which is best located clear of other floor markings. Photo: Sports Council*

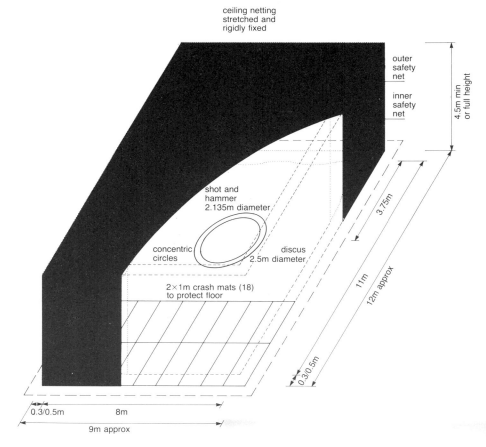

21 *Diagram of 'throws' area. A secure, heavy duty netted enclosure is essential. The outer safety net can be tensioned and weighted down but the inner netting must be free to cushion impacts and fully draped on the floor to prevent implements from breaking out. Netting must be continuous around the corners and any joint well lapped at the rear of the enclosure to allow access. Often throwing circle equipment is a luxury; a stop board can be fixed to the floor using sockets.*

*Rubber practice-grade implements should be used to safeguard the floor and avoid damage to competition grade equipment. If the latter is used, for warm-up or practice, the floor must be protected by crash mats as shown. Proprietary cages are also obtainable, **22**. For a multiple throwing facility a large single enclosure is preferable as shown in **7–10**.*

*Advice concerning javelin practice into fine arrester netting **4, 7** can be obtained from the equipment trade and British Athletics Federation. Ample space and height are also critical factors*

22 *Oval throwing cages. See also* **4**. *Photo: Sports Council*

General lighting requirements are 200 lux for training uses. For further details of lighting requirements refer to Chapter 60 and *CIBSE Lighting Guide LG4: Sports.*

3 References and further advice

Facility Advisory Group of British Athletics Federation (BAF).

British Standards Institutions, *BS 7044*, BSI, Milton Keynes. (For wear and ageing and also for multi-sports floors.)

Chapter 18 in this volume, Sportshall athletics.

Chapter 64 in this volume, Detailed design: sports floors.

Chapter 39 in Volume 1, Athletics: track and field.

Lindsay, NE and Johnson, PT, *Indoor Athletics: A Study of Tracks and Meeting Presentations*, City University, London.

Sports Council, *Arenas: A planning, design and management guide*, Sports Council, London (1989). (Includes detailed requirements and data for competition tracks.)

23,24 There are three possible forms of storage area:

- Small secure undercroft spaces for hurdles trollies, cleaners, line markers, **23**
- Tall and lengthy equipment such as that for pole vault and high jump stands, poles and bars which need protection and considerable turning space to manoeuvre to and from storage, **7**

The amount of storage space will depend on:

- Whether the centre will cover all athletics disciplines, including storage for outdoor events, **24**
- The extent of any existing storage, eg a sports hall or weights store
- Foam-filled equipment bulk storage in a fire resistant area(s), particularly in multi-sports provision, **7, 11**
- Whether equipment will be 'stored-out-in-use', particularly the bulky beds, **3, 7–9, 17, 18.**

As a space guide for a multi-sports area allow approximately 15–20% of the total activity areas for general and athletics storage. However, in the bulk foam stores volume and height of space is as important as area. A pole vault and high jump bed needs about 50 cu m of space and cannot be stored closer than 1.5 m from fire sprinkler nozzles. If 'stored-out-in-use', storage space may be reduced to about 10% of the athletics floor area. Photos: Sports Council and AT7 Coventry, **23** and Puma–Wigan Sports Complex, **24**

71
Billiards and snooker

Peter Ackroyd

1 Critical factors

- Overall area, including where appropriate officials' sitting-out space around the tables
- A firm floor level and surface
- Tables must not be moved once they have been set up and adequately protected when not in use
- Match tables need adequate space for players and elevated spectators
- Uniform, shadow-free illumination provided by special separate lighting for each table
- Good ventilation.

1.1 Space

Critical dimensions and the shape of the space required are shown in **2**. The overall size of a full-sized billiard table is approximately 4 × 2 m (approx 12 × 6 ft) depending on the particular design. The Billiards and Snooker Control Council (B&SCC) introduced (with world agreement) the 'B&SCC 3.50 m standard table' and for the first time this specifies the actual *playing area* size (3.50 × 1.75 m) *within* the cushion faces in place of the overall table size. These metric recommendations have been largely ignored and are rarely used, even in major competitions. The existing table standards will also be valid until at least 2000.

A clear playing space of 2 m (approx 6.6 ft) all round the table is desirable, so that a clear floor space of 8 × 6 m (approx 26 × 20 ft) is required for actual play. There is never any need for a greater playing area than this but if matches are to be televised the cameras will require additional space.

Seating must be positioned outside this area. If the clear playing space around the table is reduced to the absolute minimum of 1.6 m (approx 5 ft), the total playing area can be reduced to a minimum of 7.0 × 5.2 m (approx 23 × 17 ft).

1.2 Table weight and installation

The weight of a full-size traditionally designed billiard table is approximately 1.5 tonne spread over eight legs. The cost of delivery and erection of a billiard table depends on the situation and distance it has to be carried, particularly if it is to be installed upstairs or in a basement. The best situation is at ground level with good vehicle access.

1 *Photo: Alan Edwards*

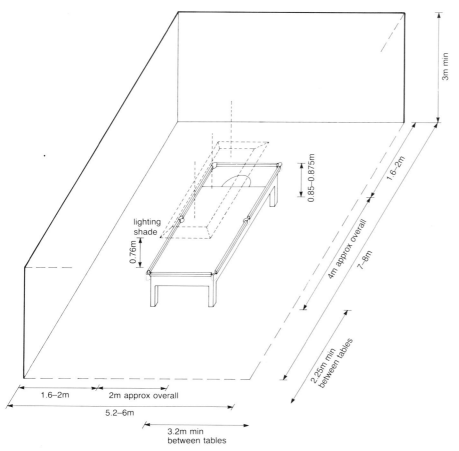

2 *Space diagram showing a type of light containing tungsten filament lamps commonly used over tables*

3 *Snooker at Crystal Palace NSC. Photo: Mark Shearman*

1.3 Siting and layout

Billiards and snooker enthusiasts feel their games cannot be played in a common space used for other activities at the same time and the concentration required for club and championship matches demands that a separate space be provided. For recreational play a bay off a multi-purpose games or social space would be satisfactory, provided that the bay could be cut off from the main space when necessary by means of a folding/sliding partition. Tables have to be plumbed and levelled accurately before use and therefore cannot be moved to make room for other activities.

For championships, exhibition or other special matches it is preferable that only one table be in play at a time, permanently positioned to allow for it to be surrounded by elevated spectators (see below). Other tables are then closed down for the match and room lights turned off or dimmed.

It is best to arrange the tables end to end to limit the possible obstruction between players at adjacent tables. Where tables have to be placed side-by-side the minimum spacing apart is given in **2**.

1.4 Spectator facilities

Spectator seating, if required, should be provided around at least three sides of one table but sufficiently distant from it to allow ample space for the players, **2**. Permanent or removable seating is acceptable.

1.5 Flooring

A firm level floor finish is essential for the table to withstand the point loads of the legs and be absolutely level.

1.6 Environmental services

For general details of environmental services recommendations refer to Chapters 60 and 61.

Heating and ventilation

A minimum background temperature of 15–16°C is desirable and adequate ventilation should also be provided to control humidity and maintain a comfortable, pleasant environment.

Lighting

The table must be uniformly illuminated so that the player can follow the movement of the ball throughout its travel. The lighting should be shadow free and enable the player to distinguish the colour of the balls.

Suitable illumination is normally provided by a purpose made canopy containing several light sources. General lighting should be provided to the surrounding areas. Detailed guidance on lighting is provided in the *CIBSE Lighting Guide LG4: Sports* from which the following table of recommendations is taken.

Standard of play/ application	Illuminance, E_m (lux)	Plane of measurement	Uniformity ratio
Recreational	500	Horizontal on table	0.8
Club	750	Horizontal on table	0.8
International	1000	Horizontal on table	0.8

Mounting height 0.8–1.0 m (approx 3 ft) above table
The scoreboard should be illuminated separately.

Acoustics

Games of billiards and snooker do not generate much noise, but the degree of concentration required to play them properly calls for a measure of sound insulation to prevent disturbance from noise outside the playing area.

1.7 Equipment: fixtures and storage

The games require the provision of a score board approximately 900 × 600 × 50 mm (approx 3 ft × 2 ft × 2 in thick) screwed to the wall, close to the table.

Storage will be required for a soft table cover and if, as usual, some cues are supplied for general use security considerations suggest that they should be stored and issued at the booking point. If stored in the playing area provision should be made for one common wall-mounted cue rack, the siting of which depends on the layout of the tables. It should be fixed well away from any heat source.

2 References and further advice

Billiards and Snooker Control Council.
Billiards Trade Association Group.
Chartered Institution of Building Services Engineers, *CIBSE Lighting Guide LG4: Sports*, CIBSE, London.

72

Indoor bowls halls and clubs

Colin Jepson and Kit Campbell

1 Background information

Facilities for indoor bowls may be provided either permanently in the form of a purpose-designed hall or club or on a temporary basis by the use of 'roll-out' carpets in any suitably sized multi-purpose area. The latter – which can range from facilities for carpet bowls to full size rinks – do not require special design features other than a level floor. They are described in Chapter 21 in this volume; this chapter relates to purpose-built facilities.

Unlike outdoor flat green bowls, where play takes place along and across the green in order to give the natural turf time to recover after wear, in the indoor game play is always along the green. For this reason there is no requirement for it to be square. Instead the number of rinks comprising a green should be related to:

- The anticipated demand from the likely catchment area
- The levels of competition it is planned to stage.

1.1 Anticipated demand and catchment area

Indoor bowls grew rapidly in popularity in the UK during the 1970s and 1980s. As a result, at the start of the 1990s there were approximately 370 centres/clubs in the UK with more planned or under construction. The number of rinks required in a particular centre can be related to the estimated number of members by assuming a figure of 100 to 125 members per rink. One rink on an indoor green can therefore accommodate approximately the same number of members as a six-rink outdoor green.

Early guidelines derived in the mid-1970s suggested that one six-rink indoor green was likely to be needed for populations of about 85,000–100,000. With the increased popularity of the game, and its growing appeal to a wider age range of players than in the past, it is clear that this standard was conservative. In the initial stages of assessing the potential demand for a project it is probably reasonable to assume that a six-rink green is now required for a population of 60,000–80,000 within about half an hour journey time. It will nevertheless always be sensible to undertake a more comprehensive local demand assessment before deciding to proceed with a particular project.

1.2 Levels of competition

Although only six rinks are required for international competition, it is normal for centres with an eight-rink green to be preferred and the additional space used for temporary spectator stands. Similarly national and regional championships tend to be played on the larger greens. For district and local championships the minimum green size is normally four rinks.

2 Schedule of accommodation

In addition to the green itself there will normally be a need for a range of ancillary areas. Where the green is part of a larger centre it may be possible for bowlers to share at least some of them with participants in other activities. However, many indoor bowls facilities are largely self-contained and therefore provided with some ancillary areas for bowlers only. The areas noted below, or access to them, will be required at most centres.

2.1 Male and female changing rooms and toilets

A total of approximately 5 sq m of changing space will be required per rink. As most bowlers remove only their outer clothing and change their shoes, changing areas need contain only benching, coat hooks (at least eight per rink) and a mirror. For matches players change completely and so it should not be possible to see directly into changing rooms from adjacent areas. It is desirable that changing rooms and sufficient toilets and wash hand basins are provided for both sexes with some flexibility in changing to accommodate all-male or all-female competitions. Consideration must be given to adequate provision of facilities for disabled users – both bowlers and spectators.

2.2 Refreshment area

At the minimum, bowlers will wish to be able to purchase snacks and hot drinks although a more sophisticated bar and lounge will be preferred by many. If a bar serving alcoholic drinks is provided it is desirable that it is separable from the general refreshment area. The size of the refreshment area(s) and ancillaries should be related to the capacity of the green assuming eight players per rink and a similar number spectating or waiting. If it is intended that spectator events or social use will be encouraged then refreshment areas should be increased in size accordingly. Subject to the Licensing Laws refreshment areas may be open directly to the surround of the green.

2.3 Casual spectator seating

Spectator space is not really necessary for those centres designed to fulfil a community purpose, but adequate surround seating should be provided on the basis of 16 seats per rink to allow bowlers to sit between 'ends' and for those who come early or stay on after their playing session. The spectator seating can be split between both ends of the rink.

2.4 Club or meeting room

A club or meeting room is generally required only when the building is managed by a club or other independent body. A typical club will require one office of about 15 sq m for the Club Secretary.

2.5 Reception/control area

The control point may be in the form of a pay box or similar area where users pay green fees and book rinks. It may also contain space for clerical staff (usually not more than one person) and should overlook both the green and the entrance and be linked to the office accommodation (if any). It is desirable that there should be a small safe or lockable cupboard for storage of cash and all lighting should be controlled from this area.

2.6 Storage space

Storage space related directly to the green is needed for equipment and furniture such as chairs, tables, a vacuum cleaner and other items. A space of about 3–5 sq m per rink should be adequate but the area required should be assessed in relation to storage for particular circumstances.

2.7 Other ancillary accommodation
Plant areas, bottle stores and general cleaners' stores need not differ in any way from those provided for other elements of recreational buildings.

2.8 Spectator provision
At centres where major events are likely to be staged it will be necessary to allow for a considerable number of spectators who will usually be seated along the sides of the green. International matches may attract up to about 1250 people and national and major regional championships as many as 500 to 1000. Major spectator provision will only be required at a very few centres and reference should be made to the appropriate regional specialist strategy (in England) or the appropriate Sports Council (in the remainder of the UK). For details of seating provision see Chapter 50 in this volume, and *Arenas*. For special events some temporary spectator seating can be provided on the green provided the surface is adequately protected.

2.9 Spatial relationships
The desirable relationship between the above areas and the green is indicated in **1**. Wherever possible ancillary accommodation should be grouped so that there is the minimum of distraction for bowlers.

3 Detailed design

3.1 Configuration of the green
Play on the indoor green is always in one direction. As with the outdoor game the indoor green is divided into sections called rinks. The following dimensions will be acceptable to all national indoor bowling associations:

- Length   preferred 36.58 m (120 ft)
- Width (inner rinks)   preferred 4.57 m (15 ft)
- Width (outer rinks)   preferred 5.18 m (17 ft)

Thus, for example, a six rink green should be (4 × 4.57 m) + (2 × 5.18 m) = 28.64 m (approx. 94 ft) wide.

These are the recommended dimensions for *all* new greens. Individual national bowling associations may accept minor variations from them and if designers wish details they should consult the appropriate national association for advice. Clubs using greens which do not

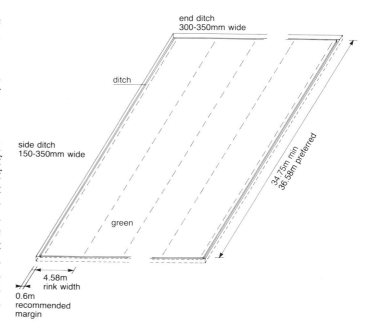

2 *Layout of a four rink green*

meet the minimum requirements of the appropriate governing body may not be able to affiliate to them.

3.2 The ditch and bank
The green should be surrounded by a ditch on all four sides which, at the ends, should be 300–350 mm (12–14 in) wide and 100–200 mm (4–8 in) deep. At the sides it may be only 150–200 mm (6–8 in) wide although it is usually simplest to have the same ditch width all round the green. The ditch dimensions are additional to the desirable rink size given above. The ditch must be so designed as to prevent bowls entering it being damaged and in practice the playing surface material is usually dressed into the ditch and up the bank. It is common and desirable to provide a method of deflecting bowls downward into the end ditches to prevent them rebounding on to the playing surface. Padding of the end banks (see below) beneath the surface material dressing helps to limit damage to bowls.

On all four sides the ditch must be enclosed by banks. At the ends of the green the banks must be not less than 229 mm (9 in) above the playing surface. Whilst there is no specified minimum height for side banks it is desirable for them to be the same height as the end banks because this

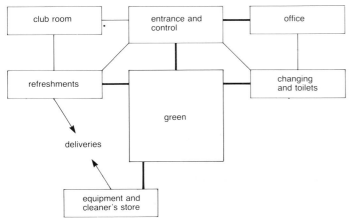

1 *Spatial relationships of the main areas of an indoor bowls centre*

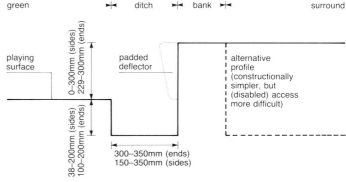

3 *Section through the ditch and bank around the green*

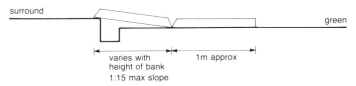

4 *Ramp for wheelchair access to green*

allows the banks to form a level circulation path all round the green. This path should be not less than 1.5 m (5 ft) wide and ideally wider at the ends to allow space for bowlers and score stands. It is recommended that the construction height of end banks should be 250 mm (10 in) above the level of the base to allow for the thickness of the playing surface and underlay.

End ditches must have a holding surface other than the surface material. Bottle corks were commonly used at one time but created problems for the cleaning of ditches. More recently a flame retardant profiled (egg carton type) ditch foam has proved to be highly popular and is easily removed for cleaning purposes.

3.3 Playing surface

The principal performance requirements for a bowling surface are rolling resistance and resistance to set, indendation or permanent deformation and wear. It must also have acceptable bowling characteristics such as speed and bias and generally be comparable with the characteristics provided by a first class turf green. Indoor surfaces, often referred to as 'carpets', are laid in panels at right angles to the direction of play to ensure that seams do not affect the true path of a bowl. Various seaming methods have been used but almost all surfaces are now seamed by use of specially designed sewing machines. Most indoor surfaces are laid over a separate underlay (rubber, felt or other textile material) which plays an important part in determining the playing characteristics of a green.

3.4 Types of surface

Jute matting and wool felt were the original indoor surfaces. More recently the development of needle-punch and woven synthetic surfaces in wider panels requiring fewer seams and with greater life potential has seen jute virtually eliminated and a rapid decline in the number of new and more costly felt surfaces.

Current major surfaces are:

- *Needle-punch synthetic textiles* – introduced about 1970 and available in wide rolls made on specialised textile machinery. Needle-punch carpets have a good record in terms of life and playability. Although they have a tendency to fibre-shedding (fluffing) and bowl tracking, recent developments have seen these problems eliminated by at least one manufacturer. Needlepunch carpets were the first type of surface to be machine seamed.
- *Woven synthetic textiles* – initially introduced to combat the rapid demise of jute matting, this type of surface has proved to be successful in terms of life and playability. It is usually made from polypropylene fibres and has been well received by bowlers.

The life and cost of a playing surface are extremely important and it is reasonable to expect a minimum life of 10 years. The amount of usage is obviously a major factor but most manufacturers should be happy to confirm the viability of their product provided that recommended

5 *Gosling Indoor Bowls Centre, Welwyn Garden City*

maintenance procedures are followed. Appearance is also important as it can have an effect on the lighting required for the playing area.

Assuming sympathetic use all bowling surfaces should require little maintenance during the playing season apart from regular vacuuming. Retensioning and periodic repositioning of end panels helps not only to keep a surface in good condition but also to ensure that maximum life is obtained. An incorrectly tensioned surface will wear faster.

3.5 Construction of the substructure

It is essential that suppliers of the selected finish are consulted on the detailed design of the complete flooring system. In many instances bowling greens have been less than satisfactory owing to inaccuracies in the levels of the base beneath the playing surface.

It is vital that the laying of the final base floor be carried out by a specialist contractor who can achieve the required tolerances. An overall tolerance of ±3 mm (1/8 in) relative to a fixed datum is essential whilst localised tolerance should be 3 mm (1/8 in) under a 3 m (10 ft) straightedge.

Various construction methods are used including: sand cement screeds; granolithic and timber tiles set on a sand cement screed overlaid with insulation boards; timber bases; and mesh reinforced concrete screed. The most successful in recent times has been the concrete screed where the top surface is float finished to required levels. Care must obviously be taken to ensure that the base substructure is suitably consolidated and guaranteed against settlement although a timber subfloor incorporating levelling wedges has been used successfully in areas where subsidence is likely. In terms of total contract cost, savings achieved on base construction are relatively minor and ill advised. Whilst overall cost is obviously an important factor, an incorrectly constructed base can only lead to unsatisfactory bowling and usually greater expense than achieved by the original saving.

3.6 Sunlight and daylight

It should not be possible for sunlight or daylight to strike the green as unsatisfactory playing conditions will result. Sunlight can also lead to deterioration of and loss of colour from the finish. If ancillary accommodation is provided care should be taken to ensure that glare is not caused by any windows which can be seen from the green.

3.7 Ceiling height

The height of the ceiling is conditioned by the need to provide even glare-free lighting on the green and the value judgement of the designer relating to the proportions of the space. A ceiling height of 3.5–4.5 m (approx 12–15 ft) above the green is usually adequate except in cases where other out of season activities take place. In such cases these other activities may dictate the clear height required. The ceiling may be of any form and does not have to be flat.

3.8 Facilities for people with disabilities

Indoor bowls is an activity in which people with disabilities can compete either amongst themselves or on equal terms with those who are able-bodied. For this reason indoor bowls centres must always be designed to be suitable for use by people with disabilities, particularly those in wheelchairs. Apart from the normal requirements of ramped entrances, special toilet facilities and the like no special facilities need be included. To allow disabled people to participate a small movable ramp is used to let wheelchairs cross the ditch and reach the level of the green. The actual bowling surface is normally protected by means of a roll-out carpet or other sheet material which is laid over the surface and removed when no longer required. A typical ramp is shown in 4. A raised surround around the green is also common and access points must be provided through this edge detail.

4 Environmental services

For general details of environmental services recommendations see Chapters 60 and 61.

4.1 Artificial lighting

For general details of artificial lighting see Chapter 60 in this volume and the *CIBSE Lighting Guide LG4: Sports*.

The spacing of fittings is dependent on the ceiling height and is determined by the need to avoid glare and ensure even illumination of the green surface. In addition to ensuring freedom from glare it should also be remembered that many bowlers wear spectacles (particularly bifocals). A minimum average illuminance of 500 lux at a uniformity ratio of 0.8 should be provided over the whole of playing area.

4.2 Heating and ventilation

Although smoking is never permitted on a green because of the possibility of damage to the surface, it is likely that there will be a considerable ventilation load as a result of non-participants smoking around the perimeter. A ventilation system is therefore required and in order to keep bowling areas as free of smoke as possible air is best supplied over the green and extracted over the perimeter circulation areas.

The minimum fresh air requirement should be calculated by reference to the estimated number of occupants of the building allowing eight players per rink and a supply rate of 12 litres per second per person. If the hall is heated by warm air the plant should be sized on the winter heating requirement unless the centre is also designed to be in regular use in summer. In this case the ventilation requirement to maintain a reasonable temperature should also be considered.

The general ambient temperature on the green itself should be 16–18°C, but if possible this should be increased to 18–21°C in circulation and ancillary areas because of the popularity of the game with older people. It may therefore be necessary to provide additional sources of heat for these areas.

5 Equipment

The following items of equipment should always be included:

- Lockers, on the basis of one locker per member or 100 per rink. Each locker should be approximately 300 × 300 × 300 mm (12 × 12 × 12 in) with a lockable door. It must be suitable for storing four woods and a pair of bowling shoes so ventilation slots are desirable.
- Coat hooks, situated either around the green in full view of the players or in a cloakroom. Hooks around the green should be provided at the sides rather than the ends of rinks. At most centres 15–20 hooks per rink should be adequate.
- Notice boards at the entrance to the green. Because most indoor bowls is competitive and centred around organised leagues as much notice board space as possible should be provided.
- Scoreboards – at most centres it is desirable to have a major scoreboard mounted on an end wall. For normal play, however, the use of portable stands with each individual rink are adequate.

6 Car parking

Eight car park spaces per rink should be provided for use by participants. Where spectator events are to be staged this number may need to be increased. Spaces reserved for disabled bowlers and spectators should be near the entrance and the access to the building designed to avoid kerbs or steps.

7 References and further advice

Chartered Institution of Building Services Engineers, *CIBSE Lighting Guide LG4: Sports*, CIBSE, London.
National Indoor Bowls Associations.

73
Climbing walls

Roger Payne

1 Introduction

General

In Britain there are an expanding number of well designed, well managed and very popular climbing walls and towers. They serve as valuable training facilities throughout the year, particularly in the winter months, and provide important meeting places for climbers. Correct location is vital to the success of a climbing wall.

History

As the sport of rock climbing advanced in the early 1970s there was considerable interest within the climbing community to develop training regimes which would enhance climbing performance. Many of the climbing walls from that period were depressingly unimaginative and poorly located. However, climbers who were keen to develop their skills and frustrated by lack of facilities or bad weather regularly frequented these walls. Today, as technical climbing standards and the use of climbing walls has increased, climbing on structures has become a recognised sport in itself. In the first ever World Cup Circuit of climbers competing on artificial walls, British climber Simon Nadin became the first climbing World Champion.

Background

The British Mountaineering Council (BMC) has a specialist committee which deals specifically with climbing walls and another which deals with competition climbing. The Climbing Wall Committee jointly with the Sports Council has produced a manual called *Climbing Walls* which gives technical information to architects, leisure managers and climbers and covers the development, design and management of climbing walls.

The BMC also runs a computerised data-base of climbing wall facilities and regularly publishes the *Climbing Wall Guide*, a listing of the best 100 or so walls throughout the UK. With this information and through its system of area committees, the BMC produces a regional and national strategic plan for the development of both new facilities and improvements to existing ones. The Climbing Wall Committee is made up of representatives from each of the BMC areas who can give local advice and represent their area committee. The BMC has a full time Development Officer with responsibility for climbing walls and through them and the area representatives the BMC can offer advice on all aspects of wall design, location and management. It is obviously essential that any provider considering the inclusion of a climbing wall should consult the above mentioned documents and make early contact with the BMC.

Climbing surfaces

In the UK there are many climbing wall manufacturers and importers, a number of which have been established for a long time. They can all offer some form of design service and the finished product can be extremely varied – this is preferable for a sustained level of interest – but it is imperative they conform to any mandatory standards for the safe construction of climbing walls and operate to a professional level. There is also a Climbing Wall Manufacturers Association (CWMA) open to any manufacturer that complies with the above. The BMC can provide contacts for professional manufacturers and CWMA.

2 Location of walls

General

The ideal situation for a climbing wall is for it to be positioned in an independent use area with a combination of a section of low level wall for unroped climbing and a section of higher wall for roped climbing. The climbing should be suitable for experts and novices and the area should be well lit, reasonably ventilated and possibly include a shock absorbing surface beneath the wall. How the wall is managed will greatly influence its success and the number of users and visits it will attract. From a design point of view there are several fairly simple considerations which will ensure that there is adequate space for the activity to take place.

Types of wall

The BMC's Climbing Wall Committee have identified three main sizes and a number of provisions required in each facility (listed below) but there is no need to rigidly

1 *A steeply overhanging, moulded wall in Newcastle which contains some moveable holds. Photo: Bendecrete*

3 *A climbing wall made of coated panels. Photo: DR Climbing Walls*

2 *A climbing wall utilising adjustable handholds erected especially for a competition at an exhibition in London. Photo: Bendecrete*

adhere to them. An important additional consideration concerning the location of a wall is its potential to provide an interesting and unusual visual focal point within a centre. A well designed and well located climbing wall can add a very dramatic backdrop and, where creative use of colour and texture are used, introduce a pleasing environmental element.

Small wall (local)

This general training facility would be relatively small, often made to fit the available space, perhaps being housed in a redundant squash court or similar or using spare space in a new building design. Aimed at a local base of climbers and with a diversity of designs. Can be a combination of low-level and high wall but lack of space usually means it is better to concentrate on one type. There are many walls of this type throughout the country that have good sustained usage. There is also the possibility of developing 'adventure walls' aimed at beginners and groups, with facilities for abseiling. This type of wall can also cater specifically for disabled needs.

Medium wall (regional)

A wall that caters for a more regional base of climbers with a combination of wall types. A low-level wall of ideally at least 100 sq. metres surface area and a taller wall of at least 10 m in height and sufficiently wide with a variety of steepness to cater for differing abilities without crowding. Unrestricted access is vitally important to ensure popularity so a self-contained area is almost imperative. To meet

the needs of competition events there are more specific requirements that can be obtained from the BMC office.

Larger wall (national)

These should be centres of excellence on a larger scale than regional walls. Major dedicated facilities are envisaged with no access problems. The site should be suitable for training for regional and national competitions. The competition standard tall wall should be at least 15 m wide overhanging by at least 6 m, and able to accommodate a minimum vertical route length of 15 m. To meet the needs of competition events there are more specific requirements that can be obtained from the BMC office. There should also be a wide range of less steep walls in the 10–15 m height range.

The bouldering wall should offer at least 150 sq. metres of surface with a variety of angles and features. There would be another self-contained area away from the competition wall with bouldering/warm-up facilities to serve as the isolation zone during competitions.

There should be an on-going development programme incorporating new ideas, eg hydraulically controlled sections, panels in new materials, different surface finishes, bolt-on holds, and the regular changing of these should be budgeted for. The venue should have other relevant training facilities (weights rooms, fingerboards) and medical support, eg sports injury clinic.

The BMC has identified approximate styles of structure, but these need not be rigidly adhered to and can easily overlap. The most important factor is that the facility caters for the market it is aimed at. Whichever facility is

4 *Climbing walls need to be interesting and pleasant to climb, with a variety of physical challenges. Photo: DR Climbing Walls*

5 *A very robust and very well used outdoor climbing wall in Birmingham. Photo: DR Climbing Walls*

6 *A climbing wall utilising tiles that can be rotated, and panels which incorporate moveable holds. Photo: Entreprise*

7 *A simple panel system with many moveable holds which can offer a great number of variations for the climber. Photo: Entreprise*

provided it is important that access be unrestricted and management be in accordance with the BMC's guidelines.

Indoor or outdoor
Climbing on a wall out of doors can be much more pleasurable than climbing on an indoor structure. The vagaries of the weather will limit the amount of use of outdoor walls by even dedicated climbers during the winter months. However, well sited and well illuminated outdoor walls, particularly in areas distant from natural cliffs, can enjoy high levels of year round use.

2.1 Design of walls

General
Much of the design work of the specialist climbing wall consultants will be constrained by the position and space made available for the climbing structure(s). Early contact with specialist climbing wall consultants is strongly recommended.

Space
Apart from having adequate height, width and depth for a climbing wall there must also be enough space for people to stand, talk and observe. Climbing walls provide a natural focal point and social meeting place for climbers. Typically a climber may use a wall for a period of around 2 hours. However, it is unlikely that more than one-third of that time will be spent actually climbing on the wall, so adequate space for participants to rest and talk should be considered essential. Good refreshments facilities are also likely to enjoy high patronage from climbers.

8 *The use of shape and angle makes a climbing wall interesting and challenging to climbers and pleasing to look at. Photo: Entreprise*

9 *Size and variation in the climbing surface make this French indoor 'cliff' an exciting wall to climb on. Photo: Entreprise*

10 *A panel system with moveable holds especially erected for an international competition in Britain. Photo: Entreprise*

11 *Grand prix competition, Birmingham 1991. Entreprise wall*

Flooring

Thought needs to be given to the choice of floor finish beneath a climbing wall. On high areas of wall where climbers should always be protected by ropes a general purpose sports floor will be suitable. Some form of shock absorbing flooring beneath lower areas of climbing walls where climbers commonly climb without the protection of ropes will allow greater use of such areas. Continuous surfaces are the best option and can be poured mixes, tiles or mats.

2.2 Environmental services

For general details of environmental services recommendations refer to Chapters 60 and 61.

Lighting

Outdoor walls need to be illuminated during the hours of darkness but it is also important that indoor walls are properly illuminated. From climbers' point of view the need is simply for the wall to be lit clearly and evenly in such a way that the lighting does not interfere with the climbing. The choice of light fittings and their position should seek to avoid strong shadows on the wall surface and glare which might affect climbers' vision.

Table 73.1: Recommended illumination levels on wall surface

Recreation and training	200 lux
Club and regional	300 lux
National and international	500 lux

Ventilation

Climbers use chalk on their hands to improve grip and this can lead to problems without regular floor cleaning. The top part of a climbing wall can also become unpleasantly warm and claustrophobic without reasonable ventilation. Climbers prefer to climb on artificial structures wearing lightweight clothes, but it is wrong to think that the climbing area needs to be kept particularly warm. In fact, a reasonably ventilated, below average room temperature (around 12–14°C) atmosphere should be regarded as ideal. In the case of a purpose designed ventilation system the air flow patterns can be utilised to draw chalk dust down to floor level.

2.3 Types of wall construction

General

Climbing walls can be constructed in a variety of ways depending upon the available budget. The method(s) of construction should be considered when the climbing area is being designed. Depending on size and shape most climbing structures usually require strengthened walls or floors to support them and it is more cost effective to incorporate this at the design stage. It is also important that the climbing area should allow for the future addition of further climbing surfaces or incorporate aspects of interchangeability.

Moulded concrete

There are several systems for applying concrete mixes to steel framework. These systems allow for the construction of unique shapes. It is possible for changeable hold systems to be incorporated into these structures.

Panel systems

Panel systems come in both fixed and changeable forms. Changeable panel systems allow for a high degree of versatility, but the panels are made up from a set number of variations and, although there may be many permutations on how the panels are put together, there is obviously a limit. The panels are typically made from resins and fibreglass or coated wood and usually contain a system of changeable internal and external holds.

Rock insertions

The insertion of concrete or similar blocks which contain recesses or projections of natural rock are an established and proven method of climbing wall construction. Such blocks can be built into the fabric of a building as it is constructed.

Bolt-on holds

There are a very wide range of bolt-on holds available. These are made from resin and fibreglass and can be an inexpensive and versatile way to extend a larger facility or create a smaller one. The holds are normally attached to the fabric of the building or to a panel system by the use of bolts.

Temporary structures

An artificial climbing structure can easily be erected to create an additional activity or focal point for some event. International and major national competitions take place on climbing walls specially erected for the event. The specialist climbing wall consultants have systems suitable for the above.

2.3 Management policy

The BMC strongly advises the involvement of local climbers, local clubs and the BMC Area Committee in the running of a climbing wall. In the past, good walls have been underused because of inappropriate management. One of the major concerns by managers is that climbing is a dangerous sport and hence it needs to be strictly controlled. In fact there are very few injuries caused on climbing walls by accidental slips and falls. On matters of management the BMC is always willing to advise.

74
Cricket schools

Peter Sutcliffe

1 Introduction

Several indoor cricket halls have been built in recent years, notably at Lords (MCC), Headingley (Yorkshire CCC) and Wigan (Wigan MBC). All were constructed, principally, to provide for indoor net practice out of season. Such specialist halls are expensive to build and, without alternative use during off-peak periods, expensive to maintain. Developments in competitive indoor cricket, both eight-a-side and six-a-side provide an attractive alternative use. (See Chapter 23 in this volume.) However, both games are predominantly winter activities and, because of the space and playing environment required, are not mutually compatible. Either game is compatible with net practice given one or two adaptations to the net layout and tracking.

It is desirable, therefore, that indoor cricket schools should be designed with multiple use in mind, especially during the summer months, for example, for archery, golf driving or bowls. This factor will affect the design of both the cricket hall and the ancillary areas, making the production of a comprehensive design brief an essential part of the planning stage.

2 Critical factors

- A hardwearing floor with good playing characteristics
- The best level of lighting that can be afforded
- An efficient system of net tracking giving adequate width and height
- Canvas blinkers
- Bowling machines
- A well lit back wall
- Adequate storage
- Bar/social area overlooking the cricket hall
- Adequate changing and toilet provision
- A suitably positioned and secure booking and control point
- Ancillary rooms, first aid, meeting/lecture.

Although both maximum and minimum levels and dimensions are quoted below, it must be stressed that it is prudent to provide a facility to the best specification possible.

2.1 Space requirements

The overall dimensions of a cricket hall will be based on the number of net bays to be provided for net practice. The dimensions of a single bay are:

	Minimum	Recommended maximum
Width	3.66 m	4 m
Length	29.12 m	33.12 m
Height of horizontal top net	4 m	4.5 m
Safety margin surrounds	1 m	

In addition, the outside and back netting must be suspended to give a minimum of one metre clear space between the netting and the walls of the building to allow for access and safety, **1**.

Thus a two bay area, **2**, would be:

	Minimum	Maximum
Width	(3.66 × 2) + 2 = 9.32m	(4 × 2) + 2 = 10 m
Length	29.12 + 2 = 31.12 m	33.12 + 2 = 35.12 m
Height	Unchanged, as above	

The dimensions for indoor cricket eight-a-side and six-a-side games are:

	Minimum	Maximum
Eight-a-side		
Width	10.3 m	11 m
Length	27 m	30 m
Height	4 m	4.5 m
Six-a-side		
Width	18.3 m	25–30.4 m
Length	30.4 m	35–36.5 m
Height	6.1 m	7.6 m

From these dimensions it can be seen that both games can be accommodated in a cricket school if the appropriate number of bays are provided. Three side by side practice bays will also accommodate eight-a-side cricket and six practice bays, six-a-side cricket. For further details refer to Chapter 23 in this volume.

2.2 Overall size

The size of the cricket school will depend on both capital and revenue costs. A facility to accommodate net practice and eight-a-side should be built up in three practice bay units. A facility to accommodate net practice and six-a-side should be built up in six bay units. Some cricket clubs prefer to hire nets in pairs so in a hall with an odd number of practice bays one net may be empty. The most practicable size, therefore, is a six-bay hall. Nevertheless, a three-bay hall allows for both net practice and the eight-a-side game and may prove an acceptable compromise.

Recommended layout
Six retractable nets, on independent tracking suspended within a high tensioned net cage, with a centre tension net dividing the area into two side by side three-bay areas, **3**.

2.3 Floor

The choice of floor surface is critical. Above all else, it should be chosen according to its cricket characteristics. It should perform well in terms of resilience, stiffness, friction, spin and resistance to wear. It should provide an overall, integral covering rather than be a series of mats rolled out on to a subsurface. In case of local wear, a problem in a cricket hall, the flooring material should be capable of repair or replacement without affecting its playing characteristics, ie spin or pace.

The flooring may be a polymer sheeting laid on to a concrete screed or a carpet. The wear characteristics of sheeting are generally superior to those of carpets. A polymer can be varied in terms of thickness and density to give different playing characteristics which is an added advantage.

Should there be no alternative to laying mats on a subsurface, it should be firm and without any cushioning otherwise the combination of mat and subsurface will

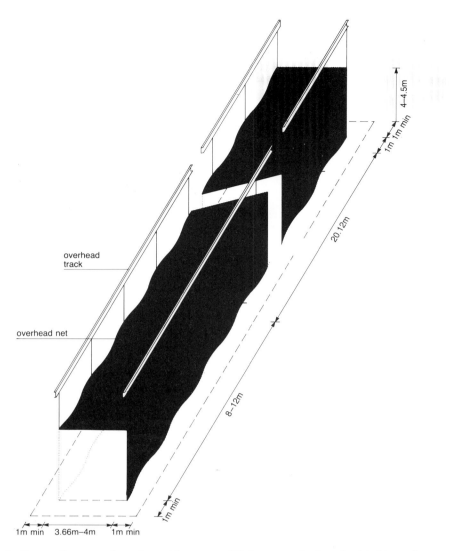

1 *Space diagram of netting with canvas blinkers attached and with integral over roof net*

overhead track

overhead net

20.12m

8–12m

4–4.5m

1m min

1m

1m min

1m min

3.66m–4m

1m min

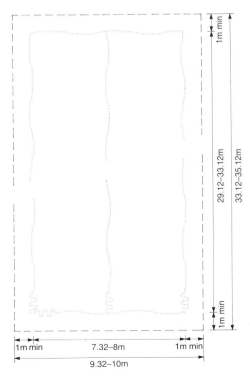

2 *Net dimensions for a two-net bay area*

1m min

29.12–33.12m

33.12–35.12m

1m min

1m min

7.32–8m

1m min

9.32–10m

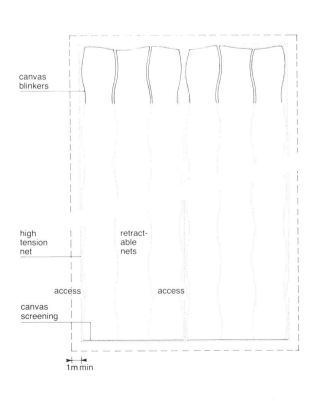

3 *Suggested layout of nets*

canvas blinkers

high tension net

retractable nets

access

access

canvas screening

1m min

4 *General view of players using nets. Photo: Peter Sutcliffe*

5 *Player batting to illustrate 'blinkers'. Photo: Peter Sutcliffe*

seriously affect the bounce of the ball. Wherever practicable, it is desirable to include extra cushioning at the bowler's end to avoid jarring. This should extend back from the popping crease to a distance of 2 m behind the bowling crease.

2.4 Floor markings

Crease markings for net and practice at the batting and bowling ends should be in white, 4.

Crease markings for either the six-a-side or eight-a-side games should be red/orange. All lines should be 38 mm (1.5 in) wide.

It is advisable to avoid all other permanent floor markings. However, the surface should be able to take temporary markings, for example chalk, for coaching purposes which can be easily and totally removed.

2.5 Netting

Suspended netting

Each bay is divided from adjoining bays by tracked side nets which extend from end to end. Independent overhead tracking provides the most efficient system, allowing each run of net to be drawn out independently. It also gives greater flexibility of use. However this system requires an independent overhead net, under which the tracking is fixed. There must be no space between the roof net and the tracking through which the ball could escape from net to net.

The net tracking system has to be adapted for each game. Eight-a-side requires the game area to be enclosed in a tension net; thus the netting for each practice bay is suspended within the surrounding tension net. For six-a-side, the height requirement means that the practice bay netting has to include an integral roof net which can be retracted with the side netting so as not to interfere with the game. However, if the roof net is fixed to the side net, the side nets cannot be drawn out independently. This arrangement may be necessary if the tracking has to be fixed to roof joists well above the normal height requirement for roof netting: otherwise it should be avoided.

The side netting should be sufficiently long for at least 0.3 m (1 ft) to rest on the floor in order to give added weight and prevent the net billowing to the side when struck by the ball thus interfering with the adjacent bay. Additional weighting of the net with lead line is desirable, 5.

Blinkers

Heavy canvas blinkers (white) *must be* fitted to all practice bays. They are canvas sheets suspended on the side and rear net, around the batsman. They should extend a minimum of 3 m (approx 10 ft) in front of the batsman – that is a distance of 5 m (16.5 ft) from the rear net, and be a minimum of 1.8 m (6 ft) high, 5.

Similar canvas sheeting is recommended for the back netting behind the bowler to provide a good visual background and prevent distractions from spectators moving behind the bowler's arm.

Cricket net practice in multi-sports halls

See Chapter 23 in this volume, for net practice in multi-sports halls.

Stowage of nets

If the cricket hall is to be used for other activities it may be necessary to stow the nets away. The netting, once fully retracted, can be raised from the ground by pulley system and stored neatly in suspended plastic holders. Stowage is more difficult if the hall is fitted with high tension netting for eight-a-side cricket. However, long vertical zips in line with the tracking in the end tension net allow the nets, when fully retracted, to be stowed outside the tension net. It is easier to stow the nets at the batting end because of the canvas blinkers.

2.4 Internal environment

For general details of environmental recommendations refer to Chapters 60 and 61 and the *CIBSE Lighting Guide LG4: Sports.*

6 *Bowling practice. Photo: Peter Sutcliffe*

Lighting

Good light levels are essential. The batsman and the bowler must be able to follow the movement of the ball, which can travel at speeds up to 80 mph, either when bowled by the bowler or struck by the batsman. Thus the bowler must have a clear view of the pitch and the batsman must be able to see the bowler clearly in his approach run and delivery action. He must then be able to track the flight of the ball. Neither must be distracted by glare nor by the brightness of the light sources in their sight lines.

These requirements are generally met by a lighting system comprising a number of horizontally mounted, fluorescent luminaires fitted with reflectors, mounted at right angles to the pitch. The reflectors must screen both batsman and bowler from a direct view of the light source. An even illumination is required throughout the hall, both transversely and longitudinally. The lighting can often be improved considerably if the rear wall behind the bowler is lit by diffuse spots mounted towards the back of the hall on the side walls, thus eliminating all shadows.

Lighting levels

It is a mistake to economise on lighting. Because cricket schools are specialist buildings they will attract players of a good standard. Lighting levels, therefore, must be higher than in multi-purpose sports halls fitted with cricket nets. The following illuminances, which are minimum maintained average horizontal values measured at floor level, are recommended:

	Illuminance	Plane of measurement	Uniformity ratio (min/ave.)	Minimum mounting height
Recreational	750 lux	Horizontal on pitch	0.8	4.5 m
Club/county	1000 lux	pitch	0.8	4.5 m
National/ international	1500 lux	Horizontal on pitch Horizontal on pitch	0.8	4.5m

2.5 Internal wall finishes

Rear wall

The wall behind bowlers should be as clear of supports and obstructions as possible and painted white.

Side walls

These should also be painted white, or alternatively pastel blue or green.

2.6 Ancillary accommodation

Storage

A secure store room adjacent to the cricket hall is essential for both playing kit (bats, balls and wickets) and for technical coaching aids such as bowling machines and video. Storage requirements usually increase with time.

Equipment

Although most adult players provide their own equipment, school use and eight-a-side cricket dictate the need to provide a complete range of playing equipment.

Bowling machines are essential, 7, and video is highly desirable. If eight-a-side or six-a-side cricket is to be played electronic score boards are needed for each playing area.

7 *Bowling machine in action. Photo: Peter Sutcliffe*

Changing accommodation

The provision for changing will depend on the number of practice bays. Calculations should be based on up to 6 or 7 players per net, that is 18 players in a three-bay hall. Although it is unusual to have an overlap of players in the changing area at changeover times. Sufficient clothes and bag storage space should be provided for at least double the number of players the hall can accommodate, ie 36 spaces for a three-bay hall. Male changing will predominate, but female changing will also be needed if mixed school coaching or multi-use is envisaged. Separate changing is recommended for coaches and officials (umpires) on the basis of one space per practice bay. All changing areas must make adequate locker, showering, toilet and washing provision.

Reception point

The reception desk should control entry to the building. It need not be elaborate since user groups usually pre-book. However, it should be large enough to house a till behind a secure counter, plus an office with appropriate furniture such as a safe, desk, telephone, typewriter and filing cabinet.

Social area

The provision of a bar/refreshment area is highly desirable. Two types of customer should be provided for: players wishing to purchase drinks after practice and spectators who may be team supporters or parents who have brought children for coaching. Wherever possible social areas should overlook the cricket hall. Secure storage is essential. Male, female and disabled toilets should be provided in addition to those in the changing areas.

First aid

A small first aid room is required with easy access both to the cricket hall and to an external door.

Lecture room

Courses for players and coaches provide a useful source of income for cricket schools. Lecture accommodation which can double up for meetings is invaluable. Such rooms should be equipped with white or blackboards, video playback facilities and a small screen plus flexible seating for up to 20.

Fitness room

A fitness room can provide a secondary source of income as well as a useful aid for players. This is an aspect of cricket training likely to increase in demand in the future.

3 References and further advice

Chapter 23 in this volume, Cricket: six-a-side and eight-a-side games and net practice.

Chartered Institution of Building Services Engineers, *CIBSE Lighting Guide LG4: Sports*, CIBSE, London.

National Cricket Association.

75
Cycling - indoor velodromes

Ken Farnes

1 Size of tracks

Championships

To qualify as a venue for the World Championships, Olympic or Commonwealth Games, a track must be built to a minimum circumference of 250 m. The three recognised sizes which have been used for most recently constructed tracks are 250 m, 285.714 m and 333.33 m.

The British Cycling Federation (BCF), like the organisations in most countries, prefers to hold its National Championships on tracks of similar dimensions to those used for World Championships to enable UK riders to experience similar conditions to riders from other nations.

The compromise size of 285.714 m (3.5 laps per kilometre) is not considered ideal as some events will involve starting and finishing at different marks. This can be confusing for both competitors and spectators.

Smaller tracks

Championship length tracks are also used for most forms of cycling event, but where space is restricted smaller indoor tracks are equally popular in Europe for the promotion of professional events such as 6-day races. They are frequently built into a multi-purpose building. In many instances the bankings of the tracks are built in place on a permanent basis whilst the straights can be demountable. Such tracks vary from 166 to 250 m. A track of say 200 m circumference leaves an arena size capable of staging most indoor sports including show jumping or ice skating.

Still smaller are the completely demountable tracks. These can be built to suit most venues and are designed to be easily transported. The track used for many years for the 6-day race at the Wembley Arena in London has a circumference of 160 m, but has been reduced to 142 m for one European venue. The basic track structure can be transported on two 12-m supertrailers.

Such small tracks could never be the venue for a World Championship but they do serve a very useful purpose as a shop window for the sport. A small track is also helpful as an indoor facility when lack of funds precludes the building of a purpose-built venue but an empty, medium-sized building is available in the area.

Training

There is also a high priority within the sport for covered training tracks with limited spectator facilities. Ideally they should be 250 m to enable riders to experience the tactics and techniques involved in championship racing but shorter circumferences may be considered in existing structures.

1.2 British Cycling Federation goals

A major goal of the BCF is to encourage the development of a number of 250 m indoor tracks. This will enable meetings to be promoted in inclement weather and provide year-round training venues. Indoor venues are also considered essential to guarantee television coverage of major meetings, thereby enabling the BCF and promoters to attract commercial sponsorship.

The BCF envisage these indoor tracks becoming regional centres for international and national track competition whilst also acting as a focus for their Regional Centres of Excellence and offering a regular pattern of local coaching. They would welcome tracks within multi-use arenas provided guarantees can be given that sufficient time will be allocated for cycling competition and training.

1.3 Shared use

The space in the centre of a cycle track forms a large clear space available for a wide range of sports and entertainment uses.

A number of the main European sports and entertainment venues such as the Olympiahalle, Munich, and Palais Omnisport de Paris are built around cycle tracks and used as the venue for championships in other sports and as major entertainment venues. Their layout particularly emphasises the amphitheatre nature of the banked cycle track. Such a mix of major entertainment uses implies limited use for cycling and would not in the short term be compatible with the BCF's anticipated use for cycling purposes in the initial series of indoor velodromes to be developed.

It must however be anticipated that an indoor cycle track will involve shared use either with other sports or entertainment.

Sports compatible with velodrome cycling (with hanging nets around the infield for safety) are tennis, hockey, wrestling, martial arts, gymnastics, handball, five-a-side football, volleyball, basketball, fencing, boxing, table tennis and movement and dance. A clear rectangular area of approximately 40 × 62 m is available for these sports within a 250 m cycle track and it is not difficult to encourage use of the track centre at all times except when actual competitions are taking place on the track by the installation of a system of nets around the infield area.

The space inside a 250 m circuit is too tight to accommodate a 200 m athletics track. Additionally, cycling and athletics tracks are geometrically incompatible because of the respective transition curves between banks and straights and difficult sightlines. Where cycling and athletics are incorporated in an arena this is normally achieved by making all or part of each track demountable.

An arena built around a cycle track with spectator facilities will constitute one of the largest clear span buildings in its region. It is therefore attractive to promoters of other spectator sports, concerts, meetings and conventions. Many of these involve spectator seating in the track centre. Sponsors of velodromes which envisage such seating provision must plan for this from the outset since up to 5000 additional spectators can be accommodated in the track centre and over the straights of the track. The issues connected with access and egress are discussed below.

Columns in the inner area are most unsatisfactory as they restrict vision of the cycling track and the arena and are very limiting to other sporting uses in the central area. Such a solution should therefore only be considered in exceptional circumstances where an existing building is being adapted.

1.4 Track design

Unlike athletics there is no fixed geometry for a cycle track. Each track is theoretically designed to accommodate the design speed for the events to be staged on the track and accommodate specific track centre uses or planning constraints. Tracks which stage motor paced racing must be designed to accommodate a design speed of 110 km per hour. Other tracks must be designed to a speed of at least 80 km per hour.

The track surface must allow adhesion when the rider is at an inclination of up to 30° either side of a right angle to the track surface (see below). The coefficient of adhesion will therefore also have an influence on the geometry of the track.

Any track which hopes to stage European or national championships must be designed to accommodate motorpaced racing. The BCF or equivalent national body will advise on those tracks where it would expect motor paced racing to be staged.

The effect of the differing design speeds is that motorpaced tracks have a lower width to length ratio whilst tracks designed primarily for sprinting will be longer and thinner, 1. Whilst the theoretical range of ratios of axial length/width is between 1:1.7 and 1:3.2, in practice the majority of recently constructed tracks fall in the range 1:2.0 to 1:2.5. The actual geometric shape of the track depends upon the design, but one can generally assume that the footprint required for a 250 m track is 110 × 60 m and for a 333. 33 m track, 145 × 75 m (see 2).

Figure 2 shows the basic geometry of a track. The angle of the banking for international standard tracks varies from 38–42° for a 333.33 m track to 40–45° for a track of 250 m. The midpoint of the straights will have an inclination of 10–13°. The track design and acceptance of the venue by the riders will be particularly judged by the quality of the transitions from the banking to the central part of the straights, before rising again.

The Union Cycliste Internationale (UCI) require that any track which stages the World Championships should have a width of at least 7 m. A minimum width of 6 m might be considered for training tracks but this can present difficulties for motor paced racing and large bunch races. There is little cost benefit in reducing track widths. There is equally little benefit in tracks wider than 8 m from a racing point of view.

Immediately inside the track is an area called the 'Cote d'Azur'. This level area with a minimum width of 600 mm,

but preferably wider, is contiguous with the inner edge of the track and is used by the cyclists when moving slowly or in emergency. The transition from the banked track to the 'Cote d'Azur' must therefore be very carefully designed and constructed.

1.5 Construction of the track

The track should be designed and constructed under the supervision of a specialist experienced in track building and the procurement of the necessary materials. Failure to use experienced designers and constructors has on occasions resulted in poor installations which become unpopular with riders and promoters and quickly fall out of use.

Tracks can be constructed and surfaced in concrete or wood. In indoor situations concrete should be discounted because of cost and the loss of flexibility in the use of the building.

Wooden tracks can be permanently constructed and shaped accurately in timber (as shown in 3) or steel framework, as for example at Stuttgart.

Timber tracks are extremely fast and coveted by racing cyclists and attractive to spectators. Siberian pine is the preferred, and highly recommended, timber for the surface of indoor tracks. The correct shapes, curves and transitions can be readily achieved provided the basic track design is correct. The natural grain of the wood and minor spaces between the longitudinal strips gives the necessary friction, the material has a degree of 'give' in use and has a safe finish. The surface is formed by laying lathes of timber longitudinally to the circumference of the track, each lathe being nailed to the next through the side. The surface must be laid to allow it to move on the supporting structure, 3. Timber tracks can be constructed by local labour supervised and assisted by experienced track builders. The surface is easily maintained and repaired and replacement of small areas is relatively easier than with concrete surfaces. Where demountable sections of track are envisaged care must be taken to ensure a continuous smooth running surface each time the sections are replaced.

Balustrade

The balustrade or safety fence surrounding the track is an essential safety feature and must be designed as an integral part of the track. Although, fortunately, accidents on the outside of the track are not frequent the balustrade must be able to withstand the force of a collision which might include the weight of a motor cycle travelling at speed.

The balustrade should be continuous and at least 900 mm high but need not be solid for the top 250 mm. See 4 for the most recent type of balustrade featuring a solid base and double railing top to prevent spectators leaning over the track. It also guides cyclists inwards without their pedals catching the balustrade. A small gate for access by VIPs and the jury should be incorporated in the design.

The solid area should be designed so that advertisements can be easily fixed.

Measurement

The markings of the track are specifically defined by the UCI and the BCF or equivalent national body will advise on the requirements. The circumference is marked by a measurement line which must be the exact circumference required without being unequally located on any part of the geometry of the track.

All other markings relate to the measurement line.

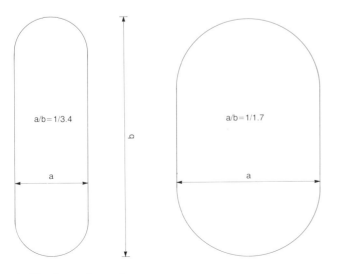

1 *Track configurations*

a/b=1/3.4

a/b=1/1.7

a

b

a

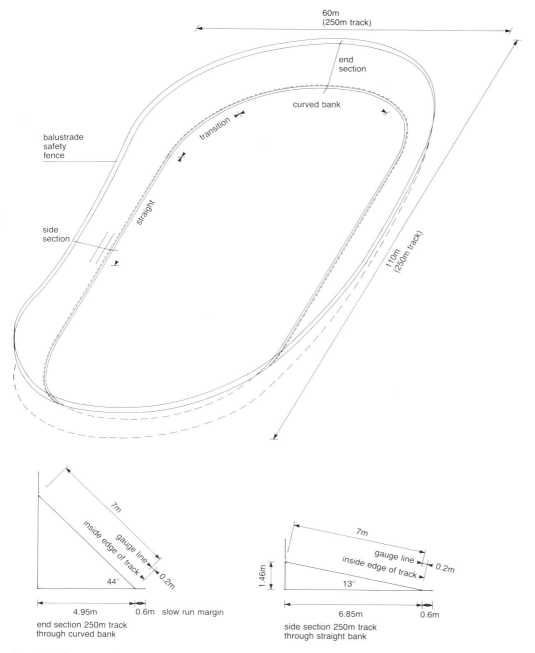

2 *Typical track cycling space diagram*

1.6 Access
One of the planning issues in the design of a new track will be the means of access to the track centre. A tunnel wide enough for two trolleys to pass, running from the dressing room area to one end or side of the track centre, is the preferred access for competitors, officials and race equipment.

An alternative is a bridge but this causes certain parts of the track to be obscured for spectators and officials and should not be utilised where a new facility is being planned.

Where extensive use of the track centre for sports and entertainment is envisaged there is considerable advantage in providing a wide access for trucks and tractors through the track. This can be by means of a section of the track which lifts mechanically, as at Olympiahalle, Munich, or a sliding section of track as at Hans Martin Schleyer Halle, Stuttgart. An alternative although less flexible means of access is a hydraulic lift from an undercroft area directly into the track centre.

1.7 Equipment and storage
The storage facilities and specialist equipment required for track cycling include:

- Two storage rooms each 20 sq m with hanging space for bikes and wheels
- A 30 sq m workshop with large work bench
- Transportable bike racks, for use in the track centre
- Two air lines at 10 bar (150 psi)
- Storage for track equipment.

1.8 Ancillary accommodation for events
The ancillary accommodation required at any arena for sports events is also required for cycling promotions (see *Arenas* in References and further advice). Extra and specific requirements for cycling events are:

- Where the track is demountable a high volume storage space must be incorporated in the design or nearby for storage of the track.

3 *Carpenters laying the surface on the 250 m cycle track in the National Cycling Centre at Manchester. Photo: R V Webb*

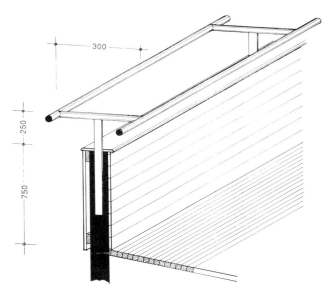

4 *Balustrade (track safety fence)*

- Administration and meetings space.
- Changing rooms – permanent facilities for 100 competitors. Suggested dimensions for units to change 20–25 riders are shown in **6**. Cyclists usually take their bikes with them into the changing units. Additional space must be found at major events for up to 200 additional

competitors in temporary team cabins located indoors or in a secure outdoor enclosure.
- Warm-up areas – an indoor area approximately 35 × 10 m is required adjacent to the track access tunnel; for major events an additional outdoor space of approximately 40 × 40 m (which may be in a secure section of the parking or service area). Alternatively riders may warm up inside the arena, circulating in the track centre or using rollers for static warm-up.
- Drug testing unit in specifically designed rooms.
- Medical facilities – including a massage room per unit of 25 riders.
- Hospitality facilities – many tracks have VIP facilities at an upper level providing a view of the track. VIP catering modules are also placed within the track centre at major events and 6-day races (see **5**). Electricity and plug-in water supplies and drainage connections are needed to service these to avoid the considerable disadvantage of bulky tanked servicing. The plug-in points should be carefully located around the inside of the track to receive flexible connections.
- Media facilities (refer also to Chapter 50 in this volume).
- Vehicle parking – secure off-loading and parking facilities are required for large estate cars, and mini-buses used by teams and for long workshop and trade vehicles.

Spectators

Figure 7 shows a series of configurations which might be used for spectator seating in a velodrome. The final choice will depend on the topography of the site, the number of spectators and whether the facility is for national or regional use.

Because of the geometry of the bankings good visibility is difficult to achieve from seats at the ends of the track. As many seats as possible should be located along the straights. Rather than provide seats above the bankings two or three levels of standing accommodation might be included at the ends of the track.

It is recommended that spectators should have a sightline to a point 500 mm above the inner edge of the track along the whole circumference. In practice some seats at the ends of straights will not achieve this but all seats should be able to see over 90% of the track.

The spectator capacity of an indoor velodrome in the UK should be at least:

5 *The National Cycling Centre, Manchester showing the use of the central area for dining and hospitality*

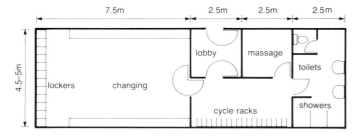

6 *A layout for a changing/storage unit for 20–25 riders*

National facility	3000–5000+
Regional facility	1000–3000
Training facility	300–1000.

These numbers could vary for other countries depending on the level of provision and frequency of events.

It should be possible to increase these numbers with temporary seating for major events.

Columns within spectator seating areas should be avoided since they create a number of seats with inferior vision and the management problems associated with ensuring customer satisfaction.

Apart from seating for training tracks it is generally not advisable to locate all spectator seating on one side of the track since this creates a poor atmosphere during competitions.

During 6-day cycle races and for many other sporting and entertainment uses spectators will be allowed to use the track centre area. Figure **8** shows the Hans Martin Schleyer Halle, Stuttgart, laid out for boxing, concert or conference purposes. This increases the capacity of the venue from 5000 permanent seats to a total capacity of 10,000. The additional uses for the arena must be defined at an early stage so that entrance and egress for all configurations can be planned in the design stage. Note particularly at Hans Martin Schleyer Halle that the lateral gangways for permanent and temporary seats are contiguous and that there are additional wide exits from the semicircular areas at each end of the track centre.

Most arenas which envisage additional seating on a regular basis use specifically designed seating units which can be readily assembled and dismantled for specific configurations. Where seating is located over the track this must be on units which completely span the track and do not rest on the track structure.

Where seating units are envisaged convenient high volume storage for these units must be incorporated in the design or provided nearby with easy access for tractors and trailers to stores and track centre.

A feature of many major continental 6-day races and championships is the social occasion associated with the event. Restaurants and catering facilities which overlook the track are therefore a common feature in indoor velodromes.

1.9 Design and engineering issues
For general details of environmental services recommendations refer to Chapters 60 and 61.

In addition to the specific design of cycling facilities the following design issues will be encountered when designing an indoor velodrome:

- It can be seen from the discussion of the building configuration that the architectural and structural design are inextricably linked. Given the large spans involved it is most important that the architect and structural

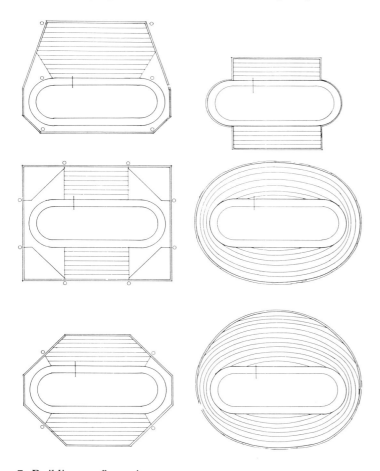

7 *Building configurations*

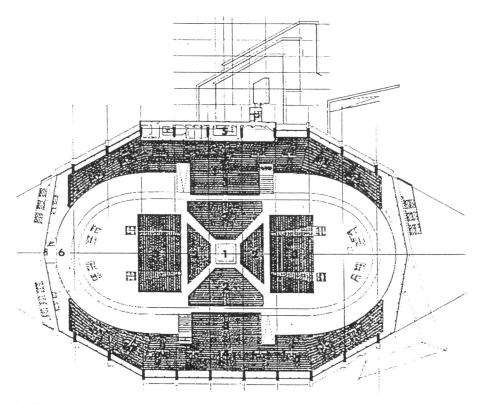

8 *Hans Martin Schleyer Halle, Stuttgart*

engineer work together to devise a building design that achieves the optimum integration of structure and arena design.

- The heating and ventilation issues should not be overlooked. The heating or cooling load for a concert with 6000 spectators in mid-winter or mid-summer will be substantial. The air-handling units for the arena will require careful design to ensure that air input and extract can handle the required air changes and large volumes of air involved without causing spectator discomfort. On the other hand, the system must be sufficiently flexible to deal with limited air change when the building is in use for training with no spectators.
- The ideal temperature for cycling is 20–21°C. Excessive cooling will affect the performance of the cyclists.
- Lighting levels at the track surface should be:
  - 300 lux for training
  - 500 lux for competition
  - 750 lux for international meetings
  - 1200 lux for televised meetings.
- Care must be taken in the design of the lighting installation to ensure that 'black spots' and excessive shadow are avoided since these can cause accidents when competitors are moving at high speed.
- The level of lighting and facilities to be permanently provided for television and conversely room for any supplementary installation to be provided by the television companies.
- The level of servicing and drainage to be provided to the track centre.
- The scoreboard and information systems to be incorporated in the design.

- The optimum level for the track centre and entrances relative to the ground level.
- Whether any natural lighting of the arena area will be incorporated in the design. Natural lighting is not mandatory but may secure energy savings during times of low use.
- Whether the thermal performance of the building envelope is to be enhanced to achieve economies in energy costs.
- Whether heating and cooling will take advantage of heat transfer and re-use to reduce energy costs.

2 References and further advice

Union Cycliste Internationale.
British Cycling Federation.
Other national governing bodies.
British Cycling Federation, *British Cycling Federation Handbook*, BCF.
Impianti per il ciclismo: Dossier, Spaziosport, **VI**(3), Italian National Olympic Committee (September 1987). Impianti per il ciclismo: Dossier. (A whole issue devoted to the history, development and design for all cycling disciplines, particularly indoor velodromes.)
City of Sheffield Recreation Department in association with the British Cycling Federation and the Sports Council, *A Velodrome for Sheffield. Initial Feasibility Study (in Relation to 1991 World Student Games)* (1987).
IAKS, *Installations de Sports Cyclistes – Elements de Planification*, IAKS, Koln (1980).
Hans-Martin-Schleyer-Halle in Stuttgart, Technik am Bau (3 March 1984).
Sports Council, *Arenas*, Sports Council, London.

76
Darts

Peter Ackroyd

1 Background information

The game is played by several players throwing darts from a standing position at a circular board, all in conformity with the dimensions and distances given below. The darts themselves must not exceed an overall length of 305 mm (12 in) nor weigh more than 50 grams.

2 Critical factors

- A safe location away from other activities with the oche (throw lines) and boards nowhere near doorways or around corners
- Standardised dimensions, distances and safety screening
- Location of spectators
- Choice of wall surface (irrespective of boxed dart boards)
- Lighting that provides adequate illumination of the board but does not cause glare
- Noise absorption for spectator events.

2.1 Space

For the dartboard diameter, height above floor and distance between player and dartboard see **2** and **3**. The distance between adjacent dartboards must be at least 2.4 m (8 ft) centre-to-centre if there are no separating screens; and at least 1.83 m (6 ft) if there is a projecting screen 1.98 m (6 ft) high and 914 mm (3 ft) wide to the right-hand side of the board. Avoid hanging dartboards adjacent to doorways or unscreened corners.

1 *Photograph: Arup Associates*

The distance between the toe side of the oche and the table that cordons off the playing area must be 1.22 m (4 ft).

Multi-purpose use of space
Darts is safest when sited away from other activities, but the space may be multi-purpose when the game is not being played. In view of the wall finish (see below) the space can also be used for displays and promotions.

Spectator facilities
Spectators should be seated at tables, on linked chairs or mobile units behind the players. They should not be seated between throw lanes in championship events because movement will distract the players.

2.2 Enclosing surfaces and finishes

The wall surface on which a dartboard is hung should be faced with a material which will not be defaced by stray darts or damage the points of the darts. A fibre-board or similar lining is therefore recommended, fixed by clip and screw fastening to allow eventual renewal of worn surrounds. The floor beneath the board also needs to be protected for the same reason, **2**.

For match play and championships it is advisable to isolate the space by means of a curtain or sliding/folding partition to ensure that players' concentration is not affected by outside noise.

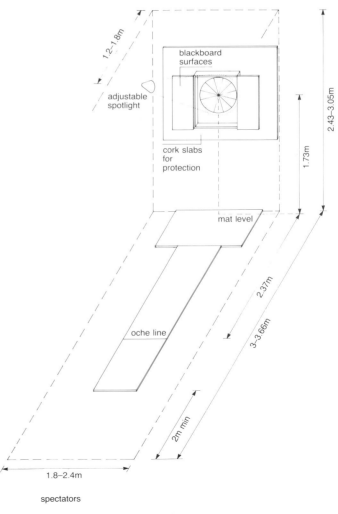

2 *Space diagram showing lighting*

299

2.3 Internal environment

For general details of environmental services recommendations refer to Chapters 60 and 61.

- A minimum background temperature of 16°C is desirable and ventilation may be required to cope with players' bouts of concentrated smoking.
- Adequate illumination of the board is essential, but the lighting must be designed and located so as not to create glare for participants or spectators, **2**. See the table below for recommended illumination levels.
- In match play situations, a noisy surrounding environment is sometimes created by spectators and other players. A reasonable degree of insulation against transmission of sound and the provision of absorbent surfaces within the dart-playing space are therefore needed.

2.4 Storage

The dart board, often contained within a box, is generally a fixture and needs no storage. The mat is rolled up and needs to be stored. It measures approximately 0.6 m long x 0.3 m diameter when rolled up and weighs about 15 kg.

3 References and further advice

The main promoter of darts is the British Darts Organisation (BDO) Ltd, which organises area and national championships. Further specialist advice can be obtained from the BDO.

Table 76.1: Recommended levels of illumination

Standard of play	Horizontal illuminance on Oche (lux)	Vertical illuminance on target board (lux)
International and national	200	750
Regional and club	100	500
Recreational and training	50	300

77
Fives: Rugby fives

Peter Ackroyd

Table 77.1: Space table

Feature	Dimensions	
	Metric	*Imperial*
Length of court	8.53 m	28 ft
Width of court (and of board fixed to front wall)	5.49 m	18 ft
Height of top edge of board above floor	0.76 m	2.5 ft
Projection of board from wall	22 mm	0.875 in
Height of front wall	4.57 m	15 ft
Height of back wall	1.82 m	6 ft
Height of level section of side walls (see 2)	4.57 m	15 ft
Height of side walls at lowest point at rear of court (see 2)	1.82 m	6 ft

1 Background information

Rugby fives is one of the oldest of all games. From the time the ball was invented people began to devise games based on knocking it against a wall or the angles of walls on all sorts of improvised courts such as castle keeps and churchyards. Rugby fives is a handball game which developed from these origins. It resembles squash rackets except that the court is smaller and the game is played with gloved hands and not a racket; hence the 17th century name 'fives' meaning 'five fingers'. Played with a hard and lively ball, the walls and floor must be built to exacting standards (see below).

2 Critical factors

- The precise specifications (see References and further advice) and required quality of construction by specialist tradesmen
- All playing surfaces must be durable, hard, smooth and flat; completely true and unaffected by moisture, light or the impact of the ball
- Finishes on playing surfaces must be of low frictional coefficient, but definitely not slippery
- All doors, fittings and the like must be flush with the wall
- No overhead projection must penetrate the two 'ceiling planes' connecting at 5.5 m from the front wall and bounded by heights of 5.6 m and 4 m on the front and back wall respectively
- Lighting and background.

Detailed specifications regarding all of the following are available from the Rugby Fives Association.

2.1 Dimensions

Dimensions of rugby fives courts are given in Table 77.1.

1 *Photo: St Paul's School, London*

2.2 Floor

The floor must be level and comprise a concrete base slab plus topping with the latter laid by specialist craftsmen as 'average' standards of trueness will not be acceptable. The topping may be 15 mm granolithic monolithically placed within 2.75 hours of laying the base slab; 25 mm granolithic laid later and bonded to the slab; or a neo-Bickley finish laid a month or more after the slab. The floor should be pigmented a deep iron red colour that will be fast in all conditions of friction, light, heat and moisture.

2.3 Walls

The walls must be 90° to the level floor. Cavity walls will help ensure that the court is not prone to undue damp penetration or condensation. They should be plastered by a specialist 'fives' plasterer, to absolutely true, flat and smooth surfaces; and painted matt black or charcoal. The exception is the wall area beneath the board on the front wall, which must be off-white, and the board itself, which must be signal red. Doors are the same colour as the surrounding wall.

Windows to the viewing area or gallery should be opening, double glazed and impact resistant. Hardwood doors should be dense, hard and extremely durable. A custom-designed internal handle may be necessary to ensure flushness.

Markings

The cavetto play-line which marks the effective height of the walls must be 50 mm (2 in) wide and painted signal red 537 gloss emulsion or applied in the form of a bonded red strip.

There may also be a requirement for 'image definition lines' to assist clear judgement of depth and form when games are televised or recorded. These are not yet standardised and the Rugby Fives Association should be contacted for advice.

2.4 Ceiling

The ceiling should be impact-resistant and woodwool slabs painted off-white are recommended.

2.5 Spectators

A court with a transparent back wall will have a viewing gallery which should be about 3 m (10 ft) deep, **2**.

2.6 Storage

A storage room or cupboard containing a tap, basin, water heater, towel rails, shelving, first-aid kit, vacuum cleaner, broom and brush-pan, cleaning materials and the like is recommended.

2.7 Environment

For general details of environmental services recommendations refer to Chapters 60 and 61.

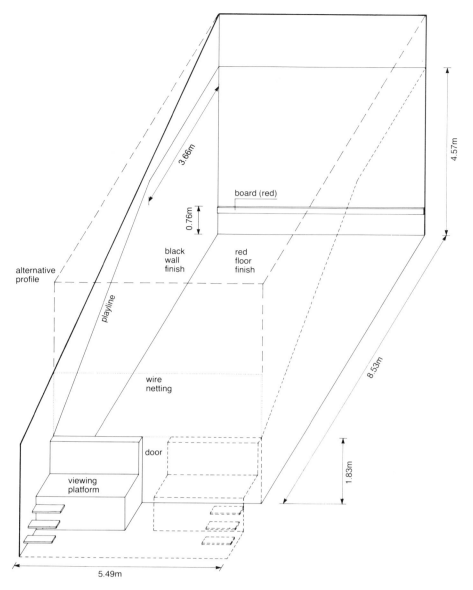

3.66m

4.57m

board (red)

0.76m

black
wall
finish

red
floor
finish

alternative
profile

playline

8.53m

wire
netting

door

1.83m

viewing
platform

5.49m

2 *A standard rugby fives court has four walls with no buttresses and is used for both singles and doubles play*

It is important that all items of equipment are impact-resistant and designed so as not to damage or trap the ball. All items within the playing zone must be flush-mounted.

Lighting
Good quality lighting is essential and it is recommended that a minimum average illuminance of 300 lux is maintained with a uniformity ratio of 0.8 or better. Horizontal illuminance at floor level will probably be the most critical value but it will also be important to achieve vertical illuminances of about 250 lux on all playing surfaces.

Temperature
The ideal temperature for playing is around 12–13°C and this should be maintained as a minimum value.

Ventilation
Good ventilation is important to avoid condensation and remove odours. A ventilation rate of six air changes per hour is recommended.

3 References and further advice
For Eton fives see Volume 1, Chapter 51.
Rugby Fives Association (RFA).
Specifications and recommendations pertaining to the construction of the fives court (available from the RFA).

78
Gymnastics training halls

Christopher Harper

1 General

The most significant development in the teaching of gymnastics has been the use of sunken pits filled with resilient material to cushion landings. The presence of floor pits and the time taken to erect and dismantle apparatus has resulted in the development of specialised training halls, **1**. This section describes the apparatus used by gymnasts together with a range of hall sizes and associated accommodation. Refer to Chapter 29 in this volume for competition gymnastics.

Gymnastics apparatus and equipment
Men gymnasts compete on the vaulting horse, pommel horse, horizontal bars, parallel bars and floor and women compete on the vaulting horse, beam, asymmetrical bars and floor.

Training takes place on these pieces of apparatus, ideally combined with pits, on floor mats and on various specialised items of training equipment, such as trampolines, trampettes and 'mushrooms', **2**.

Scales of provision
Gymnastics training halls can be grouped into three broad types:

- National training centres, **3**
- Regional training centres
- Local centres – these may share facilities with other sports, but it should be emphasised that pits in multi-use activity spaces are an impractical solution. The specialised nature of the sport, the chalk-dust and resin used

1 *Interior of King George VI hall at Lilleshall National Gymnastics Training Centre. Photo: Roger Price Photographic Ltd*

by gymnasts and the weight of any form of cover designed for the floor openings rule against shared use with other sports.

1.1 Converting existing buildings
The layout of fixed equipment is influenced by the existing structure and clear dimensions and it is not always possible to excavate for pits although raised pits (podium pits) may be considered if clear height permits. An advantage of utilising a redundant building, **4**, apart from the economies which can result from this approach, is that the site is often in a densely populated area where recreational needs for the young are difficult to meet. The most important point to be considered when surveying an existing structure with gymnastics training in mind is whether safety standards can be met. Safe clearances around and above apparatus are essential and where any possible obstruction might occur then structural profiles must be modified or protected with padding.

1.2 Gymnastics landing pits
The 'traditional' pit is 1.8–2.0 m (approx 6–6.5 ft) deep, of waterproof concrete construction filled with scrap foam, on a base foam mat to provide a safe and progressive deceleration in the landing area, **5**.

Pit plan configurations are designed to support apparatus with its legs resting on projecting but protected piers and provide a safe landing zone from vaulting and tumbling run ups, sprung floors and trampettes.

This design allows for other than feet-first landing, does not restrict rotation and offers maximum protection to the gymnast learning new skills, reducing the stress factor inherent in repetitive training. They also remove fear, the greatest inhibitor to acquiring new skills and improving performance. Where ground conditions are poor or in conversions of existing buildings with high ceilings, podium pits have been installed. They are less convenient than sunken pits as they form a physical barrier across the hall and have to be of substantial construction in order to take the loads from both the apparatus posts and the restraining cables. Perimeter walkways and access stairs must be protected with balustrade railing.

Pit infill
Although the configuration of pit construction has changed little in over 20 years, the method of infilling has been subject to constant research and development prompted by the requirements of safety both for trainees and in the sense of minimising the chance of fire. *Fire resistant foam* must now be used for pit infill, edge protection and for loose mats laid about the training areas. For further details refer to the Sports Council Fact Sheet and the relevant British Standards and Home Office Circular.

Because of the potential dangers of using open celled foam and the tendency for the current fire retarded grades to lose their protective characteristics over time a sprung membrane surfaced pit has been developed. The 'slung' pit or 'semi-slung' type, a compromise utilising a layer of foam over the membrane, offer an alternative to traditional infilling even if their cushioning characteristics are different, **6** and **7**.

1.3 Hall construction and specification
Overall dimensions will be determined by the number of apparatus stations, run-ups and floor exercise area selected, **8**. A minimum clear height of 6.5 m (approx 21 ft) below any obstruction is required over the training hall. A clear span structure will give more planning flexibility

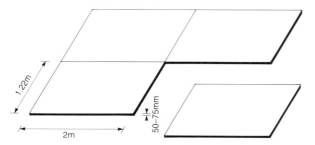

1.22m

50-75mm

2m

Double flex floor area for ground work

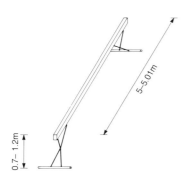

5-5.01m

0.7- 1.2m

Women's balance beam

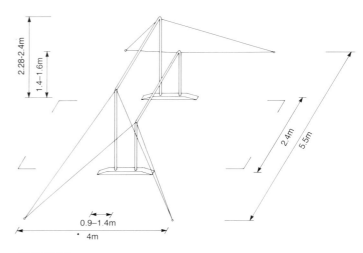

2.28-2.4m

1.4-1.6m

2.4m

5.5m

0.9-1.4m

4m

Asymmetric bars

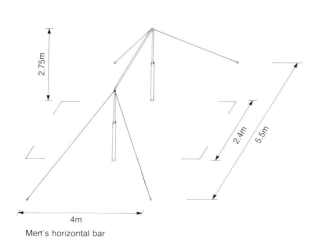

2.75m

2.4m

5.5m

4m

Men's horizontal bar

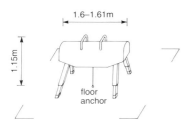

1.6-1.61m

1.15m

floor
anchor

Mens's pommel horse

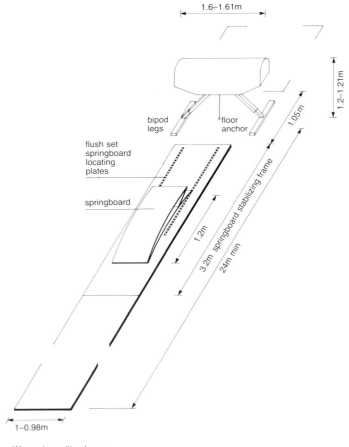

1.6-1.61m

1.2-1.21m

bipod
legs

floor
anchor

1.05m

flush set
springboard
locating
plates

springboard

1.2m

3.2m springboard stabilizing frame

24m min

1-0.98m

Women's vaulting horse

2 *Gymnastics apparatus diagrams*

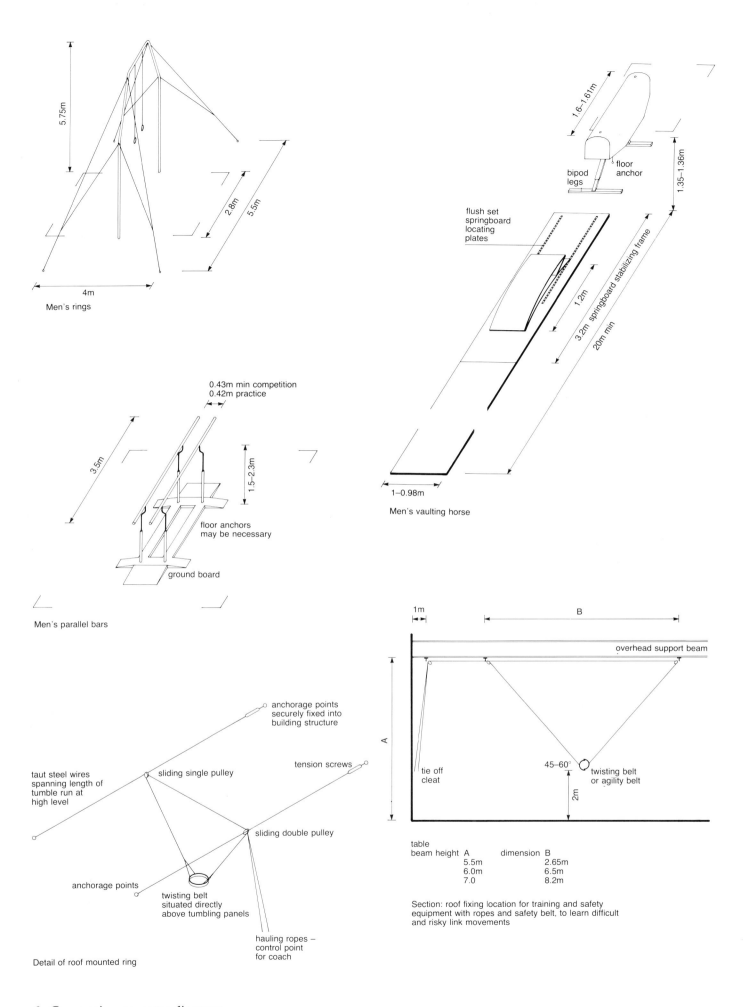

5.75m

4m

Men's rings

0.43m min competition
0.42m practice

3.5m

1.5–2.3m

floor anchors
may be necessary

ground board

Men's parallel bars

2.8m

5.5m

1.6–1.61m

1.35–1.36m

floor
anchor

bipod
legs

flush set
springboard
locating
plates

1.2m

3.2m springboard stabilizing frame

20m min

1–0.98m

Men's vaulting horse

1m

B

overhead support beam

A

tie off
cleat

45–60°

twisting belt
or agility belt

2m

table
beam height A   dimension B
        5.5m   2.65m
        6.0m   6.5m
        7.0   8.2m

Section: roof fixing location for training and safety
equipment with ropes and safety belt, to learn difficult
and risky link movements

anchorage points
securely fixed into
building structure

tension screws

taut steel wires
spanning length of
tumble run at
high level

sliding single pulley

sliding double pulley

anchorage points

twisting belt
situated directly
above tumbling panels

hauling ropes –
control point
for coach

Detail of roof mounted ring

2 *Gymnastics apparatus diagrams*

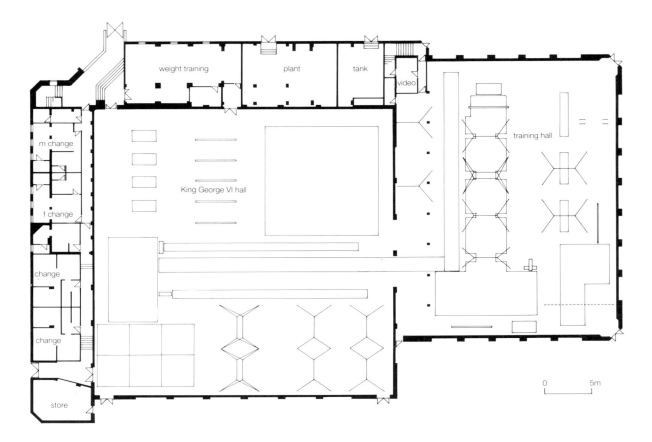

3 *Plan of Lilleshall. Note the openings between the two training halls for a run-up, a feature that can be used in local centres with restricted dimensions*

4 *A converted church for Greenhead Gymnastics Club, Huddersfield. Photo: Greenhead GC*

but it is possible for intermediate columns to be accommodated resulting in possible cost savings. Roof structure design must take account of the additional loading imposed by travelling, spotting and dismount rigs. Flush wall surfaces should be specified wherever possible and projections must be avoided whenever over-run impact is possible. If natural lighting is required the position of windows should be carefully considered. Views out are not regarded as important as they can distract from the high degree of concentration required for this sport. Any upper wall level or roof glazing must be carefully located so as to avoid blinding glare, potentially hazardous when gymnasts are involved in split second turning and catching action.

Any hard wearing, non-dusting and easily cleaned finish is suitable for the floor, large areas of which are usually covered with crash mats. Timber, traditionally hardwood or alternatively sealed softwood is preferred. Pit edge protection must be firmly fixed, with its top surface level with the floor lining mats. Fair faced masonry or timber lining are suitable wall finishes. Fittings will include wall bars and mirrors, black and white marker boards and pin board for notices and charts.

1.4 Internal environment

For general details of engineering services recommendations refer to Chapters 60 and 61.

Good levels of heating are essential to prevent gymnasts from incurring muscle injury and ensure the comfort of trainees awaiting their turn on the apparatus. A minimum level of 18°C is recommended.

Minimum lighting levels of 200 lux should be provided from ceiling mounted luminaires or alternatively (and more expensively) from uplighters. The light source should not contrast too markedly with the background so a light coloured ceiling is preferable. Good levels of ventilation are needed to ensure reasonable comfort conditions in summer time; 1–1.5 air changes per hour are recommended.

Smoke or fire detectors and an emergency lighting system are essential and their number and layout will be agreed with the Fire Officer and building control along with means of escape requirements.

Power socket outlets should be placed at convenient perimeter locations to prevent excessive lengths of trailed cable. Vacuum cleaning is the only way to prevent the successive accumulation of chalk dust. Sockets will also be required for audio equipment used in association with the floor exercise area. The acoustic performance of the hall should be considered at construction stage and the

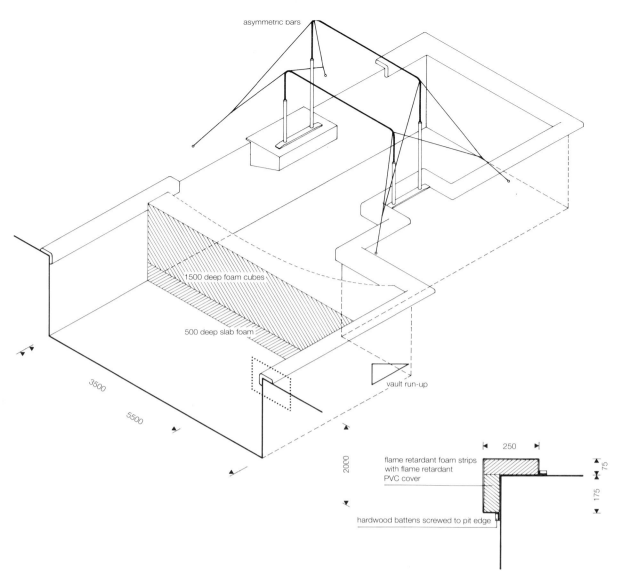

asymmetric bars

1500 deep foam cubes

500 deep slab foam

3500

5500

2000

vault run-up

250

flame retardant foam strips
with flame retardant
PVC cover

75

175

hardwood battens screwed to pit edge

5 *Profiles of a typical landing pit with a detail of the pit edge protection*

6 *Traditional pit infill with blocks of foam. Photo: En-tout-cas plc*

7 *A slung pit installation showing the membrane cover. Pit depth can be reduced to 1.2 m (approx 4 ft). Photo: En-tout-cas plc*

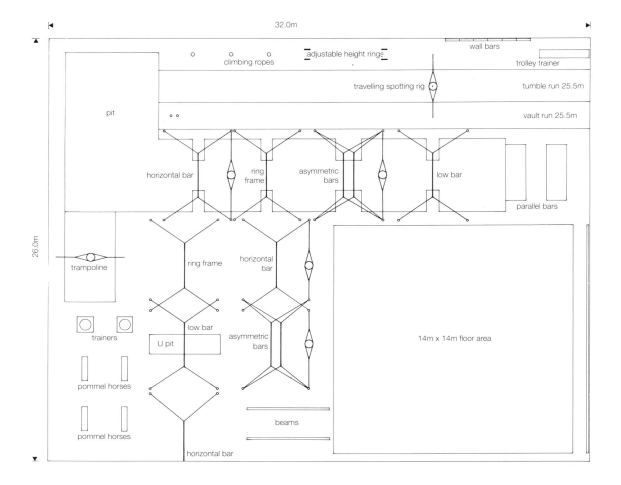

8 *Hypothetical plan for a regional training hall prepared by Continental Sports Ltd, Huddersfield*

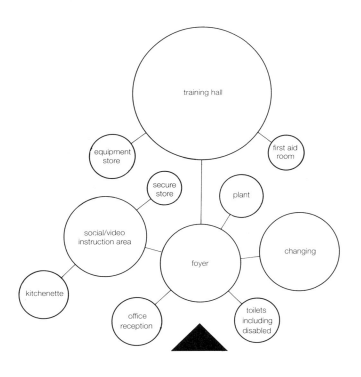

9 *Gymnastics training centre: spatial relationships diagram*

appropriate sound absorbent surfaces incorporated whenever possible.

1.5 Ancillary accommodation

The accompanying diagram confirms the range and relationship of accommodation to complement a regional training hall, with a capacity of 100 trainees, coaches and visitors. It includes a foyer, office/reception, WCs, disabled persons WC, changing rooms, plant room, first aid room, equipment store and a social and video instruction area, served by vending machines and/or a kitchenette. A small fitness and sauna suite might also be considered. This accommodation should be grouped together to one end or one side of the training hall, **9**.

2 References and further advice

Refer to the following for further information on cellular foam:

British Standards Institution, *BS 5852: Parts 1 and 2*, BSI, Milton Keynes (regarding fire tests and ignition standards).

Home Office, *Fire Hazards Associated with the Use of Cellular Foam in Sports and Recreational Facilities (Fire Services Circular No 1/1988)*, HMSO, London (1988).

The Sports Council's fact sheet and video.

79
Irish handball

Peter Ackroyd

1 Introduction

In the late 1880s the traditional Irish handball court was open-air and different examples had varying dimensions. Today's modern four wall indoor court, with its ceiling, flush lighting, hardwood floor, glass back wall and central heating, appears more like a squash or fives court.

Court or Irish handball is a ball game played by two players (singles), **1**, or two pairs (doubles). The ball is struck with a gloved hand with the object of making it difficult for the opponent to make a good return. The four walls and ceiling of the court are all playing surfaces. The game is played mainly in Ireland, the USA, Canada, Mexico, Spain and Australia. For basic coaching, practice or recreational use one and two wall courts may be marked out in any large hall which has suitable floor and wall finishes. In the USA a form of one-wall handball is played in many YMCAs, **2**.

2 *American handball court, Central YMCA, London*

2 Critical factors

- A flush ceiling: it is a playing surface
- A high standard of hard plaster on the playing walls
- A good quality hardwood floor
- Adequate illumination.

2.1 Space requirements

An Irish Handball Association international handball court has a playing area with internal dimensions of 12.192×6.098 m (40×20 ft) $\times 6.098$ m (20 ft) high. Most new courts are provided with a glass back wall which allows spectators to sit and watch the game on stepped benching or retractable tiers. A glass back court with adjacent spectator area requires an overall space approximately 19 m long $\times 6.1$ m wide internally (62×20 ft). If the court has a solid back wall spectators can be accommodated in a first floor gallery overlooking the back wall underneath which can be housed changing and toilet facilities.

The court for the four-wall game must conform to the measurements shown in **3**.

2.2 Floor

Flooring should consist of Birdseye maple, Whiterock maple or other light coloured tongued and grooved hardwood flooring laid on 75×50 mm (3×2 in) battens, Hilti nailed to a 150 mm (6 in) reinforced and damp-proofed concrete slab. The underside of the floor should be ventilated to prevent rot. The top (playing) surface should be given a single light coat of a proprietary sealer to make the floor resistant to marking; a slippery polished surface must not be created.

Court markings
The lines on the floor should be red or bright orange and 38 mm (1.5 in) wide.

2.3 Walls

External load-bearing brick walls should consist of a 112 mm (4.5 in) outer skin, a 75 mm (3 in) cavity with approved insulation and an inner skin of 225 mm (9 in) brick or concrete block, reinforced every fourth course.

Internal dividing walls between adjacent courts should consist of at least 225 mm (9 in) brickwork or blockwork.

1 *Photo: Belfast Telegraph*

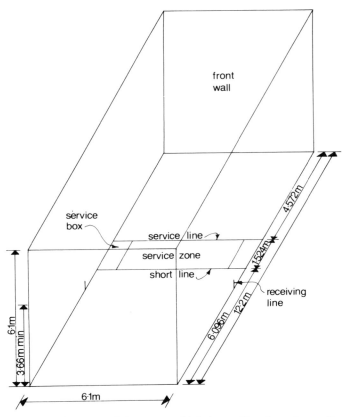

front
wall

service
box

service line

service zone

short line

receiving
line

4.572m

1.524m

6.096m

1.22m

6.1m

6.1m min

3.66m min

3 *Space diagram of the court which is smaller than the earlier traditional court*

Glass back wall

This should consist of a 12 mm (approx 0.5 in) toughened (tempered) glass fixed to a metal or timber frame with a 0.76 m (2.5 ft) centrally placed toughened (tempered) glass door similar to that used in squash courts. The minimum height of the glass back wall should be 3.658 m (12 ft). It may have to be braced with glass fins at about 1.22 m (4 ft) centres. For a detailed specification consult the Irish Handball Association.

Internal wall finishes

Wall surfaces should have a sand and cement render finished with a steel trowel; alternatively a squash court plaster finish will give an improved surface. A vee joint should be formed vertically in the long walls immediately outside the back wall of the playing area. All walls should be given three coats of a white co-polymer paint.

2.4 Ceiling

The ceiling in standard courts is flat with recessed lighting as it is a playing surface. It need extend only over the playing area and should consist of 12 mm (approx 0.5 in) chipboard or plywood fixed to the roof joists at 450 mm (approx 18 in) centres. All joints should be taped and a 3 mm (0.125 in) movement gap left between sheets.

A 10 mm (approx 0.4 in) gap should be left around the court perimeter. Adequate roof insulation should be laid between the roof joists at ceiling level and impact-resistant lighting panels fixed to finish flush with the ceiling.

2.5 Internal environment

For general details of enirnomental services recommendations refer to Chapters 60 and 61 and the *CIBSE Lighting Guide LG4: Sports* for further details of lighting recommendations.

The lighting levels required are similar to those for squash: 150 lux at floor level for recreational use; 300 lux for club and county competitions; and 500 lux for national and international play.

In larger centres, discussion with television companies should be held prior to court design in order to incorporate facilities inside the courts which will allow a game to be televised using supplementary lighting.

The ventilation system should provide four air changes per hour.

Sufficient background heating is required to enable the court temperature to be maintained at approximately 13°C. Two 3-kw fan heaters are normally considered sufficient to provide background heating to both the court and viewing area. They can be swivel mounted on the side walls of the court immediately behind the glass back wall.

3 References and further advice

General advice on court construction can be obtained from the Irish Handball Council.
Sports Council for Northern Ireland.

80
Pelota

Peter Ackroyd

1 *Photo: Federacion Espanola de Pelota*

1 Background

Pelota is a fast ball game played in a three-walled court (fronton) by two players or by several teams of players. Players attempt to hit a ball (pelota) with a wicker basket (cesta) against the front wall (frontis) so that their opponents will be unable to return it and lose a point. The game originated in northern Spain. The rules given here are for the game now played in the USA.

Pelota is played in many forms. The following types are officially recognised in international competitions:

- *Fronton largo* on a large court 50–70 m long and 10–12 m wide
- *Fronton corto* using a short, small court 30–40 m long and 10 m wide
- *Trinquete* using a court with a right and left-hand side wall
- *Plaze libre* still played only in Spain and France.

All other variations have in common the open or closed court known as the *fronton*.

2 The court

The court has three walls, **1**. The front wall is called the frontis, the back wall the rebote, and the side wall the lateral.

The frontis is made of granite blocks while the rebote, lateral, and floor are made of gunite, a pressurized cement.

The fourth side of the court has a clear screen through which spectators watch the game. To comply with UK safety factors this would need to consist of shatter-proof and possibly fire-proof glazing.

The court is divided into 15 numbered areas. The serving zone is the space between areas 4 and 7, **2**.

2.2 Internal environment

For general details of environmental services recommendations refer to Chapters 60 and 61.

3 References and further advice

Federacion Espanola de Pelota, *Proyecto-Tipo de Fronton Corto Cubierto*.
IAKS, Reclams Sportfuhrer.
Rules of the Game, Diagram Visual Information Ltd.

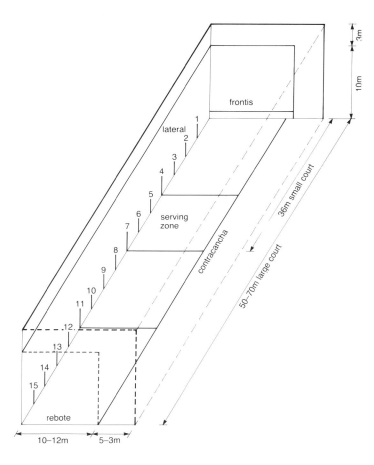

2 *Space diagram. From F to R a strong net or reinforced-glass wall must protect spectators*

81
Rackets

Peter Ackroyd

1 *Photo: Peter Smith and Stanley Paul and Co Ltd*

1 Background

This is another racket-and-ball game played in the UK, the USA and Canada, **1**. Two or four players participate in a court enclosed by four walls, the lay-out of which is similar to that of its modern and more widely popular offshoot, squash rackets, although the dimensions are larger.

2 Critical factors

- Floor and wall surface finishes
- Lighting.

2.1 Dimensions

The floor area generally is 18.3 × 9.1 m (60 × 30 ft). The surrounding walls are 9.1 m (30 ft) high and the service line on the front wall is 2.9 m (9.5 ft) from the floor. The back wall is 4.12 m (13.5 ft) high.

2.2 Markings

The front or main wall facing the players as they enter the court is traversed by two horizontal lines.

- The higher or service line is the 'cut' line. The service must be struck above it.
- The play line, near floor-level and formed by a board fastened to the wall, which determines the lower limit on the front wall to which all returns must be directed.

2.3 Spectators

Spectators must be seated above the back wall out of court line.

2.4 Finishes

The floor may be of stone, asphalt, composition (to a 'Bickley formula') or epoxy resin.

Wall surfaces must be very smooth and this requires hand plastering.

2.5 Internal environment

For general details of environmental services recommendations refer to Chapters 60 and 61. See also Chapter 87.

3 References and further advice

Tennis and Rackets Association.

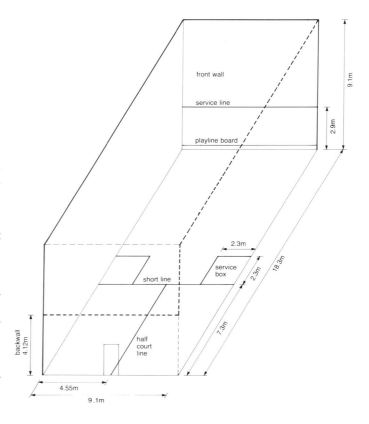

2 *Space diagram*

82
Racquetball and racketball

Peter Ackroyd

1 Background

Racquetball originated in the USA in the 1960s and was first played in Britain in 1975, where there is now an adapted version known as racketball. Both games are a variant of squash. Racketball is played on a standard (international) squash court and is therefore complementary to squash; racquetball needs a somewhat larger court.

While being fast and competitive, both games are less dependent on strength and fitness than squash, can be played to suit the needs of players and can be picked up by absolute beginners in about an hour. They are sociable sports and therefore attractive to families, being suitable for both sexes, all ages and people with disabilities. For these reasons, racquetball has rapidly become very popular and is now represented in over 50 countries on five continents with over 12 million players. In the UK racketball is played at many leisure centres, squash clubs and schools.

The principal differences between racquetball and squash are that in racquetball the ball must be bounced before being served; and the racquetball ball, which is made of hollow rubber and 57 mm (2.25 in) in diameter is twice as large as a squash one, much bouncier and does not need warming up. A racketball ball is softer than a racquetball one.

2 Critical factors

- Racquetball is played off all enclosing surfaces, including the ceiling
- Trueness of wall and floor surfaces
- Protection of recessed lights.

2.1 Space

Racquetball is played on a court approximately 12.2 × 6.1 m (40 × 20 ft). Overall height is 6.1 m (20 ft) and the back wall must be at least 3.66 m (12 ft), but not more than 6.1 m (20 ft) high, **2**.

In the UK racketball is played in a standard squash court. See Chapter 87 in this volume.

2.2 Racquetball surfaces

The hollow, high bouncing ball does not mark the enclosing surfaces.

Floor

The floor must be hard, smooth, resilient and non-slip. It must be level to within 6 mm (approx 1/4 in) in any 3 m (10 ft) radius.

Any joint must be plane to within 1.5 mm (approx 1/16 in) and open joints must not be more than 8 mm (approx 1/3 in) wide, except that an expansion gap of not more than 16 mm (approx 5/8 in) is recommended at the junction of the floor and walls.

The floor colour should be light and uniform. If the court is to be used for TV coverage a hardwood floor may be bleached white.

Walls

Walls must be plumb to within 25 mm (approx 1 in) in 6.1 m (approx 20 ft) at any place on the court; and must be plane and smooth without indentations, holes or open joints more than 2.4 mm (approx 3/32 in) in any dimension and have no variations more than 3 mm (approx 1/8 in) in 305 mm (approx 12 in) from the true surface.

1 *Photo: Sports Council*

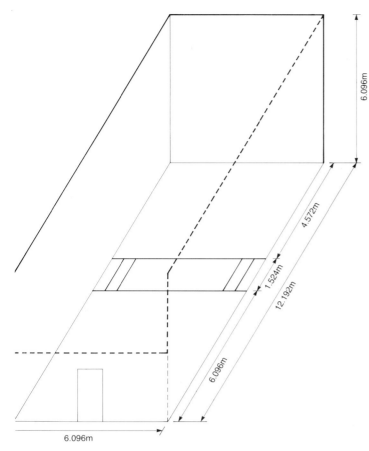

6.096m

4.572m

1.524m

12.192m

6.096m

6.096m

2 Space diagram of a racquetball court. For tournaments there must be space for a linesman and referee behind the plane of the back wall. They must be able to see the whole of the court and hear the play and the players and be heard by them

If windows are placed in rear walls they must be flush with the surface and constructed of safety materials. The recommended minimum window height above the floor is 760 mm (2 ft 6 in). Surfaces behind a window or glass wall must not be darker than the floor of the court to minimise reflections.

Doors to the court must not be more than 1.07 m (3 ft 6 in) wide and 2.13 m (7 ft) high. They must be flush with the wall surface, of the same colour and texture and have a playable surface with the same rebound characteristics as the wall. The door handle must also be flush; and the door, which opens into the court, must have a restraining device to prevent it from hitting the court wall when opened.

Ceiling

For racquetball this rebound surface must also be firm, hard and smooth without indentations, holes or open joints, except for the flush built-in lights which must be protected with shatterproof, glare-free translucent covers.

For racketball the ceiling space above the zone of play should be similar to squash. See Chapter 87 in this volume.

1.4 Markings

Racquetball line markings are shown in **2**. All lines are 38 mm (1.5 in) wide, bright red or, as alternative choices, white or black. All lines are solid except the 'receiving line' which is broken.

For racketball all the court markings for squash apply except that the cut line across the front wall is ignored.

1.5 Spectators

Spectator areas may be located behind the plane of any of the walls of a racquetball court.

1.6 Internal environment

For general details of environmental services recommendations refer to Chapters 60 and 61. See also Chapter 87 in this volume.

1.7 Other requirements

For racketball refer to Chapter 87 in this volume.

2 References and further advice
British Racketball Association (BRA).
The Great Britain Racquetball Federation.

83
Real tennis

Peter Ackroyd

1 Background

Tennis originated in France in the 12th century when French nobles began to use their hands to hit a ball over a net in a game they called *jeu de paume* (game of the fist), **1**. Later they started using rackets. The strange shape of the court is thought to have derived from the courtyards in which the game was first played. The walls, floor and sloping roof of the 'penthouse' at the hazard end of the court and along one side of it, beneath which are viewing galleries, are all playing surfaces, **2**. The game has affinities with fives, rackets and squash.

A variant of the game, played outdoors on grass under the name 'lawn tennis', developed in the mid 18th century (when softer, more bouncy rubber balls became available) and rapidly became more popular than the original. Today the word 'tennis' is almost invariably taken to mean lawn tennis. But 'real tennis', as the older game is now called, survives and there are at least 20 active courts in the UK, **3**. Real tennis differs from lawn tennis in that it is played in an enclosed hall, has a drooping net, with a hard ball which bounces fast and true on the stone or concrete floor.

2 Critical factors

- A hard, smooth floor and walls
- Certain defined projecting features from the walls
- Projecting viewing galleries with sloping roof which form part of the playing surface
- Dimensions are still laid down in imperial measure.

2.1 Dimensions

The dimensions of real tennis courts are not precisely uniform, but the playing area at floor level is approximately 29.3 m long × 10 m wide (approx 96 × 33 ft). Above the penthouses it becomes 33.5 × 11.9 m (approx 110 × 39 ft). The roof is usually about 9 m (30 ft) above the floor. Sometimes the court is naturally top lit, **2**.

2.2 Floors

The floors of courts are made of stone or concrete composition. The most favoured stones are limestone and Caen stone; the cement is Portland cement or Bickley's patent non-sweating composition. Floors may also be wood composition block or epoxy resin. They are normally black or red. Lamp-black diluted with bullock's blood and ox-galls is the traditional recipe for blackening floors and walls but 20th century redecoration usually makes use of synthetic stone paint and matt emulsion paint.

2.3 Walls

Walls are of stone or brick, coated with the same composition as the floor, colour black or slate grey.

2.4 Internal environment

For general details of environmental services recommendations refer to Chapters 60 and 61. Environmental

1 *An early French real tennis court. With acknowledgements to the Tennis and Rackets Association and the early Royal Courts of France*

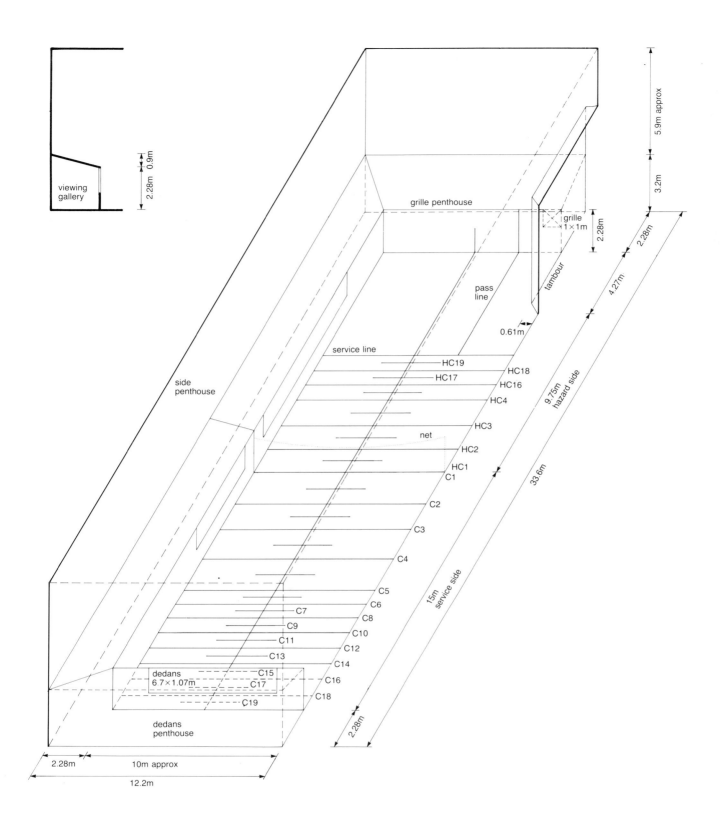

2 *Diagram of court with section through side and ends – the original penthouse. Numbered lines on the service side of the net have the following conventional designations: C1 chase the line, C2 chase first gallery, C3 chase the door, C4 chase second gallery, C5 chase a yard worse than last gallery, C6 chase last gallery, C7 chase half a yard worse than six, C8 chase six, C9 chase five and six, C10 chase five, C11 chase four and five, C12 chase four, C13 chase three and four, C14 chase three, C15 chase two and three, C16 chase two, C17 chase one and two, C18 chase one yard, C19 chase half a yard. Lines are numberd correspondingly on the hazard side. HC Hazard chase*

3 *Real tennis at Hampton Court. The original English 16th century indoor court*

requirements are generally similar to those for indoor tennis (see Chapter 88).

2.5 Some UK examples to visit
- The Queen's Club, Palliser Road, London W14.
- The Oratory School, Woodcote, Reading. Opened 1990.
- Canford School, Wimborne Minster, Dorset.
- Hatfield House Tennis Club, Old Hatfield, Hertfordshire.
- Sun Court Hotel, 19 Crosbie Road, Troon, Ayrshire.
- The Manchester Tennis and Raquet Club, 33 Blackfriars Road, Salford 3, Manchester.
- Cambridge University Tennis Court, Grange Road, Cambridge.

3 Reference and further advice
Tennis and Rackets Association.

84

Riding and indoor equestrianism

Peter Ackroyd

1 Introduction

There are a number of indoor riding activities and disciplines for which facilities are needed for local use or major events. These include at least three distinct types of equestrian establishment:

- Livery stables that provide facilities for general recreation (for which access to the countryside is important), training for competitions and possibly hunting
- Riding centres or schools that cater for either basic riding school customers, career training or training to top competition standards in various riding disciplines
- Competitive centres where events are held; these centres are often combined with the above types.

The main requirements are outlined and shown below. However, indoor and outdoor facilities are best provided together wherever possible. Also, at almost all riding establishments some open-air land is required for grazing and exercise (rather than for nutrition), for competition warm-up and horse box parking. A most-weather area, often called a *manege*, is an added advantage.

This section should be read with outdoor requirements and disciplines outlined in Volume 1, Chapter 69. For further advice consult the horse organisations and technical references given at the end of both chapters.

2 Critical factors

- Early and full consultations, particularly with land-owners and for planning permissions. (NB: consult Structure and Local Plans in relationship to land use policies for horse based activities, landscape quality and proximity of local community.)
- Site location and area (including sufficient rotation grazing land)
- Integrated indoor and outdoor facilities
- Suitable approach roads and site access
- Adequate parking and on-site turning circles for heavy vehicles
- Fire precautions, particularly a fire break between bale storage and other accommodation
- Health and hygiene provisions for horses, staff and riders
- Minimum space dimensions and horse lanes between elements of accommodation
- Minimum 4 m clear headroom for horses below obstructions and any overhang
- Manure skips for frequent collection.

2.1 Space

The following data includes the British Horse Society (BHS) recommended elements for a riding centre, but may be varied according to the nature of the centre.

Instructional
- A covered riding school, **1–3**. Desirable but not essential in areas of high quality landscape.
- A show jumping arena (usually the covered school area), **4** and **5**.
- Adjoining collecting ring.
- An outdoor manege (see **2** in Volume 1, Chapter 69), ideally floodlit. An important open-air all-weather schooling and exercise area.

Administrative
- Staff living accommodation ideally for at least two people
- Stables for horses and ponies, **6** – allow 4 or 5 stabled horses per groom/instructor

1 *Photo: Monty, Birmingham*

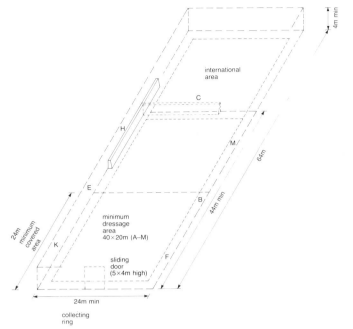

4 *Showjumping in the indoor school at National Equestrian Centre, Stoneleigh. Photo: Findlay Davidson*

- Reception/bookings
- Manager's office
- Toilets and washing facilities
- First aid
- Club room/lectures
- Canteen
- Viewing/tuition gallery or balcony (with clear views over the kicking board)
- Plant and services spaces
- Car and horse box park (for offloading space, see **9** in Volume 1, Chapter 69).

Larger centres also may need:

- Farrier's workshop
- Clipping box
- Tack and foodstuffs shop
- Stables for up to 50 horses and ponies, with proportionally larger back-up accommodation
- Separate car parking
- Male and female riders' changing rooms.

2 *Riding school and jumping areas. The broken line indicates the clear area inside the kicking boards. The BSJA preferred arena size is about 49–52 × 24–26 m. The FEI rules for indoor international CSIO and CSI events require that 'the area of the arena must be as near as possible a minimum of 2500 square metres'. Practice jump and collecting areas and a control/judges box are also required. For major dressage and show jumping events indoors an arena of 60 × 30–40 m is recommended,* **5**

2.2 A covered riding school

To provide an all-weather area for riding, it will be found that covered facilities of some sort are almost essential.

Covered schools are of many different standards. The BHS's British Equestrian Centre, **1**, consists of a riding surface 61 × 24.4 m – large enough to contain an international size arena in which to hold dressage and most show jumping events. Seating for 300 has been provided along one side. At the small end of the scale, it is possible to provide a suitable area under a Dutch barn, of which the sides are only clad for 3 m from the eaves and wattle hurdles enclose the riding surface.

Whatever the standard of the building, it is essential that the indoor riding space should be at least 24 × 44 m, which is the minimum size required for an ordinary dressage arena and equestrian centre indoor show jumping. The full size spaces for different uses are shown in **2**. Sizes include a space of 2 m which must be left all around the riding area.

There are few dimensional requirements for show jumping, **5**. For example, the British Show Jumping Association (BSJA) Rules and Year Book stipulate that for knock-out competitions the surface areas must be at least 60 × 24 m (was 30 m). For details of those

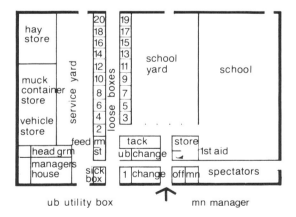

ub utility box   mn manager

3 *Plan of Lea Bridge Riding School (Architects: Lee Valley Region Park Authority)*

- Five stalls for resting ponies between hacks (rides) out, each with width to untack a pony
- Isolation box(s)
- Stable yard, **3**
- Saddle or tack room, **7**
- Forage store, **8**
- Bale barn and fire breaks
- General storage

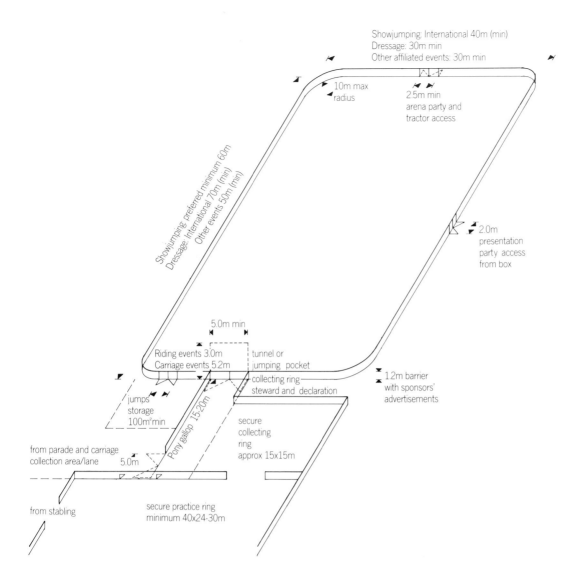

Showjumping: International 40m (min)
Dressage: 30m min
Other affiliated events: 30m min

10m max
radius

2.5m min
arena party and
tractor access

Showjumping: preferred minimum 60m
Dressage: International 70m (min)
Other events 50m (min)

2.0m
presentation
party access
from box

5.0m min

Riding events 3.0m
Carriage events 5.2m

tunnel or
jumping pocket

collecting ring
steward and declaration

1.2m barrier
with sponsors'
advertisements

jumps
storage
100m²min

Pony gallop 15-20m

secure
collecting
ring
approx 15x15m

from parade and carriage
collection area/lane

5.0m

from stabling

secure practice ring
minimum 40x24-30m

5 *Show jumping space diagram. The 60 m length for show jumping is preferred to allow the course builder to set a number of obstacles along one side, including a triple element jump, all safely spaced apart and away from the corners (for less experienced horses to turn at speed). The arena entrance from the collecting area can be positioned anywhere around the perimeter, but an end location is often nearest to the warm-up ring. Adequate pony gallop space through the entrance, secure collecting and practice rings, parade and carriage collection lanes are required. Wherever possible, tractors should use a separate route. An ideal circulation is to use both corners at one end with equipment storage between. Alternatively, storage space adjacent to the four corners has many advantages. This diagram is reprinted from* Arenas, *see References and further advice*

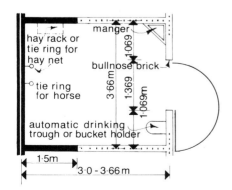

hay rack or
tie ring for
hay net

manger

bullnose brick

tie ring
for horse

1·069

3·66m

1·369

1·069m

automatic drinking
trough or bucket holder

1·5m

3·0 - 3·66m

6 *Plan of typical loose box. A horse ideally requires a floor area of 3.66 × 4.27 m (12 × 14 ft) with minimum headroom of 4.27 m (14 ft). A pony stall may be reduced to 3.05 × 3.66 m (10 × 12 ft)*

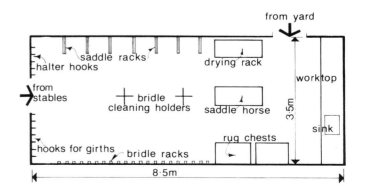

from yard

saddle racks

drying rack

halter hooks

from
stables

bridle
cleaning holders

saddle horse

worktop

3·5m

sink

hooks for girths

bridle racks

rug chests

8·5m

7 *Tack room plan and details. An adjoining rugs store is preferable to damp prone chests*

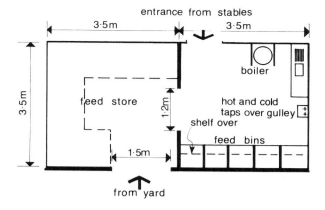

8 *Plan of feed store*

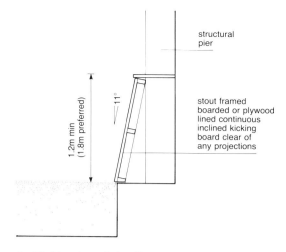

9 *Kicking board detail*

requirements for national competitions and horse grades A and B classes, refer to *Arenas* (see References and further advice). Show jumping makes very heavy demands on warm-up space and ancillary accommodation.

Dressage events require two arenas for affiliated competitions, **5**. Pony club mounted games, showing classes and indoor carriage driving events require large areas for warming up and collecting, usually outdoors.

A fundamental consideration is the proposed and permitted degree of use as an indoor competition venue, which may be limited by horse traffic generation, environmental controls, town and country planning and other space factors.

- Adequate traffic management and parking for many large vehicles (some with day-living units) may be required. A large enclosed parking area should be provided adjacent to the entrance into the warm-up areas (see below). This compound may require at least 0.4 hectares (1 acre) of well-lit, flat hardstanding. Permanent toilets are essential and showers may be useful.
- Changing rooms – riders and competitors normally change in their horse vehicle or caravan. Horses are 'tacked-up' at their vehicle or stable (see 'Stables' above).
- Warm-up area – see **2** and **5**; a practice ring is necessary to enable horses to exercise and jump one or two practice fences in an area preferably 60 × 20–30 m (30 × 20 m is the absolute minimum). Additionally, a collecting and demounting ring of approximately 30 × 20 m is required off the arena horse entrance. If the collecting ring is indoors the riding surface should be 'soft', preferably surfaced as in the arena.
- Drug testing and medical facilities may be required for top competitors (as for other sports); a dope-testing box for horse samples is part of a veterinary unit.

The most popular spectator equestrian sport indoors is show jumping.

- Spectator seating for up to 500 may be required.
- A standing only gallery near to the horse entrance is desirable for owners and grooms to watch their charges compete before quickly returning to the horse exit to aid dismounting.

2.3 Kicking boards

These are a basic functional requirement around all sides of the indoor school, **9**. A light coloured finish best reflects natural top light and provides a useful contrasting back-ground to facilitate observation of the horse's leg movements and riders' aids, particularly during transitions. The minimum height is normally 1.2 m (4 ft) and preferably 1.8 m (6 ft) and the boards are inclined outwards with an 11° rake from the vertical. In front of the spectators, kicking boards are reduced to a height of 914 mm.

Riding floor surface
The floor of the school is of great importance. Provided the surface of the ground is hard, flat and well drained, a covering of 50 or 75 mm fine sand well rolled in and mixed with commercial salt, to which 25 mm of wood shavings may be added from time to time, provides an excellent working surface. Care should be taken to ensure that the covering is not too deep at the start. The surface should be first rolled or ridden in, and then harrowed regularly. Unless watering facilities are easily available, the use of salt will avoid dust. Wood fibre specialist surfaces are also available, and fibresand surfaces are developing. It is strongly recommended that qualified advice should be sought at the outline design stage. See also References and further advice.

In the loose boxes, straw or wood chippings are normal bedding materials, and are thus a fire hazard. Organic proprietary surfaces which recycle as gardening compost or topping are also available.

Equipment
Fences and other obstacles are all free standing and require no floor fixtures or anchor points. However, the components of sets of schooling elements and show jumps are all heavy, vary in shape and size and require considerable storage space alongside the arena and preferably adjacent to each corner. There must also be ample space for tractors, harrows and trailers, **5**.

Markings
The only set pieces are for dressage as set out in **2**. Show jumping start and finish 'lines' are electronic timing beams of light and therefore mobile. If space allows it may be helpful to mark on the walls setting-out markers for six lanes for mounted games and start and finish lines.

2.4 Internal environment

For general details of environmental services requirements see Chapters 60 and 61.

The general space should be maintained at around 16°C and adequately ventilated (approximately 1.5 air changes per hour should be adequate).

Lighting

Lighting

Illumination is provided to enable the safe movement of both horse and rider appropriate to the standard of participation. The actions of both must be clearly discernible by spectators, riders, officials and trainers.

The illumination must be adequate to enable safe progress for horse and rider during all aspects of equestrian sport. It is important that a high degree of uniformity is achieved with sufficient luminaires to remove shadowing and glare around showjumping fences.

The eye level of a rider is typically between 2 and 2.5 m above ground level and may significantly increase when jumps are taken.

This should be considered when determining a suitable mounting height. Background illumination should be provided for spectator areas.

3 Arena polo

A new form of polo is becoming popular, called arena polo, which is played on an artificial surface, either indoors or outdoors. The game is normally played three-a-side but can be in pairs. The ball size should not be less than 315 mm (12.5 in) or more than 380 mm (15 in) in circumference and weight between 170 and 182 gram. In a balance test from 2.7 m (9 ft) on concrete at 70°F, the rebound should be a minimum of 1.37 m (4 ft 6 in) and maximum of 1.63 m (5 ft 4 in) at the inflation rate specified by the manufacturers.

The playing area should be at least 46 × 23 m (50 × 25 yds) and ideally 92 × 46 m (100 × 50 yds). The ground is surrounded by a boarded wall of not less than 1.83 m (6 ft) in height. The goals are 3 m (10 ft) in width and 3.66 m (12 ft) in height.

4 References and further advice

Arena Polo: Hurlingham Polo Association.

Biathlon: Modern Pentathlon Association of Great Britain: Showjumping and one other element from pentathlon.

British Horse Society (BHS).

Carriage driving: British Driving Society, BHS.

Dressage: BHS.

Table 84.1: Recommended illuminances

Application	Illuminance (lux)	Plane of measurement	Uniformity ratio (minimum /average)	Mounting height (m)
Schooling (supervised practice and training)				
Showjumping	300	Horizontal on ground	0.8	6 (min)
Dressage	200	Horizontal on ground	0.8	6 (min)
Competition				
Showjumping	500	Horizontal on ground	0.8	6 (min)
Dressage	300	Horizontal on ground	0.8	6 (min)

Horseball (mounted 'basketball'): British Horseball Association.

Mounted Games: The Pony Club (PC), BHS.

Outdoor riding and equestrianism: Volume 1, Chapter 69.

Penthalon: Modern Penthathlon Association of Great Britain. Five element sports, showjumping, shooting, running, fencing, swimming.

Riding establishments, schools and stables: BHS.

Riders with disabilities: Riding for the Disabled Association.

Show Jumping: British Show Jumping Association (BSJA) and Pony Club.

Showing: BHS, British Show Pony Society and breed associations.

Bishop, J M V and Quinton, M G, *Neufert Architects' Data*, Section 9 Riding Schools, 2nd international edn (1980).

BHS and East Sussex County Planning Department, *Horseriding in East Sussex* (December 1987) (fold-out fact sheet).

BHS publications, including: Lovatt Smith F D and BHS, *Notes on the Construction of All-weather Arenas and Surfaces* (1988).

Bradbeer, F, *New Metric Handbook*, Section 28 Stables, Architectural Press, Oxford.

Smith, P, *The Design and Construction of Stables and Ancillary Buildings*, J A Allen & Co, London (1986).

Sports Council, *Arenas*, Sports Council, London.

85
Roller skating and roller skate hockey

Christopher Harper

1 Critical factors

1.1 Rink location
The majority of skaters are in the 12–18 years age group and the selection of a site for a skating rink should therefore be influenced by the availability of good transport facilities. The Federation of Roller Skating (FRS) recommends two rules of thumb to assess the catchment area necessary to support a viable indoor roller rink: 220,000 people within a 5 mile radius of the site or 300,000 people within a 45 minute journey time. These figures are offered for general guidance and may have to be modified in the light of competing facilities, ease of access, age structure of the catchment population and similar factors. A preferred site will be close to where young people congregate and away from quiet residential areas.

1 *General skating. Photo: Richard Gardner*

1.2 Planning and accommodation
The sports falls into two main categories:

- Public recreational skating
- Skilled skating – which in turn divides into:
  (a) artistic skating (figures and dance),
  (b) speed skating,
  (c) roller skate hockey.

Artistic skating and roller hockey ideally require a rink size of 45 × 25 m (approx 148 × 82 ft) with a minimum size of 40 × 20 m (approx 131 × 67 ft). The maximum size for artistic skating at international level is 60 × 30 m (approx 197 × 98 ft). Speed skating takes places on a 200 m (approx 656 ft) oval track with 40 m (approx 131 ft) straights and end curves with an internal radius of 10 m (approx 33 ft), **2**.

The basic schedule of accommodation necessary to support a 45 × 25 m (approx 148 × 82 ft) rink is likely to be:

- Entrance foyer
- Skate shop
- Reception and office
- Clothes storage
- Skate store
- Boot change area
- First aid room
- Rink surround with seating
- General store
- Club room
- Cafeteria
- Plant room.

In addition, a bar may be provided for adult patrons. Permanent spectator seating may also be required. In assessing occupancy levels, one skater per 2.5–3.0 sq m (approx 27–32 sq ft) of rink area is the maximum level for reasonable freedom of movement. A figure of one person per 1 sq m (approx 10.7 sq ft) rink area may be used as a rule of thumb to cater for peak use with skaters packed on to the rink and calculate the maximum capacity of the building.

A primary planning requirement is to recognise the flow sequence from entrance to cloakroom or lockers, boot hire counter and changing benches, the rink and social areas, **3**. Another is to arrange accommodation so as to avoid bottlenecks and to permit supervision by the minimum number of staff.

Rink entrance
The rink entrance should be recessed or provided with a canopy to protect skaters assembling prior to admission. The layout and floor finishes must ensure that water and dirt do not get carried through to the skating surface. The reception/ticket counter should be detailed to provide security for staff, takings and equipment.

Manager's office
The office should be provided with a screened view over the rink and easily accessible from the entrance and control desk. A separate office for a secretary, or clerk, may also be considered. Good sound insulation is important.

Skate equipment shop
A small shop and display window is an essential amenity of roller rinks as well as being a source of income. It is not necessary to staff the shop on a permanent basis but it should be open at regular hours. Linking it with reception

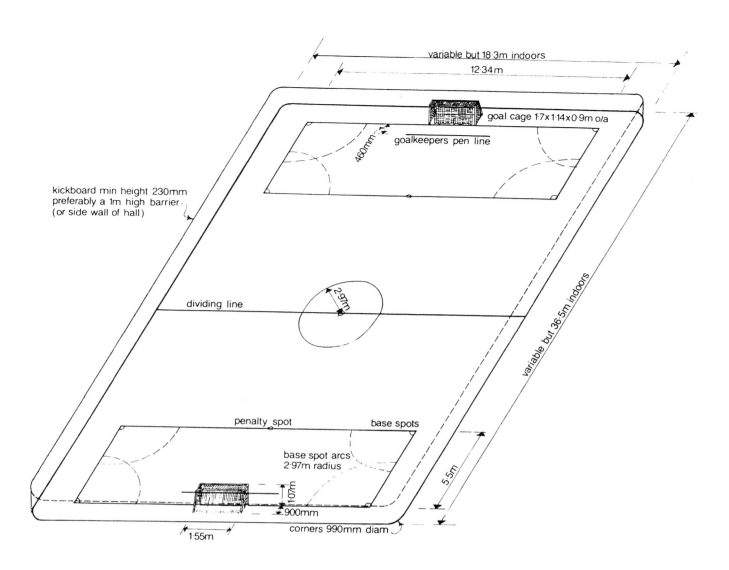

variable but 18·3m indoors

12·34m

goal cage 1·7 x 1·14 x 0·9m o/a

460mm

goalkeepers pen line

kickboard min height 230mm
preferably a 1m high barrier
(or side wall of hall)

variable but 36·5m indoors

dividing line

2·97m

penalty spot   base spots

base spot arcs
2·97m radius

5·5m

1·07m

900mm

1·55m

corners 990mm diam

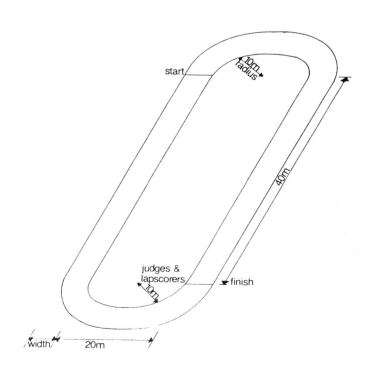

start

10m radius

40m

judges &
lapscorers

10m

finish

width   20m

2 *Dimensions for roller hockey (**a**) and speed skating (**b**).*

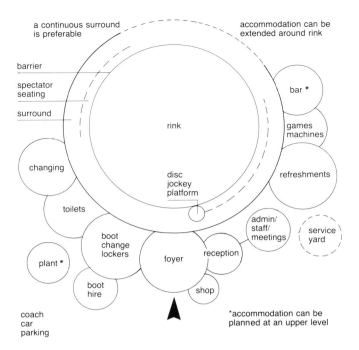

3 *Spatial relationship diagram*

can provide the opportunity for staffing economy. The shop may also be used for taking bookings for lessons with the rink instructors.

Cloakroom/personal storage
Locker storage for shoes, coats and bags must be provided close to the skate hire and changing areas with extra lockers for skaters with their own boots beside the rink surround.

Skate hire
The issue counter and skate store shelves should be arranged to permit quick, efficient issue by a minimum number of staff. The skate storage area should be equipped with a small work bench and tool cupboard for carrying out repairs such as replacing bearings or renewing boots.

Skate change area
Benches or seats should be located close to the hire counter, 4. Space standards must be adequate to ensure uninterrupted throughput at times of peak use when congestion is most likely to occur. One skate hire operative

4 *Boot changing near to self-service locker banks. Photo: C J Harper*

can issue between three and four pairs of boots a minute. An average time to change into roller boots may be 3 minutes, giving a relationship of between nine and twelve changing spaces to each issue point. Rinkside seating can be utilised by patrons bringing their own skates.

Public toilets
Male, female and disabled persons' toilets should be located adjacent to changing facilities with entrances readily visible to staff. All fittings must be of robust construction with concealed pipework and tough easily cleaned floor finishes with good slip resistant properties are essential.

Changing rooms
Changing should be sized for roller hockey teams and can also double as staff/instructors' and public changing rooms. Two rooms, each with a 4–5 m run of changing bench, are recommended. Snub pattern coat hooks and self-service lockers should be included, two per changing space. Showers, toilets and wash hand basins will be planned en-suite.

First aid room
Sprains (and occasionally fractures) are not uncommon. A first aid facility must be provided close to the rink and preferably with direct access to an ambulance layby.

Surround
The surround should extend along at least one side and one end of the rink for ease of access and for fire escape purposes and be separated from the rink with a one metre high barrier. It will also provide team bench and officials' space for roller hockey and for judges at artistic skating competitions. Overall seating provision must take account of skaters sitting out in addition to any changing benches in the surround area.

Cafeteria
The cafeteria should have direct access from the rinkside and a good view of the rink. It is an essential amenity and can contribute substantially to revenue. Planning should permit rapid service of drinks, snacks and possibly light meals. Seating should be arranged so as to be segregated from the general rink surround seating. A carefully co-ordinated layout of waste receptacles is essential to inhibit litter.

Bar
A bar can provide substantial income and will widen the rink's appeal as a social venue amongst adults. A first floor, or mezzanine location, emphasises that this area is for spectators and for skaters who have changed from boots into normal footwear. It also makes it easier for staff to control access to the licensed area.

Club/committee room
A multi-purpose space with adequate sound insulation is essential for club and staff meetings and interviews. It can also be used by instructors and off-duty staff. Fittings should comprise lockable cupboards and visual aids wall panels. A location close to a refreshments area is desirable. This room, or the manager's office, will be used by judges of artistic roller competitions and at speed skating meetings.

Music centre
A raised platform located at the rink side is required for a disc jockey or compere whose role is to control the public

skating programme and ensure safe and secure operation of the rink. The platform should be positioned at the start of one of the long straights and must have an unobstructed view of the entire rink and surrounding areas. It will be fitted with audio equipment and consoles for controlling the light, sound and public address systems, **5**.

Rink store
Storage is essential for rink equipment and other items. The storage schedule will include hockey goals, rink and surround cleaning equipment, portable furniture and barrier mats for short course speed skating. The mats must be secured in a fire proof compartment. A scissor lift for light fitting maintenance will also normally be included.

Spectator seating
Rinks of regional or national status will require additional spectator seating which can be either permanent or temporary. Bleacher (fold-out) seating may be particularly applicable as it can utilise the generous circulation spaces required for public skating.

1.3 Conversions
Many wide span buildings, particularly in urban locations, are potentially suitable for conversion to rink use. An unobstructed floor space is preferable but not essential. It will often be less costly to convert a suitable existing building for roller skating than to purpose-build a new rink, **6**.

Successful recreational rinks have been established in buildings where columns occur within the skating area

5 *The audio control platform: 'making a request'. Photo: C J Harper*

and, although not ideal, columns can be accepted providing they are in the central area and do not obstruct the perimeter skating circuit. They must be adequately protected by being surrounded with an 'island' or sheathed in resilient fire resistant material with a durable decorative cover. Ideally even recreational skating rinks should be rectangular in plan, preferably with length/width ratios of approximately 2:1. Rectangular plans automatically slow skaters at corners; square or circular rinks produce a monotonous gyratory skating pattern and are reputed to be more difficult to control. Free form rinks must be carefully designed to avoid cross-circulation and other potential collision points.

It is possible to stage roller events and championships in sports arenas or exhibition halls, particularly when large numbers of spectator seats are required. An arena floor, when cleaned and sealed, may be suitable for roller skating or alternatively a prefabricated floor of sealed particle board or hardwood panels can be laid.

When a roller skating programme is being considered for sports centres, the adequacy of circulation routes, the durability of the hall floor and the safety of wall detailing will need carefully to be assessed.

1.4 Outdoor roller rinks
Outdoor rinks are a popular attraction at many seaside and tourist centres. Skate surfaces are generally concrete terrazzo, **7**, or asphalt but as a flat level surface is essential storm water has to be dispersed by stewards using squeegees direct to perimeter drains located behind the barrier line.

1.5 Roller skating in multi-sports spaces
New sports centres which include roller skating in the design brief, **8**, should incorporate the following features:

- Foyers large enough to accommodate skaters assembling prior to the session.
- Lockers which are easily accessible to skaters. This means locating some or all clothes storage lockers on a circulation route between the foyer and sports hall entrance.
- Toilets with direct access from a main circulation route and not within changing rooms.
- All areas accessible to skaters should be clearly defined for ease of supervision and designed with appropriate finishes. Handhold rails should be considered and skirtings are essential.
- Lighting and sound are important to the success of public skating. The engineering brief for the sports hall should include appropriate audio, and 'mood' lighting systems, or have sufficient services provision for temporary installations.
- Ventilation rates which take account of this strenuous and popular activity.
- Skate storage and hire facilities within the sports hall store.
- Demountable barriers to define a boot changing and sitting out zone at the end of the sports hall.

1.6 Rink floor construction
A successful rink floor must satisfy the following performance criteria:

- Sufficient frictional resistance to give traction to the skate and prevent lateral slipping. Too high a frictional resistance will cause wheels to 'stick' and will reduce glide distance.

6 *Rollerbury: conversion of a former railway goods depot, Bury St Edmunds*

7 *Skating outdoors on terrazzo at Great Yarmouth. Photo: C J Harper*

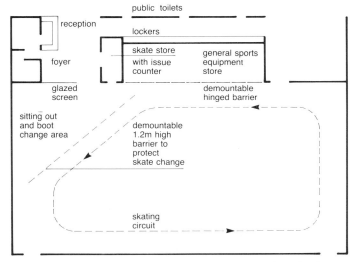

8 *Plan of a sports hall with modifications for roller skating: a SASH centre*

- Minimal rolling resistance to permit free forward and backwards movement.
- Resistance to surface deformation – a smooth, level surface is essential.
- Resistance to wear through abrasion, tearing and impact with continual tracking around the perimeter zone of the rink.

The development of plastic roller skate wheels has enabled several types of surface to meet these requirements and cater for both recreational and skilled skating. These include the following.

- *Hardwood*: Maple floors are the preferred specialist surface. Narrow strips should be laid so that skaters travel with the direction of grain, preferably with a fan or rotunda configuration at the ends of the rink to prolong board life. The surface should be constructed on a solid base to prevent drumming and ensure constant support. With batten supports it is advisable to fill the inter-batten spaces with rock wool to provide sound damping with board ends tongued and grooved to joinery standard or supported on cross-battens. Adequate movement tolerances must be incorporated during construction between boards and particularly around the rink perimeter. North American Maple has been widely and successfully used for top specification rinks but European beech with similar durable qualities may also be considered. Maintenance consists of washing and occasional sanding. The application of sealers may be considered but is not essential.
- *Terrazzo*: terrazzo tiles provide an excellent and extremely smooth surface for roller skating for both indoor and outdoor rinks. As with hardwood, these floors are of good appearance and are particularly popular in Mediterranean countries where they are also used as a general multi-sports surface. In indoor rinks terrazzo surfaces can be sealed to prevent dusting and reduce maintenance. Cleaning materials must be specified with care to prevent these surfaces from becoming dangerously slippery.
- *Concrete*: a plain power floated finish to a dense reinforced concrete slab is an inexpensive and acceptable roller surface. Granite particles added to the concrete as a topping or in an applied screed provide a most durable surface which can be decorated, if required, with heavy duty acrylic or epoxy paint. A paint or seal is essential for indoor concrete floors to prevent dusting.
- *Asphalt*: good quality asphalt flooring is another inexpensive roller surface, most applicable to outdoor rinks. Another type of finish, suitable for low cost roller rink surfaces, is a screed of modified bitumen with sand/cement and granite aggregate, developed originally for paletted warehouse floors. It is laid by trowel on a concrete slab and can be finished with roller applied epoxy, polyurethane or coloured polymer finishes.
- *Composition block*: blocks or tiles manufactured from wood particles and cement have been used extensively as a heavy duty flooring. Weekly maintenance involves brushing and washing while sealing must be carried out methodically at regular intervals to prevent dusting, a potential problem even with modern skate wheels. The selection of a suitable sealing fluid is therefore essential.
- *Polymeric floors*: these floors, laid as a plastic cast on concrete, are hard and durable with relatively low maintenance characteristics. A variety of colours are available.
- *Vinyl and plastic materials*: a wide range of sheet floorings are available but many products have frictional levels that are too high for skating. Rubber flooring is an example of an unsuitable finish.

Floor markings for hockey and set figure patterns can be laid in a number of ways. On timber surfaces it is considered best to stain on the markings with a water soluble dye. On other surfaces hard wearing paint finishes may be used and on composition block floors inlaid polymer markings offer the most maintenance free solution. If taped markings are used they should be protected with a clear polyurethane finish but will still require periodic replacement.

With any skating surface it is essential that the rink and surrounding floor surfaces are kept clean and grit free and patrons' own skates are clean and in good condition. Black toe stops (and black hockey balls) will mark surfaces and should be excluded in favour of coloured accessories.

1.7 Other floor and surface finishes

All areas accessible to skaters must be surfaced with high friction material to restrict movement. A synthetic carpet with pile or a coir mat will slow skaters down immediately at rink exits. Hard wearing synthetic carpet may be considered for all rink side and circulation areas.

Alternative surfaces which may be considered, particularly in areas where liquid spillage is likely to occur, are welded synthetic flooring with non-slip characteristics. All internal fair faced masonry walls should be clear sealed or painted. This is important as hard particles of dust abraded from the surface will quickly break down protective rink floor sealants. Skirtings are essential throughout, either applied or formed by the floor finish swept up to 200–250 mm (approx 8–10 in) high. Hand hold rails should also be considered both for safety and to reduce the frequency of maintenance.

1.8 Specialist fittings

In detailing rinks the designer must remember that many normal vertical dimensional requirements for users wearing skates are increased 50–80 mm (approx 2–3 in). This influences not only skirting height but also the height of counters, tables, sanitary fittings and even door openings.

Rink barrier

Rinks must be surrounded with a barrier one metre minimum high with tightly radiussed corners. It must be designed to resist high horizontal impact loads but may be of either open or solid construction. Open post and rail barriers are preferable and are acceptable for roller hockey when backed with heavy duty netting, **9**.

Access must be provided opposite the skate change and refreshment areas and exits provided adjacent to fire escape doors. In hockey rinks openings in the barrier should have lift off panels or gates designed to open outwards through 180° and be secured with drop bolts. All fire escape doors from the building must have ramped and not stepped thresholds.

The barrier must have a flush internal face with a smooth continuous capping rail. Demountable barriers have to be detailed to preserve these characteristics and ensure stability. Additional protection is required at the ends and preferably also at the sides of the rink for roller hockey. Suspended tracked netting or polycarbonate panels mounted to a minimum height of 1.5 m (approx 5 ft) above the barrier are the usual methods of providing this safety screening against balls which can travel at 130 kph (80 mph).

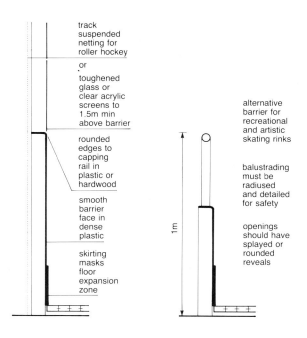

9 *The rink barrier*

Skate issue counter and store
Roller boots are stored on tilting open shelves or in racks, slatted and open backed to allow thorough cross ventilation. The hire counter must be detailed with an impact resistant, easily maintained finish and set on a recessed plinth.

1.9 Internal environment

For general details of engineering services recommendations refer to Chapters 60 and 61.

The rink designer must strive to create an agreeable, lively interior combined with durable finishes. The amount of glazing to the rink hall should be strictly controlled both to prevent solar gain, excessive heat loss and distraction to users and enable the interior to be blacked out for disco and roller dance.

Rink lighting
Lighting will normally consist of a layout of fittings to give uniform, overall average illuminance of 300 lux together with an emergency lighting system. Where high level competition and/or competitive roller hockey is be be catered for the average illuminance may need to be increased to 500 lux. In addition a system of coloured lights capable of being synchronised with dance music is an essential feature of roller rinks. Where competitions are held and matches played, higher lighting standards will be required with light intensities to give an appropriate modelling of participants for spectator viewing. Refer to the Ice Skating section of the *CIBSE Lighting Guide LG4: Sports*, for recommended levels. Lighting design in ancillary areas must be appropriate to the function of each particular space. For example, the boot store lighting layout should be centred on aisles between storage racks to give good shadow-free illumination of the fittings. Major rinks may televise events and where installed illumination levels fall short of TV requirements additional power sockets should be installed to permit additional specialist lighting.

Heating and mechanical ventilation
Heating and ventilation must be appropriate to a strenuous activity in a space with high occupancy levels. The building envelope should be well insulated and the use of glazing carefully controlled. An overall heating level of 12–15°C will be adequate for the skating area but higher levels will be required for the spectator and off-rink areas. Mechanical ventilation is essential to replace vitiated air and remove body odours, particularly important in a rink where most skaters wear normal and not sports clothing. Ventilation rates must also be assessed to control humidity levels and maintain reasonable conditions of comfort in summertime. Specific ancillary areas should be heated and ventilated in accordance with their function.

In addition there is the need to heat and ventilate effectively the skate boot store to ensure that boots dry out between hires and odours are removed at source.

Audio and acoustics
Interior finishes, particularly at high level, should be selected to reduce reverberation time. Good quality sound is particularly important for artistic skating where orchestral music must be reproduced accurately and heard clearly by the performers. A reverberation time of between one and two seconds is recommended. High volume dance and disco music is also required and the design of the building envelope, together with applied acoustic treatments, should minimise sound leakage.

Signage
Signage is most important. Apart from adding vitality to the interior, good graphics are essential for information in a space which is often dimly lit when most crowded. Other areas of applied design may be suspended ceiling baffles to reduce reverberation time and the possible inclusion of carefully controlled advertising panels, illuminated if desired.

1.10 Rink exterior

The exterior should emphasise the rink's function as a recreational building even if the design is based, for example, on a light industrial building type. Good graphics, the use of colour and lighting will all contribute to an animated exterior with emphasis concentrated on the main entrance. Low level finishes in trafficked areas must be resistant to damage and site lighting should be positioned to ensure safe passage and easy control of the building's immediate environs after dark.

Car parking will be to the standard required by local planning authorities and will be influenced by occupancy levels, the quality of nearby public transport services and the availability of existing car parking space. Coach parties will account for a substantial proportion of patrons in some rinks and it is essential to provide some coach parking bays on or adjacent to the rink site.

Shooting ranges

Christopher Harper

1 The requirements of shooting

It is essential that the possible dangers inherent in any rifle/pistol range are fully realised early in the design stage. They arise not only from the potentially lethal aspect of shooting and the need to prevent ricochet of bullets but also from lead pollution, present to some degree in all ranges.

Shooting with cartridge firearms is the only projectile sport which cannot take place in a suitably screened common sports area. Air gun competitions can be held in a cordoned off area of a multi-sports space as long as the firing points back on to any other activity. However, if shooting is among the sports being planned for in a sports centre, consideration must always be given to providing a separate, specialist range.

1.1 Special considerations
Special attention must be given to:

- Avoiding ledges or other dust traps
- Specifying easily cleaned finishes
- Providing a high standard of mechanical ventilation to remove contamination as it is produced.

For specialist details, refer to the National Small Bore Rifle Association (NSRA) or the National Rifle Association (NRA) who will also advise on design matters.

1.2 Statutory requirements
Apart from the need to obtain planning permission and building regulation approval, rifle/pistol ranges need the approval of the Ministry of Defence, although this does not apply to air guns. This approval is sought through the NSRA or NRA who should be consulted at the earliest design stage. In addition, it is recommended that the local Environmental Health Department and the Health and Safety Executive are consulted on current methods of combating lead pollution.

1.3 Structure
All internal projections should be avoided – columns or piers should occur within the wall thickness or be external to the range. Walls and ceilings must be proofed against rifle and pistol shots within an area surrounding the targets; this is particularly important if any lightweight or modular form of construction system is being contemplated for conversion to range use. Downstand beams can be lined with acoustically absorbent materials forming baffles to diminish reverberation time. Any steel beams or roof/ceiling components occurring within the target area must be lined with a minimum of 25 mm timber, on 25 mm battens, to avoid backsplash (ricochet of stray bullets). The thermal insulating properties of the structure should also meet any minimum statutory requirements.

1.4 Surrounding surfaces or enclosure
- *Floor* – no special requirements.
- *Walls* – the side walls should be flush faced and preferably be of imperforable construction. The target end wall must be imperforable and 'proofed' against occasional stray shots. If the end of the side walls come within the 7° flank of lines of fire they too should be proofed. Any projections from the wall faces which could produce ricochets should also be timber faced.
- *Ceilings* – All vulnerable projections, including light fittings, should be protected if they are within the flank lines of fire.

1.5 Armoury
If firearms are kept on the premises they will require separate storage in an armoury. The armoury can either be designed as a walk-in store with steel cabinets for each club's equipment or as a series of separate cells opening off a common area. There are no statutory requirements governing the construction of armouries and designers are therefore advised to consult with the NSRA or the NRA for current design and specification recommendations. The construction must be agreed with the local police during the design stage. Firearms certificates are issued to clubs or individuals and normally specify the arrangements for safe storage of firearms and ammunition at an identified location.

1.6 Special fittings
The bullet catcher and target mount must be designed to absorb shots and not cause ricochets or splashback. In some instances an absorbent material is placed behind the target within the bullet catcher. Tables or benches of approximately 1 m (3.3 ft) high are required for pistol shooting.

1.7 Internal environment
For general details of environmental services recommendations refer to Chapters 60 and 61.

- *Heating* – 13–16°C at and behind firing line.
- *Ventilation* – design of an efficient extract system is of the utmost importance. In multi-sports centres, the system should be completely independent from the centre's general ventilation provisions and include the following features:
  (a) Air input at the firing end of sufficient velocity and through grilles of sufficient size to ensure thorough removal of vapourised and minute lead particles. The intake can incorporate heater elements.
  (b) Extracts at the target end creating a down range air velocity, discharging into a safe, external area via filters.
  (c) The range extraction system should be fitted with an overrun, so that ventilation can continue after firing has ceased. The fans should also be switched on the same circuit as the target lights (and range warning lights) to ensure that shooting cannot take place without all safety systems being brought into operation.
- *Lighting* – targets can be illuminated from the floor or ceiling by spotlights or fluorescent tubes in inclined reflectors, but the lighting must be protected from shots. Illuminance on the targets should be between 700 and 100 lux. General lighting is required to provide 200 lux within the range and 200 lux on and behind the firing lines. The lights should be individually switched so that levels can be altered to suit competition requirements. It

is preferable that walls and ceilings are decorated in light colours.

1.8 Floor markings
The different firing lines should be painted or taped on the floor.

1.9 Club ancillary facilities
For general details of ancillary accommodation, planning and specification refer to Chapters 95 to 103 inclusive in this volume.

The range should be planned so as to be entirely separate from other accommodation which could include a foyer, male, female and disabled persons' toilet, an armoury store, office/club meetings room, and a cleaner's store.

2 References and further advice
National Small Bore Rifle Association (NSRA).
The National Rifle Association.

**Squash Rackets Association and
Kit Campbell**

1 Background information

Squash evolved from the earlier game of rackets in the 19th century, primarily in England. Players occupy the same area of the rectangular court (there is no net) and strike the ball alternately towards a front or play wall to hit it above the playboard or 'tin' and below an out of court line, **1**. The ball may be hit towards any of the four walls of the court - that is, directly towards the front, back or either side wall - provided it hits the front wall before the floor.

There are two versions: 'softball', played in most countries in the world, and 'hardball', played in North America. The courts are slightly different with the hardball court being slightly longer and narrower and having slightly different markings. The hardball game is slowly giving way to the softball and most projects will involve only softball or international courts. The US Squash Association should be contacted for details of hardball courts; this chapter deals only with those for softball.

1.1 Types of court

Most courts are permanent structures although the final rounds of professional events are now often played on demountable glass or 'Perspex' courts, **2**. Traditional plastered masonry construction – provided the plaster finish is in good condition – is generally regarded as providing the best playing conditions but there are several prefabricated or panel court systems on the market which also give good playing conditions. Traditionally courts have been provided with a viewing balcony or gallery at first floor level behind the back wall but since the mid-1970s increasing numbers have had a toughened glass back wall, **3**.

While for several decades most squash has been singles, there is growing interest in doubles using a court which is 1.2 m (4 ft) wider than for singles. Many such courts are likely to be purpose-built although one manufacturer offers a motorised sliding wall which allows singles courts to be converted to doubles or for other activities such as aerobics.

There is also growing interest in a 'micro-court' for juniors (a response by squash to the popularity of short tennis) which is designed to be demountable and so is not discussed in this chapter.

Squash provides intensive exercise within a short time; most courts are booked for periods of 30–45 minutes. In Australia and the UK its popularity increased dramatically in the 1970s; in Europe and many other parts of the world significant growth took place slightly later. It remains one of the few sports in which many facilities are run commercially, particularly in continental Europe, North America, the Far East and Australia.

1.2 Levels of provision

Various provision guidelines have been suggested from time to time but the need for squash courts, as all other indoor sports facilities, relates primarily to local patterns of demand and fashion. Providers should consult the appropriate national governing body for up to date information. The most useful and consistent guideline is that clubs should aim for about 100-125 members per court. Below this number a club may not be viable; above it members will probably find it difficult to book sufficient court time to justify their membership fees.

In facilities designed to serve the needs of small communities a squash court can also be used for other activities such as table tennis or aerobics.

1.3 Court capacity

Estimating court usage is the essential first step in assessing revenue and viability. The peak hours at most centres – in which about 80–90% of total use is likely to be concentrated – are midweek lunchtimes, midweek evenings (Fridays usually less so than Mondays to Thursdays), and Saturdays and Sundays from about 11.00–18.00. This gives about 45 peak hour use per week or a total of about 55 hours total use per week. Multiplying this figure by the income per hour (taking account of the length of the booking period) will allow gross income to be estimated.

1.4 Planning

The following factors should be assessed in considering squash provision:

- Objectives of the scheme (social and/or financial)
- Location
- Size of population and catchment area – present and future
- Nature of population and its age and socio-economic structure
- Existing facilities within the area
- Availability of land
- Methods of promotion available
- Staffing requirements
- Provision of additional facilities (sport or social).

In the UK, promoters should consult the national or regional Sports Council and the appropriate squash association.

1.5 Location

The vast majority of squash players are between the ages of about 12 and 45 years, with participation generally being highest amongst males in their twenties and those in non-manual occupations. Car ownership is normally high amongst squash players and therefore accessibility by car and the provision of car parking are important. This can increase the amount of land required for a centre significantly.

With very few exceptions, squash centres are not highly profitable. Land costs are an important element in development costs and in many countries it is fairly common for centres to be provided within industrial units, on suburban sites or as part of complexes in urban fringe locations.

1.6 Car parking

A very rough guide to the number of car parking spaces which should be provided for players at a squash centre is six times the number of courts. This factor is derived by allowing two players per court and assuming that three

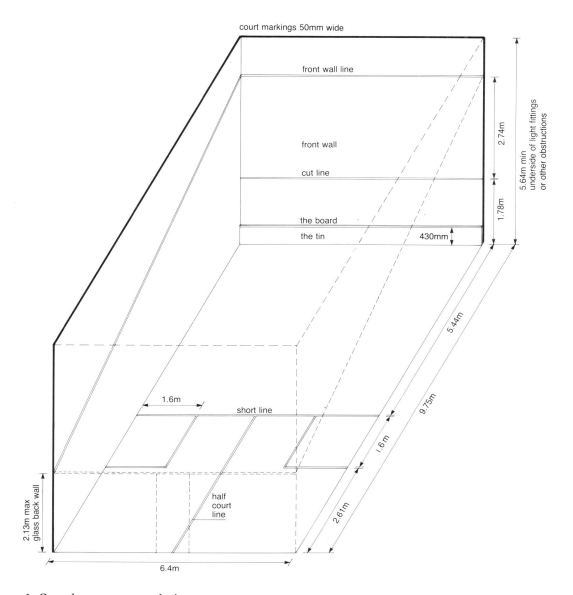

court markings 50mm wide

front wall line

front wall

cut line

the board

the tin

430mm

2.74m

1.78m

5.64m min underside of light fittings or other obstructions

5.44m

9.75m

1.6m

short line

1.6m

half court line

2.61m

2.13m max glass back wall

6.4m

1 *Squash court – general view*

2 *Demountable court with four transparent walls used for the later rounds of major professional and other competitions*

pairs of players will be present in the centre at any one time – those changing before playing, those on court and those changing after playing. In addition there will be a need for additional parking for social users, spectators and staff.

In some areas a slightly lower level of provision may be acceptable because players may travel two to a car or use other forms of transport.

2 Types of centre

Squash centres can be grouped into two broad categories:

- Commercial centres
- Local or community facilities.

2.1 Commercial centres

Commercial centres usually depend for their viability on the economies of scale in operating costs which are possible when six, eight, ten or more courts are grouped together. Because a singles court is only occupied by two players at a time, however, the total hourly throughput of centres with only squash courts is low. European squash centres, in particular, tend to have a range of other facilities which both encourage players to stay in the club

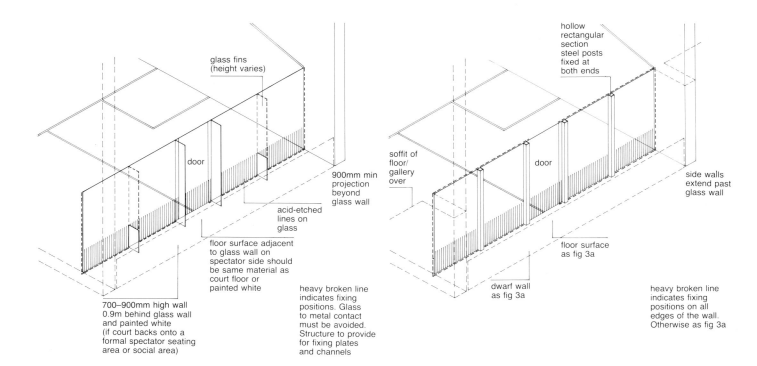

Labels in left diagram:
glass fins (height varies)

door

900mm min projection beyond glass wall

acid-etched lines on glass

floor surface adjacent to glass wall on spectator side should be same material as court floor or painted white

heavy broken line indicates fixing positions. Glass to metal contact must be avoided. Structure to provide for fixing plates and channels

700–900mm high wall 0.9m behind glass wall and painted white (if court backs onto a formal spectator seating area or social area)

Labels in right diagram:
hollow rectangular section steel posts fixed at both ends

soffit of floor/ gallery over

door

side walls extend past glass wall

floor surface as fig 3a

dwarf wall as fig 3a

heavy broken line indicates fixing positions on all edges of the wall. Otherwise as fig 3a

3 *Glass back walled court*

for a reasonable length of time after playing or visit it for other activities such as fitness training or sauna.

Squash can also be an integral component of hotel-linked or commercial sports clubs. In addition to squash courts and fitness areas, these clubs may have a small swimming pool, indoor or outdoor tennis courts, an aerobics/dance studio, snooker room, a creche and a bar and high quality refreshment facilities. They will also have a good range of support accommodation including management offices and a shop or display counter linked to reception. Most users of these centres travel by car and therefore adequate parking is essential.

In commercial centres glass back walls are usually the preferred form of provision for most courts.

2.2 Local or community facilities
Local facilities for squash can take several forms, including:

- As an integral part of a local authority sports or leisure centre
- Linked to other club facilities, for example a rugby or tennis club
- As part of community facilities in a joint use centre on a school site.

Local competitions require a minimum of two to three courts although local demand may require additional courts. If they cannot be provided at the outset space should be allowed on site for future expansion. Space for expansion is in any case always desirable .

2.3 Competition facilities
As in other sports, competitive squash covers many levels of play from club leagues to world championships. Competition courts are exactly the same size as those for local use but more courts may be required and the specification will normally be upgraded in terms of:

- Lighting
- Spectator facilities
- TV facilities.

It will normally be sensible to plan a hierarchy of competition facilities over an area rather than try to make every centre suitable for major events. The range of accommodation required in competition centres is normally dictated by the level of competition it is planned to stage. To cater for high level competitions it is usually necessary to provide between four and eight courts. Temporary spectator accommodation for between 50 and 100 people can be provided at low cost behind a glass back wall in social or circulation areas. Where larger numbers of spectators are to be accommodated tiered seating and therefore greater headroom will be required. Typically space for 200–300 spectators will be required behind most designated spectator courts and this will be suitable for the preliminary rounds of major tournaments.

The later rounds of many world, national and professional championships are now staged in glass or 'Perspex' courts, often erected specially for the purpose in conference centres or exhibition halls. These courts allow viewing through all four walls and have the twin advantages of providing accommodation for a large number of spectators and making effective TV coverage possible.

In a limited number of specialist competition centres a permanent 'centre court' has been provided with either three or four glass walls. Where such courts are under consideration there should be close liaison over their installation with both manufacturers and TV companies.

2.4 Accommodation for match officials
The development of glass walls and high profile professional events has increased the popularity of the game as a spectator sport. There are also many local competitions and league matches. Squash matches are controlled by a referee and a marker, although for local events one official

may perform both roles. The officials must be able to see every part of the court and all of the playing surfaces; hear the play; and communicate with the players.

If there is a gallery behind the court (see below), the match officals will stand or sit in in the front row of spectators and there will be no difficulty. There are also the advantages of a gallery for casual viewing and enabling small groups of players to be given instruction in the game, although the problem of the coach outside the court speaking to the players inside does remain. The gallery should be open to the court.

The positioning of match officials in glass back wall courts is not so simple. With a freestanding glass back wall the best arrangement is to have them on a platform immediately above and behind the centre of it, accessed by a ladder. This provides the minimum obstruction to the view of spectators and TV cameras and it is better than forcing the officials to sit well behind the wall where they are remote from the play and players. In courts where the glass wall is taken up to ceiling level and therefore encloses the court fully the officials sit behind the wall, sometimes on a high chair. In such courts it is necessary to provide a microphone and speaker system to allow the officials to be heard by the players.

3 The design of squash centres

The main factors which determine the eventual layout and cost of a squash centre are:

- The number of courts and range of other sports and ancillary facilities required
- Whether formal spectator courts are required
- Whether to have an 'open plan' or 'cellular' layout of courts and other accommodation; the former consists primarily of glass back walled courts immediately adjacent to and viewed from social areas while in the latter type of centre the squash courts and social areas are separated
- Whether to have one or two (or more) levels: single storey solutions tend to have a more open and relaxed atmosphere
- Making provision for expansion.

The key decision, however, is the number of glass back walled courts. Glass back walls can be thought of in several ways:

- As a means of providing a facility for spectators – in which case it is sensible to provide tiered seating behind the wall
- As a means of of creating a more informal club layout and design than is possible with fully enclosed courts
- As a means of allowing casual viewing (for example from social areas)
- As an aid to club/centre supervision and control.

While glass walls are more expensive than plastered masonry or solid panels their use can often result in cost savings if it is not necessary to provide an upper floor and staircases.

Casual viewing through glass back walls can take place from refreshment areas, wide circulation areas or even from other activity spaces. The factors to consider are:

- Will there be distraction to the squash players?
- Will the circulation areas be obstructed?
- Will the lighting and noise of squash courts be a distraction to other areas?

In the UK the most common solution for buildings containing a number of courts is to have the majority with a solid or traditional back wall (offering privacy for beginners) and one or two glass back walled courts with spectator facilities. In other parts of Europe at many centres most of the courts have glass back walls and a more 'open plan' arrangement which both makes supervision easy and creates a lively atmosphere.

4 The design of courts

4.1 Dimensions
The clear height should be measured from the finished floor level to the underside of the lowest projection, normally the light fittings. The World Squash Federation (WSF) requires a minimum clear height of 5.64 m (approx 18.5 ft) in courts to be used for championship play and this standard has been adopted by most countries.

4.2 Types of construction
The principal methods of construction for squash courts are:

- Solid walls with plastered or similar surfaces
- Prefabricated panel systems.

All of the panel systems can be erected and installed in an existing building; they are entirely of dry construction and, if necessary, insulation can be incorporated to minimise condensation.

Solid walls with plastered surfaces This type of construction is the most commonly used and consists of a dense inner leaf usually at least 200 mm (approx 8 in) thick and a 112 mm (approx 4.5 in) outer leaf with a 50 mm (approx 2 in) cavity. Building and other regulations can determine the thickness and detailing and in the UK court walls have to comply with *Codes of Practice CP 111/121* or *BS 5628 Part 1: 1978: Code of Practice Structural Use of Unreinforced Masonry*. Professional advice on any proposed structure should be obtained from an engineer.

The inner (court side) face of the structural wall should be continuous and uninterrupted by changes of material, construction or movement joints. This is necessary to provide a consistent backing material for plastering. A common mistake is to incorporate structural columns or beams in a masonry wall. This invariably leads to cracking of the plaster finish and should be avoided.

For brickwork clay commons should be used but never in kiln-fresh condition (see *BR Digests 65* and *66* in relation to irreversible moisture expansion). Bricks for internal court walls should be stacked dry under cover on site for at least seven days before being used.

Dense aggregate concrete blocks to BS 6073: Part 1 having a minimum compressive strength of 7 N/sq mm may be used as an alternative to bricks providing they have undergone their initial shrinkage and are not susceptible to moisture movement. The Cement and Concrete Association should be contacted for details of suppliers of suitable blocks, construction details and the specification of suitable mortars. Lightweight blocks or bricks of a shrinkable material are not suitable and should not be used because failure of the plaster playing finish will result. Like bricks, blocks should be stored dry until used.

Timber or steel-framed courts faced with small prefabricated panels A number of systems on the market use prefabricated panels of various thicknesses which are small and light enough to be man-handled (usually about 2.4 x 1.2 m or 8 x 4 ft). They are secret fixed to a self-supporting timber or steel frame or strapped to a structural wall or frame. Most are designed for the dry fitting out of a weatherproof shell but there is one system which is intended to be clad to provide a complete dry construction building on a prepared site slab.

The most common panel systems use a particle board corestock faced on both sides with a melamine veneer which is claimed to be very durable. The panels are grooved on all four edges and tightly butted together. They are aligned and fixed to the framing using loose tongues or 'Z' or 'H' metal sections which ensure their accurate alignment and a flush playing surface.

A more recent development utilizes a melamine type finish on a resin based core material using a 'Z' or channel section steel supporting system. The panels are held in position by steel clips which are locked into horizontal members fixed to the steel supports.

A further system consists of 176×50 mm (approx 7×2 in) redwood timber frames at 600 mm (approx 2 ft) centres for outside walls and 150×50 mm (approx 6×2 in) redwood timber frames at 600 mm (approx 2 ft) centres for partition walls between the courts. The courts are lined on the inside with a sandwich panel faced with 12 mm (approx 0.5 in) fully compressed asbestos cement sheeting with 2 mm (approx 0.08 in) of plastic sound-deadening material; there is also a balancing layer on the inside against the framing. The external walls are lined with fibre glass and clad externally with masonry, timber or profiled metal sheeting. The timber frames to the playwalls are built in jigs in a workshop and delivered to site ready for erection.

Gaps are left between sheets which are sealed with a nitrile sealant after erection. This material is soft to apply but hardens within 48 hours enabling the joints to be smoothed off with a carborundum wheel.

Large compressed wood chip or fibre based panels on 'Z' or channel sections   There is also a large panel system using 'Z' or channel section vertical framing with sole and head members, clad on both faces with a compressed woodchip or fibre based core. After erection the voids are filled with a silica sand to provide a solid background. The outer faces of the panels are then painted with a resin based paint. Movable walls operated by overhead electric motors acting on steel framing are an optional feature.

4.3 Finishes

Wall finishes
The walls of the court below the out of court lines are playing surfaces and must be true, hard, smooth and plumb. Ideally they should be white or a very light colour, able to withstand impact without sustaining damage and absorb a certain amount of condensation. They should also have a smooth finish in order to minimise marking by the ball and rackets and facilitate cleaning.

Walls above the playing surface should also be white or light coloured and of even texture. There should be little change of contrast because players view the ball against both the 'out of court' areas and the playing surfaces.

The heating and ventilation of squash courts to reduce the risk of condensation is of prime importance and is covered below.

Specialist plasters
There are several specialist plaster finishes available on the market. As a general rule, the plaster suppliers either provide an application service themselves or have designated 'approved applicators' trained in the use of their material; sometimes a guarantee is offered. It will rarely be desirable to use a non-specialist contractor and normally it is sensible to contact the plaster manufacturer to check the specification requirements for the structural walling material before a court is built.

The main materials are available in most parts of the world and include:

- Specialist plasters based on a retarded plaster formulation containing polymeric additives. This is the most commonly used group of finishes. Most materials in this group have the advantage that the base screed and finishing coat may be applied the same day ensuring a good bond between the two coats. As the plasters are self-coloured they should not be painted; this also helps to retain a limited amount of moisture absorption capability.
- A cement-based screed with fine white aggregate and glass fibre. This product is applied in two coats, the base coat 8 mm (approx 0.33 in) thick followed by a finish coat of a finer material 2 mm (approx 0.1 in) thick which has fewer glass fibres and a white marble aggregate. It is essential that the material is cured in accordance with the manufacturer's recommendations.
- A resin coated white sand and white cement with additives.

Glass back walls
Glass back walls should be 12 mm thick toughened glass with a central glass door. They are installed after plastering is complete and there are several types available, the main ones being:

- The freestanding two-panel or 'Championship' wall with a 2134 mm (approx 7 ft) high panel either side of a central door. The panel is supported by toughened glass fins which are cantilevered up from the structural floor and fixed to it using metal angles. The court is open to the area behind it over the top of the wall.
- The four panel or 'Club' wall. This is fixed on all four edges and therefore requires a continuous soffit fixing at the top, normally at a height of 2134 mm (7 ft) from court floor level. There are also rectangular hollow steel section supports in place of the fins on a freestanding wall which require a fixing at top and bottom.
- A hinged back wall which can be swung open to open the court up to the adjacent viewing area.

The method of installation must avoid glass to metal or concrete contact and provision will have to be made in the structure for fixing plates and channels. Wall manufacturers should be consulted when courts are designed. For the two-panel type it is also important to ensure that it will be possible to move 2.3×2.8 m (approx 7.5×9.2 ft) glass panels into the building to the back of the court; they are too large to go through a standard single doorway.

Both types of wall can be extended to a height greater than 2134 mm (7 ft) if required by the use of composite glass panels. If this is done the back wall line is marked horizontally on the glass with red tape at a height of 2134 mm (7 ft) to the bottom edge.

In order to make it as easy as possible for players to sight the dark ball against the base of the glass walls in some types acid etched vertical white lines are formed on the glass. Other types have a grid of white lines on the inside surface. Both provide adequate playing conditions provided:

- The lighting has the same intensity inside the court and immediately behind it. This prevents the glass rear wall acting as a mirror when viewed from inside the court.
- The floor finish immediately outside the wall is either of the same material as the court floor or similarly light in colour for a distance of about 900 mm (approx 3 ft). Where the court is adjacent to a formal spectator or busy social area a light coloured upstand board or dwarf wall 700–900 mm (approx 2.5–3 ft) high should be positioned up to 900 mm (approx 3 ft) behind the wall.

In formal spectator courts it is also desirable that the side walls of the court should extend about 900 mm beyond the glass wall and be finished in the same colour as the court walls. Alternatively, hinged folding or removable screens can be provided.

The floor

The floor should be hard, smooth, true, as light as possible in colour and able to absorb a limited amount of moisture such as drips of perspiration from players. Semi-sprung light coloured hardwood is generally regarded as the best finish but must have even grain and be splinter-free. The floor strips or boards should always be laid parallel to the side walls.

A typical flooring specification is 25 mm (approx 1 in) nominal hardwood tongued and grooved strips, secret nailed to 50 × 50 mm (2 × 2 in) softwood battens on resilient pads of rubber or polyurethane foam laid on the subfloor. First grade Canadian Rock Maple is laid on battens spaced at 300 mm (12 in) centres. Pre-finished beech flooring, supplied in double width strips, is laid on battens spaced at 411 mm (approx 16 in) centres. Both types of flooring should be laid with gaps to allow for expansion, particularly across the grain of the timber. Court floors should have a slight rough surface and be left unsealed.

It is essential to provide either a sandwich damp proof membrane or an oversite membrane before the floor is laid. If a base screed is not included the structural concrete slab must be carefully levelled.

The ceiling

The ceiling should provide a light coloured background against which the players can easily follow the flight of the ball. If a suspended ceiling is specified, a pvc-faced plaster board in an aluminium or white finished lay-in grid system will provide a finished surface which requires no initial or subsequent decoration. Lightweight panels should be fixed firmly in place because they can be dislodged if hit by the ball. Painted wood-wool slabs do not provide a sufficiently light background and are also liable continually to shed small particles of dust and debris which affects the floor surface. In addition any metal channel edges or hangers can lead to cold bridging and condensation which drips on to the floor. Beams or trusses which project below the ceiling surface should be avoided.

For the design principles of a flat roof refer to *BRE Digest 180*.

5 Standard details

5.1 Court markings

All court markings are 50 mm (approx 2 in) wide and coloured bright red.

5.2 The playboard or 'tin'

The playboard (commonly referred to as 'the tin') covers the front wall to a height of 480 mm. The top surface must be splayed so that any ball striking it is deflected upwards. Figure 4 shows the standard detail for courts of traditional construction. Proprietary plastic extrusions are also available instead of the hardwood battens at the top and bottom of the playboard. The manufacturers of panel system courts provide a playboard as part of their standard package.

5.3 Back wall sounding board

In courts with a solid back wall there should be a horizontal sounding board to give an audible indication when the ball hits the wall on or above the back wall line (in squash lines are 'out', ie the playing area excludes the lines). The board is fixed across the rear wall along and above the play line at a height of 2130 mm above finished floor level to the bottom edge. It may extend to any height above the line but should not be less than 200 mm high. Figure 5 shows a typical detail.

There is no back wall sounding board with glass walls. Either the wall stops at 2130 mm from floor level or a 50 mm red line is taped to the glass above this height.

5.4 Out of court lines

The out of court lines on the front and side walls (ie the front and side wall lines) should be concave or splayed so as to deflect any ball hitting them. This can be achieved by using a timber batten or plastic extrusion. Figure 6 shows the standard detail.

5.5 Wall/floor junction

There is no skirting in squash courts. Instead, the wall finish – which is applied before the floor is laid – is taken down to just above the structural floor level and then the floor finish laid with a gap of about 6–8 mm (approx 0.25–0.3 in) between it and the wall. This allows the floor to expand and move slightly. Figure 7 shows the standard detail of the wall/floor junction in courts of traditional construction.

5.6 The court door

Entry and exit to the court should be through a 762 mm wide x 2134 mm high door on the centre line of the rear wall of the court and open into it. The door should be hung on a hardwood frame which must be securely fixed to the structural wall. The inner face of the frame and the surface of the door must also be flush with the face of the wall surfacing material. There are no architraves on the court side of the door frame.

In courts with solid back walls the door should be a 44 mm thick plywood faced solid core type, hung on concealed hinges (SOSS pattern) and fitted with a flush drop ring handle on the inner face. A door viewer and an overhead closer should also be fitted. The inner face of the door and frame should be painted to match the court wall surfaces. Figure 8 shows a standard detail of the door frame in courts of traditional construction.

5.7 Balustrade

If a spectator viewing balcony or gallery is provided, the balustrade should have a broad flat timber shelf to enable spectators to look down into the court. Tiered stands will increase the number of spectators and enable them to see the majority of the court playing area, although a glass wall will usually provide a better spectator facility. A toughened glass balustrade will increase the view of the court for normal spectating and also when the court is being used

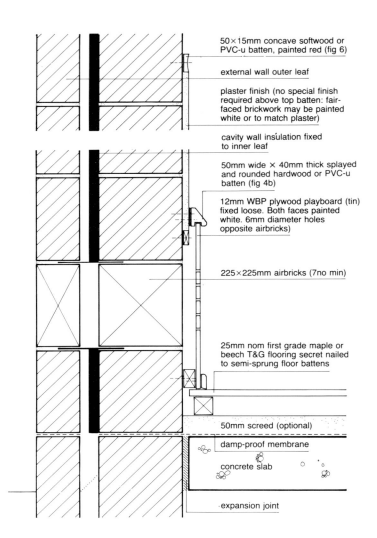

50×15mm concave softwood or PVC-u batten, painted red (fig 6)

external wall outer leaf

plaster finish (no special finish required above top batten: fair-faced brickwork may be painted white or to match plaster)

cavity wall insulation fixed to inner leaf

50mm wide × 40mm thick splayed and rounded hardwood or PVC-u batten (fig 4b)

12mm WBP plywood playboard (tin) fixed loose. Both faces painted white. 6mm diameter holes opposite airbricks)

225×225mm airbricks (7no min)

25mm nom first grade maple or beech T&G flooring secret nailed to semi-sprung floor battens

50mm screed (optional)

damp-proof membrane

concrete slab

expansion joint

4 *Standard detail: the playboard or 'tin' on the front wall*

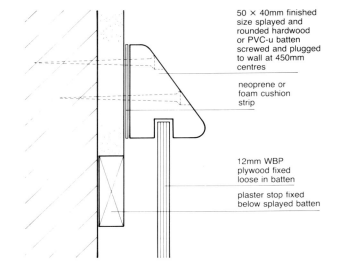

50 × 40mm finished size splayed and rounded hardwood or PVC-u batten screwed and plugged to wall at 450mm centres

neoprene or foam cushion strip

12mm WBP plywood fixed loose in batten

plaster stop fixed below splayed batten

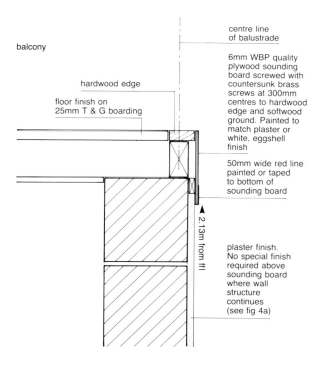

balcony

hardwood edge

floor finish on 25mm T & G boarding

centre line of balustrade

6mm WBP quality plywood sounding board screwed with countersunk brass screws at 300mm centres to hardwood edge and softwood ground. Painted to match plaster or white, eggshell finish

50mm wide red line painted or taped to bottom of sounding board

2.13m from ffl

plaster finish. No special finish required above sounding board where wall structure continues (see fig 4a)

5 *Standard detail: the back wall sounding board*

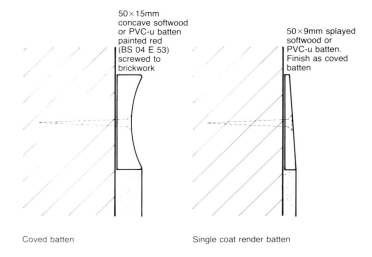

50×15mm concave softwood or PVC-u batten painted red (BS 04 E 53) screwed to brickwork

50×9mm splayed softwood or PVC-u batten. Finish as coved batten

Coved batten

Single coat render batten

6 *Standard detail: out of court lines on the front and side walls*

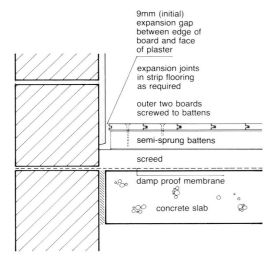

9mm (initial)
expansion gap
between edge of
board and face
of plaster

expansion joints
in strip flooring
as required

outer two boards
screwed to battens

semi-sprung battens

screed

damp proof membrane

concrete slab

7 *Standard detail: wall/floor junction*

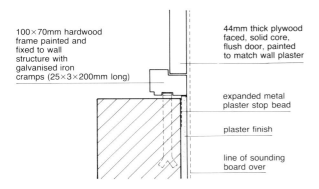

100×70mm hardwood
frame painted and
fixed to wall
structure with
galvanised iron
cramps (25×3×200mm long)

44mm thick plywood
faced, solid core,
flush door, painted
to match wall plaster

expanded metal
plaster stop bead

plaster finish

line of sounding
board over

8 *Standard detail: court door frame*

for tuition. The most effective design of gallery is one with the floor as low as possible and the front as open as is consistent with safety.

Ideally the floor of balconies should slope slightly towards the court and there should be a continuous 50 mm (approx 2 in) gap at the bottom of the balustrade. This will allow balls which are hit into the gallery area to roll back into the court.

6 Environmental requirements

For general details of environmental services recommendations refer to Chapters 60 and 61.

6.1 Ventilation

A good mechanical ventilation system is necessary to remove moisture and body odours from players and keep the courts, especially the walls, free from condensation. There should be at least one fan per court, fitted with a variable speed controller, and ideally the fan circuit should be linked to the court lighting. In centres with several courts, however, it may make control easier if the starters are taken to a central point, for example the cash desk. Alternatively, if local control is required, fan motor starters

may be in a locked box mounted on a wall outside the court.

The simplest and most effective system consists of propeller extract fans with the blades suitably guarded and mounted centrally at high level in the rear wall of the gallery or in the roof above the rear of the court. The fans should draw air through the court from air bricks behind the playboard (which can be perforated to ensure a good air flow – see Section 6.2) and discharge it to the atmosphere.

Fan noise must not intrude upon the game or distract the players. Background noise levels of less than 45 NR should be specified.

When squash courts form an integral part of a large complex care must be taken to ensure that air drawn into the courts does not come from high humidity areas such as showers, changing rooms or a bar. Where condensation is likely to be a severe problem, courts should have permanent mechanical ventilation; up to four air changes per hour may be needed.

Extract fans should be controlled so that they run on for a 15 minute period after the courts have been used to ensure that all stale air is removed.

If there is a spectator gallery, the rate of ventilation may have to be based upon its maximum occupancy.

6.2 Heating

Squash courts should be provided with a heating system which will maintain a temperature of between 16–18°C (60–65°F) in winter. In warm countries air conditioning may be necessary to keep the court air temperature at this level and control humidity.

The most common forms of heating are:

- Radiant panels heated by a low pressure hot water system
- Gas fired infra-red heaters sited along the centre line of the court and at high level above it
- Quartz radiant heaters sited at high level at the rear of the courts on the side walls
- Storage heaters or low pressure hot water radiators in the gallery area or on the court side of the balustrade.

Various other methods may be adopted if the courts form part of a larger sports complex with an air handling heating and ventilation system. The heating to the court area will then depend on the method adopted for the sports hall or adjacent areas.

If spectator accommodation is to be provided, the temperature in these areas should be 18°C. Where the courts are isolated and do not form part of a multi-sports facility, however, it is desirable to heat them in order to protect the building fabric.

6.3 Lighting

Natural light is not recommended in squash for the following reasons:

- Extra building costs
- Problems of glare and shadow
- Glass is a black background at night (squash balls are usually black or dark green)
- Loss of heat
- Risk of condensation or breakage and water penetration which could damage the floor
- Possible unauthorised use of the court – in many centres court fees are collected by means of coin in the slot light meters.

If daylight is required for some reason it should be in the form of rooflights fitted with toughened glass. It must be impossible for sunlight to enter the court.

All courts must have an artificial lighting system and, as noted above, light coloured finishes to the out of court areas on the walls and ceilings.

The level of illumination required will depend upon the standard of play:

- A minimum maintained average horizontal illumination of approximately 500 lux at 1 m above finished floor level should be regarded as the minimum acceptable. Details of how this standard is usually achieved are given below.
- Where formal spectator facilities such as a glass wall with tiered seating are provided a maintained average illumination of 500 to 750 lux over the area of the court is required.
- For championship courts where televised matches may be played a maintained average illumination of 1000 lux or more may be required. For details of lighting for TV refer to the *CIBSE Lighting Guide LG4: Sports and CIE Guides 67 and 83*.

In all cases a minimum uniformity ratio (minimum to average) of 0.7 is recommended. The walls of the court must also be evenly illuminated. Figure **9** shows a typical layout of fluorescent fittings – which are almost invariably used and give the best distribution of light. The fittings set parallel to the front wall should be angle reflectors with open ends and plain slotted reflectors for the other fittings. In order to achieve higher levels of illumination it is necessary to increase the number of fittings.

Slotted reflectors will help to illuminate the ceiling. Unprotected tubes may shatter if hit by the ball and therefore fittings should be protected.

Consideration should be given to the use of high frequency fittings and lamps which ensure that stroboscopic effects are entirely eliminated.

If meter switching is not used lighting switches should be taken to a central point for ease of control. Separate switches should be provided for each court.

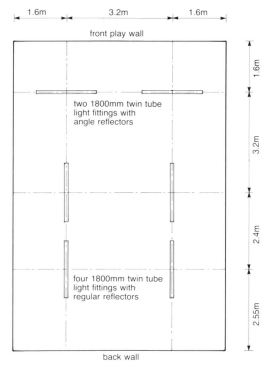

9 *Typical layout of light fittings for club courts*

For further details of lighting requirements see Chapter 60 in this volume and the *CIBSE Lighting Guide LG4: Sports*.

6.4 Clocks

In nearly all centres courts are booked for a defined time period. As a result there should a clock visible from each court. In commercial or large centres the clocks should be slaves controlled from a master clock at the control desk.

88
Indoor tennis centres

David Carpenter and Christopher Harper

1 Introduction

Purpose built indoor tennis provision is a relatively new development in the UK although in continental Europe and the eastern seaboard of the USA, in particular, indoor courts were the basis for rapid expansion of the sport in the late 1970s and early 1980s. By 1991 the UK had 460 indoor courts compared with over 5000 in France and 2600 in Germany.

2 Forms of provision

Indoor tennis courts can be successful in the commercial, statutory (public authority) or voluntary sectors.

In the commercial sector indoor courts, preferably a minimum of eight, will normally be supplemented by other profit centres such as those listed in the diagram of the Riverside Centre in West London, **1**. The 'club' will also normally be organised on a membership basis where members pay an initiation or joining fee plus an annual subscription, monthly dues and/or facility booking fees.

The public sector will normally provide indoor courts on a 'pay and play' basis with a preferential booking system for local residents or target groups. The indoor centre will act as a focal point for tennis and be integrated into an overall tennis development plan for the area, also encompassing outdoor provision. In the UK the Indoor Tennis Initiative (ITI), a joint venture between the Lawn Tennis Association, the All England Lawn Tennis and Croquet Club and The Sports Council, had, by the end of 1991, successfully provided 19 'pay and play' tennis centres. The planning design and operation of these centres was very much based on extensive research relating to overseas facilities.

Voluntary clubs may also provide indoor courts. Most voluntary club facilities are low cost air-supported structures intended primarily for winter play by members. They may also offer opportunities for coaching and instruction for non-members as a way of generating interest in the club and attracting members.

3 Feasibility studies

A feasibility study, consisting of an objective examination of all the factors that will impact upon the scheme, is essential when considering the provision of indoor tennis. It should include:

- Site analysis – size, accessibility, visibility
- Market analysis – catchment area, demographic and socio-economic analysis, potential user groups, existing participation and facilities
- Market research – to test the idea and assess demand and pricing
- Market evaluation – to determine the scope, scale and likely utilisation of a centre

- Financial analysis – capital expenditure, funding sources, projected revenue income and expenditure, cash flow and balance sheet.

Assuming a positive outcome, there are other key aspects to consider in the development phase.

Desirable facilities

Tennis is a sport enjoyed by men and women, young and old, able bodied and people with disabilities. The common linkage is that most play the sport to have fun. Research has shown that it is essential for key elements of the indoor centre such as court surfaces (medium paced are preferable), lighting and background heating/ventilation to match the users aspirations. A good tennis development programme is also an essential as again research shows that as many as 40% of players attracted to an indoor centre may be new to the game. A clear programme of instruction and events is required to maintain interest on an annual, monthly and even weekly basis.

Ideally outdoor courts with a similar playing surface to that of the indoor courts should be provided to prevent an exodus of players in the summer months. The provision of floodlighting also provides a further user option at peak times when indoor courts are fully booked.

A hot and cold food service together with a bar with emphasis on cold soft drinks and tea/coffee is also essential, but a full restaurant facility is not required. The bar/social area should be located at or near ground floor level to allow users to view play on the adjacent courts but, more importantly, so that all users pass through the area in an effort to maximise potential revenue.

Careful attention should also be paid to the design of indoor tennis centres to permit the minimum number of staff to be employed. In small centres with three or four courts, there will be times when the facility might be operated by only one person and this requires close linkage of the reception and social facilities.

4 Planning and design

Tennis centres differ from other sports buildings principally in the size of their play areas in relation to ancillary accommodation. The large and lofty tennis halls are the dominant feature and there is seldom the opportunity for breaking up their silhouette with smaller appendages. Indoor centres are also invariably grouped with outdoor courts. The requirements of a suitable playing environment can also be met with various forms of lightweight space enclosures, which are seldom considered applicable to other types of sports provision. Air hall and membrane buildings have both been used successfully for indoor courts, although problems can be encountered when combining support accommodation with proprietary long span, lightweight systems.

The tennis hall

The accompanying diagrams and table give details of critical dimensions for indoor tennis and court markings.

Structure and construction

The most usual and economic forms of conventional construction are based on portal or arched frame structures, **2**, either in steel or laminated timber. The structural grid should be designed to relate to the court layout and the intervening strips of roof lights. In lower budget projects and for established clubs, air halls or membrane buildings are frequently utilised. Refer to Chapter 66 in this volume.

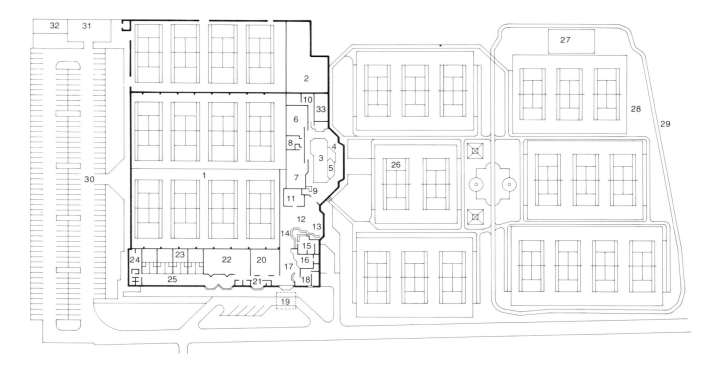

1	tennis hall	12	club room	23	squash courts
2	changing and beauty facilities	13	restaurant	24	changing
3	20m swimming pool	14	bar	25	viewing
4	whirlpool bath	15	kitchen	26	tennis courts
5	children's pool	16	sports shop	27	basketball court and tennis practice wall
6	male changing	17	reception	28	golf driving nets
7	female changing	18	office	29	jogging track
8	sauna/steam room	19	main entrance	30	parking
9	pool side bar	20	aerobics/dance studio	31	service yard
10	laundry	21	crèche	32	workshop
11	meetings room	22	fitness gym	33	plant

1 *Site layout of the Riverside Club, Chiswick*

Natural lighting

It is strongly recommended that halls receive some daylighting via double skin sealed roof lights run between each court, carefully designed and located to minimise glare. Supplementary daylighting and visual contact with the outdoor courts can be provided by low level glazing to one or both end walls. Fully glazed gables, even with a northerly aspect (in the northern hemisphere), tend to produce unacceptable high levels of glare.

2 *Portal frame structure at the ITI Batchwood Centre, St Albans. Photo: C J Harper*

Spectator seating

Some permanent spectator seating should be considered for all but the smallest, three- or four-court centres. In schemes of conventional construction, casual viewing should be provided from the reception and lounge areas. These areas can be expanded in larger centres or supplemented with gallery seating at first floor or mezzanine level along the ends of courts in either open balconies or partially glazed galleries. For specific events or tournaments, additional portable seating can be introduced around a temporary show court where access and dimensions permit.

Storage

The hall or halls should have direct access to a fully fitted store which will contain balls, rackets, practice ball machines, short tennis equipment and floor cleaning machines and materials, **3**.

Finishes and fittings

Floors The base for the playing surface should consist of a flush, level concrete slab with a maximum level tolerance of 6 mm ($\frac{1}{4}$ in) under a 3 m (approx 10 ft) straight edge up to a maximum of approx 7.5 mm (approx 5/16 in) over the whole area. Finishes fall into three main categories:

- Textile carpets
- Polymeric (rubberised) compounds
- Cushioned and uncushioned acrylics.

The choice of finish will be determined by the type of facility and intended level of play. Performance criteria to

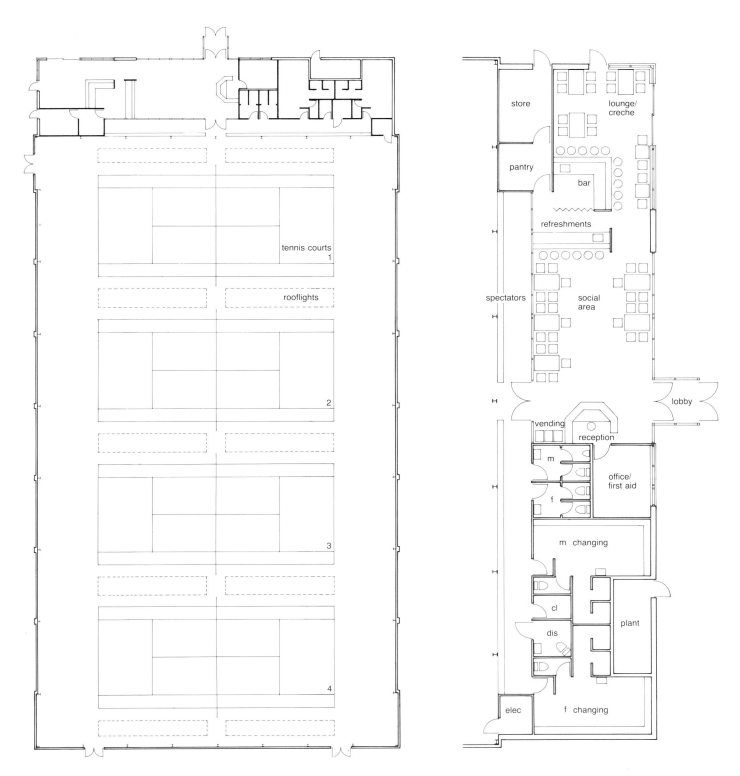

3 *Plan of the four court ITI centre at Swindon, a compact design*

The plan includes the following labels:

store, lounge/creche, pantry, bar, refreshments, spectators, social area, tennis courts 1, rooflights, tennis courts 2, 3, 4, lobby, vending, reception, m, f, office/first aid, m changing, cl, dis, plant, elec, f changing

be used include the speed of court; height and trueness of ball bounce; and the degree of topspin and slice achievable. Player requirements will also lead to consideration of the amount of slide afforded and the degrees of slipperiness and resilience. The Lawn Tennis Association's Facilities Department can be contacted for advice on a range of surfaces.

Walls Side wall construction is partly or fully masked with stop netting or fabric and occasionally by display panels. The gable structure and construction is generally exposed and may need to be decorated or clear sealed to prevent dust and grit from damaging the tennis floor.

Ceiling Lining panels must be resistant to damage and distortion from stray ball shots and structural details should be designed so as to avoid creating traps and ledges where balls can become lodged.

Fittings Back stop netting is hung as a continuous band (except for fire escape openings) along the ends of the courts. Panels of fabric are an alternative method of arresting balls and preventing them from bouncing back onto the court. Nets or fabric can be run to the full height of the side walls to create a neat, uninterrupted plane of a consistent colour, which offers less distraction to players. If the backstop material is fixed rather than being track suspended, access slots need to be formed for power sockets and fire exit signs.

Structural protection Columns or piers behind the back line require protective padding even when plan dimensions accord with current recommendations. This should be taken to 2 m (6.5 ft) approx height irrespective of whether the structure is in front of or behind the netting line.

Display or advertising panels A modular system of coordinated panels can be considered above the ends of the court and opposite any spectator seating. When required, panels should be set at eaves height directly between the ceiling and the top of the back stop material. A white/pale grey or beige background will help to relate them to the ceiling plane, and discordant colours should be avoided.

Protection of fittings
All exposed wall and ceiling fittings must be resistant to stray ball shots or protected by steel mesh cages. These fittings may include clocks, thermostats, loudspeakers and luminaires; the latter must have secure and positively located diffusers or grilles.

Sockets The tennis floor will contain sockets for posts which should be capable of being fitted with flush cover plates.

Practice wall A practice rebound wall can be considered and if required structural centres may have to be increased locally to provide adequate support stiffness. Various proprietary freestanding systems are also obtainable.

4.1 Multi use
Tennis halls are seldom used for other indoor sports. Tennis demand invariably rules out consideration of other activities as does their restrictive eaves height dimension and the types of lighting and finishes specified. The one exception is badminton where 2–3 courts can be laid out within and at right angles to a tennis court without unduly compromising the badminton clear height requirements. Lighting arrangements will, however, prove unsatisfactory unless additional pull-down badminton light clusters are fitted. Daylighting designed for tennis will also cause problems for badminton players.

4.2 Internal environment
For general details of environmental services recommendations refer to Chapters 60 and 61.

Heating
A minimum temperature of 12°C is normally considered adequate although higher temperatures can be provided. Controls should then ensure that different levels can be set. Wall mounted fan convectors have proved to be a simple and cost effective method of hall heating. Air supported structures will normally have heating elements incorporated within the blower units at the end of the hall.

Ventilation
A minimum of 0.5 air changes per hour should be provided. Internal air movement should be maintained within the range of 0.1 to 0.5 m per second (approx 0.3 to 1.65 ft per second) in order not to disrupt play.

Lighting
For detailed recommendatons regarding lighting refer to *CIBSE Lighting Guide LG4: Sports.*

Satisfactory lighting is critical to the success of the hall. A well proven system has luminaires located between and not directly over courts and related to the transverse bands of roof glazing. A uniform illuminance level of 500 lux is required over the court (the principal playing area) for levels of play up to club standard. The illuminance between the base line and rear wall and on the side run-offs (ie the total playing area) should be 400 lux. Surface reflectance values should be:

Back wall behind courts	0.2–0.4
Side walls	0.4–0.6
Ceiling	0.6–0.9
Floor	0.2–0.4

A consistent overall colour is not necessary for the floor; differently coloured court and surround areas can provide more visual interest and spatial definition without distracting players. All light fittings must be fitted with protective covers (preferably diffusers) or mesh cages securely fixed to the unit's base.

Power
One power socket should be located behind each alternate court.

4.2 Ancillary accommodation
The extent of tennis hall accommodation will vary from project to project. Each centre will have core accommodation consisting of a foyer/lobby, office, male and female changing rooms and toilets plus a disabled persons' toilet and a tennis equipment store. In addition, different types of centre might have additional accommodation as follows:

- *Tennis club*: club room, with vending refreshments, or a permanent drinks and snacks servery with provisions store.
- *Pay and play centre*: tennis development office, lounge with refreshments counter and licensed bar, crèche, and first aid facility incorporated independently or as part of an office cleaner's store, and possibly a shop. Additional spectator seating and a fitness room might also be considered, as well as an outdoor viewing area.
- *Commercial tennis centres*: the additions outlined for pay and play centres, plus any or all of a fully equipped sport shop and stockroom, squash and badminton courts, a fitness suite, a fitness/fun pool, dance/exercise studio/ restaurant and meetings rooms. There will also be an external seating terrace accessible from the bar.

The accompanying diagram, 4, suggests how various levels of support accommodation relate to play areas and the following notes confirm design requirements for tennis. Refer to Chapters 54 to 61 in this volume for further details of planning, specification and services.

Foyer/lobby
This nominal entrance space can be expanded to include a reception counter, displays, seating and refreshment facilities. It should also provide access to and a view of the courts and in larger schemes may be developed into an open plan lounge area.

Office
Offices and reception should be combined for economy of operation irrespective of the centre's size. It may also be possible to incorporate a refreshments/bar counter as an extension of the reception counter as a further develop-

4 *Combining reception with the refreshments counter can lead to staff economies and present a pleasant informality*

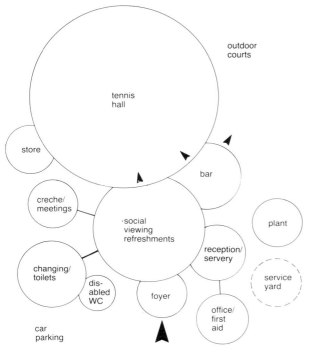

5 *Spatial relationship diagram*

ment of this philosophy. In most schemes, a separate office for tennis development personnel can be justified.

Toilets and changing
Numbers of fittings, bench spaces and lockers should relate to the standards normally provided for indoor sports: ie changing spaces will be calculated on the number of courts × 4 players × 2 for overlap. An established tradition for outdoor courts is that players arrive ready changed and it is recommended that, in most circumstances, only a token provision of two extra changing spaces plus two lockers are provided for each outdoor court.

Refreshments and bar
These areas should be linked or closely related to the main reception counter, and backed up with appropriate food/snack preparation areas, store rooms and a bar store. Proper external provision must be provided for servicing and refuse, screened from the main entrance.

4.3 Site layout and outdoor courts
The main determinants in planning new tennis complexes are correct orientation of the outdoor courts, economic access routes and proximity of services. Any surrounding residential or other sensitive uses must be taken into account because of the scale of indoor halls and the need to floodlight outdoor courts. In locations where tournaments might be held, an outdoor show court with up to 5000 tiered seats can be considered along with extensive overspill parking areas. Refer to Volume 1, Chapter 65 for outdoor tennis and Volume 1, Chapter 18 for floodlighting.

5 References and further advice
Carpenter, D, *Indoor Tennis: Review of Developments in Indoor Tennis Provision 1980–84 and Planning Guidelines for Future Development*, Sports Council, London (1984).
Lawn Tennis Association Publications List.
Lawn Tennis Association, *Court Surfaces Policy*, LTA, London (1990).
Sandilands, P and Carpenter, D, *A Guide to Community Tennis: Activity and Operations Manuals (Indoor Tennis Initiative)*, Lawn Tennis Association, London (1990).
Sports Council, *Outdoor Lawn Tennis*, Sports Council, London (1984).
The Indoor Tennis Initiative, *Indoor Tennis Centres: Scheme Planning and Model Specification: Traditional Building, Lightweight Structures and Airhalls*, Lawn Tennis Association/Sports Council, London (1991).
Trickey, C, *Tennis Courts*, Lawn Tennis Association, London (1991).

89
Ten pin bowling centres

Peter Ackroyd and Maritz Vandenberg in association with AMF Bowling Inc UK

1 Background information

After a period of declining popularity in Britain (due perhaps to the slightly seedy image of some bowling alleys) ten pin bowling has gone 'up-market' and is flourishing. Britain now has 3000 lanes in over 200 centres, and the figure is rising rapidly. The smart new centres (no longer 'alleys') are usually set in impressive premises and cater for the family. They are more expensive than before but offer cleanliness and comfort, sophisticated equipment with electronic scoring, and facilities which may include bars and restaurants, a nursery, even conference or meetings rooms.

2 Critical factors
- Consult specialist company
- Car parking provision
- Overall space requirements as shown in the guide and table below
- Control of noise
- Lighting
- Ventilation.

2.1 Planning the centre

From the outset of a project, consider possible future expansion and allow sufficient space to do so. A centre should be located where it is accessible from, though not directly on, main traffic arteries. It should have ample parking facilities and several entrances and exits.

The following must be considered:

- The location, size and zoning of the property.
- Environmental factors and the form of construction.
- Efficient locations for, and local regulations for:
  (a) Food and drinks service
  (b) Retail sales area: pro shop, other merchandise
  (c) Coin operated games area
  (d) Nursery and meeting rooms
  (e) Billiards and snooker area
  (f) Other recreational areas
  (g) Storage for pins and other equipment
  (h) Mechanics' work area.
- Facilities for those with disabilities, in the car park, at the entrance, cloakrooms and toilets and bowling areas.
- Requirements for bowls, control and scoring systems.
- Practical provisions for security.
- Expansion review and space allowances.

2.2 Space

As a 'rule of thumb' guide allow approximately 94 sq m (1000 sq ft) of building area per lane, or for 16 lanes or more allow at least 85 sq m (900 sq ft) per lane.

1 Photo: World of Tenpin

Parking can be critical for success. Allow 3 to 5 cars per lane, of 33.4 sq m (360 sq ft) space per car to include ingress, egress, driving lanes and parking spaces.

Table 89.1 quantifies lane area and overall building area for numbers of lanes:

2.3 Schedule of accommodation

A centre consists of multiple parallel bowling lanes (for dimensions see 2 and Table 89.1), plus the following ancillary spaces to serve the lanes:

- *Concourse.* This is essentially a passageway for access to the lanes and other bowling centre facilities. The larger the number of lanes, the shallower the concourse need be, but 3.65 m is a minimum. The concourse may also be used for tables and chairs (allow 2.5 m for each row of these), for food and vending drink sales, and for payphones. Unless the centre is specifically planned as a tournament centre spectator seating is not recommended here. See also Food and bar lounge, below.
- *Retail sales area and ball drilling.* Provide a glassed-in area for the sale of bowling balls and other supplies. Install modern merchandising display systems. The sales facility should enhance the product being promoted and be located so that it faces potential retail customers. Power requirements for a ball driller are two 15–20 amp mains voltage circuits.
- *Bowlers' seating area.* This is situated at the 'front end' of the bowling lanes and opening off the concourse. It should be at least 3.66 m deep and 0.15 m below concourse level. This contains the automatic scoring and control systems.
- *Ball racks.* A space behind the bowlers' seating area for the ball racks. Width must be at least 0.36 m, increased

Table 89.1: Bowling centre dimensions (Note: width excludes any columns)

No. of lanes	Width	Side aisles	Total width	Length seating to rear wall	Minimum building interior (total sq m)	Recommended building interior (total sq m)
2	3.46	1	4.36	32.15 (1)	165 (2)	195 (2)
4	6.85	1	7.75	32.15 (1)	375	395
6	10.23	1	11.13	31.15	510	575
8	13.62	1	14.52	31.15	675	760
10	17.01	2	18.81	31.15	820	940
12	20.40	2	22.20	31.15	985	1130
14	23.78	2	25.58	31.15	1150	1315
16	27.17	2	28.97	31.15	1310	1500
18	30.56	2	32.36	31.15	1475	1690
20	33.95	2	35.75	31.15	1640	1880
22	37.33	2	39.13	31.15	1800	2065
24	40.72	2	42.52	31.15	1965	2255

Note (1): In two and four lane centres the seasting to rear wall length is increased by 1 m to provide an extra deep service aisle and compensate for minimum building width.
Note (2): The minimum and recommended areas for two lane centres excludes food and drinks service.

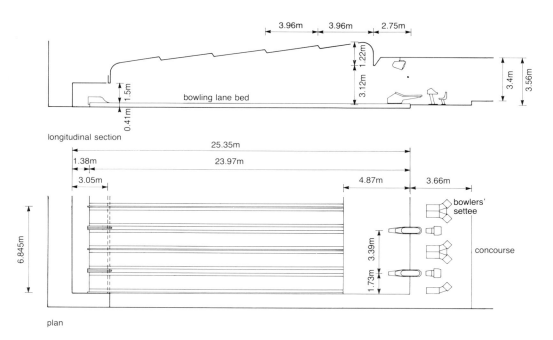

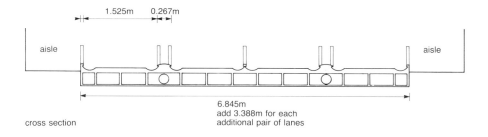

2 *Diagram of bowling lanes and related spaces. AMF and SC*

if the racks are on the same level as the bowler seating area. Racks may be 16-ball mobile storage racks, or fixed built-in racks.
- *Coat racks.* These may be incorporated in the same area as ball storage, or provided for in a special 'check room' near the control counter.
- *Pinspotter service area.* This is at the far end of the bowling lanes. This should accommodate storage of pins and other supplies, plus a service aisle at least 1.8 m wide for maintenance personnel. Ideally a large service room and a mechanic's workshop should be accessible from this service area.

- *Aisle.* A 0.9 m wide aisle, for mechanic's access, running from the front to the rear of the lanes. Smaller centres may have one aisle only; but for larger centres there may be two, one adjoining the first lane and the other adjoining the last lane.
- *Bowling pin maintenance area.* This may adjoin the service area (see above) in which case excellent ventilation and extractor fans must be provided for fume extraction.

In addition to the above, most or all of the following *administrative and social facilities* will be necessary:

- *A manager's office.* This should be large enough for the back office elements of an automated business system. In larger centres there may be more than one room, to allow for a private managerial meetings room as well as an administrative office for the counter assistants and book-keeper. The office size is dependent upon the size of the establishment and its administrative requirements. In many cases, a small private office apart from one for counter help and book-keeper/secretary is preferable for dealing with personnel, discussions with league officers and handling other confidential matters. Sufficient space should be provided for the back office elements of the automated business system as well as ample electrical points for that and other business machinery.

- *Control counter.* This is rather like the bridge of a ship, and the floor must be raised to give the control clerk a commanding view of all entrances, all lanes, and the video area, regardless of the flow of traffic. The counter should accommodate all the sophisticated electronic scoring and business equipment which forms part of a modern centre, and must therefore have ample electrical points. A display area for rental show racking and other merchandise may be included.

- *Food and bar lounge.* A whole range of attractive facilities of high quality are essential in a modern 'up-market' bowling centre. These should at least include a bar and a fast-food outlet with limited but good quality menu. A separate outside sales entrance may be considered to bring in new business. The lounge should be designed to invite bowlers in. Where permitted a pass-through service window to the concourse should be provided for waitress service to the concourse. Storage and access to an outside loading bay must be provided for all these facilities.

- *Video games.* There may be much waiting for free lanes in a busy centre, and coin-operated games help pass the time. Properly supervised and controlled video games and coin operated amusement machines contribute support for the operation and a welcome diversion for waiting list bowlers during peak periods. They should be concentrated in an area unobtrusive to bowlers on the lanes but in full view of the control counter.

- *All-purpose room(s).* This may operate at times as a nursery room for young children (therefore storage for toys and play equipment is necessary), at other times as a club and league meeting room, a function room, or a special event room. If not on the bar floor level, provide a dumb-waiter for service from the bar/snacks.

- *Media room.* In large centres where televised events may be held, a special media room may be required; but normally the 'all purpose room' above will suffice.

- *Billiards and snooker.* A billiards and snooker club or an 'open' facility, providing at least as many tables as bowling lanes is not uncommon, **4.** See also Chapter 71 in this volume.

- *Toilets.* To keep up-market clients happy these must be well-designed and finished (eg ceramic wall tiles from wall to ceiling), have excellent ventilation to prevent odours, and must be designed for excellent maintenance (coved corners, wash-down floors with drainage outlet, etc). They must be located for easy supervision. Provision must be calculated for five persons per lane at peak periods, following local authority regulations.

3 *Scoring control system in the bowlers' seating area. Photo: AMF*

Include a women's powder room lounge, well furnished and decorated.

- *Lockers.* There should be rental lockers, probably near the toilets or opening off the concourse, where customers of both sexes can store clothes and belongings. Five lockers per lane are recommended.

- *Bulletin boards.* There must be ample, easily accessible bulletin board space for posting of lane assignments, current team standings, special events and the like.

- *Staff rest room.* Facilities to comply with the Health and Safety at Work requirements.

- *Storage and utility spaces.* There must be adequate space for heating and air conditioning plant, utilities meters, cleaning equipment and supplies storage for all service, management and amenity rooms.

2.4 Finishes

Floor finishes
Bowling lane beds are built using selected tongued and grooved maple and pine boards or laminates, dense particle board and particle board approved and tested to Federation Internationale des Quilleurs (FIQ) standards and from specialist suppliers. Concourses and circulation areas are usually carpeted. Heavy circulation areas such as the step up from sitting to concourse, control counter, entrances, game and vending areas, sitting area are usually vinyl or rubber sheeting.

Wall finishes
High quality, attractive, but easily maintained surfaces are important. The acoustic properties of soft furnishings should be considered.

Ceiling finishes
Sound absorption must be provided to ensure that average noise levels are kept down, following specialist advice. A sprinkler installation is advisable.

2.5 Internal environment
For general details of environmental services recommendations refer to Chapters 60 and 61.

Acoustics
It is important that the noise created by the activity is contained by utilising sound absorbent material on the walls and ceiling surrounding the lanes.

Lighting

Lighting of 200 lux should be maintained over the lane area at floor level and 500 lux vertical illuminance provided over the pins. Illumination of all other areas should be subdued in comparison and may employ decorative or feature lighting. Care should be taken not to overilluminate the automatic scoring monitors.

Heating, ventilation and air conditioning

The ideal summer and winter conditions are 20–23°C with a relative humidity of 35–45%. Wide and rapid temperature and humidity fluctuations within the centre cause adverse bowling conditions and may be harmful to the bowling equipment. Air cooling provides summer comfort and humidity stability and is desirable. However, it is recognised that the British climate is usually temperate and air cooling costs may over-ride its benefits.

3 References and further advice

AMF Bowling Inc UK (a specialist company).

AMF Bowling Inc, *Designing the Facility – ideas from AMF* (an architectural guide for planning a bowling centre).

British Tenpin Bowling Association.

Designs on Leisure: Tenpin Reborn, (Sep/Oct 1991) (Sport and Leisure magazine of the Sports Council).

Life in the Fast Lane, *Leisure Week* (11 January 1991).

Tenpin on a New Wave, *Interior Design* (May 1989).

90
Weight training

Peter Ackroyd and Maritz Vandenberg

1 General

There are two distinctions to note. Firstly between weight lifting (a competitive sport covered in Chapter 45 in this volume) and weight training, which is a method of body development. Any space designed for strength training should cater for both, but within such a facility certain areas should be separated from each other (see below). In such dual-purpose provision, the installation of fixed equipment should not be allowed to take over too much space.

Secondly, there is little compatibility between the training equipment used by heavy athletes and lightweight training for health and general fitness purposes using machines and light free-weights. Machines are of no use for certain types of training and if they occupy too much of the available floor area (as often happens) the usefulness of the hall is impaired. For fitness facilities, refer to Chapter 91 in this volume.

1 *Photo: Motivation Techniques*

with adequate safety margins around each user (see below).
- Good ventilation is essential and air conditioning may need to be considered.
- Storage.

2 Critical factors

- There must a clear separation between spaces devoted to weight-lifting machines (the apparatus area) and spaces devoted to free-weight activity (the free-weight area) and powerlifting, **1** and **2**.
- All equipment and machines should be permanently sited in the apparatus area, and in the UK supervised by staff qualified to British Amateur Weight Lifting Association (BAWLA) standards if users are to get full benefit from the facility.
- In the free-weight area there must be enough space for uncluttered movement with bar-bells and dumb-bells,

2.1 Space

Weight training facilities must not share space with other sports. Free-weight use has increased in popularity, therefore enough space should be provided to allow uncluttered dynamic exercise with barbells and dumb-bells. Very heavy lifting areas for weight lifters, power lifters and heavy athletes should ideally be provided in separate rooms, **3**.

There must be enough space to allow free movement with weights without risk of injury to others. This means a clear space of at least 1 m at each end of the bar in bar-bell and dumb-bell areas, **2**.

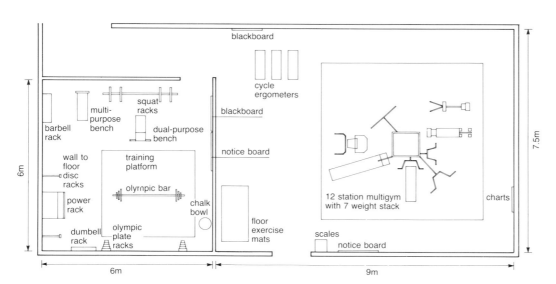

2 *Layout showing clear separation between conditioning and weight training areas. Bunyan Recreation Centre, Bedford*

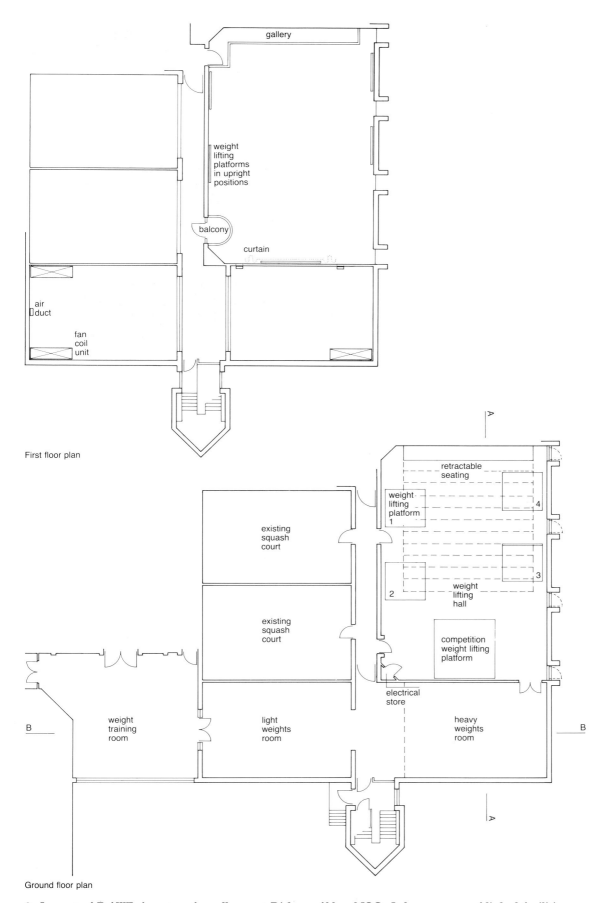

gallery

weight
lifting
platforms
in upright
positions

balcony

curtain

air
duct

fan
coil
unit

First floor plan

existing
squash
court

existing
squash
court

weight
training
room

light
weights
room

retractable
seating

weight
lifting
platform
1

4

weight
lifting
hall

2

3

competition
weight lifting
platform

electrical
store

heavy
weights
room

A

A

B

B

Ground floor plan

3 *Layout of BAWLA centre-of-excellence at Bisham Abbey NSC. It has a range of linked facilities:*
- *lightweight training room*
- *weights training area*
- *warm-up space and heavy weights room, in a converted squash court*
- *competition space (lifting with seating, judging equipment, scoreboard etc.).*
*This converted squash court is designed also for multi-use. Points of particular interest are the fold-down weight lifting platforms, **3** to **5**, and the special floor in the heavy weights room*

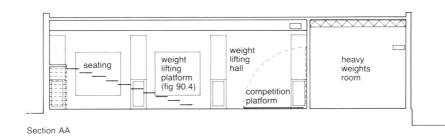

Section AA

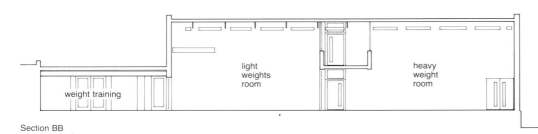

Section BB

3 *Layout of BAWLA centre-of-excellence at Bisham Abbey NSC. It has a range of linked facilities: (cont'd)*

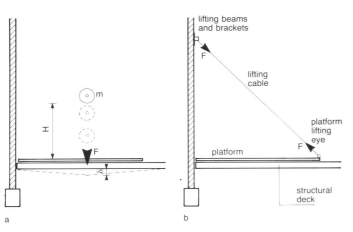

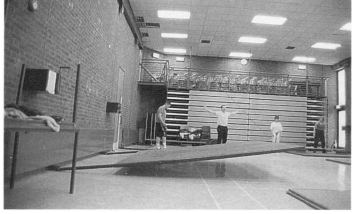

4 *Detail of fold-down platform (Bisham Abbey NSC). The calculation of loads applied to the weightlifting platform and structural deck from dropped weights (**a**) and also applied from the lifting operation to the platform framework, wall beams and brackets (**b**) takes into account: F, forces (kN); G, acceleration due to gravity (9.81 m/s²); H, height over which apparatus is dropped (m); M, mass of apparatus being dropped (kg); V, velocity of apparatus as it hits the platform (m/s); D, total deflection of platform and deck (mm). Architects: SC TUS and YRM Anthony Hunt Associates*

5 *Fold-down platform at Bisham Abbey NSC. Photo: Robin Wilson*

2.2 Equipment

Basic equipment to be provided is listed below. Some items must be kept separate (see Critical factors above):

- Lifting platforms (4 x 4 m for competitions, 3 x 3 m for practice), 4 and 5.
- International 200 kg set of weights, plus extra 62.5 kg discs. Both are essential for weight-lifting training and competition.
- Comprehensive selection of barbells, dumb-bells and weights.
- Squat stands.
- Benches.
- Multi-station weight training machine. Note that separate exercise machines are preferable to multi-station.

Other forms of apparatus are coming on to the market (but note that many of these are suitable mainly for home use, and not for multi-person usage).

2.3 Storage

After use, weights should be stored clear of the floor area either in racks or in a storage room. This is for safety and security as much as tidiness. If foam-filled mats are used, they must be stored in a separate fire-resistant store.

2.4 Finishes

Floor

A level and resilient non-slip surface is required. Where loose weights are used the floor must additionally be able to resist failure or indentation when heavy weights are dropped. This means the floor should spread the impact on the substrate by acting as a cushion and the substrate too should not be completely inflexible, 5. Use of a solid inflexible substrate could lead to a fracture of the flooring system. Older flooring installations of wooden block have now generally been superseded by artificial materials such as a battleship lino laid on asphalt and modern synthetic surfaces.

Surrounding surfaces
At least one wall must be strong enough to support the mounting of equipment such as pulling machines and weight storage-racks.

2.5 Internal environment
For general details of environmental services recommendations refer to Chapters 60 and 61.

Heating and ventilation
A good ventilation system is essential in order to control the temperature and humidity and maintain a comfortable environment. A temperature of around 12–14°C is recommended with a ventilation rate of about 10–12 air changes per hour. Higher temperatures may be acceptable in summer but air-conditioning may need to be considered where heat gains are very high or strict temperature control is needed.

Lighting
The lighting system should provide an overall minimum average illuminance of 300 lux with a good uniformity ratio (minimum 0.8) and good control of glare. For further details of lighting recommendations, see Chapter 60 and the *CIBSE Lighting Guide LG4: Sports.*

Acoustics
Control of noise within the room itself is not usually critical but it is advisable to control noise breakout to other areas.

3 References and further advice
British Amateur Weight-lifter's Association (BAWLA).
BAWLA, *Weight training*, BAWLA.
BAWLA safety booklet.

91
Fitness facilities

Jim Clough

1 Types of fitness facility

There are several fundamentally different types of fitness facility. Accordingly, providers should set clear objectives at the outset relating to their target markets and the range of facilities to be provided together with the required quality and 'image'. Dedicated fitness facilities may be:

- A key element in a fitness and health club
- A self-contained unit which complements other indoor sports facilities in a multi-sports complex
- A training unit for people involved in specific sports (eg in a rugby club)
- A corporate unit provided and maintained by a company or other employer for the use of employees and possibly also their families.

Fitness facilities can also be categorised by the type of equipment provided:

- General fitness, with mainly multigym type equipment
- Executive fitness, with mainly cardiovascular equipment such as bicycle ergometers or rowing machines
- Luxury club, with state of the art equipment
- Women only with a relaxation emphasis and fairly light exercise equipment
- Bodybuilders' 'sweatshop' with heavy equipment consisting mainly of loose weights, racks and benches.

These categories are not mutually exclusive and some facilities will be a mixture of different types. Nevertheless, problems may arise if providers seek to satisfy too many different user groups in one complex. It is for this reason that clarity of objectives from the outset is one key to success.

The following recommendations relate primarily to newbuild projects but can be adapted for conversions. The more specific the initial brief the better the finished result should be. Owners and managers may otherwise attempt to adapt, add to or alter the end product to accommodate things forgotten or not fully considered, often in an untidy or unsafe manner.

1.1 Schedule of accommodation

This section describes the requirements of the main fitness facilities in a typical stand-alone club and how they impinge on other aspects of the complex. It should be fairly simple to adapt these guidelines to the requirements of a corporate or other type of facility.

The following areas are normally considered to be essential:

- Reception/office (see Chapter 54 in this volume)
- Gymnasium (see below)
- Exercise studio (see below)
- Changing rooms (see Chapter 57 in this volume)

- Relaxation, lounge or snack area.

Clubs may also have one or more of the following, some of which are very common:

- Beauty and hair salon
- Treatment/massage rooms
- Sun beds (may be incorporated into changing rooms)
- Swimming pool
- Squash courts (see Chapter 87 in this volume)
- Shop
- Training/meeting room
- Staff room
- Fitness assessment area – usually an enclosed area of at least 3 × 2.5 m off the main gymnasium area will be adequate.

1.2 Fitness gymnasia

Shape and dimensions
The shape of fitness gymnasia is not critical; far more important is that they should be easy to clean and supervise. Simple shapes work best with a rectangle being better than a square. It is inadvisable to exceed a length/width ratio of 3:1 and designers should allow about 2.5 sq m per user (gym only; 5 m^2 for overall facility). Additional space can be made by the use of galleries and mezzanines and may be particularly suitable for cardio-vascular equipment such as treadmills, bicycles, rowing and climbing machines.

With one or two exceptions, exercise machines (both cardiovascular and resistance) function within their base

1 *Free weight equipment may seem to take up little space, but this is deceptive. A lot of ancillary space is needed for benches, stands, storage and carriage to and from storage. Photo: Jim Clough*

2 *Exercise machines require less space. The equipment shown here is an example of modern 'resistance' equipment: big, heavy and high-tech. Photo: Jim Clough*

area. At least 1 m should be allowed around machines except where they are placed back to back or against walls.

Free weight equipment requires a greater area than may at first appear. Space is required for storage racks, carriage to and from storage racks, benches, stands and use. Designers should allow about 3 sq m per exerciser in addition to bench and rack equipment.

There is usually no functional requirement for a high ceiling. Ceiling height will depend upon the need to make the space appear generous rather than cramped, avoid feelings of 'stuffiness' and provide adequate clearances for equipment delivery and use. A minimum height of 3 m is suggested.

Floor finishes
- Generally avoid use of platforms and split levels (other than galleries and mezzanines). Any height changes may result in falls, rolling weights and twisted ankles; they also make moving heavy equipment unnecessarily difficult and possibly dangerous.
- Assess floor loadings carefully: exercise machines may weigh several hundred kilograms and each user may weigh an additional 100 kg.
- Consider shock/vibration – dropping weights, weight stacks, vibration and shock from treadmills.
- Few items require floor fixing, but some do.
- The floor finish should be non-slip with high traction, durable and non-brittle as weights may be dropped on to it. It must also withstand heavy cleaning and the use of cleansing agents. Heavy duty carpet on a good quality underlay is often specified. Free weight areas are usually covered with high density rubber matting.

Wall finishes
- Consider the need for bolt fixings for wall mounted equipment. Fixed equipment can result in high forces on the wall and may require 75 mm bolts.
- Consider the need for large mirrored areas. (Note: a user can see their whole body in a mirror half their height; 1 m mirrors should suffice.)
- Wall finishes should be smooth, easily cleaned, durable and free of projections.
- Space for charts, notice boards and pictures should be 'designed in'.

1.3 Studios

Dimensions
Studios have become an integral part of fitness facilities. They are used for aerobics and activities such as yoga, pre- and post-natal classes, martial arts and the like. The best proportions are between a square and a 3:2 rectangle.

See also Chapters 51 and 52 in this volume.

Floor finishes
The following should be considered:

- The floor finish should be light in colour, resilient and sprung: timber such as maple or beech is common and probably the best finish. Cushioned surfaces which are deformable but not resilient have been tried but are not popular.
- The floor area should be rectangular and completely clear of projections, protruding shapes and or columns.
- Hi-fi equipment and speakers should not sit on the floor. They can be wall mounted, inset or fixed in a cupboard.
- A non-porous surface is best for swift dry and wet cleaning.
- The noise and vibration beneath a studio used for aerobics can be considerable. It may be necessary to provide sound proofing.

Walls
The following should be considered:

- Large (possibly floor to ceiling) mirrors on one wall
- Fixing of ballet barre to one or more walls
- Door(s) should open out from the studio
- Non-abrasive surface.

1.4 Internal environment
For general details of environmental services recommendations refer to Chapters 60 and 61. Environmental requirements are likely to be similar to weight training (see Chapter 90).

Lighting
- Exercise areas should be brightly lit with no harsh direct lights such as spot lamps shining in users' faces. Lighting design should take account of the large amount of mirrored surface.
- Dimmer switches are useful for yoga, antenatal and relaxation classes. Some clubs may require more exotic lighting systems (eg colours or strobes linked to music) for certain classes, demonstrations, competitions and social events.
- Lighting controls should be accessible to staff only.
- Basement spaces can require particularly careful lighting design.

Ventilation
Ventilation systems for fitness areas pose a particular design problem and must cope with considerable metabolic heat, body odours and humidity. Temperature and humidity controls must be capable of wider variation than normal and have the capacity to react swiftly.

1.5 Changing rooms
Space is often a limited commodity but in health clubs and gyms there is a tendency to give insufficient space to the gym and changing rooms, especially the latter. It is important to provide generous and well fitted changing rooms. If space allows female changing rooms should be allowed a little more space than male.

92
Sports medicine centres and sports injury clinics

Rose Macdonald and Geraint John

1 Introduction

This kind of specialist centre for the treatment of sports injuries is a new and developing type of facility. It can be provided as part of a national or regional sports centre, a stadium, arena or in any other suitable location. Alternative names are a Sports Medicine Centre or Sports Injury Clinic.

1.1 Location

A ground floor situation is the most suitable for easy access by people with injuries. Alternatively lift access must be provided.

Centres or clinics must always be fully accessible to people with disabilities and should therefore have ramped access and wide (ideally single leaf) doors. Front door access should be controlled from the reception point.

1.2 Accommodation

The facilities should include:

- Reception/office
- Waiting area
- Changing rooms (male and female)
- Storage room
- Consulting rooms
- Treatment area
- Gymnasium
- Wet room
- Free exercise area
- Director's office
- Office accommodation for staff.

Figure 1 indicates the desirable relationship between these areas.

Reception and office
The office should be large enough for two to three people and equipped with desks, filing cabinets, computer equipment, built-in storage cupboards (lockable) and worktop space for photocopier and other office equipment. A receptionist work station is required, built in to the reception desk, with easy access to the door opening button, cash register, safe, telephone, panic button, alarm setting, music control and emergency loud speaker. Space needs to be provided under the reception desk for appointment and statistics books and other records.

Waiting area
The waiting area should be under the direct supervision of the receptionist and equipped with comfortable chairs, coffee table, magazine and pamphlet racks on the walls and

a hot and cold drinks machine. There should also be a display case for items to be sold.

Changing rooms
Separate areas will be needed for men and women and both should be equipped with hand/hair driers. They should be fully accessible for patients in wheelchairs and this may affect the design of toilet and shower areas. They should have fixed benches and coat hooks on the walls with lockers large enough for sports bags and clothing and a good ventilation and loudspeaker system should also be provided. Floors should be laid to fall to drainage outlets.

Treatment area
This should be designed as an 'open plan' area. it should be large enough for a minimum of six couches, built-in cupboards, counter-top for physiotherapeutic electric modalities, laser, ultra-sound and other machines, **2**. There should be space to move equipment about within the area.

The treatment area should include:

- Two desks with telephone points
- Double socket outlets at waist height on all walls
- Glass walls giving a view into the wet room, gym and free exercise area
- Carpet in the floor for sound absorption
- Built-in magazine racks
- Built-in cupboards for storage
- Wall racks for holding equipment accessories
- Wash basins.

Free exercise area
This should be large enough to accommodate a treadmill and at least two treatment plinths plus room for at least two people to stretch and perform free exercises.

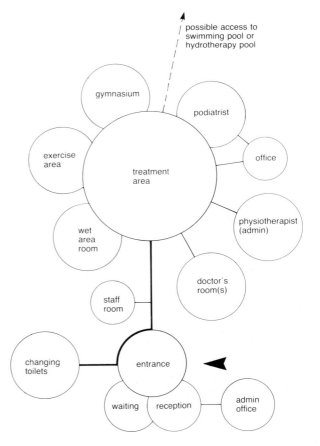

1 *Planning diagram of relationships between various areas*

Gymnasium area

This should be large enough to accommodate all the proposed equipment with adequate ceiling height for movement of air. The main features are:

- Good air extraction system
- Solid walls for fixed equipment attachment, eg wall bars, pulley systems
- Double doors for equipment movement
- Solid floor for heavy equipment, some of which will be fixed to the floor, eg weight machines
- Carpet on floor to deaden and absorb noise
- Waterproof material under bicycle ergometers
- A plentiful supply of double socket outlets at waist height
- Electric clock, cardiac monitors, mirrors and portable mirror
- Glass walls above waist level for clear visibility by physiotherapists without allowing noise to filter into the treatment area.

Wet room

This room should be provided with a water-resistant floor graded to drainage outlets. It should be large enough for an ice bed at workable height for casting orthotics or taping, and the room should be equipped with:

- Built-in sunken faradic foot baths with shelf for battery-operated machines
- Ultrasound sink at waist height
- Large ice machine
- Whirlpool with stepdown transformer
- Hydrocollator
- Washer and dryer
- Fitted drying rack for ice towels
- Sink with separate hot and cold (drinking water) taps and worktop
- Storage cupboard
- A good supply of waist high double socket outlets.

Physiological testing laboratory

This does not need to be very large but should have office accommodation for the staff. It should be equipped with a sink and small worktop and appropriate physiological testing equipment. There should be good air extraction or air-conditioning equipment.

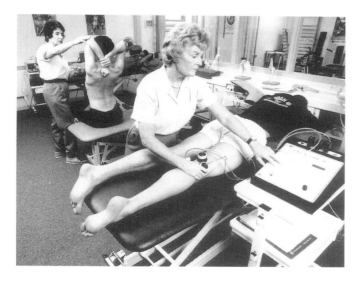

2 *Patients being treated at Crystal Palace National Sports Centre, London*

Consulting rooms for doctors/podiatrists

Two or three rooms will be required, each large enough for a desk, chair and examination couch, patients' chairs and built-in cupboard (lockable). Each room should have a refrigerator (lockable), wash hand basin and hand towel dispenser, several double socket outlets, a telephone point, X-ray viewing box, implement trolley and slot for the name of the doctor on the door.

Director (superintendent physiotherapist office)

This rooms needs windows through which to view the clinic, gym and wet room. It should be large enough for a desk, chair, visitors' chairs, coffee table, built-in cupboards and book case with glass panels and filing cabinets. There should also be a name slot on the door, several double socket outlets and a telephone point.

Staff office

This should be large enough for two to three desks and chairs with built-in cupboards for records and books, filing cabinets, several double socket outlets and a telephone point.

Staff room

This should be attractively designed, light and spacious with a good extractor system to stop food odours permeating the clinic. The main area should be large enough for staff meetings. There should be a *kitchen area* with built-in cupboards above and below the sink, a fridge/freezer, plenty of counter-top and several double socket outlets at waist level. The *changing area* should have lockers for clothing and the *seating area* comfortable chairs, a table and chairs in the eating area, coffee table, desk and telephone points.

1.3 Detail design points

- Working areas must be bright and airy with good lighting.
- External windows should be fitted with opaque glass and ideally not face the sun through the hottest part of the day; external sunblinds are an alternative. Vertical blinds are useful for providing shade and to black out an area – particularly the staff room – for lectures.
- Roller blinds should be provided on glass door panels for privacy.
- The air temperature must be high enough for patients to be treated wearing minimal clothing. The system should be designed to avoid draughts.
- Speakers should be provided throughout the clinic, preferably in the ceiling, for emergency announcements or music.

1.4 Additional accommodation

Depending on the type of centre, the design brief may include a lecture room large enough for 30–40 seats with provision for a teaching wall. There should be provision for slide and overhead projection, TV and video facilities. Windows should be provided with a blackout or good quality blinds.

Access to a swimming or hydrotherapy pool will be a great bonus; it should be as easy and convenient as possible. Access to facilities such as an athletics track or football pitch will also be an advantage.

1.5 Internal environment

For general details of environmental services recommendations refer to Chapters 60 and 61.

93
Doping control facilities

Geraint John and Michele Verroken

Facilities are needed at major stadia and arenas for doping control. They must provide privacy for competitors and security for the collection procedure.

A Doping Control Station is now an essential feature of any modern stadium or arena used for sports events. The following recommended room sizes and facilities will help to achieve the necessary privacy and security. It should be situated close to the competitors' exit into the competition or training area. Two interconnecting rooms are needed, an administration room and waiting room, together with an area for sample collection.

The administration room (of at least 12 sq m) should contain table and chairs, a wash basin, the sample containers, suitable materials for sealing containers and writing materials. It should be adjacent to a WC with space for two people. Two WCs are needed to speed sample taking and separate sample collection areas should be provided for each sex being tested at mixed events. A lockable freezer or refrigerator for storage of samples should also be available in this room.

The waiting area (with an area of 20–30 sq m) should be equipped with chairs, clothes hangers and hooks, possibly some magazines and an adequate supply of drinks which must be in unopened containers. A domestic refrigerator is also advisable, located in the waiting room for the immediate supply of liquid inducement. In smaller arenas, the drug testing waiting room can be a shared facility with the medical waiting room. However, separate administration and collection areas are needed.

Doping control facilities should be clearly signposted. The facilities should be capable of being locked.

Analysis of samples taken at the doping control centre will take place at specialist laboratories which are likely to be set up at a separate location.

The Sports Council publication *Doping Control Information Manual* includes recommendations for sample collection facilities. An extract is reproduced below. The designer is also advised to check with the International Amateur Athletics Federation.

Extract from the *Doping Control Information Manual* (copyright © The Sports Council 1991)

Facilities for Doping Control should provide privacy for competitors and security for the collection procedures. It [sic] should be situated close to the competition or training area. Access to the Doping Control Station is restricted to authorised personnel only (ie ISOs [Independent Sampling Officers], selected competitors and their accompanying officials, Governing Body doping control official). The entry door to the Doping Control Station must be secure.

Within the station three areas are required, a waiting area, administration area and an area for sample collection. [Ideally there should be at least two inter-connecting rooms.]

The waiting area should be equipped with chairs, clothes hangers and hooks, space for an adequate supply of non-alcoholic drinks (still and carbonated) in unopened containers and a rubbish bin. In addition reading materials, television or radio are helpful to create a relaxed atmosphere.

The administration area should contain table and chairs, wash basin, soap and towels. At major events involving sample collection over several days, a lockable freezer or refrigerator for storage of samples is useful. At least one WC is required in the sample collection area and separate sample collection areas should be provided for each sex being tested. Sufficient space is needed to accommodate the ISO and competitor in this area.

Index